Crime and Its
Treatment in Canada

CONTRIBUTORS

JOHN D. ARMSTRONG
Psychiatrist, North York General Hospital Mental Health Clinic, Willowdale, Ontario, and Associate Professor, Department of Psychiatry, University of Toronto

J. ALEX. EDMISON, Q.C.
Member, National Parole Board

J. V. FORNATARO
Assistant Professor, School of Social Work, University of British Columbia

P. J. GIFFEN
Associate Professor, Department of Sociology, University of Toronto

TADEUSZ GRYGIER
Professor, School of Social Work, University of Toronto

W. H. KELLY
Assistant Commissioner, Royal Canadian Mounted Police

A. M. KIRKPATRICK
Executive Director, John Howard Society of Ontario

A. J. MACLEOD, Q.C.
Commissioner of Penitentiaries, Department of Justice

ST. JOHN MADELEY
Staff Supervisor, Provincial Probation Service, British Columbia

W. T. MCGRATH
Executive Secretary, Canadian Corrections Association

FRANK P. MILLER
Executive Director, National Parole Service

DOUGLAS PENFOLD
Assistant Deputy-Minister, Department of Reform Institutions, Ontario

GORDON W. RUSSON
Senior Psychiatrist, Corrections Branch, Department of Social Welfare and Rehabilitation, Saskatchewan

STUART RYAN, Q.C.
Professor, Faculty of Law, Queen's University

DONALD SINCLAIR
Executive Director of the Ontario Division, Canadian Mental Health Association

R. E. TURNER
Director, Forensic Clinic of the Toronto Psychiatric Hospital, and Assistant Professor, Department of Psychiatry, University of Toronto

Crime and Its Treatment in Canada

edited by W. T. McGrath

1965

Macmillan of Canada   Toronto

St. Martin's Press   New York

Library of Congress Catalogue Card No. 66 - 12924

Printed in Canada by McCorquodale and Blades Printers Limited
for The Macmillan Company of Canada Limited, 70 Bond Street, Toronto

Foreword

'The mood and temper of the public in regard to the treatment of crime and criminals is one of the most unfailing tests of the civilization of any country.' So said Winston Churchill in 1910.

Today, men have escaped from the pull of the earth's gravity and circled the globe at speeds of more than 17,000 miles per hour. Drugs have been found that effectively combat some of the most dreaded diseases. Yet in the field of corrections, in the treatment of crime and criminals, the words and deeds of pioneers have had a relatively minor impact. The public appears only recently to have become aware of the problems and of the necessity for a rationalized, scientific way of affording protection both to victim and offender.

When one takes cognizance of the works and efforts of Beccaria, Bentham, Chadwick, John Howard, Ferri, and Piaget, one may well wonder why it has taken so long for their theories and principles to interest the public even slightly – if not to influence its thinking. Perhaps it is because the natural tendency of human beings living in a community is to seek self-protection at practically any price, and without regard for the law-breaker.

But there are signs of change. On April 9, 1965, when the Minister of Justice of Canada announced the government's intention to establish a Committee of Inquiry, he set forth its purpose in the following terms:

> To study the broad field of corrections, in its widest sense, from the initial investigation of an offence through to the final discharge of a prisoner from imprisonment or parole, including such steps and measures as arrest, summonsing, bail, representation in Court, conviction, probation, sentencing, training, medical and psychiatric attention, release, parole, pardon, post release supervision and guidance and rehabilitation; to recommend as conclusions are reached, what changes, if any, should be made in the law and practice relating to these matters.

These are, in effect, the topics covered by the sixteen authors of *Crime and Its Treatment in Canada*. I believe that, for the sake of enlightenment, this book should be given the widest circulation, not only among students of criminology, but in all law-enforcement agencies and correctional institutions, and among the general public.

As W. T. McGrath points out in Chapter 1, 'Until we reach agreement on the basic principles of our approach to corrections, we cannot plan with confidence nor will there be uniformity of development.' Perhaps this book will bring agreement and uniformity a step closer.

THE HONOURABLE ROGER OUIMET

Judge of the Superior Court of the
Province of Quebec

Chairman of the Canadian Committee
on Corrections, appointed by
the Minister of Justice, 1965

Contents

tive powers; the judiciary; the territories; national legislation affecting the criminal courts. How the courts are organized.

System of Canadian Criminal Courts – Courts with jurisdiction over persons charged with indictable offences. Courts with jurisdiction over persons charged with summary offences. Work of trial courts: scope of jurisdiction of magistrates; implications of extended jurisdiction of magistrates. Work of appellate courts. Judicial attitudes and tendencies: attitude of the legal profession. Territorial application of criminal law. Territorial jurisdiction of courts. Administrative responsibility for criminal justice. The national Department of Justice. The provincial Attorney-General's department: the Attorney-General's agent; coroners; justices of the peace. Classification of criminal offences from the point of view of procedure. Characteristics of Canadian criminal procedure: the indigent accused; limitations on police powers; initiation of criminal process; summons or warrant; search-warrants; arrest without warrant; treatment of persons in custody pending hearing; remedies for false imprisonment and other illegal treatment of prisoners; remand for medical examination; the sentencing process. Outline of procedure on charges of offences in various classes. Conclusion.

and tradition-making importance. The significant year of 1880. Conclusion.
Appendix.

Preface

This book is addressed primarily to university students in the various disciplines involved in the control of illegal behaviour, such as criminology, law, medicine, psychology, social work, sociology, and theology, and to students in the many in-service training-courses offered by the police and correctional services across the country.

It has, however, a second purpose. Interest among politicians and public alike in the problems associated with crime and delinquency is greater today than at any time in the past. Church groups, service clubs, and citizen organizations of many kinds have formed study groups and are pressing for penal reform, and this activity is supported and stimulated by official studies undertaken by royal commissions and similar bodies. It is hoped the general survey of the field presented here will prove useful to those engaged in these official and unofficial studies.

The reader will be struck by the differences of opinion expressed by the authors of different chapters. This may be confusing but it is better to face the uncertainties that exist in the field than to subscribe to a uniformity that carries no conviction. Disagreement will stimulate the search for sounder knowledge.

I would like to express appreciation to the authors of individual chapters. All are busy men who took on this assignment at some personal sacrifice.

W. T. M.

Crime and Its
Treatment in Canada

1

Crime and the
Correctional Services

W. T. McGRATH

WHAT IS CRIME?

What constitutes crime varies from time to time and from place to place according to the views of particular societies or the necessities of particular régimes. Accordingly, we can define the term only on the basis of legislation existing here and now. In its generally accepted legal sense, it refers to acts or omissions that violate the provisions of criminal legislation. Criminal legislation comprises all the laws forbidding specific acts or demanding the performance of specific tasks (such as paying income tax) and providing penalties for non-compliance.

In Canada, this definition of criminal law is not fully applicable, since under the terms of the British North America Act, criminal law is the exclusive prerogative of the federal government, and therefore no provincial statute may be classed as criminal. However, many of the responsibilities allocated to the provinces, such as the control of liquor and traffic, and the regulation of hunting and fishing, can be discharged only by the use of legislation that operates like criminal legislation. For our purposes, then, in looking at the crime problem, the distinction between federal and provincial legislation is a merely formal one, and it matters little whether an offence is dealt with under federal or provincial law.

Juvenile delinquency is a special problem, but it must be considered a subdivision of crime. The basic legislation permitting special treatment of juveniles who have committed an offence is federal, and forms part of the general criminal jurisdiction of the federal government.

Crime can also be defined in sociological terms. Our codified criminal

1

legislation is a formalized statement of the kinds of prohibition and requirement that any social group, no matter how primitive, lays down for its members. In primitive societies such rules are verbal only, and it is not until society grows complex that it becomes necessary to write them down.

CORRECTIONS

The term 'corrections' (or 'correction' as it sometimes appears) encompasses the body of knowledge and practice related to society's handling of people – either adults or children – who have been convicted of an offence. It also extends into the area of prevention, since any successful effort in that area reduces the number of people who become involved in delinquency or crime. The term is not a very good one, since it does not contain within itself any indication of its meaning in this context – we attempt to correct many things besides people who have antisocial tendencies. It is used only in English-speaking North America and in Australia.

Penologists in the United States selected it deliberately to replace the older term 'penology', which had fallen into some disrepute since it shares a common root with the word 'penalty' and has no connotation of treatment.

A distinction is drawn between criminology, which refers to the academic study of problems associated with crime and delinquency, and corrections, which refers to the practical operation of services. In French-speaking Canada and in the rest of the world, the meaning of criminology is extended to cover the whole area.

Although it is often suggested that it should be abandoned because it is awkward and non-descriptive, the term 'corrections' is in common use. Several provinces have an official called the director of corrections; the federal government set up a Correctional Planning Committee in 1958; and the national co-ordinating body is called, in English, the Canadian Corrections Association. In French it is La Société Canadienne de Criminologie.

THE CORRECTIONAL SERVICES

The following are generally recognized as the services falling in whole or in part within the scope of corrections. They are separated here under juvenile and adult headings to avoid confusion in the meaning of some of the terms.

JUVENILE	ADULT
Prevention	Prevention
Police	Police
Detention Homes	Jails and Lock-ups
Juvenile Courts	Family Courts
	Criminal Courts
Probation	Probation
Training-schools	Prisons (penitentiaries, reformatories, and special institutions)
	Parole
After-care	After-care

Also part of the correctional system, and underlying and affecting all these services, are legislation, staff training, and research.

It is difficult to say which of the preventive services should be considered part of corrections. Anything that strengthens community and family life probably tends to reduce crime and delinquency, but usually only those services that are specifically aimed at the reduction of delinquency or crime are included. The extent to which the preventive services are regarded as forming part of corrections tends to vary from one situation to another.

Only what might be called the social part of police work, such as the handling of arrested persons, can be considered as falling within the field of corrections. Such technical matters as determining who committed a crime, or maintaining traffic control, are excluded. The same selectivity must be applied to the work of the courts. Activities directly related to treatment – sentencing, for instance – are considered part of corrections, while such technicalities as the sifting of evidence are not.

It is a fact, however, that the moment of his arrest by the police marks the beginning of the rehabilitation of the criminal offender. His treatment in the police lock-up, the manner in which the police take statements, the way evidence is collected and presented to the court, all have an effect on his attitude towards authority, and will have an important influence on his final adjustment. And though some of the activities of the courts are not regarded as correctional, their work as a whole must be seen as part of the over-all rehabilitative process. If a man feels he has been treated fairly by the courts he will be an easier subject for rehabilitation.

Criminal legislation forms part of corrections, because the operation of most correctional services is controlled directly by the laws under which they are established. Federal examples are the Penitentiaries Act and the Parole Act; provincial examples are the acts controlling probation and training-schools for juvenile delinquents. Also, by setting out procedures, and by defining crimes and attaching penalties to them, the legislation determines who will come under the care of the correctional services and under what conditions. If the laws are good the services are given a manageable task; if they are poor, the difficulties faced by the services are increased accordingly.

Staff training is considered an integral part of corrections because the major facility through which the correctional services can change criminal attitudes and behaviour is the interpersonal relationship between staff member and offender. Staff must therefore be of high quality and well trained.

It is only from research that we can eventually get the knowledge we now lack on many aspects of crime – knowledge that is essential if our efforts are to achieve their maximum effectiveness. It is therefore an important part of corrections.

NEED FOR UNITY

This listing of the services that make it up indicates the complicated nature of the correctional system. When we take into account as well the division of responsibility among various levels of government, and considerations of geography, we see that there is a serious problem – the danger of fragmentation. In the past, there has been a lack of understanding and even some mutual distrust between the staffs of the various services, and between workers in the field in different parts of the country. These difficulties are overcome as the individuals involved get to understand each other's attitudes and problems. With understanding comes mutual respect. The need for co-operation among the services intensifies as treatment comes to be recognized as a legitimate aim of corrections. The services can be fragmented administratively, but the individual offender cannot be; if treatment is the goal then all the services that deal with him must work together.

THE AIMS OF CORRECTIONS

One of the fundamental issues facing those in the corrections field in Canada today is the lack of agreement as to what our aim should be in our dealings with convicted offenders. Different people see different objectives. Some believe that the aim should be to make the criminal suffer, either to repay him for the harm he has done or to frighten potential criminals into being good; others believe that treatment should be the aim. These aims are incompatible. Suffering may be an unavoidable part of treatment, but it is a different matter to inflict suffering deliberately for its own sake. Any service whose aim is deliberately to cause suffering is a most unlikely channel for treatment.

The kind of services we build will depend on which of these two aims we finally adopt. It may be that we should adopt a mixture of both. If so, we should determine how much weight is to be given to each. At any rate, there is an urgent need to be clear what our aim is. Because of the lack of clarity in this basic matter, we have no real over-all plan for corrections in this country. Progress is hindered because we are working at cross purposes and because there are contradictions all down the line.

HISTORY OF PUNISHMENT

The history of punishment for crime is a fascinating one, but any lengthy consideration of it would be out of place in a book devoted to current corrections. In primitive societies, acts interpreted as being offensive to the spirit-world were considered more serious than secular offences, since they might bring down divine wrath on the whole community. Some of the earliest recorded instances of capital punishment among the Jewish tribes were the executions ordered by Moses for the breaking of ritual law. In this context punishment becomes a form of social purification and divine appeasement.

Secular crimes, on the other hand, even serious ones like murder, were usually dealt with as private wrongs, to be avenged by the family or other social group to which the victim belonged. Violent revenge was gradually replaced by monetary compensation, with the scale laid down by the society. As stronger central government developed, crime came to be seen as a breaking of the king's peace, and revenge, or punishment, became the right of the leader.

The punishments meted out were based on the assumption that every person was in possession of a free will, and that a crime was the result of a deliberate intent to do wrong. Punishment was therefore crude, direct, and sufficient, it was hoped, to deter further crime. It took the form of physical damage of the most brutal order. The death penalty was in force for almost all crimes, even minor ones like petty theft. At one time in England over two hundred crimes were punishable by death.[1] The result was a shockingly high number of executions. Capital punishment was supplemented by various kinds of torture and mutilation – branding a T on the brow of a thief, for instance, or cutting off a man's ears, nose, or hands.

There has been a gradual move away from violent punishment. Most

[1]L. Radzinowicz, *History of the English Criminal Law*, London: Stevens & Sons, 1940.

of the advanced countries use neither capital nor corporal punishment, although for some reason the English-speaking countries are among the slower in abandoning them. In Canada, legislation passed in 1961 limits the death penalty to some forms of treason, piracy that involves murder or attempted murder or that endangers the life of some person, and murder that is either 'planned or deliberate' or that occurs during the commission of one of a specified list of crimes. It is probable that under this law not more than two or three will be executed each year in Canada. Judicial sentences of torture are now limited to the laying on of the lash or the strap, and these instruments too are falling into disuse. Between fifteen and thirty-five Canadians receive such sentences each year.[2]

We have probably reached the closing phases of the use of violent punishment for crime. Today we rely on prison sentences, on fines and similar punishments, and on devices such as probation that are frankly intended as treatment.

THEORIES OF PUNISHMENT

What, then, should be our guiding principles as we draw up legislation to protect ourselves against crime, and as we develop our correctional services? Down through the centuries, various theories have held sway, and they influence our thinking now.

The first of these is the theory of *retribution*. This is the oldest of the theories, and is based on the belief that the criminal should suffer for what he has done, that he owes a debt to society that must be paid. This belief sometimes gains support from a religious interpretation of crime, and the need to appease divinity.

The symbol of the theory of retribution is the statue of Themis, the Greek goddess of justice, which stands over many of our court-houses. She is blindfold against extraneous issues such as pity, and she holds in her hands the eternal scales of justice. The idea is to place the offence in one scale, and in the other an amount of punishment that will re-establish the balance. But this immediately poses the problem of assessing the amount of punishment that will balance any particular offence. As we read Chapter 3 of this book, 'Sources of Illegal Behaviour', we are led to ask whether the individual is alone responsible for his crime. Can a person who has grown up under difficult circumstances be held as responsible for his evil actions as one who has had the advantage of

---

[2]Canada, Dominion Bureau of Statistics, *Statistics of Criminal and Other Offences*, Ottawa: Queen's Printer (annual).

6

favourable circumstances? Can the situation in which a child grows be bad enough to remove all responsibility from him?

The problem of free will has been inconclusively debated through the centuries. It may be that the individual has a degree of self-determination left to him no matter what his experiences have been. We like to think that this is so, but our desire that it should be may itself be the product of the kind of training we receive in our society.

Whatever element of free will remains to an individual, social science has established that he is, at least in large part, the product of the environment in which he has developed. The individual cannot be held responsible for the home and community situation into which he was born. Responsibility for failure to provide the kind of environment that gives a child a chance to grow into a happy and law-abiding adult rests with the community as a whole. We are all responsible for the conditions under which he lives and we all share his guilt if he later turns to crime. Obviously, we must maintain some forms of punishment for our own protection until we can find a way to remove the sources of crime; but when punishment is inflicted, every member of the community, instead of feeling a sense of satisfaction that the wrongdoer has suffered his just deserts, should have a deep feeling of remorse and failure. Such an attitude would make the retention of any form of vindictive punishment impossible. We take what steps we must to protect ourselves from danger, but there is no justification in social science for what amounts to a form of mass revenge; and religion combines with social science to convince us that revenge is unacceptable as the basis of one of our major social services.

However, many people who support the theory of retribution maintain that this is not a fair presentation of the theory. They say that the offender must be punished, not from any desire for vengeance, but so that an instinctive abhorrence of the offence may be built up in the minds of the members of the community. If, for instance, every time a murder is committed the murderer is hanged, then abhorrence of the crime of murder will be fostered in the minds of the public. This idea must be kept distinct from the concept of deterrence. Deterrence is a more direct effect operating on an individual who fears a specific punishment for a specific crime.

It would be most difficult to demonstrate that the attitude of the public towards various crimes bears any ratio to the punishment traditionally meted out for them. We have an instinctive abhorrence of many actions – striking a parent, for instance – that in practice may not bring severe punishment. Public aversion towards a murderer, whose crime

7

is traditionally punishable by hanging, is likely to be less than that towards the sexual seducer of a child, for whose offence the courts have traditionally given a light sentence.

Another argument offered in support of vengeful punishment is that it serves as a community catharsis. All members of the community have antisocial feelings, and in payment for suppressing such feelings the law-abiding citizen demands satisfaction of his desire for revenge against those who do offend. Thus the socially-minded are given a further incentive to continue to suppress undesirable tendencies.

Although there is undoubtedly some truth in this contention, it would be most difficult to measure how much. Will the arrest and public denouncement of the criminal suffice, or must actual punishment be inflicted? If the argument were carried to its extreme, we might be back hanging even minor offenders.

The arguments in support of the theory of retribution still carry weight with a great many people, but no large body of informed opinion could be found today to defend it on any theoretical grounds.

The second theory of punishment is that of *deterrence,* based on the belief that a person contemplating a crime will be deterred by the suffering of those previously condemned for similar acts, and that those who have suffered punishment will be less likely to offend again because of the fear of further penalties.

With our present knowledge, it is impossible to assess the deterrent effect of judicial punishments. It is true that the average motorist is less likely to go through a red light if he fears a twenty-dollar fine. However, the average motorist is probably a reasonably well adjusted person. Also, going through a red light does not normally carry the psychological implications of more serious crime (although it may do so sometimes – in the case of a rebellious youngster, for instance). The research done on capital and corporal punishment suggests that neither carries any special deterrent effect. Why expect more from other kinds of punishment?

It appears that the deterrent effect lies in the probability of detection and conviction, rather than in the kind or amount of punishment that may follow conviction. For a well-established member of the community, the real punishment would be discovery, and public disgrace for himself and his family. If this consideration will not deter him, neither will fear of an uncertain sentence following possible conviction. The risk of prison is part of the way of life of the professional criminal. His concern, too, is with not getting caught.

One danger of the deterrence theory is that in making an example of an individual offender in order to deter others, we may cause him to become more bitter, and therefore more perilous to society than he was already. Another stems from an unjustified amount of reliance on deterrence. If it does not work, we will have committed our hopes to an illusion while delaying the search for more effective means of meeting the situation.

The extent to which judicial punishment is effective as a deterrent is a more urgent subject for research than any other in the field of corrections. The issue is too important and too basic for us to rely on guesswork. We need facts.

A third theory, now getting increasing support from medical and social research, is that of *reformation*. According to this, the function of the judicial and correctional process should be to return offenders to normal and law-abiding lives as quickly and expeditiously as possible. It is recognized that the basic purpose of the process is to protect the public from illegal activity, but it is maintained that the only real protection lies in reforming the individual. If the discharged offender goes back to the community as dangerous as he was at the time of his conviction, or even more dangerous, society has obviously been given little protection.

Part of the trouble in putting this theory into practice is that we do not have the skills to ensure that all convicted criminals will, if given treatment, lead law-abiding lives. It is true that in this area, theory is well ahead of practice, and we could do a great deal more along treatment lines than we are now doing, but there are still many criminals beyond the reach of present knowledge. With such criminals, segregation is about all we can offer.

Besides, it is an unanswered philosophical question whether the state has the right to force personality change (treatment) on the individual, and under what circumstances it has that right. Levying a traditional punishment like imprisonment can be a relatively clear-cut provision, but how does one assess the more subtle levying of personality change? Little question would be raised in regard to a dangerous criminal, but where is the line to be drawn? If a person is guilty of a minor theft, should the state be permitted to change his personality as it sees fit? We have already reached this stage in the juvenile field. It does not matter whether it is a serious offence like armed robbery or a minor one like truancy that brings a child before the juvenile court. Once there, he is found guilty, not of the specific act, but of being a delinquent. From then on, the status of all offenders is exactly the same, and the court has very great powers over them until they reach the age of twenty-one. If

9

this policy were followed in the adult field, the state would be empowered to order whatever kind of treatment it deemed wise over a long period of time, even for petty theft and minor traffic offences.

Apart from these theories, *segregation* of the criminal element is often claimed as one of the advantages of holding offenders in prison. There are obviously dangerous criminals who cannot safely be left at large, and some of them will not respond to our present treatment skills. There can be no doubt that keeping these people where they can do no harm is useful, and if they can be held through the most active years of their lives they may sometimes be safely released. Our legislation for indeterminate sentence tries to express this policy.

We have placed undue faith, however, in the possibility of segregating the criminal population as a whole. New crimes are constantly being committed, and offenders who have completed terms of imprisonment are constantly re-entering the community. The flow into our Canadian prisons, year by year, is about the same as the flow out. Thus, only a part of the criminal population is segregated at any time.

WHAT SHOULD BE OUR GUIDE?

Among these various schools of thought, it is difficult to decide what our approach should be. Despite the objections to the theory of retribution, it represents justice to many people. It has been said that not only must justice be done, but it must be seen to be done, both by the offender and by the public. For example, there is a seeming fairness to equal sentences for equal crimes, if the deeper factors of causality are ignored. If two men commit the same crime, and one is sentenced to five years in prison while the other is sentenced to only one year, we cannot be surprised if the one given the longer sentence claims that he has suffered an injustice. Nor can we be surprised if our attempts to rehabilitate this man are blocked by his resentment. Inequality of sentence is one of the most difficult problems with which prison officials have to deal.

It is also true that in many instances the theory of retribution limits punishment more than does that of reformation. 'An eye for an eye and a tooth for a tooth' seems a harsh principle; but as well as *not less than,* it also says, in effect, *not more than* an eye for an eye and *not more than* a tooth for a tooth. The theory of reformation allows much greater latitude; the uselessness of punishment as a treatment device is recognized sufficiently, however, to remove much of the danger in this – though we must remember that what we call treatment may appear as punishment to the recipient.

At the same time, it is obvious that there is pragmatic value in varying the sentence according to the personality of the offender so as to guard against the risk of repetition. It is also true that the cause of justice in the final sense is better served when the individual's whole history is taken into consideration. The difficulty lies in explaining this to the offender and to the public.

Nor is there an obvious solution to the conflict between deterrence and reformation. A recent example may illustrate this quandary. A member of the federal parliament was convicted of accepting a bribe, and the court awarded a suspended sentence. Was the court's action wise? In all probability the 'treatment' requirements of the offending member of parliament were met by this sentence. No doubt the publicity surrounding the incident was more than sufficient punishment. But did the court have another and more pressing responsibility? This country seems to be facing an increasing number of crimes related to betrayal of trust by public officials, and one of the most alarming aspects of the trend is the apparent apathy of the public. Should the opportunity have been taken to stress, through the medium of a prison sentence, that this kind of thing will not be tolerated in Canada? Should the need for public condemnation of the act have taken precedence over the needs of the individual offender?

It may also be doubted whether civic officials who indulge in graft are in need of treatment in the same sense as are maladjusted persons whose criminal activity is symptomatic of an underlying social or psychological uncertainty. It may well be that deterrent punishment is more effective with the white-collar offender; yet we reserve our sternest sentences for the violent criminal.

One thing is certain. Until we reach agreement on the basic principles of our approach to corrections, we cannot plan with confidence, nor will there be uniformity of development.

Further Reading

BRILLINGER, H. ROY. 'The Judge and the Psychiatrist', *Canadian Journal of Corrections,* vol. 1, no. 2 (January 1959).

BROWN, E. W. H. 'A Layman Looks at Magistrates', *Canadian Journal of Corrections,* vol. 1, no. 3 (April 1959).

CANADA. Committee to Inquire into the Principles and Procedures Followed in the Remission Service of the Department of Justice of Canada. *Report* (Fauteux Report). Ottawa: Queen's Printer, 1956.

————. Royal Commission to Investigate the Penal System of Canada. *Report* (Archambault Report). Ottawa: King's Printer, 1938.

COHEN, RONALD. 'Custody and Treatment: an Anthropological View', *Canadian Journal of Corrections,* vol. 3, no. 2 (April 1961).

GIBBONS, DON C. 'Comment on the Efficacy of Criminal Treatment', *Canadian Journal of Corrections,* vol. 2, no. 2 (April 1960).

GUTTMACHER, M. S. 'Individualization of Sentence', *Canadian Journal of Corrections,* vol. 3, no. 3 (July 1961).

JAFFARY, STUART KING. *Sentencing of Adults in Canada.* Toronto: University of Toronto Press, 1963.

KATZ, SIDNEY. 'Do Our Courts Dispense True Justice?', *Maclean's* Magazine, August 1, 1959 (Reprinted in Paul Fox, *Politics: Canada.* Toronto: McGraw-Hill, 1963).

KIRKPATRICK, A. M. 'Correcting Corrections', *Criminal Law Quarterly,* vol. 2, no. 4 (February 1959-60).

MCGILL UNIVERSITY, Department of Psychiatry, Forensic Clinic. 'Some Psychological Aspects of Sentencing', *Canadian Journal of Corrections,* vol. 3, no. 1 (January 1961).

MCGRATH, W. T. 'The New Criminal Code', *Queen's Quarterly,* vol. LX, no. 2 (Summer 1953).

————. *Planning Canada's Correctional System.* Toronto: John Howard Society of Ontario, 1960.

MCRUER, J. C. 'Sentencing', *Canadian Journal of Corrections,* vol. 3, no. 3 (July 1961).

MORTON, J. D. *The Function of Criminal Law in 1962.* Toronto: Canadian Broadcasting Corporation, 1962.

PHILLIPS, ALAN. 'A Modern Manual of Graft in Civic Office', *Maclean's* Magazine, March 10, 1962.

QUEEN'S UNIVERSITY. *Proceedings of the Seminar on the Sentencing of Offenders.* Kingston, 1962.

ROYAL CANADIAN MOUNTED POLICE. *Law and Order in Canadian Democracy.* Ottawa: King's Printer, 1952.

SASKATCHEWAN. Penal Commission. *Report* (Laycock Report). Regina: King's Printer, 1946.

SCOTT, G. W. 'Sentencing', *Canadian Journal of Corrections,* vol. 1, no. 3 (April 1959).

SZABO, DENIS. 'Criminologie et Sociologie', *Revue Canadienne de Criminologie,* vol. 1, no. 5 (October 1959).

2

Crime and Society

TADEUSZ GRYGIER

Definitions and Concepts

CRIME AND CORRECTIONS: OUR DEFINITIONS DON'T FIT

Crime is an act prohibited by the criminal law, says the definition stated in the first chapter of this volume; to a lawyer this is not only a good definition, but possibly the only acceptable one.

The function of corrections, as of the criminal law itself, is to eradicate crime; this would certainly be the view of a criminologist or a specialist in corrections.

Both statements are obvious to the point of being trivial. The only trouble is that they are incompatible, unless we are prepared to keep logic on a short leash, which is an old English custom. Let us release the leash, analyse what we have said, and see where the logic will lead us. If we do not like the conclusions, is there, perhaps, something wrong with our premises?

Let us look at the situation, first of all, as modern scientists would, and accept, with Einstein, that things and events are always relative to the co-ordinate system in space-time, and thus relative to the observer. In our case we have three observers and three points of view.

If we take, first, the point of view of the law enforcement agent, the criminal law is an ultimate criterion, an arbiter of values, a set of sacred rules that maintain society's order and ensure its protection. Crime upsets the existing order. The law is there, dignified and immobile; then the criminal comes and breaks it.

An expanded version of this chapter will appear in a forthcoming book by Tadeusz Grygier on *Concepts of Crime and their Practical Consequences*. The other chapters of the book will trace the historical development of concepts of crime and juvenile delinquency, and the impact of modern science, medicine, and the welfare state.

To the criminal the situation does not appear the same way. From his point of view he is engaged in his activities under pressures from his physical, social, and emotional needs, and of his family, his group, and society as a whole. He is society's product and its victim; he does what he can, in the only way he knows, to survive and to enjoy life. His act, until it is interfered with, is not a crime; it is an innocent act, a part of natural social processes and of individual free will. In this context, social processes and individual acts take precedence; the criminal law creates unwarranted interference in human affairs.

If we now take the third possible position, that of an 'impartial' observer of the conflict between the offender and the law, it becomes clear that crime is not, of itself, a fact; it is a relation between an act and a piece of legislation. If we say that we want to eradicate crime, we are trying to do away with something that has two interrelated components. Without a conflict between the two there is no crime. We can destroy crime by destroying either of the components. It would be ineffective to try to interfere with natural social processes; it would be much cheaper and more effective to abolish the criminal law. In this way all crime would disappear overnight, but would society be better off?

It now becomes apparent that our purpose, the purpose of corrections, must be not the eradication of crime but the eradication of undesirable behaviour. What the criminal law does is only to provide a framework and a set of limits.

LEGAL AND SOCIAL FUNCTIONS OF SENTENCING

Sentencing is both a legal act and a social function. The legal aspect determines its limits: no sentence can be passed outside the confines of the law, but within these limits all sentences are legally valid. Their social validity presents a different problem and could vary from action to action and from one offender to another.

We may say that the purpose of sentencing is to apply legal sanctions and thus to enforce the law; or we may say that the sentence should fit the offender and not the offence. But we cannot make both these statements in one breath and hold that both are true – they are incompatible. Legal sanctions are attached to prohibited acts (crimes) and not to offenders. Moreover, as H. L. A. Hart says, all laws consist of general rules, applicable to courses of action, not single actions, and to multitudes of men, not single individuals.[1] For this reason the fundamental principle

---

[1]H. L. A. Hart, 'Positivism and the Separation of Law and Morals', *Harvard Law Review*, vol. 71 (1958), pp. 593-629.

of law is to treat like cases alike. But cases which are alike in law are not necessarily alike in psychodynamics.[2] We follow the rule of law in some cases and follow the principles of psychiatry, psychology, and social work in other cases; but we must be able to distinguish between the two sets of principles and realize the danger of either confusing them or making one of them universal and applicable to all acts and all people. If we want to adopt one principle, one criterion which would tell us the proper balance, we must extend our thinking beyond the accepted framework of jurisprudence.

MULTIPLE AIMS OF SENTENCING

In an address at Queen's University (June 20, 1963) to the conference on alcoholism and drug addiction, Mr. Justice Kelly came close to the present writer's concept of relativity. He defined 'law' as a means of engendering and maintaining desirable relationships between individuals and the state, and between individuals in the state. In order to achieve its objective, he said, law is 'retributive, punitive, exemplary, and corrective'.

This view, though inspired by positive aims, is still harsh and negative when it comes to means. Even the word 'corrective' is nearer, in emotional undertones, to a surgeon's scalpel than to the rehabilitative, patient, and understanding approach of a welfare worker in corrections. Can the criminal law have more positive aims? Can there be a general principle above the multiplicity of aims?[3] Can we simply add rehabilitation and treatment to the means outlined by Mr. Justice Kelly and accepted by most judges throughout the world as the aims rather than the means? Or is it true, as stated in the first chapter of this book, that punitive and rehabilitative aims are incompatible?

If they are compatible, they certainly come frequently into conflict, and we are told that it is up to the court to make a judicious blending of all the principles of modern justice. In one case it would seem to be a pound of retribution, a ton of deterrence, and an ounce of reformation, mixed together and put over a slow fire in a vat of segregation. In another the proportions are different and possibly the vat is not used. What the best mixture is we are never told; this is to be judged individually, from case to case. But it is impossible to evaluate such judging if no criteria are stated and no *general* principle is involved.

2Psychodynamics is defined as the science of mental processes.
3Henry M. Hart does not think so. See 'The Aims of the Criminal Law', *Law and Contemporary Problems*, vol. 23 (1958), pp. 401-11.

Tadeusz Grygier

NEED FOR PRINCIPLES

We clearly need a general principle and a positive idea in order to reconcile our needs: to prohibit and to allow, to punish and to reform, to avenge and to forgive. To say that we can reconcile these aims by maintaining a sense of perspective and a balance of aims and methods is not enough; we all have different ideas of what the right perspective and the right balance are.

We sometimes try to find rescue in a multiplicity of principles, but it is the view of the writer that we already have too many principles, as we have too many laws, and in this he is in agreement with some of his Canadian legal colleagues,[4] who postulate that there should be as little law enforcement and as little judging as possible.

Introducing a new law, especially a harsh law, is never an innocent affair. Every rule has some effect, not only on the problem with which it deals, but also, indirectly, on all other problems and on all other laws. If we treat a particular type of offence harshly, the effect of punishment on all other offences is correspondingly reduced.

The situation is analogous to clinical judgment in diagnosis. If we ascribe a condition to several causes, of which only one is the true cause, the introduction of irrelevant factors detracts from the value of the relevant one. Treatment based on such diagnosis has little chance of success.

Introducing an additional purpose or principle of sentencing is equally harmful. It detracts from the already existing aims and principles, adds further confusion to a field that has never been distinguished by clarity, and allows more room for personal bias and prejudice in the administration of justice. As we know from social psychology, prejudice is stronger the more confused the issue is.

NEED FOR PARSIMONY IN LAW AND JURISPRUDENCE

What we need is not a multiplication of principles but their reduction. The same trend has been well established in the physical sciences, where new scientific laws tend to replace a greater number of existing laws and to accommodate a still greater number of actual observations. This laudable parsimony is singularly absent in legislation; it is also absent in criminological thought. 'Philosophy, it is said, springs from wonder, and the dialogues of Plato show that the first inclusive wondering was largely con-

---

[4]Alan Mewett, 'The Proper Scope and Function of the Criminal Law', *Criminal Law Quarterly*, vol. 3 (1960), pp. 371-91. J. D. Morton, *The Function of Criminal Law in 1962*, Toronto: C.B.C., 1962; 'Crime and the Law', *The Globe and Mail*, May 1 and 2, 1962.

16

cerned with legal-political problems. From Plato to Hegel, the period covered in Huntington Cairns's notable history, law continued to be important, if not always central, in philosophical thought. Then specialization set in. Philosophy suffered fragmentation, jurisprudence became the province of legal scholars, and social science was departmentalized.'[5]

We should end multiplicity and fragmentation, and reintroduce simplicity and integration. If we did, the administration of justice might cease to be merely a philosophy of law and become a part of the philosophy of science.

In face of the apparent conflict between the legal and the social concepts of crime, let us see whether we can formulate a legal concept of crime filled with social and psychological content. Our concept should be wide enough to accommodate both the seemingly incompatible notions that have dominated past and present correctional philosophy, namely punishment and treatment. In this writer's opinion the conflict, still raging in Canada,[6] is entirely illusory. There is no problem of punishment versus treatment, infliction of deliberate suffering versus welfare. Punishment may be the best treatment – in some cases. Treatment may involve hardship. Any conviction, and even a court appearance, inflicts harm and, therefore, punishment. The main problem is ensuring *rational interference* by the government and its agents, and setting the legal limits of that interference to safeguard both the freedom of the individual and the well-being of society.[7]

---

[5] Jerome Hall, 'Reason and Reality in Jurisprudence', *Buffalo Law Review*, vol. 7 (1958), p. 351.

[6] R. I. Cheffins, 'Preparation for Effective Sentencing', *Canadian Bar Journal*, vol. 3 (1960), pp. 287-96. Stuart K. Jaffary, 'Canada's Penal System', *Canadian Welfare*, vol. 24 (1949), pp. 23-6; 'Punishment *vs.* Treatment in the Prisons', *The Globe and Mail*, January 4, 1963; *Sentencing of Adults in Canada*, Toronto: University of Toronto Press, 1963; 'What's Wrong with our Penal System?', *The Globe and Mail*, March 7, 1964. A. M. Kirkpatrick, 'Correcting Corrections', *Criminal Law Quarterly*, vol. 2 (1960), pp. 420-36; 'Prisoners' Aid and Penal Reform', *Crime and Delinquency*, vol. 6 (1960), pp. 383-90; 'Prisons and their Products', *Canadian Journal of Corrections*, vol. 4 (1962), pp. 160-78. Joseph McCulley, 'Some Present Problems in Corrections', address to John Howard Society, London, Ontario, March 14, 1958; 'Now is the Time', address to John Howard Society, St. Catharines, Ontario, March 6, 1959.

[7] On the principles of punishment, see a lucid and well-ordered exposition by H. L. A. Hart, 'Prolegomenon to the Principles of Punishment', Presidential address to the Aristotelian Society, London, October 19, 1949. On the concept of sanction, or 'an enforcement of obedience', see John Austin, *The Province of Jurisprudence Determined* (1832) and *The Uses of the Study of Jurisprudence* (1863), with an introduction by H. L. A. Hart, London: The Library of Ideas, Weidenfeld and Nicholson, 1954. According to Austin, punishments are 'only a *class* of sanctions, the term being too narrow to express the meaning adequately', p. 15.

Tadeusz Grygier

WELFARE AND PUNISHMENT RECONCILED IN ONE DEFINITION

If our concept of crime were wide enough, it could include punishment as one of the possible measures, but not the only measure, to be taken by the authorities in cases of legally defined antisocial behaviour. Such a concept would be linked with the concept of tolerance of all behaviour not listed as criminal and with the concept of freedom to act, within legal limits, whatever the majority of the group might think and whatever they might desire. On the other hand it should not be dependent, as is our present concept, on the concept of responsibility; it could thus avoid the contradictions inherent in the choice between deterministic and indeterministic approaches to criminal behaviour, and could therefore reconcile the indeterministic criminal legislation with the largely deterministic criminological thought. The following definition is proposed:

> *A crime is an act for which criminal legislation prescribes sanctions aimed at the protection of society, which includes the offender.*

In this definition, (a) there is no crime without prohibition expressed in criminal legislation, (b) prohibition is made effective by sanctions, (c) there are no sanctions unless there is both a prohibited act and a legal provision permitting the organs of the state to interfere, (d) in law, the term 'act' includes 'omission', (e) the aim of the sanctions is protection of society, and (f) society includes the offender.

CONSEQUENCES OF THE DEFINITION

Having stated a definition, let us analyse its components and examine the consequences.

1. The first part implies that there is no crime unless a prohibited act has taken place. The definition is not so wide as to include all acts that are dangerous or otherwise antisocial. It is confined to acts clearly prohibited under the sanctions of the criminal law; but prohibition and sanctions do not necessarily imply punishment.

The principle that there should be no punishment without a law allowing the state to punish does not necessarily mean that there is no crime without the sanction of punishment. In modern times punishment is not the only sanction and certainly not the only consequence of a crime. Some modern correctional methods, such as probation, conditional and unconditional discharge, and even medical treatment, are also the consequences of criminal acts and are part of a wide range of modern sanctions.

2. There is a basic difference between the concept of protection of society, including the offender, and the concept of social defence, which excludes

18

the offender from society. Whatever may be the modification aimed at reconciling the concept of social defence with the principle of human rights, the concept of defence implies the existence of an enemy who is to be defeated and, if necessary, annihilated. It is not accidental that Enrico Ferri, who originally developed the concept of social defence, was in favour of capital punishment as the ultimate measure.[8] The concept of protection is, in the present state of knowledge, incompatible with capital punishment.

3. The idea that the offender remains a part of society may be difficult to accept until we face the fact that, given the circumstances, we are all offenders. We usually think that the criminal is somebody else, somebody unlike ourselves and unrelated to us. There are good psychological grounds for this distinction between a law-abiding citizen and a criminal, but there is little logic in it. No one is a full-time criminal or a full-time honest man. Is a 'white-collar criminal' a criminal or a businessman? Is he a danger to society, or are his actions a part of the current practice? Is he simply a robber, or is he a modern Rob Roy who steals money from his competitors, shareholders, suppliers, and workers, but often gives it away to charity? Is a citizen who avoids paying taxes no longer a citizen because he has broken the law? Or is he a citizen if his accountant is clever enough, but the enemy of society if his accountant is stupid? Is the neglected child, abandoned by his parents and in need of correctional treatment, an enemy of society and an aggressor, or is he a victim? Is he merely a victim if his chronological age is fifteen years and eleven months, but a criminal if caught two months later? Of all the consequences of the definition presented, recognition of the offender as a part of society is the most important.

THE OFFENDER AS A PART OF THE SOCIAL SYSTEM

In his paper 'Society, Social Pathology and Mental Ills', Professor John R. Seeley shows vividly and lucidly the extent to which the offender is not only a part of the social system, but possibly a necessary part.[9] When about ninety per cent of offenders come from a small area that year by year yields up its quota of offenders, when one generation of offenders is succeeded by another, and juvenile delinquents turn into hardened criminals with unfailing regularity, the word 'guilty' loses its meaning.

In this context, the guilty and the innocent are just as much a part of

[8]Enrico Ferri, *Criminal Sociology*, Boston: Little, Brown, 1917.
[9]John Seeley, 'Society, Social Pathology and Mental Ills', McCuaig Lecture, Queen's University, Kingston, April 30, 1962.

the system as the winning and losing horses in a race. The Shah of Persia was alleged to have said at Ascot while explaining to King Edward why he preferred to look at the women rather than at the horses: 'In Persia everybody knows that one horse can run faster than another – who cares which one?'

In our present system, many criminals are like the losing horses at Ascot. In a recent investigation of chronic petty offenders, the author found that none of the 109 subjects was able to compete successfully in a technologically advanced society. They were all losing the battle with life, and the reformatory was to them not a punishment but a refuge. They were treated as if they were outside the social system, although in fact they were its inevitable product. As Professor Seeley says in his paper, if twelve virgins are to be sacrificed annually to the dragon, it is more helpful to find out why we have dragons and why they need sacrifice than to devise a selection system which determines the choice of the virgins.

THE TRIAL AS A MORALITY PLAY

Even supposing that the criminal law and the administration of justice are no more than selection devices, there may be some purpose in having such a selection. In his W. M. Martin Lectures at the University of Saskatchewan, Professor J. D. Morton advanced the idea that the trial is a contemporary morality play that is necessary as a conditioning technique.[10] In his view, this technique is directed at the non-criminal member of society rather than at the criminal; it is certainly more effective in supporting the consciences of law-abiding citizens who have little inclination to engage in crime than it is in creating a conscience in the criminal to whom it is directly applied. Unfortunately, seen in this light, the administration of justice presents a play in which a discriminating audience might believe in the plot, but would not believe in the message of justice. This is the more so if we accept the fact that in many cases punishment, or even treatment, especially institutional treatment, does the offender more harm and makes him a less productive member of society than does a lack of any intervention, whether punitive or therapeutic in intention. Is a morality play necessary, and is it effective? Whatever else a criminal trial is, its dramatic aspect cannot be disregarded.

USES AND ABUSES OF PSYCHOPATHOLOGY

Seeley argues that, whatever the consequences for the individual, the

---

[10]J. D. Morton, 'The Crises in Criminal Law', W. M. Martin Lectures, University of Saskatchewan, January 23-5, 1963.

morality play (in his own words, 'the selection of sacrificial virgins') is either a necessary or at least a frequently employed device. As intimated earlier by Durkheim, it is a device that fosters conscience and mental health in most of us, at the expense of those who are treated – or punished – and thereby harmed. Society utilizes the fact that the equilibrium of the whole is dependent on the illness of the parts. The stability of the social system may rest, as Seeley says, on the mutually supporting instabilities (illnesses) of the parts. To some extent, we are all like certain cases of alcoholism in which any reduction of pathology in one spouse increases the mental pathology and alcoholism of the other. In this context not only are the offenders part of the social system but, as Seeley says, the social system needs the psychopathology of us all.

There is no need to go here as far as Seeley and Morton have gone, not because what they say is untrue, but because going as far as they do is not necessary to the present argument. Even if the trial is a play and its participants wear masks, it does not follow that the play is performed for the sake of conditioning. As Santayana says, 'I would not say that substance exists for the sake of appearance or faces for the sake of masks, or the passions for the sake of poetry and virtue. Nothing arises in nature for the sake of anything else. All these phrases and products are equally involved in the round of existence.'[11]

Does this view imply that we should remain impartial observers, an uninvolved audience, looking at the rituals of justice and corrections and not caring about their tragic and inevitable consequences? If one were to advocate this, one might be said to follow the Canadian academic tradition in which, as Professor Harry Johnson suggests, professors are expected to discuss politics with sarcasm but are not allowed to debate policies with sincerity.[12] But we should be positive rather than cynical, and the first step in the right direction would be a limitation of the scope of the criminal law.

HOW TO REDUCE THE SCOPE OF THE CRIMINAL LAW

We must first decide what types of human behaviour are really and truly undesirable, in that they are harmful to individuals or society as a whole, or they endanger the well-being of either.

If we disapprove of behaviour, it does not follow that we must prohibit it. We should never prohibit any behaviour that society as a whole approves of; if we do – and we do at times – our prohibitions do not work.

11George Santayana, *Soliloquies in England*, New York: Scribner, 1922.
12Harry Gordon Johnson, *The Canadian Quandary*, Toronto: McGraw-Hill, 1963.

We have on our books laws so seldom enforced that they merely put other laws in disrepute.

We should examine very carefully the harm brought about by the behaviour we wish to prohibit. If there is no harm, there should be no prohibition. A legal system that would forbid any acts just because the majority of people regard them as distasteful would put an end to our freedoms and to the development of our civilization. In the end there would be only popular art, popular actions, and popular thoughts.

We must examine the effect of our prohibitions on human behaviour. If the aim of a prohibition is to eradicate a type of behaviour or, at least, to limit its extent, we must see that this objective is achieved. Some prohibitions, as any parent knows, only irritate, and add taste to the forbidden fruit. To examine the effects of the prohibitions, and therefore of the criminal law, would not be a simple intellectual exercise; it would require careful empirical research. Under close scrutiny many of our laws may prove redundant; if they are redundant, they not only impose unnecessary restrictions on our freedoms, but also weaken the force of other, necessary laws. It is an accepted principle of education that too many prohibitions weaken discipline.

THE ARSENAL OF SANCTIONS

When we know that a law is necessary and enforceable, we must turn our attention to the arsenal of sanctions. We used to talk purely in terms of penal sanctions. We then discovered treatment and assumed it to be more humane, more modern, and more scientific than punishment. This is a questionable assumption.

Treatment is not more humane than punishment if in fact it imposes more pain, restricts more freedoms for a longer period, and produces no effects that are accepted by the 'patient' as desirable. 'Modern' does not mean new; it means in keeping with progress, and we must always be chary of acclaiming anything as true progress merely because it is new. 'Scientific' does not mean approved by scientists; it can only mean supported by scientific evidence. How many of our treatments have been supported by scientific evidence based on proper experimental design?

Once we have accepted that treatment is not necessarily pleasant and effective, we may be prepared to see that what we call punishment may sometimes be less painful and more effective. The apparent superiority of treatment over punishment is often an illusion. Moreover, the distinction itself is illusory; our sanctions, more often than not, contain both elements, penal and therapeutic.

MEASURES OF EFFECTIVENESS AS A CRITERION

So, instead of thinking of punishment versus treatment, we should think of the arsenal of sanctions and examine their effectiveness. If they are not effective, they merely contribute to unhappiness and expense, and they foster crime instead of limiting its scope. If there are no effective sanctions, there can be no effective prohibitions of the criminal law. Only morality can be effective without any clearly defined and enforceable sanctions.

In his W. M. Martin Lectures, Professor Morton postulates that the concept of crime and the criminal process aim at keeping certain kinds of antisocial behaviour at a tolerable level. He suggests two tests for determining which behaviour should be categorized as criminal:

1. Can society tolerate it? If so, it should not be made criminal unless there is fear that it may soon reach intolerable levels.

2. Will the criminal process assist in controlling it? Is it an apt area for interference by means of this awful process?[13]

The present writer would like to add another test:

3. Would some other process be equally or more efficient (less wasteful or more effective or both)? If so, the criminal process should be avoided.

These three tests are all empirical, that is, dependent only on the results of observation and experiment. They are thus consistent with our concept of the purpose of the criminal law in social rather than in moral terms. If we accept the definition of crime that is central to our discussion, the criminal law provides only a specific machinery of protection, which has to be justified by its efficiency, to serve what is essentially a welfare purpose. In this context, the need for research is as self-evident as the need for a fair trial, and the main task of criminology is to test the efficiency of the legal machinery and correctional practice.

THE MORAL PURPOSE OF THE LAW

We may, however, conceive the purpose of the criminal law as moral rather than social. In this concept, the goal of the administration of justice is the affirmation of philosophically and legally defined principles of behaviour. The goal is achieved through punishment and moral condemnation of the offender, and the causes of criminal behaviour need not, indeed should not, be studied – they lie in the criminal intent, the free choice of evil made by the offender. To study his social background, or his

---

[13]Morton, 'The Crises in Criminal Law', *op. cit.*

psychological make-up, is not only irrelevant but positively dangerous, for if we accept that social or psychological forces may be the basis of criminal behaviour, we undermine the concept of free will and of criminal intent, and we may be accused of undermining the moral fibre of society as well.

The author conceives a broadly defined social purpose as essentially moral, but this conception is opposed to enforcement of public morality unless such enforcement serves directly an individual or social end. It is only when we define the function of the criminal law in moral rather than social terms that criminology ceases to be a science, and the criminologist need not, in fact should not, be a scientist. In this concept criminology and corrections would have to remain apart. Instead of interdisciplinary co-operation we might, at best, have interdisciplinary co-existence. What would be progress for criminology would be regressive and reactionary for corrections.[14]

The Enforcement of Morals

THE ENFORCEMENT OF MORALS INTRODUCED

The idea that the enforcement of morals is the main function of the criminal law is cogently stated in Sir Patrick Devlin's Maccabaean Lecture in Jurisprudence of the British Academy, given in 1959, which has not ceased to be the subject of controversy. Sir Patrick (later Lord Devlin) suggests that a complete separation of crime from sin 'would not be good for the moral law and might be disastrous for the criminal', and that 'the criminal law as we know it is based upon moral principle. In a number of crimes its function is simply to enforce a moral principle and nothing else.' This, in his view, is necessary for the preservation of society:

> What makes a society of any sort is community of ideas, not only political ideas but also about the way its members should behave and govern their lives; these latter ideas are its morals. ... For society is not something that is kept together physically; it is held by invisible bonds of common thought. If the bonds were too far relaxed, the members would drift apart. A common morality is part of the bondage. The bondage is part of the price of society; and mankind, which needs society, must pay its price.

In this context, an offence against public morality is an offence against

---

[14]Compare an excellent exposition of these views and their practical consequences by Edward J. Sachar, 'Behavioral Science and Criminal Law', *Scientific American*, vol. 209 (1963), pp. 38-45, and H. M. Hart, *op. cit.*

society itself, and a rebellion. But 'society cannot tolerate rebellion; it will not allow argument about the rightness of the cause.' Following this argument, Sir Patrick declares that

> if society has no right to make judgments on morals, the law must find some special justification for entering the field of morality: if homosexuality and prostitution are not in themselves wrong, then the onus is very clearly on the lawgiver who wants to frame a law against certain aspects of them to justify the exceptional treatment. But if society has the right to make a judgment and has it on the basis that a recognized morality is as necessary to society as, say, a recognized government, then society may use the law to preserve morality in the same way as it uses it to safeguard anything else that is essential to its existence. If therefore the first proposition is securely established with all its implications, *prima facie* society has the right to legislate against immorality as such.[15]

THE ENFORCEMENT OF MORALS CRITICIZED

There are several flaws in the above argument. First, it is not true that society will not tolerate rebellion. It often does, and in fact the whole of society may be rebellious against an oppressive government, either foreign or even its own; it is only the governments that cannot tolerate rebellion.

Neither is it true that the need of society to preserve morality necessitates the enforcement of morals. On the contrary, it is part of modern morality that it is immoral to enforce morals as such. Some norms of behaviour must be enforced, but the circumstances under which this is practical, desirable, or even moral are exceedingly complex. We may agree with Sir Patrick Devlin that an established morality is as necessary as good government to the welfare of society. Welfare itself is also necessary, but it does not follow that it must be enforced. As Richard Wollheim says, it has been characteristic of the civilized parts of Europe to develop, over the last three centuries, a theory of politics according to which the identity and the continuity of society resides not in the common possession of a single morality, but in the mutual toleration of different moralities.[16]

PUBLIC MORALITY AND INDIVIDUAL FREEDOMS

In the author's view, the democratic doctrine of government is still essen-

15Sir Patrick Devlin (now Lord Devlin), *The Enforcement of Morals*, Maccabaean Lecture in Jurisprudence of the British Academy, London: Oxford University Press, 1959.
16Richard Wollheim, 'Crime, Sin, and Mr. Justice Devlin', *Encounter*, vol. 13, no. 5 (November 1959), pp. 34-40.

tially liberal, and the principle first formulated by John Stuart Mill in his essay 'On Liberty' still applies:

> The only purpose for which power can be rightfully exercised over any member of a civilized community against his will is to prevent harm to others. His own good, either physical or moral, is not a sufficient warrant. He cannot rightfully be compelled to do or forbear . . . because in the opinion of others to do so would be wise or even right.[17]

It must be said that Sir Patrick Devlin does, to some extent, water down his own argument. He does not say that all sin must be punished to preserve public morality and thereby society as a whole; he merely states no limits to the right of society to enforce its morals. But, as Professor H. L. A. Hart says in a review of Mr. Justice Devlin's lecture, we run a grave risk if we allow the common man, the man on the top of the Clapham omnibus, as Sir Patrick calls him, to dictate our moral standards, and tell him that 'if only he feels sick enough about what other people do in private to demand its suppression by law, no theoretical criticism can be made of his demand'.[18]

PUBLIC ORDER AND DECENCY VERSUS PRIVATE MORALITY

The modern counterpart of Mill's principles of liberty, the *Report* of the Committee on Homosexual Offences and Prostitution (generally known as the Wolfenden Committee Report), is also watered down and full of contradictions. The Committee states that the function of the criminal law is

> to preserve public order and decency, to protect the citizen from what is offensive or injurious, and to provide sufficient safeguards against exploitation and corruption of others, particularly those who are especially vulnerable because they are young, weak in body or mind, inexperienced, or in a state of special physical, official or economic dependence. . . . It is not, in our view, the function of the law to intervene in the private lives of citizens, or to seek to enforce any particular pattern of behaviour, further than is necessary to carry out the purposes we have outlined.[19]

If the enforcement of morals is not the function of the criminal law, how is the citizen going to be protected from immorality? How can he be sure that he or his children will not become contaminated? Perhaps the

[17]John Stuart Mill, *On Liberty*, London: Oxford University Press, 1963.
[18]H. L. A. Hart, *The Listener*, July 30, 1959.
[19]United Kingdom (Home Office and Scottish Home Department), *Report* of the Committee on Homosexual Offences and Prostitution (Wolfenden Committee Report), London: H.M.S.O., 1957.

Wolfenden Committee's aim 'to preserve public order and decency' is not very far from the enforcement of morals.

THE NATURE OF MORALS

In his Maccabaean Lecture, Mr. Justice Devlin is not content to state a case for the enforcement of morals; he also discusses the nature of morals. He postulates that no moral code 'can claim any validity except by virtue of the religion on which it is based', and argues further that a 'state which refuses to enforce Christian beliefs has lost the right to enforce Christian morals'.[20] In other words Christian beliefs must be enforced too.

Any theory of morality is, of necessity, a theory of mind, and here Sir Patrick's theory falls down. No presumption is valid if there is clear evidence to the contrary, and all psychological evidence is contrary to Sir Patrick's hypothesis.

Whether one accepts Freud's theory and the clinical evidence of his followers, or Pavlovian and behaviouristic theory and the experimental evidence on conditioning, or Piaget's concepts and his observations on morality and law as expressions of the rules of the game, all the data painstakingly collected in this century speak against the idea that morality has its origin in religion. Sociological and anthropological evidence point in the same direction. A link there is, since many moral commands are implicitly a part of religious dogma; but it is impossible to say which moral principles have come into public morality from religion, and which – especially in primitive societies – have acquired religious sanctions because legal sanctions were found to be insufficient. The relationship between religious and moral beliefs is not that of cause and effect but of mutual reflection and reinforcement.

If Sir Patrick were wrong only about the origin of public morality, it would not necessarily affect his further reasoning. Unfortunately, his assumption about the basis of morality implies that he would like to enforce religious morality, and this is clearly impossible unless we have only one religion. Of course, Sir Patrick may think that there is only one true religion, but this is a thought foreign to modern legal thinking and to the function of law in present society. Sir Patrick does not say that one or any religion should be enforced by law; he is able, like many of us, to keep his logic on a short leash. But if one wants to follow a piece of jurisprudence that appears to be based on logical argument, it is sometimes useful, as we discovered in the opening section of this chapter, to release the leash and see where the logic will run. Sir Patrick's logic would run not forward but

[20]Devlin, *op. cit.*

backward, into the primitive societies of the shamans and the religious persecutions of the Dark Ages.

PUBLIC MORALITY AND PUBLIC OPINION

Just as it is sometimes difficult to distinguish between private and public morality, it is often equally difficult to find more than a shade of difference between public morality and public opinion. In some countries, in which relatively authoritarian attitudes predominate, the laws tend to create public opinion. Thus Hermann Mannheim quotes a famous German lawyer and penologist of more than a century ago, C. J. A. Mittermaier, who said that public opinion in Germany 'regards infamy not as a consequence of crime but as the result of certain penalties'.[21] Erich Fromm, in his discussion of the origin of ethics, with particular reference to Nazi Germany,[22] gives full support to Mittermaier and analyses the psychodynamics involved. To some extent laws always foster or create public opinion,[23] and yet they are themselves the product of such opinion. As with religious and moral beliefs, the relationship between law and public opinion is not that of simple cause and effect; it is a relationship of mutual reflection and reinforcement. We make laws in order to preserve values of our society,[24] but by making a law we also affect the value system; what is prohibited is felt as more immoral just because it is linked with the threat of public exposure and sanctions.

SOCIAL CONSEQUENCES OF ILLEGAL ACTS

The fact that acts are disapproved by society or forbidden by law has

[21]Hermann Mannheim, 'Criminal Law and Penology', in *Law and Public Opinion in England in the 20th Century,* ed. by Morris Ginsberg, London: Stevens, 1959. The same point is made in an excellent Norwegian play, Helga Krog's *Break-up,* reminiscent of Ibsen's *John Gabriel Borkman.* The case stated by Karl, a fraudulent lawyer, is somewhat different from Borkman's self-defence (or Raskolnikov's in Dostoyevsky's *Crime and Punishment*). In Karl's case the justification comes not from a special mission or ability of the hero, but from the breakdown of the moral system itself: 'The prevalent moral standard is the system of do's and don'ts that best insures the retention of the *status quo* for those who benefit by it. They are the ones who make the law and the law determines the moral standard. . . . An act is not punishable because it is immoral, it is immoral because it is punishable.'

[22]Erich Fromm, *The Fear of Freedom,* London: Routledge and Kegan Paul, 1942; 'Hitler and the Nazi Authoritarian Character Structure', in *Readings in Social Psychology,* ed. by T. M. Newcomb and E. L. Hartley, New York: Holt, 1947; *Man for Himself: An Enquiry into the Psychology of Ethics,* London: Routledge and Kegan Paul, 1948.

[23]Mannheim, *op. cit.,* p. 267.

[24]Hermann Mannheim, 'Penalties To Fit the Crime', *The Times,* London, November 27, 1957.

some consequences not only in terms of sanctions. The knowledge that the act is disapproved changes the quality of the act itself in the mind of the doer. Homosexuality is permitted in some societies. It was permitted and even approved in ancient Greece; for that reason it was an innocent act. But the very fact that it is disapproved and regarded as immoral in Western society means that it is no longer innocent. The fact of disapproval must produce internal (mental) conflict and to some extent a conflict between the homosexual and society, whether any formal sanctions are applied or not.

This ability of the law to foster or create public opinion and the value system of the society makes it imperative that any existing and any proposed legislation should be subject not only to legal scrutiny, but also to the scientific analysis of the social scientists, who are more competent than the lawyers to assess the social consequences of legislation and court practice. This does not imply that social scientists should sit in judgment over lawyers; the only sensible solution is an interdisciplinary framework in which both can profitably work together.

LAW AS IT IS AND LAW AS IT OUGHT TO BE

The necessity to develop an over-all strategy, including legislation, brings us to another distinction – that between law as it is and law as it ought to be. As Austin says: 'The existence of law is one thing; its merit or demerit is another. Whether it be or be not is one enquiry; whether it be or be not conformable to an assumed standard, is a different enquiry. A law, which actually exists, is a law....'[25]

Distinguishing between law as it is and law as it ought to be, admirable in theory, frequently breaks down in practice. The law may be incomplete, unclear, or internally inconsistent; when the judges have to apply it to a particular case, careful reading and logical analysis may be misleading. The judges may decide that they do not know what the law is in this case; they may therefore decide what the law ought to be, and by their decision make a new law.

This problem is most lucidly discussed in a dispute between Professors H. L. A. Hart of Oxford[26] and Lon Fuller of Harvard.[27] Unfortunately, Professor Hart confuses (and Professor Fuller fails to separate) two separate issues: one is indicated by the title of his paper, which is on 'the

25 Austin, *op. cit.*, p. 184.
26 H. L. A. Hart, 'Positivism and the Separation of Law and Morals', *op. cit.*
27 Lon L. Fuller, 'Positivism and Fidelity to Law: a Reply to Professor Hart', *Harvard Law Review*, vol. 71 (1958), pp. 630-72.

separation of law and morals', and the other, with which he deals mainly in the text, is the distinction between law as it is and law as it ought to be. The confusion is probably due to semantics – the word 'ought' implies moral judgment. But if I think I ought to join issue with Professor Hart, am I really compelled by moral considerations? The law as it ought to be implies not necessarily higher moral values, but such pedestrian considerations as effectiveness, simplicity, certainty, and even low cost of administration. The concept of desirable law does *not* imply the desirability of enforcing morals. It may imply the desirability of enforcing psychiatry or social work. By introducing law as it ought to be into law as it is, the judges do not necessarily introduce morals; similarly, postulating the desirability of the distinction, the need for law reform, or the requirements of science, expresses an intellectual rather than a moral judgment.

SEPARATION OF LAW AND MORALS

The distinction between law as it is and law as it ought to be is desirable, though often difficult in practice to maintain; *separation* of the two is both undesirable and impracticable. Distinction is necessary because it is impossible to improve on the existing legislation without knowing that it is not what it ought to be; separation is harmful because no law should be formulated or enforced in complete disregard of what is desirable. The distinction between law and morals presents relatively little difficulty, but separation of the two is always difficult. Nevertheless, it may be necessary to separate them, especially in heterogeneous countries such as Canada, in which different religions and different cultural and moral standards have to exist side by side if the existing social and political structure is to be maintained. The principle of enforcement of morals immediately poses the question: which morals? In Sir Patrick Devlin's exposition it ultimately leads to enforcement of religion; thus it is logically untenable in countries with many religions, including England.[28] Any attempt to use the law as the arm of morals not only leads to confusion, but in the final analysis undermines both the legal and the moral system. This would be particularly so in Canada, where the main moral principle appears to be not a fear of God or a melting of cultures into a uniform Canadian way of life, but tolerance for many gods and a variety of cultures and standards of behaviour.

Living for a short time in Nazi-occupied Poland and, later, deported by the Russians to remote regions of the U.S.S.R., the author faced a practical test of a conflict between law and morals. On more than one occasion,

[28]English courts, in defiance of logic, do enforce morals, as Sir Patrick is well aware.

when faced with conflict between the demands of his private morality and the demands of the law, he deliberately chose to disregard the law. It did not follow that he regarded Nazi law or Soviet law as non-law, just because it was in conflict with his conscience.

The Enforcement of Welfare

THE LIMITS OF RETRIBUTION AND
THE ENFORCEMENT OF WELFARE

Juvenile delinquency legislation is particularly prone to enforce morality regardless of the social consequences of such enforcement; but it differs from ordinary criminal legislation in that it confuses the enforcement of morals with the enforcement of welfare. For instance, the first step taken by Canada towards the present juvenile delinquency legislation was the Children's Protection Act, passed by the Ontario legislature in 1893. Similarly, the Swedish Child Welfare and Youth Protection Act, 1924, applies sanctions that are penal in their effect on children who, 'because of their parents' immorality, carelessness, or inability to bring them up properly, are in danger of becoming delinquent'.[29] The present Juvenile Delinquents Act of Canada defines as a delinquent any child who violates any provision of the Criminal Code, or any federal or provincial statute, or any by-law or ordinance of any municipality; a child 'who is guilty of sexual immorality or any similar form of vice' (a condition that, according to Freud, would include all normal children); and a child 'liable by reason of any other act to be committed to an industrial school or juvenile reformatory under the provisions of any Dominion or Provincial statute' (and that includes a great many children, even those *accused* of petty crime).[30]

CANADIAN JUVENILE DELINQUENCY LEGISLATION CRITICIZED

This situation was criticized in a number of 'briefs' to the Committee on

29Ola Nyquist, *Juvenile Justice: A Comparative Study with Special Reference to the Swedish Child Welfare Board and the California Juvenile Court System*, London: Macmillan, 1960.
30Section 7.1(f) of the Ontario Training Schools Act, 1960. A completely new Act, formulated by a committee of which the author was a member, was introduced by the Ontario government and approved by the legislature after this chapter had been written; the new Act is consistent with the principles of jurisprudence as outlined in this chapter. On the concept of 'the state of delinquency' and its practical consequences, see Tadeusz Grygier, 'The Concept of the "State of Delinquency" and its Legal and Social Consequences', *Wayne Law Review*, vol. 11, no. 3 (1965); and 'The Concept of Social Progression', in *Criminology in Transition*, ed. by T. Grygier, H. Jones and J. Spencer, London: Tavistock Publications, 1965.

Juvenile Delinquency, appointed by the Minister of Justice of Canada on January 18, 1962. One of them, submitted by the Canadian Corrections Association, says:

> We believe no child should be categorized as 'delinquent' in general terms. Also, we believe that the power the court may exercise over the convicted child should bear some relationship to his offence, so that a child who has committed only an infraction of a municipal by-law cannot be taken from his parents or sent to a training-school.
>
> To bring this about, instead of being charged with a delinquency, the child should be charged with the specific offence against the applicable federal, provincial or municipal legislation. The court should have the same authority over the child convicted of a relatively serious offence as it now has over a child judged delinquent. However, there should be some limitation on the authority of the court over the child who has committed the by-law kind of offence. If the minor infraction is committed by a child who is thought to be in need of further care, proceedings should be instituted under the provincial child protection legislation.

THE LIMITS OF RETRIBUTION AND
THE ENFORCEMENT OF WELFARE

The above proposal may sound, to some sensitive ears, as retrograde and reactionary; in the author's opinion it is not. The proposal, admittedly, implies the concept of retribution; but retribution does not necessarily mean revenge, and its adoption in the law does not mean that every criminal act committed by a child must involve retributive sanctions.

The function of the criminal law is not to declare what suffering *must* be inflicted upon the offender in *all* circumstances, but merely to prescribe what state interference *can* occur in *some* circumstances. Some offenders inevitably will escape detection, others – with the help of our law of evidence – will escape conviction; some state intervention may be unprofitable, even if permissible; other sanctions would not be fair. The law can only set the limits beyond which the courts must not go.

Thus, although sharing the views of the Canadian Corrections Association, and favouring the theory of retribution, I do not mean – nor, surely, does it mean – that punishment *must* be inflicted in proportion to the gravity of the offence. I mean only that the intervention of the state, which is not wanted by the offender and is therefore regarded by him as punishment, should not be out of proportion to the gravity of his offence. This general principle applies also to juvenile justice. If three years' imprisonment is too harsh a sentence for the adult crime of stealing an apple, let us not 'adjudicate' by sending the child who has committed the same crime to an institution for a similar period of time, whether or not this is 'treatment and not punishment', and whether or not he can be released earlier as 'cured'. 'Cure' often means that a bed is needed for the next patient, just as 'parole' may mean that the prison is over-crowded.

THE USES AND LIMITS OF DETERRENCE

The author also favours deterrence, but not in the sense that we inflict punishment solely to deter others. Punishment not for the offence but as a warning to others is equivalent to punishment for no offence at all. The unpleasant consequences of the offence may have a deterrent effect on the offender and on others; but it would be against one's sense of justice to inflict more harm – whatever the express intention of the sentence – than is justified by the gravity of the offence. Most of all, punishment out of proportion to the gravity of the offence creates a sense of injustice in the very minds we wish to reform; it therefore defeats its own purpose and fails to protect society as well as the offender.

We already suffer from too many laws and too much judging, too much punishment and too much treatment – in fact, too much state interference and too little evidence that its declared objectives are achieved. We are prone to exclaim in indignation 'This cannot be permitted!', without trying to ascertain whether the evil we see will in fact be curtailed by prohibition, or whether perhaps it will be enhanced by penal sanctions and accompanied by more evils such as are inherent in any oppressive measure.[31]

JUVENILE JUSTICE ABROAD

The situation abroad is no better than in Canada. In a paper published in 1962, we are told that in the United States 'juvenile justice should be a mixture of adequate legal disposition and advanced social welfare practice',[32] yet the very same paper criticizes many aspects of the inquisitorial procedure in the juvenile courts and the fact that 'hearsay evidence is not only admitted in court but rigorously sought after'. We are told, of course, that 'the juvenile court is not a criminal court; a hearing is held, not a trial, delinquents are adjudicated, not convicted. It is not the State versus

---

[31]For empirical evidence on social and psychological consequences of deterrent and other oppressive measures, see Tadeusz Grygier, *Oppression: A Study in Social and Criminal Psychology*, London: Routledge and Kegan Paul, 1954.

[32]Lewis Yablonsky, 'The Role of Law and Social Science in the Juvenile Court', *Journal of Criminal Law, Criminology and Police Science*, vol. 53 (1962), pp. 426-36.

John Doe, but the State *in the interest* of Johnny Doe that dominates juvenile hearings'.[33] At other times it is pointed out that the juvenile court has its origin in Chancery as well as in criminal law, and that the state or its agent, the court, is the ultimate parent of the delinquent child;[34] but the Chancery procedure appears to prevail and, in the words of Professor Tappan, it provides the power to incarcerate children without any visible manifestations of due process.[35] In this way children 'become adult criminals, too, in thankless disregard of the state's good intentions as *parens patriae*'.[36] The situation in Europe, which I have recently had an opportunity to survey, is essentially similar; in the Soviet Union it is worse.[37] Moreover, most 'welfare' systems concerned with juvenile justice define dependent, neglected, and delinquent children in very vague terms, full of moral overtones. The original set of definitions that distinguished delinquency from crime, and affected subsequent legislation throughout North America, was formulated by the state of Illinois in 1899 in such terms that the Act appears to be a harangue rather than a piece of legislation. It refers to 'houses of ill-fame' and to 'vicious and disreputable persons'; mixes neglect with depravity and with association with 'thieves, vicious or immoral persons'; lists jumping 'onto any moving train', 'indecent or lascivious conduct'; and so on.

MORAL EXHORTATION AND HYPOCRISY
AS THE BACKBONE OF OUR JUVENILE LAWS

The value of moral exhortation of children is open to question. There is no doubt about its frequency in courts, churches, schools, and households; but its psychological consequences are assumed rather than measured.

Theoretical considerations would be against using this method in court, even if we assumed that what is communicated by the judge is clearly and objectively understood by the child – a questionable assumption, not shared by those who combine professional qualifications in social work

---

[33]Donald J. Newman, 'Legal Aspects of Juvenile Delinquency', in *Juvenile Delinquency*, ed. by Joseph S. Roucek, New York: Philosophical Library, 1958, p. 35.

[34]Harry Elmer Barnes and Negley K. Teeters, *New Horizons in Criminology*, New York: Prentice-Hall, 1943, pp. 922-30. Juvenile Court of Cook County, Illinois, *Fiftieth Annual Report*, Chicago: Inland Press, 1950, pp. 13-16. Herbert H. Lou, *Juvenile Courts in the United States*, Chapel Hill: University of North Carolina Press, 1927, pp. 2-5.

[35]Paul W. Tappan, *Juvenile Delinquency*, New York: McGraw-Hill, 1949, p. 205.

[36]*Ibid.*

[37]Tadeusz Grygier, 'The Concept of the "State of Delinquency" and its Legal and Social Consequences', *op. cit.*

with experience on the bench.[38] If we accept one of the most popular psychological theories of the origins of moral behaviour, that of conditioning, exhortation should have little effect; according to this theory, consequences in terms of reward or punishment are the main factor in shaping attitudes and behaviour, including moral attitude and behaviour. If we accept the psychoanalytical school of thought, the method fares even worse; by exhortation we increase the distance between the person who reprimands and the one who has to listen, and therefore we make what is called 'identification' more difficult. According to the psychoanalysts, the best way to become a moral person is to acquire a feeling of oneness with a model of behaviour, a person who is close to us, whom we can love and admire, and to incorporate his values as our values. An exaggerated repudiation by the possible idol reduces the chances of identification with him and of incorporation of his values. When we indulge in exhortation we may think that we show the culprit how to behave; in fact, we merely show how unworthy he is and we pretend that we are superior. We do not raise the moral standards of the listener; we merely indulge in moral smugness, in exhibitionistic pronouncement of our own moral superiority.

The hypocrisy of our law and of our system of administering justice to our children can hardly go further. We use terms so vague that any child whose behaviour we dislike can easily be branded as a juvenile delinquent, but we are careful not to use the word 'crime' even with respect to most serious antisocial acts. We use a language full of moral indignation and utter condemnation, and then pretend that we never convict children – we merely 'adjudicate'. We take decisions that separate children from their parents and submit them to a variety of measures that, because of their unpleasant character and clear connection with the offence committed, can only be viewed by the children as punishment for their crimes. Then we call their punishment 'welfare', and add – not without justification, but often without evidence – that we act in the interest of the children.

THE EFFECT OF DOUBLE MORALITY ON CHILDREN

Children are most unwilling to take us at our word. In 1961, the author had excellent evidence of their mistrust in a study in Ontario Training Schools, conducted by the University of Toronto School of Social Work.

---

[38] W. E. Cavenagh, *The Child and the Court*, London: Victor Gollancz, 1959. Eileen Younghusband, 'The Juvenile Court and the Child', *British Journal of Delinquency*, vol. 7 (1957), pp. 181-95.

The children were told that the aim of the study was to understand their problems better and so improve services in accordance with their emotional needs. But, despite their co-operation in taking personality[39] and sociometric tests that asked them very personal questions, they did not accept the object of the study as valid. To them psychological understanding and social services in the school were of but minor importance. As far as they were concerned, the main problem was neither diagnosis nor treatment, but the reason they were sent to a training-school at all. According to them, nobody had told them clearly of what they were accused. They did not know what the conviction meant, but they knew they were 'convicted'; and they had never heard the word 'adjudicated' or 'adjudged', used by the legislators and probably quoted by the judge. They felt they had an 'indefinite sentence for nothing', and 'indefinite is worse than life'. They did not resent the treatment they received at the school; they resented the fact that their judicial disposition did not represent justice. It is difficult to treat and rehabilitate when this feeling of resentment is so strong, and one's own position, both legally and morally, so weak.

We have been deceiving ourselves in claiming that our legislation and our judicial decisions are moral. It is true that they are usually based on good intentions and that they are in accordance with values. This, in the light of our modern, scientific approach, is insufficient. Moral action is not simply action in accordance with values; it must mean action in accordance with the *probability* of achieving values. In that sense, action based on good intentions alone is not only irrational; it is also immoral. Our present juvenile justice is full of good intentions, but it commands little respect from those who are subjected to it and who, despite their youth and limited education, are able to gain insight into its moral and legal weakness.

Any treatment, however well planned, starts with a handicap if the 'patient' regards it as punishment. If treatment is an unpleasant consequence of a crime, it is seen as punishment for the crime; and if it does not fit the crime and does not follow any clearly defined rules of law, it is likely to be seen as unjust.

THE DANGERS OF PREDICTION AND INDIVIDUAL PREVENTION

Prevention directed at individuals who are likely to commit crimes, especially when it is based on inaccurate predictions, is even more dangerous than treatment of crime without proper legal safeguards. The

[39]Tadeusz Grygier, *The Likes and Interests Test*, London: National Foundation for Educational Research, 1960.

inability of experts, acting on their professional judgment, to predict human behaviour with any degree of precision is well known and admitted.[40] Statistical prediction does not fare much better, although – according to *statistical* evidence – it is more valid than subjective judgment.[41] Owing to a fault in methodology, the best known prediction tables, by Sheldon and Eleanor Glueck,[42] would have led, if taken seriously, to over ninety per cent wrong decisions.[43] By contrast, a bland assumption that a child who has not been found guilty of an offence will never become a juvenile delinquent (defined, as by the Gluecks, in terms of having been submitted to institutional corrective treatment) would lead to ninety-six to ninety-eight per cent correct decisions. Of course, by taking preventive action we can save some children, but many children who might otherwise have saved themselves may conform to our worst expectations.[44]

To say this is not to be against prevention, nor indeed against prediction. On the contrary, one can accept these facts and yet see the scientific control of criminal behaviour as the main theoretical and practical problem before us.[45] Such control must entail the ability to foresee the consequences of our actions; and this, in turn, requires not only vision, but also prediction methodology, careful experimentation, and statistical analysis. One may hope that scientific and humane control can, better than any other, reconcile the offender with society, of which he is a part. After all, without prediction no rational decisions can be made.

[40]Marcel Frym, 'What Psychiatry Can Do for Criminology', *Bulletin of the Menninger Clinic,* vol. 25 (1961), pp. 196-205.

[41]P. E. Meehl, *Clinical* vs. *Statistical Prediction,* Minneapolis: University of Minnesota Press, 1954.

[42]Sheldon and Eleanor Glueck, *Unraveling Juvenile Delinquency,* New York: The Commonwealth Fund, 1950; and *Predicting Delinquency and Crime,* Cambridge, Mass.: Harvard University Press, 1959.

[43]D. H. Stott, 'The Prediction of Delinquency from Non-Delinquent Behaviour', *British Journal of Delinquency,* vol. 10 (1960), pp. 195-210. A. A. Walters, 'Research Note; A Note on Statistical Methods of Predicting Delinquency', *British Journal of Delinquency,* vol. 6 (1956), pp. 297-302.

[44]The same view was expressed in a statement made by the Council of the Society for the Psychological Study of Social Issues, referring to the prediction study carried out by New York City Youth Board. See Council Statement dated January 31, 1960, on the New York City Youth Board's Report, 'An Experiment in Predicting Juvenile Delinquency', *SPSSI Newsletter,* April 1960.

[45]Tadeusz Grygier, 'Staff Development and Education in Criminology and Corrections', *Criminal Law Quarterly,* vol. 5 (1962), pp. 220-47; and 'The Teaching of Criminology as Part of the Curriculum of a Department of Psychology', *The Canadian Psychologist,* vol. 5a (1964), pp. 35-40.

Law and Welfare in the Modern State

We have now made a complete circle and returned to the first paragraphs of this chapter. On the way, we found intricate problems where truths appeared self-evident, and we found conflicts where harmony of law and society might easily be taken for granted. We are now ready to summarize the argument and to strive for a balanced outlook that will allow crime and society to co-exist. We also need co-existence between law and morality, and between law and science.

The essential element of the legal concept of crime is that nothing is a crime that is not legally defined, nothing is a crime that is not pronounced as such by the legal authorities as a result of the proper judicial process, and that the consequences of a crime are also legal whether we apply sanctions of punishment or facilities of compulsory treatment. But to some extent, the theory of law is also the theory of government and the theory of the state; and the purpose of government and the purpose of the state coincide with the purpose of law. This applies to the civil law as to the criminal law: it was the civil Roman code that defined the purpose of the law as 'to render to each man his own'. The problem is, as Plato knew so well, what is 'his own'. As Harold Laski used to say in his lectures at the London School of Economics, this depends on the kind of society we live in, whether it is liberal, socialist, feudal, slave, or other. Contemporary society is becoming increasingly a welfare society.

We need criminal sanctions even in a welfare state. The cardinal principle of welfare is protection of the individual and of society as a whole, and in some cases sanctions are necessary to ensure that protection; in most cases, however, it can be ensured without them. A study of the social and emotional needs of chronic petty offenders conducted by the author shows the application of the concept of protection to a particular problem.[46] Such offenders are, to a large extent, victims of technological progress and of our neglect of the human aspect of a changing civilization. Instead of punishing them we should try to integrate them in society. For electronic computers, we plan programs consisting of long series of simple tasks, each within the capacity of the computer. We must now start programming equally simple tasks for simple, uneducated people. The simpler each task, however, the more complex is the planning of the whole. This solution is outside the framework of the criminal law and is not consistent with the traditional aims of the administration of justice, but it is consistent with the concept of society that includes the offender.

[46]Tadeusz Grygier, 'The Chronic Petty Offender: Law Enforcement of Welfare Problem', *Journal of Research in Crime and Delinquency*, vol. 1 (1964), pp. 155-70.

CRIMINALS EXPLOITED — FOR PEACE AND MORALITY

At times we fail to protect the offenders. On the contrary, we exploit them. We exploit them in prison labour, which sacrifices constructive work and rehabilitation for the sake of peace on the labour front. Instead of productive work, which of course would compete with trade-union labour in the open market, and for which prisoners could be paid proper wages, we impose on them endless cleaning and maintenance tasks for which there is no pay.

We exploit them for the sake of deterrence, since without criminals we cannot safely test the limits of our freedoms. To a large extent, we need the concept of crime and the criminal law because we need limits to permissible behaviour. When we have limits, our freedom is restricted. Without limits our freedoms would be illusory and life impossible. We need criminals because we cannot appreciate the limits without forever testing them and getting hurt, directly or by proxy. The criminals do the testing for us and allow us to learn our lessons at their expense.

At times we may feel justified by thinking that the good of society overrides the principle of protection of the individual. We sacrifice one offender to deter the others, and at least we try to do him as little harm as possible. At times, together with deterrence, we apply rehabilitation and welfare; we cannot advance this as an argument, however, except in religious terms (to save the offender's soul) when we hang him by the neck.

DETERRENT LAWS AND THE REIGN OF TERROR

Capital punishment does, no doubt, produce fear. But fear does not always have a restraining effect; do we not sometimes hit, verbally or even physically, those whom we fear? The principle of capital punishment is one of deterrence — the actual restricting effect of terror. But terror and deterrence are different things. Terror breeds rebellion and violence, as well as restraint on the part of the individual, and the deterrent effect of capital punishment is merely alleged and not proven. In the scientific sense it is actually disproved, since the evidence for it has been examined by numerous investigators and found lacking. If we merely say in the circumstances that the evidence is inconclusive and that the case is open, we ought to accept with the same logic that no hypothesis for which insufficient evidence is offered is ever to be rejected, and therefore that no defendants are to be acquitted. In science, as in court, we must arrive at decisions in accordance with the principle of the onus of proof.

Thus we invoke alleged deterrence to uphold the law, and merely

Tadeusz Grygier

create terror, which itself is a negation of law and of the democratic form of government. And we often behave like a man in a general brawl who is not satisfied with incapacitating the man who has just hit him; he must kill the aggressor to feel safe, and so does not think of the total effect of his action. But the other participants are apt to react violently. More often than not he could save his skin if he were less ruthless himself.

HUMANITARIAN LAWS AND THE PRINCIPLES OF WELFARE REUNITED

Could we be safer if we were less ruthless? This is a general question, not limited to capital punishment. Correctional practice is certainly changing in this direction. It is changing in its form, which is becoming less cruel, and in its purpose, which is a welfare rather than a punitive purpose. And, perhaps, if we try to see criminals as victims of natural social processes, and the concept of crime and punishment as the means to ensure the efficiency of our own self-control, it may be easier for us to accept the later chapters of this book and the humanitarian principles of correctional treatment.

In our discussion, we have abandoned a number of traditional concepts of crime and corrections as inadequate, incompatible with each other, and out of place in a modern society. Instead of the multiplicity of aims of the criminal law, with another set of aims for corrections, we have developed an overriding concept which embraces law, corrections, criminology, the administration of justice, and all the functions of the modern state. That concept is the protection of society, including the offender.

Seen in this light, the criminal law and corrections are not in conflict. The traditional aims of the criminal law change their character and become the means necessary to attain a purpose of a higher order. If they are no longer the aims but the means, we have a clear criterion by which we can judge them: the criterion of utility (as Austin or Bentham would say) or efficiency (as present-day researchers and administrators would prefer to call it). This criterion will tell us, *provided we develop and use empirical tests,* which laws we need and which correctional methods we should choose in each case. When in doubt, we are better off without the compulsion of the law.

3

Sources of
Illegal Behaviour

DOUGLAS PENFOLD

The title of this chapter might better have been 'Theories of Causation' or something similar. To cover the subject 'Sources of Illegal Behaviour' in anything like an adequate manner would require a good deal more space. The material of the chapter, therefore, will be confined to an overview of some factors and major theories of causation. Further, there will be no attempt to relate Canadian criminal statistics to these factors and theories, nor will there be a review of any attempts at theory development in Canada. There is no reason to suppose that criminal behaviour in Canada is essentially any different from criminal behaviour in the rest of the Western world; and within the knowledge of this author, no theory developed in Canada has yet gained international acceptance. Those interested in more comprehensive treatment of the subject are referred to the bibliography at the end of the chapter.

HEREDITY AND ENVIRONMENT

All behaviour is a function of the interaction of heredity and environment. The question of which is the more important in determining certain kinds of behaviour used to be a popular subject for debating clubs, and it was often contended that one or the other was all-important. Such assertions, of course, are nonsense. One cannot have any effect without the other. Any organism is a product of both. The organism grows within an environment and within the limits set by the characteristics it receives from its ancestors. A bird's ability to fly is differentiated from a cat's lack of ability to fly by hereditary characteristics. A bird cannot

41

fly unless the proper environment has been present so that the inherited organs for flying could properly develop. A cat cannot fly no matter what type of livable environment it happens to inhabit. It simply has not inherited the necessary organs for flying. The best we can say, therefore, is that heredity sets the limits within which an organism *can* develop. Environment determines to what extent, *within the limits set by heredity,* the organism *will* develop.

PHYSIOLOGICAL FACTORS AND THEORIES OF CRIME

Heredity theories of causation state, in effect, that illegal behaviour is determined largely by a heredity that at the very least predisposes an individual toward it. While some of these theories do state that environmental factors affecting an individual may have some effect on illegal behaviour, they hold that the predominating influences are genetic or hereditary factors.

By and large, the contribution of constitutional, biological, and hereditary factors in determining illegal behaviour has been ignored by the majority of modern criminological theorists. This tendency is unfortunate in view of recent advances in brain physiology and its relationships to behaviour. While nothing conclusive about neuro-physiological correlates of illegal behaviour can be learned from any of the more recent studies of brain function and behaviour, enough progress has been made to suggest that recent attempts in criminology to ignore hereditary and biological determinants of illegal behaviour may be premature, to say the least. The tendency to over-emphasize the environmental theories has gained ground. This has occurred in spite of warnings by certain personality and behavioural theorists. In 1949, Hebb stated, in part, 'we do *not* know that juvenile delinquency, associated with broken homes, is due to the home environment and not just as much to the *inheritance* of the same emotional instability that broke up the home' (italics mine).[1] In 1950, Cattell stated that one has to account for the fact that 'heredity is somehow a very important determiner' of criminality.[2] However, the present-day emphasis on the correction and rehabilitation of offenders probably has had a great deal to do with the growing acceptance of more positive psycho-sociological theories. If the causes are psycho-sociological rather than hereditary or biological, then the possibility of correcting illegal behaviour more readily obtains. Even scientists are sometimes deficient in objectivity, and a theory may be rejected, not for its possible

[1]D. O. Hebb, *The Organization of Behavior*, New York: John Wiley, 1949, p. 265.
[2]R. B. Cattell, *Personality*, New York: McGraw-Hill, 1950, p. 130.

faults, but because it conflicts either with established practice or with whatever the rejector would like practice to be.

The more satisfactory method of determining the relative effects of heredity and environment involves keeping one constant and varying the other. It is impossible, however, to hold environmental factors constant. No two people have experienced the same environmental stimuli from the moment of conception. At any moment, therefore, even if it were possible to expose two people to identical environmental stimuli, they would respond differently – their responses depending on previous environment and possibly different heredity.

Investigators have sometimes contended erroneously that environments can be similar. We do not know that they are similar in any particular set of circumstances. Even what appear to be minute variations in environmental stimulation may be critical in their differential effects on organisms. It seems reasonable to suppose that much of the variance in experiments in which environmental factors have allegedly been held constant was due to a large number of such minute variations in stimulation. In the view of this writer, therefore, we can never fully rely on results obtained by allegedly holding certain environmental factors constant. The best that can be said of such results is that they are suggestive or not suggestive – depending on the direction of the results. The only alternative, then, is to try to hold heredity constant.

There is one situation where this is possible. Since monozygotic or 'identical' twins are identical genetically, the assumption of the same hereditary predispositions is valid, and it remains only to find identical twins who have engaged in illegal behaviour. Here, some problems arise. We cannot be certain that twins who happen to look alike are also identical in heredity; they may not have developed from the same ovum. Further, although we can be certain that environments are not precisely the same, they may be sufficiently alike to contain major contributing factors to illegal behaviour. Some investigators claim that identical twins are more likely to receive similar kinds of environmental stimulation than, say, fraternal twins or other siblings within the same household. Yet, despite the uncontrolled variables involved, results of studies in this area are certainly worthy of close examination.

Montagu reviewed and summarized some studies in this area.[3] Totalling the numbers in each of four categories, he found that, with identical twins, 67 per cent were concordant, that is, they were similar 'with

[3]Ashley Montagu, 'The Biologist Looks at Crime', *Annals of the American Academy of Political and Social Science,* September, 1941.

respect to the commission of one or more crimes', whereas 33 per cent were discordant, that is, they had dissimilar careers. With fraternal twins, the opposite ratio obtained: 33 per cent were concordant and 67 per cent were discordant. These are rather impressive differences, but the criticisms mentioned in the preceding paragraph apply.

Among the early 'biological' theorists, one who had considerable impact on criminological thinking was Lombroso (1835-1909), an Italian physician. Lombroso spent years in analysing data obtained from studies of Italian prisoners. These data involved anthropological and physical measurements of many kinds. Lombroso concluded that some people are 'born criminals', that they possess certain physical and mental characteristics in common with the savage. He did not discard the role of environmental forces entirely. He felt that within the very tight limits set by biological forces, environment has some effect. He believed that the 'born criminal' could be differentiated from the non-criminal by various anatomical measurements, particularly those of the skull. 'Such for example, are: the slight development of the pilar system; low cranial capacity; retreating forehead; highly developed frontal sinuses . . .; greater pigmentation of the skin; tufted and crispy hair; and large ears.'[4] Further, he felt that the organic factor in crime amounts 'to 35 per cent or even 40 per cent'. Studying what he calls the 'causes of crime', or the non-organic factors, convinced him that these could only be described as the 'last determinants' and that the organic factors are paramount.

Later in his career, Lombroso digressed somewhat from his earlier insistence upon biological determiners of illegal behaviour. Among other things, he considered the possibility that disease and other environmental factors might affect development to such an extent that constitutional states are brought about similar to those produced by heredity. He also became aware of the fact that some kinds of illegal behaviour and some types of criminals appear to be produced without signs of hereditary determination. Nevertheless, Lombroso is thought of to a large extent as a constitutional or biological theorist in criminology.

Probably Lombroso's greatest contribution was in his use of the scientific method in his investigations – inadequate though his techniques may have been. The most serious criticism one can make of these techniques is that he failed to use control groups. Later investigators of the Lombrosian tradition remedied this defect to some extent. Goring used a

---

[4]Cesare Lombroso, 'The Criminal – A Born Type', from *Criminology, A Book of Readings*, C. B. Vedder, S. Koenig, and Robert E. Clark, editors, New York: Holt, 1953, p. 139.

sample of over 3,000 convicts in English prisons and compared them to control groups of non-criminals.[5] Although the control groups were not 'normal' in that they were not truly representative of the general population, at least they were non-criminals. Goring found no essential differences between sub-groups of the criminal sample, nor between the criminal and the non-criminal groups. He certainly found no evidence for the anthropological conclusions of Lombroso. He did note that certain criminal types tended to be physically inferior in some ways – notably shorter in stature and lighter in weight. These physical deficiencies, however, may have been due to poor socio-economic backgrounds and not at all due to hereditary factors.

Many writers on criminological theory refer to the work of Hooton in the United States as a contribution to constitutional theories.[6] He 'measured and observed' and analysed a total of 17,076 people, including 1,976 'sane civilians' and 1,227 'insane civilians'. He took some twenty-two 'standard anthropometric measurements' on head and body. He found definite differences between the criminal and non-criminal samples, and also noted some differences among various classifications of offenders. He concluded that, 'On the whole, the biological superiority of the civilian to the delinquent is quite as certain as his sociological superiority.'[7] He felt that individuals who were inherently inferior would succumb more readily to 'the adversities or temptations of their social environment and fall into antisocial behaviour.'[8]

Regardless of how one feels about biological determinism with respect to criminal behaviour, one cannot ignore Hooton's findings. One can disagree, however, with some of his recommendations. He suggested developing reservations for paroled delinquents and allowing the inhabitants to become self-governing. Some of these reservations, he felt, might become quite prosperous after 'a generation or two'.

Of much greater significance for biological or constitutional theories of criminality is the work of Sheldon.[9] Sheldon developed a type theory of personality based on bodily characteristics, corresponding in many ways to the earlier work of Kretschmer. Sheldon postulated three basic body types, the endomorph, the ectomorph, and the mesomorph. Hardly

[5]Charles Goring, *The English Convict,* London: His Majesty's Stationery Office, 1913.
[6]Ernest A. Hooton, *Crime and the Man,* Cambridge, Mass.: Harvard University Press, 1939.
[7]*Ibid.,* p. 376.
[8]*Ibid.,* p. 388.
[9]Wm. H. Sheldon, *et al., Varieties of Delinquent Youth,* New York: Harper and Brothers, 1956.

anyone is a pure body type, but individual bodies are composites of the three basic body types. The endomorph is characterized by the prominence of the intestines and other visceral organs and has a tendency to fat. The mesomorph is characterized by a predominance of muscle and bone. The ectomorph is delicate and thin, and has a larger height-to-weight ratio than either of the other two. The endomorph is characteristically sociable, likes food, and craves affection. The mesomorph is energetic, has a desire for muscular activity, and is very direct in his manner. The ectomorph tends to withdraw from people, and is prone to sensitivity and anxiety. Sheldon classified each individual on a seven-point scale in accordance with the proportion of each body type in his make-up.

Sheldon's body-type theory was used by both Sheldon himself and by the Gluecks[10] in their investigations of delinquent behaviour. Sheldon studied 200 delinquent young adults from the Boston area. He found that this sample of delinquents tended to mesomorphy, and that the more delinquent the individual, the greater the tendency to mesomorphy. Aside from this tendency, Sheldon's results were far from decisive. The Gluecks found similar tendencies using a large group of delinquents and control groups. As Sheldon did, the Gluecks concluded that mesomorphy, as a component characteristic, was an important factor in the causation of delinquency.

The fact that delinquents, as a group, tend to muscular activity, are outgoing in temperament, are aggressive, and so on, does not mean that these factors are causal. As is the case with any positive correlation between two variables, the relationship may be due to a third factor or a group of factors, and one variable may not necessarily be causal to the other. There is no adequate justification, therefore, from the facts elicited by Sheldon or the Gluecks, for assigning a causal role to body-type. It might equally be argued that an outgoing person who is direct in manner and who likes muscular activity will indulge in muscular activity and will develop a physique with a large measure of the mesomorphic component; and that the same type of temperament likes the kind of adventurous activity represented by delinquent behaviour. There is no evidence to suggest that delinquent individuals do not possess a love for daring and adventurous activity in itself, delinquent activity being just one avenue of expression. Whatever the case, nothing of a conclusive nature can be adjudged from the evidence of Sheldon or the Gluecks –

[10]Sheldon and Eleanor Glueck, *Physique and Delinquency*, New York: Harper and Brothers, 1956.

despite the fact that their approaches were a major advance over those of Hooton and Lombroso.

In a study of 1,000 delinquents, Healy found that approximately one-seventh possessed some physical defects.[11] He concluded that this sample was also biased toward mental abnormality. In other words, of the one-seventh of his sample who had physical abnormalities, a large proportion also had mental abnormalities of some sort. He felt that, with this group removed from his sample, the remainder showed no greater incidence of physical abnormality than do the general population.

Endocrinologists have shown that secretions of the ductless glands can have profound effects on behaviour. Podolsky suggests from prior studies that hypoglycemia, an inability of the body to maintain an adequate supply of blood-sugar due to defective endocrine operation, has something to do with criminal behaviour.[12] He stated, 'The lower the sugar level falls, the greater is the tendency to commit a criminal act.' However, most of these studies of endocrine deficiencies have been conducted within prison walls. A correlation between certain types of endocrine deficiencies and emotional disturbance has been noted. Here again, we are faced with the problem of causal relationships. The atmosphere of prisons may have created emotional disturbances along with their endocrinological correlates. Even if such studies were conducted on individuals not in prison, emotional disturbances associated with arrest, court arraignment, punishment, and so on, could well be causal factors in endocrinological changes.

Some mention should be made in this section of two other factors, namely sex and age. The Dominion Bureau of Statistics reported that, in 1960, eighty-nine per cent of delinquents in Canada between seven and fifteen years old, inclusive, were boys.[13] This figure coincides well with figures in the United States and in certain other countries, although in some countries the proportion is much higher. The Bureau did not give figures for older age groups, but there is no reason to suppose that the proportion varies appreciably. We cannot, however, conclude that differences in criminal rates of the sexes are due to biological differences in themselves. As Sutherland and Cressey show, they are likely due to differences 'in the social positions and traditions of the two sexes'.[14] In areas

11Wm. Healy, *The Individual Delinquent,* New York: Little, Brown, 1915, p. 146.

12Edward Podolsky, 'The Chemical Brew of Criminal Behaviour', *Journal of Criminal Law, Criminology, and Police Science,* vol. 45 (March-April, 1955).

13Dominion Bureau of Statistics, *Canada Year Book, 1962,* Ottawa: Queen's Printer, p. 370.

14Edwin H. Sutherland and Donald R. Cressey, *Principles of Criminology,* 6th Edition, Philadelphia: J. B. Lippincott Company, 1960, p. 112.

where the social positions and certain aspects of role are similar, sex differences in delinquency rates are relatively small. Age also appears to be a factor in frequency and type of criminal behaviour, but there is a danger in taking over-all figures as possessing meaning that would not be justified if they were analysed in detail. Although the general tendency in most countries seems to be for the maximum rate of criminal behaviour to occur during or near adolescence, this depends to a large extent on such factors as the type of crime, criminal reporting procedures, and the like. In addition to this, the Gluecks found that approximately forty per cent of their group who were involved in delinquent activity as adolescents no longer were involved by their late twenties.[15]

PSYCHOLOGICAL FACTORS AND THEORIES

With the development of the Binet-type intelligence scales, prior to World War I, a great deal of intelligence testing of prison groups was undertaken by psychologists practically everywhere in the Western world, but most notably in the United States. The results of these early studies led investigators to conclude that delinquent and criminal behaviour was largely associated with low intelligence. Some early reports indicated that over half the prison populations tested scored at the feeble-minded level, and the conclusions based on these studies gained general acceptance at that time. However, later improvements and refinements in testing intelligence and abilities led to considerably different results. With the large-scale measurement of the intelligence of American Army personnel during World War I, a much better standard of comparison for other adult groups became available. It was generally found that prisoners within institutions scored at about the same level as American Army personnel. Wechsler, an authority on the measurement of intelligence, pointed out that the army sample was much more representative of the general population than were the samples upon which earlier tests were standardized.[16] Consequently, many investigators revised their earlier estimates of large differences between delinquents and samples of the general population. Healy and Bronner, in their studies in 1936, found that 'carefully conducted and intensive psychological testing resulted, quite unexpectedly, in establishing no signs of differentiation between the mental equipment of the delinquents and the controls in our series'.[17]

[15]Sheldon and Eleanor Glueck, *Juvenile Delinquents Grown Up*, Cambridge: Harvard University Press, 1940.
[16]David Wechsler, *Measurement of Adult Intelligence*, 3rd Edition, Baltimore: Williams and Wilkins, 1944.
[17]Wm. Healy and Augusta F. Bronner, *New Light on Delinquency and Its Treatment*, New Haven: Yale University Press, p. 61.

Despite the fact that significantly large differences are no longer obtained in most studies of intelligence, some differences, however small, are found in some studies. Over a ten-year period, the author has found mean differences between groups of inmates in Ontario reformatories and standardizing samples to be as much as ten I.Q. points. Such distributions have been skewed, usually, in such a manner as to indicate an even greater proportion below the average than the mean indicated. However, these differences may be due to any or all of the following:

1. Poor motivation. Many of the studies have been done on prison populations. It probably would be generally agreed among those who have tested prisoners to any extent that many of them are not motivated to do their best. Probably fewer of them than of the control groups are so motivated.

2. From the general population, probably a greater proportion of individuals of below-average intelligence get into trouble with the law than do those with average or above-average intelligence. They are more easily influenced by delinquent examples and tend to be more easily caught. Further, those of very low intelligence have failed to learn the values of society to the same degree as those with better intelligence, and are therefore more likely to commit criminal acts.

3. Lombroso's earlier theory of the relationship between mental deficiency and criminality would, even if partly true, provide an explanation for a lower mean level of intelligence in criminals.

Many studies finding differences in intelligence in favour of non-criminal groups have used tests of intelligence that depend heavily on verbal material. Some studies, including those of the Gluecks, have found that delinquents do less well on verbal than on non-verbal material.[18] Using the Wechsler-Bellevue test, an individually administered test of intelligence, the Gluecks found that their delinquent group had less verbal facility than the non-delinquent controls, but scored somewhat higher on two of the non-verbal or performance sub-tests. The delinquents had a 'tendency toward direct and concrete ways of mental expression'.[19] The author has found, in an institution for selected male offenders that contains relatively few with below-normal intelligence as measured by a group test of intelligence, a tendency to below-average performance on the verbal reasoning, language usage, and arithmetic test of the Differential Aptitude Battery. The same group showed an academic retardation of almost two years. From these results alone, however, it is impossible

18Sheldon and Eleanor Glueck, *Unraveling Juvenile Delinquency*, Cambridge: Harvard University Press, 1950, p. 199.
19*Ibid.*, p. 276.

to say whether the relatively poor performance on verbal material was due to failure to achieve in school, or whether failure to achieve in school was due to a lower level of verbal fluency, or whether some third factor, or combination of factors, was responsible for both.

Since intelligence is one aspect of personality, it is not surprising that some of these findings in the intelligence area are consonant with findings in other areas of personality. On the basis of Rorschach testing and psychiatric interviews, the Gluecks found their delinquent group to be more outgoing, aggressive, and adventurous, more extroverted, hostile, defiant, and suspicious than non-delinquents.[20] They were also less dependent, less submissive to authority, more stubborn, and less critical of themselves. Further, according to the results of the Rorschach tests, the delinquent group showed less tendency to neuroticism.

The Glueck work, as well as the findings of others, points to the existence of emotional disturbance and conflict in a large percentage of the delinquent population. This does not mean, however, that the presence of emotional conflict and disturbance necessarily leads to delinquent behaviour. As Tappan states, most people who are emotionally unstable do not become delinquents, but the emotional instability, along with suggestibility, may 'facilitate the expression of antisocial and aggressive impulses'.[21] The Gluecks found a fairly strong tendency to extroversion in delinquents as a group. It may well be that delinquents tend to turn their emotional conflicts outward and against society, whereas non-delinquents tend to internalize theirs and to work them out through various kinds of ego-defence mechanisms such as fantasy and repression. Tappan points out that, though the delinquents' method of working out problems in an outward and aggressive way may be mentally healthier, it is bound to bring them into more frequent and serious conflict with legal authorities.[22]

It should be emphasized here that not all delinquents in the Glueck study showed emotional conflict. Approximately one-quarter of them did not.[23] We may assume from this and other studies that a significant number of delinquents and criminals do not show signs of emotional disturbance or conflict beyond what one might expect from any so-called 'normal' group. This is fairly strong evidence that a certain proportion of delinquency may well be within the range of normal expression of

20*Ibid.*, p. 275.
21Paul W. Tappan, *Crime, Justice and Correction*, New York: McGraw-Hill, 1960, p. 152.
22*Ibid.*
23Glueck, *op. cit.*, p. 247.

tendencies quite acceptable to society generally. Further, there are certain strata of society that, to varying degrees, accept certain types of illegal behaviour as 'normal' and as quite reasonable ways of satisfying materialistic needs as long as one is not 'caught'. For example, in certain neighbourhoods in large Canadian and American cities, it is quite acceptable to commit some forms of theft if one can get away with it.

Some types of criminal behaviour may in certain circumstances be considered free of emotional disturbance and particularly excessive conflict – depending on the mores of the groups in which the individual finds himself. For example, homosexuality is almost universally frowned upon as a form of sexual outlet. Yet there are groups within Western culture in which homosexuality is acceptable behaviour. Further, in prisons and in some isolated military units during wartime when women are not available, the incidence of homosexuality is far greater than that found in the general population. The conflict and the disturbance arise, in some cases, when those who practise homosexuality run foul of the law. There are some situations in which homosexuality is adjustive behaviour, however criminal.

A formulation of Jenkins might be useful to consider here.[24] He concluded, as did the Gluecks, that delinquents as a group are less likely to be neurotic than non-delinquents. He divided delinquents into the 'adaptive' and the 'maladaptive' types. The adaptive delinquent is characterized by goal-oriented behaviour and is motivated by the same factors 'which keep our competitive economic system ticking'. The successful criminal career is adaptive. Typically, an adaptive delinquent or criminal possesses vigour, an aggressive attitude, and a 'good musculature'. He has received sufficient maternal care to develop social responsiveness, but has lacked effective paternal guidance. The delinquent's home is usually crowded and unattractive. As a consequence, the associations that primarily influence his attitudes and behaviour are those of delinquent companions of the street. The behaviour of the maladaptive delinquent, on the other hand, is the result of frustration and is stereotyped. It is not goal-oriented but, in fact, involves the renunciation of any goal. Punishment only serves to worsen the situation and the delinquent reacts to it with increased hostility and 'a reduced capacity for either adjustment or self-control'. This conception has implications for treatment. Obviously the corrective environment for the adaptive delinquent should be quite different from that for the maladaptive delinquent.

24Richard L. Jenkins, 'Adaptive and Maladaptive Delinquency', *The Nervous Child*, 11, October 1955, p. 9.

Douglas Penfold

SOCIOLOGICAL FACTORS AND THEORIES

An immense amount of material has been written about various sociological theories of crime, and many studies have been done on social factors and their relationships to criminal behaviour. In view of space limitations, the discussion in this chapter will be confined to a few theories and to a brief consideration of some of the social factors that have been found to be, or thought to be, related to criminal behaviour. Sociologists, of one type or another, undoubtedly have contributed more to theories of causation than any other group, and to give anything but a thorough review of their contributions is probably an injustice from the start. Much more comprehensive studies of the subject (see Further Reading) vary a good deal in their treatment of the material, and in many cases do not cite, or otherwise refer to, the same material. This is no doubt due not only to differences in theoretical orientation but also to differences in organization of the subject matter.

In a number of studies, the family situation has been found to be a significant factor. The Gluecks noted that their delinquent group as a whole came from homes that were physically and emotionally less adequate than those of the non-delinquent group. They found that, where financial assistance to families was necessary, the providers of the delinquent families were less ready to assume their responsibilities than the providers of the non-delinquent families, among whom the need for assistance stemmed largely from 'unforeseeable conditions', usually economic.[25] They also found that the environment in which the delinquents were raised was less likely to produce 'healthy, happy, and law-abiding children' than that in which the non-delinquent controls were raised.[26] Many studies of delinquents in training-schools of Ontario and elsewhere indicate a higher proportion of 'broken' homes – broken psychologically or otherwise – than can be expected in the background of non-delinquents. It has often been noted that figures from training-school populations are usually biased because of the greater tendency for delinquent children from broken homes to be committed to training-school. Nevertheless, the incidence of family inadequacy in the background of delinquents generally exceeds that of the non-delinquent 'normal' controls.

One of the more important ecological studies of delinquency has been that of Shaw and collaborators in Chicago.[27] Burgess had previously hypothesized that the greatest incidence of delinquency could be found

[25]Glueck, *op cit.*, p. 107.
[26]*Ibid.*, p. 115.
[27]Clifford R. Shaw, Frederick M. Zorbaugh, Henry D. McKay, and Leonard S. Cottrell, *Delinquency Areas,* Chicago: University of Chicago Press, 1929.

in the 'interstitial' areas of a city – areas in transition from residential to business and industrial use. Shaw found this to be so in Chicago. In a study covering eight years, he and his collaborators found that in the zones that had been disorganized socially by the encroachment of business and industry, and where physical deterioration had taken place, the highest incidence of crime and delinquency obtained. There was a progressive decline in incidence from these inner zones to the periphery or suburbs of the city. Similar findings obtained in other American cities, although in some cities 'gaps' in the general tendency were found where, within depressed areas, there were pockets with low rates of delinquency. Nevertheless, the general finding seems to be that the more deteriorated the area, both physically and socially, the greater the incidence of delinquency. Moreover, the incidence in such areas in Chicago remained relatively stable for over thirty years.

It cannot be assumed from these studies that the deterioration found in the depressed areas was causal to the high rate of delinquency. It might well be that these areas were settled by inadequate individuals who could not compete by normal means for better living conditions, and that some of the same traits that were causal to social deterioration generally were causal also to delinquent behaviour. Further, high-delinquency-rate areas are not by any means entirely delinquent; a significant number of children are non-delinquent and have few contacts and sympathies with the delinquent groups. This seems to indicate that factors other than those inherent to the area itself are operative.

The effects of gang activity on delinquent behaviour have been the subject of much discussion. At the outset, distinctions should be made between gangs in overcrowded delinquency areas and gangs in other areas more fortunate socially. Thrasher studied over 1,300 gangs in Chicago and found that delinquent gangs existed wherever there were overcrowding, poverty, and slum conditions.[28] Park states that 'it is the habitat which determines whether or not their activities . . . become a menace to the community'.[29] Many gang activities, depending on the nature of the gang, either are beneficial to the community or do not constitute a serious menace to community life. The Gluecks found that fifty-six per cent of their delinquents, as against less than one per cent of their non-delinquents, belonged to gangs.[30] However, there appears to be no

[28]F. M. Thrasher, *The Gang. A Study of 1,313 Gangs in Chicago*, Chicago: University of Chicago Press, 1927.
[29]F. M. Thrasher, *The Gang*, 2nd Edition, Chicago: University of Chicago Press, 1936, p. xi.
[30]Glueck, *op. cit.*, p. 103.

evidence to conclude that gang activity in itself is causal to delinquency, though given a fertile environment for its development the gang structure may amplify delinquent tendencies already present and result in greater delinquent activity.

Some authors have a good deal to say about the breakdown of social norms and values in our society as a contributory factor to delinquent behaviour. Tappan quotes Merton's statement that some types of deviant behaviour increasingly have become successful behaviour – successful in terms of the achievement of materialistic goals – and that this success of deviant ways of goal-achievement tends to 'eliminate the legitimacy of the institutional norms for others in the system'.[31] Individuals who are otherwise unable, through lack of opportunity, through inability, or for other reasons, to achieve the goals that they deem desirable do so through methods not in consonance with the norms and values of society. This process is encouraged by increased mobility and anonymity within urban society and by the fact that others are tending to operate in a similar manner with, in many cases, a good deal of success. There seems little doubt that there has been a 'weakening' of our traditional norms and values but, as Tappan points out, there is danger of over-emphasizing this. Some values are still relatively unchanged. 'The value attached to human life and personal liberties is probably no less strong than it was in the last century.'[32] Further, new norms have arisen to replace the old. Probably the best we can say at present is that the 'weakening' of traditional norms and values, without clear-cut and adequate replacement, is no doubt a contributing factor to criminal behaviour.

Sutherland developed a theory of criminal behaviour known as 'differential association'.[33] To Sutherland, criminal behaviour is largely the result of a learning process. An individual becomes a criminal because he has associations which favour the development of criminal behaviour, whereas the non-criminal has associations from which he learns 'an excess of definitions favourable' to non-criminal behaviour. To a large extent, criminal behaviour develops from an excess, both in frequency and consistency, of associations and contacts with criminal behaviour. Systematic criminal behaviour is caused by social disorganization. Differential association and social disorganization as hypotheses are counterparts and are 'consistent with each other'.[34] Sutherland saw social disorganization

[31]Tappan, *op. cit.*, p. 176.
[32]*Ibid.*
[33]Sutherland and Cressey, *op. cit.*, p. 8.
[34]Edwin H. Sutherland, *White Collar Crime*, New York: Holt, Rinehart and Winston, 1949, p. 254.

54

of two types: 'social disorganization may appear in the form of lack of standards' (anomie) or 'conflict of standards' (culture conflict).[35]

Since Sutherland's theory is probably the most elegant of criminological theories to date, it would probably be useful to quote the main points of the latest revision of his 'genetic theory of criminal behaviour' as given by Sutherland and Cressey in *Principles of Criminology*:

1. Criminal behaviour is learned.
2. Criminal behaviour is learned in interaction with other persons in a process of communication.
3. The principle part of the learning of criminal behaviour occurs within intimate personal groups.
4. When criminal behaviour is learned, the learning includes (a) techniques of committing the crime, which are sometimes very complicated, sometimes very simple; (b) the specific direction of motives, drives, rationalizations, and attitudes.
5. The specific direction of motives and drives is learned from definitions of the legal codes as favourable or unfavourable.
6. A person becomes delinquent because of an excess of definitions favourable to violation of law over definitions unfavourable to violation of law. This is the principle of differential association.
7. Differential associations may vary in frequency, duration, priority, and intensity.
8. The process of learning criminal behaviour by association with criminal and anti-criminal patterns involves all of the mechanisms that are involved in any other learning.
9. While criminal behaviour is an expression of general needs and values, it is not explained by those general needs and values, since non-criminal behaviour is an expression of the same needs and values.[36]

Sutherland used this theory in his explanation of white-collar crime. Korn and McCorkle state, in an excellent review of his contributions, that his analysis of white-collar crime produced evidence most damaging to his theory.[37] They claim that much white-collar crime (such as some cases of embezzlement) 'cannot be accounted for in terms of contacts with other embezzlers or white-collar offenders'.[38] Rightly enough, they state that many white-collar criminals have been law-abiding citizens, have rarely had associates from the criminal world, and have worked secretly and alone, and that often the offence seems to be the result of some 'per-

35*Ibid.*
36Edwin H. Sutherland and Donald R. Cressey, *Principles of Criminology*, 6th Edition, copyright 1960, Philadelphia: J. B. Lippincott Co., pp. 77-9.
37Richard R. Korn and Lloyd W. McCorkle, *Criminology and Penology*, New York: Henry Holt, 1959, p. 299.
38*Ibid.*

sonal crisis'.[39] However, such statements, as Sutherland points out, often ignore the associations with non-criminal patterns. Further, personality traits are included in the 'concept of differential association'.[40] Despite the fact that a person who commits a crime for the first time may not have had any direct associations with 'criminal elements', he has had associations with individuals who have committed criminal acts, since the entire population probably have committed criminal acts. Further, learning arises from more than direct contact. In Sutherland's terms, the number of definitions favourable to law-breaking may have been previously just below the level of definitions unfavourable to law-breaking. A series of events could quite suddenly have changed the balance. Regardless of whether one accepts Sutherland's notions, they cannot be discarded on the grounds that an individual who suddenly commits a crime did not have the required associations. We cannot trace the associations, using the term in the broad sense, of any individual with any degree of accuracy. What may seem petty and incidental may actually be critical.

Conclusion

What can one make of the vast amount of data on criminal and delinquent behaviour that have accrued from all the approaches to the study of human behaviour? The situation in criminology is essentially no different from the state of affairs found in the behavioural sciences generally, where some feel that more data should be collected at the behavioural level with less emphasis at the present time on theory construction, while others believe that the construction of theories with the subsequent generation of hypotheses for testing constitutes the best approach. And so it is in criminology as well. There are those, particularly those in practice, who feel that no one theory can possibly explain all the delinquent cases they encounter. They feel that a particular set of circumstances that can explain delinquent behaviour in the case of one individual is inadequate to explain what appears to be similar behaviour in another. These devotees of the so-called 'multiple factor' approach usually shun as much as possible association with any particular theoretical approach in order to avoid theoretical bias. At one end of the continuum, if there is a continuum, are those who insist on collections of facts and relationships without any present attempt to explain them. At the other end are those who take a cavalier approach to the mere collection of data and who are so devoted

39*Ibid.*
40Sutherland, *op. cit.*, p. 265.

56

to a particular theory that they sometimes behave as if their theoretical assumptions were facts.

Considering the present state of the behavioural sciences, including criminology, we probably need the work of both the fact-collectors and the theory-constructors. Eventually both camps must come together, but the time is not yet ripe nor will it be in the foreseeable future. In the meantime, those who are faced every day with the necessity of trying to explain in reports the delinquent behaviour of individuals will probably continue the pragmatic approach of grasping at any explanation that happens to make sense to them. They will continue to look for what appear to them to be poor developmental conditions as antecedents to delinquent behaviour, although most of them know that correlation between a condition and delinquent behaviour does not mean, necessarily, that this condition is causal to that behaviour.

The author would like to end by quoting a paragraph from Tappan's *Crime, Justice and Correction,* which indicates a few of the basic questions one has to consider in putting the whole problem of criminality into perspective.

It has been suggested that the success and pleasure goals in our social system naturally entail some criminality. But crime derives more obviously from the means men use than from the ends they seek in social life. The problem here lies in the fact that the approved paths through which men may implement their wants have been less clearly prescribed than have the legitimate ends and, in part for that reason, these paths are not closely scrutinized. Some modes of attainment, to be sure, have been long and well defined by tradition; rewards are readily accorded the limited aristocracy of special talents that are channeled in proper ways. The leader of men, the imaginative entrepreneur, and the specialized professional are quickly acclaimed. Universally respectable avenues to high achievement are few, however, and difficult of access. There are other less clearly marked routes to material gain that accommodate a more rapidly moving, if less respectable, traffic. The law-obedient and morally conservative majority shun these dubious short cuts; but impatient, incompetent, or unregulated individuals are attracted to them. There is little curiosity about the way they have traveled and, should they attain a successful end, they may find some acclaim for their cleverness in getting through. Short of success, they may still enjoy the fruits of illegal enterprise, if they are fortunate, or they may spend a little time in prison, if they are not. Crime does pay in the short run for those who have little status or self-respect to lose, and offenders are afflicted with a short-run view. A variety of rationalizations facilitate their violations: the big shots, too, are thieves but on a greater scale; only suckers work; a fast buck will buy as much. And it is true, of course, that the coin of the ruthless businessman, the persuasive charlatan, the unscrupulous politician, the amiable gambler, the professional thief, or the anxious embezzler is as freely negotiable as any other in the market place. Who is to attach distinctions of individual worth?[41]

Further Reading

A. While there are other works that might just as well merit special consideration, the author feels that the following three books will provide the reader with an excellent overview of the subject in far more detail than that afforded by this chapter.

KORN, RICHARD R., and Lloyd W. McCorkle. *Criminology and Penology.* New York: Holt, Rinehart and Winston, 1959.

SUTHERLAND, EDWIN H., and Donald R. Cressey. *Principles of Criminology,* 6th Edition. Philadelphia: Lippincott, 1960.

TAPPAN, PAUL W. *Crime, Justice and Correction.* New York: McGraw-Hill, 1960.

B. COHEN, ALBERT R. *Delinquent Boys: the Culture of the Gang.* Glencoe: The Free Press, 1955.

GLUECK, SHELDON and ELEANOR. *Juvenile Delinquents Grown Up* (A Commonwealth Fund Book). Cambridge: Harvard University Press, 1940.

————. *Physique and Delinquency.* New York: Harper and Brothers, 1956.

————. *Unraveling Juvenile Delinquency* (A Commonwealth Fund Book). Cambridge: Harvard University Press, 1950.

HEALY, WILLIAM, and Augusta F. Bronner. *New Light on Delinquency and Its Treatment.* New Haven: Yale University Press, 1936.

RECKLESS, WALTER C. *The Etiology of Delinquent and Criminal Behaviour.* New York: Social Science Research Council, 1943.

SHAW, C. R., H. D. McKay, *et al. Juvenile Delinquency and Urban Areas.* Chicago: University of Chicago Press, 1942.

SUTHERLAND, EDWIN H. *White Collar Crime.* New York: Holt, 1953.

VEDDER, CLYDE B., *et al. Criminology, A Book of Readings.* New York: Holt, 1953.

WHYTE, WILLIAM F. *Street Corner Society.* Chicago: University of Chicago Press, 1943.

[41]From *Crime, Justice and Correction* by Paul W. Tappan, copyright 1960, McGraw-Hill Book Company, Inc., p. 173. Used by permission.

4

Rates of Crime and Delinquency

P. J. GIFFEN

It is one of the less important paradoxes of our time that most discussions of criminal statistics begin with the expression of grave doubts about the reliability of the official figures and then present these statistics in various combinations as if they faithfully portrayed the real world. Apparently nobody is happy about the state of criminal statistics, but no serious student of criminology can get along without them. There is no easy or immediate way out of this dilemma. If generalizations are to be made about the amount of crime and the number of criminals, these facts must, with rare exceptions, be derived from the statistics published by government departments. The generalizations may become less speculative as the agencies collecting the statistics bring about more adequate returns from reporting bodies, and as empirical studies yield formulae for estimating the ratio of actual to reported crime. Meanwhile, responsible writers will continue to emphasize the limitations when they present criminal statistics.

SOURCES OF CANADIAN STATISTICS

The Judicial Section of the Dominion Bureau of Statistics is responsible for collecting national statistics on crime and delinquency in Canada and for preparing the annual volumes of the various series of statistical publications.

Police Statistics, published annually from 1920 to 1959, brings together information derived from police departments throughout the country. Of direct interest to the student of crime are the tables of offences known to the police, by the type of offence and locality, as well as the information on the number of arrests or summonses and the number of prosecutions for each type of offence. Starting with the 1960 series, this information is organized in a separate bulletin, *Crime Statistics,* and the other information on police matters is published in two companion volumes, *Police Administration Statistics* and *Traffic Enforcement Statistics*. The changes are part of recent efforts by D.B.S. to improve all the annual statistics dealing with the administration of justice. A new system of uniform crime-reporting, developed in co-operation with a committee of the Canadian Association of Chiefs of Police, has resulted in more reliable information on crimes known to the police since 1962.

The steps taken to increase the proportion of police departments filing returns appear to have had some success. Whereas in 1956 only 276 police departments reported, the situation was described as follows in the Introduction to *Crime Statistics, 1960*:

> Monthly reports were received from 767 departments representing 80.6 per cent of potential contributors. There were 108 departments or 11.3 per cent who submitted less than twelve monthly reports and 77 departments or 8.1 per cent who did not report.

Reports from the Quebec Provincial Police had not been received by 1961, but, according to the Introduction to *Crime Statistics, 1961* (the latest available at the time of writing), that police force would commence reporting in 1962. Until all police departments report regularly, police statistics cannot be used to determine the amount of crime on a national basis.

The quality of the reporting also remains such as to raise doubts about the validity of the information, as the following note in the Introduction to *Crime Statistics, 1961* indicates:

> The data published in the tables of this report leave much to be desired in the way of completeness and uniformity, even though there has been some improvement in recent years.

An examination of some of the figures in the 1960 and 1961 *Crime Statistics* reveals differences between large urban centres that make sense only if interpreted as reflecting differences between police departments in the classification of offences and the adequacy of reporting. In Table I the numbers of crimes of four major types known to the police of Montreal, Toronto, and Vancouver are compared for the two years. The population reported to be under the jurisdiction of each police department in 1961 is indicated under the name of the city.

It seems unlikely that Montreal actually experienced such a dramatic increase in thefts between 1960 and 1961, since the other two cities showed a declining number. An increase in the efficiency of reporting appears to be involved; this impression is strengthened by the disproportionate increase also shown in the cases of breaking and entering and of

TABLE I

SELECTED OFFENCES 'KNOWN TO THE POLICE' OF
MONTREAL, TORONTO, AND VANCOUVER, 1960 AND 1961

Offence	Montreal (1,155,178)		Toronto (1,595,809)		Vancouver (376,808)	
	1960	*1961*	*1960*	*1961*	*1960*	*1961*
Theft	13,265	21,532	33,277	31,694	14,212	13,875
Breaking and entering	4,933	6,644	8,138	7,157	4,698	4,752
Fraud	18	6	2,536	2,836	60	50
Assault causing bodily harm	99	637	1,159	1,220	242	202

Source: Dominion Bureau of Statistics, *Crime Statistics 1960* and *1961*.

serious assaults in Montreal. The enormous discrepancy between Toronto and the other two cities in known cases of fraud points to the conclusion that similar offences may be differently classified by police departments; many offences that would be regarded as frauds in Toronto may, for example, be classified as thefts in Vancouver and Montreal. The relative rarity of 'assault causing bodily harm' in Montreal may be due to the tendency of the police to classify such offences as 'common assault'. Whatever the reason for the discrepancies, their existence makes the statistics of limited usefulness for research.

Statistics obtained from the courts are published annually by D.B.S. in two series, *Statistics of Criminal and Other Offences* and *Juvenile Delinquents*. Whereas the police statistics on offences can tell us nothing of the characteristics of offenders, the courts can provide data on the sex, age, marital status, residence, ethnic origin, and several other characteristics of the people who appear before them, as well as information on the disposition of cases. Moreover, the classification of offences can be based on the judicial process instead of on the judgment of the police.

In Canada, the value of court statistics is enhanced by a Criminal Code that applies throughout the country, and by an integrated system of court jurisdictions. The United States Bureau of Census attempted to collect court statistics from 1932 onward, but the published series, *Judicial Criminal Statistics,* came to an end in 1945 because of war conditions, 'plus the more important fact that the series as it was being conducted was not a success and could not offer reliable measurements of what the courts did'.[1] The main obstacles were the failure of many courts to report and the difficulty of interpreting the returns in the light of differences in criminal law between states.

Comparison of police statistics in Canada with the two series based on the courts shows that a higher proportion of judicial districts than police jurisdictions have reported, and that the number of judicial districts reporting has varied less over time. Although in recent years no judicial district in the country has failed to report, according to the statistics, some courts within districts have apparently been remiss. A mimeographed note provided with *Statistics of Criminal and Other Offences, 1959*, indicates this:

> The number of adults appearing before the courts charged with indictable offences in 1959 was 34,812, an apparent decrease from the 1958 figure of 38,415. This may be partially explained by the failure of several courts, including that of a large urban centre, to submit returns to the Dominion Bureau of Statistics.

Correctional institutions at various levels are a third source of information on criminal matters. Since 1937, in accordance with an agreement between D.B.S. and the Department of Justice, penitentiary statistics have been collected and tabulated by D.B.S. and published in the annual report of the Commissioner of Penitentiaries.

Prior to 1957, general information on the population of correctional institutions of all types was included in a section of *Statistics of Criminal and Other Offences*. In 1961 a separate volume entitled *Correctional Institutions Statistics, 1957-1959* appeared, containing tables on total populations and population movements by province and type of institution (but nothing on the characteristics of the prisoners). Annual volumes containing similar information have appeared since. Recently, committees of the Canadian Corrections Association have collaborated with D.B.S. in planning much more extensive annual series on institutional populations. Annual series on training-schools, adult prisons, probation, parole, and after-care are expected to result from these deliberations.

CRIMINAL STATISTICS AS SAMPLES

If criminal statistics are to be used as indices of amounts and types of crime or of numbers and characteristics of criminals, we must take into account that they describe only a sample of the universe of offences or

[1]R. H. Beattie, 'Problems of Criminal Statistics in the United States', *Journal of Criminal Law, Criminology and Police Science*, vol. 46 (July-August 1955), pp. 178-86.

offenders. The problem does not exist if we adopt a strictly legalistic position and say, in effect, that no act can be called a crime until a court of law has declared it so, and no person can be called a criminal until a court has found him guilty. Few students of the subject would be willing to observe this restrictive ordinance if it meant giving up an interest in the actual incidence of potentially punishable acts and potentially culpable perpetrators.

Unfortunately, the ratio of the known to the unknown is a mystery, and probably differs by time and place and type of offence. 'Crimes known to the police' are obviously only a portion of the total crimes committed. The vested interests of the offender, the victim, the police, and the local government may combine in various ways to determine whether the offence ever becomes part of a statistical table. It seems likely that bank robberies, for example, rarely go unreported by the victim, whereas many cases of rape, incest, and blackmail are never revealed to the police. Where the 'victim' is a willing participant, as he is usually in gambling, bootlegging, and prostitution, the appearance of the act as a 'crime known to the police' will depend largely upon the initiative of the law-enforcement authorities; policies of enforcement in these spheres are notoriously variable.

When we proceed from the official statistical debut of the act as a 'crime known to the police' to the appearance in the statistics of a conviction and the appearance of the offender as a convicted person, additional selective forces intervene. Somebody must be arrested, charged, brought to trial, and found guilty – a series of steps that involves numerous contingencies. Hence, the statistics derived from the courts are an even smaller sample than the 'crimes known'. The relative size of the sample apparently varies with the type of crime. In 1960 the thefts known to the police numbered 159,299; the number of cases concluded was 62,366, or 39.1 per cent. The number of prosecutions was in the ratio of 89 per cent of the number of arrests and summonses. In contrast, the number of concluded cases of assault causing bodily harm was in the ratio of 77 per cent of the offences known to the police, and the prosecutions were in the ratio of 93 per cent of the arrests and summonses. While these exact ratios should not be taken seriously without a thorough examination of the statistics, they do indicate a considerable difference between crimes as regards the probability of their appearing in court statistics.

The drop in numbers between the reporting of offences and the registration of court convictions is probably much greater for juveniles than for adult offenders. In dealing with juveniles the police may handle the matter without laying a charge, or the court may consider advisable the withdrawing of the charge in favour of an unrecorded disposition – that is, the matter is settled informally without a finding of delinquency being entered on the record. In 1944 an attempt was made to ascertain the frequency of the latter practice.[2] Only thirty-six courts supplied information, but the figures showed that, for every three cases given a formal hearing, four were handled informally as 'occurrences'. Changing methods of dealing with delinquents may explain many of the apparent fluctuations in rates of delinquency. In 1950 the province of Quebec passed the Schools for the Protection of Youth Act, which provided an alternative procedure to that of the Juvenile Delinquents Act. If the young person is found to be 'in need of protection', he does not appear in the statistics as a delinquent. The dramatic decrease in Quebec's delinquency rate from 202 per 100,000 in 1950 to 87 per 100,000 in 1952 may be, in large part, due to the use of this alternative. We have no way of estimating how widely alternative methods of dealing with juvenile offenders are used in other provinces, but the trend appears to be in this direction. The official statistics on delinquency may increasingly underestimate the incidence of illegal acts by juveniles.

Between the conviction of offenders and their statistical appearance in the prison population, the sample declines very sharply. Of the adults convicted in Canada in 1960 for indictable offences, 35.2 per cent were sentenced to jail, 5.3 per cent to reformatory, 0.6 per cent to training-school, and 8.3 per cent to penitentiary. The prison population is a highly select group of individuals.

While a damning case can be made for the inadequacy of criminal statistics as facts about representative samples, it does not follow that they must be abandoned for research purposes. Pending the extensive study that will be necessary to determine which statistics are most reliable and what inferences are justified, certain obvious precautions can be observed. One is to take seriously only fairly large differences in rates, and to check whether these differences agree with other evidence, including the findings in comparable jurisdictions. The statistics on other more reliably reported forms of deviant behaviour of which the rates are known to correlate with rates of crime may give clues as to the reliability of the criminal statistics. Another precaution when calculating rates is to offset the possible fluctuations in enforcement and reporting from year to year by using averages for a number of years.

[2]Reported in Nicolas Zay, 'Gaps in Available Statistics in Crime and Delinquency in Canada', *Canadian Journal of Economics and Political Science,* vol. 29 (February 1963), pp. 75-89.

THE CALCULATION OF RATES

The convention in studying criminal statistics has been to convert absolute figures to per capita rates. Although the practice is followed here, the tacit assumption that the ratio of crime to population is a measure of 'criminality' is not valid since it implies that the opportunity (or provocation, or 'temptation') is constant. The fallacy is demonstrated in Table II.

TABLE II

CONVICTIONS FOR IMPAIRED DRIVING (SUMMARY AND INDICTABLE) IN QUEBEC AND ONTARIO, 1956

	Quebec	Ontario
Convictions for impaired driving per 100,000 pop. 16 yrs. and over	105	152
Convictions per 100,000 licensed motor vehicles	360	331

Source: P. J. Giffen, 'Canadian Criminal Statistics' in *C.P.S.A. Conference on Statistics, 1960, Papers,* Toronto: University of Toronto Press, 1962, p. 80.

Since Ontario has more motor vehicles than Quebec, the use of the number of motor vehicles as the measure of opportunity gives a quite different picture of the tendency to break highway laws than does a rate based on population. In constructing rates for embezzlement or theft by conversion, to take another example, the proclivity for this form of larceny might be measured by using the number of positions of financial trust as a base. Only for crimes against the person is population clearly the measure of opportunity.

To calculate opportunity rates for many crimes, however, we would need information that is not now made available. The nature of the information contained at present in official statistics reflects the preoccupation of criminologists with the reformation or rehabilitation of the individual criminal. The implicit assumption that this is the prime or only method of coping with criminals has led to an overwhelming concern with the characteristics of criminals and a neglect of information on the nature of crimes and the situations in which they are committed. We can, for example, find in official statistics information on the sex, age, and ethnic origin of convicted thieves but nothing on what was stolen, from whom, and under what circumstances. Most criminal statistics tell us nothing about the victims of crimes, although the importance for research of this information has often been stressed. Until such data are available, we have no alternative but to use per capita rates. They are probably the most useful compromise in dealing with totals that embody a variety of crimes, each of which could conceivably have a different measure of opportunity.

Whether the rates that can be calculated are convictions per capita or convicted persons per capita will depend upon the tabulating units used in the official statistics. Since 1949, *Statistics of Criminal and Other Offences* has used 'persons convicted' as the unit for tabulating information on offenders convicted of indictable offences; this is obviously much less misleading than 'convictions', which could cause an individual to appear in a table several times. For offences punishable on summary conviction, the less serious but more numerous offences, 'convictions' are still used as the tabulating units. The unit for compiling juvenile delinquency data is a compromise between 'persons' and 'convictions' called 'appearances resulting in a finding of delinquency'. The juvenile who is convicted of several offences at one appearance is listed only once, according to the most serious offence, but if he appears in court later in the same year on another charge he becomes, statistically, an additional delinquent. In 1961, the 15,215 appearances resulting in a finding of delinquency involved 13,358 children, so that the use of this unit for compiling social data does not appear to be seriously misleading.

The conversion of absolute figures on crime to per capita rates also depends on the availability in other sources – this usually means census materials – of statistics on the general population that are organized in classes similar or convertible to those of the criminal statistics. Many per capita rates can be computed only for the years of the regular Census of Canada, held in the first year of each decade (1941, 1951, etc.). Rates by religion, birthplace, and years of education are of this type. The much more limited Census of Population and Agriculture, conducted in the fifth year after the regular census (as in 1956), provides a basis for rates by age, sex, and marital status for most of the significant geographical units. Rates by age and sex for the provinces can be calculated for the intercensal years on the basis of the *Estimates of Population*, published periodically by the Dominion Bureau of Statistics.

VARIATIONS IN RATES OF CRIME AND DELINQUENCY
Differences over Time
The alarming view that crime and delinquency, as well as other forms of deviance, are continually increasing seems to be widely accepted, but the official statistics give no indication of a dramatic increase over the last couple of decades. Figure 1 shows the average annual rates of delinquency for seven five-year periods between 1926 and 1960. Apparently rates of

delinquency went down during the depression, rose to a new high during World War II, declined to a low in 1951-5, and rose again in 1956-60. The decline during the depression and the rise during wartime appears to have been a universal phenomenon in industrialized societies. The common element among the numerous explanations is that family supervision was relatively strict during the depression period, when adults spent much time at home, and relatively lax during wartime, when work, service in the armed forces, and recreation drew people from the home. The fact that delinquency rates in Canada did not increase from 1951 to 1960 as they did in the United States may be explained in part by the increasing proportion of Canadian cases that were handled without formal adjudication.

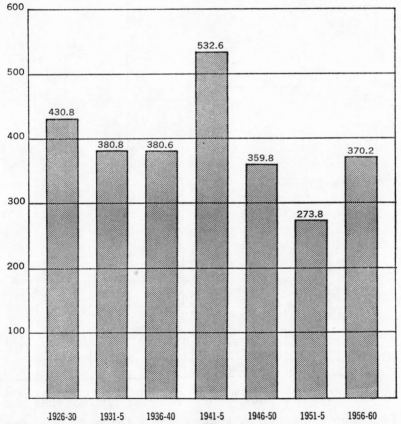

Fig. 1. Rates of juvenile delinquency, Canada, five-year averages, 1926-60. Source: D.B.S. annual publication, *Juvenile Delinquents*.

The adult rates of conviction for indictable offences for the longer period from 1901 to 1960 (see Figure 2) show an over-all trend of increase, or of better reporting, or of both. An increase over this period might legitimately be expected in view of the transformation of Canada from a predominantly rural to a predominantly urban society. The rates rose during the depression and dropped slightly during World War II, the reverse of the juvenile pattern. In recent years they appear to have been rising again.

The belief that crimes of violence have increased dramatically is not borne out by Figure 3. The rate of 'offences against the person' has re-

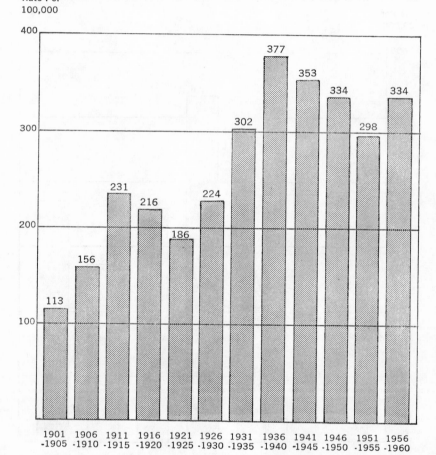

Fig. 2. Rates of conviction for indictable offences, Canada, five-year averages, 1901-60. Source: D.B.S. annual publication, *Statistics of Criminal and Other Offences.*

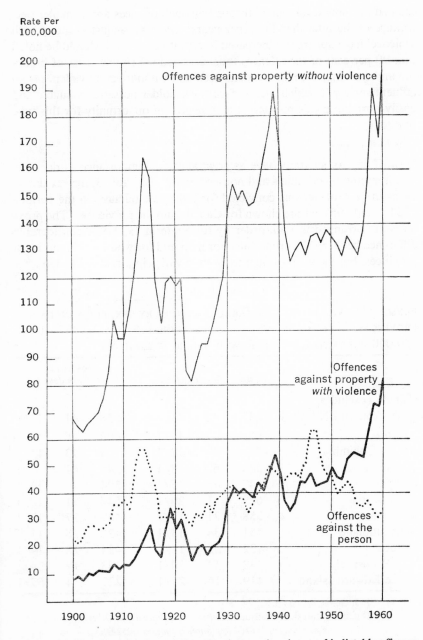

Rate Per
100,000

Offences against property *without* violence

Offences
against property
with violence

Offences
against the
person

1900   1910   1920   1930   1940   1950   1960

Fig. 3. Changes in rates of convictions for three major classes of indictable offences, Canada, 1900-60. Source: D.B.S. annual publication, *Statistics of Criminal and Other Offences.*

mained at a low level, which means that such offences are a smaller percentage of the total than in earlier years. 'Offences against property with violence' have apparently increased in recent years, but it should be noted that 90 per cent of the offences thus classified are simple cases of breaking and entering, with no weapons used and without actual violence – an affluent society in which the average householder possesses valuable and easily portable goods presents a high degree of opportunity for this type of offence.

Sex Differences

'Few, if any, other traits have as great statistical importance as does sex in differentiating criminals and non-criminals'.[3] In Table 3, the sex differences in rates of persons convicted for indictable offences in the periods 1951-6 and 1957-61 are shown for Canada and the provinces. (The provinces are arranged in rank-order by total rate in 1961.) A considerable difference between the crime-rates for men and for women is found in all provinces, but the ratio of men to women varies in a marked fashion be-

TABLE III

PERSONS CONVICTED OF INDICTABLE OFFENCES BY SEX, FOR CANADA AND PROVINCES: AVERAGE OF ANNUAL CONVICTIONS 1951-6 AND 1957-61 PER 100,000 POPULATION 16 YEARS AND OLDER OF EACH SEX

	1951-56*			1957-61†		
	Males	*Females*	*Ratio*	*Males*	*Females*	*Ratio*
Canada (excluding Yukon and N.W.T.)	537	36	15/1	558	41	14/1
Alberta	617	47	13/1	800	66	12/1
British Columbia	714	59	12/1	774	73	11/1
Manitoba	524	62	8/1	545	61	9/1
Ontario	647	43	15/1	594	46	13/1
Nova Scotia	629	31	20/1	544	31	18/1
Saskatchewan	358	21	17/1	439	27	16/1
Newfoundland	451	34	13/1	426	38	11/1
Quebec	422	25	17/1	424	22	19/1
New Brunswick	442	14	30/1	493	17	29/1
Prince Edward Island	419	16	26/1	227	4	57/1

Sources: *P. J. Giffen, *op. cit.*, p. 82.
†Dominion Bureau of Statistics, *Statistics of Criminal and Other Offences, 1957-61*; *Census of Canada, 1961*; *Population Estimates*, 1952-60.

[3]E. H. Sutherland and D. R. Cressey, *Principles of Criminology*, Philadelphia: Lippincott, 1955, p. 114.

tween provinces. In these rates, as in so many others, the figures for Canada as a whole mask a notable disparity between regions.

Since the rates for males follow, with minor exceptions, the differences between provinces in total rates, discussion of them can be left for the section on provincial differences. The female rates vary from province to province. The wide difference in sex ratios, ranging from 8/1 in Manitoba in 1951-6 to 57/1 in Prince Edward Island in 1957-61, indicates that the female rates are not simply a reflection of the general crime-rate.

No simple patterns of provincial difference in female rates are apparent from Table III. While two of the Atlantic Provinces (Prince Edward Island and New Brunswick) have low rates for women, the other two do not. Two of the Prairie Provinces have relatively high rates, but Saskatchewan does not. Quebec is an obvious exception to the generalization that high female crime-rates go with a high degree of urbanization. The high female rates in Alberta and British Columbia fit in with their pattern of rapid population growth, but the high rate in Manitoba goes together with a relatively slow population growth from 1957-61.

Several writers have pointed out that the sex ratio in convictions for crime varies with the relative status of women; as women enjoy greater freedom, and approach equality with men, they apparently commit more crimes. Some of the provincial differences in sex ratio might be explained if they were tested against statistical indices of the status of women. Following this reasoning, we might expect the rising status of women since World War I to be reflected in an increasing proportion of female offenders, but the statistics of convictions for indictable offences show no such trend. In 1919 female convictions were 12.2 per cent of total convictions. For the next 11 years, the female proportion fluctuated between 9 and 12 per cent of the total. It dropped to 8.3 per cent in 1931 and then fluctuated between 9 and 11 per cent until World War II, when the proportion rose to 15 per cent in 1942. Then the proportion of women offenders declined with minor fluctuations until a low of 5.6 per cent was reached in 1957. Since then the proportion has increased somewhat, reaching 8.1 per cent in 1961. These mystifying changes bear no apparent relationship to the changing status of women in our society.

Table IV contains information about the sex of delinquents. (The provinces are again arranged in descending order of total rates in 1961.) The rates for both boys and girls vary over a much wider range than the adult rates. This may be due, in part, to the much wider discretion exercised in deciding whether or not juveniles will be brought to court. The most highly agricultural provinces (Saskatchewan and Prince Edward Island) have unusually low rates for girls. The most urbanized provinces

71

have relatively high rates with the exception, once again, of Quebec. The differences between the extremes are sufficiently large to merit further study.

TABLE IV

SEX OF JUVENILE DELINQUENTS FOR CANADA AND PROVINCES:
ANNUAL AVERAGE 1951-6 AND 1957-61 PER 100,000 POPULATION
7-15 YEARS OF AGE

| | 1951-56* | | | 1957-61† | | |
	Boys	Girls	Ratio	Boys	Girls	Ratio
Canada (excluding Yukon and N.W.T.)	497	62	8/1	679	92	7/1
British Columbia	969	117	8/1	1035	154	8/1
Ontario	769	97	8/1	811	133	6/1
Alberta	445	69	6/1	740	112	7/1
Manitoba	523	119	4/1	839	142	6/1
Nova Scotia	649	52	13/1	641	42	15/1
New Brunswick	447	38	12/1	604	60	10/1
Newfoundland	562	26	22/1	793	73	11/1
Quebec	205	26	8/1	413	48	9/1
Prince Edward Island	426	6	74/1	357	8	45/1
Saskatchewan	77	4	18/1	172	12	14/1

Sources: *P. J. Giffen, *op. cit.*, p. 83.
†Dominion Bureau of Statistics, *Juvenile Delinquents, 1957-61*; *Census of Canada 1961*; *Population Estimates, 1952-60*.

Broad differences between males and females in the types of serious crime for which they are likely to be convicted are shown in Table V. Although males outnumber females in all offence categories, the ratio is much higher for some types of offences than for others. It is not surprising that males show a greater proclivity for more violent or physically daring predatory crimes, such as armed robbery and breaking and entering. The high ratio of men to women in sex offences reflects the fact that the physically aggressive sex offences, such as indecent assault and rape, which are characteristically male, are defined in our legal tradition as serious enough to be indictable, while common prostitution, which accounts for a considerable part of female crime, is not included in the table because it is punishable on summary conviction. Commercialized vice makes up a relatively high proportion of female indictable offences because it includes bawdy-house keeping and narcotics offences. In 1961, three times as many women as men were convicted for keeping a bawdy-house; although men exceeded women in narcotics convictions, the ratio was only 1.7 to 1.

TABLE V

NUMERICAL AND PERCENTAGE DISTRIBUTION OF INDICTABLE-OFFENCE
GROUPS* BY SEX OF PERSONS CONVICTED, CANADA, 1961

| | Number | | Ratio | Percentage | |
	Males	Females	M to F	Males	Females
All offences	35,516	3,163	11/1	100.0	100.0
Homicide	79	5	16/1	0.2	0.2
Assault offences	3,693	204	18/1	10.4	6.4
Sex offences	1,159	9	129/1	3.3	0.3
Family offences	65	47	1.4/1	0.2	1.5
Commercialized vice	929	376	2.5/1	2.6	11.9
Gainful offences with violence	7,731	132	59/1	21.8	4.2
Malicious offences against property	761	33	23/1	2.1	1.0
Theft	15,484	1,814	9/1	43.6	57.4
Fraudulent offences	3,403	439	8/1	9.6	13.9
Motor-vehicle offences	456	9	50/1	1.3	0.3
Other offences	1,756	95	18/1	4.9	3.0

Source: Dominion Bureau of Statistics, *Statistics of Criminal and Other Offences, 1961.*
*The names of offences included in each of these groups is given in P. J. Giffen, *op. cit.*, p. 104.

The differences between boys and girls in the types of offences that lead to their being convicted of juvenile delinquency, shown in Table VI, are quite marked. Although offences against property clearly predominate among the boys' convictions, girls are more likely to find themselves adjudged delinquents for a variety of misbehaviours that might be described as 'running wild'. Precocity and promiscuousness in sexual relations probably account for many of the convictions listed in the statistics as 'immorality', 'incorrigibility', and 'vagrancy', which together make up 33 per cent of the female offences. If we add to them those convictions listed as 'Liquor Control Act' (mostly drinking under age), 'disorderly conduct', and 'truancy', we have accounted for 53 per cent of the total delinquencies of girls.

Whether the property offences of boys are really rationally planned crimes for gain, or forms of 'acting-out' due to status frustration (the explanation favoured by A. K. Cohen),[4] the statistics, of course, do not tell

[4] Albert K. Cohen, *Delinquent Boys: The Culture of the Gang*, Glencoe, Illinois: Free Press, 1955.

TABLE VI

NUMERICAL AND PERCENTAGE DISTRIBUTION OF JUVENILE OFFENCES
BY SEX, CANADA, 1961

| | Number | | Ratio | Percentage | |
	Boys	Girls	B to G	Boys	Girls
All Offences	13,504	1,711	8/1	100.0	100.0
Theft	4,335	423	10/1	32.1	24.7
Breaking and entering	3,348	65	52/1	24.8	3.7
Interferences with property	1,204	44	27/1	8.9	2.6
Automobile theft	781	11	71/1	5.8	0.6
Various municipal by-laws	574	51	11/1	4.3	3.0
Highway Traffic Act offences	352	44	8/1	2.6	2.6
Incorrigibility	346	367	0.9/1	2.6	21.4
Taking motor vehicle without consent	320	4	80/1	2.4	0.2
Disorderly conduct	291	131	2.2/1	2.1	7.7
Having in possession	289	12	24/1	2.1	0.7
Assault offences	247	26	10/1	1.8	1.5
Liquor Control Act offences	222	122	1.8/1	1.6	7.1
Truancy	124	92	1.3/1	0.9	5.4
Vagrancy	93	36	2.6/1	0.7	2.1
Immorality	83	155	0.5/1	0.6	9.1
Other offences	895	128	7/1	6.6	7.5

Source: Dominion Bureau of Statistics, *Juvenile Delinquents, 1961*.

us. Certainly few of the offences labelled 'automobile theft', 'taking a motor vehicle without the owner's consent', or 'interferences with property' are acts aimed primarily at economic gain. It is also worth noting that crimes of violence against other persons are relatively rare among juvenile offences, contrary to the impression created by the mass media.

Age Differences

All countries that keep statistics report a preponderance of young people among convicted criminals. Table VII indicates that the rate declines with age in Canada, but that the decline is much sharper for males than for females. The increase in the rate for both sexes between the sixteen- and seventeen-year-old level and the eighteen- and nineteen-year-old level is an unexpected finding. In 1956 the older group of males had a rate that was 92 per cent of the rate of the younger age-grade and the females in the older group had a rate that was 97 per cent of the rate of the younger group. Although we cannot attach much significance to such a small difference without further evidence, it does raise the possibility that the young people born in the later years of World War II are less inclined to criminal acts than those born in the earlier years. If so, the trend should show up in the criminal statistics of the next few years.

TABLE VII

AGE AND SEX OF PERSONS CONVICTED OF
INDICTABLE OFFENCES, CANADA, 1961

Age in years	Rate per 100,000 population in each age-group		Rate as percentage of 16-, 17-year rate	
	Males	Females	Males	Females
16, 17	1,844	101	100.0	100.0
18, 19	1,899	119	103.0	117.8
20–24	1,336	106	72.5	105.0
25–29	760	72	41.2	71.3
30–34	524	57	28.4	56.4
35–39	411	46	22.3	45.5
40–44	311	43	16.9	42.6
45–49	240	35	13.0	34.7
50–59	169	27	9.2	26.7
60 & older	55	7	3.0	6.9

Number: Males – 35,516; Females – 3,163
Age not stated: Males – 1,589; Females – 158

Sources: Dominion Bureau of Statistics, *Statistics of Criminal and Other Offences, 1961,* and *Census of Canada, 1961.*

Urban-Rural Distribution

Tables VIII and IX contain apparent exceptions to the commonplace observation that urban communities have higher rates of crime than rural areas. In 1961 the Canadian statistics for the first time showed rural rates exceeding urban rates in some provinces. It is particularly startling to find that in British Columbia the rural rate of juvenile delinquency is over twice the urban rate. However, an examination of the 1961 census reveals that any true differences in rates are obscured by changes in the criteria for classifying the population as urban or rural. The change in 1961 from the definition used in the 1956 census resulted in the exclusion from the 1961 urban population of any non-urbanized fringes within metropolitan areas and the inclusion of the urbanized fringes of smaller cities whose total population including the urbanized fringe was 10,000 or over. If the change had resulted in a large increase in the population classified as urban, some of the relative increase in rural rates might be interpreted as a result of the narrowing of the population base used in the calculations, but the actual change in population was in the opposite direction – in Canada as a whole the urban population went down by 271,537. Only in Saskatchewan and Prince Edward Island did the rural population decrease.

The confusion is increased if we take into account that each court official who reports to D.B.S. makes his own decision in each case as to whether the offender's residence is urban or rural. The criteria he uses in marginal cases may bear no similarity to the census definition of either year.

TABLE VIII

RESIDENCE OF PERSONS CONVICTED OF INDICTABLE OFFENCES, FOR CANADA AND PROVINCES, 1956 AND 1961. RATES PER 100,000 POPULATION 16 YEARS AND OLDER

	1956*		1961†	
	Urban	Rural	Urban	Rural
Canada (excluding Yukon and N.W.T.)	283	185	361	194
Alberta	387	246	586	246
British Columbia	356	332	461	344
Manitoba	343	210	462	203
Ontario	285	204	365	186
Nova Scotia	280	205	348	223
Saskatchewan	363	126	422	129
Newfoundland	334	121	385	131
Quebec	212	142	254	162
New Brunswick	305	135	169	214
Prince Edward Island	217	56	155	19

Number: 26,844   Number: 37,347

Residence   Residence
not stated: 567   not stated: 1,332

Sources: *P. J. Giffen, *op. cit.*, p. 90.

   †Dominion Bureau of Statistics, *Statistics of Criminal and Other Offences, 1961* and *Census of Canada, 1961.*

TABLE IX

RESIDENCE OF JUVENILE DELINQUENTS, FOR CANADA AND PROVINCES, 1956 AND 1961. RATES PER 100,000 POPULATION 7-15 YEARS OF AGE

| | 1956* | | 1961† | |
	Urban	Rural	Urban	Rural
Canada (excluding Yukon and N.W.T.)	443	159	546	419
British Columbia	672	526	516	1118
Ontario	535	293	707	711
Alberta	586	85	636	381
Manitoba	681	130	706	446
Nova Scotia	467	264	499	377
New Brunswick	446	113	613	241
Newfoundland	875	49	474	305
Quebec	198	40	442	172
Prince Edward Island	760	57	302	219
Saskatchewan	90	1	359	85
	Number: 9,114		Number: 16,971	
	Residence not stated: 6		Residence not stated: 3	

Sources: *P. J. Giffen, *op. cit.*, p. 90.
    †Dominion Bureau of Statistics, *Statistics of Criminal and Other Offences, 1961* and *Census of Canada, 1961.*

Do these changes in urban and rural rates embody changes in the pattern of offences? The rates for broad offence-groups, shown in Table X, indicate some shifts in their relative importance. The gainful offences increased considerably in 1961, but the increase was much greater among urban than rural dwellers. The rates for assault offences decreased among urban residents and increased among rural residents, which brought the two rates close together.

The radical decline in motor-vehicle offences that appears to have taken place among both populations is deceptive. The decrease is due primarily to a drop in convictions for impaired driving as an indictable offence from 2,132 in 1956 to 218 in 1961, and for driving while intoxicated from 383 to 10. The Crown may proceed by way of indictment or summary conviction on either charge, and the decrease represents a greater disinclination on the part of some Crown Attorneys to charge an accused with an indictable offence. Comparing the summary convictions for the

P. J. Giffen

TABLE X

TYPES OF INDICTABLE OFFENCES COMMITTED BY URBAN AND RURAL OFFENDERS, 1956 AND 1961. RATES PER 100,000 POPULATION 16 YEARS AND OLDER

	1956*	Urban 1961†	Change	1956*	Rural 1961†	Change
Homicide	1	1	0	1	1	0
Assault offences	37	33	−4	26	28	+2
Sex offences	9	11	+2	6	7	+1
Family offences	1	1	0	1	1	0
Commercialized vice	12	14	+2	2	2	0
Gainful offences with violence	48	71	+23	28	46	+18
Malicious offences against property	5	6	+1	5	6	+1
Theft	108	166	+58	60	78	+18
Fraudulent offences	24	37	+13	14	15	+1
Motor-vehicle offences	25	3	−22	35	5	−30
Other	13	19	+5	8	9	+1

Number: 1956 – 26,846; 1961 – 37,001

Residence
not stated: 1956 – 567; 1961 – 1,678

Sources: *P. J. Giffen, *op. cit.*, p. 94.
†Dominion Bureau of Statistics, *Statistics of Criminal and Other Offences, 1961* and *Census of Canada, 1961.*

same two years, we find that the convictions for impaired driving increased from 12,059 to 23,151, and that the convictions for driving while intoxicated increased from 1,718 to 5,906 – increases far in excess of the rate of population growth.

Educational Differences

The data provided in the criminal statistics on the educational levels of persons convicted of indictable offences yield the only usable measure of socio-economic status. Although the occupations of indictable offenders and of the fathers of juvenile delinquents are stated in the official statistics, they cannot be used to calculate rates. For 1961 this is clearly out of the question because the census used a new classification of occupations while the criminal statistics continued to use the old classification. In previous census years the categories formally corresponded, but the differences in

78

rates between occupations calculated on this basis are so extreme that they cannot be taken seriously. In 1951, for example, the rate of indictable offenders classified as 'labourers' was 1,975 per 100,000 persons in that occupation, as compared with 56 per 100,000 for persons classified as 'managerial'. One suspects that the information on occupations provided by court officials is based on different criteria than those used by census enumerators and coders.

TABLE XI

EDUCATIONAL LEVEL OF PERSONS CONVICTED OF INDICTABLE OFFENCES, CANADA, 1951 AND 1961. RATE PER 100,000 POPULATION 16 YEARS AND OVER

| | 1951* | | 1961† | |
	Number	Rate	Number	Rate
No Schooling	915	462	424	242
Elementary School	17,012	361	18,533	367
High School	7,590	220	14,412	252
Above High School	882	149	499	66

Educational level not stated: 1951 – 2,576; 1961 – 4,811

Sources: *P. J. Giffen, *op. cit.*, p. 94.
    †Dominion Bureau of Statistics, *Statistics of Criminal and Other Offences, 1951* and *1961*; *Census of Canada, 1951* and *1961*.

Table XI indicates that the crime-rate declines as the level of education rises. The only obvious anomaly is that the group with no schooling has a low rate in 1961, lower than all except the 'above high school' group. But the large proportion of cases 'not stated' means that these rates might be differently ranked if the offenders whose education is not given were disproportionately distributed. Our suspicion of non-randomness is strengthened when we look at the differences among types of offences in the 12.4 per cent of the total cases where education is not stated. Of these, 43.4 per cent are motor-vehicle offenders, and 25.2 per cent are commercialized-vice offenders. In contrast, only 10.7 per cent are offenders convicted of theft, and 11.1 per cent are offenders convicted of gainful offences with violence. In so far as people of different educational levels tend to be convicted of different types of offences, this selective reporting may give an unreliable picture of the relative criminality of the four educational levels.

The information in Table XII indicates that the offence pattern does differ by educational level. Offenders with the most education appear to be least likely to engage in violent predatory offences and ordinary theft,

P. J. Giffen

TABLE XII

PERCENTAGE DISTRIBUTION OF INDICTABLE OFFENCES BY EDUCATION
OF PERSONS CONVICTED, CANADA, 1961

	No Schooling	Elementary	High School	Above High School	Not Stated
Homicide	0.7	0.3	0.2	0.0	0.2
Assault offences	19.8	10.4	8.5	8.8	13.0
Sex offences	6.8	3.0	2.9	5.8	3.0
Family offences	0.9	0.2	0.2	1.0	0.3
Commercialized vice	1.1	2.2	3.8	3.4	6.9
Gainful offences with violence	15.3	22.6	18.7	9.8	18.2
Malicious offences against property	0.9	1.9	1.9	1.6	3.2
Theft	42.7	46.3	45.3	30.8	38.8
Fraudulent offences	5.7	7.4	13.0	29.9	9.0
Motor-vehicle offences	1.1	0.6	0.8	2.4	3.9
Other	4.7	5.2	4.9	6.4	4.2
Number	424	18,533	14,412	499	4,811

Sources: Dominion Bureau of Statistics, *Statistics of Criminal and Other Offences, 1961*
and *Census of Canada, 1961.*

but more likely to get money by fraudulent means. Violence against other persons appears to be more characteristic of offenders of lower educational attainment. The drop in the total rate for persons with above-high-school education between 1951 and 1961 is due largely to the decline in motor-vehicle offences. These offences were 18 per cent of the convictions of the most educated offenders in 1956 – a much higher proportion than that found at the other three educational levels – but they declined to 2.4 per cent in 1961. This apparent decline in indictable motor-vehicle offences is due largely to the decline in the offences involving alcohol and this, in turn, is explained by a change in the policies of prosecution mentioned in a previous section. A few jurisdictions that earlier proceeded against drinking drivers by indictment have adopted the more common practice of charging them with summary offences.

Religious Differences

Little attention has been paid by criminologists to differences between adherents of the major religious groups in rates of crime. If large differences were proven to exist, they would be difficult to interpret since religious

80

differences are confounded with class and ethnic differences. Also, nominal religious affiliation masks wide differences in the extent of belief in religious dogma and in participation in religious activities.

TABLE XIII

RELIGION OF PERSONS CONVICTED OF INDICTABLE OFFENCES, 1951 AND 1961. RATE PER 100,000 POPULATION, 16 YEARS AND OLDER, FOR ALL DENOMINATIONS WITH 100 OR MORE OFFENDERS

| | 1951* | | 1961† | |
	Number	Rate	Number	Rate
Roman Catholic	13,799	356	18,979	373
United Church	4,077	203	5,087	212
Anglican	3,947	262	4,356	267
Presbyterian	1,611	267	1,309	220
Baptist	881	131	967	244
Lutheran	729	223	904	194
Greek Orthodox	453	355	425	237
Jewish	222	147	203	112
Salvation Army	139	318	218	398
Pentecostal	103	171	143	164

Other religions: 1951 – 360; 1961 – 572
No religion: 1951 – 227; 1961 – 534
Religion not stated: 1951 – 1,538; 1961 – 3,388
Protestant, not otherwise stated: 1951 – 1,194; 1961 – 1,594

Sources: *P. J. Giffen, *op. cit.*, p. 96.
†Dominion Bureau of Statistics, *Statistics of Criminal and Other Offences, 1961* and *Census of Canada, 1961*.

Table XIII seems to show that some fairly large differences in rates exist among religious groups in Canada, but a closer examination of the statistics leads to questions about their reliability. If the large number of offenders whose religion is not stated or whose Protestant denomination is not specified are not randomly distributed among the religious affiliations, the true picture may be quite different. Rates for the large 'Protestant, not otherwise stated' category of offenders cannot be calculated because the census has no comparable classification of the general population. (Census enumerators are apparently much more successful at eliciting and recording specifics of religion than are court officials.)

However, the relatively high Roman Catholic rate cannot be accounted for by the failure to report religious preferences. The rate of conviction

P. J. Giffen

of all non-Catholics plus those Catholics whose religion is not stated is still lower than the conviction rate of the Roman Catholic group. In 1961 the rate for the residual group was 237, compared with 373 for those who were listed Roman Catholics.

TABLE XIV

RELIGION OF JUVENILE DELINQUENTS, 1951 AND 1961. RATE PER 100,000 POPULATION 7-15 YEARS OF AGE, FOR ALL DENOMINATIONS WITH 100 OR MORE DELINQUENTS IN 1961.

	1951 Number	Rate	1961 Number	Rate
Roman Catholic	2,878	267	6,791	407
United Church	974	237	1,609	240
Anglican	926	343	1,402	332
Baptist	298	378	340	317
Presbyterian	299	340	328	271
Lutheran	75	121	251	255
Greek Orthodox	51	208	162	510
Salvation Army	95	721	140	684
Pentecostal	56	306	135	439

Other religions: 1951 – 187; 1961 – 430
No religion: 1951 – 14; 1961 – 55
Religion not stated: 1951 – 331; 1961 – 714
Protestant, not
    otherwise stated: 1951 – 460; 1961 – 2,858

Sources: Dominion Bureau of Statistics, *Juvenile Delinquents, 1951* and *1961*; *Census of Canada, 1951* and *1961*.

Table XIV indicates that there are also large differences among religious groups in rates of juvenile delinquency but that, once again, the figures are to be regarded with scepticism because of the numerous cases in which religious preference is not recorded. The rank-order of religious groups in delinquency-rates is markedly different from that for adult offenders. Moreover, both the juvenile and adult rates show a considerable change in the rates of some religious groups from 1951 to 1961, although such changes are much more marked among juvenile delinquents. Either there are pronounced shifts between age-groups in the likelihood of affiliates of the various religions being convicted of offences, or the reporting by the courts is highly variable. We have no way of knowing.

82

Country-of-Birth Differences

The relationship between country of birth and rates of conviction in Canada, 1951-4, has been examined in a study done for the Department of Citizenship and Immigration.[5] Figure 4, based on data from this study, shows the contrast between the rates of conviction of native-born males and those born in other countries. Whereas the rate of the native-born is

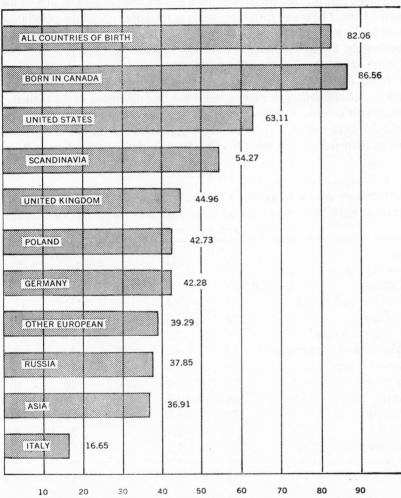

Fig. 4. Average rates of conviction in Canada per 10,000 males, 15-49 years of age, by country of birth. 1951-4.

[5]Frank G. Vallee and Mildred Schwartz, 'Report on Criminality among the Foreign-Born in Canada' in B. R. Blishen *et al., Canadian Society* (first edition), Toronto: Macmillan, 1961, pp. 560-7.

86.6, that of foreign-born males taken collectively is 42.8, or less than half. The rates for specific foreign-born groups range from 63.1 for the United States-born to 16.7 for the Italian-born.

The differences in rates may be due in some degree to differences in the age-distribution of males within those groups. A group made up to an unusual extent of old men would likely have a low rate, but if age were controlled statistically, the group might have a rate as high as that of the native-born. The use of forty-nine years as the upper age of the population base in the study lessens but does not eliminate the influence of age. Unfortunately, figures on convictions cross-classified by country of birth and age are not available in the official statistics.

If the discrepancy between native-born and foreign-born rates is not due to age differences, it may reflect a genuine difference in the tendency to commit crimes. A difference might be expected in view of the highly selective immigration policies of recent decades. In so far as the applicant for an immigration visa must have no known criminal record, must be of

TABLE XV

BIRTHPLACE OF FATHERS OF JUVENILE DELINQUENTS, 1951 AND 1961. RATE PER 10,000 MALES 25-64 YEARS OF AGE OF EACH BIRTHPLACE IN THE CANADIAN POPULATION

	1951* Number	Rate	1961† Number	Rate
Canada	4,968	3.6	11,764	3.8
England and Wales	415	9.4	211	11.7
Scotland	192	13.6	71	9.9
Northern Ireland	1	0.2	21	10.4
Other British Commonwealth	11	9.0	13	7.9
United States	116	2.6	89	11.0
Germany	21	3.1	20	3.5
Italy	74	19.6	8	0.9
Poland	73	3.2	28	3.6
Russia	84	2.7	28	3.6
Scandinavia	32	2.1	54	19.3
Other European Countries	230	5.2	59	2.8
Asiatic Countries	25	7.3	11	5.8

Father's birthplace not stated: 1951 – 401; 1961 – 90

Sources: *P. J. Giffen, *op. cit.*, p. 90.

†Dominion Bureau of Statistics, *Juvenile Delinquents, 1961* and *Census of Canada, 1961*.

good physical health and free of a diagnosed serious mental illness, and give evidence of his ability to support himself, it seems likely that many of the potential criminals are prevented from entering the country.

A part of the explanation may be that it takes time to assimilate the criminal norms, techniques, and associations of the new society; the process is at least as long and difficult as that of assimilation of the legitimate patterns, since the opportunities are weighted in favour of the latter. The relatively high conviction-rate of males born in the United States lends support to this theory, since their cultural background is closer to the dominant Canadian pattern than that of other immigrants.

The delinquency-rates of the children of foreign-born parents present a more complex picture. The second generation of a majority of the nationality groups shown in Table XV appear, in 1961, to have higher rates than the children of Canadian-born parents. But the very considerable differences between the rates in 1951 and 1961 for some groups should caution us to attach little significance to the ranking in any one year. With so few cases involved, a change of a few children in any category except 'Canadian-born parents' can make a large difference in rates. Moreover, the age distribution of males twenty-five to sixty-four years of age of each birthplace has probably changed considerably over the ten-year period, thus changing the proportion within origin-groups of men at the ages when they are most likely to be fathers of juveniles. The most surprising change in rates shown in the table is that for delinquents of Italian parentage. The number decreased by only 66 between 1951 and 1961, but this decline was sufficient to change their standing in terms of rates from by far the most delinquent group in 1951 to by far the least delinquent in 1961. The least debatable conclusion to be derived from these statistics is that children of foreign-born fathers are responsible for only a minor part of official delinquency in Canada – 20.4 per cent in 1951 and 22.2 per cent in 1961.

Provincial Differences

The apparent differences among Canadian provinces in rates of crime and delinquency are particularly intriguing because the relative standing of several of the provinces is not what one would expect on the basis of the degree of urbanization and growth of the province.

A test of the extent to which differences in urbanization account for provincial differences in rates is reported in Table XVI. The standardized rate for each province is the rate of convictions adjusted for differences in urbanization among provinces. It is the rate that a province, given its present urban and rural rates, would have if the proportion of its population living in urban centres in 1961 were the same as that of Canada as

a whole. The trustworthiness of the standardized rate is reduced by
the large number of cases in which residence is not stated and by the possibility that court officials use different criteria than census officials in classifying the residences of offenders – factors discussed above in the section
on urban-rural differences.

TABLE XVI

PROVINCIAL RATES OF CONVICTION STANDARDIZED FOR RURAL-URBAN
DISTRIBUTION OF RESIDENCE. RATES PER 100,000 POPULATION 16 YEARS
AND OLDER, 1961 (RANK-ORDER OF PROVINCES IN BRACKETS)

	Unstandardized Rate*	Standardized Rate*	Change
Canada	313	313	
Alberta	465 (1)	489 (1)	24
British Columbia	431 (2)	428 (2)	–3
Manitoba	375 (3)	389 (3)	14
Ontario	327 (4)	315 (5)	–12
Nova Scotia	292 (5)	310 (7)	18
Saskatchewan	259 (6)	339 (4)	80
Newfoundland	263 (7)	313 (6)	50
Quebec	233 (8)	228 (8)	–5
New Brunswick	184 (9)	182 (9)	–2
Prince Edward Island	64 (10)	115 (10)	50

*Using only offenders for whom residence is stated.

Sources: Dominion Bureau of Statistics, *Statistics of Criminal and Other Offences,
1961* and *Census of Canada, 1961.*

The ranking of provinces by rates of conviction is altered little by
standardizing for urbanization. This seems to indicate that provincial
differences in rates are not due to a significant extent to differences in the
proportion of their populations living in urban centres. Only in Saskatchewan, Newfoundland, and Prince Edward Island is the rate increased
very much by altering the urban-rural distribution of population. All three
provinces have a considerably more rural population than Canada as a
whole, but so has New Brunswick, whose rate is decreased slightly by
standardizing.

The census definition of 'urban' used above includes all centres of
1,000 population and over. A closer relationship between urbanization
and rates of crime might be found by looking only at proportions of provincial populations in larger urban centres. In Table XVII the ranking

86

of the provinces in conviction-rates is compared with their ranking in terms of the proportion of population in centres of 30,000 and over, and the proportion in census metropolitan areas. In addition, the provinces are ranked in terms of population increase from 1956 to 1961.

TABLE XVII

COMPARISON OF PERSONS CONVICTED OF INDICTABLE OFFENCES.
POPULATION IN CITIES AND METROPOLITAN AREAS, AND RATES OF
GROWTH, BY PROVINCES (RANK-ORDER OF PROVINCES IN BRACKETS)

	Indictable Offenders 1961*	Delinquents 1961†	Percentage of Population in Centres 30,000 +, 1961	Percentage in Census Metro Areas 1961	Percentage Increase in Population 1956 - 1961
Canada	328	449	34.9	44.8	13.4
Alberta	476 (1)	500 (3)	44.9 (1)	46.3 (5)	18.6 (2)
British Columbia	464 (2)	684 (1)	29.0 (5)	58.0 (1)	16.5 (3)
Manitoba	391 (3)	435 (4)	36.6 (4)	51.6 (3)	8.4 (6)
Ontario	337 (4)	628 (2)	37.4 (3)	52.2 (2)	35.6 (1)
Nova Scotia	296 (5)	382 (5)	23.5 (7)	25.0 (6)	6.1 (8)
Saskatchewan	293 (6)	150 (10)	26.0 (6)	—	5.1 (10)
Newfoundland	273 (7)	374 (7)	13.9 (9)	19.4 (7)	10.3 (5)
Quebec	244 (8)	270 (8)	38.8 (2)	47.0 (4)	13.6 (4)
New Brunswick	191 (9)	379 (6)	16.6 (8)	16.0 (8)	7.8 (7)
Prince Edward Island	64 (10)	243 (9)	—	—	5.4 (9)

* Rate per 100,000 population 16 years and older
† Rate per 100,000 population 7-15 years of age

Sources: Dominion Bureau of Statistics, *Statistics of Criminal and Other Offences, 1961;*
Juvenile Delinquents, 1961; Census of Canada, 1961.

A measure of statistical association applicable to such data is the Spearman rank-correlation. If the rank-order of the provinces in any two measures is completely similar, the correlation will be +1.0, and if they are completely reversed the correlation will be −1.0. Scores between these extremes indicate degrees of positive or negative relationship between the rank-orders.

The ranking of the provinces in rates of indictable offenders is positively associated with their ranking in the three measures, but the correlations are not high: +.58 rank correlation with population increase, +.54 with the proportion in census metropolitan areas (only the eight provinces with such areas are used), and +.53 with the proportion in cities of 30,000 and over.

The ranking of the provinces in juvenile-delinquency rates is fairly highly associated (+ .76) with population increase, moderately (+ .69) with the proportion of the population in census metropolitan areas (eight provinces), and hardly at all (+.29) with the proportion in centres of 30,000 persons and over.

These findings in regard to provincial differences are difficult to interpret. If we assume that all courts are equally faithful in reporting cases to the Dominion Bureau of Statistics, or at least that there are no significant differences between provinces in reporting, we are forced to conclude that the degree and type of urbanization and the rate of population increase do not have a consistent influence on crime-rates.

But when the rankings in Table XVII are examined more closely, we find that the four provinces with the highest rates of indictable offenders are all quite highly urbanized (none is less than 64-per-cent urban) and, with the exception of Manitoba, growing rapidly. At the other extreme, the very low conviction-rate of Prince Edward Island accompanies the least urban of provincial populations and a very slow rate of growth. The low rank-correlations between the series in Table XVII appears to be due

TABLE XVIII

COMPARISON OF RATES OF INDICTABLE OFFENDERS, JUVENILE DELINQUENTS, DIVORCES, ALCOHOLICS, ILLEGITIMATE BIRTHS, AND SUICIDES, BY PROVINCES, 1961 (RANK-ORDER OF PROVINCES IN BRACKETS)

	Indictable Offenders	Juvenile Delinquents	* Divorces	† Illegitimate Births	‡ Suicides	§ Alcoholics
Canada	328	449	36.0	4.5	7.5	2,140
Alberta	476[1]	500[3]	78.0[2]	6.2[4]	8.9[3]	1,550[6]
British Columbia	464[2]	684[1]	85.8[1]	6.9[1]	11.8[1]	2,380[2]
Manitoba	391[3]	435[4]	33.9[4]	6.3[3]	7.6[5]	1,970[4]
Ontario	337[4]	628[2]	43.9[3]	3.5[10]	8.8[4]	2,440[1]
Nova Scotia	296[5]	382[5]	33.2[5]	6.9[1]	5.2[7]	1,460[7]
Saskatchewan	293[6]	150[10]	27.1[7]	5.9[5]	10.2[2]	1,170[9]
Newfoundland	273[7]	374[7]	1.3[10]	4.3[8]	3.7[10]	915[10]
Quebec	244[8]	270[8]	6.6[9]	3.6[9]	4.6[9]	2,340[3]
New Brunswick	191[9]	379[6]	32.4[6]	4.4[7]	5.0[8]	1,230[8]
Prince Edward Island	64[10]	243[9]	7.6[8]	4.8[6]	6.7[6]	1,640[5]

*Rate per 100,000 population. Dominion Bureau of Statistics, *Vital Statistics, 1961.*
†Per cent of live births. *Ibid.*
‡Rate per 100,000 population. *Ibid.*
§Estimated alcoholics per 100,000 population aged 20 and over. *13th Annual Report of the Alcoholism and Drug Addiction Research Foundation of Ontario*, Toronto, 1964.

largely to the few provinces whose conviction-rates are anomalous in terms of their urbanization and growth. Quebec is the outstanding example. Although the province has a low conviction-rate, it is the second most urbanized province (using the census definition of 'urban') and it had the fourth highest rate of population increase in 1956-61. These exceptions suggest that differences in the reporting of cases may play an important role.

Clues to incongruities in the rank-order of provinces in conviction-rates might also be found by comparing these rates to their ranking in the rates for other 'social problems' that are more reliably reported or estimated. This is done in Table XVIII.

The rank correlation of indictable-offender rates with divorce-rates is +.83, with suicide-rates +.64, with illegitimacy-rates +.51, and with rates of alcoholism +.35. The rank-correlation of juvenile-delinquency rates with divorce-rates is +.87, with alcoholism-rates +.58, with suicide-rates +.42, and with rates of illegitimate births +.28. In short, only the ranking in divorce-rates correlates highly with the ranking in conviction-rates of both types.

One cannot assert that the social conditions producing high rates of crime always result in correspondingly high rates of these other types of minority behaviour (despite the consistent standing of British Columbia) since other variables are known to be involved. A predominantly Roman Catholic population, for example, is likely to have a low rate of suicide and a low rate of divorce, whatever its crime-rate. Differences in the causation of the four types of divergent behaviour are indicated by the fact that they turn out to be inconsistently correlated with each other. The highest rank-correlation is +.76, for divorce-rates and suicide-rates by provinces, and the lowest is −.06, for rates of alcoholism and illegitimacy. Although this table raises interesting questions, it cannot be used as an indication of the reliability of reporting.

ANOTHER APPROACH TO CRIMINAL STATISTICS

In this chapter certain figures reported in the official court statistics have been examined on the assumption that, converted into rates, they would tell us something about differences among major social categories in amount and in types of crime. Many anomalies for which there are no apparent explanations have emerged, and these have inevitably led to questions about the reliability of the official statistics.

A more fruitful approach might be to treat the official statistics as guilty until proven innocent. With such an approach, when a difference in rates is found, the initial assumption is that the statistics are at fault, and attention is directed to discovering differences in the faithfulness of reporting or in the methods of classification that could account for it. If nothing is uncovered, an explanation is sought in differences in the administration of justice and law enforcement. Of course the research worker may eventually be driven to the conclusion that the disparity is one of those rare cases of genuine difference in rates – a residual category particularly troublesome to explain.

This suspicious approach is more likely to produce reliable official statistics than manipulation of the figures as if they reflected the real world. The responsibility for doing such studies must rest largely with the Dominion Bureau of Statistics, however, since it alone is in a position to secure and make available much of the necessary data.

5

Criminal Legislation

A. J. MACLEOD

A person commits a crime when he does anything that the law says he must not do or fails to do something that the law says he must do, if by reason of his act or omission he becomes liable to punishment under the law.

Crime prejudices the safety and welfare of the public as a whole. The object of criminal proceedings, therefore, is to punish the offender and thereby, hopefully, to prevent any repetition of the act or omission by that offender or by any other person.[1]

Criminal legislation deals with a number of matters in relation to the social problem of crime. It defines the type of conduct that constitutes a criminal offence. It sets out the kinds and degrees of punishment that the court may impose upon a person who is convicted of an offence. It provides the procedures that are to be followed in the field of criminal law to compel the appearance of an accused in court, to determine the court by which the question of guilt or innocence is to be decided, and to ensure the attendance of witnesses at the trial. Criminal procedure is treated elsewhere in this volume. This chapter deals with criminal legislation other than laws governing matters of procedure.

OFFENCES

Under the British North America Act, the federal Parliament has exclusive jurisdiction to legislate in the field of the 'criminal law'. Parliament has, accordingly, passed the Criminal Code, the statute in which the bulk of the criminal law of this country is to be found.

---

[1]The object of civil proceedings, on the other hand, is to satisfy a person who has been damaged or injured by compelling the wrongdoer to compensate the victim for the wrong that he has suffered.

HISTORY OF CANADA'S CRIMINAL LAW

More than 360 sections of the Criminal Code define offences and set out punishments. Most of them describe conduct that is now generally regarded as morally wrong by the majority of Canadians, and much that must have been unacceptable under the customs and usages of the earliest Britons, the Romans, and the other peoples who came to live in what is now the United Kingdom.

In very ancient times the mass of the people were completely illiterate. The laws could not be reduced to writing, but were largely transmitted from generation to generation by word of mouth. This 'unwritten law' was common, or general, throughout the realm. In time it came to include the reports of the judges who presided over the courts of antiquity, and the treatises of scholars who were concerned with the law. It was law made by the courts to meet the moral and social needs of the community, as distinct from law enacted by a legislature or council that reflected the wishes of the majority of the people.

This common law of Britain was augmented over the centuries as necessity required and became the basis of the legal systems of the Commonwealth countries and the United States. Thus the original criminal law that applied in Canada was the common law of England and those statutes of the United Kingdom Parliament that extended to the New World.

Two years after Confederation, the Parliament of Canada passed five principal Acts concerning the criminal law. They were based on, or adapted largely from, similar statutes passed in the United Kingdom in 1861. In 1878 a royal commission was established in Britain to prepare for that country a draft code of criminal law. In the course of time, it reported to the government of the United Kingdom and submitted a draft code. However, the government of the day did not see fit to act upon the recommendations of the royal commission nor has any succeeding United Kingdom government. That country does not even now have a consolidation of the criminal law in one statute. Rather, the criminal law is to be found in more than one hundred and fifty individual statutes that have been enacted by Parliament.

In Canada, the first Criminal Code was submitted to and enacted by Parliament in 1892. It was based largely upon the United Kingdom draft code. Amendments to the Code began to be introduced in Parliament almost immediately, and continued to be introduced in almost every session until the revised Code came into force in 1955.

Until 1955, a person in Canada could be prosecuted for common-law offences. The revised Criminal Code, however, abolished all common-law offences. Now no person can be charged with and convicted of a criminal offence unless the conduct complained of has been declared by Parliament to be an offence. At the same time, however, the new Code preserves every rule and principle of the common law that justified or excused the conduct of an accused person or that constituted a defence to the charge against him, except in so far as Parliament, from time to time, might legislate otherwise.

Criminal Offences

The Criminal Code reflects, basically, the accepted moral standards of the day. It contains prohibitions and punishments concerning such matters as these:
– offences against public order (treason, sedition, piracy, prize-fights);
– offences against the administration of law and justice (bribery, breach of trust, corruption of officials, perjury, false accusations);
– sexual offences, offences against public morals, and disorderly conduct (rape, incest, seduction, acts of gross indecency, obscene publications);
– offences involving disorderly houses, gaming and betting (gambling, book-making, lotteries, bawdy-houses, prostitution);
– offences against the person and reputation (failure to provide necessaries of life, criminal negligence, homicide, suicide, causing bodily harm, assault, kidnapping and abduction, abortion, communicating venereal disease, bigamy, blasphemous or defamatory libel);
– offences against rights of property (theft, robbery, and extortion, breaking and entering, possession of stolen goods, obtaining by false pretences, forgery);
– fraudulent transactions relating to contracts and trade (fraud, falsification of books and documents, impersonation, forgery of trademarks and trade descriptions, criminal breach of contracts);
– wilful and forbidden acts in respect of certain property (mischief, arson, false alarms, cruelty to animals);
– offences relating to currency (counterfeiting, uttering counterfeit money).

Not all of the offences created by Parliament under the power to enact criminal law are to be found in the Criminal Code. Most of the statutes of Canada, from the Aeronautics Act to the Yukon Quartz Mining Act, contain provisions that create offences and authorize punishments. Under the Aeronautics Act, for example, it is an offence for a person to operate a commercial air service without a valid and subsisting licence issued by the Air Transport Board. Under the Yukon Quartz Mining Act, it is an offence for the holder of a mining claim to cause damage or injury to the claim of any other holder by throwing earth, clay, stones, or other material upon it.

Provincial Offences

The British North America Act authorizes each provincial legislature to impose 'punishment by fine, penalty, or imprisonment for enforcing any law of the province'. All provincial legislatures exercise this power. For example, by provincial laws relating to the use of liquor, hunting and fishing, operation of motor vehicles on the highway, public health, protection of children, and the like, they have created offences and authorized punishment for offenders. These are indeed 'provincial offences', but are not 'crimes' under the criminal law. The point to be remembered is that the criminal law is enacted by the federal Parliament and applies everywhere in Canada, while a provincial law applies only in the province where it was enacted by the legislature.

TYPES OF CRIMINAL OFFENCES

An offence under the criminal law of Canada is either an indictable offence or an offence punishable on summary conviction. Indictable offences are those that society regards as serious and, in the worst cases, deserving of substantial punishment. Where the punishment upon conviction may be heavy, a person who is accused of an indictable offence is entitled, if he wishes, to be tried by jury. Some indictable offences admit of less severe punishment, and those accused of them are not entitled to be tried by jury. These include theft or obtaining by false pretences when the amount stolen or obtained does not exceed fifty dollars, attempted theft, obstructing a police officer, keeping a common gaming-house, operating a lottery, and assaulting a police officer.

A summary conviction offence is less serious than an indictable offence and is not considered to merit heavy punishment, even in the worst cases. The policy of the law, therefore, is that the accused is not entitled to be tried by jury.

Some offences are both indictable and summary conviction, and the option whether the proceedings will be by indictment (that is, in most cases entitling the accused to elect trial by jury) or by summary conviction (that is, in every case non-jury) ordinarily rests with the Crown Attorney.

THE ELEMENTS OF CRIME

To constitute a crime there must be, as a general rule, both a 'guilty mind' and a prohibited act or omission. The criminal law does not punish a mere intention, however wrongful or blameworthy, unless it is accompanied by a prohibited act or omission. Moreover, again speaking generally, the criminal law does not punish an act or omission, however reprehensible, unless it is done with some wrongful or blameworthy (that is, criminal) intention. This 'blameworthy condition of the mind' is referred to by lawyers and judges as *mens rea*. It is a necessary ingredient of crime that must be proved by the prosecution in any serious offence.

Criminal intention is not to be confused with motive. A man's intention is his determination to follow or not to follow a particular course of conduct. His motive is his reason for reaching that determination. On the question of conviction or acquittal, the criminal law as a rule disregards the motives of the accused, although his motives may have some effect on the question of punishment. The test is whether the accused has reached the age of understanding, and is sane, sober, and free to act or refrain from acting. If so, and if it is established that he has done something that is defined as a crime, he is guilty, whatever his motive might have been, or even if he had no motive.

The law takes the view that a man's acts or omissions are the best guide in determining his intention. Accordingly, a well-known rule of law states that 'every man must be presumed to know and to intend the natural and probable consequences of his act', even if it is an act of omission. In court, however, this presumption is rebutted by proof that the accused, when he committed the act, did not have a mind capable of forming an intention. Thus no person can be convicted of an offence in respect of an act or omission on his part that occurred while he was under seven years of age. The law assumes that such a child has not yet acquired sufficient discretion to know right from wrong. Nor can a person be convicted if he was between seven and fourteen years of age at the time of the alleged offence unless 'he was competent to know the nature and consequences of his act and to appreciate that it was wrong'.

Again, the law provides that no person shall be convicted of an offence committed while he was insane. (The law presumes, however, that everyone is and has been sane until the contrary is proved by the accused or his counsel.)

A person who has committed an offence under compulsion, by threats of immediate death or grievous bodily harm from a person who was present when the offence was committed, is excused for committing the offence, if he believed that the threats would be carried out and if he was not a party to any conspiracy or association whereby he was subject to compulsion. The excuse of compulsion, however, is not available to those accused of treason, murder, piracy, attempted murder, assisting in rape, forcible abduction, robbery, causing bodily harm, or arson.

A man cannot commit a crime when he is asleep or has been thoroughly drugged, because in that condition he is not capable of forming an intention or of understanding the nature of any act that he may do. There are cases, too, where drunkenness is a defence, because the extreme degree of intoxication precludes the existence of any intent at all.

PUNISHMENT

The punishments authorized under the criminal law, depending upon the nature of the offence, are these: fine, forfeiture, suspended sentence, imprisonment, whipping, and death.

In some cases the law prescribes different degrees or kinds of punishment for an offence. For example, the Code provides that everyone who commits robbery is guilty of an indictable offence and is liable to imprisonment for life and to be whipped. In such circumstances, the punishment to be imposed and the degree of punishment are in the discretion of the court that convicts the accused. The court may sentence the offender to any term of imprisonment up to life imprisonment. It may authorize or not authorize whipping, as it sees fit. It may impose a fine in addition to imprisonment, and whipping in addition to either of them. If no previous conviction is proved against the offender, the court may suspend the passing of sentence, pending his good behaviour.

Fine

The criminal law today rarely prescribes a fine as a specific punishment for an indictable offence. It is unnecessary for the law to do so, because the Code provides that an accused who is convicted of an indictable offence punishable with imprisonment for five years or less may (except where a minimum term of imprisonment is prescribed) be fined in addition to, or instead of, any other punishment that is authorized. When an accused is convicted of an indictable offence punishable with imprisonment for more than five years, the convicted person may be fined in addition to, but not instead of, any other punishment that is authorized.

The Code authorizes a term of imprisonment to be imposed in default of payment of a fine. If a proportion of the fine is paid, the term of imprisonment is reduced by the same proportion.

There is no limit to the amount that a court may order a person to pay by way of fine upon conviction for an indictable offence under the Criminal Code. The law presumes that the courts will fix upon an amount that is reasonable but realistic. For summary conviction offences under the Code, the maximum fine is $500. It is to be noted, however, that other Acts of Parliament sometimes limit the amount of fine that may be imposed on indictment for the offences they create, and sometimes fix a maximum higher than $500 in summary conviction proceedings.

For both indictable and summary conviction cases, the Code authorizes the convicting court, subject to certain limitations, to direct that a fine shall be paid forthwith or that it shall be paid at such time and on such terms as the court may fix. The limitations are as follows: the court may not require payment forthwith unless it is satisfied that the defendant has sufficient means to pay immediately or unless, upon being asked whether he wishes time for payment, the defendant does not request time. Unless there is some special reason for not allowing time to pay, the court must allow at least fourteen days, and a warrant of committal may not be issued until the time for payment has expired. The court may, upon the defendant's application, extend the time for payment.

Where a court convicts an accused of an indictable offence, it may, upon the application of a person who has suffered loss or damage to property as a result of that offence, order the accused to pay to that person an amount by way of satisfaction or compensation.

Forfeiture

In the commission of certain offences, some article or thing is involved that, in the eyes of the law, would be dangerous or at least contrary to the public interest if it were held in private ownership, lest it be used again for the commission of a similar offence. The law therefore provides that, where there is a conviction, the court may order the article or thing to be forfeited to Her Majesty in right of the province, to be disposed of as one of Her Majesty's provincial ministers may direct. For example, an offensive weapon might, upon forfeiture, be destroyed or, if a firearm, kept in a police armoury. Money seized in connection with gaming offences usually is deposited with the provincial Treasurer. An automobile that has been used in connection with drug trafficking usually is sold at public auction, and the proceeds deposited in the government treasury.

Suspended Sentence and Probation

In some cases, the court may decide that, even though the accused is guilty of the offence, a fine or a sentence of imprisonment is neither necessary nor desirable. In such a case, instead of sentencing the offender to punishment, the court may suspend the passing of sentence. It is to be noted that it is the passing of sentence that is suspended, and not sentence itself. The court's power in this respect is by no means unlimited, however. The power does not exist where the law prescribes a minimum fine or a minimum term of imprisonment; the minimum punishment required by the law must be imposed. Nor, with certain exceptions, may sentence be suspended if it is proved that the accused has previously been convicted of an offence. The exceptions are as follows: if only one previous conviction is proved and it took place more than five years before the current offence, sentence may be suspended; even if the one previous conviction that is proved took place within the previous five years, sentence may nevertheless be suspended if the previous offence was not in the same class of offence as the current one, for example, if one was theft and the other assault.

A point to be kept in mind is that the Crown must 'prove' previous convictions. That is to say, the Crown must bring evidence before the court to establish that the accused was previously convicted. It is solely in the discretion of the Crown to prove or not to prove previous convictions, and the judge or magistrate may or may not, of his own knowledge, be aware that there were previous convictions. If the Crown does prove one or more previous convictions, the court cannot suspend the passing of sentence unless the case falls within one of the exceptions already noted. On the other hand, if the Crown does not choose to bring before the court any evidence concerning previous convictions, there is nothing to prevent the court from suspending the passing of sentence.

In determining whether or not suspended sentence is the proper remedy, the court considers the age, character, and antecedents of the accused, the nature of the offence, and any extenuating circumstances surrounding the commission of the offence.

The court will not suspend the passing of sentence unless the accused is prepared to give an undertaking that he will keep the peace and be of good behaviour during any period that is fixed by the court, and that he will appear and receive sentence when called upon to do so during that period if he commits a breach of his undertaking. The court may prescribe conditions to be set out in the undertaking that the accused gives: for instance, that he shall make restitution and reparation to any person who suffered injury or loss by his offence, and that he shall provide for his dependants. The court may impose any conditions that it considers desirable in the circumstances. The law prohibits such a recognizance to be kept in force for more than two years.

The court may, of course, require the accused to report from time to time to a person designated by it, and the accused is under the supervision of that person during the prescribed period. This aspect of suspended sentence is known as 'probation'. If the offender fails to carry out the terms of his undertaking, the supervisor must report him to the court, which may have him brought before it to be sentenced for the offence in respect of which sentence was suspended.

Imprisonment

Under the former Criminal Code, there was great disparity in the sentences that the criminal law authorized upon conviction for offences. The Criminal Code Revision Commission (1949-53) felt that the sentences provided in the former Code followed no apparent pattern or principle and, in the Commission's view, were frequently not consonant with the gravity of the offences to which they related. The Commissioners were of the opinion that there should be a few general divisions of punishment by imprisonment, each offence being assigned to one of the divisions. Accordingly, apart from cases where the sentence of death may be imposed, the present Code provides maximum sentences for indictable offences in accordance with the following pattern: life, fourteen years, ten years, five years, and two years. The new Code also establishes a standard maximum sentence for summary conviction offences, that is, imprisonment for a period not exceeding six months or a fine not exceeding $500, or both.

A section of the Criminal Code that authorizes imprisonment commonly states that a person who is guilty of an offence 'is liable to imprisonment for' two years, five years, or ten years, as the case may be. This means that two, five, or ten years is the greatest term of imprisonment that the court may impose. Of course, if the statute prescribes 'not less than two years and not more than ten', the court must impose a sentence of at least two years but it cannot exceed ten years. The 1955 revision of the Code did away with most minimum sentences in the Code itself. Other statutes still provide minimum sentences for some offences, but the only ones that remain in the Code are for the offences of driving while intoxicated, driving while ability is impaired, and theft from the mails. Under the Code, the sentence of death is mandatory upon conviction for capital murder or for certain forms of treason and piracy, and a sentence of preventive detention is mandatory where the court finds an accused to be a dangerous sexual offender.

A sentence of imprisonment commences to run immediately it is imposed, unless the statute otherwise provides or the court otherwise orders. Thus the term of a sentence to penitentiary commences to run on the day it is imposed by the court, even though the offender may be detained in a local prison for some time before being transferred to the penitentiary. Where an accused is convicted on two or more charges, the court may order the sentences to be served either consecutively or concurrently. If a convicted person is released on bail, pending an appeal, the time during which he is at large on bail does not count as part of his sentence.

A person sentenced to imprisonment for life or for a term of two years or more is required to be sentenced to a penitentiary operated by the federal government. The Province of Newfoundland provides an exception: there prisoners who are a federal responsibility are confined in a prison operated by the province. A person sentenced to imprisonment for a term of less than two years, or for two or more terms of less than two years each to be served one after the other, must be sentenced to a prison or reformatory operated by the provincial authorities in the province in which the conviction took place.

Whipping

Where whipping is an authorized punishment, the court may sentence a convicted offender to be whipped on one, two, or three occasions. The court is required to specify the number of strokes to be administered on each occasion, but there is no limit to the number of strokes that it may specify. A sentence of whipping must be carried out under the supervision of a medical officer. The cat-o'-nine-tails is to be used, unless some other instrument is specified in the sentence. The instrument most frequently used nowadays is a strap.[2] The officer in charge of the prison determines when a sentence of whipping is to be executed, but the Code requires that, whenever practicable, this shall be not less than ten days before the expiration of any term of imprisonment. The law prohibits the whipping of females.

The Penitentiary Regulations require that sentences of whipping be carried out in as humane a manner as possible in the presence of as small a group of officers as is reasonable in the circumstances.

It is a sign of the times – and of modern correctional thinking – that the list of offences for which whipping may be imposed is steadily diminishing. Generally speaking, it is now reserved for those offences that involve violence or the threat of violence: rape and attempted rape, indecent assault, armed burglary and robbery, choking or strangling or suffocating another person, administering or attempting to administer a stupefying or overpowering drug or other substance. However, it is also authorized as a punishment for incest and sexual intercourse with a female under fourteen years of age, offences in which violence is not necessarily an element.

Sentences of Death

The law requires that the sentence pronounced against a person condemned to death 'shall be that he shall be hanged by the neck until he is

[2]The cat-o'-nine-tails consists of nine strands of woven cotton cord, each strand being one-eighth of an inch in diameter and eighteen inches long, with frayed ends. The strands are attached to a thirty-inch wooden handle. The strap is smooth leather, three-sixteenths of an inch thick, fifteen inches long and three inches wide, attached to a leather handle that is twelve inches long. The strap is perforated by eight holes, each one-quarter of an inch in diameter, spaced two and one-half inches apart.

dead'. A judge who sentences a person to death must appoint for the execution of the sentence a day far enough in the future to allow sufficient time for the Governor General in Council³ to consider the case. The judge is required to make a report of the case to the Minister of Justice.

A person who is sentenced to death must be confined in a safe place within a prison, apart from all other prisoners. Only the keeper of the prison and his servants, the prison doctor, and a clergyman or minister can have access to him without written permission from a judge of the court or from the sheriff. A death sentence must be executed within prison walls in the presence of the sheriff, the keeper of the prison, the prison doctor, and any other persons required by the sheriff to be present. A clergyman or minister who wishes to attend may do so, and so may any other persons whom the sheriff considers it proper to admit.

The coroner having jurisdiction where a sentence of death is carried out must hold an inquest within twenty-four hours after the execution. Unless the Lieutenant-Governor in Council of the province otherwise orders, the body is required to be buried within the prison in which the sentence is executed.

The practice in Canada since Confederation has been to have every capital case considered by the Governor General in Council after all legal remedies on the part of the convicted person have been exhausted or abandoned. The Letters Patent constituting the office of the Governor General of Canada, issued by the Sovereign, read in part as follows:

> Our Governor General shall not pardon or reprieve any . . . offender without first receiving in capital cases the advice of our Privy Council for Canada and, in other cases, the advice of one, at least, of his Ministers.

Although it is the practice to have all capital cases considered by the Governor General in Council, this step is not legally necessary. If the minister concerned (either the Minister of Justice or the Solicitor-General) believed that there should be no interference in the sentence of death, he could merely refrain from taking any action, and the offender would be executed at the appointed time. If, on the other hand, he felt that the sentence should be commuted, he would have to seek the concurrence of his cabinet colleagues who constitute, for all practical purposes, the Privy Council. If they agreed, the order of the Governor General commuting the death sentence would issue accordingly.

THE PREROGATIVE OF MERCY

The Criminal Code authorizes the Governor General in Council to grant

---

³ The Governor General acting on the advice of the cabinet.

relief from punishment to offenders. This can be done by remitting part of a sentence of imprisonment, by granting a free pardon or conditional pardon, or by remitting, in whole or in part, a pecuniary penalty, fine, or forfeiture imposed under an Act of Parliament. However, as has been noted, nothing in the Criminal Code in any manner limits or affects Her Majesty's royal prerogative of mercy. The traditional practice in Canada has been for the Governor General, acting on the advice of one member of the cabinet, to exercise the royal prerogative of mercy where the punishment in respect of which it is sought is a punishment other than death.

Free Pardon

A free pardon may be granted by the Governor General. It is ordinarily granted only on the ground of innocence established by the applicant or admitted by the Crown. A free pardon says, in effect, that the person to whom it is granted did not commit the offence of which he was convicted, that is, that there has been a total miscarriage of justice. Not more than fifteen free pardons have been granted between 1935 and 1965.

Ordinary Pardon

In the case of an ordinary pardon, the guilt or innocence of the convicted person is not in issue. The pardon is usually granted on compassionate grounds. The Crown forgives the offender for having committed the offence, and releases him from the conviction and the penalties. It does not say that he did not commit the offence.

Ordinary pardons have been granted where the offence was of a minor nature, and the applicant had lived a law-abiding life since the conviction, in cases where the granting of the pardon would provide some benefit to the applicant and would not endanger society.

Remission of Sentence of Imprisonment

An order of remission by the Governor General remits the amount of time remaining to be served by an offender under the sentence of imprisonment. It is usually based on some compassionate ground in circumstances where parole, for one reason or another, is not a suitable remedy: for example, where the inmate has served a substantial portion of his sentence and there is illness or a death in his family. It is also granted, upon occasion, when the sentence imposed upon the offender exceeds that authorized by law, and the offender, for whatever reason, has not seen fit to seek his remedy in the courts.

Remission of a sentence of imprisonment does not involve changing the terms of the sentence passed by the court. The order is that the inmate shall be released from imprisonment forthwith.

Commutation of Sentence of Imprisonment

The prerogative of mercy includes power to commute a sentence of imprisonment to one of shorter duration, for example, to substitute a five-year for a ten-year sentence. The power has been exercised only very rarely and, indeed, has not been used at all from 1935 to the time of writing. The policy has been instead to leave the convicted person to his remedy by way of an appeal against sentence to the appropriate appeal court.

Remission of Fines and Forfeitures

Under the prerogative of mercy, the Governor General has the power to remit a fine or forfeiture in whole or in part, no matter to whom it is payable. Remission results in the return of money already paid by way of fine, or money or chattels already forfeited under the order of a criminal court.

Usually an applicant must show some compassionate ground, such as undue hardship to the offender or his family. There have been cases where the fine or forfeiture was remitted because of illegality of sentence or because of innocence of the convicted person. In the case of innocence, however, the remedy should ordinarily be by way of pardon and automatic return thereunder of the money or chattels paid or forfeited.

The power of remission has been exercised in regard to forfeitures of bail, but in such cases the traditional practice has been to refuse the remedy if the applicant is a professional bondsman.

Restoration of Driving Privileges

Where an order prohibiting driving has been made under Section 225 of the Criminal Code, the power to lift the prohibition, in whole or in part, is now vested in the Parole Board under the Parole Act. Where there is also a suspension of licence under a provincial statute, the applicant must look to the Crown in right of the province. Traditionally, the tendency has been not to grant relief except in unusual circumstances: where the prohibition results in substantial hardship, for example, it might be lifted to the extent necessary for the driver to earn his living and support his dependants.

Remission of Corporal Punishment

Remission of whipping has been granted where the physical or mental condition of the offender has been such as to indicate that the imposition of corporal punishment would do more harm than good and, therefore, should not be carried out; where the legality of the sentence was in question; where the commission of the offence involved mitigating circum-

A. J. MacLeod

stances; where the offender was a psychopath; or where exceptional reasons for compassion existed.

Punishment should be calculated, as far as possible, to reform the offender. If whipping, because of the mental or physical state of the prisoner, is likely to verge upon or achieve brutality, or for any reason is likely to make the prisoner worse rather than better, an application for remission of the sentence is justified.

OTHER ASPECTS OF CRIMINAL LAW

The Habitual Criminal

The Code provides that, where an accused has been convicted of an indictable offence and is found to be an habitual criminal, the court may, upon application by the Crown, impose a sentence of preventive detention. It is, in effect, a life sentence because under it the convicted person will remain in custody until such time as he is released on parole by the Parole Board. A condition precedent to the imposition of a sentence of preventive detention upon an habitual criminal is that the court considers such a sentence expedient for the protection of the public.

Under the Code an accused is an habitual criminal if

(a) he has previously, since attaining the age of eighteen years, on at least three separate and independent occasions been convicted of an indictable offence for which he was liable to imprisonment for five years or more, and is leading persistently a criminal life, or

(b) he has been previously sentenced to preventive detention.

An application for a sentence of preventive detention will not be heard unless

(a) the Attorney General of the province in which the accused is to be tried consents;

(b) seven clear days' notice has been given to the accused specifying the previous convictions and the other circumstances upon which it is intended to base the application, and

(c) a copy of the notice has been filed with the court.

On the question whether the accused is or is not persistently leading a criminal life, he is entitled to tender evidence as to his character and repute, but it is in the court's discretion whether to admit evidence of his character and repute on behalf of the Crown.

The Dangerous Sexual Offender

The Code makes preventive detention mandatory for the dangerous sexual offender. By definition this is 'a person who, by his conduct in any sexual matter, has shown a failure to control his sexual impulses, and who is

104

likely to cause injury, pain or other evil to any person, through failure in the future to control his sexual impulses or is likely to commit a further sexual offence'.

The Crown may apply to the court for a finding that an accused is a dangerous sexual offender if he has been convicted of rape, carnal knowledge, indecent assault, buggery, bestiality, gross indecency, or an attempt to commit any of these offences. At the hearing, the court is required to hear the evidence of at least two psychiatrists, one of whom is nominated by the provincial Attorney-General, and any other evidence that is relevant.

Where the court finds that the accused is a dangerous sexual offender, as defined, it must impose a sentence of preventive detention. In effect this is, as in the case of the habitual criminal, a life sentence. However, the law requires the Parole Board, at least once in every year, to review the condition, history, and circumstances of every person undergoing preventive detention, for the purpose of determining whether he should be permitted to be at large under parole supervision.

Identification of Criminals

The Identification of Criminals Act, Chapter 144 of the *Revised Statutes of Canada,* provides as follows:

> 2. (1) Any person in lawful custody, charged with, or under conviction of an indictable offence, or who has been apprehended under the Extradition Act or the Fugitive Offenders Act, may be subjected, by or under the direction of those in whose custody he is, to the measurements, processes and operations practised under the system for the identification of criminals commonly known as the Bertillon Signaletic System, or to any measurements, processes or operations sanctioned by the Governor in Council having the like object in view.
> (2) Such force may be used as is necessary to the effectual carrying out and application of such measurements, processes and operations.
> (3) The signaletic cards and other results thereof may be published for the purpose of affording information to officers and others engaged in the execution or administration of the law.
> 3. No one having the custody of any such person, and no one acting in his aid or under his direction, and no one concerned in such publication, shall incur any liability, civil or criminal, for anything lawfully done under this Act.

An order-in-council has been passed under Section 2 of this Act authorizing police forces to take photographs of persons to whom the Act applies.

The Identification of Criminals Act does not apply to a child who is charged with the commission of a delinquency under the Juvenile Delinquents Act and there is, therefore, no authority to fingerprint or photograph such a child. It is otherwise, of course, if the act complained of is an indictable offence and the juvenile court, in its discretion, orders the child to be proceeded against by indictment in the ordinary courts.

Extradition Act

Most of the more enlightened countries of the world have passed legislation and have entered into treaty arrangements with each other whereby persons who have been charged with or convicted of relatively serious offences may be returned from the countries to which they have fled, to stand trial or receive punishment in the countries where their offences are alleged to have been committed. Under the Extradition Act of Canada, no person is liable to be surrendered by Canada if the offence alleged to have been committed in another country is of a political character. This Act applies only to countries not within the Commonwealth.

The Fugitive Offenders Act governs the surrender by Canada of persons who have committed, elsewhere in the British Commonwealth, offences that are punishable by imprisonment for one year or more where they were committed, whether or not they would be offences if committed in Canada.

Other Criminal Legislation

Other statutes, enacted by Parliament under the criminal-law power, are discussed elsewhere in this volume. Some examples are: The Royal Canadian Mounted Police Act (Chapter 6), the Juvenile Delinquents Act (Chapter 8), the Penitentiary Act and the Prisons and Reformatories Act (Chapter 12), the Parole Act (Chapter 13), and the Narcotic Control Act (Chapter 16).

HOW CRIMINAL LAW IS MADE

A new criminal law – like any new law – starts out as an idea in the mind of some individual. This individual may be a judge, a lawyer, a peace officer, or a civil servant. More likely, he is a private individual or a representative of a group of private citizens who see a danger to the community or to some community interest, unless Parliament legislates on a certain matter.

The idea may come from a newspaper account of a local incident in which some injury or damage has been suffered by a person who, in the opinion of the reader, should not have suffered. The reader is surprised to find that the criminal law provides no means whereby the wrongdoer can be brought before the courts and punished. He thinks that wrongdoers of this kind should be punished.

Accordingly, he writes to his Member of Parliament, expressing his dissatisfaction with the state of the law and suggesting new legislation, or he may write directly to the Minister of Justice in Ottawa. In any event, his letter reaches the desk of the Minister, who then asks his departmental officials to consider the merits of the proposal. The suggestion may be referred to the Criminal Law Section of the Commissioners on Uniformity of Laws, an organization composed of all of the Deputy Attorneys-General of the provinces. It may be referred to the Criminal Justice Section of the Canadian Bar Association. The Minister may seek the views of experienced judges, lawyers, or other professional men in whose judgment he has confidence.

The Minister ultimately makes his own decision on the merits of the proposal. If he agrees with it, he will seek the concurrence of his colleagues in the cabinet. If they agree, the proposal will be contained, along with other proposals, in a bill to amend the Criminal Code or other appropriate statute. The bill will, in due course, be introduced in Parliament.

In the House of Commons, the principle of the proposal, as set out in the bill, will first be explained to the members by the Minister, and speeches on the principle will be made by those members who are interested. The proposal will then be considered in the committee of the whole House; at this time the Minister may be called on to answer questions concerning the measure, and amendments may be moved by any member. Eventually the proposal is passed, either amended or not amended, or it is defeated.

The same procedure, in effect, is followed when the bill (if it has been passed in the House) is sent to the Senate. In the Senate, however, it is customary for the bill to be referred to the Banking and Commerce Committee so that departmental officials may be questioned concerning it and, sometimes, so that interested private citizens may be called upon or given an opportunity to express their views. If there are no amendments to the proposal in the Senate, and it is passed by the Senate, it will then await royal assent by the Governor General. Upon receiving royal assent it becomes law, unless the bill itself provides that it is not to become law until some later time.

The criminal law of Canada, although taking its form from parliamentary draftsmen, and its force from the action of the legislature, owes much of its substance to the work of persons who are neither draftsmen nor parliamentarians. Especially in the last two decades or so, it has been a favourite practice of governments to refer problems in the field of criminal law to royal commissions. For example, as has been noted, the revision of the present Criminal Code was the work of a royal commission. In the mid fifties, there was a royal commission on criminal sexual psychopaths, and another on the defence of insanity in criminal causes. In 1956, the Fauteux Committee reported upon the principles and procedures followed in the Remission Service of the Department of Justice and, in so doing, made a number of recommendations that have now been incorporated in the criminal law of Canada. Changes in the criminal law also resulted from the report of the Archambault Commission in 1938, which had been appointed to inquire into the operation of Canadian penitentiaries.

Nevertheless, it should be observed that very little of the criminal law of Canada is enacted without consideration by some form of parliamentary committee. The revised Criminal Code of 1955 was considered on several occasions by special committees of the Senate and of the House of Commons. In 1955, a special committee of the Senate reported on the traffic in narcotic drugs in Canada. In 1956, a joint committee of the Senate and House of Commons reported on the questions of capital punishment, corporal punishment, and lotteries.

The device of referring questions of principle in the field of criminal law to royal commissions and parliamentary committees is advantageous in that it enables interested organizations, whether national or local, and interested individuals to make recommendations concerning the state of the law and what should be done to improve it. As evidence that the public takes advantage of such opportunities, it should be mentioned that, on the revision of the Criminal Code of 1955, the House of Commons committee alone heard oral representations from dozens of national organizations and received briefs from almost one hundred others.

Further Reading

CANADA. Criminal Code, *Statutes of Canada, 1953-4*, chapter 51. Ottawa: Queen's Printer.

————. Letters Patent Constituting the Office of Governor General of Canada, *Revised Statutes of Canada, 1952*, vol. VI. Ottawa: Queen's Printer. p. 305.

MARTIN, J. C. *Annotated Criminal Code of Canada*. Toronto: Cartwright, 1955.

6

The Police

W. H. KELLY

No public agency is of greater importance to the community than the police. Usually the police officer is the first point of contact between the citizen and the law. How the police conduct themselves and what they accomplish do much to destroy or create respect for the law. And the increasing complexity of our society, with its urbanization, industrialization, technological improvement, and mobility, has brought greater need of law and efficient police protection. The police moreover are in a strategic position to detect the causes of crime and delinquency and to prevent such acts. They are on the 'front line', and their vigour and efficiency largely determine society's reaction to violations of the law.[1]

THE POLICE AND THE LAW

The Evolution of Law

As previous chapters have explained, law is now, as it was in its beginnings, a code of conduct drawn up by society for its own protection. Today, as in ancient days, laws must be enforced by the threat of punishment to lawbreakers. Until quite recently the punishment of a transgressor was often banishment from the community and from the protection it afforded, and sometimes even death. Various degrees of punishment have now been established, but banishment in the form of a jail sentence is still common.

Law-making has also changed over the centuries. As society developed, kings or other leaders acquired the right to make the laws. Later the power of such leaders declined to the point where the people gained the right to make their own laws and to subject even the leaders to those laws. Almost

[1]Robert G. Caldwell, *Criminology*, New York: Ronald Press, 1956, p. 255.

109

700 years ago, Henry Bracton[2] stated an important constitutional principle:

> But the King himself ought not to be subject to man but subject to God and to the law, for the law makes the King. Let the King, then, attribute to the law what the law attributes to him, namely, dominion and power, for there is no King where the will and not the law has dominion.[3]

Although much of the law now in force was originally common law, law-making today in a democratic country is a legislative function. That is, the people, through their elected representatives, make the law.

The Evolution of Law Enforcement

As law-making evolved so did law enforcement. As the power of the kings increased and they made their own laws, they also enforced them, usually by means of the army or the nobility. As the power of the kings diminished and the law-making power of the people increased, the law-enforcement powers passed into the hands of the people. Today in a democracy such as Canada, the public, through its government, controls the police forces that enforce the law.

The use in England in the eighteenth century of the 'night-watch system' may be said to have marked the transition from law enforcement as an arm of the ruler to law enforcement as an arm of the people. That system, however, which required civilians to patrol city streets 'slowly and silently and now and then to listen', was inefficient for a number of reasons. It was very difficult to compel the citizens to take their turns. Since most of the watch pursued regular work during the day, sleeping while on watch was common. Such protection as the watch could provide was available only from 9 p.m. to sunrise; at no other time was there police service. Moreover, 'sunrise' depended upon the time stipulated in the local laws. This was not the same in all localities and so 'sunrise' could mean any time between 3 a.m. and 5 a.m.

The growth of communities and the resultant need for more adequate policing led to the formation of day-watches independent of the night-

---

[2]Henry Bracton, whose real name was Bratton, was an itinerant justice in England around 1250. His fame arose mainly from his attempt to systematize the body of English law by compiling early judicial decisions into one treatise, paying particular attention to decisions that he felt were precedents. His work contributed to a basis for the later establishment of case law.

[3]Quoted from Bracton's Notes in C. K. Allen, *Law in the Making*, 6th edition, Toronto: Oxford University Press, 1961.

watch. Although this advance added in some measure to the security of the citizens, it did not solve all problems. The fact that each ward had its own watches led to rivalry rather than efficiency, and an attempt to centralize the forces failed. There was also great conflict between day- and night-watches. Neither had enough men to do the job adequately, and many, members of the night-watch in particular, were more devoted to personal interest than to duty. Their shortcomings 'consisted mainly in their neglecting duty to earn extra money and then spending it whilst on the job. According to one authority, in London, the seventeenth century "nightly watch" consisted of a thousand watchmen who were paid a shilling or less per night according to their ward or parish . . . . This limited their recruitment to those least able to do their job properly . . . . For a tip of sixpence, . . . they would help a drunk to get home unharmed . . . . They spent most of their time in night cellars and dram shops.'[4] Under this system, crime flourished to such an extent that, by the early nineteenth century, the authorities estimated that in England there was one criminal in every twenty-two persons. Clearly a more effective form of organized law enforcement was essential.

In 1822 Sir Robert Peel made an abortive attempt to set up a police force in the London area. He continued his efforts in spite of opposition, and in 1829 succeeded. The move was strongly criticized in some quarters as one designed to trespass on the rights of the individual, but the speedy reduction in the number of crimes against person and property soon won favour and support for it.

Organized law enforcement in Canada and the United States began in the colonial period and was based on the night-watch system. In Canada the city of Toronto was incorporated in the year 1834. On March 11, 1835, the city council agreed to the appointment of five constables and a chief of police to operate under the direction of the High Bailiff and the City Magistrate. Two years after its formation, the police force was supplied with uniforms. The strength of six continued until 1852 when about a dozen constables were sworn in. In 1859 the force was organized as a proper police department and it had a strength of thirty-two men.

In 1844 the city of New York abolished the night-watch system and set up a form of police force consisting of approximately eight hundred men, but it was not organized as a proper police department until 1853. It has always been considered to be the oldest organized police department on the North American continent.

4Patrick Pringle, *Hue and Cry: The Birth of the British Police*, Toronto: Nelson, 1955, p. 43.

ORGANIZATION AND JURISDICTION OF
LAW-ENFORCEMENT AGENCIES IN CANADA

The organization and jurisdiction of law enforcement agencies in Canada are based on the powers conferred at Confederation upon the federal and provincial governments. The following excerpts from the British North America (B.N.A.) Act of 1867 are relevant:

> *Section 91*: It shall be lawful for the Queen, by and with the Advice and Consent of the Senate and House of Commons, to make Laws for the Peace, Order, and good Government of Canada, in relation to all Matters not coming within the Classes of Subjects by this Act assigned exclusively to the Legislatures of the Provinces; and for greater Certainty, but not so as to restrict the Generality of the foregoing Terms in this Section, it is hereby declared that (notwithstanding anything in this Act) the exclusive Legislative Authority of the Parliament of Canada extends to all Matters coming within the Classes of Subjects next hereafter enumerated; that is to say,
>
> *Sub-Section 27*: The Criminal Law, except the Constitution of Courts of Criminal Jurisdiction, but including the Procedure in Criminal Matters.
>
> *Section 92*: In each Province the Legislature may exclusively make Laws in relation to Matters coming within the Classes of Subjects next herein-after enumerated; that is to say,
>
> *Sub-Section 14*: The Administration of Justice in the Province, including the Constitution, Maintenance, and Organization of Provincial Courts, both of Civil and of Criminal Jurisdiction, and including Procedure in Civil Matters in those Courts.

In other words, the federal government has the exclusive right to make criminal law; the provincial governments must enforce it. The federal government sets down criminal procedure; the provincial governments organize and maintain the courts that carry out this procedure. Within their own areas, the provinces are also empowered to create police forces that have provincial or municipal jurisdiction.

The Federal Police Force

In Canada the federal police force is the Royal Canadian Mounted Police, which was originally formed in 1873 as a constabulary to police the Northwest Territories. Its members are appointed peace officers for the whole of Canada, and in actual practice have jurisdiction anywhere in Canada with respect to any federal statute.

In its role as the federal police force, the R.C.M.P. is concerned in the enforcement of more than fifty federal Acts including the Customs Act, Excise Act, Canada Shipping Act, Narcotic Control Act, Indian Act, and

Explosives Act. Enforcement of the Criminal Code, however, is, by authority of the B.N.A. Act, a provincial responsibility. As a matter of policy, therefore, the R.C.M.P. refrains, with very few exceptions, from active enforcement of the Criminal Code except where it also acts as a provincial or municipal police force.

The R.C.M.P. is under the control of the Minister of Justice, to whom the Commissioner of the R.C.M.P. is directly responsible. The senior officer of the divisional headquarters in each province is in turn responsible to the Commissioner at R.C.M.P. headquarters in Ottawa for administrative purposes and in matters relating to federal statutes. The sub-divisions are responsible to the Divisional Officers Commanding in the provinces. Each sub-division consists of some ten to twenty detachments, and the size of a detachment depends on the volume of police work in its area.

Section 20 of the Royal Canadian Mounted Police Act (April 1, 1960) states that the 'Minister [of Justice] may, with the approval of the Governor in Council, enter into arrangements with the government of any province or, with the approval of the Lieutenant-Governor in Council of any province, with any municipality in the province, for the use or employment of the Force or any portion thereof, in aiding the administration of justice in the province or municipality, and in carrying into effect the laws enforced therein'. By virtue of such arrangements made with the provinces, the R.C.M.P. acts as the provincial police force in British Columbia, Alberta, Saskatchewan, Manitoba, New Brunswick, Nova Scotia, Prince Edward Island, and Newfoundland. Although the Royal Northwest Mounted Police were responsible for provincial policing in Saskatchewan and Alberta from 1905 to 1917, the present arrangements have been in effect since 1928 in Saskatchewan, since 1932 in Alberta, Manitoba, New Brunswick, Nova Scotia, and Prince Edward Island, and since 1950 in British Columbia and Newfoundland. In these eight provinces, the R.C.M.P. is employed in the enforcement of the laws of the provincial legislature and in the carrying-out of certain other police duties agreed upon by the federal and provincial governments. Only Ontario and Quebec maintain their own provincial police forces.

Where the R.C.M.P. acts as the provincial police force, there must be a provision in some provincial legislation appointing members of the R.C.M.P. as peace officers for the province. In Manitoba, for example, under the provisions of the Provincial Police Act, all members of the R.C.M.P. are appointed constables for the province and are thereby given authority, which they would not have otherwise, to enforce provincial statutes. In Nova Scotia, this authority is granted to the R.C.M.P. under the Constables Act. The same procedure is followed where the R.C.M.P.

is under contract to carry out municipal police duties; provisions are contained in provincial statutes whereby members of the Force are appointed municipal constables for the purpose of enforcing municipal by-laws.

In provinces where the R.C.M.P. by agreement enforces provincial statutes and the Criminal Code, it reports directly on matters involving these to the Attorney-General of the province. Similarly in municipalities where it is responsible for law enforcement, it reports directly to the municipal authority concerned. The R.C.M.P. is the only police force in the Yukon and Northwest Territories, where it enforces all laws and ordinances. In these areas the Minister of Justice assumes the duties of a provincial Attorney-General.

The Provincial Police Forces

Provincial peace officers, including R.C.M.P. officers in the provinces where they act as the provincial police, are primarily concerned with the enforcement of the Criminal Code and provincial statutes, and their jurisdiction is generally confined to the province in which they are employed. They do not enforce the law in those municipalities that have their own police forces. The powers, jurisdiction, and regulations of provincial police forces are derived mainly from the Police Acts of the provinces concerned. For example the *Revised Statutes of Ontario,* 1960 (Chapter 298, Police Act, Sections 40-62), cover the establishment, jurisdiction, and powers of the Ontario Provincial Police Force and give statutory authority by which the Lieutenant-Governor in Council may create regulations for the administration of this force.

The authority of the provincial peace officer is also derived from many federal statutes which, in granting authority to peace officers, define 'peace officers' in terms that include municipal and provincial policemen. The Criminal Code of Canada is an example of such legislation: provincial police are peace officers under the definition in the Criminal Code, and consequently have all the authority granted to peace officers by the Code. The Criminal Code is a special case, however, because the duty of the Provincial Police to enforce it is established not only by the Code itself, through the authority given 'peace officers', but also by the constitution, which charges the provinces with the responsibility for the administration of justice. Thus enforcement of the criminal law, which is contained primarily in the Criminal Code of Canada, devolves to provincial authorities. In some federal statutes, such as the Narcotic Control Act and the Indian Act, the term 'peace officers' is used but not defined. Unless otherwise indicated, the term is taken to include peace officers appointed by the province.

Each provincial police force is headed by a Commissioner or Director, who is directly responsible to the Attorney-General of his province. In turn, the Officers commanding the various districts, divisions, and detachments are responsible to the Commissioner or Director.

The Ontario Government has recently set up a permanent Provincial Police Commission, the main function of which is to ensure adequate and competent policing throughout the province. The Commission may investigate and make recommendations to the government on any subject relating to crime conditions generally, including matters involving either provincial or municipal police forces. At the present time, the Commission consists of three men, one of whom acts as chairman.

As noted earlier, only Ontario and Quebec operate their own provincial police forces. In all other provinces the R.C.M.P. acts as the provincial police force.

The Municipal Police Forces

The municipal police forces, which include city, town, county, and township police forces, constitute the largest body of police in Canada, their total strength being more than 12,000 men. They are responsible within their own municipalities for enforcement of the Criminal Code, provincial statutes, and municipal by-laws. Municipal police generally have jurisdiction only in the municipality in which they serve as peace officers. However, certain members of most municipal forces have provincial as well as municipal jurisdiction and can thus investigate outside their own municipalities offences that occur within them.

As the Attorney-General of a province is responsible for law enforcement within the province, he exercises some degree of control over municipal policing; in some provinces, through the local Crown Attorney who gives considerable guidance to municipal police forces in his area and has wide power. Although, according to the *Revised Statutes of Ontario* (Chapter 298, Police Act, Section 2), 'every city and town is responsible for the policing of and maintenance of law and order in the municipality and for providing and maintaining an adequate Police Force in accordance with the police needs of the municipality', it is the Attorney-General who ensures that the required policing is carried out. When a municipality fails to maintain its own police force, or fails to maintain it in accordance with the provisions of the Police Act, or fails to enter into agreement with another municipality or with the Ontario Provincial Police Force for such maintenance, then 'the Commission may take such action as it deems necessary to secure the proper policing of the municipality by the Ontario Provincial Police Force and charge the municipality with the cost thereof . . . ' (Sections, 4, 5, 52, and 53, Chapter 298, *R.S.O. 1960*, as amended by Chapter 105, *R.S.O., 1961-62*).

Administratively, many of the municipal police forces are, through their chief constable, responsible to a police commission rather than to a police committee made up of council members. This commission normally has three members, at least one of whom is usually a magistrate or a county court judge, appointed by the provincial government. Often a member of city council is *ex officio* a member of the commission, thus giving the municipal government a direct voice in policy. The trend is toward removing control of the police force from a committee to a commission; the latter arrangement is more desirable from a police point of view, because a police commission is more independent in its authority than a police committee. A committee is usually made up of elected representatives in the community, and local pressures can often result in interference with police responsibilities.

Over one hundred municipalities in the provinces other than Ontario and Quebec are policed under contract by the R.C.M.P. In these municipalities, therefore, the R.C.M.P. perform a municipal, provincial, and federal role. In Ontario, the Provincial Police Force carries out municipal police duties, under contract, in addition to its provincial duties. In the Province of Quebec the provincial police also carry out municipal police duties when specially authorized by the Attorney-General.

Other Law-Enforcement Agencies

The other law-enforcement agencies in Canada, such as the railway or company police, constitute a small minority and have restricted jurisdiction. They are mainly concerned with offences committed against company property. However, members of these forces are often appointed special constables with jurisdiction to act beyond company property when dealing with crime that occurs thereon.

1. *Railway Police.* Section 456 of the Railway Act (*Revised Statutes of Canada, 1952,* Chapter 234) provides for the appointment of constables on the application of the railway company concerned to a superior or county court judge, two justices of the peace, or a stipendiary or police magistrate, within whose jurisdiction the railway runs. Section 457 of the same Act authorizes these constables to operate at railway terminals and within a quarter-mile of the tracks for the preservation of peace and the security of persons and property against unlawful acts:

    a. on railway and works belonging thereto;

    b. on and about trains, roads, wharfs, quays, landing-places, warehouses, lands, and premises belonging to the company whether in a county, town, city, parish, district, or other local jurisdiction anywhere through which the train passes. The constables have full powers of peace officers within their jurisdiction.

2. *Company Police*. The Ontario Police Act states that the Attorney-General may order a particular area to be designated a special area if abnormal conditions or special circumstances make it inequitable that responsibility for policing should be imposed on the province or any municipality. He may require any company that owns such an area to enter into an agreement with the Commissioner of the Ontario Provincial Police for its policing by constables employed by the company. If a special area has been so designated and the company refuses or neglects to enter into such an agreement, the Ontario Provincial Police will police the area and the cost may be recovered from the company as a debt due Her Majesty in right of the Province.

In some provinces, a number of company policemen are appointed constables by the Attorney-General under the Provincial Police Act and, therefore, have the same authority as any other provincial police officers.

3. *Customs and Excise Enforcement Officers and Others*. There are enforcement officers in Canada whose jurisdiction is even more limited than that of railway and company police. The powers of customs and excise enforcement officers and game-wardens are restricted to enforcement of a certain statute or group of statutes. These officers are not usually regarded as policemen, although in reality they are peace officers with limited police powers.

THE PEACE OFFICER: HIS POWERS OF ARREST AND SEARCH

The foregoing résumé of law-enforcement agencies covers most of the persons actively engaged in maintaining law and order in Canada. They are peace officers possessing the special powers of arrest and search required for the performance of their duties. According to Section 2 (30) of the Criminal Code, the term 'peace officer' includes:

(a) a mayor, warden, reeve, sheriff, deputy sheriff, sheriff's officer and justice of the peace;
(b) a warden, deputy warden, instructor, keeper, gaoler, guard and any other officer or permanent employee of a prison;
(c) a police officer, police constable, bailiff, constable, or other person employed for the preservation and maintenance of the public peace or for the service or execution of civil process; and
(d) an officer or person having the powers of a customs or excise officer when performing any duty in the administration of the Customs Act or the Excise Act.

117

Powers of Arrest

1. *Arrest without Warrant.* The peace officer's powers of arrest without warrant are governed primarily by Sections 435 and 436 of the Criminal Code of Canada. These sections provide as follows:

> 435. A peace officer may arrest without warrant
> (a) a person who has committed an indictable offence or who, on reasonable and probable grounds, he believes has committed or is about to commit an indictable offence or is about to commit suicide, or
> (b) a person whom he finds committing a criminal offence.
> 436. Anyone may arrest without warrant a person who, on reasonable and probable grounds, he believes
> (a) has committed a criminal offence, and
> (b) is (i) escaping from, and
> (ii) freshly pursued by
> persons who have lawful authority to arrest that person.

Section 435(a) refers to indictable offences only and gives the peace officer extensive powers of arrest – he needs only reasonable and probable grounds for believing that the suspect has committed or is about to commit an indictable offence. Once he has reasonable grounds, he may arrest the suspect even though no offence has, in fact, been committed or contemplated. It is worth noting that whether or not the suspected act takes place, the peace officer when arresting under these circumstances is declared by law to be 'justified', and is thus protected from criminal and civil liabilities.

Section 435(b) is confined to situations in which the peace officer finds a person actually committing a criminal offence. The term 'criminal offence' has been interpreted to mean any offence punishable on summary conviction or indictment under the Criminal Code of Canada or any other federal statute. It does not include an offence that is a violation of a provincial statute only.

Two other sections of the Criminal Code authorize arrest without warrant. Section 31 provides authority to the peace officer to arrest without warrant any person whom he finds committing a breach of the peace or whom, on reasonable and probable grounds, he believes is about to join in or renew a breach of the peace.

Section 171(2) authorizes a peace officer to arrest without warrant any person whom he finds keeping a common gaming-house, or any person found therein.

In addition to the Criminal Code, other federal and provincial statutes contain authority for peace officers to arrest without warrant for certain offences against those statutes.

2. *Arrest with Warrant.* Apart from the circumstances named above, the Criminal Code does not allow an arrest to be made without a warrant. Instead, a charge under oath is laid before a justice of the peace by the aggrieved party, or by a peace officer, against a specific person. The justice may then issue a 'warrant to apprehend', which authorizes any peace officer to arrest the person named in the warrant. Subject to two exceptions, a warrant to apprehend may be executed only within the territorial jurisdiction of the justice by whom the warrant was issued. The first exception is in the case of 'fresh pursuit', when the warrant may be executed anywhere in Canada. The second exception exists when a person is found or is suspected to be in a jurisdiction other than the one for which a warrant for his arrest was issued. In such a case, the warrant may be executed only when a justice of the peace in this jurisdiction is satisfied that the warrant is authentic. That is, someone who knows the signature of the issuing justice must swear that the signature on the warrant is actually that justice's signature.

When effecting an arrest with a warrant, the peace officer must have the warrant with him and should produce it if requested. In summary conviction offences when an arrest is made on a warrant, a copy of the warrant must be served on the person arrested, at the time of his arrest (Criminal Code, Section 700(2)). In indictable offences this procedure is not required. A warrant issued under a provincial statute cannot be executed outside of the province in which it was issued.

3. *Duty of Person Arresting.* A common-law rule states that a person must be informed immediately of the reason for his arrest, and Section 29 (2) of the Criminal Code specifically imposes a statutory duty upon any person who arrests another to inform that person of the reason for his arrest. Failure to do so may provide grounds for a civil action against the offending peace officer. Section 2 of the Canadian Bill of Rights also provides in part that 'no law of Canada shall be construed or applied so as to deprive a person who has been arrested or detained of the right to be informed promptly of the reason for his arrest or detention'.

Any peace officer who arrests a person, with or without a warrant, must not hold that person for an unreasonable length of time. If the officer intends to proceed in the courts he must take the prisoner before a justice within twenty-four hours after the arrest if a justice is available, and otherwise as soon as possible.

Although a peace officer or a private person should use force only in cases of extreme necessity, and his revolver only in the last extremity, he is authorized to use as much force as is necessary to effect a lawful arrest. A person must not use force that is intended to or is likely to cause death or grievous bodily harm, unless he believes on reasonable or probable grounds that it is necessary for the purpose of preserving himself or anyone under his protection from death or grievous bodily harm.

A peace officer 'who is proceeding lawfully to arrest, with or without a warrant, any person for an offence for which that person may be arrested without warrant, and everyone lawfully assisting the peace officer, is justified [that is, protected against civil and criminal liability] if the person to be arrested takes flight to avoid arrest, in using as much force as is necessary to prevent the escape by flight, unless the escape can be prevented by reasonable means in a less violent manner' (Criminal Code, Section 25).

It should be made clear, however, that everyone who is authorized by law (private person or peace officer) to use force is criminally responsible for any excess thereof according to the nature and quality of the act that constitutes the excess (Criminal Code, Section 26).

Also, if an arrest is not justified by law (for example, if a warrant is required and the peace officer does not have one), and the peace officer, meeting resistance, assaults the person he is attempting to arrest, then the peace officer could properly be convicted of assault on that person. Because the attempted arrest was illegal, the person had a right to resist.

4. *Search: Persons and Property.* Authority to search the person and property of an individual has been granted by Parliament and by provincial legislatures by means of enabling provisions in the federal and provincial statutes. Under most statutes, the right to search is available only to certain individuals charged with the responsibility of enforcing the statute. The Criminal Code is not so restrictive and under it any person has the right to apply to a justice of the peace for a search-warrant. Whether it is granted depends on the justice before whom the request is made. The right to search is, therefore, a statutory right, except in the case of a person arrested for an offence (see below), and the individual exercising the right must abide by the statute. Any abuse of his authority may leave him open to a civil action of trespass.

In certain cases a search may be conducted without warrant. For example, the Criminal Code authorizes a peace officer, who believes on reasonable grounds that an offence involving the possession of offensive weapons has been committed, to search without warrant a person, vehicle, or premises other than a dwelling-house for anything in connection with the offence. Section 10 (1) of the Narcotic Control Act enables a peace officer, who has reasonable cause to suspect that any drug is kept or concealed for any purpose contrary to that Act, to search without warrant any place other than a dwelling-house and any person found therein. Likewise, under the authority of Section 131 of the Customs Act, enforcement officers who have reasonable grounds of suspicion may search without warrant any package suspected of containing prohibited property or smuggled goods, and may stop, enter, and search any vessel or vehicle for such goods. Section 141 of the Customs Act provides authority to such officers to search without warrant any person entering Canada, if the officer has reasonable cause to suppose that the person searched has smuggled or prohibited goods secreted on his person.

Besides the federal statutes mentioned, many provincial statutes, particularly those concerned with liquor and game, contain provisions authorizing the search without warrant of vehicles and buildings other than dwelling-houses.

Authority is established in the common law, as well as in statutes, for peace officers to search persons without warrant after arrest.[5] The courts have held that an officer, after making an arrest, has the right to search the prisoner and to remove his clothing if necessary. The officer must take from the prisoner and hold for the disposition of the trial court any property that, in good faith, he believes to be connected with the offence charged, or which may be used as evidence against the prisoner or which may give a clue to the commission of a crime or the identification of the criminal. Any weapon or implement that might enable the prisoner to commit an act of violence or to effect his escape must also be taken from him.

The 'writ of assistance' is a document sometimes used by enforcement officers under federal statutes, particularly the Customs, Excise, and Narcotic Control Acts. The writ is similar to a blanket search-warrant sometimes issued under provincial Liquor Acts, and authorizes the holder to enter and search any premises in Canada for the purpose of detecting any offence against the particular Act for which the writ was issued. The writ is used only when there are circumstances in which, in the absence of a writ, a search-warrant could be obtained; it is left to the judgment of the person in whose name the writ is issued to decide when such circumstances exist.

The writ of assistance is issued by a judge of the Exchequer Court of Canada, usually upon application by the Attorney-General of Canada, and is granted to a particular individual. Since the writ provides fairly wide powers, the court is selective when granting it. It can be used only when a search is being effected under the particular Act for which it was granted and it must not be used imprudently.

Generally, under the Criminal Code a search-warrant is required to

---

5See also Chapter 7, *The Adult Court*, p. 136.

search any building or place for anything related to an offence that has been committed against the Code, or for evidence concerning the commission of such an offence. A search-warrant is a document, issued by a justice or a magistrate, authorizing peace officers to search premises or property. In order to obtain a search-warrant, the applicant, who may or may not be a peace officer (in the case of a search for stolen goods the applicant is usually the owner), must complete upon oath, before a justice, an 'information to obtain a search warrant'. This document must describe clearly the things to be searched for and the offence in respect of which the search is made. The applicant's reasons for believing that the goods to be searched for are in the particular premises or property must be indicated in the information.

The issuing of a search-warrant is a judicial act and, therefore, the justice or magistrate must consider the grounds upon which the request for a warrant to search is founded. If he is satisfied that there are reasonable grounds for believing that the goods in question are in the property to be searched, he may then issue the warrant. The warrant normally authorizes the applicant and peace officers to search the place for the goods in question.

In practice, the warrant to search is directed to a peace officer (constable) and the actual search is carried out by him, accompanied by the applicant whose name appears on the warrant; the applicant's presence is usually required so that he can identify the objects of the search if they are found and require identification. The warrant must be executed by day,[6] unless the justice authorizes its execution by night in specific terms. It is effective only within the territorial jurisdiction of the issuing justice, unless it is endorsed by a justice in another district, in which case it may also be executed in his jurisdiction. The person executing the warrant may break into premises to be searched if, after informing the possessor of the property of the purpose of his visit and demanding entry, he is refused admission.

There is a duty upon the person conducting the search to have the warrant or writ with him and to produce it if required. The articles to be searched for must be listed in the warrant. Nothing else may be seized except as provided for by Section 431 of the Criminal Code, which authorizes the seizure of anything that the officer executing the search believes, on reasonable grounds, to have been obtained by or used in the commission of any offence other than the offence for which the search-warrant was issued.

[6]Criminal Code definition of 'day', 6 a.m. to 9 p.m.

Parliament is particularly careful to ensure the fundamental rights of the individual. Thus when the law permits any peace officer to encroach on them, he must adhere strictly to the letter of the law. These rights are safeguarded not only by the watchfulness of the judiciary, which is quick to correct any abuse of authority, but also by the citizen's privilege of initiating a civil action against any offending officer.

We have dealt here with criminal offences, that is, the offences set out by the Criminal Code and those offences in other federal statutes to which the provisions of the Code apply.

5. *Authority to Search and Arrest under Provincial Statutes.* Many provincial statutes contain provisions authorizing specific persons to search without warrant or to effect an arrest without warrant in certain circumstances. In each instance, it is necessary to look to the particular statute for the necessary authority. Many empowering provisions under provincial statutes are limited in that only persons specified in the enactment are granted such authority.

Under the Ontario Game and Fisheries Act, for example, an officer under the Act is empowered to search without warrant vehicles and premises other than a dwelling-house when he has reasonable and probable grounds for believing that game or fish are kept illegally therein. The term 'officer' is defined in the Act to mean a member of the Ontario Provincial Police, a conservation officer, a member of the R.C.M.P., or any other person authorized to enforce the Act. Not even a village or town constable would come within the definition of 'officer' under this Act, unless specifically authorized.

In many provinces, provincial legislation provides for the granting of general powers of search to officers employed on Liquor Act enforcement. Under this legislation, individual police officers may be given a general warrant that authorizes them at any time and without any other warrant to search any premises in which they believe liquor is unlawfully kept. Section 110 (3) of the Ontario Liquor Control Act contains such a provision under which the Commissioner of the Ontario Provincial Police force may grant such power to any particular police officer.

Authority to arrest without warrant is provided by many provincial statutes and, again, the scope of the authority is determined by the provisions in the Act. Under a provision of the Highway Traffic Act of Ontario, a peace officer, as defined by that Act, has power to arrest without warrant any person who he, on reasonable and probable grounds, believes has committed certain offences that are enumerated in that provision. A similar provision appears in the Manitoba Highway Traffic Act. These are instances in which the police officer does not have a general power of arrest without warrant, but can effect an arrest in the case of certain offences.

Under the Ontario and the Manitoba Liquor Control Acts, a constable is authorized to arrest without warrant only persons whom he finds committing offences against those respective Acts.

To sum up, authority under provincial statutes to search without warrant, or to effect an arrest without warrant, depends on the provisions of individual Acts. In each case, it is necessary to review the Act and to determine if such authority is contained therein, and, if it is, which individuals are empowered by the Act to carry out the relevant provisions. The latter may usually be ascertained by referring to the definition section of the particular enactment.

It should be noted that, while there are provisions in the Criminal Code for executing search-warrants and warrants to arrest anywhere in Canada beyond the jurisdiction of the issuing justice, any such warrants issued under a provincial statute can only be executed within the province for which they were issued. There is no provision in any provincial statute to authorize the arrest of a person beyond the boundaries of the province in which the offence was committed, nor can a search-warrant be issued in a province to authorize a search in any place beyond that province.

CO-OPERATION BETWEEN POLICE FORCES

It is becoming increasingly evident that only the closest co-operation among police forces in Canada will enable them to cope with the methods of the modern criminal. Co-operation sometimes takes the form of assistance in detecting and apprehending criminals who have fled from one jurisdiction to another. Assistance is also given through aids to identification as, for example, through the R.C.M.P. Identification Branch in Ottawa, which operates a national clearing-house for records of such matters of police interest as fingerprints, tickets of leave, registration of fire-arms, fraudulent cheques and documents, and tire-tread identifications. Crime detection laboratories of the R.C.M.P. located in Ottawa, Ontario, Regina, Saskatchewan, Sackville, New Brunswick, and Vancouver, British Columbia provide scientific examination of evidence to all police forces in Canada. In Ontario and Quebec, the provincial laboratory similarly serves the police forces in those provinces.

Co-operation is likewise possible in police training, and is becoming more frequent in practice. For instance the Canadian Police College, operated by the R.C.M.P., is open to other forces, and provincial police schools are being established to assist in the training of municipal forces. Police forces also exchange advice and assistance on such matters as reorganization or the establishment of new departments.

An important factor in developing greater co-operation between police agencies is personal contact between officials. At lower levels the contact between police forces is mostly operational and consists, among other things, of the pooling of information concerning the activities of known criminals. At senior levels contact is made in various ways: for example, through bilateral meetings or through membership in such organizations as the International Association of Chiefs of Police, the Canadian Association of Chiefs of Police, and other similar regional groups.

On the international level, police forces co-operate through the International Criminal Police Organization, better known as 'Interpol'. This organization has a central co-ordinating office in Paris, France, which is responsible for setting in motion investigations when member countries report crimes of international significance. Ninety-two countries are represented in Interpol, which is not a separate police force as it is often depicted in films and on television, but a combination of police forces already in existence in the participating countries. When there is an international criminal problem, the appropriate police force of any country involved handles its own part of the problem. In Canada, the Government has designated the R.C.M.P. to carry out liaison between members of Interpol and the various Canadian police forces. An annual conference of Interpol, held in a different country each year, is attended by delegates representing the police forces that have the liaison responsibility in each country.

CO-OPERATION BETWEEN THE POLICE AND THE PUBLIC

*Responsibilities of the Public with Respect to the
Maintenance of Law and Order*

In order to understand the responsibilities of the public towards the maintenance of law and order, it is necessary to bear in mind several points. First, a police force is an organization set up by the public itself, through its political representatives, and thus a police officer, in performing his duty, is merely acting as an agent of society, enforcing those laws that society itself has made. Second, although society gives the police the powers to act on its behalf, it retains for itself the responsibility for seeing that these powers are properly used. Society's responsibility thus includes supervision of the police and of the civilian authorities that have direct control of the police. Also, and of equal importance, society has a responsibility to make its individual members aware of the function of the police and of the need for public approval of, and active support for, police actions legitimately carried out.

A public that is aware of these duties and accepts these responsibilities will help to ensure that the police operate effectively, in the best interests of citizens and police alike. In case of inefficiency, for example, the community has a duty to question, through its elected representatives, the leadership of the police organization. When the leadership is incompetent and is allowed to continue so, the community should question the civilian authority responsible for the supervision of its police force. No police force will remain incompetent if the civilian authority accepts its full responsibility.

Besides striving for a competent police force, the general public is duty-bound to support the police actively in their day-to-day operations. People often hesitate to give information or other assistance to the police, unless they can do so anonymously, usually either because they wish to avoid an appearance in court with its attendant waste of time and the possibility of undesirable publicity, or because they are afraid of appearing to be disloyal to their fellow citizens. Sometimes they fear retribution. Any such disinclination to assist the police actively, however, indicates a lack of awareness of the responsibility of the general public to help preserve law and order.

The average citizen has neither the time nor the knowledge to perform law-enforcement duties; society has assigned such duties to specially appointed members. But neither society nor the individual has ever relinquished the common-law rights of 'protecting the peace', and in fact, these rights have been incorporated into the Criminal Code. The following sections of the Criminal Code provide for the citizen to make an arrest without warrant in certain circumstances. Arrest may be made:

By any person
> 434. Anyone [meaning peace officer or citizen] may arrest without warrant a person whom he finds committing an indictable offence.

By any person on fresh pursuit
> 436. Anyone may arrest without warrant a person who, on reasonable and probable grounds, he believes
> > (a) has committed a criminal offence, and
> > (b) is (i) escaping from, and
> >   (ii) freshly pursued by
> > persons who have lawful authority to arrest that person.

By owner of property
> 437. Anyone who is
> > (a) the owner or a person in lawful possession of property, or

126

(b) a person authorized by the owner or by a person in lawful possession of property, may arrest without warrant a person whom he finds committing a criminal offence on or in relation to that property.

Under Section 30 of the Criminal Code any person who witnesses a breach of the peace may detain any person who commits or is about to join in or renew the breach of the peace, for the purpose of giving him into custody of a peace officer.

Although the peace officer's powers of arrest without warrant are slightly wider than those of an ordinary citizen, the ordinary citizen may arrest without warrant a person whom he finds actually committing an *indictable offence*, or who he is reasonably certain has committed a *criminal offence* and who is endeavouring to elude pursuers having lawful authority to make the arrest. Moreover, as Sections 25 and 30 of the Criminal Code indicate, a person making an arrest or carrying out any other law-enforcement action lawfully authorized, is 'justified' in using 'as much force as is necessary for the purpose'.

Historically and legally, then, the private citizen has a responsibility for law enforcement. The police are not the sole guardians of the law.

Responsibilities of the Police with Respect to the Public

No matter how aware the citizenry might be of the responsibilities historically and legally bestowed upon it to assist the police in the maintenance of law and order, its co-operation could scarcely be expected if, in the eyes of the public, the police themselves did not set and maintain reasonably high standards in their professional and private lives.

1. *Professional Standards.* The modern policeman is neither the dull-witted individual often characterized in motion pictures and on television, nor an exceptional being, clairvoyant in the solving of crimes. He is an intelligent individual striving for proficiency in his chosen vocation.

In Canada, police forces are very careful in their selection of a prospective policeman. The successful applicant must be a man of integrity, whose character will stand unblemished after a thorough investigation into his past life. His background is checked for any indication of a weakness that might impair his ability to perform his duties effectively. The true policeman is not motivated by an obsession to wield authority over others, nor attracted to the vocation by nice uniforms or the prospect of doing nothing but driving around in a new shiny car. He is attracted by a sincere desire to help others and, in the field of public service, to contribute to the establishment of a peaceful and law-abiding nation.

At the present time, the minimum educational requirement in most

police forces is at least a completed Grade 10. Some police forces require
a higher standing, and there is a trend throughout the country to raise the
requirement. Although a Grade 10 education may be sufficient for basic
and routine duties, and although the physique of a prospective policeman
is necessarily of considerable significance, intelligence and education are
also extremely important. There is plenty of room, and need, in police
work for men with advanced education.

Most police forces supplement the initial training of the policeman with
a well-planned educational program during his entire service. This program may consist of instructional courses varying from three-month
specialized courses to four- and five-year courses leading to a university
degree. The selection of a candidate for an advanced educational course
depends on many factors, among which his educational status at time of
engagement and his apparent desire to improve his education are of prime
importance.

The number of police personnel with university training is increasing
annually, and there is a constant demand for university graduates in most
of the larger police organizations. Law enforcement with all its intricacies
presents the graduate with a challenging opportunity to apply his knowledge to the practical aspect of police work. In spite of his university standing, it is essential that the graduate undergo normal police training and
carry out active police duties in the field, so that he will be able to appreciate fully the administrative and investigative problems associated with law
enforcement.

Success in crime prevention is necessarily linked with success in the
detection and investigation of crime. This in turn demands highly skilled
and trained personnel. Any investigation includes the gathering of information, and the gradual abandonment of less promising leads for more
promising ones, to the point where sufficient evidence is accumulated to
warrant laying a charge against a suspected person. In any investigation
of a crime, the aim is to find the person responsible and, in so doing, to
protect the innocent.

Prior to conducting any investigation, the peace officer must have a perfect knowledge of his statutory authority and of the rules of evidence.
Lack of either may result in the destruction of the entire case against the
accused, and possibly in a judgment for damages being awarded against
the peace officer, either of which misfortunes is not in the best interest of
the community.

The investigator must have keen powers of observation: his initial
examination at the scene of an offence must be thorough and complete,
since he usually has no second opportunity to obtain evidence. He must

have a basic knowledge of the scientific aids available to him, and he must make use of them. No article found at the scene of a crime is too minute to be of value. The slightest impression or stain on the smallest object, in the experienced hands of the scientist in the crime-detection laboratory, may provide a vital link in the investigation. But impressions and stains are easily obliterated, and once altered they lose their significance. The investigator must be an expert both in collecting and in protecting such evidence, for it is normally his responsibility until it reaches the laboratory.

A few examples will illustrate the skills involved in detecting crime. The expert in the laboratory, on examining a distorted piece of lead removed from the body of a man who was shot, can usually ascertain the calibre, type, and probable make of the weapon used. If the suspected fire-arm is subsequently located, further tests in the laboratory may show convincingly that it was the weapon used.

Recently in a Canadian city, investigators at the scene of a break-in found a piece of fabric containing fewer than twenty tiny yarns. The fibre expert in the police laboratory showed conclusively that the yarns in the piece of cloth had originally been part of the trousers of the suspect. In his conviction, this tiny piece of fabric was the main evidence to connect the accused with the scene of the crime.

In numerous cases, fingerprint impressions have been the only means of placing a suspect at the scene of a crime. Heel impressions preserved at the scene have also been connecting factors between the accused and the offence. In the western provinces, where safe-blowings are common, there have been a number of instances where flakes of plaster, found in the clothing of a suspected safe-blower and shown to be similar to the plaster in the blown safe, have added considerable weight to the evidence against the accused.

The police officer, having succeeded in detecting crime and in laying the necessary charges, is responsible for seeing that the person he alleges to be guilty of an offence is taken before the court and that the full facts, as he knows them, are placed before it without embellishment or prejudice. There the responsibility of the investigator ends. The task of assessing the evidence and administering justice belongs to the court.

The foregoing paragraphs describe only a few of the many and diverse duties of a policeman. It is evident, then, why police work requires men of high professional standards.

2. *Personal Standards.* Personal integrity is also important. A peace officer is continually handling situations involving the rights of individuals, and his acts may often appear to result in infringement of such rights. They may take the form of a search of property or person, or a deprivation of

liberty. They frequently, therefore, have a profound effect on the personal lives of others. A policeman should appreciate the responsibility placed upon him by society and should always act within the legal limits of his authority. It is important for him to remember, in dealing with people suspected of having committed crimes, that although he suspects guilt and indeed feels that the evidence is available to prove it, the law presumes that people charged in courts with offences of any kind are innocent until proven guilty in a court of law.

3. *Public Relations: The Police Officer on and off Duty*. Public co-operation is one of the greatest assets that the police officer can have and for this reason he must continuously cultivate and maintain it. The manner in which a police officer conducts himself on duty – whether it involves giving evidence in court, interrogating a suspected person, issuing a traffic ticket, or just speaking to someone on the street – can assist in winning the confidence of the public and can encourage support from it. The police officer must work to develop the confidence of the public to the point where it will wish to be identified with him in his enforcement of law and order.

In his relations with the public, the police officer must at all times be firm, courteous, and friendly. His friendliness, however, must not result in dereliction of duty. He must be fair, and be known to be fair, and he must not put himself in a position where he can be suspected of favouring one group or individual at the expense of another. He must carry out his duties in such a way that the public will have no valid grounds for complaint.

One source of friction between the public and the police is the use of plain-clothes men, detectives, and unidentifiable police-cars. Although the public realizes that such methods are necessary in the investigation of serious crimes, such as murder and robbery, it sometimes objects to their use in connection with lesser offences, such as infringement of traffic laws (in spite of the fact that crime arising out of the operation of motor vehicles is mounting annually and that its investigation consumes a large portion of any community's police budget). All authorities agree that, wherever possible, police should be identifiable as such; but when identification results in the lawbreaker's escaping detection, the police must take whatever steps are necessary, within the law, to bring the guilty person before the courts.

Friction may also arise from the policeman's duty to be vigilant. It is impossible for him to do his duty unless he investigates every circumstance in which he suspects that a crime has been committed. Unavoidably he will thus sometimes have to investigate an innocent person, and will thereby incur the ill will of certain members of the public. An informed public, however, will accept this thoroughness not as an infringement of the rights of the individual, but as a guarantee of the protection of the community.

Another source of friction lies in the fact that, as community life becomes more complex, more laws become necessary. The public and the police must be aware of the effect of this situation on their respective responsibilities. The public will have to realize why such additional laws are necessary; the police will have to remember that it takes time for the ordinary citizen to conform to laws with which he is not entirely familiar.

It is the duty of the police officer, when a crime has been committed, to take action that will bring a suspect, if the evidence warrants, before the courts. In the matter of minor offences, much is left to the discretion of the individual police officer, and warnings are more frequent than more severe action. Although some judicial authorities have held that only courts should have the right to decide whether a punishment or a warning is more appropriate, when a police officer tends to take even trivial offences to court, he usually becomes unpopular both with the public and with the courts. Since unpopularity might injure the police officer's effectiveness in investigating the more serious kinds of crime, particularly if he loses the co-operation of the public, it is probably better for him to be allowed to use his own discretion in minor matters, not only for the efficiency of the police force, but also for the good of the community itself. A system allowing formal warnings, recorded and approved by superiors, appears to be desirable in these matters.

Even in his time off, the policeman is responsible for maintaining law and order. Although he may consider himself 'off duty', he knows that his authority and responsibility as a peace officer are not cut off. He continues to have these twenty-four hours of the day. If, in his 'time off', he sees activity that to him indicates that the law is being infringed, he is required to take whatever action the circumstances demand. This could range from simply notifying other policemen who are 'on duty' to taking direct police action himself. In this way a policeman is never 'off duty'.

As to his own behaviour, it must at all times be above reproach if the policeman is to retain the respect of the public. Surely the community has a right to expect that anyone responsible for checking on the behaviour of its members will himself set a good example.

POLICE ROLE IN THE PREVENTION OF CRIME

Although the public is always more conscious of the police action that results in punishment than of the work that results in the prevention of crime, it has long been recognized that crime prevention is the main pur-

W. H. Kelly

pose of a police force – the true test of its efficiency. P. Colquhoun, a leading English magistrate, said, about 1800, before there were organized police forces as we know them today:

> Police in this country may be considered as a *new Science*; the properties of which consist not in the Judicial Powers which lead to *Punishment*, and which belong to Magistrates alone; but in the Prevention and Detection of Crimes, and in those other functions which relate to Internal Regulations for the well ordering and comfort of Civil Society.[7]

The detection of crime and its consequent punishment are in themselves deterrents to crime, requiring, among other things, an efficient police organization. As Robert G. Caldwell has pointed out, 'a police agency that vigorously and efficiently enforces the law operates as a definite deterrent to the commission of crime and delinquency and therefore contributes in a significant way to the prevention of those problems'.[8]

Some methods of prevention consist of warnings and advice given to persons who have committed, or who would otherwise be likely to commit, petty offences. Other methods include educational campaigns that may, for example, teach the public how to be on guard against theft, counterfeit money, and fraudulent cheques, and thus make the commission of crime more difficult. Even routine advice about adequate locks or alarm systems for business premises and dwellings, or the necessity of locking unoccupied cars, constitutes crime prevention.

The police constable on the beat, patrolling highways, city streets, and waterways, is a major deterrent to crime. Prevention takes another form in youth clubs, which the police sponsor and in which they participate in order to promote good citizenship. Club programs include lessons on such topics as road and water safety. By contributing to such clubs, a policeman is fulfilling his obligations to two sets of responsibilities: those of the peace officer, and those of the good citizen.

Intelligent law enforcement depends upon policemen who realize that the prevention of crime, not only the detection of crime, is the primary aim of any police force.

OTHER POLICE DUTIES

While the peace officer's main responsibilities are the prevention of crime and the detection of those guilty of infractions of the law, he performs many duties that do not fall into either of these categories. These duties fall upon him by reason of his position in the community and because, in

[7]P. Colquhoun, *A Treatise on the Police and Crimes of the Metropolis*, London: Longman, Rees, Orme, Brown, and Green, 1829.
[8]Robert G. Caldwell, *Criminology*, New York: Ronald Press Company, 1956.

132

the mind of the public, the very nature of the problem puts it in the police sphere.

The police are always relied upon to conduct inquiries or organize searches to locate missing persons. They are responsible for the identification of victims of drownings, fires, and motor-vehicle and aircraft accidents; sometimes police experts identify victims of accidents by their fingerprints when no other method of identification is possible. In any emergency, whatever the cause, the police force invariably assumes responsibility for controlling crowds and ensuring that those involved in handling the problem are unhampered.

Although traffic control, both pedestrian and vehicular, is somewhat apart from the main purpose of police work, except for that part of it that consists of enforcing the traffic laws, it too has become a police responsibility. The policeman on traffic duty does more than enforce the law – he assists motorists to travel safely and without delay. The police also organize and supervise school traffic-patrols, and it has been chiefly through the interest and encouragement of police forces throughout the country that the patrol program has proven such a success.

Every day, the policeman and the police-station are asked innumerable questions. People ask about the laws, particularly municipal by-laws, related to the activity of their neighbours, dogs, and children, and to innumerable other matters. They ask about the sources of particular information they require. Domestic problems are often brought to the police in the hope that they may be solved without reference to the more complex procedures of the law.

Because of his contact with the public, the policeman is often drawn into situations concerned with problems such as juvenile delinquency, desertion by husbands, and the various other types of tragedy that one finds in homes in the average community. In dealing with these, he develops a knowledge far beyond that required for the prevention and detection of crime. It is only natural, therefore, that he is called upon for advice. Often he is able to refer the individual to some other source of advice and assistance, such as a social service agency, rather than depending upon his own working knowledge of a particular situation. Very often he can advise on whether matters are of a civil or a criminal nature and can suggest the steps necessary to resolve a particular problem.

The police force is the best organized body in the community, and the best trained to deal with situations such as those mentioned above. Its members accept these responsibilities as a logical step arising out of their position in the community, and as being quite in keeping with the purpose of their existence, which is to provide service to the public.

Conclusion

In general, the standard of policing in Canada is high, but increased training is necessary to maintain high standards. There is considerable hope that the steps taken by provincial authorities to establish training facilities for municipal and provincial policemen, in addition to the federal facilities, will enable all communities to enjoy the services of well-trained and experienced peace officers. Police leaders believe that only modern training methods can equip the individual policeman to meet the challenge he faces in a society that is becoming more complex day by day.

Police forces are already co-operating closely to combat the type of crime that exists in an age when the criminal has access to new techniques in the commission of crime as well as to fast transportation and communication.

The cost of maintaining police forces is increasing as a result of the demands being made upon them by circumstances over which the community has only a relative measure of control. Some municipalities have difficulty in meeting the cost of keeping police forces up to strength, and not all communities can afford to compete with industry and commerce for the type of man with the intelligence and ability necessary to handle present-day police problems.

The police know that their work forms only a segment of the fight against crime. It is essential that all agencies engaged in the work of prevention and rehabilitation co-operate closely, and that, wherever possible, the full support of the public is obtained. The aim is not just to catch the criminal; it is to rehabilitate the offender so that he will never again become a police problem.

Further Reading

CALDWELL, ROBERT G. *Criminology*. New York: Ronald Press, 1956.

CANADA. British North America Act, 1867-1951. Ottawa: Queen's Printer.

————. Criminal Code, *Revised Statutes, 1953-4*, ch. 51. Ottawa: Queen's Printer.

————. Customs Act, *Revised Statutes, 1952*, ch. 58. Ottawa: Queen's Printer.

————. Railway Act, *Revised Statutes, 1952*, ch. 234. Ottawa: Queen's Printer.

————. R.C.M.P. Act, *Revised Statutes, 1959*, ch. 54. Ottawa: Queen's Printer.

————. *Law and Order in Canadian Democracy.* Ottawa: Queen's Printer.

MANITOBA. Highway Traffic Act, *Revised Statutes, 1954,* ch. 112. Winnipeg: Queen's Printer.

ONTARIO. Game and Fish Act, *Revised Statutes, 1961-62,* ch. 48. Toronto: Queen's Printer.

————. Liquor Control Act, *Revised Statutes, 1960,* ch. 217. Toronto: Queen's Printer.

————. Police Act, *Revised Statutes, 1960,* ch. 298, and *Revised Statutes, 1961-62,* ch. 105. Toronto: Queen's Printer.

ROLPH, C. H. *The Police and the Public.* London: Heinemann, 1962.

7

The Adult Court

STUART RYAN

Roots of Canadian Court System

The Canadian system of penal courts and their organization for the administration of penal justice both resemble and differ from those of Britain and the United States, with which they are most naturally compared. As first a colony, then a dominion, and finally a member of the Commonwealth, Canada has been much more closely under the influence of Britain than has the United States, and Canada expressly professes that her criminal law is based on that of England. At the same time, Canada is a federal state and a North American nation, whose people are closely related to those of the United States in population, social organization, culture, and attitudes, and the influence of American ideas in Canada has been continuous and is increasing. Canadian legal tradition, the training, attitudes, and methods of judges, magistrates, and lawyers, and the atmosphere of Canadian courts resemble those of England more closely than they do those of the United States, but there are subtle blendings of English and American influences with Canadian materials that have produced a result neither English nor American, but Canadian.

An important factor in Canadian legal development has been the French element. In Quebec, although, as in the rest of the country, criminal law and criminal procedure are governed by national legislation and are based on the law of England, the general legal system, the judiciary, the legal profession, the legal tradition, and the atmosphere of the courts derive their origins from France and the great romanistic system of civil law, and draw their vitality largely from the French culture prevailing in that province.

National courts are bilingual, but it must be admitted that French-Cana-

136

dian judges are more truly bilingual than their English-Canadian colleagues. Judges educated in the French tradition have a noticeable influence on the jurisprudence of the Supreme Court of Canada, the highest court of appeal for the whole country, where many important criminal cases are decided; and judgments of Quebec criminal courts, often written in French or by judges who think in French, are cited as precedents elsewhere.

The primary influence not only on Canadian penal jurisprudence but also on Canadian penal legislation has, however, been English law, and not only the common law but also the great body of English 19th-century legislation that embodied sweeping reforms in the rules of criminal law defining offences, determining responsibility, and prescribing punishments, in the system of criminal courts, and in criminal procedure. One reform that the English refused to make was adopted in Canada, namely the codification of criminal law and procedure. The substantive part of the first Canadian Criminal Code, enacted in 1892, was derived from a Canadian combination of the English draft code of 1878 with a body of earlier Canadian statutes that, in turn, had been modelled to a considerable extent upon previous English legislation. The procedural provisions, while drawing freely on English procedural reforms, were for the most part Canadian in origin. Since creating her own Code, Canada has been less inclined to follow the English lead, but has become more independent in the development of substantive law, and even more so in the creation of her own system of courts and criminal procedure. Sweeping English reforms in the 20th century have been sparingly followed in Canada.

Direct American influence in substantive law has been noticeable, chiefly in anti-combines legislation and in reference to juvenile delinquency. In the latter field, we have also borrowed our system of courts and procedure from the United States. The example of American federalism, together with our own colonial experience, gave us a developed doctrine of the nullity of *ultra vires* legislation, that is, attempted legislation beyond the jurisdiction of the legislature. Our courts have applied this principle to confine the national and provincial legislatures within their assigned spheres of legislative competency. American experience also seemed to furnish us with examples not so much of what to do as of what to avoid in distributing penal jurisdiction and responsibility between the national and provincial governments.

In principles, procedures, and techniques of sentencing, we seem to have followed the English rather than the American tradition, although our scheme of sentencing is more conservative than either the English or the American, in that we adhere more closely to the traditional punishments of death, imprisonment for the sake of custody, and fine. Our judges sometimes tend to follow American examples in imposing considerably longer sentences than their English counterparts are accustomed to do.

CONSTITUTIONAL AND LEGISLATIVE BASES FOR THE CANADIAN
SYSTEM OF ADMINISTRATION OF CRIMINAL JUSTICE

In spite of the foregoing, much in the field of substantive law, in the court system, in procedure, and in the organization for the administration of criminal justice consists of native contributions. Some features of the Canadian system are unique.

The scheme of the penal courts and of the administration of criminal justice is governed by the distribution of legislative, executive, and judicial jurisdiction, power, and authority between national and provincial governments under the British North America Act, 1867, and a series of amending acts, all given the same title, which may be referred to collectively as the B.N.A. Act.

There is only a very limited theory of 'separation of powers' in Canadian constitutional theory and practice. It is confined to two features: the independence of the judiciary, and the rule that a judicial function that ought to be exercised by a superior court cannot be given to a provincial court or other agency whose judges or members are not appointed and paid by the national government. There is no general principle of defined fields of activity assigned to the legislative, executive, and judicial branches of government, with each branch confined to its own field as is inherent in the Constitution of the United States, nor is there any body of rights formally reserved to the people.

The Canadian Bill of Rights, although in some respects similar in language and purpose to that of the United States, is a simple statute of the Parliament of Canada, subject to repeal or amendment in the ordinary way, and not, like the United States Bill of Rights, a constitutional instrument overriding all contrary legislative, executive, and judicial action. It does not purport to have any effect within the provincial sphere. In the same manner, the only provincial Bill of Rights now in force, that of Saskatchewan, and the somewhat over-advertised Ontario Human Rights Code are simply provincial statutes effective only within the scope of provincial legislative jurisdiction and subject to repeal.

There is talk of 'entrenching' the Canadian Bill of Rights in the 'constitution' by amendment of the B.N.A. Act, but until this is done, and even after it is done, the citizen's best protection against abuse of power, particularly in criminal law, rests on procedural rules. These rules, established by legislation and practice, for preventing oppression and unfair treatment of the individual by those in authority depend on the tradition of honourable dealing, fair play, and respect for the rights of the individual that our people, and through them our governments, our courts, our legal profession, and our police have inherited from Britain. Since the courts have interpreted the Canadian Bill of Rights as declaratory of existing rights rather than as creating new ones, it has not added appreciably to the previously existing safeguards of the citizen's freedom and rights. Unfortunately, the Canadian tradition of fair play and respect for the rights of the citizen has been somewhat weakened by North American influences, chiefly United States, but Canadian as well, not so much in the courts or among the legal profession as in the legislatures, government departments, and other law-enforcement agencies. In consequence, although Canada does not need an 'entrenched' Bill of Rights as badly as it has been needed in the United States, she does need one.

Most criminal prosecutions, like most state business, are conducted in the name of the Queen on behalf of the state, and are frequently said to be conducted by the Crown, which is a convenient term for the constitutional functions, property, interests, and activities of the sovereign in the state. Hence the title, '*Rex* or *Regina* v. *the accused*', usually given to criminal cases. The newcomer to the Canadian scene may be confused by the 'Crown in right of Canada' and the 'Crown in right of a province', particularly since both 'Crowns' take part in the administration of penal laws, and both are frequently involved in the same case. For example, a prosecution in Ontario of a charge of capital murder under the national Criminal Code, following investigation by local or provincial police, will be conducted in the name of the Queen in a provincial court by provincial authorities, and the Queen will be represented by a prosecutor, who is an agent of the provincial Attorney-General. If the accused is convicted, the provincially designated authorities, after all appeals have been disposed of, will have to make arrangements for his execution, and carry it out if his sentence is not commuted. The 'Queen in right of Canada', acting through the Governor General in Council, may exercise statutory powers or the common-law 'Royal Prerogative of Mercy' and commute the sentence to life imprisonment, in which case the offender will be imprisoned in a national penitentiary. The same authority can pardon him before or after conviction, or can substitute some other form of punishment. The 'Queen in right of Ontario', through the provincial Attorney-General, can halt the prosecution before conviction, but after conviction will have no power to interfere with the sentence in any way. If, however (to take a most improbable case), the sentence is commuted to one of less than two years' imprisonment or to a 'reformatory sentence', the offender will ordinarily be imprisoned in a provincial institution. Variations of this pattern are encountered in other classes of cases.

It will be part of the purpose of this chapter to explain how this division of function works. That it does work is evidence of a national capacity for co-operation and compromise. Unfortunately, however, it furnishes many excuses for failure to correct the many weaknesses of our system.

Distribution of Legislative Powers

Section 91(27) of the B.N.A. Act assigns to the national Parliament exclusive power to make laws relating to criminal law and procedure, but excludes the establishment and organization of criminal courts. Section 92(14) assigns to the provincial legislatures exclusive power to create, organize, and maintain provincial courts, both civil and criminal, and to govern the administration of justice in the provinces. The apparent simplicity of this arrangement is deceptive.

For example, Section 92(15) of the Act gives provincial legislatures the power to impose penalties for contraventions of provincial statutes. (Provinces delegate some of this power to municipalities.) Persons charged with such offences are tried under procedures established by provincial legislation. Quebec and the Atlantic Provinces have established their own codes of procedure for such prosecutions; the western provinces and Ontario have adopted the national criminal procedure, but with a number of modifications and differences varying from province to province.

As a result, although the more serious kinds of offences are created and are dealt with under national legislation, a considerable body of important penal legislation is provincial. Highway traffic, liquor, and the issuing and trading of securities are three fields in which, although the most serious offences are national, the main bodies of regulations and the greater number of offences are provincial. Of 3,180,545 convictions of all kinds in 1961, as reported by the Dominion Bureau of Statistics, the table on the next page shows the approximate distribution.

All provincial and municipal offences are punishable on summary conviction (although Newfoundland makes provision in its code of procedure for indictable provincial offences) and most of them would be called minor or petty. Virtually all conduct considered seriously criminal, except some 'white-collar' offences, is punishable under national legislation.

Thus, a system of penal laws, composed of a core of national legislation dealing mainly with the more serious crimes and broad fringes of provincial legislation, is administered chiefly by provincial authorities in a system of provincial courts. This statement, although true, is only part

Class of Offences	Number of Convictions	Approximate Percentage
Indictable offences under national legislation	71,262	2.3
Summary offences under national legislation	123,407	3.9
Provincial traffic offences	709,570	22.3
Other provincial offences	197,180	6.2
Municipal offences other than traffic and parking	52,997	1.7
Municipal traffic offences	203,724	6.3
Parking	1,822,405	57.3
Total	3,180,545	100.0

of the picture. Section 101 of the B.N.A. Act authorizes the national Parliament to create a court of appeal for the whole of Canada and to create other national courts to administer the laws of Canada. Such a court of appeal has been created in the Supreme Court of Canada, which has been made the final court of appeal in criminal as well as civil matters throughout the whole country. A national trial court of special jurisdiction, the Exchequer Court of Canada, has been given narrowly limited criminal jurisdiction in the trial of combines offences.

Under this power, it would seem possible to create national courts of general criminal jurisdiction, but to do so would upset the whole pattern of Confederation, and, since such national courts could not be given exclusive criminal jurisdiction, it is unlikely that it would be considered worth while to create them. At the same time, the creation of national criminal courts to deal with offences that imperil national security is not beyond the bounds of possibility.

Courts martial and other service tribunals under the National Defence Act, including a court of appeal known as the Court Martial Appeal Board, have jurisdiction in respect not only of service offences but also of ordinary national penal offences committed by members of the armed forces and other persons attached thereto. Service disciplinary tribunals, also created under national legislation, have certain jurisdiction over members of the Royal Canadian Mounted Police.

The Judiciary

Under Section 96 of the B.N.A. Act, the national government appoints and pays not only the judges of national courts but also those of all superior, county, and district courts of the provinces. Provincial superior courts are the most important provincial courts of civil jurisdiction and, in one sense, the most important provincial criminal courts. County and district courts are inferior courts of considerable importance in civil matters, and of somewhat less importance in criminal law.

Judges of provincial superior courts, by Section 99 of the B.N.A. Act, are guaranteed secure tenure of office during good behaviour up to a retirement age of seventy-five years. They may be removed for misconduct, but only by the Governor General in Council on a joint address of both Houses of the national Parliament. Judges of provincial county and district courts also hold office during good behaviour up to the same retirement age, but under statutory authority only; they may be removed by the Governor General in Council on an adverse report by a committee of inquiry. Whether judges of national superior courts share the guarantee given to judges of provincial superior courts, or only that lesser degree of security given to judges of provincial county and district courts, is debatable. In any event, an attempt, by legislation or otherwise, to remove any of these judges for any cause other than misbehaviour would create a constitutional crisis, and in fact they all enjoy equal security and independence. No superior court judges have been removed, and the few removals of county or district court judges appear to have been clearly necessary.

Although appointed by the national government, judges of the courts of each province are selected from the legal profession of that province. In each province, the profession is independent, fully organized, and self-governing, with full authority for training, qualifying, admitting, and disciplining all lawyers practising in the province. All members of provincial professions are entitled to practise in national courts, and the judges of national courts are selected from among their numbers. A sort of federal organization of the Supreme Court of Canada is maintained by the practice that one judge is chosen from the Atlantic Provinces, three from Quebec (as required by statute), of whom in practice at least two are French-speaking Roman Catholics and one is usually an English-speaking Protestant, three from Ontario, of whom one is usually a Roman Catholic, and two from the Western Provinces. The Chief Justices have been alternately French- and English-speaking in recent years, and this alternation may become an established pattern.

Other provincial inferior court judges, magistrates, justices of the peace, coroners, sheriffs, and other court officers of provincial courts are appointed and paid under provincial legislation and by provincial or municipal governments. Subordinate officers of national courts are appointed and paid by the national government.

Although a trend in practice towards restricting appointments of magistrates to legally qualified persons is evident, not all magistrates and juvenile or family court judges and very few justices of the peace are lawyers. Only in Nova Scotia and New Brunswick is there legislation requiring certain classes of magistrates to be lawyers.

There is a growing tendency to provide, by provincial legislation, that provincially appointed inferior court judges and magistrates are to hold office during good behaviour up to a retirement age, sometimes from the time of appointment, but more often after a period of probation. Some, however, hold office 'during pleasure', which is a most unsatisfactory tenure. As time goes on, more and more are employed on full-time appointments and paid exclusively by salary, but some are appointed only for part-time service, and some are still paid wholly or partly by fees or by salaries that vary with the court costs paid by convicted persons. Full-time, fixed-salaried employment has proved the most satisfactory arrangement.

No Canadian judges, magistrates, sheriffs, prosecutors, or court officers are elected. The legal training and capability of Canadian superior court judges are, on the whole, good; a considerable number are lawyers of very high calibre. The quality of the county and district court Bench is generally good, but uneven. Before their appointment, few superior, county, or district court judges have had any appreciable amount of training in any aspect of criminology, or any great experience or interest in criminal law or corrections. Appointments to county and district courts are usually made from among supporters of the party in power in the national government; non-political appointments are rare. In superior courts, although patronage prevails, occasional non-political appointments are made. It is said that political considerations have least importance in appointments to the Supreme Court of Canada, but retiring senior national cabinet ministers are sometimes rewarded in that way. The Minister of Justice, whose duty it is to recommend persons for appointment to all these judgeships, strives constantly to find the best men available, although he is hampered by the positive and negative pressures of patronage and by occasional refusals of leaders of the Bar to take office.

The system works reasonably well. The Canadian judiciary has been honest and honourable. It has apparently been free of bribery and corruption, and has until very recently been little spotted by scandal of any kind. At the time of writing, a criminal charge of perjury against a judge in respect of conduct before appointment to the Bench is pending, and an allegation of the receipt of certain favours by another judge, before his appointment, has been investigated. In neither case was the conduct alleged to refer to his selection or appointment.

Professional tradition and general Canadian sentiment tend to confine the effects of favouritism and prejudice to narrow limits. It is, however, unfortunate that the system provides a judiciary whose technical competence in the field of criminal law and corrections is considerably lower than in that of civil law.

The Territories

In relation to distribution of powers and functions within the federal scheme, it must be remembered that the Territories are subject exclusively to national legislative control. Parliament and the national government perform in respect of them the roles of both the national and the provincial authorities. Territorial legislatures and executives are municipal rather than provincial in nature. The national capital is not extra-provincial, being situated primarily in Ontario, but having now spread into the province of Quebec.

National Legislation Affecting the Criminal Courts

The main body of national criminal legislation is, of course, contained in the Criminal Code, the latest revision of which came into effect on April 1, 1955. On this revision, the last remaining common-law criminal offences have been abolished in Canada, but common-law principles relating to liability, justification, and excuse continue in effect, except insofar as replaced or modified by Canadian legislation. These principles, which have been created and developed and moulded by the courts, control the application of penal legislation. Through them, the courts perform an important law-making function. Other national penal statutes, such as the Narcotic Control Act, the Official Secrets Act, and over one hundred other national statutes, contain special provisions affecting liability or procedure, none of which are of any particular importance in this study; procedure in prosecutions under these statutes is otherwise governed by the Criminal Code. Evidence in trials on charges of national offences is governed by the Canada Evidence Act and, subject thereto, by the common law as modified in each province by provincial statutes. The latter alone, with the common law, govern evidence in trials on charges of provincial offences. The chief distinguishing feature of the Canadian law of evidence is the abolition of the privilege of a witness to refuse to answer a question if the answer might incriminate him in an offence in future proceedings. A provision is made that, if he objects on that ground, he must answer, but the answer may not be used against him later. This protection is of little practical value. Under the Canada Evidence Act, the accused

144

person may give evidence or not as he chooses. If he testifies, he may be cross-examined about previous convictions. Under provincial statutes in some provinces, he may be compelled to testify for the prosecution on charges of provincial offences.

The nature of a 'delinquency' and the jurisdiction of juvenile courts over children and adults are set out in Chaper 8. Where juvenile courts do not exist, children between seven and fourteen years of age are, except in Newfoundland where special legislation is in force, subject to ordinary penal laws and are tried in ordinary penal courts. This is subject to the child's being found competent to understand the nature and consequences of his conduct and, if the conduct constitutes a penal offence, being competent to appreciate that it is wrong.

Children over fourteen years of age in those parts of Canada (except Newfoundland) where the Juvenile Delinquents Act is not in force are subject to penal laws in the same manner as adults. Only in some details respecting detention pending trial, evidence, and publicity of the trial is any provision made in ordinary penal laws for persons under sixteen years of age before conviction. There are special provisions with respect to the sentences that may be imposed and where prison terms must be served. As it is, about thirty boys under sixteen, mostly from Quebec, are sentenced to penitentiary terms each year.

HOW THE COURTS ARE ORGANIZED

In describing Canadian courts of criminal jurisdiction, we may properly speak of a Canadian system, since, in respect of national offences, the courts function as a result of co-operative acts of the national Parliament and the provincial legislatures. Parliament designates classes of courts among which criminal jurisdiction is distributed. The provincial legislatures create courts of the respective classes with capacity to exercise that jurisdiction in each case, and Parliament confers jurisdiction on those courts accordingly. Provincial legislation confers jurisdiction on some of those courts to try charges of provincial offences, and in some cases creates additional courts for that purpose.

All courts may be divided into two classes: trial courts and appellate courts. Dealing first with trial courts, we may arrange them by two schemes of cross-classification – by composition or by jurisdiction.

In respect of composition, trial courts are of two kinds: those composed of judge and jury, and those composed of a judge or magistrate alone. In respect of jurisdiction, they fall into three classes: namely, superior courts of criminal jurisdiction, courts of criminal jurisdiction, and summary conviction courts. We will often call courts of the first class 'superior criminal courts', for the sake of convenience.

The system of our courts of criminal jurisdiction is described in the following tables.

The Exchequer Court of Canada and the courts of the territories are created and organized under national legislation, and their judges and staffs are appointed and paid by the national government.

In each province, the courts are created and organized under provincial legislation, and their administrative staffs are appointed and paid by the provincial government. Magistrates, justices of the peace, and all judicial officers of the same rank and status are also provincially appointed and paid; in this category are the judges of Sessions, and district and municipal judges of Quebec. The remaining judges exercising criminal jurisdiction in these courts are the superior, county, and district court judges who are appointed and paid by the national government.

System of Canadian Criminal Courts

COURTS WITH JURISDICTION OVER PERSONS
CHARGED WITH INDICTABLE OFFENCES

A. *Judicial Officers Conducting Preliminary Inquiries* (when necessary)
(i) *Magistrates,* including provincial, county, city, stipendiary, police, and deputy magistrates and, in Quebec, judges of Sessions, and district and municipal judges
(ii) *Justices of the peace,* when no magistrate acts

B. *Trial Courts for Indictable Offences*

(i) *Superior Courts of Criminal Jurisdiction* (referred to herein, for convenience, as superior criminal courts)

(a) One in each province and territory, as follows:
Quebec: Court of Queen's Bench, Trial Side (Cour du Banc de la Reine)
Manitoba and Saskatchewan: Court of Queen's Bench
Newfoundland, Nova Scotia, and British Columbia: Supreme Court
Prince Edward Island: Supreme Court of Judicature
New Brunswick: Queen's Bench Division of Supreme Court
Ontario: High Court Branch of Supreme Court
Alberta: Supreme Court, Trial Division

(b) *Organization and Composition.* Provincial courts have province-wide jurisdiction. In Quebec, the court is organized in judicial districts, and trials are presided over by judges of the Superior Court

(Cour Supérieure), which is the superior provincial court of civil jurisdiction. In other provinces, the courts have concurrent criminal and civil jurisdiction, and judges travel in circuit to county or district towns to hold trials. Territorial courts have jurisdiction throughout their respective territories.

Trials are conducted by single judges and juries of twelve, except that:

1. Juries of six sit in Alberta and the territories.
2. The accused may elect trial by judge alone in Alberta on any charge.
3. Certain Combines Act offences are triable by judge alone in any of these courts.

In Newfoundland, Nova Scotia, Prince Edward Island, and Ontario, the court includes a grand jury, and no person may be tried unless this jury, sitting in camera before trial, decides that there is enough evidence against an accused person to justify putting him on trial. In other provinces and territories, there are no grand juries.

(c) *Jurisdiction.* Territorial courts of this class may try indictable offences committed within their respective territories, while provincial superior criminal courts may try such offences committed not only within their respective provinces but also in any part of Canada that is not within a province. An indictable offence committed outside Canada and triable by a Canadian court may be tried by any of these courts before whom the accused is brought. The only accused persons who may be brought before one of these courts are those who have been committed for trial for indictable offences by magistrates or justices of the peace after preliminary hearings, or against whom indictments have been presented by the Attorney-General of the province (or in a territory, the Attorney-General of Canada), or by his direction, or with his written consent, or on order or written consent of a judge of the court.

These courts may try any indictable offence and have exclusive jurisdiction to try charges of treasonable offences, intimidation of Parliament, incitement to mutiny, piratical acts, rape, murder, being an accessory after murder, manslaughter, criminal negligence causing death, threats to kill and related attempts and conspiracies. They have jurisdiction to try Combines Act offences concurrent with that of the Exchequer Court of Canada.

(d) The Exchequer Court of Canada has nation-wide concurrent jurisdiction, on consent, to try Combines Act offences and no others.

It has no jury or grand jury. Judges sit in any capital or county or district town in Canada.

(ii) *Courts of Criminal Jurisdiction* (a technical term referring to inferior courts having jurisdiction to try indictable offences that are not within the exclusive jurisdiction of superior criminal courts)

(a) *Courts composed of judge and jury*
New Brunswick: County Court Jury Sittings (one in each county)
Ontario: Courts of General Sessions of the Peace (one in each county and judicial district)

County (and, in Ontario, district) court judges sit singly with juries of twelve. In Ontario there is a grand jury with the same role as in the superior criminal court; there is none in New Brunswick.

These courts have jurisdiction, concurrent with that of provincial superior criminal courts, to try persons charged with indictable offences not within the exclusive jurisdiction of superior criminal courts who have not elected for trial by magistrate or by judge alone, and who have been committed for trial or have been charged by indictment in the same manner as in a superior criminal court.

In the other eight provinces and the territories, where separate jury courts of this class do not exist, such persons are tried in superior criminal courts.

(b) *Courts composed of judges sitting without juries*
1. In all provinces except Quebec – county (or district) judge's criminal courts, one in each county or judicial district, each with one or more judges.
2. Also, in Newfoundland, Manitoba, Saskatchewan, Alberta, and British Columbia – a judge of a superior criminal court.
3. In Quebec – a judge of the Sessions of the Peace or district judge.
4. In each territory – the judge of the territorial court.

These courts try persons charged with indictable offences not within the exclusive jurisdiction of a superior criminal court who have elected trial by a judge without a jury, and have been committed for trial after preliminary hearing or charged on indictment in the same manner as in a superior criminal court.

Note: These courts have no grand juries. Judges of Sessions of the Peace and district judges in Quebec are appointed and paid by the provincial government, but for this purpose are classed in the Criminal Code with judges who are nationally appointed and paid.

In Ontario, a chief judge of the county court system co-ordinates the work of the county and district courts, including the courts of general sessions and county and district court judges' criminal courts. In Alberta, there are two judicial districts, each with a chief judge and a number of district judges. In Saskatchewan, the whole province is one judicial district.

(c) *Magistrates.* In each province, judicial officers known by divers names are appointed under a provincial law by which they are specially authorized to try charges of indictable offences under Part XVI of the Criminal Code, in which they are simply called magistrates. In Quebec, judges of Sessions of the Peace and district judges also have the status of magistrates.

In the autumn of 1964, the government of Ontario appointed a 'chief magistrate' to supervise and co-ordinate the operation of magistrates' courts throughout the province, with the object of increasing the efficiency of these courts and, among other things, eliminating avoidable delays in handling cases. The work of the chief judge of the county court system leads to the expectation that the chief magistrate's office will prove to be a valuable one, but at the time of writing, it is too early to make an accurate assessment of its effectiveness.

In the territories, territorial court judges and police magistrates have this status concurrently.

The jurisdiction of magistrates is twofold:

1. Absolute jurisdiction to try, with or without consent of the accused, charges of theft, obtaining or attempting to obtain by false pretences and knowingly having possession of unlawfully obtained goods involving values or amounts up to $50, attempted theft of any amount, resisting or obstructing a peace officer or his assistant performing his duty, keeping a common gaming-, betting-, or bawdy-house, lottery offences, cheating at play, driving a motor vehicle while disqualified, certain assaults, fraud relating to fares or tolls, and certain related offences.

These indictable offences are considered relatively minor and therefore the accused cannot elect to be tried by a judge and jury or judge alone, if the magistrate decides to try him for one of them. The magistrate, however, may on his own account decide whether to try the accused or not.

2. Jurisdiction to try, with consent of the accused, other indictable offences not within the exclusive jurisdiction of a superior criminal court.

When an accused comes before a magistrate charged with an indictable offence, the magistrate must first determine whether the offence charged is one which is

a. within the exclusive jurisdiction of a superior criminal court,
b. within his own absolute jurisdiction, or
c. within his consent jurisdiction.

If the offence is within class (*a*), the magistrate holds a preliminary hearing and, if he finds there is enough evidence to show that the accused may be convicted, he commits the accused for trial. If the offence is within class (*b*), the magistrate decides whether to try the accused or to hold a preliminary hearing and, if the evidence warrants it, to commit the accused for trial. If the offence is within class (*c*) the magistrate offers the accused an 'election' to be tried by a magistrate, or by a judge and jury, or by a judge without a jury. If the accused elects trial by magistrate, the magistrate may try him or remand him for trial by another magistrate.

Trial by a magistrate is 'summary'. The only pleadings are the written 'information' containing the charge or charges, together with any written particulars given by the prosecutor, and the oral pleas of 'guilty' or 'not guilty', or some special plea, made by the accused. The procedure is almost the same as on the trial of a charge of an 'offence punishable on summary conviction', but the magistrate may impose any punishment authorized for the offence he is trying, and thus for some offences he may sentence offenders to life imprisonment and whipping, and may impose in some cases a fine of any amount and in others preventive detention for life. Appeals from magistrates who have tried charges of indictable offences go to the provincial courts of appeal in the same manner as from superior criminal courts.

C. *Appellate Courts for Indictable Offences*

(i) In each province and territory, the provincial or territorial court of appeal hears appeals from acquittals or convictions and from sentences on charges of indictable offences. These courts differ amongst themselves in title and organization, but each is the highest appellate court of both civil and criminal jurisdiction in its province or territory.

In Quebec the court of appeal is the Court of Queen's Bench, Appeal Side. Although it would seem from its title to be a branch of the court whose other branch conducts trials as a superior criminal court, in practice its judges are appointed as Queen's Bench judges and sit in appeal, while trials in the Court of Queen's Bench are presided over by superior court judges.

In Newfoundland, Nova Scotia, and Prince Edward Island, the court of appeal is the Supreme Court of the province, sitting *en banc* (*in banco,* 'on the bench') at the provincial capital in panels of three or more judges, and hearing appeals from trials conducted by each other as well as from other courts. In these provinces, the superior court judges spend parts of each year travelling on 'circuit' to preside at trials at county or district centres throughout the province; during other parts of each year, they sit *en banc,* hearing appeals.

In the other provinces and territories, the court of appeal is, and is called, the provincial or territorial Court of Appeal, or Appellate Division of the Supreme Court. Judges of these courts are appointed to exercise primarily appellate jurisdiction, and do not preside at trials except under special arrangements in cases of temporary shortage of trial judges.

The regular method of disposing of appeals, both civil and criminal, in these courts is by hearing oral argument, normally presented by counsel for the parties, based on the trial pleadings and proceedings and on transcripts of the evidence taken at the trial. New evidence is rarely received. Appeals in writing by convicted persons are also heard. Somewhat more freedom is allowed in presentation of appeals against sentence than on those against conviction or acquittal.

In certain cases, as noted below, appeals from summary conviction cases can reach these courts of appeal.

The provincial courts of appeal are created and organized under provincial legislation and their subordinate staffs are appointed and paid by the governments of the respective provinces. The judges are appointed and paid by the national government. The court of appeal of Yukon Territory is composed of judges of the Supreme Court of British Columbia and the judge of the Yukon territorial court; that of the Northwest Territories is composed of judges of the Supreme Court of Alberta and the judges of both territorial courts.

(ii) The rights of appeal to the court of appeal from trials on charges of indictable offences are as follows:

(a) If the accused is sentenced to death, there is an automatic appeal against conviction and against sentence, unless the sentence is fixed by law.

(b) The accused may appeal against conviction, in any other case,

   1. on a question of law, without leave, as of right;

2. on a question of fact or of mixed law and fact, with leave of the court of appeal or on certificate by the trial judge that it is a proper case for appeal; or

3. on any other ground, with leave of the court of appeal.

(c) The provincial Attorney-General, in prosecutions conducted by provincial authorities, and the Attorney-General for Canada, in prosecutions conducted by national authorities, may appeal against acquittal on a question of law, without leave, as of right, but have no power to appeal on a question of fact or one of mixed law and fact. No appeal may be brought against a verdict of acquittal, unless some error of law occurred in the trial.

(d) Either the accused or the appropriate Attorney-General may appeal, with leave of the court of appeal, against sentence other than preventive detention, unless sentence is fixed by law. A person sentenced to preventive detention may appeal against sentence on a ground of law or fact or mixed fact and law, without leave, as of right. The Attorney-General may appeal in the same way on a point of law against refusal to impose that sentence.

(iii) The court of appeal may dismiss an appeal or allow the appeal and order a new trial or, if it appears that the accused could not be convicted on a new trial, direct an acquittal. On appeals against sentence, the court may substitute a legal for an illegal sentence, or in its discretion, increase or reduce a legal sentence that appears to be inadequate or excessive. In doing so, it may substitute one form of punishment for another.

(iv) In other than cases involving sentence of death, appeals from convictions or acquittals may be taken by the accused from provincial courts of appeal to the Supreme Court of Canada, as follows:

(a) An accused may appeal against a conviction affirmed by the court of appeal,

1. as of right, on a question of law on which a judge of the court of appeal dissents, or

2. on any other question of law on which leave to appeal is given by the Supreme Court of Canada.

(b) An accused acquitted at trial whose acquittal has been set aside by the court of appeal, or a person who was tried jointly with such an accused and was convicted and whose conviction was affirmed by the court of appeal, may appeal to the Supreme Court of Canada as of right on a question of law.

(v) A person convicted and sentenced to death whose appeal has been dismissed by the court of appeal or a person acquitted of a capital offence whose acquittal has been set aside by the court of appeal may appeal to the Supreme Court of Canada on any ground of law or fact or mixed law and fact, as of right.

(vi) The appropriate Attorney-General may appeal to the Supreme Court of Canada from a judgment of the court of appeal setting aside a conviction or dismissing an appeal,

(a) as of right, on a point of law on which a judge dissents in the court of appeal;

(b) on any other question of law on which leave to appeal is given by the Supreme Court of Canada.

No appeal on a question of fact or of mixed fact and law can be taken to the Supreme Court of Canada except by a person under sentence of death. Except on a question of law in relation to preventive detention, no appeal against sentence may be taken to that court.

COURTS WITH JURISDICTION OVER PERSONS
CHARGED WITH SUMMARY OFFENCES

A. *Trial Courts for Summary Offences*

(i) *National Offences.* Such a court is called a summary jurisdiction court, and is defined as a 'person' given jurisdiction by the terms of his appointment to try charges of offences punishable on summary conviction. Here, and in the case of a magistrate who tries indictable offences, the court is not an institution staffed by persons, but is the person of the judicial officer, and therefore special procedural provisions are required to allow, on changes of magistrate, for continuity of proceedings, which the identity of the institution provides in other courts. These courts have no juries or grand juries.

Justices of the peace are authorized to receive informations, issue summonses and warrants, grant adjournments, and issue process after trial. In some cases, it is required by the statutes creating offences that trials be conducted by a magistrate or two or more justices of the peace sitting together, and in others, the statutes authorize a single justice to try charges. In practice, whether under statutory requirement or not, outside of Quebec and the territories, the normal practice is that magistrates conduct such trials, but justices of the peace may act at the request of, or in the absence of, magistrates where the relevant statutes permit them to do so. The magistrates who have

153

power to try charges of indictable offences, as mentioned in paragraph B. (ii) (c), above, are also authorized to try charges of summary offences. Other magistrates appointed in provinces other than Ontario and Saskatchewan have jurisdiction only over summary offences. In these two provinces all magistrates have power to try both summary and indictable offences. In the territories, certain R.C.M.P. officers are justices of the peace and can try summary offences.

All these judicial officers and their staffs are appointed and paid by provincial governments, except in the territories. Their jurisdiction may extend throughout the province or territory, as in Ontario and Saskatchewan, or it may be confined to a district, county, or local municipality, as is the case for certain magistrates in British Columbia and Nova Scotia.

The words 'magistrate' and 'district magistrate' are no longer used in Quebec. They have been replaced by 'district judge', the title of a judicial officer, appointed and paid by the provincial government, having inferior civil as well as criminal jurisdiction. Some municipal judges are given the same jurisdiction in that province.

(ii) *Provincial and Municipal Offences*. Provincial legislation creating offences and authorizing the creation of municipal offences and regulating summary penal procedure generally gives jurisdiction to single justices of the peace. In practice, magistrates usually try charges of both provincial and municipal offences, as well as national offences, but justices of the peace do so under arrangements made in the absence of, or at the request of, magistrates. In Quebec, municipal judges try certain charges and others are tried by a district judge. Except in Quebec, no class of judicial officers is given power to try only provincial or only municipal offences.

B. *Appellate Courts for Summary Offences*

(i) Appeals from summary conviction courts are of two kinds. An appeal by way of 'stated case' may be brought, on points of law only, to the provincial superior criminal court, or an appeal in the form of a re-trial may be heard in a court called the 'appeal court', which must be distinguished from the provincial Court of Appeal.

(a) In each province there are a number of appeal courts, each consisting of one of the respective tribunals or judges below mentioned: *Newfoundland and Prince Edward Island*: a judge of the provincial Supreme Court

Each territory: a judge of the territorial court
Quebec: a judge of the Superior Court (Cour Supérieure)
Other provinces: a county or district court

Such re-trials are conducted by a judge without a jury, on evidence given *viva voce* or, on consent, read wholly or in part from a transcript of the evidence given at the first trial. New evidence is admissible, whether for the prosecution or the defence. The judge may acquit or convict, basing his decision on the evidence now before him, free from any findings made by the summary conviction court. If he convicts the accused, he may impose any authorized sentence – the same as, or greater or less than, the original sentence, if any.

(b) The 'stated case' is merely a report in writing by the magistrate or justice, submitted on the demand of the appellant, setting out the facts as he has found them together with his rulings on points of law, and asking the superior criminal court whether he was right in law. The points of law involved are determined on the basis of the information (charge sheet) and the stated case and no other material, before a single judge of the superior criminal court, who gives his decision and sends the case back to the magistrate or justice to dispose of accordingly. Questions of fact or mixed law and fact cannot be considered in this kind of appeal.

(ii) In certain cases, a conviction may be set aside on a 'motion to quash' made by the defendant in the superior criminal court. The procedure is somewhat different from that of the stated case, but the scope of the remedy is similar in that only points of law may be argued.

(iii) Superior courts control proceedings of summary conviction courts and other inferior courts by extraordinary remedies known as certiorari, mandamus, prohibition, and habeas corpus.

(a) *Certiorari* is an order requiring the inferior court to send up the record of a case to the superior court, where the proceedings will be reviewed, and either confirmed or quashed, on the ground that the inferior court has acted beyond its jurisdiction or that its procedure has been defective.

(b) *Mandamus* is an order by the superior court requiring the inferior court to perform a duty it has failed to perform.

(c) *Prohibition* is an order forbidding the inferior court to act beyond its jurisdiction when it threatens to do so.

(d) *Habeas corpus ad subjiciendum* is the great remedy by which

Stuart Ryan

any person having custody of a prisoner is ordered to produce the prisoner before the superior court in order that the legality of his detention may be determined. Its scope is somewhat restricted, since a warrant valid in its face is a sufficient answer to the order, but it may be supplemented by certiorari and the regularity of the proceedings behind the warrant may be examined.

(iv) In all these extraordinary procedures, an appeal to the provincial Court of Appeal, and eventually to the Supreme Court of Canada, is available. The appeal in habeas corpus applications, which is rather complicated, was created by an amendment of the Criminal Code enacted in 1965.

(v) An appeal by either party, on a question of law from an appeal court or from the decision of a superior criminal court on a stated case, may be taken to the provincial or territorial court of appeal, with leave of that court, or, in some provincial or municipal matters, on certificate of the Attorney-General that an important point of law is involved. A further appeal may be taken by either party on a point of law to the Supreme Court of Canada, with leave of that court.

WORK OF TRIAL COURTS

The table on page 141 shows that only 2.3 per cent of convictions are for indictable offences, while 57.3 per cent are for parking offences, and 40.4 per cent are for other summary offences. Almost all charges of parking offences are settled out of court by pleas of guilty. The same is true of a large number of other traffic offences. A large volume of charges of summary offences remains to be disposed of in court, and almost all of these are dealt with by magistrates. Every plea of guilty out of court requires a formal conviction by a magistrate or justice of the peace in court.

Even on charges of indictable offences that cannot be disposed of out of court, the overwhelming majority of trials are conducted by magistrates. The figures on the following page are reported by the Dominion Bureau of Statistics for the year 1961.

The disproportionate number of convictions, as compared with acquittals, in cases tried by magistrates is explained partly, at least, by the fact that a large proportion of those tried by magistrates plead guilty, while few pleas of guilty are made before judges, whether sitting with or without juries. Where the accused has the right of election, he normally elects trial by magistrate if he intends to plead guilty.

156

TRIALS OF CHARGES OF INDICTABLE OFFENCES

Method of Trial	Tried	Acquitted	Convicted	Other Disposition
Judge and jury	939	256	618	65
Judge alone	2,651	631	1,996	24
Magistrate, consent jurisdiction	20,756	1,581	19,057	118
Magistrate, absolute jurisdiction	18,815	1,705	17,008	102
Totals	43,161	4,173	38,679	309

Trial by jury is relatively most frequent and trial by judge alone is relatively least frequent in Ontario. The following figures extracted from the 1961 statistics show the distribution in that province of methods of trial:

PERSONS TRIED ON CHARGES OF INDICTABLE OFFENCES
IN ONTARIO IN 1961

Method of Trial	Number Tried	Percentage of Total Number Tried in Canada
Judge and jury	452	47.0
Judge alone	371	13.6
Magistrate, consent jurisdiction	8,642	35.2
Magistrate, absolute jurisdiction	6,733	41.1
Total number tried	16,198	37.5

Jury trial in civil actions is relatively more frequent in Ontario than anywhere else in the Commonwealth. There is probably some correlation between the two frequencies.

The relatively large number of cases throughout Canada within the absolute jurisdiction of magistrates – almost 44 per cent of the total of indictable offences – is not generally appreciated. No doubt, a large number of these are cases of theft where the amount involved is really over $50, but either the amount cannot be proved or the accused offers to plead guilty to theft of not over $50, for which the maximum penalty is two years imprisonment, and his offer is accepted. Nevertheless, it is reasonable to take the relative frequency of less grave offences into account when assessing the amount of criminality in Canada.

The 2,651 persons tried by judge alone in Canada elected to be tried in that way, since nobody can be compelled to be tried by a judge alone, unless the accused is a corporation charged under the Combines Act.

There were 939 persons tried by judge and jury; 364 persons were charged with offences within the exclusive jurisdiction of superior criminal courts. Of the latter group, twenty-three were tried in Alberta and could elect to be tried by judge alone, although the statistics do not show how they elected, and some of them may have been tried by judge alone. The remaining members of this group had no right of election. It appears therefore that the number of persons who actually elected to be tried by judge and jury was between 575 and 598.

It is evident from these figures that the magistrate is the work-horse of the administration of criminal justice. In 1961, judges, with or without juries, disposed of only 8.3 per cent of all charges of indictable offences, as against 91.7 per cent dealt with by magistrates. In relation to the totality of all criminal and penal charges, judges were involved in only 0.11 per cent in that year, and the vast majority of the others were handled by magistrates.

In relation to sentencing of offenders for serious crimes, the roles played by superior, county, and district court judges and magistrates are illustrated in part by the following figures, calculated from the Criminal Statistics (D.B.S.) for the years 1955 to 1961, inclusive:

AVERAGE NUMBERS OF PERSONS CONVICTED OF INDICTABLE
OFFENCES IN CANADA, PER ANNUM, IN YEARS 1955
TO 1961 INCLUSIVE

Classes of Courts	Average Numbers Convicted Per Annum	Approximate Percentage
Superior courts	614	2.0
County and district courts	1,320	4.3
Magistrates	28,803	93.4
Total	30,737	100.0

Ontario, with over a third of the country's population, has well over a third of the crime. During the period from 1955 to 1961 inclusive, the average numbers of persons convicted of indictable offences per annum, by or before each judge and each magistrate in Ontario, were approximately as follows:

Each high court judge	8
Each county or district court judge	7
Each magistrate	111

It is not easy to produce comparable figures for other provinces, since different court systems produce variations not shown in the statistics.

In superior criminal courts, criminal work is more or less evenly distributed among judges who travel on circuit throughout their provinces. In county and district courts, there is less uniformity of distribution of work, since there is a concentration of crime in larger centres of population, and judges of this class do not move around as much as superior court judges in the course of their duties. This concentration is reflected in the following table taken from the 1961 records of York County Court, Ontario, which includes Metropolitan Toronto:

PERSONS TRIED ON CHARGES OF INDICTABLE OFFENCES

	General Sessions (judge and jury)	*County Court Judges, Criminal Court* (no jury)
Number of persons tried	268	163
Number of persons convicted	133	122
Number of trial days	236	84

The senior county court judge of York County handles practically nothing but criminal work, in which he is assisted to a limited extent by some of his colleagues. He tries more criminal cases than any other nationally appointed Canadian judge. No other Canadian judge participates in as many convictions for indictable offences as does a full-time magistrate. Each magistrate on regular duty in Metropolitan Toronto made about 500 convictions for indictable offences in 1961, while all the supreme, county, and district court judges in the province together made only 540 convictions in that year.

It is, however, impossible to speak of the average work-load of a magistrate. There are a number of part-time magistrates with widely varying work-loads. Even among full-time magistrates, there is tremendous variation. Further, different methods of compiling statistics in the several centres make accurate comparisons impossible. Some information is, however, available.

The following approximate figures are based on information furnished by individual magistrates in smaller centres and administrators of magistrates' courts in metropolitan areas:

Metropolitan Toronto (average figures for 1960-1)

Number of magistrates	20
Charges (exclusive of parking tickets),	
approximate number per annum	500,000
Indictable offences	12,000
National summary offences	8,000
Provincial offences	154,000
Municipal offences	326,000

(Approximate number of parking tickets 600,000)

Justices of the peace dispose of an unstated number of minor traffic offences in Metropolitan Toronto.

Vancouver (1960)

Number of magistrates	8
Charges (exclusive of parking offences),	
approximate number	73,000
Traffic offences (criminal, provincial, and municipal)	50,000
Other criminal offences (indictable and summary)	5,700
Other national offences	800
Other provincial offences	12,200
Other municipal offences	4,300

(Approximate number of parking offences 110,000)

Winnipeg (1960)

Number of magistrates	5
Charges (exclusive of parking tags)	
approximate number	36,000
Traffic offences (criminal, provincial, and municipal)	25,000
Other criminal offences (indictable and summary)	1,300
Other national offences	300
Other provincial offences	900
Other municipal offences	8,500

(Approximate number of parking tags 90,000)

The following examples illustrate the variation in numbers of cases dealt with by individual magistrates. Figures given are for 1960 and are approximations based on information given by the magistrates themselves.

	Approximate number of cases in 1960
Yukon	
Full-time magistrate (200-250 of these were charges of indictable offences)	1,200
Newfoundland	
Part-time magistrate	575
Prince Edward Island	
Part-time magistrate	1,685
New Brunswick	
Part-time magistrate	1,700
Ontario (outside of Metro Toronto)	
Full-time magistrate	12,000
Full-time magistrate	3,100
Manitoba	
Part-time magistrate	1,000
Saskatchewan	
Full-time magistrate	10,575
Full-time magistrate	2,935
Alberta	
Full-time magistrate	6,555
British Columbia	
Part-time magistrate	1,865

These figures do not include parking-ticket cases. In addition, magistrates (and in a few cases justices of the peace) held at least 3,590 preliminary hearings in cases where accused persons elected to be tried by judge and jury or judge alone, or in cases triable by judge and jury without election.

Outside of metropolitan centres many magistrates sit at several places and travel extensively. Some Ontario magistrates go as far as 12,000 miles per annum to sit in five or six places. The jurisdiction of the magistrate at Whitehorse extends over the whole of the Yukon Territory and he sits in six widely separated centres.

A magistrate with power to try charges of indictable offences may sit in three capacities at one sitting. In one case, he may conduct a preliminary hearing to determine whether to commit an accused for trial by judge and jury or by judge alone. He may next sit as a 'court of criminal jurisdiction', trying a person charged with robbery or theft who has elected to be tried by him, or exercising his 'absolute' jurisdiction to try without election a person charged with attempted theft. In a third case, he may act as a 'summary conviction court', trying a person charged with committing a disturbance or a provincial offence.

The several courts in which he sits must be distinguished. A summary conviction court cannot try a charge of an indictable offence. A person charged with a summary offence cannot be tried for that offence by a superior criminal court or 'court of criminal jurisdiction'; however, a person charged with an indictable offence by the appropriate court may be found not guilty of that offence, but guilty of a lesser included summary offence. There are differences in procedure between the various kinds of trials and hearings a magistrate conducts.

Magistrates who are also juvenile or family court judges report that the work of that court takes up from ten to forty per cent of their time, proportionately restricting that available to dispose of adult offenders. Juvenile and family court cases are regarded by these magistrates as time-consuming, far out of proportion to their numbers. The student of adult corrections might wish that equal attention could be given to adult cases.

Some, but not many, magistrates report that they find their case-load excessive and that they lack time to give adequate consideration to each case. In this, they are most likely primarily concerned with the question of guilt or innocence rather than with consideration of sentence. The writer has been able to obtain an expression of opinion on this question from only one magistrate sitting in a metropolitan area, where the pressure of cases is heaviest, and where many observers have remarked on the constant heavy burden of work that compels presiding magistrates to handle cases at great speed, as if on an assembly line. He reports an average daily docket of 90 to 120 cases, none of which are charges of traffic offences. He is compelled to dispose of them at almost machine-gun speed. Recently, interest has been shown by the press in the congestion of magistrates' courts in Metropolitan Toronto, and to the evident consequent inability of magistrates to give adequate time to the consideration of individual cases. In one case reported to the writer, an accused, who was not represented by counsel, elected trial and pleaded guilty to an offence and was sentenced to life imprisonment, without any hearing of evidence, and all within less than five minutes. At a recent conference, a magistrate explained his practice in not filling out reports requested by the National Parole Board after sentence, by saying that he did not have time to learn the necessary facts about offenders in order to answer the questions in the form, although he was required to impose sometimes very severe sentences – up to life imprisonment.

In comparing the pressure of work on magistrates with that on superior, county, and district court judges, one must keep in mind the average length of the individual trial in each court. A criminal trial in a superior court is unlikely to last less than a day, and may go on for several days or weeks. Several recent trials in the Supreme Court of Ontario have lasted longer than six weeks each. In a county or district criminal court, a criminal trial is unlikely to last less than half a day, and may go on for several or many days. There are few pleas of guilty in these courts. Few trials before magistrates last over half a day and many are much shorter, lasting only a few minutes. The great majority are disposed of on pleas of guilty.

The problems involved in organizing and assessing masses of evidence introduced in long trials, and in reviewing the law and the evidence for juries in jury trials, are very complex and difficult. Such trials are exhausting for all concerned. They occupy, in the mass, a considerable amount of time in metropolitan areas. Except in Ontario, civil jury trials are rare, but in that province there are said to be more of them than in any other Commonwealth jurisdiction. The combination of civil and criminal jury trials requires long jury sittings at Toronto, with heavy backlogs of civil cases, and occasionally prolongs such sittings elsewhere. Efforts to reduce a heavy backlog of cases in each of the Court of General Sessions and in the County Court Judge's Criminal Court at Toronto have so far been unavailing. Measures proposed by the chief judge of the provincial county court system and the provision of additional court rooms in the new court house now under construction may solve the problem.

In other provinces, there does not seem to be any insuperable difficulty in handling criminal trials in superior, county, and district courts. Criminal work always has precedence in those courts, and delays owing to pressure of time are suffered chiefly by civil litigants, but would not be serious if proper steps were taken to expedite trials. The circuit system itself, and the consequent necessity of waiting for the next assizes, causes much more delay in bringing on cases for trial in superior criminal courts than the pressure of work in those courts. This delay could be overcome by an extended practice of trying cases in superior courts and transferring cases from one county to another for trial. Except in metropolitan areas, any person electing trial by a judge without a jury can be tried with fair dispatch, but those electing jury trials in courts of criminal jurisdiction must await the next jury sittings, perhaps five months away. Occasionally, and this means too often, individuals have been kept over a year in custody awaiting trial. More flexibility in fixing dates of jury sittings would easily remedy this situation, but sometimes the delay is caused by pressure of work on defence counsel. Any congestion in superior, county, or district courts, except in metropolitan areas, is not caused or appreciably contributed to by the criminal work of those courts, except occasionally and temporarily.

On the other hand, it is clear that there is constant congestion in the courts of many magistrates, particularly, but not exclusively, in metropolitan areas and other large centres. The cause of it is not hard to find. It consists principally of a combination of traffic and liquor offences. Courts that must deal annually with more than 40,000 careless driving charges, over 600,000 other provincial traffic offences, over 90,000 cases of intoxication, and over 60,000 other liquor offences, with an inadequate number of magistrates, are bound to be congested, even though the majority of them are disposed of on pleas of guilty, written or oral. Contested traffic cases often involve apparently endless delay through frequent adjournments, since the mobility of the population makes it necessary to assemble police officers, witnesses, defendants, and counsel from distant places. The trial of such a case is often as long, and the issues affecting liability are often as complex, as in many civil actions for damages, and, in fact, the charge is often contested only because of the civil consequences, particularly with respect to insurance and driving licences.

Various devices are employed to relieve the congestion. An experiment in holding 'night traffic courts' in Metropolitan Toronto has been criticized by police and court officials, but it has allowed a considerable number of defendants, who might otherwise have been compelled for economic reasons to plead guilty out of court, to attend and defend themselves, with the result that a surprising number of them have been acquitted. Other experiments in special traffic courts have been made. In Vancouver, a new building, housing three busy traffic courts, has been in operation for nearly four years. Construction of a new court house and new city hall in Toronto should provide space for magistrates' courts, now very poorly accommodated there. A 'remand court' to be introduced there should relieve other courts of much pressure.

A good deal of time could be saved in all courts, but chiefly in magistrates' courts, by reforming the law of evidence to permit documentary proof by report and certificate of many facts that must now be proved by oral evidence of witnesses. In addition to the introduction of a large class of new official documents, provision could also be made for proof of uncontested or non-controversial facts by affidavit evidence read at the trial, with a copy given to the opponent in advance, subject to the right of the opponent, on notice and at his initial expense, to require that the witness be produced for cross-examination.

Further separation of the functions of magistrates and justices of the peace would promote efficiency. Justices could not only receive informations, issue summonses and warrants, grant remands, allow bail, and complete recognizances and other documents, but also receive pleas of guilty on charges of minor offences, fix and receive payment of fines and costs, and perform other ministerial and minor judicial functions for the relief of magistrates. Several of these measures have been undertaken in some jurisdictions. Further study would bring to light other ways in which this relief could be extended, for example, by providing more clerical assistance. In some cases, legislation would be necessary: for example, a justice or a magistrate's clerk should be authorized to sign certificates of conviction or acquittal and warrants of committal on conviction, but this time-consuming work must now be done by the justice or magistrate.

Consideration of the scope of the magistrate's jurisdiction, as outlined in the next section, will suggest that it might be a good step to recognize the status of the magistrate as the most important trial judge for indictable offences, and divide his office into two – that of a 'criminal court judge', dealing with indictable offences and the more serious summary offences, and that of a 'minor-offence court judge', dealing with the less serious summary offences, each office to be filled by a different person. The number of 'criminal court judges' could be smaller than that of the present magistrates, but a larger number of 'minor-offence court judges' would be required, and the combined total of both classes of judges would be greater than that of the present number of magistrates. The salary and status of the 'criminal court judge' would have to be improved, and it would be desirable to have him appointed and paid by the national government. He could take over the criminal jurisdiction of the county and district court judges, and could sit with or without a jury as required. Outside large centres of population, he could have a fairly large district and travel extensively. It might be desirable to retain the present superior criminal court jurisdiction for the sake of public opinion. Otherwise it could be given to the new 'criminal court judges'. The 'minor-offence court judges' could be appointed and paid by provincial governments. They could handle preliminary hearings of cases to be tried by jury or by superior criminal courts.

Scope of Jurisdiction of Magistrates

It is not primarily with respect to numbers of charges disposed of that the situation resulting from the allotment of jurisdiction to Canadian magistrates is remarkable. The striking fact is that the only offences that may *not* be tried by magistrates are those in the small group of offences exclusively reserved for superior criminal courts. Of these, none occur in large numbers and only those connected with homicide and rape occur with any approach to frequency. In 1961, out of 364 persons tried on charges within the exclusive jurisdiction of superior criminal courts, 207 were convicted of the offences, with which they were charged, 71 were convicted of lesser offences, and 86 were acquitted. Magistrates may, therefore, with consent, try any of the offences normally associated with professional or habitual criminality or with the confirmed delinquent personality, such as armed robbery, armed breaking and entering, kidnapping (rare), extortion, theft, possession of goods unlawfully obtained, false pretences, frauds, bribery and corruption (except for a few rare varieties), forgery, counterfeiting and uttering, as well as all drug offences, all sexual offences except rape and its attempt, arson and other property damage, and all other non-homicidal violence, not to mention all non-fatal criminal negligence. In fact, the draft of the present Code, proposed by the Royal Commission in 1952, would have included rape and attempted rape within their consent jurisdiction, but Parliament would not go so far.

A magistrate may not only convict persons accused of any of the foregoing offences; he may also impose the maximum penalty authorized for each of them. He may sentence an offender to imprisonment for life or to preventive detention, to whipping, to forfeitures and fines and other pecuniary penalties in any amount. In short, he may impose any penalty except death.

While differences in judicial systems make comparisons with experience in other countries difficult, it appears that Canadian magistrates have much greater jurisdiction and powers than magistrates in any other common-law country. In England, magistrates can impose no term of imprisonment beyond twelve months. England, of course, retains the Quarter Sessions courts, many of which are staffed with lay justices assisted by legally qualified chairmen or clerks, but these courts have somewhat more limited jurisdiction than Canadian magistrates. Only Queen's Bench judges may impose life imprisonment and certain other penalties (except for burglary), and these judges try proportionately more criminal charges than judges do in Canada. The pattern in Australia and New Zealand appears to resemble that in England in relevant features. In the United States, trial of charges of serious offences appears to be exclusively in the hands of judges corresponding to our superior, county, and district court judges.

Implications of Extended Jurisdiction of Magistrates

The consequences of imposing so great a responsibility on so large a class of judicial officers, so diverse in background, education, experience, and outlook as the Canadian magistracy, have not been fully worked out. Not only are there wide variations in technical skill and judgment, resulting in some cases from lack of legal or other prerequisite training and in others from lack of relevant previous experience, there is also a constitutional problem of some importance which has significant practical aspects.

The device chosen by the Fathers of Confederation for securing the independence of the judiciary was the provision in the B.N.A. Act that judges of the superior, county, and district courts of the provinces must be appointed and paid by the national government, and that superior court judges should hold office during good behaviour and be removed only by an act almost as solemn as an Act of Parliament. Our superior court judges preserve their privileged position against provincial legislation appearing to encroach upon what they consider to be the proper fields of jurisdiction of superior courts by declaring that legislation purporting to entrust jurisdiction in those fields to provincial tribunals not staffed by superior, county, or district court judges is *ultra vires* and null and void. Yet under national legislative authority, over ninety per cent of all trials of charges of indictable offences (including some offences which were capital at the time of Confederation and were then within the exclusive jurisdiction of superior courts, and which are now punishable with every authorized punishment short of death) are now conducted by judges who are not federally appointed, some of whom have no legal training beyond what they pick up in the course of their work, some of whom hold office during pleasure of provincial governments, and some of whom are still paid in whole or in part by fees and are therefore dependent in part on convictions for their remuneration. No judicial officer who holds office during pleasure can be fully independent. No judicial officer whose remuneration depends to any extent on convictions can be sure of being impartial. While the practice of making appointments during good behaviour has been adopted and confirmed by statute in Ontario and, in part at least, in other provinces, evidence before the Royal Commission on Organized Crime in Ontario in 1962 and 1963 has shown that approaches that nobody would dare make to a judge are made to magistrates by leading politicians and others. Some magistrates are uncertain how to protect themselves against such proposals, being afraid, perhaps with reason, of the political influence of the intervenant, and have felt obliged to consult the Attorney-General on how to deal with the problem. Moreover, nothing was done to the intervenants about the attempts, as far as we know, while the magistrates were rebuked by the Attorney-General for seeking advice. Admittedly, the situations revealed before the Royal Commission were unusual, but nearly every magistrate could no doubt relate from his own experience more than one attempt to influence his decision. Most of these efforts are not corrupt. Many are even well meant. Most are ineffectual. Nevertheless, they are made.

In other respects, in spite of the improved status of magistrates, there is still a legacy of unfortunate attitudes to overcome. There are magistrates who appear to regard themselves, in some measure, as agents of the provincial Attorney-General, under some obligation to regard his pronouncements on enforcement policy as instructions to themselves. There have been a few recent instances that might support an inference that at least two Attorneys-General shared that opinion to some degree, to the extent of issuing instructions with respect to the conduct of courts and, in at least one case, sentencing policy. Some magistrates have, or seem to have, a too close association with the police and the Crown prosecutor to be able to be completely impartial. When the magistrate and the Crown prosecutor drive to the court house together and immediately disappear into the police office to arrange the day's docket, an accused person may well wonder whether his future is being settled before court opens. The same police officers appear before a magistrate as witnesses or prosecutors almost daily, year in and year out, and it must be hard for a magistrate not to be conditioned to regard them as fellow workers in a common cause and to accept their views of the facts and of the accused almost without question. It must be even harder for a magistrate who is a member of a police commission to be impartial.

Even where these factors do not influence the outlook of the magistrate, the name 'police magistrate', still applied to him in some jurisdictions (reminiscent of Henry Fielding and the Bow Street Runners), the name 'police court' applied to his court, the apparent domination of the court by many policemen, and his membership on the police commission where that is the case, all combine to colour the impressions made by him and his court on accused persons, witnesses, and public.

Magistrates have not achieved the same degree of withdrawal from affairs as judges, and are more subject than judges to the currents of sentiment, sympathy, and prejudice flowing through their communities. Although it is argued that such participation in the community's attitudes is an advantage to the magistrate in sentencing, the risk of a certain distortion of vision is real.

No matter what the individual magistrate may do to protect himself, all these influences, official and otherwise, make it hard for him to maintain independence of attitude. There are, however, counterbalancing influences that make the situation better than it might have been.

The increased jurisdiction of magistrates has given the magistracy enhanced prestige. Greater care in selection of magistrates and improved tenure, salaries, and conditions of work have attracted better men to the Bench, although there is room for a great deal of improvement in all three conditions, even in the best of situations, and there are considerable fallings-off from the best throughout the country. At least one former Attorney-General considered himself entitled to threaten to dismiss any magistrate who did not conform in court to his standard of conduct. Many magistrates have shown themselves determined to improve their professional qualifications and attainments generally, particularly with reference to sentencing. These advances have not been uniform throughout the country. Perhaps greater progress has been shown in Ontario than in some other provinces, since the Magistrates' Association of that province, with the support of a succession of Attorneys-General and their departments, has for a number of years conducted an organized program of study. All magistrates show much greater capacity for independence than one might expect, having regard to the disadvantages of their positions. The writer has encountered no evidence and only one suggestion of bribery or corruption.

The fact that 'leaders of the Bar' are not attracted to the magistracy is not necessarily an obstacle preventing the building up of a highly qualified magisterial Bench. The training and experience of such leaders fit them to adjudicate in civil rather than in criminal matters. Men who appear to be less highly qualified, but who are willing to engage in organized and private study in correctional fields, can make excellent magistrates. Recent experience during two two-week seminars with a number of magistrates has led the writer to the conclusion that standard legal training and qualifications, although desirable, are not indispensable, provided that the individual's background is otherwise favourable and that deficiencies resulting from lack of such training are made up by special studies in such fields as constitutional law, criminal law, procedure, evidence, and corrections.

The statistics cited above reveal great confidence in the magistracy, not only on the part of Parliament and the provincial legislatures in giving magistrates such extensive jurisdiction, but also on the part of the legal profession and accused persons in so often choosing trial by magistrate rather than by judge or jury, and on the part of Attorneys-General in not exercising their right to require trial by jury on charges of offences punishable with over five years' imprisonment. There must be reasons for this confidence, and the conclusion therefrom, that, although by no means free from defect, the magisterial courts are doing acceptable work on the whole, is confirmed by other evidence.

WORK OF APPELLATE COURTS

In 1961, appeals taken to provincial and territorial courts of appeal from courts trying charges of indictable offences were as follows:

FROM CONVICTION OR ACQUITTAL

Appeals by Accused

Dismissed	467
Appeal allowed and acquitted	170
Appeal allowed and new trial ordered	12
Appeal allowed and conviction of lesser offence substituted	5
	654

Appeals by Crown

Dismissed	17
Appeal allowed and new trial ordered	5
Appeal allowed and conviction directed	10
	32

FROM SENTENCE

Appeals by Accused

Dismissed	1,038
Appeal allowed and sentence varied	405
Appeal allowed and sentence suspended	48
	1,491

Appeals by Crown

Dismissed	2
Appeal allowed and sentence varied	20
	22

Appeals taken in that year to the Supreme Court of Canada in respect of charges of indictable offences were as follows:

FROM CONVICTION OR ACQUITTAL

Appeals by Accused

Dismissed	7
Appeal allowed and acquittal directed	9
	16

Appeals by Crown
Dismissed   1
Appeal allowed and conviction directed   1

   2

In the same year, the following numbers of appeals of all kinds were taken from courts trying summary conviction cases:

FROM CONVICTION OR ACQUITTAL
Appeals by Accused
Dismissed   658
Accused acquitted   385
New trial ordered   5
Substituted verdict   55

   1,103

Appeals by Informant (complainant)
Dismissed   82
Accused convicted   131
New trial ordered   4

   217

FROM SENTENCE
Appeals by Accused
Dismissed   63
Sentence varied   145
Sentence suspended   6

   214

Appeals by Informant (complainant)
Dismissed   18
Sentence varied   17

   35

The work of appellate courts is of importance extending greatly beyond the individual cases and far out of proportion to the number of appeals disposed of. Many judgments of appellate courts, including full reasons for judgment, are reported in 'law reports' published for use by judges and lawyers. The Supreme Court of Canada and, under its influence, the provincial and territorial courts of appeal determine judicial policy and impose significant controls on the operation of the courts, and also on the policy of those responsible for executive and administrative decisions in the enforcement of penal laws.

In dealing with individual appeals, appellate courts have wide powers. Not only may a conviction or acquittal be set aside and an acquittal or conviction ordered in its place. If a person has been wrongly convicted of a serious offence, but is guilty of a lesser included offence, the appellate court may substitute a conviction for the lesser offence. When a conviction or acquittal is set aside, the court of appeal may order a new trial if there was evidence on which the accused might have been convicted, at a properly conducted trial, of the offence charged or a lesser included offence. The power to order a new trial, which has been withheld from the English Court of Criminal Appeal except in rare cases, is considered by Canadian lawyers to be of great value, because it enables an accused to be freed from an improperly obtained conviction without automatically freeing him from criminal responsibility, if he might have been convicted had the trial been properly conducted.

JUDICIAL ATTITUDES AND TENDENCIES

The Supreme Court of Canada, within the limits of its jurisdiction, tends to promote uniformity in application of criminal legislation throughout the country. Its jurisprudence is characterized by concern for the liberty of the subject and by a desire to impose rational limits on criminal responsibility, largely through emphasis on the necessity in most cases of a 'guilty mind'. These attitudes have been reflected by provincial courts.

The judicial methods by which these aims are pursued are not all equally justifiable in theory, but they must be understood if one is to understand our courts. The historical development of our criminal law and criminal courts has caused many rules of judicial policy to be expressed in the form of rules of procedure, and especially in the form of rules for the conduct of jury trials and for the admission and effect, or the rejection, of evidence at such trials. Our law of evidence has been laboriously built up over a long period of time into an elaborate and complex system of rules of a substantive nature, as well as of a procedural nature, chiefly exclusionary, designed to allow the framing of simple questions of fact to be answered by juries of laymen, and to avoid causing confusion to them through the reception of evidence whose probative value seems to be slight when compared with its prejudicial effect on untrained minds. Moreover, during the late 18th and early 19th centuries, in an effort to mitigate the horribly confused mass of savagely punitive criminal legislation then in effect, a judicial policy was evolved that allowed the narrowest possible interpretation of the definitions of offences, demanded a very high standard of proof of guilt, and imposed all possible procedural obstacles, reasonable and unreasonable, against the prosecutor. This policy built up a judicial attitude of resistance against efforts to obtain convictions, which has left a legacy of procedural rigidity, partly enshrined in and partly remedied in our Criminal Code, and of suspicion of all legislative change, whether procedural or substantive. These characteristics of judicial attitudes have not been eliminated by codification or by extensive substantive and procedural reform. When coupled with a still rather complex procedure and a largely unreformed law of evidence, they give a strongly procedural and still somewhat ritualistic tone to our jurisprudence. Many acquittals are gained and many convictions are set aside on procedural grounds, because procedural devices are the chief weapons by which judges protect, as they believe, the liberty of the subject. This tendency is particularly noticeable when judges are faced with legislative innovations, such as provisions imposing a burden of proof of innocence on the accused or measures that seem to impose punishment divorced from fault, as in the case of preventive detention, both of which most judges tend to consider basically unjust. Although the judges have accepted from England an unjustifiable doctrine of liability without fault in certain classes of so-called welfare offences, mostly minor, our jurisprudence seems to be moving towards elimination of the theory.[1]

The lack of a national court of final appeal on questions of sentence leaves each provincial court of appeal to some extent a law unto itself in this field. Although all courts recognize the national character of criminal law and the desirability of uniformity of principles and standards throughout the country, provincial or, at least, regional differences in outlook are reflected in differences in emphasis in application of principles. No Canadian court is radical in relation to any problem. Judges who quote Bentham's theory of punishment[2] cannot be called advanced. Retribution and deterrence often outweigh reformation, in enunciation of goals of punishment. Some courts, such as those of Quebec and the Atlantic Provinces, are, however, more conservative than others. It may be that the attitude of any court is affected to some extent by the availability and quality of the provincial probation service. The country-wide development of probation services, now beginning, will no doubt influence all

1In *R. v. Piggly Wiggly Canadian Ltd.* (1933) 60 C.C.C. 104, the court held that an unwitting error in weighing bags of sugar leading to the offering for sale of bags containing less than the weight marked on them constituted an offence without proof of intentional or negligent conduct or any other fault.
2That the sole purpose of punishment is deterrence, either of the offender or of others.

courts, but judges in Quebec will probably continue to follow their own policies to a considerable degree, for two principal reasons. First, at the time of writing, there exists in Quebec no probation service and an incomplete system of provincial correctional institutions. Second, and more important, different attitudes resulting from different traditions often lead English-Canadians and French-Canadians from the same premises to different conclusions.

The legal profession has not completely ignored the correctional aspects of criminal law. Canadian law schools introduce correctional problems in teaching that subject and nearly all of them now offer elective courses in criminology.

Queen's Law Faculty, in 1962 and 1963, conducted two seminars on sentencing for judges, magistrates, and all others concerned in the administration of criminal law. Reports of the proceedings have been circulated among all Canadian judges and magistrates.

The first of what it is hoped will become a regular series of nation-wide judicial conferences on sentencing was held in Toronto in 1964, arranged by the Centre of Criminology of the University of Toronto. Judges of courts of all levels throughout Canada, including nearly all the chief justices of provincial superior courts, took part. After the conference, a statement concerning the aims of punishment, approved by the participants, was published. It was remarkable in that it was the first broadly based Canadian judicial pronouncement on punishment that did not rely on retribution. A more esoteric conference of chief justices on the same subject has since been held. It is too early to predict the effect of these conferences, but a series of them cannot fail to be of value.

The fact that judges of superior trial courts and provincial courts of appeal are usually men with extensive experience in civil law but relatively little in criminal law has been the subject of criticism by some judges as well as other persons. Proposals for creating provincial courts of criminal appeal staffed by judges with great experience and skill in prosecuting and defending criminal charges and thorough knowledge of criminal law, to which one or more teachers of criminal law might be added, have been made. While such a scheme would have highly desirable effects, it would appear to be practicable, if at all, only in Quebec, Ontario, and British Columbia, because in other provinces there are not enough criminal appeals to provide work for a special court.

It would be an error to expect too much from such an arrangement. The judges of the Supreme Courts of Newfoundland, Nova Scotia, and Prince Edward Island sit on both criminal trials and criminal appeals. Yet the criminal jurisprudence of those courts is not superior to that of other provincial courts of appeal. Admittedly, most judges have relatively little criminal law experience before appointment and hear relatively few criminal cases at trial. Something would have to be done in any event to overcome the lack of knowledge in the field of corrections. A measure to reorganize the Supreme Court of Nova Scotia along the lines of those of Alberta or Ontario has been passed by the Legislative Assembly, but at the time of writing had not been brought into effect by proclamation.

Attitude of the Legal Profession

There is a growing tendency to regard the prosecution of criminal offences as a career, concomitant with a growing practice of appointing full-time salaried prosecutors. The appointment of prosecutors has in the past been largely influenced by political patronage and is not free therefrom at present, but the office has not usually been a step in a political career. If anything, it has been regarded as leading to a possible judgeship. The defence of criminal charges does not generally in this country involve the suggestion of dishonesty that American literature and, to some extent, American professional opinion attribute to the practice in the United States. It is considered an honourable function of advocacy to defend even guilty persons, and it is not a black mark against a counsel if his client is convicted. Counsel are restricted by professional ethics and watchful courts from employing the tricks and dodges popularly associated with defence of criminal charges in American literature and drama. A few recent exceptions to the foregoing statements have been the subject of official reprimand. It is hoped that any tendency in that direction has been arrested. Economic factors limit the participation of most lawyers in criminal trials. Only a few leading counsel make any appreciable amount of money out of the practice. The others devote more or less time to it, often at a loss, depending on their own temperaments and on the demands of the more lucrative civil law side of their work.

TERRITORIAL APPLICATION OF CRIMINAL LAW

The chief principle of the application of Canadian criminal law is territorial. No provincial law can create an offence consisting of acts or omissions committed outside the province. Except where otherwise provided by national legislation, no person can be convicted in Canada for a nationally created offence committed outside Canada.

The territory of Canada for this purpose includes the territorial waters, which extend for three nautical miles from its coasts and are treated as parts of adjacent provinces. The waters of the international section of the St. Lawrence River and of the Great Lakes to the international boundary are actually within the adjacent municipalities and judicial districts of Ontario. The status of the waters of Hudson and James bays and of the Arctic Archipelago is not in all respects clear. Canadian 'customs waters' extend for twelve nautical miles from our coasts, and certain jurisdiction under the Customs Act is claimed for conduct within those waters. The effect of proposed extensions of Canadian territorial waters cannot now be predicted.

Canadian courts are given extended jurisdiction over offences committed outside Canada in the following cases:

1. Offences committed on board Canadian ships on the high seas;

2. Offences committed anywhere on board any ships by British subjects domiciled in Canada who are not members of crews of foreign ships on which the conduct occurs;

3. Offences committed against property or person out of the Queen's dominions by members or recent members of crews of Canadian ships;

4. Indictable offences committed on board Canadian aircraft;

5. Indictable offences committed on board any aircraft on flights ending in Canada;

6. Specific offences committed outside Canada:
    (a) treason;
    (b) false statements to obtain or extend passports;
    (c) piratical acts;
    (d) bigamy where a resident of Canada leaves Canada with intent to go through a bigamous marriage ceremony and does so abroad;
    (e) offences under the Canada Shipping Act;
    (f) offences triable by service tribunals of the armed forces.

TERRITORIAL JURISDICTION OF COURTS

Each criminal court has a stated territorial jurisdiction. That of the Exchequer Court of Canada is over the whole country. Provincial or territorial superior criminal courts have jurisdiction throughout their respective provinces or territories. Some courts of criminal jurisdiction and summary conviction courts, such as provincial and territorial magistrates, and all courts in Saskatchewan, have jurisdiction throughout their respective provinces or territories, while other courts of these classes have jurisdiction limited to a city or town or a county or district or group of counties or districts. Usually the territorial jurisdiction is defined in the name of the court.

Except where otherwise specifically provided, an offence committed in a province is triable only within that province. 'Newspaper libel', although committed wherever the newspaper is distributed, is triable only in the province of publication.

Under a recent amendment to the Criminal Code, a person in custody anywhere in Canada may offer to plead guilty to any offences committed by him anywhere and triable by a Canadian court, other than offences triable only by a superior criminal court. The court having jurisdiction over such offences where the accused is in custody may accept his plea of guilty and sentence him for these offences, but if any of the offences was committed in another province the consent of the Attorney-General of that province or his deputy is necessary to give the court jurisdiction. The accused is thus enabled to clear himself of all offences except the most serious, and, indeed, of practically all of which a multiple offender is likely to have been guilty except those related to homicide, and to protect himself against the device of having warrants for his arrest on charges of his old offences waiting for him outside the prison gate the moment he steps out of custody.

Offences committed in any part of Canada not in a province may be tried anywhere in Canada, but the proportion of them tried in the territory of commission is growing. A person charged with an offence committed out of Canada or on board ship or aircraft and triable within Canada may be tried where he is found or arrested or in custody.

Conduct described as an offence committed out of Canada refers to conduct that, if it had occurred within Canada, would have constituted an offence under Canadian national legislation, but where the conduct occurs on an aircraft out of Canada, it is not triable in Canada unless it is equivalent to an indictable offence under such legislation. An offence under the law of some other country cannot be tried as such by a Canadian court.

ADMINISTRATIVE RESPONSIBILITY FOR CRIMINAL JUSTICE

The responsibility for the administration of criminal justice in relation to court proceedings is divided between national and provincial authorities in a manner that seems at times surprising and illogical, but which, through co-operation, works better than one might expect. The organization is 'flexible' (that wonderful word!) in that the national authorities modify their role in each province to fit that assumed by the provincial government.

Notwithstanding Section 92(14) of the B.N.A. Act, provincial authorities do not assume responsibility for investigation and prosecution of all offences under national legislation. These roles are shared in an undefined way by national and provincial authorities, the national authorities generally handling the following:

1. Fields of criminal activity in which the Royal Canadian Mounted Police act as national security police, and other fields related to property, revenue, or affairs of the national government;

2. Prosecutions under the Combines Investigation Act;

3. Prosecutions under the Narcotic Control Act, national pure food laws, the Weights and Measures Act, the Unemployment Insurance Act, the Canada Shipping Act, and other national statutes administered by national government departments;

4. In some provinces, prosecutions under all national statutes other than the Criminal Code;

5. In Quebec, prosecutions for currency offences.

Other prosecutions are handled by provincial authorities, the arrangement in each province being a matter of agreement and custom.

In certain charges under the Criminal Code, including harbouring of deserters, bribery of judges, sending or taking an unseaworthy ship to sea, and offences committed by aliens on board ships in territorial waters or on aircraft out of Canada, the consent of the Attorney-General of Canada to the prosecution is required, although at least some of these prosecutions would be conducted by provincial authorities. On the other hand, certain steps in the course of any prosecution may require the consent of the provincial Attorney-General, no matter by whom the prosecution is conducted, and appeals are taken or contested in his name (with his consent) even when the Attorney-General for Canada is conducting the prosecution.

THE NATIONAL DEPARTMENT OF JUSTICE

The national government includes the Ministry of Justice, headed by the Minister of Justice, usually, but not always, assisted by a junior minister called the Solicitor-General. The Minister of Justice is *ex officio* Attorney-General for Canada, but, unlike his English counterpart holding the latter office, he is not selected or employed as a leading advocate appearing in court on behalf of the Crown. Whatever may have been the Minister's career before his appointment, and few of them have been really outstanding advocates, he is most unlikely to appear personally in court while in office.

Although he is the legal agent of the Crown in right of Canada in all courts, and is contemplated as being present in any court when any interest of the Crown in that right is in question, and much civil litigation on that behalf and some criminal proceedings are carried on in his name, he almost always appears by counsel, sometimes by the Deputy Attorney-General or other departmental counsel and sometimes by counsel retained *ad hoc*. The Minister is usually too busy to be a pleader, being constantly engaged not only as chief adviser to the Crown in right of Canada in legal matters, in which he resembles his English namesake, but also in being, what the English Attorney-General is not, the head of an important department of the national government, responsible for many duties that in England are performed by the Lord Chancellor, the Home Secretary, the Treasury, and other departments.

The Minister of Justice is responsible for the work of the Royal Canadian Mounted Police, the Penitentiary Service, and the National Parole Board, all of which are described in other chapters. In addition, he is responsible for the work of the Combines Investigation Commission, the agency primarily charged with the administration of the Combines Investigation Act. The work of the department in the penal field is correlated by the Criminal Justice Section, under the supervision of an assistant deputy-minister.

The extent of interference or attempted interference in the criminal work of this department by members of Parliament and other political figures, as revealed recently in the House of Commons and in evidence before the Dorion Commission, is disquieting. More disturbing is the apparent inability of all, or nearly all, of them to appreciate the harmful tendency of what they consider a legitimate activity on behalf of constituents.

In cases in which there is reason to believe that a person may have been unjustly convicted of, or sentenced for, an indictable offence, and where all rights of appeal have been exhausted or have expired, the Minister of Justice is authorized by the Criminal Code to order a new trial or to refer any question in connection with the conviction or sentence to a provincial court of appeal for hearing and determination, or for an opinion. Under recent authority, preliminary investigation of facts involved in all applications for such an order or reference is now conducted by the National Parole Board. Such applications are received by the Minister in large numbers, but very few orders or references have been made, although in some cases, but not in all, very painstaking investigation has been conducted. In 1963, following widespread public unrest, an intervention resulted in a reference to the Ontario Court of Appeal, which cut in half a twenty-four-year sentence by a magistrate. As a last resort, the Governor General in Council may refer any question to the Supreme

Court of Canada for an opinion, and this step was taken in the notorious Coffin case.[3]

The role of the provincial Attorney-General resembles that of the national Minister of Justice rather than that of the English Attorney-General. He might be called the provincial Minister of Justice, since he is the head of an important department of the provincial government, responsible primarily for the administration of justice within the province. He is responsible for advising the Crown in right of the province in legal matters, for assisting in the preparation of legislation of all kinds, for advising on policy and preparing legislation in detail in the fields of 'lawyer's law' (including the constitution, organization, jurisdiction, and operation of provincial courts and the administration of civil and criminal justice), for supervising the administrative aspects of the operation of those agencies, and for many other matters. He recommends persons for appointment as judges for inferior provincial courts, magistrates, justices of the peace, sheriffs, coroners, and court officials, and recommends conditions of employment, remuneration, scales of salary, and pensions for them. In some provinces, Attorneys-General have actively encouraged and supported a program of training for magistrates. In Quebec and Ontario, the Attorney-General is responsible through a commission for the administration of the provincial police, and in the other provinces for dealing with the detachments of Royal Canadian Mounted Police who perform the role of provincial police there. He also shares responsibility with local authorities for supervision of local police. In some provinces, his department operates 'crime laboratories' and employs pathologists, toxicologists, psychiatrists, and other experts, sometimes on full-time salaried employment, sometimes on general or special retainers of men in private practice.

[3]In *R. v. Coffin* (1956) 114 C.C.C.1, the accused had been convicted of murder by the Quebec Court of Queen's Bench, Trial Side, and his appeal had been dismissed by the Appeal Side of that court. His application for leave to appeal to the Supreme Court of Canada had been dismissed. As a result of widespread criticism, the Supreme Court of Canada was directed to hear argument on the grounds for appeal advanced on behalf of the accused, and after doing so decided that no reason for setting aside the conviction had been established. The accused was hanged, but criticism by several individuals of the conduct in that case of the police and of the prosecutor has continued. A book describing the authorities as murderers led in 1964 to a judicial investigation of the conduct of the investigations and the trial. The result of the investigation was confirmation of the result of the trial. The author was ordered to be imprisoned for contempt of court, and, at the time of writing, his appeal from this sentence is pending. It appears that proceedings may be taken against his counsel.

Although, like the Minister of Justice, the provincial Attorney-General is the legal agent in all courts of the Crown in right of the province, and many legal proceedings on that behalf are conducted in his name, and he is contemplated as being present in court on behalf of the Crown in right of the province whenever its interests are involved, he is even less likely than the Minister of Justice to be a leading advocate. In fact, at the time of writing and for a number of years, Alberta has been served by Attorneys-General who have not even been lawyers. Whatever his qualifications, he is too busy, as a rule, to appear in court in person, although some provincial Attorneys-General have appeared more or less frequently on behalf of their provincial Crowns. In most provinces, the Deputy Attorney-General, the Director of Public Prosecutions, and counsel permanently employed in the department do most of the court work in superior appellate courts, but other counsel are not infrequently employed *ad hoc*.

The degree and extent of political pressure exerted by members of provincial legislatures and other political figures on the criminal work of these departments is not less, and not less disquieting, than in the case of the Department of Justice.

The Attorney-General's Agent

In nearly all provinces, the Attorney-General regularly employs legal agents throughout the province to act for him, usually one in every county or district. In several provinces, these lawyers are known as Crown prosecutors; in others the description is simply Attorney-General's agent. In some provinces, some prosecutors are municipally employed. In Ontario, the title is Crown Attorney, and his office is a statutory one. A growing number of Crown Attorneys are employed on a full-time salaried basis, and it is the purpose of the Ontario Attorney-General's Department to make this arrangement uniform throughout the province as vacancies occur; there are still, however, a number of Crown Attorneys who are paid by fees, most of whom are employed on a part-time basis. Arrangements in other provinces follow a similar pattern, but Quebec is apparently the only province besides Ontario where the policy of full-time salaried employment has been adopted. Although not elected, Attorney-General's agents have usually been selected with regard to political factors, at least to the extent that supporters of the party in power in the province have had the best chance of appointment. Quebec has recently announced that its prosecutors are to be brought under the provincial Civil Service Act. On the whole, the system has worked reasonably well. The level of ability has been acceptable and an honourable tradition has been maintained.

Some excellent counsel have been employed on part-time retainers, and a number of the men on full-time employment have been of high calibre. Full-time service offering a career in the public service or a stepping-stone to the Bench or private practice should bring about general improvement and is apparently doing so in Ontario, but unless better salaries are offered, it will become increasingly difficult to find competent men to fill vacancies. Nearly all prosecutors share the general lack of training in correctional fields common to the legal profession as a whole.

The Attorney-General's agent, by whatever name he is known, works in conjunction with the police, advising them with reference to the investigation of offences, the laying of charges, and applying for summonses and warrants. He is not an investigator and does not employ investigators. That work is for the police. He may advise justices of the peace in connection with the forms of charges and other legal points related to the ministerial side of their work. He conducts the prosecution of all charges of indictable offences within his territory, down to trial and sentence, although the Attorney-General may appoint a special prosecutor for difficult or important cases and, if so, the Attorney-General's agent assists the prosecutor. He conducts the prosecution of summary offences on instructions from the Attorney-General or request of local authorities. On appeal to the local appeal court from a summary conviction court, the Attorney-General's agent represents the informant, unless a private informant is privately represented. Some agents are fairly frequently employed as special prosecutors throughout the province.

The agent is regularly heard by justices of the peace, magistrates, and judges on applications for bail and remand, and, in practice, seems to exercise almost a veto power over the granting of bail in lower courts. At any rate, his representations on the subject have great weight in all courts, and his proposals with respect to amount are rarely rejected. Since remand in custody can be practically assured in nearly all cases by fixing high bail, the agent's sense of fairness must be highly developed. In the cases in which prosecutions cannot be commenced without the consent of the Attorney-General of Canada or of the province, it is the agent's responsibility to obtain the consent and lay it before the court.

At trial, the agent may consent to the reduction, or even withdrawal, of a charge. He may determine the outcome of a trial by a decision relating to the presentation of evidence.

In respect of sentence, the agent is responsible for obtaining the criminal record of the accused and other apparently significant material, and placing it before the court. His views on the subject have much weight before some judges and magistrates, but others seem to prefer the prosecutor to place the facts before the court and make no representations. The increasing use of probation officers and pre-sentence reports has had the effect, in some courts, of restricting the role of the agent in matters of sentence. It is suggested that a more active policy in relation to sentencing, if based on understanding of the goals of punishment and principles of sentencing, as well as a thorough study of the individual case, would better promote the interests of justice, but the absence of vindictiveness inherent in the above-mentioned policy is praiseworthy.

The policy is in keeping with the tradition of impartiality, which representatives of the Crown are trained to maintain in all criminal proceedings, and which is, in fact, fairly well maintained. As a class they say, and are constantly admonished by the courts to believe, that their role is to bring out all the facts, favourable and adverse to each side, fully and fairly, to strive by all fair and honourable means to obtain a conviction, if the facts seem to justify one, but to take no unfair advantage of the accused, to make no effort to deceive the court, whether judge or jury, to conceal no relevant evidence favourable or unfavourable to the Crown or the accused, not to seek a conviction for a more serious offence than the facts appear to warrant, and to ask for acquittal if guilt does not appear to be established. It would be folly to assert that this code is always adhered to, but the courts are alert to exhort and, in some cases enforce, its observance.

Coroners

Coroners, who are usually but not necessarily medical practitioners, are appointed by provincial governments, except in Newfoundland and Nova Scotia, and some provinces have chief coroners to supervise the work of their colleagues. The employment of local coroners is usually on a part-time basis, with remuneration by fees. While these officers do a considerable amount of good work, they sometimes look like fifth wheels and must often feel rather futile. They are required to examine the bodies of persons who died apparently from other than natural causes, and, when instructed to do so or when they deem it necessary, to conduct, in tribunals called coroners' inquests, inquiries with juries to determine the cause of death. Coroners in some provinces may dispense with inquests, if not otherwise instructed. Since there is no rule requiring autopsies in all cases, there is some risk in the practice, and cases of murder overlooked by coroners may be later uncovered. On the other hand, a murder eluded a coroner some years ago in Ontario because of a mistaken diagnosis on autopsy. Where there is evidence of foul play or other criminal conduct, and some person is charged with homicide, or where investigation is pending and it is not desired to make the evidence public for the time being, and particularly if there is a possibility that a fair trial of some person may be prejudiced by publication of the evidence, or that a person who is accused will be called as a witness before the coroner and there compelled to answer incriminating questions, in some cases Attorneys-General have issued instructions to adjourn the inquest without taking evidence until after the conclusion of the criminal proceedings, or until it has been considered that no evidence sufficient to support the prosecution of any person has been discovered. If some person is by that time convicted of homicide, it may be decided unnecessary to proceed with the inquest. This practice, although not uniform, has much to recommend it. In Saskatchewan, by statute, the Attorney-General is required to decide whether an inquest shall be held in such circumstances, and in Alberta, he is authorized to direct that none shall be held in a case of murder.

The coroner's inquest is really the sitting of a special kind of court, and witnesses may be compelled by summons or warrant to attend and give evidence. In the conduct of inquests, coroners are usually advised by the Attorney-General's agent, and he normally questions the witnesses and suggests to the coroner how he may instruct the jury. Although inquests are open to the public, interested persons and their legal representatives have no enforceable right to attend other than as members of the public, and have no enforceable right to examine or cross-examine witnesses, except in British Columbia and Alberta, or to call witnesses, except in British Columbia. In other provinces, coroners may extend such privileges by permission. In all provinces, any person who demanded to testify would no doubt be heard, if it appeared that he might have some relevant knowledge. Proposals to have experts examined may, but need not, be acceded to. Usually questions suggested by or on behalf of interested persons are put to witnesses by the coroner or the Attorney-General's agent. In British Columbia, all persons who may be affected by the proceedings, and in Alberta, all suspected persons may be represented by counsel and may examine or cross-examine witnesses. In Saskatchewan, suspected persons cannot be compelled to give evidence and, if they do, cannot be cross-examined.

Formerly, a person accused of murder or manslaughter by a coroner's jury could be put directly on his trial. This practice was abolished in Canada in 1892, and in its place, the coroner is empowered to cause the person so accused to be arrested and brought before a justice of the peace.

In Quebec, the coroner exercises a veritable inquisitorial jurisdiction, issuing warrants or oral instructions for arrest of suspects, and others as material witnesses, on which they are held without bail for long periods of time and questioned under conditions recently the subject of severe adverse criticism. They are then compelled to give evidence at an inquest with only the uncertain protection of the Canada Evidence Act to prevent their evidence from being used against them in a later trial, if they have objected in due form at the inquest. It is said that an inquest always precedes a prosecution on a charge of homicide.

In Newfoundland, magistrates instead of coroners hold inquests. In Nova Scotia, the replacement of coroners by medical examiners is now complete, and provision is made for the holding of inquests by magistrates.

Manitoba is the only other province in which a coroner is expressly given power to issue a warrant in the first instance, instead of a summons, for arrest of a witness. In the two provinces where magistrates conduct inquests they have a similar power.

Justices of the Peace

Justices of the peace are provincial officers. Some are employed full-time and paid by salary, but a number are either officials who have other duties and are available to act as justices when required, or are on part-time employment and are paid by fees. Formerly in some provinces, the heads of all municipal councils and all municipal clerks automatically held this office, and other appointments were scattered broadcast for political reasons or as a mark of local prestige, but these practices have been or are being abolished. The trend is towards making appointments only as required according to the amount of penal work for justices to do. Unfortunately, some policemen are made justices in the name of administrative convenience. This practice is dangerous and instances of conflict of interest and duty have arisen under it.

Justices receive informations charging persons with offences, and issue summonses or warrants for arrest to compel appearance of accused persons and witnesses at preliminary hearings and trials before justices and magistrates, and receive special informations and issue warrants to search for things. In the absence of magistrates, they remand accused persons in or out of custody and grant bail, before a magistrate or higher court is 'seised' of a case, except that on a charge of an offence punishable by death, or of non-capital murder, or of certain treasonable or seditious offences, bail may be granted only by a judge of a superior criminal court. When bail is authorized by a judge or a magistrate, the recognizance may be taken by a justice. When not prohibited by provincial law, the justice may hold preliminary hearings to determine whether persons charged with indictable offences should be committed for trial or released. Under provincial laws, they are often given power to try provincial and municipal

Stuart Ryan

offences. However, magistrates have the powers of justices, and not only normally conduct all summary trials and preliminary hearings and frequently make remands and grant bail, but also, on occasion, receive informations and issue summonses and warrants. The extent of actual employment of justices varies from province to province. In Quebec, certain municipal judges perform some of their functions.

CLASSIFICATION OF CRIMINAL OFFENCES
FROM THE POINT OF VIEW OF PROCEDURE

While there are only two general classes of criminal offences, indictable and summary, they may be arranged in more detail as follows:

1. *Indictable Offences*
   (a) Offences triable only by a superior criminal court as above mentioned.
   (b) Offences triable by a court of criminal jurisdiction in respect of which the accused may elect to be tried by a magistrate authorized to hold trials under Part XVI of the Code, by a judge or by a judge and jury.
   (c) Those that a magistrate authorized as above may in his discretion try without giving the accused any election, or may refuse to try and for which he may send the accused to be tried by judge and jury.

2. *Offences Indictable or Summary at the Option of the Prosecutor*

The purpose of creating such offences is to enable the prosecutor to gauge the apparent seriousness of the individual offence and elect the mode of procedure providing an apparently adequate maximum penalty, while not cluttering up higher courts with less serious offences. An explanation of the possible consequences of the various elections open, first to the prosecutor and, second, in some cases, to the accused, would be very complicated. In practice, over ninety-nine per cent of charges of such offences are treated as summary, the total number so tried in recent years being about 13,000 per annum. Most of those treated as indictable are tried by magistrates, and nearly all are therefore tried in the same court. The chief consequences of summary trial are simplification of procedure, reduction of penalties, and a different appeal procedure.

3. *Summary Offences*

CHARACTERISTICS OF CANADIAN CRIMINAL PROCEDURE

Canadian criminal procedure, like that of all common-law countries, is basically accusatorial and adversarial rather than inquisitorial in nature.

186

In countries where criminal procedure is inquisitorial, the court assumes the initiative in investigation (in some countries even employing judicial police for the purpose), in the apprehension and questioning of suspects and witnesses under compulsion before trial, in the preparation of a dossier or record of pre-trial proceedings on which the trial will be based, and in conduct of the trial; the object throughout is defined as seeking out and ascertaining the truth. In the adversarial system, these functions, in so far as they are lawful, are performed by the police and the prosecutor, while the court awaits the submission of evidence by the prosecution and the defence, and acts as umpire during the trial and as adjudicator at the end, basing its decision on the evidence put before it through the initiative of the prosecutor and the accused or his counsel. In this system, the state, the Crown, is treated as a party to a lawsuit, occupying a special position and enjoying certain limited privileges, but subject to certain procedural disadvantages and other disabilities, and otherwise in the same position as any other party. The burden of adducing evidence to prove guilt generally rests on the prosecutor, and he can neither require the accused to give evidence at the trial (under national rules) nor, with few exceptions, compel him to make any pre-trial statement. If he wishes to prove a confession by the accused, he must, with few exceptions, show that it was made freely and voluntarily. The accused is generally entitled to be presumed to be innocent, and can ordinarily be proved guilty only by evidence satisfying the court of his guilt beyond a reasonable doubt. The accused may in most cases say nothing and offer no evidence, and make no explanation, and the court must acquit him if the prosecution evidence does not create the very high degree of probability of his guilt necessary to support a conviction. The few exceptions to each of the foregoing statements are statutory and limited.

The accused is entitled to be tried in open court, unless for good cause the court orders a trial *in camera* (in closed court), which rarely happens in adult courts; to hear the evidence against him unless he so misbehaves himself that he must be removed to permit the trial to continue, and then his counsel may remain; to be represented throughout by counsel, who may cross-examine all prosecution witnesses freely; to introduce evidence on his own behalf; and to give or not give evidence himself as he decides, upon advice of counsel. Evidence of good character may be introduced freely on his behalf. The prosecutor may not introduce evidence of bad character against him, except to rebut evidence of good character, unless proof of misconduct in another matter is directly relevant to prove his guilt of the offence charged. However, if he gives evidence himself, he may be cross-examined about previous convictions. If he denies them, they may be proved against him. This rule has kept many accused persons out of the witness-box and many lawyers consider it unfair to the accused.

The Indigent Accused

The problem of legal representation of the indigent accused is, on the whole, not very well handled. Nowhere in Canada is there a publicly appointed and paid 'public defender', as in some American jurisdictions. There has been heretofore nowhere in Canada a comprehensive state-supported scheme of paid legal aid as in Britain. Canadian lawyers are dubious about the value of the public defender, many having or professing to have reason to believe that such an officer would tend to co-operate too fully with the prosecutor, or tend to put up a *pro forma* defence in many cases, but they look with more sympathy at schemes where voluntary societies (which may be state-subsidized) employ counsel to defend indigents.

The legal professions in all provinces provide free legal aid in some form. In Newfoundland, Prince Edward Island, and the Territories, it is unorganized. In the other provinces, it is organized in various ways. In Nova Scotia, Quebec, and Ontario, participating lawyers receive no remuneration. In New Brunswick, the only remuneration is a small allowance for defence of capital charges. Elsewhere, provision is made for paid legal aid in certain classes of cases. On the whole, although the first annual report by the director of the British Columbia scheme, introduced in 1963, expressed satisfaction with it, none of these schemes results in adequate representation in criminal cases.

The work usually falls on the shoulders of a few enthusiasts, assisted by inexperienced counsel and law students, in each centre, all of whom do good work as far as they can. There are not enough of them to handle all cases where help is needed. Rules are made limiting the kinds of cases where help is given, and persons previously convicted may be refused aid or no aid may be given on appeals. In some areas, no aid is given in ordinary criminal cases. The profession has never been completely unresponsive to the needs of the indigent accused, and much unrecognized legal aid has always been given and is still given on a personal and haphazard basis. Leading counsel frequently and voluntarily defend, without fee, persons charged with homicide and certain other offences that attract a great deal of public or professional interest, but an indigent accused before the magistrate on a charge of breaking and entering or theft may have as much need of help, and may not get it because of his previous record or because counsel are not available. The Montreal Legal Aid Bureau employs two lawyers, who distribute work among members of the Bar. The latter are theoretically obliged to undertake it. In Halifax, the fifty-two junior members of the Bar are required to serve in rotation.

In Ontario, growing dissatisfaction with the voluntary unpaid scheme operated by the provincial Law Society with state-subsidized payment of out-of-pocket expenses, led to the employment, first, of one, and later, of two full-time salaried solicitors to co-ordinate the work in Metropolitan Toronto and to give assistance in penal institutions. A committee appointed by the provincial Attorney-General has recently submitted a report based on extensive study, recommending introduction of a comprehensive scheme of state-supported legal aid along the lines of the English civil legal-aid system. The scheme would be administered by the provincial Law Society in co-operation with other agencies. Lawyers volunteering for the work would be paid about seventy-five per cent of normal fees. Aided persons who are able to contribute to the cost would be required to do so according to their ability. Aid in criminal cases would cover all proceedings up to sentence on charges of indictable offences against persons without criminal records, and might be granted in special cases to recidivists and for appeals. If adopted, the scheme should bring about a great improvement in the defence of needy persons, and would have a profound effect on the work of the criminal courts. Congestion would be increased through a reduction in numbers of pleas of guilty and through longer trials. A higher proportion of trials before judges, with or without juries, could be anticipated. Legal-aid counsel would be under a heavy responsibility, both to their clients and to the cause of justice, in deciding how to advise their clients to plead. At the same time, a considerable number of recidivists would continue to lack effective representation.

Limitations on Police Powers (See also Chapter 6, The Police)

No person may be lawfully detained or compelled to go to or remain in any place, unless he is lawfully arrested with or without warrant and charged with a statutorily defined offence for which he may be lawfully arrested in that manner, in the circumstances, or unless some other person is charged with an offence and the person detained is arrested under warrant as a material witness, or unless he has been involved in a motor accident and must remain at the scene and tender help and give his name and report to the police, or unless he is obliged to report to a customs or immigration officer, or to register a firearm, or under a similar limited duty. Recently, prolonged custody without trial of persons accused of illegal entry into the country, and of persons held for deportation pending appeal, has led to apparently well-founded complaints, and a number have been released on bail, although some complaints are now reported to be unfounded.

The police may, and indeed must, in performance of their duty question witnesses and suspects, but no person is compelled to answer questions in relation to his own conduct or that of others, whether or not he is under arrest, except in certain restricted circumstances under special statutory authority: for example, if he is found in a disorderly house, or involved in a motor accident, or is a witness before a court or a royal commission, or other statutorily authorized inquiry. No person can be compelled to give any sample of blood, urine, or breath for analysis; but in Saskatchewan, if he refuses to do so, his owner's and driver's licence may be suspended. Yet, if such a sample is taken without consent, an analysis of its contents may be proved in evidence, although results of a breathalyzer test obtained in a manner disapproved by the judge were rejected in a recent case. Similarly, in several jurisdictions, although there are statutory provisions prohibiting or restricting 'wire-tapping', information gained by that means, contrary to these provisions, may be proved in evidence. In general, evidence illegally obtained is admitted at trial, if relevant. However (see page 187), confessions made to persons in authority, particularly by persons in custody, are not generally admitted in evidence unless it is proved that they were made voluntarily and not in response to any promise or threat.

Initiation of Criminal Process

Except in a few cases where no prosecution may be commenced without the authority of the Attorney-General of Canada or of the province, any person, police officer or not, may, in appropriate circumstances, initiate criminal proceedings in one way or another. Normally, of course, this step is taken by a police officer.

The first proceeding may be the laying of an information in writing before a justice of the peace by a person who completes the prescribed form and swears or affirms that he knows, or believes on reasonable grounds, that the accused person is guilty of a certain named offence. This step may be preceded by arrest without warrant, but the information must be laid as the first step in all cases or soon after, unless an indictment is brought directly before an appropriate court with the authority of the Attorney-General or a judge. In two provinces, a 'traffic ticket' may commence proceedings for a provincial traffic offence.

On receipt of the information and administering the oath or affirmation, and, if necessary, questioning the informant and any witnesses he produces, assuming that the accused person is not already under arrest, the justice must decide whether to

1. do nothing about it, if there seem to be no reasonable grounds for believing that the accused might be found guilty;
2. issue a summons to be served on the accused, requiring him to appear before the court; or
3. issue a warrant authorizing any peace officer to arrest the accused and bring him before the court.

The justice can be compelled to receive the information, to hear the evidence of the informant and his witnesses, and to decide whether or not to act and, if so, how, but he cannot be compelled to make any particular decision. The remedy for his refusal to act is persuasion and, if that fails, to seek another justice and try to persuade him to act. If the offence is indictable, an unsuccessful informant may seek the authority of the Attorney-General or the judge to present an indictment in the appropriate court. If it is summary, and no justice will issue process for an offence under a national statute, it appears to be assumed that the case must not be worth while prosecuting. There is in at least one province a way of compelling the issue of process for provincial offences, depending on the provincial law. Unfortunately, the tendency of justices is all the other way. They tend to regard themselves rather as rubber stamps, to complete and issue summonses and warrants on demand.

Summons or Warrant

Once it has been decided to proceed, the question whether to issue a summons or warrant depends on the nature of the offence and the probability or otherwise that the accused will attend to answer the charge if he is at large. For more serious offences, a warrant is almost always issued. For less serious indictable offences, there is not necessarily 'one law for the rich and one for the poor', but there is something that can look like it, since the status of the accused in the community, his reputation, and his past conduct will often decide the issue. Much may depend on the status of the complainant and the degree of probability of guilt of the accused. The Attorney-General's agent may be asked for advice. If a law enforcement officer asks for a warrant, one will normally be issued. On a private information, a summons is more likely to be issued, unless there is good reason to believe either that the accused is dangerous at large or that he is likely to run away. For summary offences, a summons is normally employed, but a warrant may be issued on cause being shown.

Search-Warrants (See also Chapter 6, The Police)

Search-Warrants are obtainable before or after the commencement of a prosecution, on information in the prescribed form, made on oath or affirmation, showing good reason to believe that anything may be found in respect of which, or on which, an offence may have been committed, or which is likely to be used for the purpose of committing an offence-against-the-person for which arrest without warrant is authorized, or which will probably furnish evidence of commission of an offence. By endorsing such a warrant, a justice anywhere in Canada may make it enforceable within his jurisdiction. Anything found while a warrant is being enforced that is reasonably believed to have been obtained by, or used in, the commission of an offence, or explosives believed to be held for an illegal purpose, may be seized, whether mentioned in the warrant or not even when related to an offence not mentioned in the information. Search by peace officers without warrant for illegally held offensive weapons is authorized by the Criminal Code. Under various national and provincial statutes, search without warrant or under blanket forms of warrant or under powers given by special forms of warrant or writs of assistance may be conducted by peace officers or other authorized persons for limited purposes, such as looking for contraband goods, narcotics, obscene matter, illegally possessed liquor, gambling or gaming instruments and records, women in bawdy-houses, records for use in enforcement of revenue laws, or evidence of combines offences. Wholesale seizure of records, as well as seizure of vessels or vehicles, may be made.

Attention has recently been directed to a number of instances of apparent abuses of these powers, particularly in relation to an allegedly obscene publication, to seizure of lawyers' files containing clients' confidential papers, and to several apparently unjustifiable invasions of private dwelling-houses in purported enforcement of liquor laws. Since there is no general rule in Canada that illegally obtained evidence cannot be used in court, and since the remedy of prosecuting or suing officers who exceed their powers is rarely exercised, and since there is no substantial evidence of disapproval by senior police officers of such abuse of authority, and virtually no disciplinary action in respect of it by police commissions, the temptation to go beyond the limits of legal authority is great. A feeling is growing, however, that some of these powers authorize morally unjustifiable interference with innocent persons.

Arrest Without Warrant (See also Chapter 6, The Police, p. 118)

Powers to arrest without warrant are very wide. A peace officer may arrest without warrant any person whom he finds committing any national offence and any person whom he suspects, on reasonable grounds, of having committed or being about to commit any indictable offence, or of having been involved or being about to be involved in a breach of the peace. Any person, peace officer or not, may arrest without warrant any person whom he finds committing an indictable offence and any person whom he believes, on reasonable grounds, to have committed any national offence and to be fleeing from and freshly pursued by persons authorized to arrest him for that offence. The owner or lawful possessor of property, or person authorized by him, may arrest without warrant any person whom he finds committing any national offence on or in relation to that property. Any person who witnesses a breach of the peace may detain any person who commits or is about to join in the breach of the peace. A private person who arrests or detains anybody must deliver him to a peace officer as soon as possible. Any person arrested with or without warrant must be brought before a justice of the peace as soon as possible, at the latest within twenty-four hours, if one is available. Peace officers in fresh pursuit may enter private premises without warrant to make an arrest, if the fugitive is an occupier of the premises or is found in the premises of another. All arrests without warrant must be made on a charge of some offence or breach of the peace. Provincial statutes give power to peace officers to arrest without warrant for certain provincial offences, such as some liquor or some traffic offences.

Treatment of Persons in Custody Pending Hearing

A person in arrest may be searched, even to the extent of looking in his mouth or ears, and perhaps using X-rays and pumping out his stomach. Anything found on or in him that is likely to be of use as evidence in relation to an offence may be taken into custody. His valuables may also be taken for safekeeping. He may be finger-printed and photographed and subjected to other identifying procedures authorized by regulation. He may be placed in line-ups and shown to witnesses with a view to identification.

He may be subjected to a medical examination, and made to perform tests with a view to determining his state of sobriety or other condition. In several recent trials, evidence of results of such tests considered by judges to be improperly made has been rejected. If there is any suspicion of illness or injury, he should be examined at once for the purpose of diagnosis and possible treatment. Occasionally a prisoner believed to be drunk dies or is discovered in a coma as a result of brain injury or other non-alcoholic cause. Such occurrences suggest that medical examinations ought to be made more often and more promptly than they are.

The prisoner may be questioned at length and subjected to various tricks or persuasive measures, short of force, to induce him to confess or make a statement. The truth of frequent complaints of the use of violence by policemen for this purpose is hard to ascertain, but such conduct is believed to be not unknown. Although a confession involuntarily made is not admissible in evidence against him in ordinary cases, information gained improperly may be used to discover evidence, such as stolen goods, instruments, and so on, which may be used against him; in certain cases, which are not universally approved, parts of statements relating to the places where things were found have been admitted in evidence.

The prisoner is entitled to refuse to answer any or all questions (except under express statutory requirement — see page 187), to consult a lawyer, and to communicate with relatives or associates for the purpose of reaching a lawyer and of arranging bail. The deprivation of the right to consult counsel is a common and frequently justified cause of complaint, and tricks and dodges to prevent communication between a person under arrest and his lawyer, until the prisoner has signed a confession, are fairly frequently employed. Bail should be reasonable under the Bill of Rights, 1689, but bail is often set at a high figure to keep a prisoner in custody.

An abuse of process that is not as common as it was, but is still unfortunately winked at, even by one Court of Appeal, is the laying of what is called a 'holding charge', that is, a fictitious charge, usually of vagrancy, followed by remanding the accused in custody without bail or subject to very high bail that he cannot provide, perhaps from week to week, in the hope that evidence for his retention on a more serious charge will come to light.

A material witness may be arrested on warrant and retained in custody, under conditions similar to those applicable to an accused person, if the witness is likely to abscond or unlikely to attend on summons or subpoena. This power may be lawfully exercised only when some other person has been charged and is being prosecuted, a limitation which recent newspaper reports suggest is not always observed.

Remedies for False Imprisonment and Other Illegal Treatment of Prisoners

The basic method of obtaining release from illegal detention is the order for production of the prisoner before the court on habeas corpus (from the great common-law writ, in Latin, meaning, 'Have the body of the prisoner before the court so that he may undergo whatsoever the court may order concerning him'). This order is made by the superior criminal court of the province or the Supreme Court of Canada. The remedy is limited in that only the regularity of the process may be inquired into, but it may be supported by another order called certiorari, which requires all the proceedings to be sent to the superior court for examination. If no legal ground for detention is shown, the prisoner will be ordered to be released. No application can be made by way of habeas corpus to fix or vary bail since other process is available for that purpose, nor may this procedure be used in place of an appeal from a conviction for an indictable offence. Recent decisions have had the practical effect of depriving the prisoner of the supposed common-law and statutory right to apply for habeas corpus to every superior court judge in turn. A uniform right of appeal in habeas corpus applications has been provided by a recent amendment to the Criminal Code (see page 156). The limited right given by statute to apply for habeas corpus to a judge of the Supreme Court of Canada is not available by way of appeal from a provincial court.

A person illegally arrested or detained has a right of civil action for damages against the responsible persons, whether public officials or not. However, if a warrant for arrest has been issued, this may excuse the officer making the arrest. A person maliciously prosecuted without reasonable grounds, and who has been acquitted, has a right of civil action for damages against the complainant and the instigator of the prosecution. A conspiracy between two or more persons to bring a false accusation of commission of a crime against another person, knowing it to be false, and to cause him to be prosecuted, is an indictable offence. Under the combined effect of the Criminal Code and the Canadian Bill of Rights, it would appear to be an indictable offence to imprison a person wilfully, knowing that no legal ground of imprisonment exists. This offence would include continuing to detain a person unlawfully after one learns of the unlawfulness of the detention, even though it appeared at first that it was lawful, and would also include any deliberate abuse of criminal process to deprive another person of liberty. Depriving a prisoner of the right to communicate with relatives or associates or of the right to consult counsel would appear also to be an indictable offence. In this situation, the police often use subterfuges to keep a suspect actually in custody without formally arresting him, and, if a police officer were charged with the offence, he would probably deny that the suspect was in arrest, although the arrest and custody were real and effective. A prisoner is entitled to be brought before a justice within twenty-four hours after his arrest, or as soon afterwards as a justice is available, and a formal charge must be laid against him at or before this appearance. Failure to comply with this requirement would appear also to be an indictable offence. The accused may be remanded from time to time pending trial or preliminary inquiry, in custody or at large, with or without bail. Each remand is to be for not more than eight days, unless the accused is out of custody and consents to a longer remand.

Remand for Medical Examination

If at any time before or during trial it is made to appear to the court by medical evidence that the accused may be mentally ill, he may be remanded in or out of custody for psychiatric examination, for up to thirty days under the Code (or in Ontario, under provincial legislation, sent to a mental hospital for up to sixty days even without previous medical evidence). On such remand, the accused may in practice be certified as mentally ill and in need of treatment in a mental hospital. If so, he will probably be confined in such an institution for treatment, although the Code is silent on this point.

This procedure may superficially be regarded as satisfactory because the accused is treated in a therapeutic institution where he should be, but the legislators probably did not have in mind – at least did not provide for in the Code – all the implications of the procedure. If the accused is certified and placed in a mental institution, the legal aspect of the case is left in the air, because the accused may not have been mentally ill at the time of the offence, or, even though mentally ill at that time, he may have not been insane within the meaning of the Code and may still be criminally responsible. An application by an inmate of an Ontario mental hospital for release on habeas corpus, from prolonged detention following such a remand and certification as a mentally ill person under provincial legislation, has recently been dismissed by the Supreme Court of Canada in a decision that is not universally regarded as a good one.

This is not the only problem confronting the accused person. If he is later discharged from the mental institution as cured, what is to happen to him? Should he then be tried for the offence? The Code furnishes no answer to this question. In practice, an administrative decision is made by the Attorney-General or his deputy, in his discretion, to have the prosecution dropped or proceeded with, but a decision not to proceed does not dispose of the charge unless it is dismissed. If the accused has been certified, he may have been legally insane and not criminally responsible, but this issue cannot be decided without a trial. If he was not legally insane, the offence may not seem important enough, upon his discharge from the institution, to require penal action, but it remains a potential threat to the accused if he is not tried. If the accused is not too mentally ill to stand trial and is not certifiable, the psychiatrists find themselves in a most awkward position. They may find the accused to be in need of psychiatric treatment, but what are they to report to the court? They cannot assume that he is guilty, because he has not been tried, and they cannot therefore recommend any particular disposition of the case. A common practice, in that situation, is to report merely that the accused is fit to stand trial, but this procedure is unsatisfactory. If the accused is tried and sentenced following such a report, without further study of the case by some qualified person, as happened in a recent case in Toronto that caused great public concern, the result may be most unhappy. Further study must be given to the foregoing problems before a satisfactory solution can be reached. As pointed out by one critic, the court cannot sentence an offender to treatment in a mental therapeutic institution anyway. The British Mental Health Act, 1959, offers an example that might, perhaps, be followed, since it permits the court to sentence a mentally ill offender to an indeterminate period of treatment in a mental hospital, rather than to a term of imprisonment.

The Sentencing Process

In describing a criminal trial, the lawyer, the judge, and the magistrate usually relate in detail the proceedings up to verdict and have little to say about what follows, while the student of corrections is likely to be greatly concerned with the sentence and its execution and too little interested in what leads up to it. We will pass over, for the time being, that part of the trial leading up to verdict and commence this part of our study with the finding of 'guilty'.

Until recently, Canadian criminal trials have reflected the lawyer's point of view, and this lack of interest in the sentencing process is exemplified by the lack of procedural provisions for that stage of the trial in the Criminal Code. In recent years, the correctional aspect of the trial has been receiving greater attention and a rather meagre jurisprudence governing the process is being developed.

Some consideration has always been given by judges and magistrates to issues affecting sentence, but, in the past, methods of informing the court of relevant facts have been rather haphazard and often perfunctorily employed. Since judicial thinking relates the appropriate punishment most closely to the offence for which sentence is being pronounced, the nature of the offender's participation, whether alone or with others, whether as leader or follower, whether with or without elements of deliberation, temptation, provocation, liquor, or similar factors, has always been considered. If not brought out before verdict, it is often asked for by the court. Past offences have normally been taken into account, but the usual methods of proof, through the Royal Canadian Mounted Police identification report or by admission of the accused or by certificate of conviction, have furnished the court with only the dry bones of the record. The inclusion in this document of charges of which the accused has not been convicted is a frequent source of complaint. A common practice has been for a police officer to give evidence relating to the foregoing issues and also concerning history, habits, associates, character, and reputation, as known to the police. Evidence of personal history, character, and reputation may be given on behalf of the offender by himself, by members of his family, and by friends and associates. Many sentences have, however, been imposed without any of this information, or even a part of it. In many cases, a few questions have satisfied the court, and the rest has been left to the initiative of the prosecutor or defence counsel. The latter, believing that his duty to his client extends to securing as much mitigation of sentence as possible, is not interested in bringing forward unfavourable evidence, and often therefore merely utters a few platitudes. The prosecutor, influenced by the belief that he should not be a persecutor, often considers that his duty requires him to say little or nothing about sentence.

At this stage of the trial, evidence is often rather informally presented. Rules excluding hearsay, opinion, character, and reputation are generally regarded as inapplicable. Written reports, statements, and opinions are freely used. Unsworn statements by the accused, by the police, and by both counsel are normally received. If any assertion is denied, or if demand is made that any person stating a fact, or relied on as authority for a fact, be produced for cross-examination, formal proof is normally made or the statement is supposed to be ignored by the court. Frequently counsel for each side is allowed to question witnesses whether they testify under oath or not.

The recent and current expansion of the work of social welfare agencies means that more information is often available for the court through social and health workers. Some claim that information they receive from their clients is privileged against disclosure. This issue is not settled. A private member's bill to protect confidentiality of these communications was introduced into the House of Commons in 1964, but made no progress. More and more use is being made of psychiatric evidence, which, if presented before verdict, is given orally under oath and subject to cross-examination, but if tendered in respect of sentence may be received either in that way or, by consent of parties, in the form of a written report.

The greatest advance in sentencing practice has been the introduction of the pre-sentence report, which is sought by most courts whenever available, at least in relation to young offenders and special cases. In some jurisdictions, such reports are not available for adult offenders, since normally the probation services have been first introduced in juvenile courts and have been gradually extended to adult courts as availability of personnel has permitted. Shortage of probation officers everywhere and pressure of responsibility for supervision of probationers and parolees make it impossible to provide a full pre-sentence report service, and priorities must be allotted. Some judges and magistrates believe that a long record speaks for itself, and, in smaller communities, some magistrates believe that they can rely on personal knowledge of offenders. The time is not far off, however, when a sentence for an indictable offence without such a report will be a rarity; and reports will probably be demanded also in dealing with chronic drunks and other chronic petty offenders.

The value of these reports depends on the training, skill, and judgment of the probation officer. Owing to the necessity of building up probation services ahead of the means of providing full professional training, the professional attainments of probation officers are still uneven, but improvement is going on all the time.

The usual practice is that copies of the report are furnished to the court, to the accused or his counsel, and to the prosecutor, and the probation officer is present in court and may be cross-examined in respect of any statement contained in the report. In some courts, the probation officer is sworn as a witness, presents his report as an exhibit, and is made available for cross-examination. Persons cited as authorities in the report can be required to be produced on demand, but such demands are rarely made.

The doctrine in some American courts that the report must be a confidential document, available only to the court and not disclosed to the prosecutor or accused, although approved by the Supreme Court of the United States notwithstanding the American Bill of Rights, has been almost instinctively rejected by Canadian courts and most Canadian lawyers. If confidentiality is not sustained, prevailing Canadian legal opinion is that the disadvantage is more than offset by maintenance of the principle that the accused is entitled to know and to hear or see the evidence against him, in respect not only of guilt but also of sentence. This attitude is adopted not only in consideration of the adverse effect of any other practice on accused persons but also for the sake of public acceptance of the justice of the sentence. An exception might be made in relation to psychiatric evidence indicating mental abnormality or disturbance on the part of the accused. Some critics have suggested a few other exceptions, but they are hard to define or to justify. If the accused is represented by counsel, no information should be withheld from the counsel.

With very few and minor exceptions, courts of appeal have insisted that only evidence given to the court in the presence of the accused or his counsel can be properly considered in sentencing. Conferences in the judge's chambers, in the absence of the accused but in the presence of his counsel, have been permitted. In a few cases, conferences by the judge with psychiatrists about the mental state of the accused have not resulted in quashing the sentence, but some appellate judges have disapproved and the cases must be regarded as exceptional. In a few other instances, the receiving of information by the judge out of court, in relation to sentence, has been regarded with disapproval, but has in the circumstances been considered not to have materially affected the result. On an appeal, the trial judge must report in writing on the trial to the court of appeal, and in several cases in which his report has shown that he received out-of-court communications that substantially affected the sentence, the court of appeal has reduced the term.

Suggestions have been made that certain evidence in relation to sentence should be received *in camera*, in the presence of the accused. There is some merit in the proposal.

OUTLINE OF PROCEDURE ON CHARGES OF
OFFENCES IN VARIOUS CLASSES

Perhaps criminal procedure can best be illustrated by several hypothetical examples, illustrating how charges of offences of various kinds are disposed of. The courts are those of Ontario. No material difference will be experienced in other provinces, except in detail.

Case 1.

John Bull was arrested under a warrant issued by Thomas Shallow, J.P., on an information, sworn by Constable Robert Peel, charging him with the capital murder of Marianne de Gaulle, who had rebuffed his amorous advances. The warrant authorized any peace officer to make the arrest, which was effected by Peel.

Bull was taken to a police station, 'booked in', and questioned about the offence. He demanded to be allowed to communicate with his solicitor, and under the Canadian Bill of Rights this facility should have been allowed him, but somehow the opportunity never occurred, and Bull was kept in the police lock-up overnight while questioning continued, and Bull signed a confession.

Next morning he was brought before Justice Shallow. The information was read to him, and he was remanded in custody in the local jail for six days until the next sitting of the magistrates' court. Bull was now allowed to communicate with his solicitor, who applied for bail to Mr. Justice Lynch of the High Court, but the application was refused because bail on murder charges is granted only in the most exceptional circumstances.

He appeared in due course before Magistrate Henry Fielding, who heard medical evidence suggesting that Bull might be mentally ill and remanded him for not more than thirty days in custody for psychiatric examination. Bull was returned to court with a report indicating insufficient mental disorder for commitment to a mental hospital, and was again remanded in custody several times, from week to week, until the witnesses necessary for the preliminary inquiry could be made available.

The preliminary inquiry, conducted by the magistrate after these remands, involved the introduction, in Bull's presence in open court, of evidence sufficient to satisfy the magistrate that Bull might reasonably be found guilty and should therefore be tried. Witnesses for the Crown were examined viva voce (orally – literally 'by living voice') by the Crown Attorney and cross-examined by defence counsel. Bull was then asked whether he wished to say anything, but made no statement; his counsel called no witnesses since he considered it better not to disclose his defence at that time.

The magistrate committed Bull for trial at the next jury sitting of the High Court, commonly called the Assizes. No further application was made for bail, since it would have been futile.

At the opening of the Assizes, the Crown prosecutor presented a document called an indictment in which Bull was charged with the capital murder of Marianne de Gaulle. The presiding judge, Mr. Justice Jeffries, read the indictment to the Grand Jury (now literally a little jury of seven persons) and briefly explained relevant parts of the law of homicide to them. The Grand Jury retired and, *in camera* and in the judge's and Bull's absence but with the assistance of the Crown prosecutor, heard evidence of witnesses sufficient to satisfy them that Bull might reasonably be found guilty. The foreman then marked the indictment a 'true bill' and the Grand Jury returned and presented it to the court.

Further proceedings then took place in open court. The charge was read to Bull, but, before he pleaded, his counsel asserted that he was now unfit to stand trial by reason of present insanity. A special jury was empanelled and heard evidence on this question, and brought in a verdict that Bull was sane enough to be tried. Bull was then called upon to plead and pleaded 'not guilty'. (Nobody has ever lawfully pleaded 'innocent' in an English or Canadian court, notwithstanding all the newspaper reports in the world to the contrary.) His counsel indicated that, among other issues, he would raise the question whether Bull was at the time of the homicide so insane as to be entitled to a verdict of 'not guilty because of insanity'.

By a process that might seem a little long to an English lawyer, but would seem incredibly short to his American counterpart, a *petit* (small) or trial jury of twelve men and women was empanelled and sworn. This stage of the trial lasted about an hour. Evidence, including psychiatric evidence, was given for both the Crown and the defence, each witness being fully examined and cross-examined in turn. The confession signed by Bull was rejected by the judge as involuntary. Bull, after discussion with his counsel, decided not to give evidence. No comment on his not doing so could be made by the judge or by the prosecutor.

First Bull's counsel, then the prosecutor, and finally the judge addressed the jury. The judge commented fully on the evidence, explaining the issues and what evidence was relevant to each, and what findings and verdicts were open to the jury. Both counsel objected to several points in the judge's charge to the jury but he refused to change it.

The jury rejected the defence of insanity, and brought in a verdict of 'not guilty of capital murder but guilty of non-capital murder'. The judge had no choice, and was compelled to sentence Bull to life imprisonment. If the verdict had been 'guilty of capital murder', the judge would have been compelled to sentence Bull to death. Since the sentence was fixed by law, there was nothing to be said by either counsel about sentence and no point in hearing evidence on the subject.

Bull appealed to the Court of Appeal against conviction on several points of law, and, with leave of that court, on several points of mixed law and fact, alleging that the verdict should have been 'not guilty of murder but guilty of manslaughter'. The appeal was dismissed. Bull could have appealed to the Supreme Court of Canada on points of law, with leave of that court, but did not do so.

Bull was kept in the local jail until the time for appeal to the Supreme Court of Canada expired, and was then transferred to Kingston Penitentiary to serve his sentence.

Case 2.

Richard Turpin was arrested without warrant by Constables Dogberry and Verges on a charge of robbery. Constable Dogberry then swore an information charging Turpin with the offence. Turpin's experience was similar to that of Bull until he arrived before the magistrate, except that the justice of the peace could have granted bail, but refused to do so in his discretion on representation by the Crown Attorney that, when Turpin had last been at large on bail, he had committed another robbery. The magistrate did not remand Turpin for psychiatric examination, there being no suggestion that he might be mentally ill.

When the magistrate read the charge to Turpin, he told him that he could elect to be tried by a judge and jury, by a judge without a jury, or by a magistrate without a jury. Turpin elected to be tried by judge and jury. A preliminary hearing was held in the same manner as in Bull's case, and Turpin was committed for trial at the next court of competent jurisdiction. The magistrate refused bail, as did a county court judge to whom application was made.

Turpin could have been tried at the Assizes, but the next competent court in point of time was the Court of General Sessions of the Peace presided over by Judge Doe of the county court. Turpin was therefore tried by that court under the same procedure as at Bull's trial, except that no question of insanity was raised. The jury found him guilty, and, since the maximum penalty for robbery is life imprisonment and whipping and no minimum is fixed, Turpin was remanded for two weeks for sentence, and on his reappearance evidence and representations on the question of sentence were heard.

The R.C.M.P. record, showing two previous convictions for robbery, was shown to Turpin's counsel, who, after checking it with Turpin, consented to its being read by the judge. A pre-sentence report was presented by the probation officer who had prepared it, and who was now sworn as a witness. Copies of the report had been furnished in advance to the prosecutor and Turpin's counsel. The latter cross-examined the probation officer on several points. Additional factual and character evidence, including psychiatric evidence, both first-hand and hearsay, could have been given by either side, but Crown counsel had nothing to say and defence counsel contented himself with an address in mitigation of sentence. The judge imposed a sentence of fifteen years' imprisonment and twenty lashes.

Turpin appealed against conviction and sentence, with leave of the Court of Appeal. That court confirmed the conviction, but varied the sentence by deleting the order for lashes. Although Turpin was kept in the local jail until the time for appeal to the Supreme Court of Canada expired, his sentence ran from the day when it was first imposed and not from the day of his transfer to penitentiary.

Turpin might have elected to be tried by a judge without a jury, in which case he would have been tried in the County Judge's Criminal Court by similar procedure.

Case 3.

William Sykes, charged with indecent assault on a young girl, underwent the same experience as Turpin until he appeared before the magistrate. There he elected to be tried by the magistrate, pleaded guilty, and was remanded in custody for sentence. Upon reading a pre-sentence report and hearing conflicting psychiatric evidence, the magistrate decided that Sykes had committed the offence during a period of temporary emotional stress, but was not mentally ill, would not be a menace at large, and would respond favourably to psychiatric treatment. He therefore, over the protests of the Crown Attorney, put Sykes on probation under suspended sentence for two years, on condition that he regularly submit to outpatient psychiatric treatment as long as required. A week later the Attorney-General gave notice of application for leave to appeal to the Court of Appeal against sentence. The Court of Appeal granted leave, allowed the appeal, and substituted a reformatory sentence of six months determinate and twelve months indeterminate for the sentence of probation.

Case 4.

Bunty Fagin, charged with theft of not over $50, was treated in the same manner as Turpin until he appeared before the magistrate. The latter said: 'This case comes within my absolute jurisdiction. You have no right to elect how you will be tried. How do you plead?'

Fagin pleaded guilty and was remanded for sentence. His record and the pre-sentence report showed that he was now thirty-five, and that since his sixteenth year he had been constantly engaged in theft and had been convicted thirty-three times previously of theft of not over $25. The magistrate sentenced him to a reformatory sentence of two years less one day determinate and two years less one day indeterminate. This was a most unusual sentence for the offence in question, which, although often committed by professional or habitual offenders, is usually treated as a relatively minor offence. However, there was no appeal.

Case 5.

Solomon Grundy, charged with driving a motor vehicle while intoxicated, underwent an experience similar to Turpin's prior to his appearance before the magistrate, except that he was examined by a physician shortly after his arrest and voluntarily submitted to a breathalyzer test, administered by a police officer.

On Grundy's appearance before the magistrate, the prosecutor asked the court to proceed summarily.

Grundy had no 'election' and therefore had to plead at once. He pleaded 'not guilty', and the trial proceeded. Evidence of the medical examination and the result of the breathalyzer test was received. He was found guilty and sentenced to the minimum term of seven days' imprisonment in the local jail, and an order was made prohibiting him from driving a motor vehicle in Canada for three years. Grundy appealed against conviction and sentence. The appeal took the form of a re-trial in the county court, where he was found not guilty of driving while intoxicated but guilty of driving while his ability was impaired by alcohol. He was sentenced to a fine of $100 and costs, and the period of prohibition of driving was reduced to one year.

Case 6.

Soames Forsyte, a merchant, was served with a summons charging him with selling a firearm to a boy under fourteen years of age, and issued on an information sworn by the boy's father. He appeared before the magistrate on the day fixed by the summons and pleaded 'not guilty'. Evidence was heard proving the sale and showing that Forsyte had reason to believe that the boy was under fourteen. Forsyte was found guilty and fined $50 and costs, which he paid.

Conclusion

The Canadian court system has many good features and works reasonably well and causes little public dissatisfaction. The last statement is due only in part to the merits of the system. The Canadian public is too poorly informed, too little concerned, and too easily satisfied. While generally satisfied with the system, the Bench and the Bar are conscious of many weaknesses and are constantly making proposals for improvement in detail. Their proposals are not bold enough in concept. The system has faults, resulting from its rather haphazard and inconsistent development, from its partly illogical structure, from half-reformed procedure, from the defects in correctional education shared by judges, magistrates, lawyers, and other officials, from the piling of too great a mass of miscellaneous work on the magistrates, and from inadequate provision of subordinate staffs, particularly in magistrates' courts and the probation service. By and large, its faults have not resulted from bad faith, dishonesty, or greed. There have been a few magistrates and justices of the peace whose hunger for fees has led them to injustice and oppression, but they and their works have been eliminated in most parts of the country. The effects of their abuse of power have been almost entirely confined to minor offences.

The wrongs that are done in Canadian courts, and some wrongs are done, are occasionally the result of prejudice, but chiefly the result of human errors, of overwork, of too ready satisfaction by the judge or magistrate that he is fully informed or that he understands the evidence or the law, and similar causes. It is in the lower courts that injustice is most frequent and hardest to combat: it is unintentionally inflicted and the problems are often misunderstood not only by the court but also by all others directly concerned, and usually by the public as well. The sufferers are usually poor, depressed, and of bad reputation, or badly confused young persons; most of them are not legally represented and are rather helpless. It would be wrong to exaggerate the incidence of injustice, but it occurs. It would be wrong to sing paeans of praise about the system, but it deserves credit for merit.

Further Reading

CANADA. Criminal Code, *Statutes of Canada, 1953-4*, 2 & 3 Elizabeth II, chapter 51, in force from April 1st, 1955, amended by several later statutes; best studied in annotated editions noted below. Ottawa: Queen's Printer.

FRIEDLAND, MARTIN L. (Professor, Faculty of Law, University of Toronto). *Detention before Trial.* Toronto: University Press, 1965.

LAGARDE, IRENEE, J.S.P. *Nouveau Code Criminel Annoté.* (L'auteur est Professeur de Droit Criminel, Université de Montréal.) De valeur non seulement pour les lecteurs canadiens-français mais aussi pour tous les étudiants, maintenu à jour par un supplément à feuilles mobiles. Montréal: Wilson et Lafleur Ltée, 1959.

MARTIN, J. C., Q.C. *Martin's Criminal Code.* (The author was formerly Provincial Magistrate for Saskatchewan, then research counsel for the Royal Commission to revise the Criminal Code, 1947-52, and latterly a member of the national Department of Justice.) Contains valuable historical and exegetical material, including text of former Code in 'parallel' arrangement, concordance of old and new Codes, and notes of selected reported decisions. Kept up to date by annual volume (edited by Dr. A. W. Mewett) containing consolidated text of Code with all amendments to date of publication, reference to recently decided cases, and texts of Canada Evidence Act and Canadian Bill of Rights. Toronto: Canada Law Book Co. Ltd., 1955.

POPPLE, A. E., LL.B. (ed. Criminal Reports (Canada)). *Crankshaw's Criminal Code of Canada.* 7th edition. Contains reference to nearly every reported Canadian decision on criminal law and many from other countries as well as articles on selected subjects and texts of Canada Evidence Act, Canadian Bill of Rights, Excise Act, Identification of Criminals Act, Juvenile Delinquents Act, Lord's Day Act, Money Lenders Act, Narcotic Control Act, Newfoundland Act, Northwest Territories Act, Official Secrets Act, Parole Act, Pawnbrokers Act, Penitentiary Act, and Yukon Act. A comprehensive and complete current text, kept up to date by loose-leaf supplement. Toronto: Carswell, 1959.

————. *Snow's Criminal Code of Canada. 6th edition.* A 'concise edition', with selected case references, texts of several other statutes and precedents for forms, kept up to date by cumulative supplement. New edition being prepared. Toronto: Carswell, 1955.

————. *Criminal Procedure Manual.* Practitioner's handbook. 2nd edition. Toronto: Carswell, 1956.

————. *Daly's Canadian Criminal Procedure and Practice.* An older work on procedure, but still valuable for some purposes. 3rd edition. Toronto: Carswell, 1936.

ROGERS, A. W., Q.C., W. B. Common, Q.C. (retired Deputy Attorney-General of Ontario), and C. R. Magone, Q.C. (formerly Deputy Attorney-General of Ontario). *Seager's Criminal Procedure Before Magistrates.* An older work, but still valuable. 3rd edition. Toronto: Canada Law Book Co. Ltd., 1932.

RYAN, LEONARD J. *Tremeear's Criminal Code.* 6th edition. Very full but quite different in treatment from Crankshaw. Toronto: Carswell, 1964.

ARTICLES

BULL, H. H., Q.C. (Crown Attorney, York County, Ontario). 'The Career Prosecutor of Canada', *Journal of Criminal Law, Criminology and Police Science,* vol. 53 (1962), p. 89.

MACKAY, R. S., LL.M. (Assistant to Commissioner, Ontario Commission on Civil Rights). 'Some Reflections on the New Criminal Code', *University of Toronto Law Journal,* vol. 12 (1958), p. 206.

Canadian Bar Review

ADAMSON, HON. J. E. (formerly Justice, Manitoba Court of Queen's Bench). 'Judicial Sentencing', vol. 11 (1933), p. 681.

CROUSE, G. H. 'Critique of Canadian Criminal Legislation', vol. 12 (1934), pp. 545, 601.

MACLEOD, A. J. (Commissioner of Penitentiaries), and J. C. Martin, Q.C. 'Offences and Punishments under the New Criminal Code', vol. 33 (1955), p. 21.

————. 'Procedure under the New Criminal Code', vol. 33 (1955), p. 41.

MCRUER, HON. J. C. (Chief Justice, Ontario High Court). 'Sentencing', vol. 27 (1949), p. 1001.

MEWETT, A. W., S.J.D. (Professor of Law, Osgoode Hall Law School). 'Criminal Law, 1948-1958', vol. 36 (1958), p. 445.

O'HALLORAN, HON. C. H. (formerly Justice, British Columbia Court of Appeal). 'Punishment of Criminal Offenders', vol. 23 (1945), p. 555.

Stuart Ryan

———. 'Criminal Law and the Supreme Court of Canada', vol. 26 (1948), p. 158.

SEDGWICK, JOSEPH, Q.C. (recently Treasurer, Law Society of Upper Canada). 'Comments and Criticisms of the New Criminal Code', vol. 33 (1955), p. 63.

TURNER, KEITH (Manitoba Law School). 'The Role of Crown Counsel in Canadian Prosecutions', vol. 40 (1962), p. 439.

'Symposium on Inequalities in the Criminal Law', vol. 34 (1956), p. 245.

Criminal Law Quarterly

HAINES, HON. E. L. (Justice, Ontario High Court). 'The Case for the Training of Magistrates', vol. 2 (1959-60), p. 207.

MCINNES, HON. H. W. (Justice, British Columbia Supreme Court). 'Criminal Law as a Career', vol. 1 (1958-9), p. 162.

MALONEY, ARTHUR, Q.C. 'The Court and the Police Functions in the Developing of Effective Canadian Corrections', vol. 2 (1959-60), p. 164.

ORKIN, M. M. 'Defence of One Known to Be Guilty', vol. 2 (1959-60), p. 170.

SAVAGE, C. C., Q.C. (Crown Attorney, Middlesex County, Ontario). 'The Duties and Conduct of Crown and Defence Counsel in a Criminal Trial', vol. 1 (1958-9), p. 164.

Canadian Bar Journal

COMMON, W. B., Q.C. (retired Deputy Attorney-General of Ontario). 'Uniform Application of Principles of Punishment', vol. 1 (1958), 5, p. 49.

HOPKINS, D. W. (retired Ontario Provincial Magistrate). 'Sentencing', vol. 1 (1958), 5, p. 53.

8

The Juvenile and Family Courts

W. T. McGRATH

The juvenile court and the family court share a common remedial philosophy and the common purpose of so dealing with legal problems that affect the members of a family that the family will be maintained or reestablished as a functioning unit. However, not all provinces have family courts, and it will therefore be more convenient to deal with each type of court separately.

THE JUVENILE COURT

All provinces, as well as the Yukon and the Northwest Territories, have juvenile courts, although not necessarily under that name. In British Columbia they are called children's courts. In Quebec the social welfare courts perform all the functions of a juvenile court, some of the functions of a family court, and some additional functions of a social nature, such as appeals under public-assistance legislation.

Not all parts of all provinces have the advantage of juvenile courts. The legislation provides that a province may establish juvenile courts for selected cities or areas, while leaving other areas without such service. The areas not covered are shrinking rapidly, however, and for the most part now include only isolated districts. Where no juvenile court exists, children are subject to the same procedures as adults.

Historical Background

Special legal provisions for dealing with children charged with or convicted of a criminal offence can be traced back many centuries. The common law provided that a child under seven years of age be considered incapable of committing a crime; a child between eight and fourteen was assumed not to have reached the age of criminal responsibility, although this assumption could be rebutted by evidence of malice. The old Equity Courts[1] took a special interest in children, sometimes serving as guardians. Special criminal legislation dealing with children existed in some of the Canadian provinces over a century ago.

Canada's first national legislation in dealing with child offenders was passed in 1894. It provided for the private trial of children under sixteen and for their detention apart from older prisoners. For Ontario only, it required that in the case of a boy under twelve or a girl under thirteen, the court should consult the local children's aid society; instead of sentencing the child, the court could order him placed in a foster-home or an industrial school.

The first federal legislation, however, that dealt with delinquency in modern terms was the Juvenile Delinquents Act passed in 1908. A number of minor amendments were made over the years and then, in 1928, the Minister of Justice called a federal conference to advise him on amending the Act. This conference drew up a draft bill that, with a few changes, became law on June 4, 1929. This Act is now known as the Juvenile Delinquents Act, 1929, and is Chapter 46 of the *Statutes* of that year. Some amendments have since been passed, but they are matters of detail and do not affect the general principles of the legislation. The Act does not apply to Newfoundland. Juvenile courts were established there under the provisions of the Child Welfare Act, 1944, prior to union with Canada. Under the terms of union, the provincial legislation remains in force.

On January 8, 1962, the Minister of Justice announced that a departmental committee had been set up to study all aspects of delinquency in Canada, including the legislation. Many organizations and individuals have submitted briefs to that committee, suggesting changes. The result of the committee's work is still being awaited as this is being written. Presumably major changes in the legislation will result.

The Juvenile Delinquents Act

One of the chief difficulties in framing the Juvenile Delinquents Act was keeping it within the legislative jurisdiction of the federal Parliament. Although the fact that crime is within the exclusive jurisdiction of the federal legislature makes possible a measure applicable to the whole of Canada, the civil status of the person, on the other hand, is within the exclusive jurisdiction of the provincial legislatures. It is not possible, therefore, in a federal Act to define delinquency as a state or condition as has been done in

[1]These courts were set up in the 14th century to mitigate the harsh technicalities of the common law. They disappeared as separate courts in most jurisdictions towards the end of the nineteenth century, although their function was assumed by other courts.

most jurisdictions in the United States. The members of the 1928 federal conference thought this definition highly desirable, however, and so in drawing up their draft bill they treated delinquency as an act and made it an offence, but made it look like a state or condition. The Act says:

> 2. (1) (h) 'juvenile delinquent' means any child who violates any provision of the Criminal Code or of any Dominion or provincial statute, or of any by-law or ordinance of any municipality, or who is guilty of sexual immorality or any similar form of vice, or who is liable by reason of any other act to be committed to an industrial school or juvenile reformatory under the provisions of any Dominion or provincial statute; . . .
>
> 3. (1) The commission by a child of any of the acts enumerated in paragraph (h) of subsection (1) of section 2, constitutes an offence to be known as a delinquency, and shall be dealt with as hereinafter provided.
>
> (2) Where a child is adjudged to have committed a delinquency he shall be dealt with, not as an offender, but as one in a condition of delinquency and therefore requiring help and guidance and proper supervision.

There are several objections to these provisions, quite apart from the difficulty in identifying a form of vice that is similar to sexual immorality. It makes no difference what action brings a child before the juvenile court; he is, on conviction, found guilty of having committed a delinquency. No legal distinction is made between a child involved in a serious offence such as armed robbery and one involved in an infraction of a by-law, such as driving a bicycle without a licence. The power of the court over the child is the same in both instances.

Since delinquency is defined as far as possible as a state or condition, the child is looked upon as having a tendency to antisocial behaviour rather than as having committed one undesirable act. Perhaps some children may properly be so classified, but many of those declared delinquent, particularly those who have committed only minor or isolated offences, show no such habit pattern. Probably no child should be categorized 'delinquent' in general terms, and certainly there should be some legal distinction between offences of various degrees of gravity. This distinction could be provided by charging the child, not with a delinquency, but with the specific offence against the applicable federal, provincial, or municipal legislation. The very broad definition of delinquency was written into the 1929 Act to assist a child who is technically guilty of a minor offence, but whose primary problem is a lack of proper care from his parents. The delinquency is often easier to prove than the neglect, and through the juvenile-probation staff the child gets the care he needs. However, a child in this situation should be reached through provincial child-welfare legislation rather than through perversion of criminal legislation.

The Act gives each province the power to set anywhere between sixteen and eighteen as the upper age limit used in defining a juvenile. British Columbia, Manitoba, and Quebec have set it at eighteen; Alberta, at eighteen for girls but sixteen for boys; Saskatchewan, Ontario, New Brunswick, Prince Edward Island, and Nova Scotia, at sixteen. It is also sixteen in the Yukon and the Northwest Territories. In Newfoundland, where the Act does not apply, it is seventeen. This Act is federal legislation, and it seems improper that it does not apply equally to all Canadians. It is difficult to justify the fact that a youth of seventeen who commits an offence in one part of Canada is treated as a child, while he would be treated as an adult if he were elsewhere in the country. In the opinion of the writer, the age limit should be uniform across Canada. There is a great deal of disagreement on the age at which it should be set, but eighteen seems to have the widest support.

The philosophy that guides the juvenile court is set out in Section 38 of the Act:

> This Act shall be liberally construed to the end that its purpose may be carried out, namely, that the care and custody and discipline of a juvenile delinquent shall approximate as nearly as may be that which should be given by its parents, and that as far as practicable every juvenile delinquent shall be treated, not as a criminal, but as a misdirected and misguided child, and one needing aid, encouragement, help and assistance.

Section 17 provides that a trial in the juvenile court 'may be as informal as the circumstances will permit, consistently with a due regard for a proper administration of justice'. The juvenile court must function primarily as a court, receiving only proper evidence and adhering strictly to the provisions of the law; but informality is encouraged in order that the child and his parents may understand the procedures and feel that the aim of the court is to help the child and not to apply social vengeance.

Confidentiality is provided for. No news media may publish the name of a child before the court, or any other information that may identify him. This is intended to protect the child from harmful publicity at the time, and from a reputation that may stay with him all his life. Court records are available only to those involved in his treatment program.

The question of the confidentiality of juvenile court records later in the juvenile's life, when, for instance, he is applying for a job or for a visa to another country, is a troublesome one. It is obvious that a mistake, or even a series of mistakes, on the part of a juvenile should not be permitted to hinder his later adjustment; usually the desirable thing is to have the whole incident forgotten as soon as possible. Technically, the record remains confidential, but the information in it can often be obtained from other sources. Neighbours usually know about the incident, and personal inquiries will normally uncover the facts. Also, application forms for employment or for visas often contain questions phrased in such a way that the individual discloses his own juvenile record. The question whether the juvenile record should be made available to the adult court if the individual is later convicted there poses a special problem. If we expect the judge of the adult court to sentence intelligently, he must know the individual's history, but many people feel that even here the juvenile's record should be protected, as it is at present.

Children awaiting trial are to be held apart from adult offenders, according to the Act, and a detention facility must be provided. Unfortunately, many courts still do not have such facilities and have to resort to compromises such as using one wing of the adult jail.

Section 20 of the Act lays out the various courses open to the court in dealing with a child who has been found delinquent:

> In the case of a child adjudged to be a juvenile delinquent the court may, in its discretion, take either one or more of the several courses of action hereinafter in this section set out, as it may in its judgment deem proper in the circumstances of the case:
>
> (a) suspend final disposition;
> (b) adjourn the hearing or disposition of the case from time to time for any definite or indefinite period;
> (c) impose a fine not exceeding twenty-five dollars, which may be paid in periodical amounts or otherwise;
> (d) commit the child to the care or custody of a probation officer or of any other suitable person;
> (e) allow the child to remain in its home, subject to the visitation of a probation officer, such child to report to the court or to the probation officer as often as may be required;
> (f) cause the child to be placed in a suitable family home as a foster home, subject to the friendly supervision of a probation officer and the further order of the court;
> (g) impose upon the delinquent such further or other conditions as may be deemed advisable;
> (h) commit the child to the charge of any children's aid society, duly organized under an Act of legislature of the province and approved by the Lieutenant-Governor in Council, or, in any municipality in which there is no children's aid society, to the charge of the superintendent,[2] if one there be; or

[2]The superintendent is defined in the Act as the director of child welfare in each province, or the official who performs these functions, whatever his title.

    (i) commit the child to an industrial school duly approved by the Lieutenant-Governor in Council.

It will be seen that the judge of the juvenile court has very great powers over a child adjudged delinquent. This kind of authority is necessary, but surely it ought not to apply to a child who has only broken a municipal by-law. The extent of the judge's powers underlines strongly the need to separate the minor from the serious offenders.

Once a child has been declared delinquent, he remains under the care of the court until he reaches the age of twenty-one; it may recall him at any time and change the disposition of his case without the necessity of hearing further evidence. There is no provision in the Act permitting the court to end its authority over him. It would seem wise to include such a provision so that the child could be discharged completely upon reaching the appropriate stage in his development.

There is provision, however, for the provincial Secretary, if he sees fit, to prescribe that when a child is committed to a children's aid society, or to the superintendent, or to an industrial school, the province will assume responsibility for him; in this event, the court's authority will end.

Section 9 provides for the transfer to the adult court of a child who has reached the age of fourteen, and who is charged with an indictable offence, if, in the opinion of the juvenile court judge, 'the good of the child and the interest of the community demand it'. When this is done, the child is dealt with as an adult and loses all the protection provided by the Juvenile Delinquents Act. This procedure is intended for the unusual child who is so confirmed in his dangerous habit patterns that he could not be handled in the facilities set up for delinquents. Application of the section varies. In some provinces, for instance, children charged with murder are automatically transferred to adult court; in others, transfer is not at all automatic, and charges of murder are quite frequently heard as delinquencies in the juvenile courts.

The juvenile court is empowered to deal with an adult who 'aids, causes, abets or connives at the commission by a child of a delinquency, or does any act producing, promoting, or contributing to a child's being or becoming a juvenile delinquent or likely to make any child a juvenile delinquent'. Usually such charges centre around sexual activity either involving a child or in his presence, or drunkenness or the use of foul language before a child.

Many juvenile courts deal with some children as 'occurrences'. In these cases the probation staff act informally as consultants to parents in dealing with a difficult child, without a court appearance, and without having the child adjudged delinquent. In some courts more children are dealt with as occurrences than as delinquents.

As pointed out in Chapter 1, the British North America Act places jurisdiction for criminal legislation with the federal government, but makes the setting up and administration of all courts, adult and juvenile, a provincial responsibility. Thus each province has its own juvenile court legislation. The juvenile courts come under the Department of the Attorney-General in all provinces except Nova Scotia and Newfoundland. In those two provinces, they come under the Department of Public Welfare. In the Yukon and Northwest Territories, the federal Minister of Justice functions as Attorney-General, and these courts come under his department.

Neglected Children

In addition to dealing with children charged with delinquencies, the juvenile court hears cases under provincial child-welfare legislation, such as Children's Protection and Children of Unmarried Parents Acts. The legislation varies from province to province, as does the extent of the jurisdiction of the juvenile courts in the field of child welfare. The hearings involve applications from child-care authorities to have wardship removed from parents and invested in the child-care authorities, on either a temporary or permanent basis, and suits to determine paternity. The court is involved only in hearing applications and handing down decisions. Carrying out the decisions is not the duty of the staff of the court, but of the child-welfare authorities.

A number of provinces prefer to deal with a child suspected of having committed a delinqency as neglected under provincial child-welfare legislation, rather than as delinquent under the Juvenile Delinquents Act. This avoids the stigma of delinquency. The extent to which this policy is followed affects the official statistics of the incidence of delinquency.

Court Personnel and Facilities

The judge has general responsibility for the operation of the juvenile court. Not only does he preside at court hearings, but he has direction of the probation and administrative staff, the detention facilities, and the clinical staff where these services are part of the court.

No formal qualifications are laid down for the judge, except in the province of Quebec, where the judge of the social welfare court must be a lawyer with ten years' experience. The result is that people come to the juvenile bench with widely varying backgrounds. Little is provided in the way of induction training for new juvenile court judges.

In urban areas it is usual for appointments to be made on a full-time basis, and in the larger centres there may be several full-time judges. In many rural areas the magistrate of the local adult court serves as juvenile court judge on days set aside for that court. Some provinces provide circuit courts in rural areas so that the services of a full-time judge will be available.

In some provinces the judge's salary and the other expenses of the court are a provincial responsibility. In others they are met by the municipality. The latter system has its drawbacks: it is contrary to the established concepts of the dignity and independence of the Bench that a judge of the juvenile court should have to defend his request for proper facilities before local municipal councils; and uniformity of facilities, personnel, salaries, and procedures is easier to obtain through provincial financing. The province pays the major share of expenses of other courts, and there seems to be no logical reason for this exception.

Similarly, the probation staff are hired and paid by the province in some parts of the country, but by the municipality elsewhere. In some provinces the probation staff serving rural areas are paid by the province, while the larger municipalities employ and pay probation staff for their own courts.

The probation officer has two major functions. When requested by the court, he prepares a pre-sentence report to help the judge determine the best disposition. Since children are involved, such reports put great emphasis on family relationships. His second function is the supervision of children placed on probation by the court; again, the child's family is closely involved. Most of the probation officer's time goes to the supervision of probationers.

The administrative staff are responsible for court stenography, and for keeping the court records and protecting their confidentiality.

The detention facility, where one exists, is intended to hold children who for some reason cannot be left in the community pending trial or sentence. The aim is to keep them away from older prisoners, and to provide a setting as non-punitive and positive as possible. It is also used occasionally for special purposes, such as holding a child who has run away from his home in another part of the country until he can be returned to his own municipality. While a child is in detention, he can be examined by the clinical staff and the probation officer who prepare pre-sentence reports, but the proper purpose of the detention facility should be kept in mind, and a child should not be held there just for the convenience of the staff. Obviously, the lack of good detention facilities for so many of our juvenile courts is a serious handicap to good service. The services of a mental-health clinic, staffed by psychiatrists, psychologists, and social workers, should be available to the juvenile court to help in personality assessment. Such services are available to most courts on a part-time basis, but few are as generously served as they would like to be.

Treatment centres are needed for emotionally disturbed children. Such centres, operated by the public-health services or by private agencies, do exist in some of the major cities, but the number of children who are known by the medical practitioners and the social agencies to need such care is much larger than the centres can accommodate. Outside the major cities, such centres are seldom available. The court is thus left in a real and tragic position of trying to deal with a child who is technically delinquent, but whose main problem is emotional disturbance.

The courts also need to be able to provide alternative living arrangements for children who cannot be returned to their own home. Foster-homes help fill this need. So do hostels where a child can live under supervision while going out to a local school or to employment. Such facilities would reduce the danger of a child's being sent to training-school just because there is nothing else available for him. Again, although some of the major cities do have such hostels, many courts have to operate without this resource.

We have created the juvenile court and put it in a position where it often has to take on the difficult task of assessing the special requirements of an individual delinquent and determining, and sometimes providing, a course of treatment that will make it possible for him to live a normal life in the normal community; but we have not provided the court with the facilities necessary for such a task. This is false economy. Many of the failures of the juvenile court could have been prevented if money had been provided for proper facilities and, expensive though such facilities are, they are far cheaper than dealing with the life-time criminal career that might result. This kind of failure not only involves the individual in tragedy, but it brings the whole juvenile court into disrepute.

THE FAMILY COURT

Family courts are in operation only in British Columbia, Alberta, Manitoba, Ontario, Nova Scotia, and Newfoundland. However, the juvenile courts in New Brunswick administer some legislation of the kind that family courts deal with, such as that concerning deserted wives and children. The social-welfare courts of Quebec are not family courts in the sense in which we are using the term here, since they have no power of coercion. They may, for instance, advise quarrelling spouses, but they cannot take measures to enforce their advice.

Function

Generally speaking, the development of the family court represents an extension of the methods of the juvenile court to include other cases involving children and family life. Essentially, it is a special court that is given jurisdiction over family matters not assigned to a juvenile court by the Juvenile Delinquents Act.

The family court has family counsellors or probation officers, who meet in a confidential setting with married couples who are in conflict to try to remove the source of conflict and bring about reconciliation. It is better if this attempt is made before an appearance in court, because things may be said in court that make reconciliation more difficult. Sometimes the couple can be referred to a community agency, sometimes the family counsellor carries the case himself. If this process fails, or if the couple insist from the beginning on a formal appearance, the case is heard before a judge. Even here, the possibility of reconciliation should be kept always in mind, but once the case has reached the stage of a court appearance, reconciliation is unlikely.

In cases of desertion or non-support, the court may make an order against the husband for the support of his wife and children. In some courts he is ordered to make the payments to the court to be passed on to the wife; in other courts he is ordered to make the payments direct to his wife, but she has the right to take further action against him if he does not keep up the payments. A reciprocal agreement among the provinces makes it difficult for the husband to avoid his responsibilities by moving to another province. Children may also be ordered to support their parents in some instances, but such cases are rare.

When one member of the family is convicted of assault against another member of the family, and reconciliation seems unlikely, the court may order the offending person to stay out of the home or may send him to prison. Such action, however, is reserved for serious cases, since it usually ends any hope of rebuilding the family.

Legislation

Unlike the juvenile court, the family courts are based on provincial legislation, although they do handle certain federal offences, such as some under the Criminal Code that involve members of the same family. Just what comes under their jurisdiction varies from province to province, but the major work comes from legislation affecting deserted wives and children, and from assault charges laid under the Criminal Code. They do not handle divorce cases. This is just as well, considering all the legal difficulties surrounding a divorce hearing; the added load would make it more difficult to achieve the primary purpose of the courts. Besides, the function of these courts is to keep families together, not to separate them.

Administration

In most provinces, the family courts were created by extending the functions of the already existing juvenile courts. In these instances no distinction is made between the two and they function as a single unified court. In others, where the family court was set up separately, a distinction is maintained, but the two function closely together, sharing the same facilities and same personnel.

CONCLUSION

The juvenile and family courts are the newest experiment in our court system, and probably the most specialized. In a sense, they are the courts most basic to our social well-being, since they lay stress on the importance of children and on the need to keep families functioning at a level where they can fulfil their responsibilities to children. Their chief function is a dual one: they operate as a legal tribunal in applying the law and ensuring justice, while at the same time they try to place what is best in the legal tradition at the service of children and of families. In addition, they serve as treatment agencies for children placed on probation, and as counselling agencies to married couples undergoing a period of marital strain.

It remains to be seen what they will contribute to the developing philosophy of other criminal courts, but the success they have had so far in their work with children and with families cannot be ignored in any discussion of the efficacy of the remedial approach.

Further Reading

The Child Offender and the Law. Ottawa: Canadian Corrections Association, 1963.
The Family Court in Canada. Ottawa: Canadian Corrections Association, 1960.
The Juvenile Court in Law. Ottawa: Canadian Welfare Council, 1952.
JOSIE, SVANHUIT. *The Purpose and Legal Status of the Family Court* (Published in the 1953 annual report of the Delinquency and Crime Division). Ottawa: Canadian Welfare Council, 1953.
STEWART, V. LORNE. 'The Juvenile and Family Court', in *A Manual for Ontario Magistrates,* edited by S. Tupper Bigelow. Toronto: Queen's Printer, 1962.

9

Probation

ST. JOHN MADELEY

DEFINITION

Every practitioner in the field of probation – and probably every probationer too – has a different idea about the meaning of the term 'probation'. Related professions such as law and the police also have their own concepts of the meaning of probation. The *Concise Oxford Dictionary* defines it as:

> ... testing of conduct or character of a person especially a candidate for membership in a religious body; moral trial or discipline; system of releasing young criminals, especially first offenders, on suspended sentence during good behaviour under supervision of a person (probation officer) acting as friend and adviser.

We are concerned here, of course, with the last mentioned shade of meaning. Note that there are four elements: conviction, suspended sentence, good conduct, and supervision.

Some of the most common conceptions of probation in the public mind are discussed by Tappan in *Contemporary Corrections*.[1] These are:

1. *Probation is a device to escape punishment.* This is a hang-over from the concept that justice should be blind – that for every offence there should be a set punishment. This concept negates the modern idea of reformation of the offender and relies solely on the punitive and deterrent effects of imprisonment, effects that have been proven somewhat ineffective in preventing crime. Without going into specific figures, we are all aware that our prisons are populated by large numbers of repeaters or

---

[1]Paul W. Tappan, ed., *Contemporary Corrections*, New York: McGraw-Hill, 1951, pp. 384-5.

recidivists. In Canadian law, we have officially abandoned the concept that justice should be blind, because our criminal laws for the most part allow the courts discretion in the imposition of sentence, by setting only maximum penalties for offences. Seldom is a penalty defined as a minimum sentence or one with upper and lower limits, for example, not less than two nor more than five years imprisonment. If we accept the concept that every offence should carry a set penalty, then we might as well employ machines for the imposition of sentence, but we could not then take into account the circumstances surrounding the commission of an offence or treat the deliberate offender differently from the accidental offender.

2. *Probation is leniency.* This assumes that probation is dictated primarily by sympathy to prevent 'contamination' of the offender, particularly the young offender, by contact with other criminals in jails. Historically this concept was the forerunner of probation as it is known today, but as the sciences of psychology, psychiatry, and social work have progressed and given us a measure of insight into the development of personality and the treatment of personality disorders, we are forced to the conclusion that sympathy is a poor substitute for enlightened understanding in preventing recurrence of the crime and thus protecting the public. These are the basic considerations of our whole system of law, courts, prisons, and penalties. It is true that probation is more lenient than imprisonment, but where the criterion for its choice is sympathy, we exclude a great body of scientific knowledge from affecting, as it rightfully should, the decisions of our courts in relation to the granting of probation.

3. *Probation is punishment.* There are many who argue that the conditions of probation – the obligation to report, and the publicity – actually make the offender regard probation as a form of punishment, though legally it is a form of suspended sentence and hence no punishment. It is true that the restrictions and obligations are onerous to many probationers, but we must not forget that these are imposed with the primary object, not of punishing the offender, but of helping him to modify his behaviour so that society is protected from further offences. The chief aim of probation is to change the offender so that crime is no longer a necessary part of his behaviour pattern, rather than to punish him for his offence.

4. *Probation is a policing device.* This implies that the primary function of the probation officer is to watch the offender and wait for a breach, and then to bring him back before the court for sentence. It ignores the probationer's need for help to modify his behaviour and attitudes, and implies that there is some magic in the term 'probation' that will inspire or frighten the offender into conformity. Where heavy case-loads prevent the

221

St. John Madeley

effective use of casework techniques in modifying behaviour, probation
frequently degenerates into this type of approach, and many police – and
even some judges and magistrates – regard the threat of a breach as the
principal deterrent to further criminality.

5. *Probation is treatment.* This has the twin objectives of protection of
society and rehabilitation of the offender to useful citizenship through
changing his attitudes, modifying his patterns of conduct, and leading him
to choose new goals and embark upon a plan of living acceptable to
society. The two objectives are not incompatible if the supervising probation officer has the necessary skill and the ability to generate a desire
for change in the probationer. This involves a knowledge of personality
and behaviour and the capacity to assist people in their own efforts to seek
satisfactory and socially acceptable solutions to their problems, whether
they are problems caused by physical defect, personality, educational
limitation, employment, family relationships, or economic difficulties. The
concept has been succinctly stated in a Canadian manual for probation
officers as 'treatment directed toward the rehabilitation of the offender
to the end that he may be responsible to the community as one capable of
developing a personally satisfying method of living, as a constructive and
productive member of society.'[2]

HISTORICAL BACKGROUND

For centuries, death had followed conviction for any serious crime, as
surely as night followed day. During the eighteenth century, however,
there was a ferment of new ideas, having its first dramatic expression in
the French revolution. Democracy and the rights and dignity of man
began to receive recognition, and it was in the aftermath of the social
revolution that took place in the eighteenth and early nineteenth centuries
that probation had its start in England. As early as the fourteenth century,
the English common law gave recognition to the principle of judicial reprieve – the withholding of sentence during good behaviour. This was
usually achieved by the appointment of a surety, who had power to enforce conditions and a duty to return the offender for sentence if he failed
in the conditions or committed further crimes. The device was sparingly
used and did not receive statutory recognition until the Criminal Law Consolidation Act of 1861 and the Summary Jurisdiction Act of 1879.

In England, the emergence of rudimentary ideas for social treatment
bore fruit in prison reform and in more extensive use of judicial reprieve,

[2]Saskatchewan, *Manual of Policies and Procedures*, Department of Social Welfare and
Rehabilitation, Corrections Branch, Regina: Queen's Printer, January 1, 1960, p. 2.

222

or binding over to keep the peace, especially in the case of young children and first offenders. It became the custom for magistrates to call for volunteers to act as sureties, and this growing need was met by the Church of England Temperance Society, which first appointed court missionaries in 1876. Prior to this, however, the value of probation was established by a Warwickshire magistrate, Matthew Davenport Hill, who, in 1841, began keeping records of those placed on probation of good conduct. He so placed 484 of whom only seventy-eight, or sixteen per cent, had to be returned to the court for sentence. Recorder Cox of Portsmouth also followed this practice and noted only two failures over a twelve-year period. Cox maintained a register and had occasional inquiries made by the police as to the progress of probationers.

The court missionaries gradually won the support and confidence of magistrates and police and their use increased. In 1890 there were thirty-six, and by 1907, 143 were so employed. These missionaries proved the value of the supervisory element of probation, and so successful was this experiment that the state made provision by law in 1907 for the appointment of salaried probation officers. The use of probation officers was not, however, mandatory until 1925, when under far-reaching provisions for training and subsidy, probation officers were required for all jurisdictions.

In the United States, the pattern of development was very similar, with probation emerging from the provisions for binding over to keep the peace, which the newly established independent country adopted from the English common law. However, legal recognition of the practice was achieved in the United States earlier than in England, and various statutes regulating the release of offenders on probation of good conduct, with sureties, were passed in 1865 and 1869. In 1841, Augustus John, a bootmaker by trade, began a sustained service to the Boston courts, acting as surety for offenders and agreeing to befriend and supervise those released on suspended sentence. During the first ten years of his service, he had pledged bail to a total amount of $99,464 for 1,102 persons, of whom 674 were males and 428 were females. Almost half of his cases came from the municipal court and slightly more than half from the police court.[3] Up to 1858, a year before his death, he had bailed out 1,946 persons.[4] Quite a one-man crusade!

As his work proved its value, Augustus John found many supporters. He did not live to see the tree he planted come to full fruit. Others, how-

[3]C. L. Chute and M. Bell, *Crime, Courts and Probation*, New York: Macmillan, 1956, p. 44; quoted from 'A Report of the Labours of Augustus John', published by the *Christian World*, 1848.
[4]*Ibid.*, p. 44; quoted from a later report.

ever, carried on his work, and the value of the 'friend and adviser' to the probationer was officially recognized by the State of Massachusetts in the statute of 1869 referred to above. This law provided for the appointment of a visiting agent to be attached to the Board of State Charities. This was the first instance of a state agency empowered to investigate and to take charge of delinquent children brought before the court. Though the law did not expressly authorize it, many such children were placed on a foster-home basis. The following year the statute was amended to require the attendance of the 'visiting agent' at court in nearly all delinquent-children cases throughout the state. So successful was this early experiment that, in 1878, the state legislature authorized the city of Boston to appoint a probation officer for adults, and two years later, in 1880, the legislature authorized the appointment of adult probation officers in every city and town in the state.

It should be noted that whereas the success of Augustus John stimulated events in England, the Americans were the first to enact probation legislation.

THE CASEWORK PROCESS AT WORK

An understanding of the casework process is an essential part of the probation officer's training. Charlotte Towle in *Common Human Needs* has given us these seven steps:

1. Observation and gathering of facts – both tangible and psychological.
2. Scrutinizing the facts in the light of our professional knowledge of human behaviour and personality development.
3. Formulation of a tentative hypothesis or diagnosis.
4. Testing of the hypothesis through further inquiry.
5. Formulation of an interpretive or diagnostic statement.
6. Action recommended or taken on the basis of the diagnosis, which is further tested and revised in accordance with the results of this action.
7. Continuous self-appraisal by the worker to discount his own bias.[5]

These steps are separated for analysis only and in practice several steps may be occurring simultaneously. However, since the objective of the process is change in the individual, it is more relevant to look at the techniques producing motivation for change in the probationer, than to analyse the probation officer's method.

Those techniques include such things as:

1. Accepting and understanding the probationer without condoning his

[5]As quoted by Helen V. White in 'Recording: A Dynamic in Casework', *Family*, October 1943.

actions. Warmth, empathy, and a knowledge of personality development are important here.
2. Helping the probationer to discharge inhibiting emotions by expressing them in a permissive, non-directive setting.
3. Giving the probationer insight into why he feels the way he does.
4. Suggesting ways to control or re-channel harmful emotional reactions.
5. Supporting and recognizing his efforts to change.
6. Helping him to define problem areas in his life and the implications
of these problems.
7. Broadening his viewpoint through exploring ways to improve his
adjustment to society.
8. Helping him to face reality and to work out acceptable methods of
dealing with reality.
9. Referring him to other appropriate agencies for help with special
problems, for example, to psychiatric clinics for help with personality
disorders, to employers or employment agencies for suitable work,
to Alcoholics Anonymous for a drinking problem.
10. Helping the probationer to build, with his own unique resources, a
more satisfying life, not by giving him orders, but by enriching his
own plan and relating it to reality.
11. Interpreting the probationer to others with whom he must deal so that
demands made on him will not produce harmful stresses.
12. Exploring specific relationship problems and helping him to deal
wisely with them.
13. Building his self-respect and feeling of self-worth.
14. Manipulating environmental factors where they are contributing to
maladjustment.

The integrity and warmth of the probation officer are important in the
formation of a constructive relationship between him and his client. All the
probation officer's activities too must take place within an authoritative
framework, for he has a duty to ensure the observance of the conditions
imposed by the court and to report non-observance of the conditions. He
must be aware of the probationer's activities, not only through what the
probationer tells him, but through other sources of information.

The probation officer must have the ability to organize his time, to
write meaningful reports for the court and for his own records, and to
stimulate the community towards the provision of programs, oriented to
crime prevention, such as improved recreational facilities, better mental-
health services, hostels, community centres, urban redevelopment to
eliminate slum areas, etc. The real rewards of the job come from his ability
to stimulate constructive changes in his client and in the community.

St. John Madeley

HOW SUCCESSFUL IS PROBATION?

A number of studies indicate a success-rate for probation of approximately eighty per cent. There are, of course, different definitions of success, such as:

1. Successful completion of the actual period of probation;
2. Avoidance of criminal activity for a stated term after the end of the probation period; or
3. Success measured in terms of an index purporting to measure positive movement towards emotional maturity.

Suffice it to say that the yardstick chosen will influence the results. A recent survey undertaken in British Columbia points to a success-rate of between seventy-seven and eighty-seven per cent. In this study, every tenth case between 1947 and 1960 was reviewed and followed up by a check through records of provincial institutions. The follow-up period varied from thirteen years to one year. No check was made, however, of correctional institutions in other provinces or in the federal field. The follow-up would not disclose offences dealt with by way of fine unless there was default in the fine and consequent imprisonment.

In other words, to assess success figures, we need to know not only the definition of 'success' used for the study, but also what flaws exist when the chosen yardstick is applied to the problem. Other factors are operative here too. Any person put on probation is a member of a select group, through, for example, such considerations as:

1. The opinions (and even prejudices) of the magistrate or judge;
2. The pre-sentence investigation;
3. The social or economic status of the offender;
4. The type of offence committed; and
5. The community climate in relation to the offence.

The list is not intended to be exhaustive, but merely to suggest the kind of factors that have a bearing on the selection of cases for probation.

There is no question of the substantial cash savings to the community when one compares a daily cost of forty cents per person on probation with over $8 for imprisonment, even though the period on probation would normally be considerably longer than the period of imprisonment.[6] In addition, there are intangible values, both to the individual whose attitudes are changed and to society as a whole.

6British Columbia figures quoted at a refresher course for probation officers, February 1963.

226

LEGAL IMPLICATIONS

With this background, we may now look at the Canadian scene. Canada, of course, inherited English law and customs, and also has been greatly influenced by developments in her neighbour, the United States. In Canada, it is the federal government's responsibility to legislate on criminal matters, but the provinces' responsibility to staff and organize the lower courts. The three sections of the Criminal Code of Canada dealing with the suspended sentence are Sections 638, 639, and 640, and these are quoted in full.[7]

Section 638

1. Where an accused is convicted of an offence and no previous conviction is proved against him, and it appears to the court that convicts him or that hears an appeal that, having regard to his age, character and antecedents, to the nature of the offence and to any extenuating circumstances surrounding the commission of the offence, it is expedient that the accused be released on probation, the court may, except where a minimum punishment is prescribed by law, instead of sentencing him to punishment, suspend the passing of sentence and direct that he be released upon entering into a recognizance in Form 28, with or without sureties,
(a) to keep the peace and be of good behaviour during any period that is fixed by the court, and
(b) to appear and to receive sentence when called upon to do so during the period fixed under paragraph (a), upon breach of his recognizance.
2. A court that suspends the passing of sentence may prescribe as conditions of the recognizance that
(a) the accused shall make restitution and reparation to any person aggrieved or injured for the actual loss or damage caused by the commission of the offence, and
(b) the accused shall provide for the support of his wife and any other dependents whom he is liable to support, and the court may impose such further conditions as it considers desirable in the circumstances and may from time to time change the conditions and increase or decrease the period of the recognizance, but no such recognizance shall be kept in force for more than two years.
3. A court that suspends the passing of sentence may require as a condition of the recognizance that the accused shall report from time to time, as it may prescribe, to a person designated by the court, and the accused shall be under supervision of that person during the prescribed period.

[7]A recent amendment to the Criminal Code broadens the provisions of Section 637, dealing with 'binding over to keep the peace'. It now permits the imposition of probation-reporting in lieu of (summary conviction offences), or in addition to (indictable offences), any other sentence imposed by the Court.

4. The person designated by the court under Sub-section 3 shall report to the court if the accused does not carry out the terms on which the passing of sentence was suspended, and the court may order that the accused be brought before it to be sentenced.

5. Where one previous conviction and no more is proved against an accused who is convicted, but the previous conviction took place more than five years before the time of the commission of the offence of which he is convicted, or was for an offence that is not related in character to the offence of which he is convicted, the court may, notwithstanding Sub-section 1, suspend the passing of sentence and make the direction mentioned in Sub-section 1.

Section 639

1. A court that has suspended the passing of sentence or a justice having jurisdiction in the territorial division in which a recognizance was taken under Section 638 may, upon being satisfied by information on oath that the accused has failed to observe a condition of the recognizance, issue a summons to compel his appearance or a warrant for his arrest.

2. A summons under Sub-section 1 is returnable before the court and an accused who is arrested under a warrant issued under Sub-section 1 shall be brought before the court or a justice.

3. A justice before whom a warrant under Sub-section 1 is returned may remand the accused to appear before the court or admit him to bail upon recognizance, with or without sureties, conditioned upon such appearance.

4. The court may, upon the appearance of the accused pursuant to this Section or Sub-section 4 of Section 638 and upon being satisfied that the accused has failed to observe a condition of his recognizance, sentence him for the offence of which he was convicted.

5. Where the passing of sentence is suspended by a magistrate acting under Part XVI or Part XXIV or by a judge, and thereafter he dies or is for any reason unable to act, his powers under this section may be exercised by any other magistrate or judge, as the case may be, who has equivalent jurisdiction in the same territorial division.

Section 640

For the purposes of Sections 638 and 639, 'court' means

(a) a superior court of criminal jurisdiction,

(b) a court of criminal jurisdiction,

(c) a magistrate acting as a summary conviction court under Part XXIV, or

(d) a court that hears an appeal.

These sections of the Criminal Code deal only with adults or those children raised to the ordinary courts under Section 9 of the Juvenile Delinquents Act. The Code as it relates to probation is permissive legislation and confers no right on the offender. Eligibility is restricted quite severely, to first offenders, or to those with a clear record for five years, or if there is a conviction within this period, to those whose previous offence is unrelated to the current one. In Great Britain and in many jurisdictions in the United States, there is no such limitation. Amongst practitioners in the field, there is a considerable body of opinion favouring removal of the eligibility restrictions imposed by the Code.

While Section 638 of the Code does not expressly authorize a presentence investigation, it gives tacit approval to such by the words 'having regard to the age, character and antecedents, to the nature of the offence, and to any extenuating circumstances surrounding the commission of the offence'. The section authorizes various forms of suspended sentence in addition to probation, and empowers the court to impose conditions, to vary the conditions from time to time, and to shorten or lengthen the period of probation, provided the two-year limitation is not exceeded. Offences for which the law provides a minimum punishment are specifically excluded. The court may designate the person to whom the probationer is to report, and imposes an obligation on such persons to report failure of the probationer to observe the conditions of his probation.

Such failure is brought to the attention of the court through a sworn complaint called a breach of recognizance, subject to proof in the same manner as an ordinary complaint. The court may sentence because of a breach, but this is not mandatory, and the sentence then imposed is for the original offence, not the breach. Section 639 also provides for the eventuality that the original magistrate or judge is no longer in a position to act when the breach is laid and sets out the procedure to be followed.

Some weaknesses are apparent. The provision of probation services is not mandatory and no obligation is imposed on a province to provide a probation service. There is, of course, no federal system of probation as in the United States. There is no legal provision for transfer of responsibility if the probationer moves to another province. Informal reciprocal arrangements do exist between provinces, but, for the most part, these are not even authorized by provincial legislation. The procedure for bringing a defaulting probationer before the court and of proving the breach in cases where he has removed to another jurisdiction are expensive and cumbersome, unnecessarily so in the opinion of this writer. In England – a small, compact, and densely populated country – returning the probationer to the original court for sentence on a breach does not impose any great problems, but in a country the size of Canada, with a large mobile population (because of the high proportion of seasonal work), there would appear to be justification for working out a new procedure whereby the probationer could be brought before the court where the breach occurred for sentence or for change in the probation terms and conditions. Documentary proof of the original conviction and placement on probation could be supplied to the court processing the breach. It can readily be seen that considerable expense is involved if, for example, a probationer from a British Columbia court, who has moved with permission to Ontario, commits a breach in Ontario. There is the cost of transporting the prisoner and his escort to British Columbia, and if a plea of not guilty is entered to the breach, witnesses also may have to be brought from Ontario. Under such circumstances, the breach would seldom be processed, with resultant unfairness and loss of respect for probation. In fact, very few are returned for breach from any great distance unless the R.C.M.P. are involved. City and metropolitan forces are reluctant to spend the money.

The term 'previous conviction' is not defined and this gives rise to a variety of interpretations and consequent unfairness. Some magistrates interpret it to mean previous conviction under the Criminal Code, some to mean previous conviction under the Code or under any federal statute, and some to mean any previous conviction whatever. If the second interpretation is used by one magistrate, an Indian who had a previous conviction for a liquor offence under the Indian Act (a federal statute) would not be eligible for probation, whereas a non-Indian who had a previous conviction under a provincial liquor law would be eligible. It would seem a simple matter to eliminate this possible source of discriminatory treatment of an offender by defining 'previous conviction'.

Juvenile probation in Canada is governed, in the main, by provisions of the Juvenile Delinquents Act, also a federal statute. Like the Criminal Code, the act imposes no obligation on the provinces to establish probation services for juveniles. The reader is referred to Chapter 8 for details of this legislation.

HOW PROBATION IS ORGANIZED IN CANADA

With ten Canadian provinces, varying greatly in size, population, economy, and political climate, it is only natural to find variety in the way in which probation is organized. To get the necessary factual information for this chapter, the writer prepared questionnaires in 1960 and 1964 that were sent to all provinces. These are the source of all figures quoted in the succeeding sections dealing with each province. Unfortunately, some replies to the questionnaire were incomplete, and some provinces failed to supply any information. Hence, it has been impossible to give complete information, and the variety of systems of organization has made comparisons difficult or impossible.

230

Probation in British Columbia

The Probation Service in British Columbia is part of the Corrections Branch of the Attorney-General's Department. The Director of Correction is also Chief Probation Officer. A Probation Act[8] was first passed in 1946, although the service antedates the legislation by some four years.

Probation officers provide supervision and pre-sentence service to the courts for both adults and juveniles. The service also handles parole supervision and pre-release planning for the British Columbia Parole Board, and in some areas, parole supervision at the request of the National Parole Board. Administratively, the province is divided into regions under regional supervisors. Although the service is nominally province-wide, there are some gaps in remote areas of the province where the Department of Social Welfare co-operates with the Family and Children's Court judges in providing supervision of juveniles and some counselling for parents of juveniles appearing in court. Vancouver has its own Family and Children's Court and employs its own probation officers for juveniles. Victoria and Surrey also have established such courts but the province staffs them with probation officers, charging for this service. Other areas of the province are in process of establishing their own municipally operated family courts with financial assistance from the province through provincially employed probation officers assigned to these courts.

A recent development of interest is the Family and Children's Court Act,[9] which became effective July, 1963. It made broad sweeping changes in juvenile and family courts and authorized probation officers to 'solve family problems without the intervention of a judge' (Section 7(2)). At the time of writing, no new courts have been established under the Act, but several proposals are pending, including one involving a circuit court covering several cities in the Okanagan Valley. To implement fully the provisions of the Act will require substantial expansion of probation services in this province. An increase in authorized establishment of probation staff (excluding clerical staff) from 64 to 102 in the 1965-6 fiscal year, gives evidence that the government intends to make increasing use of probation services.

During 1963-4, 2,257 cases were placed on probation to the Provincial Probation Service, 414 were released under parole supervision, and 365 were receiving a voluntary service, that is reporting to a probation officer after the end of a formal probation period, or without a court order to report. During the same year probation officers also prepared 2,467 pre-

[8]British Columbia, *Revised Statutes, 1960,* Victoria: Queen's Printer, Ch. 301.
[9]British Columbia, *Statutes, 1963,* Victoria: Queen's Printer, Ch. 70.

sentence reports for the courts in which some disposition other than probation was made.

The budget was $562,924 for 1964-5 and over $900,000 for 1965-6. Staff as at October 31, 1964 numbered sixty-four. Case-loads averaged fifty-nine at March 31, 1964. This level limits intensive supervision of cases and the effectiveness of the probation officer is further reduced by time devoted to pre-sentence reports.

Some idea of the rate of growth of the service can be obtained from the following figures for the number of probation officers employed (provincial service only):

1945	1950	1955	1960	October 31, 1964
1	6	17	37	64

The service provides for in-service training and staff development through regional and province-wide staff meetings, with periodic refresher courses and institutes on special aspects of the work. In individual cases, time off to attend special university courses has been granted. There is provision for educational leave, without pay but with substantial assistance from the federal-provincial welfare training-grants and Canada fellowships. Educational leave is also granted on an individual basis. Educational standards have been high for new staff members, who now require university graduation as a prerequisite for employment as probation officers. A recent analysis of the sixty-four professional staff shows seventeen with Bachelor or Master of Social Work degrees and other Master or higher degrees, and thirty with other Bachelor degrees.

The service is actively engaged in a number of research projects and has been experimenting with group techniques for some time. There is a small library available to staff members but funds for its expansion are limited.

Psychiatric consultation is not generally available to probation officers, but a study is being made to determine the type of psychiatric service best suited to the field of corrections. Teams from the mental-health clinic, to which cases may be referred, operate throughout most of the province.

Probation in Alberta

Alberta's probation services also operate within the Attorney-General's Department. There are two probation branches, both under the same superintendent – the Juvenile Offenders and Probation Branch, and the Adult Probation Branch. The first named is responsible for juvenile courts and juvenile delinquency on a provincial level, with family courts at Ed-

232

monton, Red Deer, Calgary, Lethbridge, and Medicine Hat. The Adult
Probation Branch provides probation services for all the criminal courts
in the province. Alberta sets the dividing age between juveniles and adults
at sixteen for boys, and eighteen for girls. In addition to the provincial
services, a number of the larger municipalities employ their own probation officers. Thus there are fifty-five provincially employed probation
officers and a further twenty-eight employed by municipalities. The Salvation Army provides probation services for a limited number of selected
cases from police courts in Edmonton and Calgary.

The 1964-5 budget total for probation was $682,540. There is sufficient
staff to maintain fairly low case-loads – fifty-five for provincial staff, but
somewhat higher for municipally employed probation officers.

Probation services have been provided in Alberta since 1940, but were
not organized provincially until 1952. There were twelve probation officers
in the provincial service in 1955, thirty-five in 1960, and fifty-five in
October 1964, so growth has been fairly rapid.

The probation branches hold annual staff meetings as a means of in-
service training and periodically organize institutes. There is a system of
educational leave for staff and substantial financial assistance is given in
approved cases. Recently educational leave has been increased, and
this has served to increase the proportion of professionally trained staff
in the provincial services. The proportion is somewhat higher among
municipally employed probation officers than among those employed provincially. The lack of a School of Social Work in the province no doubt
has limited the number of professionally trained probation officers and has
added to the expense of financial assistance for educational leave. In an
effort to improve the quality of staff, the province has under study an in-
service training-course, which will eventually reach all staff as well as new
employees.

The provincial service has only a limited professional library available
for staff and no regular budget for library acquisitions. The province has
undertaken no research project and none is planned at the time of writing.

Probation in Saskatchewan
In Saskatchewan, both adult and juvenile probation come under the Department of Social Welfare and Rehabilitation. The provincial Corrections
Act was passed in 1953 and its preamble gives expression to the remedial
rather than punitive philosophy of the department.[10] A formal adult probation service was first established in 1949 in Regina and Saskatoon.
Owing to lack of trained staff, expansion was slow and not until 1958 was

[10]Saskatchewan, *Statutes, 1953*, Regina: Queen's Printer, ch. 240, p. 3654.

service accorded to courts in Moose Jaw. During the next two years, services were extended to the courts in North Battleford and Prince Albert. In other areas, selected cases are carried by social workers in the welfare services, and plans are going ahead to extend probation service to rural courts throughout the province.

Although adult and juvenile probation are under the same department, they are separated for administration. The Corrections Branch handles adult probation, while juvenile probation is handled as part of the generalized case-load of the provincial welfare workers. Thus juvenile probation is available in all nine regions of the province, but adult probation is not yet available in all areas. Pre-sentence investigation is part of the service in both fields. Since the cost of juvenile probation is included in the cost of welfare services generally, it is not possible to give over-all figures for the cost of probation in this province. The number of staff members has increased slowly; there was one probation officer for adults in 1950, there were three in 1955, five in 1960, and twelve at the end of 1964. Supervisory staff are not included in these figures.

Bursaries are available for educational leave. The staff is highly qualified professionally, with all but one adult probation officer having a university degree. Case-loads vary from a low of fourteen to a high of 108, with a provincial average of forty-six.

The departmental library comprises some 1,500 volumes and fourteen periodicals, and has an annual budget of $2,000 for acquisitions. The library serves the whole department, and provides an example of the way facilities provided by the administration of the whole department enrich the probation service. It has been estimated that the equivalent of more than twenty-five per cent of one staff member's time is devoted to research. Psychiatric consultation is available to probation officers, and resident or travelling mental-health clinics are available for assessment of individual cases.

Probation officers are provided with a well-prepared manual of instructions. Saskatchewan differs from other provinces in that the probation officer is not an officer of the court, but more of a consultant assisting the courts in the complex task of sentencing.

Probation in Manitoba

Moving eastward to the next province, we find probation services once again set in the administrative framework of the Attorney-General's Department. The Director of Corrections has over-all responsibility and administers probation services, both adult and juvenile, through the Chief Probation Officer, who is also responsible for the Juvenile Detention

Centre. Though its name might suggest municipal involvement, the Winnipeg Juvenile and Family Court is a unit of the Provincial Probation Service and is headed by the Director of Court Services. Thus all probation officers in the province are civil servants.

Juvenile probation in Manitoba started in 1909 with the establishment of the Winnipeg Juvenile and Family Court. Adult probation services did not begin until February 1, 1957, when the Provincial Probation Service was started. Probation services have now been expanded to provide both adult and juvenile probation in all but isolated areas of the province, with expenditures of $420,000 in 1964-5.

There is no Probation Act in this province. The Child Welfare Act makes provision for probation officers for juveniles, but does not set out, in detail, their duties and responsibilities. Probation officers for adults are presumed to be authorized under the provisions of Section 638(3) of the Criminal Code.

A staff of thirty-four probation officers and supervisors is employed on probation duties. Of these, eighteen have a B.A. degree, seven are Bachelors of Social Work, and four are Masters of Social Work. The remaining five have completed at least senior matriculation plus the prescribed departmental in-service training-course. At the time of writing five staff members were on educational leave; three were working towards B.S.W. degrees and two towards M.S.W. degrees. Recruitment policy now requires a minimum of university graduation for probation officers. (These figures are quoted from a letter to the writer dated November 26, 1964.) Thus in the educational qualification of its probation staff, Manitoba compares favourably with the other provinces.

There is sufficient staff to keep case-loads down to sixty or less as an average. A small intake unit, attached to the Winnipeg Juvenile and Family Court, does not have case-supervision duties and has been excluded in the calculation of the average mentioned. At the end of September 1964, 499 adults were under probation or parole supervision, 484 juveniles reported to officers serving courts outside metropolitan Winnipeg, and 350 juveniles were under the supervision of the Winnipeg Juvenile Court officers.

While no formal research project is now in progress, there has been experimentation in the use of group therapy in a summer-camp program, and in foster-home placement. Diagnostic and consultative psychiatric services are provided by a full-time psychiatrist and a psychologist, responsible to the Director of Correction. These services are supplemented by child-guidance clinics attached to the Brandon and Selkirk mental hospitals.

A manual for probation officers was completed in 1963 and has done much to standardize practice throughout the service as well as to assist new officers in understanding their duties.

Probation in Ontario

Ontario has the oldest and largest probation service in Canada. The history of juvenile probation goes back to 1893, when a form of probation was first authorized by the Children's Protection Act, Chapter 45.[11] Adult probation has been offered since 1922 when the Ontario Probation Act was passed. Administratively, probation is organized under a Director of Probation in the Attorney-General's Department. Some seventeen supervisors and 163 probation officers cover the province. In addition, Ottawa, Toronto, and Windsor have municipal probation staffs attached to juvenile and family courts.

The province is well served with juvenile and family courts, organized to serve every county and district of the province. All these courts have probation officers attached to them. Provincial probation officers also serve magistrates' and superior courts. The 1964-5 Ontario government budget for probation was $1,582,000. Some idea of the extensive use of probation in this province can be gained from the figures at the end of September 1964: 5,580 adult and 2,002 juvenile probationers, 171 parolees – a total of 7,753. The probation staff prepared 6,808 social histories, pre-sentence, and pre-release reports in the first nine months of 1964. Staff growth in terms of numbers employed by the province has been phenomenal since 1950, as evidenced by the following figures:

			October 31,
1950	*1955*	*1960*	*1964*
14	105	150	180

In addition to a six-week training-course for new probation officers and a two-week advanced course for experienced officers and supervisors, the probation service provides monthly and annual staff meetings and periodic institutes with outside discussion leaders. After two years of service, probation officers may be granted educational leave with some financial assistance as an outright grant. Some nine per cent of the staff have social-work degrees and a further forty-five per cent have university graduation or better.

Work-loads appear well controlled, varying from forty-eight to 132

---

[11]C. L. Chute and M. Bell, *Crime, Courts and Probation,* New York: Macmillan, 1956, p. 30.

with the average (in 1963) at sixty-eight units, counting a case for supervision as one unit, a pre-sentence report or social history as two units.

Although no person on staff is fully employed on research, a number of research projects have been undertaken by branch headquarters staff, as well as the Probation Officers' Association, Ontario. Both supervisory staff and field-staff have been involved in a number of these projects.

Probation in Quebec

In our survey of Canada from west to east, we have so far found both adult and juvenile probation services provided by government departments; in Quebec we find government services in the juvenile field only, with adult probation handled by private agencies.

The department of government involved in juvenile probation is the Family and Social Welfare Department. This controls the Youth Protection Services, which provide not only probation, but industrial or training-schools, clinics, and reception homes. Thus all related services come under one director, giving an opportunity for unified control and administration. The 1964-5 budget was about $835,000, with 12,578 cases under supervision at the end of October 1964. According to the staff figures provided, probation services for juveniles have expanded fairly rapidly.

1940	*1945*	*1950*	*1955*	*1960*	*October 31,* *1964*
15	25	30	40	65	116

Organized probation services in Quebec date from 1950 when the social-welfare courts were established, replacing juvenile courts in that province. Prior to 1950, there were volunteer services under the aegis of the Catholic Church and the Catholic Young Workers. The Youth Protection Services were created in 1959 to co-ordinate all services to juveniles.

Staff training is carried out by means of weekly staff meetings and quarterly half-day meetings. Orientation and in-service training are provided by Les Centres du Socio-Pédagogie, which provide training for all branches of the Youth Protection Services. In addition, there is provision for educational leave, with government assistance on a loan basis, after two years' service.

The proportion of professionally trained staff, including all university graduates, is less than twenty-five per cent. Salaries were lower than those in other provinces and case-loads were high by modern standards, averaging 125 cases per probation officer in October 1964.

Quebec is one of the provinces doing research in the field of probation, and it is interesting to note that the possibility of introducing group-counselling techniques is being seriously considered at the time of writing. Psychiatric consultation is extensively used.

Probation services provided include pre-sentence investigation.

Probation in New Brunswick

New Brunswick entered the adult probation field in 1959 and now has ten probation officers and a supervisor serving the province. Probation services come under the Attorney-General's Department with the supervisor reporting through the Inspector of Penal Institutions.

Offices are located at Bathurst, Campbellton, Edmundston, Fredericton, Moncton, Newcastle, St. Andrews, and Saint John. Pre-sentence investigation is provided for all courts, as well as parole supervision of those released from New Brunswick Training School, by the New Brunswick Parole Board, and by the National Parole Board. Case-loads as at December 31, 1964, average eighty-two, a heavy load for an officer also involved in pre-sentence investigations which average seventy-six per officer per year. Staff training facilities are limited.

Probation in Nova Scotia

Adult and juvenile probation services are separately organized in this province; adult services are administered by the Attorney-General's Department through the Director of Probation, while the Department of Public Welfare provides juvenile probation services.

It was only in October 1961 that the Juvenile Delinquents Act became applicable throughout Nova Scotia, and juvenile court facilities were extended to cover the entire province. Where there are no juvenile probation officers attached to a juvenile court, probation services are provided by the local Children's Aid Society. The dividing age between adults and juveniles is sixteen. Adult probation services have been in existence only since the fall of 1954. There are now ten juvenile probation officers in the province and fourteen adult probation officers.

The responsible department provides pre-sentence investigation for the courts, and co-operates with the National Parole Board by undertaking parole supervision on request. Psychiatric facilities are available through the Victoria General Hospital at Halifax, the Nova Scotia Hospital at Dartmouth (both operated by the provincial government), and also through mental-health centres located at strategic points.

Case-load figures indicate an average of fifty-eight per adult probation officer as at October 1964. No information on staff training, educational leave, library facilities, and so on, was supplied.

There are no family courts in Nova Scotia.

Probation in Prince Edward Island

Adult and juvenile probation services are not organized by the provincial government in this province. We have no information on any private agencies offering a probation service there.

Probation in Newfoundland

Newfoundland has no formal government probation service for adults, but its Public Welfare Department does undertake supervision of cases referred by other provinces. Some adult probation supervision is also extended by that department to those placed on probation by the family court at St. John's. However, the John Howard Society in the St. John's area and the Salvation Army and other churches provide informal probation supervision to the magistrates' courts.

Probation services to juveniles are the responsibility of the Public Welfare Department, which has two officers specializing in probation in St. John's, and one each in Conception Bay, Central Newfoundland, and Corner Brook. Probation services for juveniles in other areas are supplied by Welfare Department staff members as part of their regular duties.

We have no information on case-loads, staff training, or educational leave policies for this province.

Probation in the Yukon and Northwest Territories

Probation services for the Yukon Territory were established in June 1964, but so far no services exist in the Northwest Territories. There is one probation officer, stationed in Whitehorse, for the whole of the Yukon. Cases in remote areas are supervised by volunteers or report by mail. In the first year of operation, seventy-five pre-sentence reports were prepared for the courts and the case-load grew to thirty-five.

Summary and Conclusions

Most provinces place adult probation services within the administrative framework of the Attorney-General's Department, but one (Saskatchewan, see page 233) puts them under the Department of Social Welfare and Rehabilitation. Four provinces put juvenile probation in the Welfare Department. All provinces where probation services are offered provide a pre-sentence service to the appropriate courts.

The following table summarizes the textual material on the various provinces and gives a limited opportunity for comparison. It is unfortunate that not all provinces provided all information in sufficient detail to permit a more meaningful comparison.

	B.C.	Alta.	Sask.	Man.	Ont.	Que.	N.B.	N.S.	P.E.I.	Nfld.
1. Administration:										
(a) By the Attorney-General's Dept.										
(i) Juvenile	x	x	–	x	x	–	x	–	–	–
(ii) Adult	x	x	–	x	x	–	x	x	–	–
(b) By the Social Welfare Dept.										
(i) Juvenile	–	–	x	–	–	x	–	x	–	x
(ii) Adult	–	–	x	–	–	–	–	–	–	–
2. Provides pre-sentence service to courts	x	x	x	x	x	x	x	x	–	?
3. Probation Act	x	–	x	–	x	–	–	–	–	–
4. Case-loads (average)										
(a) 50 or less	–	x	x	–	–	–	–	–	–	–
(b) 50-9	x	–	–	–	–	–	–	x	–	–
(c) 60-9	–	–	–	x	x	–	–	–	–	–
(d) over 70	–	–	–	–	–	x	x	–	–	–
(e) no figures supplied	–	–	–	–	–	–	–	–	–	x
5. Has system of educational leave	x	x	x	x	x	x	?	?	–	?

No survey of probation services in Canada would be complete without a look at the statistics. At the time of writing, there is no over-all statistical analysis, but the Dominion Bureau of Statistics does give figures on those over sixteen placed on probation, with supervision, following conviction for an indictable offence.[12] The latest figures available to this author were for 1961, and are reproduced in the table on page 241.

It is difficult to explain the wide differences among the figures in column 2, though differences between predominantly rural provinces, such as Saskatchewan and Prince Edward Island, and those which are predominantly industrial, such as Ontario, have an important bearing. However, this does not explain why Alberta, for example, has a much higher rate

[12]Canada, Dominion Bureau of Statistics, *Canada Year Book 1963-4*, Ottawa: Queen's Printer, pp. 388, 391, 392.

Province	Persons over 16 convicted of indictable offences (1)	Rate per 100,000 over 16 years of age (2)	Number placed on probation (3)	Per cent (3) as % of (1)* (4)
British Columbia	5,092	465	757	14.9
Alberta	4,012	477	551	13.7
Saskatchewan	1,743	293	214	12.3
Manitoba	2,368	391	380	16.0
Ontario	13,985	339	3,175	22.8
Quebec	8,064	245	1,043	12.9
New Brunswick	1,038	290	97	9.3
Nova Scotia	1,383	297	269	19.4
Prince Edward Island	42	65	–	0
Newfoundland	703	274	50	5.6
Yukon and Northwest Territories	249	1,103	5	2.0
Canada	38,679	330	6,541	16.9

*The author's calculations.

per 100,000 than Saskatchewan, though both are rural provinces, or why the difference between Ontario and Saskatchewan is relatively small. Variations in police efficiency are undoubtedly responsible, at least partly, for some of the differences. It is apparent from the figures in column 4 that one's chance of receiving a suspended sentence with probation is largely dependent on where one lives. This needs correction.

Few probation departments are actively involved in evaluative research. Even published figures on success-rates lack uniformity in the definition of 'success'. There seems to be general agreement on a success-rate of eighty per cent or better. A British Columbia study of 880 cases (a random ten per cent sample) showed that eighty-eight per cent successfully completed probation and that eighty-two per cent were not re-sentenced to a British Columbia institution during a six-year follow-up period.[13]

Case-loads in some provinces are so high that they preclude effective casework, and without casework there is not likely to be any real change in the probationer's attitude. Hence, society is not getting the best possible protection. A system of federal grants to provinces that conform to reasonable case-load standards would be worth studying as a method of improving the quality of probation services.

No information on salaries was included because constant changes

13Director of Correction, *1962-63 Annual Report*, Victoria: Queen's Printer, p. T13.

would soon make such information obsolete. Probation officers' salaries have increased substantially during the past five years; however, there is wide divergence between salaries offered by the various provinces. In the final analysis, salaries have a bearing on the quality of staff the work is able to attract, as does promotional opportunity. At the moment, salary increments are limited to four to six years by civil service grading and classification. Thus a probation officer must move into supervisory and administrative areas if he is to move toward salary levels achieved by other professions.

Few probation departments appear to have a positive attitude to public relations; yet in this as in any other field, increased public support will result in increased appropriations. The public must be convinced that probation is worth while, and that it is worth spending money on the prevention of crime.

Recent research in sociology has resulted in many new concepts of value to the field of probation, and there is a need for an imaginative approach to test these concepts and to evolve new methods and techniques and apply them to probation. A system of federal subsidy to encourage provinces to be experimental and to share their findings with other provinces would be a constructive step. Such a program, coupled with federally supported training-grants to improve the educational qualifications of probation officers, would do much to make the field more attractive as a career for promising young people, and would, I believe, help to overcome the shortage of qualified staff, and to prevent the loss of staff to other fields by providing the vital challenge of professional stimulation in a growing profession.

Supervision as a tool for professional growth has not as yet been fully exploited. Many supervisors are responsible for ten or more probation officers and find their effectiveness reduced by the fact they can afford to spend only limited time discussing cases with individual staff members. Many good men are lost to the profession through the lack of stimulation, which good supervision can provide.

In summary, it is apparent that the following conditions are required to improve probation services in Canada:

1. Uniformity of legislation and standards.
2. Legal recognition of transfer of cases between provinces, and a scheme to enable a breach of probation to be processed by a court other than the original court if great expense would be involved in returning a probationer to the original court for sentence.
3. Better training for probation officers and improvement of standards of supervision.

4. Improved public relations and community involvement.
5. More research, and more funds provided by the federal government to stimulate research.
6. Control of case-loads, and reduction to the point where effective case-work can be done by the probation officer.
7. An imaginative approach to evolve new techniques useful to the field of probation.

This list is not intended to be exhaustive, but these are demonstrably important.

10

Training-Schools in Canada

DONALD SINCLAIR

DONALD SINCLAIR

LEGISLATION AND ADMINISTRATION

Section 3(2) of the Juvenile Delinquents Act reads:

> where a child is adjudged to have committed a delinquency he shall be dealt with not as an offender but as one in a condition of delinquency and therefore requiring help and guidance and proper supervision.

It is worth noting that the chief purpose of the court in implementing this Act is not to administer punishment or even to determine the degree of guilt of the offender; it is to take whatever action is considered to be necessary in the best interests of the child. At the same time the court may act in the child's interest only after he is found to be an offender in that he has committed a special kind of offence known as a delinquency, a point to which further reference will be made.

Section 2(1)(h) defines a juvenile delinquent as being, among other things,

> any child who violates any provision of the Criminal Code or of any Dominion or provincial statute or of any by-law or ordinance of any municipality. . . .

While provincial statutes differ in detail, they all make provision for children to be brought before the court not only by reason of being accused of a criminal offence, but also by reason of their living in circumstances that expose them to danger. For example, the Ontario Training School Act, R.S.O. 1960, ch. 404, provides for bringing before the court a child who is found destitute through being an orphan or through having a parent undergoing imprisonment, or one who, through his parents' neglect, is growing up without salutary parental control and education.

244

In brief, then, the cases that come before juvenile courts can be broadly classified in three groups:
1. Cases resulting from offences that, were they to be committed by an adult, would be punishable by a fine or imprisonment;
2. Cases resulting from problem behaviour peculiar to children, for example, playing truant from school, being unmanageable at home, running away from home;
3. Cases resulting from children being neglected or in need of care and protection.

In all cases, if the court feels that institutional training or treatment is advisable, the child is likely to be committed to a training-school. Thus the training-school works not only with delinquent children, but also with neglected children and those in need of protection. It has been contended that it is unwise to house dependent children together with those who have offended. The counter-view is that '. . . it is a mistake to regard all children in need of care or protection as innocent victims of circumstances and the delinquents as necessarily more depraved. Adolescent girls . . . who are beyond the control of their parents and already having promiscuous sexual relations with men are not legally delinquent since they have not broken the law, but nevertheless they are generally more depraved, and more difficult to handle, than the average young law breaker.'[1] This view is supported by many training-school superintendents, who claim that the neglected child is often a bigger problem in the institution than the young offender.

The case for separating the neglected or dependent child should not, however, be lightly dismissed. Not all children in these categories are culpable in the manner of the adolescent girl in the argument quoted and the danger of contamination may be real. Many may well 'give trouble' upon admission to a training-school simply because they are rebelling against a system that in their view is unfair, even though society says it is acting in their best interests. Finally the argument for separation would seem to be stronger in those provinces where training-schools form a branch of a Department of Correction or Reform than in those where they fall under the administration of a Department of Welfare. It is argued that when the child leaves the school and searches for work, if inquiries necessarily made by employers reveal that he was in a school administered by a Department of Reforms, the employers are likely to conclude that he is a 'young criminal'. Such a stigma, it is contended, is less likely to attach to a child educated in an institution under the surveillance of a Welfare Department.

[1] W. Elkins, *The English Penal System*, London: Pelican Books, 1957, p. 65.

The fact that the juvenile court judge, under present legislation, must deal with all three classes of child – the delinquent, the neglected, and the dependent – tends to confuse the issue as to whether juvenile courts are primarily moral agencies or treatment agencies. To the child before the court it matters little which they are; should he be removed from his home and committed to a training-school, he will view this as punishment. It may be called treatment. It may be in the child's interest. To him, however, it is punishment. We must face the fact that, in general, the court too looks upon committal as punishment. Why else does the court so often warn a child that if he continues acting in his present fashion he will have to be sent away? Why else does the court sometimes paint a picture of training-school as a place it is well to stay clear of, where the staff 'will not take your kind of nonsense'? The attitude of the court can, of course, change from one case to another. If the child has given no evidence of being delinquent, but is sorely in need of protection, the court is likely to be sympathetic and may represent the training-school not as the ultimate sanction that can be imposed, but as a warm and friendly place with a swimming-pool, a gymnasium, and good food. A certain amount of hypocrisy seems almost unavoidable when the same disposition has to be made in vastly different circumstances.

Within the three broad classes of children are many sub-divisions, and there is justification for the often-voiced complaint of training-school staffs that their schools are little more than catch-basins for all sorts and conditions of children whose only common denominator is that other agencies in society have failed to meet their needs. This complaint is reinforced by the existence of such a provision as that which was contained in the Ontario Training Schools Act until its revision in 1965. Section 10(a) of the Act stated:

> The Minister may order that a boy or girl who has been made a ward of a Children's Aid Society . . . or any other boy or girl one of whose parents or guardians consents thereto . . . and who in the opinion of the Minister is in need of the training and discipline offered by a training school shall be admitted to a training school.

Legislation of this nature brings into sharp focus the question whether the normal judicial safeguards can safely be bypassed in the supposed interests of the child. The social worker's argument in favour of such legislation is that it provides her with a powerful preventive weapon; others may well fear that something less than justice is done when a child is admitted to a training-school without the benefit of a court hearing. Take the case of a fifteen-year-old girl who keeps late hours, who comes home with her clothing disarrayed, and whose parents have found contraceptives in her handbag. Suspicions are strong but unconfirmed. The social worker may claim that intervention is immediately necessary to avoid a tragedy such as disease or pregnancy; her concern is more with what the child *is* than with what the child may or may not have *done*. The opposing view is that committal to a training-school may be a grave miscarriage of justice, because the suspicions, however strong, may prove to be unjustified. Suspicions are not evidence.

The revised Ontario Training Schools Act removes the power of the Minister to admit children to training-schools and requires that all commitments to the schools must be by judicial order. The protection of a judicial hearing is obviously a welcome and overdue provision, but it is contended that the revision could have given the child additional protection by making it mandatory for the court to provide him with independent legal representation. The need for such representation is evident when consideration is given to the fact that the interests of the child and those of his parents (or welfare agency) making an application for commitment are in opposition. Almost certainly the child's interest is to stay in the community, and the fact that an application has been made is proof that the parents' interest is to have the child removed to a training-school.

Administrative practices as well as the governing legislation differ from one province to another. In British Columbia, training-schools fall under the jurisdiction of the Department of Health and Welfare; in Alberta under the Department of the Attorney-General; in Ontario under the Department of Reform Institutions. In British Columbia, Saskatchewan, and New Brunswick, all the schools are operated and administered by government departments; in Quebec, all the schools with one exception are operated by private agencies with financial support from the government; in the other provinces, there are both privately operated and government operated schools. In Ontario, the school must accept those children whom the court commits to it; in Quebec, because the schools are private institutions, a school can accept or refuse admission to a child and, should it refuse, the onus of finding another school that will accept the child rests with the court.

To increase the confusion, some of the nomenclature in the Juvenile Delinquents Act is outdated and some of the stipulations in the Act are ignored in several provinces of the country. The terms 'industrial school' and 'detention home' do not as satisfactorily describe the institutions to which they are applied as do the terms that have superseded them in general use – 'training-school' and 'observation home'. The Act makes it mandatory for the juvenile court to establish detention homes, but in practice few courts have done so since, unfortunately, the Act does not stipulate who is to be responsible for the cost of providing and maintaining such homes. It is also mandatory for the court to appoint from among the citizens a juvenile court committee. Few of these committees are, in effect, working committees and, of course, it is not possible to compel a judge to utilize their services.

Finally, there are different legislative provisions governing the licensing of institutions in the different provinces. In Alberta, Nova Scotia, Ontario, and Newfoundland, all children's institutions must have a licence; in British Columbia, all except Children's Aid Society shelters and institutions must be licensed; other provinces either require no licensing or require it for some institutions and not for others.

The picture, then, is a complex one and seems to provide evidence that an Act written to meet the needs of twenty-two years ago now stands in need of revision.

THE CHANGING CONCEPTS OF INSTITUTIONAL CARE

The first major step forward in the care of children in institutions probably occurred with the realization that child offenders needed to be housed in separate institutions from those used for adult offenders. Before this time the attitude was that all were equally offenders and that the proper place for offenders was prison.

The first institutions for delinquent children were in general large and had few staff; regimentation was the order of the day and work was the basic program. While diligence and obedience were stressed, the keynote was cost; the more economically the children could be fed and clothed, the better. Physical punishment was frequently used, not through any desire to be cruel, but merely because it was genuinely believed that to spare the rod was to spoil the child. Although the methods then in vogue may now be looked on as cruel, quaint, or even bizarre, we cannot question the intentions or the sincerity of our predecessors.

Changes in community attitudes brought changes in the institutions. No longer was it considered enough merely to remove the delinquent from society and lock him up, thus exacting retribution and at the same time punishing him so as to deter him from repeating his offence. He now had to be 'given a trade' so that he would have the dignity and satisfaction of his work to sustain him on his return; he had to be 'educated to the limit of his potential' so that he would realize the folly of breaking the law. Perhaps in these attitudes of the community there is reflected the belief that it was mainly the unemployed, the lazy, and the illiterate who committed offences. Be that as it may, we introduced and then gradually broadened programs of academic, vocational, and recreational activities.

248

The expansion and increased variety of program content brought in turn a reduction in the amount of regimentation, simply because it was no longer possible for everyone to do the same thing at the same time. Very broad individual differences had to be recognized, for some inmates were found fit for one aspect of the program, some for another. More attention was focused on what happened to children when they left the institution, and basic follow-up services were established. These changes constituted another big step forward. One feature, however, remained unchanged: the institution made little attempt to adjust its program to meet the needs of the child; the child was still expected to adjust to the institution, to fit into its program, and to conform to fairly rigidly applied rules, routines, and standards.

The rate of change in community attitudes to the delinquent has accelerated since the Second World War. Changing attitudes have brought change in administrative goals. More community interest has meant larger budgets, better facilities, and more hope of stressing the re-education of the individual rather than the containment and conformity of the mass. Changes in administrative goals have in turn brought changes in staff attitudes; now the answer to 'what is expected of me?' is not what it once was, and the question 'what kind of person is this child?' is having to be more frequently raised. Even the child's role is changing.

All these factors have a direct impact on the content of the institution's program. The chain began with the change in community attitudes to the offender; it would be interesting, if space permitted, to trace how this came about. One important contributing factor was the development of child analysis. The early analysts realized that a separate environment had to be created for children whose disturbance was rooted in the home environment, and their experience in treating such children in residences away from their homes opened new approaches and helped to make the community more aware of the problems of children in institutions. Increased community interest gave a further impetus to treatment.

The position today is that while a survey of institutions in Canada discloses great variation in the methods used, most schools appear to fall into one of two classifications. The first of these we might call the 'common-sense type': this phrase is intended to describe the institution where therapy in the clinical sense is not contemplated. The emphasis is placed on a humane approach, on understanding, on common-sense handling. The intention is to give the child the opportunity to learn how to get along with his fellows, accept authority, develop his ability, and widen his interests.

An examination of this type of institution would, one suspects, show that the hope for success does not lie in the academic classes, in the trade shops, in the recreation programs, or in any other part of the program, but in the fact that the children are given the opportunity to identify with an adult. To the child who has to live away from his home, every person with whom he comes into contact has either a positive or a negative meaning for him, and the selection of staff should be made with this in mind. From this point, however, there is much groping in the dark because it is not known in what circumstances, or under what conditions, the right identifications will occur. There is no guarantee that another child will not be the identification figure chosen. It cannot categorically be stated with a background of proven scientific data that, 'if this boy is put into B house and allowed to pursue the trade of carpentry, this or that identification will follow'. All too often, although the effects of such moves are seen – an interest captured, a realization born, an insight achieved – there has been no awareness of the process taking place; only the effect is seen. The reverse is equally true; the process of maturation can be seen to be halted or retarded, and yet it is not possible to point a finger at the cause.

The second type of institution might be called 'specialist oriented'. In a sense such a term is a complete misnomer, but what is meant is that the institution has a complement of psychiatrist, psychologist, caseworker, and group-worker. Trained personnel of this kind may be engaged either as a result of public pressure or in the belief that their contribution will facilitate rehabilitation. If the former, they are likely to be accepted by the staff with a great deal of reluctance; if the latter, they are often expected to perform little less than the miraculous. In either case problems arise. Their relationship with the house-staff is made more complex because of the reasons behind their introduction. The staff may look upon them with suspicion, fearing that their own jobs are going to be made more difficult, and that they themselves are going to become mere sources of information rather than important cogs in the wheel. Staff members who at first welcome the therapist may complain later that they are not being brought sufficiently into the picture and that the therapist lays too great a stress on the secrecy of his material. In schools where specialist staff work in a clinic or centre set apart for the purpose, the role of the clinician as being someone different, special, and apart, is apt to be emphasized in the eyes of house-staff. Conflict arises as to methods to be used, and the greater the conflict becomes, the more firmly entrenched each side becomes in its belief that the other is misguided and naïve. In other words, to lay a veneer of treatment upon the existing surface of training will not work – the material will not adhere unless the surface is properly prepared to receive it.

This may seem a gloomy picture to present of those schools that have bravely introduced therapists into their organization and it needs to be said that it is not a complete one. The advent of such people has brought about certain changes that have been most advantageous, such as, for example, the speedier identification of the seriously disturbed child, the very real help that is given to such a child, the gradual change in attitudes to their work, however reluctant initially, on the part of the house-staff, and the increasing demand by the house-staff to be trained in the principles of child care.

It is regrettable that training-school administrators have made little attempt to explore the possibility of breaking completely from past methods and traditions. The Boscoville School in the province of Quebec has done so and its program might best be described as one of 'total staff involvement' in that its aim is to involve house-staff directly in treatment practice and to consider the duty of the house-staff as being more than merely 'holding' the boy between one interview and the next. The costs of operating an institution on these lines are likely to be in excess of costs in the other schools. Staff-pupil ratios must be high. Staff must be well trained; they must be very willing to lay bare their own feelings and explain their own attitudes in daily staff tutorials; they must have a clear picture of their exact role in the total structure, a role that is part teacher, part social worker, part therapist; they must be able to absorb a good deal of hostility and aggression, and must be able to recognize when they are satisfying their own needs rather than those of the child.

To examine some of the more recently developed methods and techniques of child care is to realize how much more stress than formerly is being placed on treatment. Those who consider that treatment in the correctional setting needs still more emphasis must first define what they mean. It has been said that we have progressed in that our methods were first retributive, then repressive, then permissive, then oriented in some degree towards treatment, and now stress the therapeutic, community approach. This seems a strange way of looking at things, for not all those who come into care need treatment in the clinical sense: some need controls, some need permissiveness, some need custody, and *all*, simply because they are children, need training. What the variations in methods and the variations in theories do point up is the need for a variety of institutions that are purposely planned in order that the differing needs of different children can be met in the best and most satisfying way. This variety will be fully possible only in the larger provinces that have a number of institutions, but in those provinces a reception or assessment centre

251

will be necessary to ensure that each child can be placed in the school most likely to meet his needs.

THE CHILDREN IN THE SCHOOLS

Elsewhere in this book, the causes of crime are discussed at length. The causes of juvenile delinquency do not differ from those of crime in general. One might add that the confusion and conflict surrounding the question of causation do not differ either, for it is possible, in analysing the literature and the research work in the area of juvenile delinquency, to find support for almost any viewpoint; there are almost as many conflicting theories about causation as there are delinquents. In the light of all that has been said, it is not surprising that the majority of workers in the field today have come to accept that at the root of delinquency there is an infinite variety of causes. They would concur with Grunhut's contention that 'the outstanding fact in juvenile delinquency is its "multiple causation", whether we are considering it as a social phenomenon in a smaller or larger community, or considering the criminal career of an individual.'[2]

This multiplicity of causes is paralleled by a multiplicity of maladies and malfunctions evident in the children who are served in training-schools. The difficulties with which the training-school staffs have to cope may be evidenced from a survey conducted by the author in 1959 at a school for girls with a population of less than 200. This examination disclosed the following wide assortment of children: those who were openly acting out and those who were withdrawn, both groups including a proportion of emotionally disturbed children; mentally retarded girls awaiting a vacancy to occur at a school equipped specifically to deal with them; girls subject to epileptic attacks; pregnant girls; girls classified as schizophrenics who, in the author's estimation based on past experience with conflicting diagnoses, would spend a considerable amount of time being transferred from training-school to mental hospital and back again; girls with venereal disease; girls adjudged to be psychopathic. In addition to all of these there were what might be called the 'purely delinquent' – those who were mentally normal, who functioned adequately on a social level, and gave no evidence of being in a state of imbalance emotionally. They had been fully aware of what they were doing at the time they committed their offences; they weighed the consequences, took the chance – and were caught.

Each of these groups could be further classified. Some of the children had a high degree of intelligence, but because of truancy were retarded as

[2]M. Grunhut, *Penal Reform*, Oxford: Oxford University Press, 1948, p. 347.

much as three grades, and the problems of teaching a very bright fifteen-year-old who is grouped in an average Grade Seven class need no elaboration. Conversely there were some of subnormal intelligence who had been 'promoted' in community schools on the basis of age alone. There were girls found to have been prostituting themselves for more than two years, and girls whose only crime was to be deprived of both parents and incapable of adjusting to the demands of their several foster-parents. There were relatively naïve seventeen-year-olds and there were thirteen-year-olds whose sophistication was startling but pathetic.

Beyond all these differences there was evidence that there were two basic groups with vastly differing needs. On the one hand there were children who needed to establish acceptable personal habits and work-habits, to develop certain interests and skills, and to learn to live at peace with the rules and the standards of the school in order that they might learn to live with the laws of society that govern behaviour. On the other hand there were children in need of treatment rather than training, whose past offences and present attitudes and conduct were symptomatic of emotional disturbances, the causes of which needed to be ascertained.

It cannot be denied that there are children in training-schools who should not be there. There are three main reasons for this, the first of which is the absence in the community of variant forms of care. This obstacle could be largely overcome if the courts were to increase the extent to which they use foster-care, but it will not be practicable for them to do so until a more positive and wholehearted attempt is made to find good foster-homes; this, in turn, is likely to happen only when the present remuneration to foster-parents is substantially increased. Payments are at present completely inadequate, and appear particularly low when compared to the costs of maintaining a child in institutional care. The time has surely come to acknowledge that foster-families render an important service. Though no one would wish that maintenance rates were such as to make this a profitable enterprise, equally no one would wish to see families financially penalized for accepting a heavy responsibility and acting as good citizens should.

The second reason for children being in training-schools who should not be there is the tendency to look at the symptom rather than the cause. The third is the tendency to think in terms of administrative convenience rather than in terms of the child's need, so that he is viewed as being primarily a 'health' problem, a 'welfare' problem, a 'reform' problem, and only secondarily as a child in need of special care. In the case of a pregnant girl, for example, the fact of pregnancy rather than the fact of delinquency should be the prime consideration; such cases could be better cared for in the same fashion as girls who are found to be pregnant but not adjudged delinquent. In one sense all unmarried mothers are delinquent, and unless there are exceptional circumstances it is unfair that some are committed to training-schools while others are treated in the community. Similarly with the mentally ill and the retarded: there may be insufficient hospital facilities; the court may be reluctant to place children in hospitals designed for adults; or it may be easier for the court to get a child into a training-school than into a mental hospital. But none of these difficulties excuses the practice of using the training-school as a substitute mental hospital.

It is suggested that there are basically four classes of children whom the courts should commit to training-schools: children who must be committed for the protection of the community or for their own protection; those for whom institutional care is indicated as a result of a thorough clinical and diagnostic evaluation; those who need the security of consistently applied and easily assimilated rules and regulations; and those whose experience in their parental relationships has been such as to make it difficult for them to establish positive relationships with adults, towards whom they are hostile or suspicious, and whose need is for an environment where close personal relationships will not be demanded of them.

The training-schools directly administered by departments of government cannot control intake, as can their private counterparts; they must accept all the children committed by the courts. So long as this situation exists, so long as there is an absence of community facilities to deal with severely maladjusted children, so long as appropriate and specialized care is not available to treat the cause rather than the symptom, the training-school staffs will continue to struggle against the tide and will see a gradual reduction in the effectiveness of their total program.

It may be argued that a classification program within a provincial network of institutions will go far to alleviate the problem. This is true, but not every province has a population large enough to warrant such a program. Ontario, which has eight training-schools that are the direct responsibility of a government department, has a classification system for boys and one for girls, but arrangements like this are plainly not possible in provinces where the total number of children committed is too small to allow a variety of institutions. As the population increases, however, the need for more institutions will be evident, and it is likely that an increasing amount of consideration will have to be given to the relative merits of different forms and degrees of classification.

At present there are two forms of classification in operation in all provinces: children are separated according to sex and according to religious beliefs, the Catholics being separated from the non-Catholics. One can detect no evidence that there is likely to be change in these two areas. The growing number of workers in the field who believe that co-educational training-schools have decided advantages over those that deal with a single sex have, of course, some weighty arguments. The atmosphere is a more natural one, and an opportunity is provided to teach boys and girls how to appreciate and co-operate with each other in a healthy and desirable association. Certainly a strong case has been made for co-educational schools for younger children in order that brothers and sisters may be kept together; since separation from parents can be an overwhelming experience for a child, it is surely inhuman to separate brother and sister as well.[3] These arguments, however, are apparently of insufficient weight to convince administrators, who have grave doubts whether they are not more than outweighed by the problems that would arise, whether the cost of the necessary additional supervision could be justified, and – on surer grounds – whether community attitudes are sufficiently advanced to allow the provision of a co-educational training-school.

Ontario is the only province in which classification in any extended form is apparent. As indicated already, boys are separated from girls and Catholics from non-Catholics as in the other provinces, and then boys and girls are subject to different systems of classification. Girls are classified by a single criterion, namely, the degree of supervision that each child is thought to require; the four girls' schools range from a small maximum-security unit at one end of the scale to a school (Port Bolster) that approximates a group foster-home at the other where children are truly part of the local community and have a great deal of freedom and unsupervised time. Between these two extremes are two larger schools (Galt and Lindsay), which have different degrees of control and supervision. The classification takes place at a reception centre where a social history of each girl is compiled and she is given a battery of psychological tests and sometimes a psychiatric examination. On the basis of the data compiled, plus the observations of the supervisory staff, she is allocated to the appropriate school. A girl can be transferred from one school to another if it appears that an environmental change will help her.

The system for boys is based on several criteria: younger boys are separated from older boys and are housed at one school (Cobourg); older boys with an academic bent are sent to a second school (Simcoe); those who appear likely to profit from a vocational training are sent to a third (Bowmanville); the fourth school (Guelph) is a small maximum-security

[3]*Standards of Foster Care for Children in Institutions,* New York: Child Welfare League of America, 1947.

unit to which boys may be transferred from one of the other schools if they have given evidence of being completely unable to adjust there. The last school contains the persistent absconder, the violent aggressive boy who has assaulted other boys or disrupted the school program by his constant acting-out behaviour, and the boy whose offence has been such that the protection of the community makes maximum security necessary (at the time of writing, there are four murderers in a total population of forty).

In the province of Quebec, classification in the over-all planned sense does not exist, since each school is privately operated and works independently of the others, but Quebec has advantages not possessed by the remaining eight provinces in that certain schools specialize in one or more aspects of treatment or training. One school (Boscoville) places great emphasis on a unique relationship that is fostered between the 'éducateur' and the boy, and on group therapy; another (Mont St. Antoine) has a remarkable vocational-training program; another (Shawbridge) concentrates on training boys in the practice of farming.

FACILITIES AND PROGRAMS IN THE SCHOOLS

Physical Facilities

The schools and their facilities vary a great deal in kind and nature, as could be expected. The largest, Mont St. Antoine, has a capacity of 450; among the smaller schools, the Saskatchewan Home for Boys and the Ontario Training School for Girls, at Port Bolster, each has fewer than twenty pupils in residence. Most larger schools are of the cottage type, in which each school is divided into separate houses or cottages, while the smaller schools are 'one-roof' establishments. Most are open, that is with no special emphasis on custody, but two schools of maximum security have been built in the last seven years: the Ontario Training School for Boys, at Guelph, which has capacity for forty-eight boys, and Centre Bertholet at Rivière des Prairies, Quebec, which is capable of accommodating ninety boys and sixty girls. The latter is not in any sense co-educational as there is no free mixing of boys and girls, the two units being quite separate.

Some say that to build a maximum-security institution for juveniles is to admit defeat, but this contention is hard to defend. It must be recognized that some individuals, for the sake of the community, must be contained until it appears unlikely that they will repeat their offences. In 1960-1, for instance, two juveniles in Ontario were found guilty of murder; for them, the only alternative to a children's maximum-security institution would have been the penitentiary or the reformatory, with the obvious attendant disadvantages. There are also juveniles who have not only failed to respond to the care and treatment provided in the open training-school, but have had a disrupting effect upon the development of others. Finally, there are the persistent absconders who only seem able to settle down and come to grips with their problems when the temptation to abscond has been removed.

In the absence of any research data, one can only say that experience so far would tend to support the belief that the physical security of the closed school seems to make a positive contribution towards solving the emotional insecurity of some juveniles. On the other hand, there are very real dangers. The existence of the maximum-security school as a place to which children can be transferred can become a crutch for the ineffective superintendent at an open school; the child inmate's feeling of dependency can be increased, so that he becomes 'institutionalized' and less capable of standing on his own feet; the transition from the tightly closed school to the open world outside may place too heavy a burden upon the insecure adolescent; and the emphasis on custody can have a deleterious effect upon the treatment program. The open school offers more hope for the eventual re-education of children because it provides more opportunity for integration with local communities, and because children can be more easily encouraged to develop self-reliance, independence, and a sense of responsibility in a setting where they are placed in the position of making choices and decisions for themselves.

The open school must always, by its very nature, face the problem of hostile community feelings that arise when children abscond. If children are given the opportunity of running away, as indeed they must be, then some are going to take that opportunity. Staff members worry about a young child being on his own without money and perhaps a long way from friends, but they are anxious too lest he commit a further offence by stealing money to buy food and clothing or by stealing a car to make good his escape. These offences are most likely to occur within the local community, and goodwill between the community and the school can evaporate quickly when local residents discover that absconders have driven away in their cars. It is therefore essential that there be a good public-relations program that includes the interpretation of this problem to the community. There is no doubt that communities can be helped to realize that the number of absconders is in itself no indication of the success or failure of a school. A low rate of absconding does indeed indicate that the school is adequately fulfilling one of its functions, the custody of the child, but it is quite possible for such a rate to result from the sacrifice of training to the demand for custody.

While the 'open' institutions are built without bolts, bars, or high walls,

257

Donald Sinclair

there is actually a varying degree of custody within this apparent 'openness'. At some schools that claim to be open, when one is shown around one soon discovers that every door is kept locked and is unlocked only by a staff member; others can truly claim that the doors are never locked. This distinction, however, may not in itself be an accurate measure of the custodial nature of the school, since custody is more a matter of staff attitudes and expectations than of material restrictions.

Although as stated earlier, facilities vary greatly across the country, many of the schools are extremely well equipped, particularly in comparison with their counterparts in other countries. Swimming-pools and gymnasia can be seen in many; those at St. Joseph's Training School, Alfred, Ontario, and at Notre Dame de Laval, Laval des Rapides, Quebec, are splendid examples of such facilities. Vocational training of one kind or another is available in most schools; its calibre and extent vary but it is probably seen at its best at Mont St. Antoine in Montreal. Among the schools that have a program of farm training are those at Shawbridge, Quebec, and at Bowmanville, Ontario. All the Roman Catholic schools have excellent facilities for worship; the remainder all have daily or weekly worship, but many have no church or chapel and these hold services in auditoria or classrooms.

Programs in the Schools

In most schools an analysis of the program would reveal that training is of a fivefold nature: academic, vocational, recreational, social, and spiritual. If the program is to be concerned with treatment as well as training, clinical personnel must also be available who are able to diagnose a child's problem and help him by counselling and by therapeutic measures to solve it. While many schools claim that their programs are treatment oriented, these claims, unfortunately, are not correct unless the word treatment is used in an unusual way; for example, it is misleading to talk of treatment in the Ontario Training Schools when some of the schools employ neither social worker nor psychologist; others employ one but not the other and none of them have full-time psychiatric service. Certainly all schools encourage the child to develop good work-habits, acceptable personal habits, a measure of self-control, and an ability to keep the rules. Treatment, however, is much more than this, since its concern is not with fitting the child into a mould. Those treating the child must attempt to diagnose the root cause of his inability to adjust in his own home and in his own community, must search for the fundamental motives of his behaviour, and within the school must plan a program tailored to fit his needs.

258

If any of the provincial government departments that are responsible for training-schools intend to establish a program of treatment for each child, they will need to emphasize the importance of the initial work that is done with the child immediately upon reception. Clinical personnel would receive reports from agencies that have previously been concerned with the child, and the comments of teachers, probation officers, parents, and others would be carefully studied. The school psychologist would give the child intelligence, aptitude, and personality tests; the social worker would compile a social history; where necessary a psychiatric examination would be ordered; the child would receive a thorough medical examination; his attitude and conduct during these first few important days would be observed closely by staff. On the basis of the information compiled during the reception period, certain important decisions would be made. The needs of the child determined during this period may dictate, for example, whether he sleeps in a dormitory or in a single room; whether he moves in an academic or a vocational stream; whether he is placed in a cottage with older boys, younger boys, or those his own age; whether he is put under the care of this supervisor or that one; and they will indicate whether he needs remedial teaching, and whether he should be a member of a small cottage where almost individual attention can be given to him or whether initially he will benefit more from the anonymity that a larger group can provide. In short, a plan would be conceived that will be of real help to the child; it would need to be communicated to all the staff who work with him, so that all may work together towards the same goal; it would need to be flexible, so that as the child matures and develops a sense of self-adequacy and grows more confident in his relationships with others, changes can be made accordingly.

In most training-schools a child placed in an academic program will find that the curriculum and standards of education are those of his community school. In general, he will find that the classes are somewhat smaller and that he is therefore given more individual attention. While in the great majority of schools, academic classes are held on the premises, in some, students in Grade Ten and higher attend the local high school.

The boy who is advised to follow a course of vocational training will have a wide range of occupations to choose from if he is committed to one of the larger institutions such as Mont St. Antoine or Bowmanville, but may have little choice, if any, at a smaller one. At some schools, the instruction in certain trades is of the quality necessary to develop highly skilled workers – the machine-shop course at Guelph is an example – but this is not generally the aim of vocational training, nor should it be. For one thing, the time available for training is too short. Vocational training is used to give a boy a sense of achievement, to awaken an interest, develop a skill, co-ordinate hand and eye, and make the boy familiar with the use of basic tools, rather than to give him a trade. Unfortunately, the standards of teaching in the vocational training are rarely comparable to those in the academic program: there is an urgent need for short-term, intensive teacher-training courses for the technical instructors.

There is much less vocational training for girls. It may be that this is a lingering reflection of the former state of affairs in society generally. Usually, only some form of domestic training – laundering, sewing, cooking, and the like – and some commercial training are available, though an occasional school provides a course in hairdressing.

The standards of recreational and social education, perhaps surprisingly, are somewhat disappointing. The emphasis, naturally, is on team games, but though the clichés of the give-and-take of games and the development of team spirit are often aired, the observer may be excused for wondering whether the recreational period is any more than an opportunity for staff to relax while keeping the children active. In some schools it appears to be assumed that leisure-time activity is more a matter of the staff's leisure than of the children's. The result is that the natural athletes continue to shine while those who are reluctant, perhaps afraid, to take part and who need to be encouraged are either forced to participate – in which case they merely go through the motions – or are left out of things 'because they will spoil it for others'. Outdoor recreation, however, in spite of its general lack of direction and organization, is of a higher standard than the indoor. Television – a good educative tool in certain circumstances – has become a refuge for the inadequate supervisor who lacks ideas of his own and for the lazy supervisor who cannot be bothered to plan his evening's program. In this, as in other matters, there are exceptions among the schools, but they are few. In fairness to staff, however, it must be strongly emphasized that nearly all the schools are overcrowded, with the result that each staff member must supervise so many children that it is almost impossible to provide adequate recreational programming.

Setting high standards in the academic, vocational, recreational, and spiritual re-education of the child will not of itself guarantee progress. Excellent facilities and an excellent program on paper may amount to little in effect, unless the climate of the school is such that it will help nurture the child's personal growth. Where the general atmosphere is friendly and accepting and where staff members show, by their attitudes and by the interest they take, that they are genuinely interested in helping the children, rich benefits will be reaped from the program. On the other hand, no wealth of variety and specialization in programming can offset the effect of the supervisor who is unable to handle his own hostility, who sees the children as 'young punks who need to be taught a lesson', who uses his position to meet his own needs rather than theirs, or who cannot in his own daily conduct live up to the precepts he quotes to the children.

The child's progress through the school is noted and reported on to varying degrees. In some schools he is interviewed at intervals by a board of review composed of key staff members; in others the interview is with the superintendent alone, though he is furnished with reports from staff members. There remain a few schools in which little systematic note of the effect of the school upon the child appears to be taken, and where, consequently, he receives little guidance regarding his progress. Where regular reports are submitted to the superintendent, a survey shows that though there is the expected variation between schools, six points are considered to be important in assessing the extent of the progress made: attitude to authority, relationship with other children, general attitude and conduct, personal habits, work-habits, and the degree to which the child has been able to develop a system of values.

Ideally, the length of time spent by the child in an institution would be governed by the extent of his response to the plan of treatment and training. When the response is maximum, the point has been reached when he can return to the community, because now he can exercise self-control, can get along with his peers, is not hostile to those in authority, and has given evidence of a growing sense of confidence and self-reliance. There are, however, many factors that make the ideal almost impossible to achieve. Overcrowding is the primary one; it can upset the most carefully conceived plan. Most schools are forced to release children who are far from prepared for the transition, simply to make room for others who have been committed. Secondly, there are still cases where the child is committed to a definite sentence though this is entirely contrary to the spirit of the Juvenile Delinquents Act. Thirdly, in some provinces the consent of the court that committed the child must be obtained before he can be released. Finally, some children, despite the best intentions of everyone, appear quite incapable of responding to the treatment and training provided.

There comes a point in a child's progress when he is ready to leave the school and there is a danger that beyond this point deterioration may set in. Yet there are additional factors that every superintendent must consider. The child may be ready in the middle of a school term and his education may be set back a year by his inability to make the necessary difficult adjustment when he goes out; a job having been found for him, the school may be informed at the last moment that it has now been filled; home circumstances may take a sudden change. The possibilities are endless, and due weight must be given to every reason for and against the child's departure at this point.

A good deal of lip-service is paid to the principle that while the child is being prepared for his return to the community, preparations must also be made with the community school, the home, and other agencies to receive him, but practice falls short of honouring this principle. The duty of visiting the child's home while he is in the school should obviously be carried out by an after-care officer who is to be responsible for supervising him when he is released. Unfortunately, after-care workers suffer, as do their colleagues in the schools, from case-loads that are much too heavy. As an example, in 1963, one after-care worker at the Ontario Training School for Boys, Cobourg, had a case-load of ninety-two boys who had been released and who were being directly supervised by him; in addition the worker was expected to develop a relationship with those boys presently in the school who would eventually be his responsibility upon release. During the same year, a staff of three after-care workers at St. John's Training School, Uxbridge, were supervising a total case-load of nearly three hundred boys and again were faced with the almost impossible task of not only doing so, but of attempting to become acquainted with the problems of those boys presently undergoing training who would form the future case-load.

As with other aspects of the system, the pattern for after-care varies across the country. In some provinces it is carried out by the same department of government that administers the school, or by the same private agency; in others, by court probation officers; in some schools the after-care workers are based in the school; in other schools the workers are based in different localities throughout the province. Where the worker is based in the school, he has the advantage of being provided with an opportunity of getting to know the child, but suffers from the disadvantage of having little opportunity to develop contacts in the community from which the child comes. Where the worker is based in the community the reverse applies.

Finding foster-homes is an important part of the after-care worker's job and is becoming increasingly difficult in all parts of the country. Among the factors that make it difficult are the following: an increasing number of women are working outside their homes and are reluctant to assume further domestic responsibilities; the maintenance rates paid to foster-parents provide hardly sufficient money for the child's upkeep let alone a payment for services; some potential foster-parents fear interference by the child's natural parents; others fear interference from the placing agency, which periodically inspects the homes and which offers advice on how the child should be handled. Because of the shortage of foster-homes, unfortunately some homes are used that are doubtful providers of the nourishment children need most – stability and affection.

The time may well have arrived when the schools ought to examine the possibility of establishing group foster-homes, staffing them with foster-parents chosen for their suitability and paid a reasonable salary for their services. The group home would not only ease the problems caused by the shortage of normal foster-homes, it would also benefit children who are ready to leave the institution but who are not yet able to adapt comfortably to a situation in which they are the 'only' children in a home, who cannot accept the intensely personal relationship in such a situation, but who can accept the less personal nature of relationships in a group home.

Some schools (for instance, Marymound, the Roman Catholic School for Girls, in Winnipeg) have experimented with a form of 'halfway house', a separate institutional facility where the child is given many of the benefits of home life while still being under the supervision of the institution. Such a plan can be seen to have great potential, but it is, of course, no substitute for the foster-home, because when the child leaves the halfway house the problem of finding a home still remains to be solved.

PUNISHMENT AND DISCIPLINE

The nature of the controls that a school imposes, the form of the punishments it uses, and the extent to which it can develop a system of discipline that both protects the child and helps to prevent him from offending against the social order of the institution are major factors in its administration. Few would disagree with the following statement from one of the more admirable publications on training-school standards:

> Not only is the question of discipline and punishment a crucial treatment consideration, it is also the crux of the administrative problem of conducting a training-school program.[4]

The core of the problem of punishment might best be summed up in this way: how can the school teach a child to accept the responsibility for his own actions without using forms of punishment that only embitter him or further aggravate his problem?

The viewpoint is sometimes expressed that children themselves would

[4]Children's Bureau, United States Department of Health, Education and Welfare, *Institutions Serving Delinquent Children,* Washington: Government Printing Office, 1957, p. 98.

263

rather be punished by old-fashioned methods that are now outlawed than be counselled and prompted into achieving some insight into the reasons for their misconduct. This view neglects some important factors. Admittedly, some children seem to take punishment gladly, but their motives for doing so need to be known. For some, punishment purges the offence; the slate is wiped clean, the debt is paid – and more debts can now be accumulated without uncomfortable pangs of conscience. One child will seek punishment because he has accepted on his shoulders the burden of responsibility for the disturbed family life from which he has come; children are prone to indulge in such self-censure to an extent that is often underestimated. Another will seek to be punished in order to strengthen his belief that adults in authority are enemies.

To acknowledge that such cases exist is not to say that children should never be punished. What is indicated, however, is that before any punishment is given several factors should be considered, including: the exact nature of the offence, the circumstances that provoked it, the child's needs, his possible motives if he should be seeking punishment, the adult's possible motives in awarding it, and the degree to which the child is responsible for his own actions. It has already been made clear in this chapter that there are some children in training-schools who cannot be held responsible for their actions. For them punishment is no answer. At the other end of the scale are those who break society's rules deliberately, in full realization of what they are doing. These must take responsibility for their actions. Acceptance of responsibility for any action means basically that one must suffer or enjoy its consequences. Not only must the child who deliberately breaks rules, fully aware of what he does, suffer the consequences, but the consequences should be such as are likely to deter repetition of the act. No knowledge of the wrongdoer's history, environment, heredity, and so on must affect the inevitability of the consequences (though they should affect the nature of the consequences) once his responsibility is established. The saying 'To know all is to forgive all' may be true; our social structure is not at present based on this, however, but on the assumption that each must be held responsible for himself unless he is adjudged insane.

Two difficulties bedevil the training-school in this question of punishment. First, between the above two extremes is the whole range of degrees of responsibility; we do not as yet know how it can be determined how much responsibility exists in each case. Secondly, there is no certainty that punishment will prove to have any deterrent value. In this area we have little knowledge but many suspicions: we suspect that for the unpleasant consequences to be effective they must be directly connected in the mind of the youngster with his part in the prohibited action; we suspect that their long-term effectiveness depends upon the memory of the present unpleasant situation carrying over to a future temptation; we suspect that they will not be effective unless there is a distinction in the child's mind between the individual who awards the punishment and the actual cause of the punishment. We are sure of one thing, the carry-over value does not depend upon the severity of the punishment; this much, past history and modern research have both made clear.

Punishment there may have to be, but punishment alone is not enough. Indeed, as has been intimated, it can be endured – or even enjoyed – proudly or triumphantly. Schools where it is borne in mind, however, that youngsters, and especially youngsters in training-schools, need the approval, admiration, and affection of those they admire and respect manage to turn this need to the children's advantage. What deters the child from repeating his offence is not that he has lost this privilege or that, not that he has lost the company of his friends, but that he has lost some of his supervisor's feeling for him by letting his supervisor down. The good supervisor can make it obvious to him that his misconduct has damaged their relationship, but he must be careful to make it equally obvious that, though it has been damaged, it has not been destroyed. In other words, it is made clear to the child that, though he has for the time being lost some of the supervisor's goodwill, there is still some remaining and the relationship can be restored to its former level. However outrageous an offence may be, the supervisor disapproves but does not reject. He is mature enough to recognize that the child will come round if the measure taken and the disapproval indicated were fair, just, and deserved and that, although the child's immaturity will cause the supervisor to be temporarily upset, the child will realize that the door has not been completely closed on him.

However, although disapproval or a temporary lessening of good feeling is sufficient in many cases, additional corrective measures will be indicated in others. Some of the measures which have been used or are still in use in Canadian training-schools are examined in the following paragraphs.

In 1946, when Albert Deutsch published his findings of the punitive practices he found in use in some training-schools in the United States, the American public was shocked to discover how sadistic these practices were.[5] In 1947, and again in 1959, the British public was equally shocked by revelations of conditions in some of their approved schools; a teacher was shot and killed by a boy at Standon Farm School in 1947, and a

[5] A. Deutsch, *Our Rejected Youth*, New York: Little, Brown, 1950.

mass outbreak and disturbance occurred at Carlton School in 1959. In the British cases the official enquiries showed that hitting, slapping, and kicking of boys by the staff were not uncommon and that other ineffective and punitive devices were also resorted to.[6] Canadian schools have been fortunate to date to escape the notoriety that attends this type of incident or inquiry, and indeed it is extremely unlikely that an inquiry would reveal practices similar to those Deutsch found. The fact remains, however, that there are schools in Canada that use one or more of three forms of punishment that, while none is sadistic nor as devilishly ingenious as some of those Deutsch describes, can have a demoralizing effect upon a child.

The first of these is to allow one or more senior children to apply corrective measures. This step places a burden of responsibility on the senior child that he should not be expected to carry, and can be quite disastrous. Inevitably, it results in the 'strong man' of the group assuming a judge's role and being more than kind to his friends and less than kind to the remainder. Scapegoats are quickly found for any offence; in such circumstances the existence of the passive, withdrawn child is pitiful. In general, the measures invoked by the children themselves are much harsher than any that adults would devise, and decisions that appear to the children to be just and fair often bear little relation to the needs of the individual offender. In addition, a child who accepts this sort of authority with the best of intentions can hardly help becoming an intermediary between the supervisor and his fellows; it often happens that the group first looks upon him with suspicion and then isolates him.

In the second form of punishment, the group is punished for the misdeeds of one member. This is used in some institutions when an offence has been committed to which the culprit will not own up. The group becomes the scapegoat. Apart from the obvious unfairness to the innocent, the choice is quickly recognized by the group as a measure of desperation. To use it at all is foolish, since it inevitably leads to a battle between the group's loyalty and the staff's pride, but the foolishness becomes criminality when the staff blackmails the group into ganging up on the luckless culprit. When tactics of this kind are resorted to, any gap that may exist already between staff and youngsters becomes an unbridgeable gulf. The 'we' that signifies the whole school community immediately divides into 'we' and 'they'.

The third form, corporal punishment, is one on which most people

[6]Report of Committee of Enquiry into the Conduct of Standon Farm Approved School, London: H.M.S.O., 1947, and *Disturbances at the Carlton Approved School*, London: H.M.S.O., 1959.

have very definite views, but they are nearly always views that spring from emotional, rather than from rational, grounds. Knowledge of the revengeful or sadistic motives, which in the past often led to its imposition, and of the harshness and severity with which it was sometimes administered has led to a revulsion against its use today either in institutions or the home setting. Some parents question whether this reaction has not resulted in the baby being thrown out with the bath water. They reason that not to use corporal punishment merely because it has been abused in the past is comparable to banning the use of morphia or heroin for the same reason. Whatever advantages, however, it may have when applied by parents to young children at home, its use with older children in an institutional setting is fraught with danger. It is difficult to control; the mildest form of hitting or slapping cannot be tolerated, since the point at which a cuff becomes a blow is difficult to determine. It is precisely what some youngsters want to see, because it reinforces their feelings about the hostility of adults and because it gives them the satisfaction of seeing the staff use the child's weapon. All too often its use indicates a lack of self-control on the part of the adult concerned, or is clear evidence that he has not learned his job properly and is taking what he considers the easy way out. It is frequently no more than a relief-vent for the angry or exasperated adult, and in such a case it can be both cruel and humiliating. Few people, even some with years of experience, seem to realize fully to what extent children coming into institutions fear being hit. In many cases, this is the first topic of inquiry when they meet their fellows – a very understandable inquiry, especially for those who have had many beatings in the past.

Two forms of punishment that do not have the demoralizing effect of those described above, but the values of which are very open to question, are practised quite widely. In one of these the school uses a system of merit and demerit marks that are tied to certain rewards and punishments. Usually the marks are related to 'stages' in the school: having compiled so many marks a child is promoted to a second stage; acquisition of a further fixed number results in promotion to a third stage; finally, when the requisite total is obtained, he is released. With young children, there appears to be a very real value in this system but with the older ones it has mixed results. In a large school it is not easy to administer, and the merits or demerits can only be 'audited' on a weekly or monthly basis. In some cases, this results in a child being punished long after the offence, so the relationship of the punishment to the offence, in the child's mind, is slight. In other cases, a child may feel that having accumulated certain demerits he may as well be killed for a sheep as for a lamb, and so he offends further to make his punishment 'worth while'. Another difficulty ensues from relating the number of marks earned to a release date; there is a point in the youngster's progress when he is ready for release, but if the required marks have not been earned release must be denied. Conversely, a child who has earned the requisite number of marks for release may show obvious indications that he is not yet ready for this step. Finally, the greatest weakness of this system is that while it may be initiated with the best intentions of assessing progress in many areas of the children's development, it is so cumbersome to administer that behaviour, or misbehaviour, inevitably becomes the single criterion on which marks are assigned; the system falls down because the child who conforms will quickly earn his release, although conformity in itself is no indication of successful rehabilitation.

In the second of these two forms of punishment, offenders are assigned to a 'punishment group' whose task it is to perform all the arduous and unpleasant tasks that are part and parcel of everyday life in the school. It should not be employed without careful consideration. It creates a very real danger that some boys will come to equate all hard or distasteful work with punishment. If one of the aims of the training-school is the inculcation of good work-habits, that aim is unlikely to succeed if hard work is looked upon only as the natural consequence of misbehaviour.

Two further punitive practices deserve specific mention. One of these, segregation of the child from the remainder of his group, appears to be almost universally used in institutions. When limits have been overstepped, the use of segregation is a clear demonstration to the child that unacceptable behaviour has unpleasant consequences. When a child has obviously lost control and is liable to do damage to himself or to staff, or when he is becoming so excited that he needs to cool off, segregation is protective both to himself and to the group. In instances when a child is ready to give in but dare not because he fears the scorn, contempt, or sarcasm of the group more than he fears the adults' response, it is an excellent face-saving device. Like corporal punishment, however, it can become a crutch for the less efficient staff member, and so certain safeguards need to be erected around its use. The period of segregation should be no longer than is absolutely necessary. Nothing is more frustrating to the hyperactive child than to be shut in his room with no outlets for his bursting energy; nothing is less therapeutic to the withdrawn child than to be denied the company of others – as a punishment this is comparable to being refused a visit to the dentist. It is wise not to fix in advance the duration of the period of segregation, but to allow the child to rejoin the group when the time is ripe. Any child in segregation should be visited regularly, preferably by an adult with whom he has a good relationship; and he should be given opportunities to talk over the action that led to his being segregated. Sometimes, following the segregation of one individual, it is important that the group be encouraged to discuss the affair, since it is essential that the group view the absent member neither as a hero nor as a scapegoat. In every case, the re-entry into the group should be made as easy as possible, both for the group and for the child.

Finally, one of the most common corrective measures in use in training-schools is deprival of privileges. It is probably true to say that it carries fewer dangers than other measures do, and it can be effective without being damaging to the child. Properly used, it can be easily understood by the wrongdoer as a logical consequence of unacceptable behaviour. If a child misconducts himself during a ball-game he may be denied further participation in the game; if he refuses to get up in the morning he may have to go to bed earlier at night; if he fails to do his homework one night he may be deprived of recreation the next night. He can readily understand these consequences as being fair and just. For this measure to be successful, there must necessarily be a wealth of privileges in the program, and as with any other measure, it needs to be applied immediately so that it can be easily related by the child to the incident concerned. It is obviously of no benefit if the withdrawn privilege is not considered a privilege by the child. In other words, it is useless to deprive him of something which he feels has no value, and it is essential that what constitutes a privilege, as distinct from a pleasant aspect of the regular program, should be clearly defined. Letters and visits, for example, should be considered integral parts of the program, not privileges; to deny a child these is not only to cut off one way of working with him, but it is also unfair to others, because parents and friends may suffer. The only time denying a visit from parents is justified is when there is a sound therapeutic reason.

Each of the measures outlined is a tool that can fall into the wrong hands. The severest of measures when used by a competent adult who understands the child can be more effective – or do less damage to the child's personality – than the mildest of measures used by someone without understanding. Some schools, aware of this, place in the hands of the superintendent alone all responsibility for deciding which measure is most appropriate. While there is much to be said for this method, there is surely as much to be said for training the person working directly with the child to use the sanctions wisely himself. If it is true that the key to rehabilitation lies in the relationship of the supervisor to the child, then it follows that breaches of discipline should be handled by the supervisor. Referring the matter to the superintendent may be sometimes wise, but it can result in

269

a time-lag between the offence and the punishment. It also may be no more than an excuse to dump into the superintendent's lap a problem that perhaps has been created by the worker; this can cause the child to lose respect for the worker.

Some schools have been able to evolve a compromise between these two approaches. The supervisor is given the authority and the responsibility to deal with situations as they arise, and only refers to the superintendent those incidents that (1) give evidence that the child is seriously disturbed, (2) endanger the treatment and training of other children, (3) are likely to prejudice community opinion against the school, or (4) on the surface appear to warrant segregation.

Punishment may be defined, whichever form is used, as any action taken, after an offence is committed, with the intention of restoring the social balance that the offence disturbed and of dissuading the offender from repeating his offence. Discipline, on the other hand, is a constant and continous process; its aim is to produce in the individual that measure of self-control, self-organization, and respect for the needs and rights of others that makes for orderly living. It may well be that the most important tasks in a training-school are to establish controls, encourage relationships, and to provide facilities that will help the children achieve and maintain a sense of order and purpose in their lives.

Controls

The school must set controls, both to establish orderly behaviour of the group and to protect the individual. The child requires help in positively directing his natural aggressiveness, in learning to restrain his desires and impulses, and in recognizing the needs of others, since he is neither strong enough nor wise enough to make final judgments about himself or about his conduct. One or two schools attempt to foster an extremely permissive climate, perhaps in reaction to the concepts of earlier days when institutions repressed children by imposing rigid controls and demanding obedience and conformity for their own sake. The older concepts gave little of lasting value to the child, but the benefits of swinging to the other extreme are also questionable. The question for any training-school is not whether permissiveness or conformity should prevail, but rather what degree of permissiveness is best for any one child at any given point in his development.

The sanction for controls should lie not in a written list of rules and regulations so much as in the implied and expressed expectations of staff. Some rules are necessary, but they should be kept to the minimum consistent with the needs of the children; they should be intelligible to all the children, by whom they must be recognized as being reasonable and in their own interests; they should be fairly administered by people whom the children respect; and they should be constantly checked to ensure that they have not outlived their usefulness.

However few and wise the rules, they will be broken. A child acting under the power of an influence he cannot control, or reacting to an overwhelming situation, is almost certain to break rules; but so, too, will the least disturbed and the best behaved of children out of sheer desire to test the limits. Limit-testing is an essential step in the process of growth, for it is only thus that children will learn to set their own limits as they grow increasingly independent. Much of the so-called misconduct in a training-school is really no more than a testing of limits. It is not suggested that, being recognized, it should be ignored, any more than that it should be repressed. Some misconduct should be ignored, but when this is advisable, and the extent to which attention should be paid to it, will vary with individual children and with the circumstances.

This may not be welcome reading to those who work in schools where it is believed that the only principle necessary to achieve good discipline is that of being 'firm and fair'; but the phrase 'firm and fair' is often only something to hide behind and it means different things to different people. To some, firmness means treading hard on all infractions, and fairness means dealing with all like offences in exactly the same way, that is, using standard punishments for the different offences. Such a viewpoint pays heed neither to the child's accountability nor to the circumstances surrounding the offence.

To what extent, however, can programs be individualized so that a child's accountability can be roughly assessed? Obviously there is more hope in the smaller schools. In the larger schools the view is sometimes taken that such a degree of individual attention not only is impossible, but would be of doubtful value. The argument is that if one child's action is ignored at a particular stage in his development because it is considered good that it should be, while another child is punished for a similar misdemeanour, the supervisor can be accused of favouritism. The answer to this argument, however, is that if the relationship between the supervisor and the children concerned is a healthy one favouritism is not likely to be suspected.

Relationships between Staff and Children
The nature of the relationship between the staff and the children is probably the most important factor in the establishment not only of a positive system of discipline, but also of a healthy climate within the schools. Vital

to this relationship is the manner in which the child is dealt with; to repeat any mismanagement he has experienced previously is fatal. Extreme rigidity and extreme permissiveness are both bad, but inconsistency is even worse.

Consistency in dealing with a group of delinquent children is not easy to achieve. It is more easily achieved in a smaller school, or in one, large or small, that has a clearly defined policy wholeheartedly supported by the staff. The supervisor's philosophy is reflected in his attitude to the child and in his conduct in the school. If children find him to lie or evade the truth, if he acts on the principle of 'do as I say, not as I do', if he tries to come down to the child's level but still expects obedience when he asks for it, he will be resented.

If the supervisor has no firm beliefs to govern his attitude and conduct, he will judge each situation as it arises, on the spur of the moment, and cannot avoid being inconsistent. Nor will he be able to inspire in the children the trust and respect that is essential. Children are no different from adults in that, though they have to take orders from their superiors, their self-esteem is damaged only when the order comes from one whom they can neither trust nor respect. Not only will the supervisor who has the respect of the group have his orders obeyed, but the group will not feel that they are losing face or demeaning themselves by obeying them.

Unless the supervisor's philosophy is based on respect for each individual and his worth, there is the further danger that he will use his work to give himself certain emotional satisfactions and to meet his own needs rather than those of the children. The need to be liked and admired, for example, is common to all, but the training-school is no place for staff to meet this need within themselves. The seeker of popularity is a nuisance who is doomed to fail. Young people, realizing that a supervisor will allow them to have things their own way because he cannot face the unpopularity that may ensue from denying them, increase their demands from day to day until the point is reached where someone has to clamp down. The boys rightly view this as inconsistency. Before the clamping down, the supervisor has probably used promises or threats in an effort both to exact obedience and to remain popular; this makes for poor discipline, particularly when the promises cannot be kept and the threats cannot be followed through. The unfulfilled promise is bound to earn a child's distrust just as the threat that is not implemented when it is unheeded is bound to lose his respect. The search for popularity is not always easily detected. It is being pursued by the supervisor who remains silent when a fellow staff member is being criticized by children, and by the supervisor who condones with a smile a glaring example of unmannerly behaviour or cheap humour. Even the habit of some staff of adopting the jargon of the children is a mild expression of the same fault.

Another way in which many training-school workers seek to meet their own needs through their work is in their use of authority. Adults caring for children in a training-school not only have a great responsibility, they also have a great deal of power, and there is no doubt that some sadistic satisfaction can be obtained from a malicious exploitation of that power. The dictatorial supervisor who enjoys the power, authority, and control that he can exercise over young people is not respecting the dignity of the individual. He is not educating his charges, but exploiting them in the interests of his own vanity. This type of worker not only abuses his authority, but often compounds his offence by implying that he is right and that others are misguided. To say 'When you are with me, you will do it my way' is to reflect upon other staff, apart from constituting a direct challenge to young people.

It is usually recognized that it is vital for the supervisor to gain and to hold the respect of the children, but less often that this respect will not be forthcoming unless the children themselves are first respected. In young people respect is like affection or trust; they cannot give it unless and until they have received it themselves. Without respecting a boy it is possible to make him obey or conform, but obedience and conformity ought not to be the goal. It should not be the function of the schools to produce slaves or robots, best prepared, perhaps, to obey a gang-leader or conform to a gang-code, but rather to produce children trained to be self-reliant, self-respecting, and self-disciplined. The supervisor must show his respect for the child in innumerable small ways: the way he listens to him with courtesy and attention; the way he speaks to him without scorn or sarcasm; the way he recognizes his individual characteristics; the way he handles his problems and his requests, with patience, tact, and honesty.

In brief, the relationship between the adults and the children constitutes the single most important factor affecting discipline within the school; and this relationship is dependent to a large extent upon the strength of each adult's character, the example he sets, his willingness and ability to learn, and his recognition that he must be accepting and friendly in his attitude towards the children and must deal with them as consistently as is possible.

TRAINING-SCHOOL STAFF

In order to nurture the total growth of the child it is necessary for the training-school to employ individuals with different skills and abilities, for example, cooks, gardeners, teachers, social workers, psychologists. Ironically, those who work most closely with the children, the houseparents or supervisors, are more often than not the only staff members appointed without having had either training or experience in the job they have to do.

The work of the supervisor encompasses four broad areas. He must develop a positive relationship with each child, and do so in such a manner that he is consistent but pays heed to individual differences. He must protect and control the child, yet allow him to express himself to the degree necessary for his development. He must be able to organize the daily life of the children in such a manner that, although a sense of order and security prevails, they are given the opportunity to adventure and experiment in a program infinite in its variety. He must integrate his efforts with those of other staff so that the techniques and methods essential to successful fulfilment of each child's treatment plan are applied consistently by all.

Whether he can succeed in these four areas will depend upon several factors, the most important of which are:

1. The number of children for whom he is directly responsible;
2. His own qualities – his knowledge of children and his skill at working with them in addition to his personal attributes;
3. The extent to which the school trains and develops him;
4. The extent to which the policy and philosophy of the school are clearly defined and made known to him;
5. The availability of funds to implement the policy;
6. The amount of conflict between individual staff members in a variety of roles, some of whom may see their own roles as more important than those of their fellows; and
7. The pressures of community attitudes, particularly those of the locality in which the school is situated.

The number of supervisory staff differs with the size of the school and the school's purpose. If a school sees its purpose as no more than the temporary detention of children, the ratio of staff to children can be much smaller than is possible in a school that is intent upon providing the maximum degree of training and treatment for each child. While in general, schools employ far too few staff, there are some notable exceptions. The Ontario Training School for Boys, at Guelph, for instance, has two staff members for every three children, and the school at Port Bolster, Ontario, has a slightly higher proportion than this. It should be recognized, however, that these are both very small schools, that the figures given are those for the total staff employed, not merely the child-care or supervisory staff, that supervision is exercised on a 24-hours-a-day basis all year round, and that when vacation time and week-ends off are taken into consideration the actual working ratios are far less imposing. At Guelph, for example, the number of children supervised by one staff member is usually never more than twelve.

In the larger schools it is not unusual to find more than forty children supervised by one staff member. It is questionable whether in these circumstances much recognition can be given to individual differences. It is not surprising that the charge is often levelled at training-schools that they place undue emphasis on conformity, for faced with direct responsibility for such numbers of children, the average supervisor quickly realizes that control is most easily achieved by the simple device of having everyone engage in the same activity at the same time. It is unlikely that any school will agree that conformity is one of its goals, but it is true that conformity receives emphasis simply because it is a means of achieving control, which is an acknowledged goal. That control can be achieved without emphasis on conformity is evident in smaller institutions where the staff has a group, rather than a mass, of children to work with, but any attempt to minimize conformity is likely to fail unless it is accompanied by a reduction in the number of children for whom any single staff member is held responsible. It is extremely difficult in the larger schools to establish controls without undue regimentation.

While there are many able and talented supervisors employed in the schools, superintendents in general believe that they do not attract a sufficient number of high calibre. The reasons are probably similar to those reported in the United States where there is a like shortage. One study cited low salaries, lack of recognition of competence, the effect of political appointments on the continuity of professional programs, and the effect of civil service restrictions on the mobility of employment.[7] Another held that, in any field of endeavour, if able people are to be attracted three conditions must be fulfilled: the prestige and status of the job must be high in the eyes of the community; the salary structure must be adequate in relation to the responsibilities; the job itself must be defined and organized in such a way as to challenge and use effectively the interest of talented people.[8] The fact must be faced that these conditions do not now obtain in Canada.

If suitably trained or suitably experienced people cannot be attracted, then it remains for each school to acquire the best recruits it can and subsequently attempt to provide them with in-service training. The need for training is acknowledged in all provinces, but there are problems yet to

[7]U.S. Department of Health, Education and Welfare, *Training Personnel for Work with Juvenile Delinquents,* Washington: Government Printing Office, 1954.
[8]*Teachers for Tomorrow,* New York: Ford Foundation, 1955.

be overcome before all schools can make provision for it. In some schools the nature of the work and the number of staff are such that it is felt to be impossible to set time apart for training, and some do not have personnel capable of instructing, while at the same time they are out of reach of university or other suitable resources. Where it is possible to provide for in-service training, the problems that arise centre around the following:

1. The form and the content of training;
2. The difficulties inherent in attempting to give the same course to people with varying academic backgrounds;
3. Translation of the learning process into on-the-job practice; and
4. The evaluation of training and the selection of criteria for evaluation.

Although the subject of staff-training is dealt with elsewhere in this book, it may be salutary to emphasize two points here, one relating to the form and content of training and the other to its use in minimizing role-conflicts.

There are two broad approaches to training. In one, the aim is to provide the basic theoretical background considered essential for those working with children in need; in the other, the concern is with practical problems that arise in an institution, and training is geared to solving them. The first kind may take the form of a series of university extension courses given inside or outside the institution, intended to give the worker an understanding of human growth and behaviour, a knowledge of counselling, and of methods of working with groups. In the second, the training is conducted within the institution and can take such forms as case conferences on individual children, staff meetings, or the introduction of outside 'experts'; but whatever the form, the object is to solve a problem that has become evident in the school.

Each of these two types of training has serious disadvantages. The university extension course has an obvious limitation in that it cannot provide supervision of the worker on the job – perhaps the most important ingredient of successful training. Because of this, it is possible for some participants, learning only theory, to be harmed rather than helped. Also, unless the course is most carefully planned and presented, it is possible for it to result in harm to children, because a little learning being at least potentially dangerous, a worker may fail to recognize when he is out of his depth and, with disastrous consequences, neglect to hand a child over to the appropriate clinical worker.

The practical problem-solving approach, if it is to be successful, needs to be co-ordinated by a training-officer, who is himself qualified by training and experience. His role is more than that of a catalysing agent; he needs to know each worker individually and to have such a relationship with him that the worker feels free to discuss his fears, anxieties, and prejudices, and his hostilities towards those for whom he is responsible. Without supervision of this kind, it is extremely doubtful whether training by means of solving problems can ever be effective. Even should it happen to be so in certain cases, the question arises whether the insight and experience gained from solving one particular problem can be given theoretical form so that it can be passed on to other schools or to other workers in the same school. The average worker in an institution has developed many skills and acquired much knowledge as a result of many years' experience, but unless these skills and this knowledge can be formulated and presented in such a manner that they can be understood by a recruit, he too must wait for years of experience before he can be of real benefit.

The two kinds of approach, it is contended, should not be regarded as mutually exclusive, as though there were no choice but to follow one or the other. Apart from the inherent disadvantages in each, it is obviously absurd to teach theory as though practice were irrelevant, or to teach practice as though theory did not exist.

The advent of the clinical worker has been marked by conflict in the majority of schools, very often simply because the trained clinical worker and the untrained supervisor have different perspectives. On the one hand, we have a group of workers with similar training and educational background who are concerned at least as much with the root causes of behaviour as with its manifestation, who generally work in a one-to-one relationship with the client, and whose job-security and job-mobility are established by the fact that they are few in numbers and the demand for their services is great. On the other hand there are workers from widely differing backgrounds who must be as concerned with control of the many as with treatment of the individual, whose work demands focusing of attention on overt behaviour whatever its underlying cause may be, whose job-security may depend upon their ability to exercise control, and whose job-mobility is non-existent because of their lack of training.

If a course of training is to be effective, it must recognize this conflict and must aim at encouraging staff, particularly those with different roles, to complement rather than compete with each other's work. The school can further this aim by very clearly defining the respective responsibilities and authorities that each role carries, by establishing lines of direct communication between staff, and by selecting clinical workers who are just as capable of handling the anxieties, hostilities, and suspicions of their untrained colleagues as those of the children.

Summary

The degree to which the training-schools in Canada are able to fulfil the goal of successful rehabilitation of the young delinquent is limited by several factors. These limitations may be removed in the future if consideration is given by federal and provincial governments to effecting the following changes:

1. Placing the responsibility for care and treatment of neglected, dependent, and delinquent children on the Child Welfare Departments of the provinces;
2. Committing to training-schools only children who need the type of care these schools provide.
3. Developing a wider range of alternative forms of care, such as group foster-homes, and extending the present use of foster-care.
4. Providing appropriate hospitals for children who are mentally ill or seriously disturbed emotionally, and adequate maternity homes for pregnant girls; and ceasing to commit these children to training-schools.
5. Reducing the size of training-schools and drastically reducing the number of children for whom each houseparent or supervisor is responsible.
6. Establishing juvenile courts on a regional basis and providing them with adequate clinical facilities for thorough assessment and observation of a child before disposition of his case.
7. Providing an after-care service that can effectively work with the family of a delinquent while he is receiving training.
8. Providing adequate training-programs for training-school staffs.
9. Intensifying the drive to attract well-trained clinical workers to the schools.

At the federal level, certain changes in the present legislation are needed. Indications of the type of change desirable have been given briefly earlier in this chapter, but the reader is referred to *The Child Offender and the Law* for an excellent and searching examination of the defects in present legislation.[9] The time is ripe, indeed, for the federal government to assume more responsibility in this entire area than merely that of passing the necessary legislation. Leadership of the kind that in the United States is provided by the Children's Bureau is needed at the national level. Recommendations to this effect have been made to the Department of Justice committee that has recently completed its examination of the problem of juvenile delinquency.

[9]Canadian Corrections Association, *The Child Offender and the Law,* Ottawa: Canadian Welfare Council, 1962.

11

Some Aspects of Nineteenth-Century Canadian Prisons

J. ALEX. EDMISON

PIONEER PRISONS

In 1836 the magistrates of the Home District (afterwards called the County of York) reported to the Lieutenant-Governor of Upper Canada as follows:

> In the early settlement of the Province, and from the thin and scattered state of the population of the Home District, as well as the comparative absence of crime and infrequent detention of prisoners in custody on civil process for debt, the safekeeping of criminals and others was perhaps but a secondary consideration. A known place for their reception under the proper officers was at such a period all that was found to be indispensably necessary, and for many years without any serious inconvenience being found to result. An ordinary building, constructed almost in the rudest manner, with a common enclosure marking its precincts, was found sufficient for the existing wants.[1]

This description would have been true of most other prison establishments in Canada during the pioneer period. The phrase 'a secondary consideration' is a meaningful one. It explains the great difficulties experienced by pioneer jailers in obtaining government grants adequate to pay their own salaries, to feed the prisoners, and to maintain the institutions.

A physical description is extant of the jail at Niagara. A traveller, John M. Duncan, who wrote a two-volume account of his experiences in the United States and Canada in 1818-19, describes it as follows:

[1]Report of the Magistrates of the Home District to the Lieutenant-Governor of Upper Canada, 1836, Upper Canada Records, Queen's Park, Toronto.

279

The cells surround and open from the hall, which leads to the court room. The partitions and doors of the cells are composed of pieces of oak firmly bolted together; the doors are about 9 inches thick, consisting of 2 thicknesses of wood with a sheet of iron between them. Some of the debtors' apartments have a small window, but the criminals have no light but from a small semi-circular opening in the doors. Debtors' cells have fireplaces, but criminals have only a stove in the hall, from which no perceptible warmth can reach them.[2]

Perhaps, as the magistrates suggested, the reason our forebears did not consider jail construction of major importance was the relative freedom from crime of pioneer Canada. A good illustration of this condition can be found in the *Canadian Settler's Guide* by Mrs. Catherine Parr Traill of Peterborough County, Upper Canada, published in 1857. The following quotation is almost nostalgic, especially when read by those contending with or frustrated by present-day delinquency and crime:

There is one thing which can hardly fail to strike an emigrant from the Old Country, on his arrival in Canada. It is this – the feelings of complete security which he enjoys whether in his own dwelling or in his journeys abroad through the land. He sees no fear – he need see none. This is a country where the inhabitants are essentially honest – Here you may sleep with your door unbarred for years. Your confidence is rarely, if ever, abused; your hospitality never violated – It is delightful, this conscious-ness of perfect security; your hand is against no man, and no man's hand is against you.

As population increased and the growth of towns brought new and more serious crime problems, unplanned provisions no longer sufficed. Deficiencies were constantly brought to light in the reports of grand juries. In the early 1830s the Lieutenant-Governor of Upper Canada, Sir John Colborne, took cognizance of grand-jury criticisms and dispatched a letter to the sheriff of each district asking for a report on the number of prisoners in each institution, their sex and age, their crimes, their daily food allot-ment, and on the facilities for light and heat. The compilation of the replies to this directive revealed wide discrepancies. In some districts chil-dren imprisoned with their parents (a practice followed when there was no one else to care for them) had no food allowance and had to be fed from outside sources. In some, mattresses and blankets were supplied; in others they were not.

There was much resentment among the magistrates against what they

2Quoted from John M. Duncan, *Travels Through the United States and Part of Canada*, pp. 107-8, in C. W. Jefferys, *The Picture Gallery of Canadian History*, vol. II, Toronto: Ryerson, 1945, p. 247.

considered meddling on the part of the Lieutenant-Governor. Grand juries continued to be critical, however, and included in their condemnation the intermingling of all types of prisoners, including children, debtors, and the insane, along with dangerous criminals.

In Lower Canada and the maritime colonies, events followed much the same course. This commentary on the difficulties associated with the Montreal Gaol appeared in the *Montreal Transcript* on November 8, 1838:

> The Grand Jury have visited the prison, and hope that its state may be represented in the proper quarter. They understand that it is customary (for want of room, perhaps), to mix untried persons who are presumed by the law to be innocent, with convicted offenders; to put the poor child who has committed his first offence, and who, perhaps, sincerely repents of it, into the same apartment with the most hardened and profligate, there to be perfected in all that is evil, and contaminated by idleness and intimate intercourse with the most abandoned villains. Society can never lack a plentiful supply of offenders, as long as a public prison that is made a seminary of vice, exists. The Grand Jury earnestly wish to see proper classification of offenders introduced into the public prison, religious and moral instruction brought to bear more effectually, especially upon young prisoners, and employment provided for all classes, in order that some may have a chance of improving, by the punishment which the law imposes, instead of coming out worse members of society than they go in, as is now invariably the case. The Jailor represents to the Grand Jury, the propriety of providing ... labour for the prisoners, as nothing tends so much to render them evil disposed, refractory, and drunken as idleness. The money earned by labour might be advantageously laid out in providing clothing for the prisoners, who are now, many of them, in a state of nakedness. The Grand Jury are sorry to learn from Mr. Wand, that he is unable to prevent the clandestine introduction of liquor.

The process was much the same in the West, but occurred at a later period. Originally, law enforcement was in the hands of the Hudson's Bay Company, and dealt with relatively minor problems, such as disobedience, insolence, or assaulting an officer of the company. Capital cases were transferred to England or to Upper Canada. It was not until a sizable group of settlers established the Red River Settlement in 1812 that the need for a regular jail was recognized by Lord Selkirk. Even then, action was delayed until 1835 when an institution was started at Fort Garry. (The justice that was administered meanwhile has been described as 'easy-going' with fines and forfeitures predominating.) The charter of the company gave the governor and his council power to enact fines and 'other punishments' as long as these were not repugnant to the laws of England.

J. Alex. Edmison

Also chief factors in isolated places could try criminal cases and award fines or punishment. As the population of Canada grew, the establishment of larger and more formally organized penitentiaries became imperative. These did not necessarily lead to the improvement hoped for, as we shall see.

ALTERNATIVES TO IMPRISONMENT

It may be useful to digress at this point to consider the alternatives to imprisonment available to the early-nineteenth-century courts. Modern alternatives, such as probation, had not been developed. The alternatives that then existed in Canada have long since been discarded.

The Pillory

One of these alternatives was the pillory. It was made of a solid frame of wood punctured with holes through which were thrust the head and hands of the offender. When the wooden frame was closed, these openings fitted snugly around the neck and wrists, holding the victim secure. The whole machine was mounted on a pivot so that the person being punished could be made to face in any desired direction. This punishment was imposed in public, and often citizens of the community showered the culprit with rotten eggs and similar refuse. The hangman was usually in attendance with a whip to force the victim to face his tormentors. An hour spent in the constrained position of the pillory could have disastrous effects, and the victim often suffered physically long after. The pillory was not, apparently, used in Upper Canada but it did play a part in the administration of justice in Lower Canada. The one in the open Montreal market was resorted to frequently, with or without the infliction of a sentence of thirty-nine stripes. The culprits ordinarily stood in the pillory for one hour, usually between the hours of ten and eleven in the forenoon, and were thereafter discharged. As late as 1829, a man stood in the Montreal pillory for passing bad French crowns, as an utterer of counterfeit money had a year earlier. The pillory was abolished in Canada by statute in 1842.

The Stocks

The stocks, on the other hand, were used in Upper Canada, but no reports have been found on their use in Lower Canada. They were a wooden contraption with holes for arms and legs, in which the offenders could be seated, sometimes two at a time. In 1804, a woman was sentenced to them for the space of two hours on two different market days. William Lyon Mackenzie, first mayor of Toronto, presiding over the mayor's court in 1834, gave this sentence to a man convicted of larceny: 'to stand one hour to-morrow, and one hour to-morrow week, in the common stocks, and to

282

be banished from the Home District for twelve months'.[3] The stocks were located in the market-place in early York. The date of the last use of the stocks in Canada cannot be stated definitely, but it was probably long before 1872, the year of their last recorded use in England.

Branding

It is perhaps not generally known that branding had a period of use in Canada. It is on record that the chief justice of Upper Canada in 1798 had criminals branded in open court. The practice was abolished in the province by statute in 1802 'save for the crime of manslaughter'.[4] In Lower Canada the records of the old Montreal Prison reveal branding-sentences until at least 1826, in which year two men were branded on the hands for manslaughter and one was branded for murder.[5]

Branding fell into disuse in England during the reign of George III and was finally abolished there in 1829. The writer has come across no Canadian cases after that date, except those of soldiers who were convicted under the Mutiny Act, or who were deserters. Branding in such cases was continued until at least the end of the 1840s.

Banishment

In 1802 legislation was passed in Upper Canada providing for the banishment of people convicted of crime. The banished person was ordered to depart the province at his or her own expense and peril. For instance, in 1829 a man pleading guilty of larceny was sentenced to banishment from Upper Canada for seven years and 'to be allowed 8 days, this day included, to leave the Province'; and in 1831 a man was sentenced to be banished from Upper Canada for life 'and to be allowed 7 days to leave'.[6] On January 10, 1834, in Montreal, a convicted burglar, sentenced to be hanged, was pardoned on condition that he leave Lower Canada. In 1841 the Canadian Parliament ruled that anyone returning from banishment would be imprisoned for at least four years and afterwards transported. (Newfoundland had its own system of banishment. Convicted persons were simply put on an out-going boat, and eventually found themselves in Prince Edward Island, Nova Scotia, or New York State, there to fend for themselves. When immigration laws were tightened, this practice proved to be impractical and in 1902 was finally abolished.)

Technically, banishment in the old sense has long since disappeared in

[3]James Edmund Jones, *Pioneer Crimes and Punishments,* Toronto: George N. Morany, 1924.
[4]*Ibid.*
[5]J. Douglas Borthwick, *History of Montreal Prison*, Montreal: 1886.
[6]Jones, *op. cit.*

Canada. Nevertheless a 'reasonable facsimile of same' would seem to survive in the current practice of some magistrates who say: 'Guilty, 30 days, but sentence suspended provided you leave town within 24 hours.'

Transportation

This sentence was levied frequently. In the 1843 nominal roll of prisoners in the penitentiary at Kingston, there were three awaiting transportation. In Montreal during 1826 and 1827, one woman and three men, condemned to death for the crimes of burglary and horse-stealing, had their sentences commuted to transportation to 'the Bermudas'. On March 9, 1836, Sir Francis Bond Head, Lieutenant-Governor of Upper Canada, issued an official proclamation directing that 'any offenders convicted of Felony in this Province and being under sentence or order of transportation, shall be sent first to England, and thence to New South Wales, or Van Diemen's Land, as His Majesty shall direct'.[7] Deserters from the British garrisons in Canada were frequently transported to one of these two penal colonies. Many of the political prisoners convicted following the 1837 rebellion were sentenced to transportation; fifty-eight from Lower Canada were transported to New South Wales, and ninety-two from Upper Canada to Van Diemen's Land (now Tasmania). Some died on the sea journey, which sometimes took as long as eighteen weeks, and many perished in the penal colonies. Some of the survivors were given full pardon in 1842, but others did not win freedom until several years later. The *Colonial Times* of Australia reported on April 7, 1840: 'We learn that the Canadian political convicts are men of good sense and good conduct, and are anything but in their proper position in gangs on public roads.' Indeed, some assisted 'in the pursuit and capture of bush rangers and this was recorded in order that it might be taken into favorable consideration in applications for indulgence'.[8] A great deal remains to be learned of the experience of these political prisoners, and it is to be hoped that diaries and other material recently uncovered in Australia will throw considerable light on the episode.

Transportation out of Canada came to an end in 1853, but the subject of transportation was not altogether forgotten in Canada. In 1859 a movement was afoot to persuade England to make Hudson's Bay Territory into a penal colony to which convicts could be transported. The inspectors of Kingston Penitentiary in their report for 1857 had advocated a thorough exploration of such a proposal. They quoted the *Quebec Gazette* as saying:

[7]*The British Whig*, Kingston, Upper Canada, March 9, 1836.
[8]'Canadian Political Prisoners in Tasmania', Memorandum to J. Alex. Edmison from Honourable R. F. Fagan, Attorney-General of Tasmania, 1961.

A Siberia to the North of Canada would be of incalculable advantage to this Province, and we trust will be entertained; Rome was originally a collection of malefactors, and what else was Venice?[9]

As late as 1887, when the American Penal Congress met in Toronto, several speakers referred to the possible advantages of having penal colonies established in the northern regions of Canada and Alaska.

KINGSTON PENITENTIARY – IN HISTORICAL RETROSPECT
AND TRADITION-MAKING IMPORTANCE

At the time of Confederation in 1867, there were three provincial penitentiaries: at Kingston, Ontario; Saint John, New Brunswick; and Halifax, Nova Scotia. All became federal pentitentiaries at Confederation, but the last two reverted to provincial use after the building of the federal penitentiary at Dorchester, New Brunswick, in 1880. (Newfoundland in 1867 had Her Majesty's Penitentiary. It is still so designated. Since the union with Canada in 1949, it continues to be operated as a provincial institution, although holding federal prisoners by a special arrangement with Ottawa.) By the Act of Union in 1840, the penitentiary in Kingston had been designated for the incarceration of convicts from both Lower and Upper Canada. This arrangement continued until the opening of St. Vincent de Paul Penitentiary in the Province of Quebec in 1873, when 119 Quebec prisoners were transferred there by steamboat from Kingston.

As the country developed, other federal penitentiaries were opened: at Stony Mountain, Manitoba, in 1876; at New Westminster, British Columbia, in 1878; and at Prince Albert, Saskatchewan, in 1911. A penitentiary was opened at Edmonton, Alberta, in 1906, but closed as a federal institution in 1920. No further penitentiaries were built until Collins Bay, Ontario, was opened in 1930.

The oldest penitentiary in the country is the one at Kingston, and we can learn a great deal about early penology in Canada by a study of the vicissitudes of this institution. The penitentiary 'near the Town of Kingston' was opened on June 1, 1835, when six convicts were received, five of them from Toronto. The institution was built on the plan of the Auburn Prison, New York, and the deputy-keeper of Auburn, William Powers, was hired first as building superintendent and later as deputy-warden. The first warden was Henry Smith. Discord and turbulence marked the

[9]This and following references to Kingston Penitentiary are from the Penitentiary Records, Upper Canada Records, Queen's Park, Toronto, and for references after 1867 from the Public Archives, Ottawa.

administration in the early years. Warden Smith seems to have quarrelled with most of his associates. In 1840 Powers was dismissed, as was his successor as deputy-warden, Edward Utting, six years later. In 1846 the warden, through the influence of his son (afterwards Sir Henry Smith), conveniently the member of the Legislature for Kingston, had his own salary increased and those of the surgeon, the chaplain, and the architect – all three of whom had criticized him severely – correspondingly reduced. At this date the penitentiary population was 480.

On October 22, 1836, the inspectors of Kingston Penitentiary published the Rules and Regulations of the institution. These were pretty strenuous for staff and inmates alike. The warden had 'to attend constantly at the prison'. The guards were to be on duty from five in the morning until six-thirty in the evening, seven days a week, from the beginning of April to the end of September. 'During the remainder of the year, the hours for continuing the Prison open, shall embrace all day light.' The standard wage for guards was £37 10s. a year. Some of the guards were illiterate and signed receipts and depositions by their marks, as is shown in the contemporary annual reports of the penitentiary. They had to 'preserve unbroken silence' among the inmates, who 'must not exchange a word with one another under any pretence whatever'. The convicts also 'must not exchange looks, wink, laugh, nod or gesticulate to each other'. When the bell rang for them to go to mess-hall, they were to come out of their cells 'in regular order and march with their faces inclined' in one direction. At chapel they were to be seated so 'as to confront the Minister, without looking into each other's faces'. The convicts were to yield 'perfect obedience and submission to their keepers', and were at all times 'to labor diligently'. Over them always hung this final threat, no idle one, as we shall see: 'for the wilful violation of any of these duties, corporal punishment will be instantly inflicted'. The prison was always open for the citizens of Kingston to visit: 'male adults, 1s. 3d. each, females and children 7½d. each'.

The prison administration encountered such criticism that, on May 26, 1848, a five-man commission was appointed to 'investigate into the Conduct, Discipline and Management of the Provincial Penitentiary at Kingston'. The appointment was made by Lord Elgin, Governor General of British North America, and was signed by Robert Baldwin, Attorney-General. The specific allegations of official wrong-doing that culminated in the inquiry were made by the prison physician, Dr. James Sampson, later first Dean of Medicine at Queen's University, and several times mayor of Kingston. The commission forthwith set up headquarters in the

British American Hotel in Kingston and began to hear evidence. While its chairman was the Honourable Adam Fergusson, member of the Legislative Council, the dominating figure was its secretary, George Brown, editor of the Toronto *Globe* and afterwards one of the Fathers of Confederation.

What has since been called the 'Brown Report' was completed in May 1849. The eighty-four double pages are crammed with charges of graft, corruption, cruelty, and sinister politics. The commissioners were very severe in their condemnation of the treatment of child convicts. They pointed out the case of convict Peter Charbonneau, who was committed on May 4, 1845, for seven years, when he was ten years old. They said: 'The Table shows that Charbonneau's offences [in prison] were of the most trifling description, such as were to be expected of a child of ten or eleven (like staring, winking and laughing); and that for these he was stripped to the shirt, and publicly lashed 57 times in 8½ months.' Then there was the case of convict Antoine Beauche, committed November 7, 1845, for three years. 'The Table', says the report, 'shows that this 8-year-old child received the lash within a week of his arrival and that he had no fewer than 47 corporal punishments in 9 months, and all for offences of the most childish character. Your Commissioners regard this as another case of revolting inhumanity.' They cite other cases of the same description, and observe, 'It is horrifying to think of these little children being lacerated with the lash before 500 grown men; to say nothing of the cruelty, the effect of such a scene, so often repeated, which must have been to the last degree brutalizing.' Even the language question comes up in these sordid revelations; it was found that a French-Canadian boy convict named Alec Lafleur, aged eleven years, was on Christmas Eve 1844 given twelve strokes of the rawhide for speaking French. The Commissioners also investigated the practice of flogging women in the penitentiary. One perhaps should not refer to Sarah O'Connor as a woman; she was only fourteen when she was flogged on five occasions in three months. Elizabeth Breen was only twelve when she was flogged on five occasions in four months. We can agree with the Commissioners when they say: 'We are of the opinion that the practice of flogging women is utterly indefensible.'

So the report goes on, revealing barbarity after barbarity, as well as corruption and inefficiency on a large scale. One may suppose that the state of affairs had been unknown to most of the citizens of Kingston. Perhaps their suspicions, if any, had been lulled by the tribute paid by Charles Dickens, who, after a visit to the town in May 1840, wrote in complimentary terms about the penitentiary management.[10] It deserves to be remembered, however, that these unspeakable happenings were not approved by all the penitentiary officers. Some had spoken out against them and had been dismissed on trumped-up charges; others, as previously noted, had had their salaries sharply reduced.

As a result of the work of this commission, many of the unsuitable prison officials were dismissed, or they resigned under fire. Warden Henry Smith was one of the first to be affected. The sequence of events in his case can be learned from a letter sent to him by the penitentiary inspectors under date of July 9, 1852. In forwarding Smith a cheque for £700, they stated that it was his back-pay entitlement ' . . . from the date of your suspension, 19th day of November 1848 to the 13th of April 1850, the

[10]Charles Dickens in his *American Notes* described the penitentiary: 'There is an admirable jail here, well and wisely governed, and excellently regulated, in every respect. The men were employed as shoemakers, ropemakers, blacksmiths, tailors, carpenters, and stonecutters; and in building a new prison, which was pretty far advanced toward completion. The female prisoners were occupied in needlework. Among them was a beautiful girl of twenty, who had been there nearly three years. She acted as bearer of secret dispatches for the self-styled patriots of Navy Island, during the Canadian Insurrection; sometimes dressing as a girl, and carrying them in her stays; sometimes attiring herself as a boy, and secreting them in the lining of her hat. In the latter character she always rode as a boy would, which was nothing to her, for she could govern any horse that any man could ride, and could drive a four-in-hand with the best whip in those parts. Setting forth on one of her patriotic missions, she appropriated to herself the first horse she could lay her hands on; and this offense brought her where I saw her. She had quite a lovely face, though, as the reader may suppose from this sketch of her history, there was a lurking devil in her bright eye, which looked pretty sharply from between her prison bars.'

Almost certainly the young lady intriguingly referred to in this paragraph is the same as the one listed in the following entry in the official report of the penitentiary for the year ending October 1, 1842. The entry appears under the general heading 'Return of Convicts Discharged from the Provincial Penitentiary at Kingston':

'No. 349 — Eunice Whiting'

Aged:	17 (on conviction)
Height:	5' 1½''
Eyes:	Dark grey
Hair:	Auburn
Complexion:	Fair
District:	Gore (Hamilton)
Crime:	Horse Stealing
When Sentenced:	June 8, 1839
Length of Sentence:	3 years
When Discharged:	June 8, 1842.'

Reasonable accuracy may be assumed in this identification when it is noted that it is of record that at the time of Charles Dickens' visit there were nine females in the institution, only one condemned for horse-stealing, and only one serving three years.

date of your final removal in terms of the decision of His Excellency in Council.' Of Smith the commissioners had reported: '. . . We have found the Warden guilty on all (20) the charges preferred against him; and the case is so fully established – whether as regards indifference to the success of the institution – neglect of his duties – incapacity – mismanagement – cruelty – falsehood – peculation – that the only course left us, is to recommend Mr. Smith's permanent removal from the Wardenship of the Penitentiary.' The ex-warden, however, was not without his political supporters, and John A. Macdonald, the member for Kingston, was one of these. He repeatedly brought up 'Smith's cause' in Parliament and finally, in 1856, succeeded in having a parliamentary committee investigate the Brown Report and especially Brown's role during the 1848-9 inquiry. The finding of this Committee, on June 5, 1856, was not very conclusive, but gave what has been described as a mild rebuke to Macdonald.[11] Authorities now seem to agree that the deep personal animosity between Macdonald and Brown had its origin in the charges and countercharges these two leading statesmen threw at each other in what became well known in political circles as 'the Smith case'.

To provide useful work for inmates was a pressing problem from the earliest days of Kingston Penitentiary, as it is today in most of our modern prisons. Civilian workmen in Kingston resisted any convict labour that might hazard their own livings. Efforts to solve the question by granting concessions to outside contractors proved in the long run impractical. It was difficult for civilian foremen to come in and direct convict workmen. There were incidents of contraband being smuggled in and unauthorized letters going out. Efforts to operate under contract such penitentiary enterprises as cabinet-making and shoe-making proved unsatisfactory, uneconomic, and bad for general public relations. All these factors helped to inspire a strong movement to relocate the penitentiary where adequate projects for convict labour could be assured. In summarizing the basic documentation on this abortive project, one can note the contentious issues which survive to this day.

---

[11] The member for Kingston continued to take an interest in his home-town prison. In the institutional day-book are recorded his occasional visits and evidence of his general interest. In January 1871 he was instrumental in having his old school friend, John Creighton, appointed as warden. (Mr. Creighton had been mayor of Kingston and police magistrate. His civic career had been in every way admirable, as was his record as warden. He died in office in 1885.) On October 25, 1871, Warden Creighton wrote to Sir John A. Macdonald, then the Prime Minister, about his experiences as warden. Sir John A. replied in a letter on October 31, 1871, and his comments will be of interest to all involved in corrections. His letter in reply (previously unpublished) is appended to this chapter.

J. Alex. Edmison

The penitentiary had been operating for only a few years when agitation arose to have it moved to Marmora in Hastings County, Ontario. The Honourable Peter McGill of Montreal was willing to sell the Marmora Iron Works for £25,000. Two of the three commissioners appointed by the legislature to study the question reported that such a move was feasible and that the iron-works could be operated by the convicts at an annual profit of £13,037 7s. 6d. However, the third commissioner, Isaac Fraser of Ernestown, put in a minority report (dated February 20, 1839) stating:

> The principal object of transferring the Penitentiary from Kingston to Marmora, would seem to be the employment of convict labour so as not to interfere with the pursuits of the honest mechanics of the Province; but if this object can be equally well attained at the present establishment, it is evident that the loss of the large amount already expended on it will be avoided, and the necessity of a further large outlay would be prevented.

Mr. Fraser was eloquently supported in his viewpoint by a communication from Mr. William Powers, building superintendent of Kingston Penitentiary. Mr. Powers wrote, in part:

> I have been informed that a proposition was once made by some person to bring water to the Town of Kingston in pipes or an aqueduct, the Town being mostly supplied from the lake, drawn by carters; and the proposition was objected to by some, because (they said) it would injure the carters by throwing them out of employ. The objection in the case above is precisely the same in principle as those made by the mechanics against the Penitentiary, which principle, if universally allowed and carried into effect, would annihilate the arts and sciences, change the plough for the spade or the mattock, and bring mankind to a state of barbarism.
>
> It is said, likewise, that learning the convicts a trade, which they may follow when they are set at liberty, will disgrace the honest mechanic. I cannot see why mechanics should be disgraced by the occupation at mechanical labour, of those who had been convicts, than the farmer would be disgraced, should they follow the plough. If there is any reason at all in this objection, it will apply with equal force against all labour by one who had been guilty of crime, and the divine precept, 'let him that stole steal no more, but rather let him labour,' would be wrong. Of all complaints made or grievances imagined, those of the mechanics against the Penitentiary are, in my opinion, the most preposterous. As well might the physician complain of any measure to preserve the public health, or tavernkeepers, distillers, and ginshops, of efforts for the promotion of temperance.

The annual reports of Kingston Penitentiary are a mine of material on

290

the penology of the times and on the difficulties encountered by prison administrators in the nineteenth century in Canada. The comments of the wardens, chaplains, and physicians are frequently most revealing. Some of these men went out of their way to advocate reforms and displayed an insight into the causes and treatment of crime much in advance of the general thinking of the periods in which they wrote.

The report for 1856 is typical. It provides a variety of statistics on the 668 persons then confined, for instance: their crimes (including forty-two cases of horse-stealing and one of oxen-stealing); where they were convicted (Montreal leads with 115, Toronto is next with 96); and their occupations (373 were labourers, 49 seamstresses, one a law student, and one a medical student). The return on the seamstresses indicates that there were forty-nine female inmates, as for quite a number of years all females were so designated. The Protestant chaplain also presents figures. He lists the crimes committed by inmates of each Protestant denomination, and the resulting data is so similar as to provide comfort for no denominational analyst. He then breaks down the crimes of his communicants by their countries of origin (here the return appears to indicate that the Scots in Canada were less prone to murder than those of other origins). The zealous padre interrogated each member of his flock discharged during the year. He asked the question he was required to do before discharge: 'Do you go out a better or a worse man?' From the answers he compiled the following summary:

> 55 – go out improved morally
> 7 – go out much better
> 1 – better in prudence
> 1 – inclined for the better
> 1 – not much better
> 1 – not better
> 2 – neither better nor worse
> 1 – about the same
> 1 – better in a great many ways
> 1 – not any worse
> 3 – cannot say whether improved
> 1 – is not better
> 2 – go out worse
> 5 – no definite answer.

All this was obviously pleasing to the padre, for he adds: 'These answers make it evident ... that the discharged convicts, generally, leave prison morally benefitted.' We may question his assurance on this point when we note his additional observation on the effect of prison life on young offenders. He records that in his charge are seventy-five inmates between the ages of ten and twenty, and adds:

> The absence of all classification of Convicts, and the association of numerous young offenders with old, skilful, and confirmed villains, cannot have a good effect. The majority, indeed nearly all of these young offenders, were guilty only of small offences – of larceny and the like; and it seems incongruous, almost an infatuation, to place them in an Institution among hardened, expert, and experienced robbers, burglars, murderers, and others, with the view of making these young Criminals good members of society .... A House of Reformation, therefore, is imperatively called for in the Province to reform these young offenders.

The Roman Catholic chaplain in his turn brings up a matter that has always been of importance and concern to spiritual advisors in prisons.

> As the Penitentiary Bill must be re-enacted during the ensuing Session of the Legislature, I take the liberty of calling your attention to that part of the oath, by which all Officers of the Institution are bound to report to the Warden every infraction of the Rules which will come to their knowledge, which the Chaplains cannot take without exposing themselves to lose all influence over the Convicts, and to be considered by them not as their spiritual guides, but as so many paid spies over their conduct. I think that the Government should place sufficient confidence in the Chaplains to believe them incapable of concealing any serious infraction of which they might become cognizant, without binding them to do so under the obligation of an oath.

Although the warden says 'the treatment of convicts I consider to be humane', the Punishment Chart shows 1,600 deprivations of bed with concurrent bread-and-water diet, 735 confinements in the dark cell, 111 punishments by water-hose, and numerous lashings, including that of one convict who was given eighty-four strokes of the cat in the month of March 1856. (Nevertheless the total is considerably less than the 6,000 punishments meted out the year before the Brown Report, to a smaller prison population.)

The inspectors in this 1856 report are pleased with the new matron of the Female Department, Mrs. Martha Walker: 'admirably adapted for the office ... able ... zealous ... [with] much ability ... [she] secures an unusually large share of the confidence and friendship of the convicts ... appreciates the importance of a system containing elements of encouragement.' The warden (Angus Macdonell, who took over from Warden Smith in 1850) agrees with all these compliments for his new matron, but significantly adds: 'I respectfully call the attention to the following circumstances: here is a female of education entitled to every mark of respect, and having a serious responsibility, which she never leaves; this person is not so well paid as a guard or keeper of this Prison.'

The prison physician makes an observation on the Canadian Indian that might be endorsed by modern research: ' . . . with respect to the Indian there is no class of inmate whose state of incarceration differs so much from his previous free mode of life as his does; therefore from his first admission to the Prison till the day of his release, he carries on his aspect strong manifestations of dejection and despondency.'

The inspectors devote a section of their report to discharged convicts. 'Every effort', they say, 'is made to place them in a position that they may not easily be recognized, by giving them a dress that all working men may, and usually do wear, plain and decent, and to prevent them lounging about Kingston, where there is such a number of vile resorts for the vicious, where they are induced to remain carousing . . . until their money is spent, when they are thrust into the street to beg, starve or steal.' The inspectors then announce a remedy. They instruct the warden to have released convicts conveyed to the railway station, and to pay the fare to their destination at a cost of one penny per mile. By this means the inspectors thought the discharged prisoners would 'escape the toils of the harpies ever on the watch for them'.

Ordinarily only those sentenced to two years or more were incarcerated in Kingston Penitentiary. During the period when Kingston was a British garrison town, however, it was also used for military offenders serving shorter sentences. It is strange to read the convict lists of a hundred years ago and see the name of a soldier serving twenty days for drunkenness next to that of a man serving thirty years for manslaughter or rape. Sometimes military personnel were held in the institution pending transportation. Many committal papers record that the soldier had been branded on the hand with a D to indicate that he was a deserter, or with a BC for bad conduct. The *British Whig,* a Kingston newspaper, in an editorial on February 25, 1848, talked about the 'impropriety of sending soldiers to the penitentiary at Kingston for breaches of discipline'. It declared that this practice was much too common and went on: 'when a soldier loses his self-esteem he is a lost man . . . one hour's confinement among the murderers and thieves of the Penitentiary is enough to degrade a man in his own eyes forever.'

THE SIGNIFICANT YEAR OF 1880

The problems and special features of Canada's other penitentiaries can be discerned from the reports to the Minister of Justice of 1880. This was indeed a pivotal year. In the six or seven years before, new federal institutions had been opened in Quebec, Manitoba, and British Columbia. During 1880 occurred the opening of the penitentiary at Dorchester, New Brunswick, and the closing of those at Saint John, New Brunswick, and Halifax, Nova Scotia.

Certainly there has never been, before or since, in Canada, so much major penitentiary expansion in so short a period. The central figure in these developments was J. G. Moylan, Inspector of Penitentiaries for Canada since 1872. He had become known for the clarity of his reports and for his forthright opinions on all matters penological. His praise and his anger were dispensed with impartiality, as can be readily seen from his 1880 report to his Minister. Inspector Moylan was not enamoured of the Public Works Department and condemns 'the many and culpable defects in the new Penitentiaries of Manitoba and British Columbia'. The gross blunders or worse committed at Stony Mountain and New Westminster would have been avoided if the construction had been 'subject to the control of, and responsible to, the Department of Justice'. He deplores the lack of segregation facilities:

> Our penitentiaries being architecturally designed to suit the plan of indiscriminate 'association', it unfortunately happens that they are liable to become, more or less, schools of corruption, and tend to the propagation rather than the diminution of criminality; gross injustice being thus rendered possible as well to the prisoners themselves, as to the community at large, when they may be turnd out, after the expiration of their sentence, in a more debased and dangerous condition than before.[12]

He goes out of his way to compliment the Roman Catholic chaplain at St. Vincent de Paul, Father Joseph W. Leclerc, who 'more than any other, gives himself heart and soul to his work'. He is not able to comment much more about St. Vincent de Paul pending the result of a recent investigation there during which '130 witnesses had been examined and 5,000 folios of evidence written'. However he does permit himself to condemn the use of staff members in 'the contemptible role of spies upon their comrades . . . . Better the riddance of a dozen Wardens rather than permit them to degrade the character of the institution which they are expected to improve and exalt.' (Two years later Inspector Moylan was to report that St. Vincent de Paul Penitentiary ' . . . has given more trouble and annoyance to Ministers and Deputy Ministers of Justice, to Directors and Inspectors,

[12]James G. Moylan was appointed in August 1872 by Sir John A. Macdonald as one of the three Directors of Penitentiaries and in 1873 became 'Secretary-Director' with responsibility for preparing annual reports. In 1875 the Board of Directors was dissolved and J. G. Moylan became Inspector of Penitentiaries, and continued in this office until his retirement in the spring of 1895.

for the ten years of its existence, than all of the other Penitentiaries together, for the same space of time.')

He expresses pleasure that the penitentiary at Saint John, New Brunswick, has been dispensed with:

> It might have answered well enough for a common gaol – and a very common one at that – but it was utterly unsuited for a Penitentiary. There was not a solitary object or feature in the place, physically speaking, calculated to cheer, to elevate, or to produce a softening influence upon the hapless 'détenu' during his dreary term of confinement. All was grim and dismal.

He admits, however, that the physical health of the prisoners at Saint John had been good because of the location 'on the edge of the Bay of Fundy, where the inmates had the benefit of a superabundance of invigorating saline air'.

In giving his official notice of the closing of the Halifax institution he also pays tribute to 'the pure and health-giving sea air from the broad Atlantic all the year round'. He enjoyed his visits to Halifax, and had a good understanding with its officers. Nothing 'of an unpleasant or censurable nature occurred, save once. Then, pardon followed censure, and there was no wrongdoing any more.' All the prisoners had been removed to Dorchester, except two females who (as also in the case of two females at Saint John) could not be moved to the new institution because of 'no proper accommodation'. The inspector in his 'valedictory' for Halifax Penitentiary pays this rather moving tribute to its medical officer, Dr. R. S. Black,

> ... who has been attending this Penitentiary for the last thirty-six years, has been most punctual and unremitting in his attention to those who required his professional aid. Few understood better the protean character, the whims and peculiarities of our convicts in their innumerable devices to impose upon the doctor, or could more successfully deal with the impostors, without exciting their ill will or wrath, than this veteran physician. Few, too, of the officers or convicts who have passed through the institution down by the sea since 1844, have left it without a pleasing recollection of and a friendly feeling towards the amiable and kind-hearted gentleman who, while attending to their bodily ailments, did not fail to administer, by way of advice and consolation, the healing anodyne to their aching and wounded hearts. My official and personal relations with Dr. Black have always been of the most agreeable nature and I regret they are at an end.

Mr. Moylan was not as pleased with the weather experienced at Manitoba Penitentiary as with that in the Maritimes:

J. Alex. Edmison

The ex-Minister of Public Works received repeated applications for
appropriations for heating, for necessary repairs and improvements, for
officers' tenements and prison out-buildings. The four walls of the Penitentiary – encircling as many defects as could well be included in a building of the same character and size – seem to have been considered quite
adequate to meet all the requirements of an institution intended for the
safe custody and proper employment of criminals. On the bleak prairie,
with the mercury ranging between 30° and 40° below zero, a few dilapi-
dated stoves were judged sufficient to impart heat and comfort to the
shivering inmates of the Stony Mountain Penitentiary. The Surgeon's
report of pneumonia, bronchitis, influenza, rheumatism, coughs and
catarrhs and such other ailments, as cannot be attributed to a well regulated warm temperature, but contrariwise, though transmitted with
forcible appeals from the Minister of Justice of the day – especially by
Mr. Blake – for necessary action, met with no favorable response.

The Inspector notes that corporal punishment has been resorted to in
certain instances at Stony Mountain and states that he is asking for the
reasons in each case because 'when an official return exhibits flagellation
has been employed as a means of punishment, the reading public would
be, naturally enough, curious to know the reason'. This is important, he
believes, in Canada, where some of the institutions are at 'a great distance
from the Seat of Government', causing 'the Wardens of our penitentiaries
to be vested with larger powers, in this respect, than are conferred under
the British system'. He wants fewer delays henceforth from Public Works
'in view of the gradual increase in the number of convicts and of the rapidly
growing population of the Province' (Manitoba), necessitating in the near
future another wing to be added to the present building.

Mr. Moylan finds 'a rather strange state of affairs' at British Columbia
Penitentiary. He cannot understand the complaints of the warden about
the unsatisfactory conduct of the convicts during the past year. The Inspector comments:

I cannot shut my eyes to the palpable fact that there must have been some
laxity and remissness in enforcing observance of the rules and regulations,
some want of administrative ability when it is found necessary to report
that *thirty-three* convicts cannot be kept in order by the warden and his
staff.

There are, he admits, difficulties such as 'the want of a fence and consequent temptation to escape . . . circumstances calculated to keep convicts
in a continual state of excitement'; also, 'the Penitentiary is situated on the
outskirts of an impenetrable forest which invites evasion and renders
recapture extremely difficult'. He makes reference to the unoccupied 'Old
Government House' and grounds on the penitentiary reserve and says that

'it appears very strange, indeed, that there should be any let or hindrance to the building being occupied for suitable purpose in connection with the institution . . . instead of . . . being reserved and thrown open for "picnic parties" '. He had made previous requests to Public Works in this connection and he is more convinced than ever that 'the exigencies of the Penitentiary imperatively call for the cession' which he had recommended.

Inspector J. G. Moylan deserves an honoured place among those who held office in corrections in Canada during the nineteenth century. He was in advance of his time in many of his recommendations. In his 1880 report, for instance, he laid stress on 'that primary and permanent principle which is the duty of the State to enforce, namely that none shall leave a prison a worse member of the community than when entering it.' Far too little recognition has been given to men of his courage, insight, and humanity who toiled in the prison service. They worked often under what would now be considered as exceedingly difficult conditions, with scant understanding from the public, and not always with support from their superiors.

Conclusion

It is difficult to describe Canadian penology in the nineteenth century by any easy turn of word or phrase. Changes came about with the emergence of the country from pioneer status. The opening up of Canada 'from sea to sea' brought its own problems, as did the sharp increase in population. Prison reform as we now understand the term was not a continuing major issue. It is true that individual officials and others raised their voices to protest abuses and to suggest that there be treatment of inmates instead of only a strictly punitive approach. Attempts were made here and there to provide prison after-care, but lack of funds crippled such work, and ambitious projects and associations petered out. A few groups interested in penal reform passed resolutions but these seldom were acted upon, at least at the federal government level.

More hopeful signs appeared as the century drew to a close, however. Provincial authorities, especially in Ontario, were introducing progressive treatment measures, particularly in relation to child offenders, and were taking cognizance of reformation procedures that had been tried and found useful in Great Britain or the United States. In 1892 an assembly representing many organizations, including the Roman Catholic Church and most of the Protestant churches, came together in Toronto. Delegates were present from the Salvation Army, the Y.M.C.A., the children's aid societies, and many other charitable groups. The Trades and Labor Council was represented, as were the Bench and the Bar, and the Law and Order League of Toronto. In all, thirty-nine public bodies joined in a statement pressing for penal reform. The chairman of this conference was the Honourable S. H. Blake, president of the Prisoners' Aid Association of Canada, which presented its eighteenth annual report during the conference sessions. Mr. Blake said, in part:

> We have now reached what appears to be a turning point in . . . this prison reform movement. We must either relax our efforts and lose much that has been gained . . . or we must appeal for help . . . until practical effect is given to the reforms for which we are contending.[13] . . . We have put our hand to the plough but it rests with the Government and with the public at large whether we shall call a halt or retreat, or whether we shall order an advance all along the line.

Appendix

COPY OF A LETTER FROM SIR JOHN A. MACDONALD
TO JOHN CREIGHTON, WARDEN OF KINGSTON PENITENTIARY

Ottawa, October 31st, 1871.

Private

My dear Creighton –

I have yours of the 25th which I have read with all the attention you bespeak. I can quite appreciate your anxieties in your office, it is a most responsible one, not without care but as you remark, it has also its bright side. I never had any doubt of and do not now doubt your ultimate success in making the Penitentiary a school of reform, as well as a place of punishment, of course you feel that inexperience at first, that everyone does in a new situation. My only fear is that your natural kindness of disposition may lead you to forget that the primary [purpose] of the penitentiary is punishment and the incidental one reformation.

You say that you desire to feel that you are the means of making five or six hundred of your fellow creatures more happy than they have previously been in the Penitentiary. I could quite sympathize with your desire if it were to make them less miserable than they have been previously

---

[13]There were eleven so-called 'Prison Reform Principles' of the Prisoners' Aid Association, which had been endorsed by this and earlier conferences. These included: compulsory education; adoption of a probation system like Massachusetts; reformatories 'not [to] be considered as places for punishment . . . but wholly for the reformation of character'; classification of offenders; industrial training in institutions; the removal of prison labour 'from the arena of party politics'; and the recommendation that prison officers 'should be carefully selected, preferably by a system of examination and promotion, and without reference to party or social influence'.

rather than more happy – happiness and punishment cannot and ought not to go together. There is such a thing as making a prison too comfortable and prisoners too happy.

You have no doubt read David Copperfield where Dickens so successfully portrays the comforts of the model prison to which those worthies, Uriah Heap and Littimer were consigned – pray read the chapter again. I am pleased to think that I have in any way strengthened your hands by the release of some prisoners, the power of release should however be exercised very sparingly. Certainty of punishment and more especially, certainty that the sentence pronounced will be carried out is of more consequence in the prevention of crime than the severity of sentence.

I believe that one great cause of the prevalence of crime in the United States is the ease with which pardons can be obtained from the Governors of the several States through the political pressure of the friends of the convicts.

Now, as regards Grace Marks[14] – before getting your letter, indeed

14Grace Marks was a sixteen-year-old Irish emigrant who in 1843 conspired with an older fellow-servant, one Macdermot, to murder their employer, Captain Kinnaird, and his housekeeper, Hannah Montgomery, at the captain's farm some thirty miles from Toronto. The employer was shot to death and his housekeeper dispatched with an axe. The guilty pair fled by steamboat from Toronto with the captain's money and plate, and were captured at Niagara. Macdermot was executed, but the death sentence on Grace Marks was commuted to life imprisonment. The Kingston Penitentiary records show she was admitted on November 13, 1843, and released therefrom by pardon on August 6, 1872. The case was given sensational press treatment. Many visitors to the penitentiary asked to 'have a look' at Grace Marks. One of these, in 1849, was the celebrated author Susanna Moodie, who in her *Life in the Clearings* (1853) gives a lengthy account of the double murder and its principals. She mentions that she afterwards came across Grace Marks when visiting the mental asylum in Toronto. The penitentiary records confirm that the inmate, in May 1852, was removed to the asylum for treatment but was returned to Kingston on August 1, 1853. What happened to her following her final release from penitentiary is not known. That Grace Marks was the object of sympathy as well as curiosity can be deduced from this entry for September 12, 1859, in the prison day-book: 'Grace Marks scalded herself, in the face as well as one of her legs. This poor being is sufficiently unfortunate without being made more so.' Even after nearly thirty years' imprisonment, there were both people strongly in favour and people strongly against pardon for the offender. Mrs. Moodie describes Grace Marks as good looking, with a fine figure, but with perhaps too firm and pointed a chin, and Macdermot as a dissolute son of a good family, a deserter from the British Army. The authoress wonders which culprit incited the other. Was the motive robbery or did the 'overbearing' conduct of Hannah Montgomery towards the under-servants provide a revenge motive? Or was Captain Kinnaird's evident affection for the 'handsome' Hannah a strong enough jealousy factor? Mrs. Moodie's questions remain unanswered to this day. One cannot help but feel that had this case originated in Britain it would long since have been chronicled in *Notable British Trials*.

J. Alex. Edmison

the day after my return from Kingston, I placed all the papers in the hands of Lord Lisgar. He is, as you are aware, a very kind-hearted man and is besides opposed to long imprisonments. I gave the papers to him with a request that he would carefully read them and form his own opinion without any remarks from me. He will, of course, see in the papers the reports of several attorneys general and crown officers against a further commutation of the sentence.

Guard the salaries of the officers!

I had a meeting with the directors a week ago on the subject but did not conclude the matter. I hope in a day or two to be able to resume the work and finally adjust it.

Believe me,

Yours sincerely,

John Creighton, Esq. Kingston.

(signed) John A. Macdonald.

Further Reading

ANDERSON, FRANK W. 'Prisons and Prison Reforms in the Old Canadian West'. *Canadian Journal of Corrections,* April 1960.

ANDREWS, WILLIAM. *Punishments in Olden Time.* Hull, England: William Andrews & Co., 1881.

———. *Old Time Punishments.* Hull, England: William Andrews & Co., 1890.

BORTHWICK, J. DOUGLAS. *History of Montreal Prison.* Montreal: 1886.

CARELESS, J. M. S. *Brown of The Globe.* Toronto: Macmillan, 1959.

CREIGHTON, DONALD. *John A. Macdonald.* Toronto: Macmillan, 1955.

EDMISON, J. ALEX. 'The History of Kingston Penitentiary', published in *Historic Kingston* by the Kingston Historical Society, 1954.

FAGAN, JOHN. 'Early Prison Customs in Newfoundland'. *The R.C.M.P. Quarterly,* July 1962.

GUILLET, EDWIN C. *The Lives and Times of the Patriots.* Toronto: Nelson, 1938.

JONES, JAMES EDMUND. *Pioneer Crimes and Punishments.* Toronto: George N. Morany, 1924.

KIDMAN, JOHN. *The Canadian Prison.* Toronto: Ryerson Press, 1947.

KIRKPATRICK, A. M. 'Jails in Historical Perspective'. *Canadian Journal of Corrections,* October 1964.

ONTARIO. *Prison and Reformatory System of Ontario,* Report of a Royal Commission, 1891.

300

————. Report of Commission to Investigate the Provincial Penitentiary at Kingston, 1849 (George Brown, Secretary). Upper Canada Records, Queen's Park, Toronto.

SPLANE, RICHARD B. *Social Welfare in Ontario, 1791-1893*. Toronto: University Press, 1965.

TOPPING, C. W. *Canadian Penal Institutions*. Toronto: Ryerson Press, 1929. Revised Edition, 1943.

12

Canadian Prisons Today

JOHN V. FORNATARO

'Prisons' means buildings, for most of us. Generally, we consider them among the most ugly, unpleasant, and unwelcome structures in the whole community. This idea persists in spite of the current publicity about new kinds of prisons and different ways of using them. The important fact about a prison, however, is not its physical design nor its officially described use. Its importance lies in its human components: inmates and officials, who must find some way of living together under highly unnatural circumstances.

This chapter will attempt to describe that steadily growing segment of Canadian life that constitutes its prisons, and the way in which we now organize this part of our community.

ORGANIZATION OF THE PRISON SYSTEMS IN CANADA

There is no single Canadian prison system. There are, in reality, at least eleven prison systems in this country as a consequence of our federal system of government. The British North America Act defines the respective jurisdictions of the Dominion government and the provinces in penal administration.[1] The division of responsibility is purely arbitrary and has its explanation in historical tradition rather than in logic or in a scientifically deduced plan. The Government of Canada administers prisons officially designated as penitentiaries, to which persons sentenced to prison terms of two years or longer are committed. The provinces are responsible for the custody of persons sentenced to prison for terms of less than two years.

[1]British North America Act, 1867, Sections 91 (28), and 92 (6).

302

The report of the Fauteux Committee[2] recommended an extension of the Dominion government's jurisdiction in the interest of achieving a greater degree of uniformity among Canadian penal institutions. The presumption apparently is that somehow uniformity is prerequisite to efficacy.

Several meetings between officials of the Dominion government and of the provinces have been convened to explore some of the implications of this recommendation. Public statements convey the impression that there is a general but not unanimous consensus favouring the extension of Dominion jurisdiction to include responsibility for prisoners with sentences of one year or more. At the same time, a recommendation for the abolition of sentences of over six months and under one year has been accorded general official support. Whether or when these recommendations will become operative is still a matter of speculation. In any event, they seem to be based on no more clearly reasoned design than are the prevailing jurisdictional provisions.

The penitentiaries are administered by the Department of Justice through its Commissioner of Penitentiaries. Penitentiary wardens are the chief executives of their respective institutions and until 1962 each was directly responsible to the Commissioner. In that year two Regional Directors were appointed for Ontario and Quebec respectively, and in 1963 a Regional Director for the Western provinces was appointed. The Regional Director has direct oversight over wardens in his territory.

Technical activities such as medical services, agricultural operations, training-programs, and fiscal management have come under the general supervision of deputy commissioners and assistant commissioners, who have been under the Commissioner's direction.

Recent public statements promise further decentralization of authority within the Penitentiary Service. To what extent this can take place effectively within the near future is a debatable matter. Although a discussion of the issues is not timely here, it does appear relevant to draw attention to the fact that such a complex administrative reorganization cannot be accomplished simply by issuing an official order.

The institutions administered by the provinces are known by various

---

[2]Committee to Inquire into the Principles and Procedures Followed in the Remission Service of the Department of Justice of Canada, *Report* (Fauteux Report), Ottawa: Queen's Printer, 1956. The committee was established by the Government of Canada to examine the 'principles and procedures' by which the Remission Service administered the legal provisions for clemency. The committee considered it necessary to explore and to make recommendations concerning related aspects of penal organization and administration. The present National Parole Board replaces the former Remission Service.

designations: jails (or the archaic 'gaols'), reformatories, prison farms, and correctional institutions. Much of this variation simply reflects historic tradition – or pious hope. In reality the differences exist more in the names than in the objectives and social structures of these institutions. They are all for the confinement of persons with prison sentences of less than two years, as well as for the detention of persons awaiting trial, sentence, deportation, or execution. In the neighbourhood of sixty per cent of the inmates are detained for periods of a few months, and may be described as minor or petty offenders.

Real differences do exist, of course, between provincial institutions, but these tend to reflect varieties of approach in the different jurisdictions rather than marked deviation from common goals. The nomenclature rarely provides a reliable clue to the character of the institution.

The term 'jails', for example, may be used for the main institutions providing province-wide service, such as those in the three Prairie Provinces. The same term is applied to the many county, municipal, and judicial-district institutions to be found in the Atlantic Provinces, Quebec, and Ontario. Some of these fulfil the same general functions as provincial prisons; others, notably in Ontario, may be limited to detaining prisoners with shorter sentences and those awaiting trial. It would no doubt astound most Canadians to learn that in many parts of Canada an offender serves his sentence (as long, perhaps, as two years less one day) in a primitive building provided by local authorities for as few as half a dozen inmates, while his counterpart in another province, perhaps within the same province, is housed in a huge, complex, provincially administered prison.

Diversity of structure is one of the most obvious characteristics of Canada's provincial penal organization, and one that has been viewed as unfortunate by many, including the Archambault Commission[3] and the Fauteux Committee. Admittedly there are palpable and gross disparities that appear unjustifiable and pernicious from any point of view. On the other hand, the provincial administrations have, on the whole, done more useful experimentation and pioneering than has the highly standardized Penitentiary Service. It is only within very recent times, long after several provinces had proven their feasibility, that the Penitentiary Service has introduced the use of some minimum-security camp establishments.

A compromise at some point between chaos and conformity is surely desirable and possible. The objective of a neat and rigorously uniform chain of prison establishments may be one that betrays how profoundly we have ignored prisons as human communities with an impact upon

[3]Royal Commission to Investigate the Penal System of Canada, *Report* (Archambault Report), Ottawa: King's Printer, 1938.

people's lives infinitely more significant than the tidiness of an organization chart.

THE PRISON AS RESIDENCE

Heterogeneity in physical design and in living arrangements parallels the diversity of organizational structure among Canadian prisons.

The vast majority of these institutions, under whatever jurisdiction, are of maximum-security construction or incorporate features (such as perimeter fences, towers, and patrols manned by rifle-armed guards) that make them virtually maximum-security establishments. Some facilities constructed within the past decade have dispensed with most or all of the features that characterize maximum-security conditions. A few older, custodially designed prisons have undergone both physical and management changes that have resulted in their becoming frankly medium- or even minimum-security institutions; these are, however, a distinct minority.

Canadian prisons, new and old, reflect a persistent American influence. Older penitentiaries and provincial prisons reproduce the old Auburn type of construction, with 'inside' cells ranged back-to-back down the centre of the cell block. Thus prisoners have no access to outside windows for ventilation or light. Between the rows of cells a catwalk provides a means of observing individual inmates through a small peep-hole at the rear of each cell. Cell blocks generally rise in height from two to four tiers. Such structures necessitate feeding the inmates in their cells. Some provide only single-cell occupancy, but overpopulation has led to considerable doubling up in recent years.

Newer architecture continues to reflect American influence in the form of large building complexes providing for industrial, maintenance, training, recreational, and housing areas. Housing tends to consist of dormitories accommodating up to fifty or more per unit, with even less opportunity for privacy than is afforded by the old grill-fronted cells. Mass involvement and anonymity appear to be the intention and the inevitable outcome of these designs.

THE PRISON'S SOCIAL SYSTEM

What is it like in prison? In recent years more citizens than ever before in Canada believe they know the answer to this provocative question because they have made one or more prison visits. This is a great illusion. If a person inspects a house with a view to buying it he learns something about the more apparent parts of the structure. He is presumptuous, how-

305

ever, if he thinks that his examination has made him knowledgeable about the *home*, the life that goes on at that address. Similarly, visits may dispel some of the mystery about what prisons look like on the inside, but they do not inform the visitors about prison life.

On the other hand, many people who have worked in prisons for years have little appreciation of the nature of prison life and of the influences that affect it. It is not true that 'all cons are the same', or that 'all screws are the same'. This over-simplification into stereotypes is a common phenomenon in prisons and points to one of the most important facts of prison life: there is sharp segregation within prison society.

The lines are most decisively drawn between the resident inmate population and the non-resident officer population: the former group does not have access to the wider general community outside the prison; the latter group has. Although the prison worker's shift of duty may differ from any other activity and set of relationships with which he is familiar, at the end of his eight hours he returns home. He is free to shed the prison – its unique values and culture. He can dilute the unnatural influences of the institution with normalcy. He can, in short, preserve his self-image as a normal human being in a normal society. The inmate, on the other hand, is effectively sealed off from the normal community of human beings outside. He is limited to token communication even with the members of his immediate family. A dispassionate observer would suppose that Canadians place very little importance upon marital and parent-child relationships, so grossly are they discouraged by prison practice.[4]

In spite of the humanitarian or even self-interested wish on the part of each of these populations for a tolerable association with the other, the fact remains that their difference occurs at a point so crucial to the individual's humanity that a profound chasm of separation results. Genuine, spontaneous, mutual respect between inmates and officers is very rare indeed, and should its occurrence be recognized, it draws the suspicion of officers and inmates alike – and sometimes their outraged punishments.

The studies of Donald Clemmer,[5] Erving Goffman,[6] and Gresham Sykes[7] give scientifically credible grounds for the 'prisonizing' process,

[4]Ruth Shonle Cavan and Eugene S. Zemans, 'Marital Relationships of Prisoners in Twenty-Eight Countries', *Journal of Criminal Law, Criminology, and Police Science*, July-August 1958.

[5]Donald Clemmer, *The Prison Community* (reissue), New York: Rinehart and Co., 1958.

[6]Erving Goffman, 'The Characteristics of Total Institutions', *Symposium on Preventive and Social Psychiatry*, Washington: Walter Reed Army Institute of Research, 1957, pp. 43-84.

[7]Gresham Sykes, *The Society of Captives*, a study of a maximum-security prison, Princeton University Press, 1958, p. 41.

described in a Canadian context by Maurice O'Connor[8] and by Bruno Cormier.[9] This process is characterized by the social and emotional regression of the inmate, and his progressive capitulation to a system that erodes his individuality. He assumes anonymity because it is virtually impossible to do otherwise. Similarly, he ceases to make decisions on his own behalf. The range of discretion left to him is so insignificant as to make it cynical to admonish him, 'You must learn to be responsible for yourself.'

Even in prison, however, the urge to survive persists. The individual is compelled to discover ways of adapting his usual survival techniques to cope with the grossly abnormal conditions of prison life. The prevailing culture is that of the inmates. Officials represent a minority whose power is not nearly so absolute as the uninitiated may suppose.[10] Survival as a person, then, tends to depend upon one's skill in *appearing* to come to terms appropriately with the social expectations of two antithetical populations. The claims of the inmate culture are more insistent, if only because they are constant, twenty-four hours a day, every day of the week, with no holidays.

The first-timer whose orientation has previously been largely pro-social finds himself identified with an anti-authority group. His values may correspond more closely with those of the officials, but the officials hold him at arm's length because 'he's a con'. Moreover, familiarity between inmate and official may result in both being suspect in the eyes of the other prisoners and officers. As a protection to both parties, many institutions still try to enforce no-fraternization rules; ironically, well-enforced rules of this kind are often the lesser evil, in view of other common prevailing prison deficiencies. Many of the pro-social values of the new inmate appear to be irrelevant at best, and hazardous more often than not, as long as he remains in prison. Veneration of authority is culturally taboo; diligent application to work, protection of the weak, truthful communication, and respect for other people's property is for 'nuts' and lickspittles. On the other hand, self-determination and private initiative are, in effect, proscribed by the official authorities as inimical to good security.

An endurable existence thus depends either upon ability – or a natural tendency – to slink into a corner out of sight as much as possible, or

[8]Maurice O'Connor, 'Impressions Concerning Adaptation to Imprisonment', *Proceedings,* Canadian Congress of Corrections, 1957, pp. 110ff.
[9]Bruno Cormier, 'The Psychological Effects of the Deprivation of Liberty on the Offender', *Proceedings,* Canadian Congress of Corrections, 1957, pp. 137ff.
[10]Gresham Sykes, *op. cit.,* Chapter 3.

John V. Fornataro

upon skill in becoming an adaptable role-player. The latter, more common adaptation may be described as 'doing your own time', or as 'conniving' or 'deceiving', depending upon one's perspective. The social system of the prison in Canada has remained substantially unchanged despite official pronouncements of 'new deals' and the introduction of some changes calculated to improve the work of prisons. In some respects, certain innovations (many only at the level of jargon or of description) have made the problem of prison reform more difficult. At times, they have camouflaged issues, and often the simple substitution of one term for another has allowed officials and public alike to suppose that the substance also has been changed. Prisoners remain strangely like the legendary man from Missouri, and must be *shown*, not merely told, that the purpose and the methods of the prison have been changed to serve the best interests of the inmate, as a rational way of protecting the community in the long run. No great progress can be achieved as long as each part of the prison population sees the other as ever intent on deception.

CLASSIFICATION AND SEGREGATION

In spite of the ease with which many prison workers declare 'all cons are the same', in practice most of them reject such a simple notion. Very significant differences exist among men in prison as they do among men outside it. Prisons contain a few very dangerous men and a great many inadequate, bothersome, irresponsible, but otherwise relatively innocuous men. Most Canadian prisons have been constructed to provide the maximum custodial restraints necessary for the dangerous minority. This fact alone has contributed heavily to the deteriorating social system (described above) into which the offenders, the majority of whom are relatively harmless, are plunged. Some are never as harmless again until age makes them so.

The concept of classification rests on the premise that differences between prisoners are sufficiently critical and vital to demand differential ways of working with them. If all inmates were the same, there would be no grounds for distinguishing between them as to housing, custody, or program. The *Handbook on Classification in Correctional Institutions*[11] describes classification as 'a method that will assure co-ordination in diagnosis, training and treatment throughout the correctional process'. This is in essence a description to which penologists generally have subscribed. Operationally, however, there is not so much uniformity in applying the concept.

[11]*Handbook on Classification in Correctional Institutions,* New York: American Prison Association, 1947, p. 3.

The method of classification logically calls for four connected activities: a thorough appraisal of the inmate, oriented towards an understanding of the nature and extent of the disorder underlying his committal; the planning of an appropriate, integrated way of dealing with him – from his housing to his use of program resources – based on the results of the appraisal; the use of procedures and administrative organization so as to give effect to the authorized plan; and continuous evaluation of the effects of the plan, and modification as needed. The last step is sometimes referred to as reclassification, but it seems proper to include it as an integral part of classification if the description above is to be accepted.

Clearly, the processes implied in this outline demand a high degree of professional teamwork, general staff consensus on means and ends, and enlightened, imaginative administrative leadership. Rarely do Canadian prisons have the good fortune to possess all of these simultaneously. The overwhelming majority do not employ anything approaching classification, in spite of their use of the term in describing certain activities and in job titles.

A thoroughgoing adoption of classification practices offers at least two significant benefits, apart from the possible attainment of the therapeutic goal. First, it may be a means of eventually winning the inmate's genuine, direct participation in the correctional process, which is unmistakably concerned with *his* interests. No lasting gains are likely to be made in this direction simply by treatment gimmicks and catch-phrases. Secondly, the systematic collating of data and the habit of evaluating different methods of handling different inmates should encourage research and provide it with pertinent raw materials.

In 1947 the Penitentiary Service began establishing positions for Classification Officers and later for Classification Assistants. Major provincial prisons in Ontario, Saskatchewan, and British Columbia have had similar positions since 1950. Even in provincial institutions where no such titles are used, procedures are frequently employed that do not differ essentially from those formally described as classification. But the most prevalent activity is more likely to consist of allotting inmates to housing and work. In a few institutions, and with a few inmates, an approximation of classification is pursued with some rigour. Apart from these exceptions it is virtually impossible to implement the process under prevailing conditions. The ratio between inmate population and persons allocated to classification work does not permit the general employment of classification, even if personnel were all appropriately qualified for such work; at the time of writing, about seventeen years after the first establishment in Canada of such positions, people are being appointed Classification

John V. Fornataro

Officers and Classification Assistants who have no more-specialized qualifications than several years 'man management' experience obtained in military, police, or security forces, or a fresh B.A. degree. This compromise is by no means desired by most penal administrators, but the extent of its futility is not reduced by explanations that usually betray a deficient grasp of important concepts and a dearth of imaginative resourcefulness.

Sometimes there is a tendency to equate classification with segregation (an instance of the conceptual deficiency mentioned above). Segregation is the practice of allocating different categories of inmates to separate areas of the prison or to separate institutional units within the prison system. It may be employed to simplify certain housekeeping or administrative tasks, or to create maximum opportunity for giving effect to treatment plans formulated in the process of classification.

Very large prison systems are in the best position to segregate among institutions. Ontario has long possessed the largest assortment of diversified institutions calculated to leave each one with a reasonably homogeneous population. Some developments in this direction have occurred since the late 1940s in the provincial systems of New Brunswick, Saskatchewan, Alberta, and British Columbia. In a relatively recent development, the Penitentiary Service has begun to diversify institutions in order to provide for a degree of constructive segregation.

With the exception of institutional programs developed around the special needs of alcoholics, drug addicts, and inmates approaching release, systems of segregation appear to be related primarily to criteria such as age, length of sentence, and criminal history. These criteria yield prison populations who share some surface characteristics but who may be susceptible to totally different regimens of treatment. In Canada today, both internal segregation (within the same prison) and segregation among prisons primarily serve administrative and custodial expediency, rather than the object of resocializing inmates. To say this is to state a fact of administration rather than to make a judgment.

PRISON PROGRAM

A poll of Canadian opinion about what inmates do in prison would undoubtedly yield considerable variety. Some statutes still include 'hard labour' as part of the specification for punishment, and some judges are as uninformed as many lay people in thinking that such a sentence results in the offender's encounter with a rock pile.

The bitter truth is that prisons, as well as the outside community, endure unemployment as one of their most acute problems. Those who

310

may be inclined to pity offenders for the 'hard labour' element in their sentences would do better to exercise an active concern over the deadly·'·' idleness or the meaningless make-work to which inmates are consigned much of the time. Hard labour was conceived originally as an appropriate penalty. Apart from the desire to inflict punishment for crime, it was no doubt believed that persons required to perform manual labour would find this so objectionable that they would avoid the kind of behaviour that resulted in such a penalty. One wonders at the naïvety of legislators who drafted such penalties: if their reasoning worked out in practice, of course, the offender would be deterred not only from a life of crime, but also from doing any work – the ultimate penalty.

As long ago as March 1925, a few people interested in penal reform were concerned about the problems of idleness in prisons. During that month Miss Agnes Macphail, M.P., introduced a resolution in Parliament for the provision of a more adequate program of employment.[12]

The resolution included the idea that a system of payments for work should become a normal part of the prison's work program, with some earnings being sent to dependants. This was perceived by some prison-reform people of the day as a logical minimum approach to the task of preparing men to assume the normal responsibilities of citzenship. Nevertheless, the resolution was debated out of existence; it might well suffer a similar fate today. The principal objection is that the prisoner might enjoy advantages (of employment and earnings) that would seem to condone law-breaking and place a premium upon a prison sentence. This perspective upon the issue betrays not only how well preserved is the Elizabethan Poor Law principle of 'less eligibility'[13] but how deficient in imagination we are in our approach to the resolution of many social problems.

We know now that, far from being a form of punishment, work helps to satisfy our basic human needs. In our culture it is the most common means by which we procure our physical requirements. Beyond its economic value, however, work has become one of the most important means by which a man establishes his identity, experiences a sense of satisfaction and accomplishment, and wins the esteem of others. It may not be an exaggeration, then, to observe that an adequate work experience provides a man with one of his most valuable sources of self-respect. If this is accepted, work (of an appropriate sort) must be regarded as one of the

---

12Reported in John Kidman, *The Canadian Prison*, Toronto: Ryerson Press, 1947, p. 69.
13This principle in the Poor Law required that recipients of public charity should not enjoy a standard of living as good as the most destitute persons who were not in receipt of public charity. In effect, it should pay to be independent, though miserable.

most indispensable ingredients of a correctional program, and deficiencies in this respect must be given diligent and early remedy.

The vast majority of Canadian prison administrators continually attempt to ensure that every inmate is constructively occupied during the day. But generally speaking, prisons have developed a limited range of occupational activities that have become almost a stereotype of prison programs. Work activities may include industries, institutional production and services, and shop-work associated with vocational training. Some large institutions, such as the Ontario Reformatory at Guelph and the penitentiaries at Kingston and Collins Bay, carry on extensive industries, the products of which are consumed within the government service; even in smaller institutions industrial production is common. Institutional services commonly include housekeeping services covering a wide range: from cooking to painting, from mopping floors to maintaining the boiler-plant or the electrical system. In addition there are usually a number of prestigious 'cushy' paper jobs, frequently of doubtful usefulness, which are prized by inmates not only for their white-collar quality but for their close association with centres of information and influence. As one might expect, they are usually held by persuasive inmates possessing vast experience in institutions. The institution's farm is a common source of work of which the product is consumed by the institution itself.

Contemporary interest in utilizing educational methods in prison is reflected in the designation of some activities as partly vocational training and partly employment. This is often the case in mechanical or machine shops, in the manufacture of clothing, and in carpentry and allied shops. Some activities of this kind provide valuable instruction at a very high level of excellence, while others are so bad, both in the training they offer and in the work they produce, that they would not be tolerated outside of a prison. This is but one example of the limitation of official labels; they convey the official expectations or the image to be projected to the public, but they do not necessarily describe the reality. Despite the amount of publicity given to the vocational training activities of prisons, Canadian institutions on the whole provide limited opportunities of this sort. The Commissioner of Penitentiaries, for example, reported that at the end of 1960 there were 333 inmates engaged in training-courses.[14] This number was smaller than the number of first offenders under twenty-one years of age (375), which group might logically be expected to be most appropriately engaged in such programs. The other prison systems present no brighter picture, except in isolated cases of institutions where

[14]Commissioner of Penitentiaries, *Annual Report*, year ending March 31, 1960, Ottawa: Queen's Printer, 1960, pp. 15ff.

special efforts and resources have been devoted to strengthening training-programs in volume and in quality.

Academic instruction has also become part of the regular program of a number of Canadian prisons. Again, there is considerable danger of being grossly misinformed by the amount and kind of publicity given to these activities. This is evident when a judge on the one hand sentences an offender to a particular institution 'where you can learn a trade' or 'further your education', and on the other hand castigates a repeater for having failed to utilize his previous sentence in the advancement of his education. In the main, such a judge will speak in good faith but with deficient knowledge of the facts. A few young offenders may be offered a bona fide course of academic study in possibly half the provinces of Canada – if they have sufficient time in prison, and if they are committed to prisons with sound programs of education and qualified teachers. In the outside community there is a painful awareness that education must increasingly come to be regarded as a continuous process, especially in view of the impact of technology upon industry and upon the character of human relationships generally. The benefits of our new insights tend to be withheld from prisons for several generations; this tendency is not likely to be quickly reversed in order to equip inmates, by means of education, for more effective social functioning in the larger community.

Correspondence courses prepared under the auspices of the Department of Veterans Affairs for veterans of the Second World War provided some of the early impetus to academic study programs in Canadian prisons. As the initial requirements of veterans diminished, the Department acceded to requests from prison authorities for the use of course materials. In some instances these became the entire content of the prison's educational offering. Provincial departments of education generally extend to prison inmates the benefits of their correspondence-school courses, together with certification upon the successful completion of courses. A few inmates can persist in such programs of education with minimum help, but most need the tutoring and the encouragement of a competent instructor if they are to take full advantage of them. Only in a minority of Canadian prisons are these most favourable arrangements made. A few prisons in New Brunswick, Ontario, Saskatchewan, Alberta, and British Columbia have employed competent full-time teachers who provide substantial educational programs. At the present, however, these programs are so highly restricted in terms of the proportion of the prison population they serve that they might best be recognized as pilot or demonstration projects.

Since the early 1950s, changes in Canadian prison programs have perhaps been more evident in the use of leisure time than in any other single area of activity. It would be difficult to appraise the importance of these changes in relation to others that have been introduced, but the unique character of the prison's social structure tends to lend special importance to the way leisure time is employed – for leisure is bound up intimately with the distribution and use of privileges.

Time not spent in work, in Canadian prisons under all levels of government, has traditionally been dead time. It was the usual practice to confine inmates to their cells during this time. Some prison regulations stipulated that each inmate must be allowed exercise for thirty minutes or one hour daily. Very commonly this kind of rule was observed by parading men to the 'bull pen', a small and barren outdoor area bounded by a wall. Here inmates 'exercised' by shuffling around in a circle, or in some institutions by more informal and independently contrived activity or inactivity, until the prescribed time had elapsed. It was a credible reproduction of the aimless and bored hanging-around that characterizes the way in which many inmates spend much of their time on the outside. In prison, however, with its artificially homogeneous population and its aggravated tensions, exercise periods functioned as important occasions for communication and for barters, pay-offs, and similar unofficial and unauthorized transactions. On the whole, leisure time in Canada's prisons has in the past been neglected and empty time; the effects of it have been demoralizing and degenerative more than anything else. The problem has been all the more critical because of the inadequate programs of employment.

Since the Second World War, and especially since 1947, when the Department of Justice first publicized a 'new deal' in the penitentiaries, various activities have been sporadically undertaken in most prison systems, their object being to 'rehabilitate' the inmates. Without attempting an evaluation of this tendency here, it may fairly be observed that a large proportion of these activities have been directed towards the modification of the use of leisure time. The introduction of competitive team sports to prison programs, especially when they have involved participation in outside leagues, has provided the general public with one of the most graphic symbols of the 'new penology'. If, in fact, the public perception of contemporary Canadian correctional effort is symbolized thus, the explosion at frequent intervals of reactions against the 'molly-coddling' and indulgence of offenders should not be surprising.

Other leisure-time activities that are becoming increasingly typical include the learning of hand crafts and the individual production of hand-craft articles, and participation in a variety of small or special groups ranging from chapters of Alcoholics Anonymous to play and entertainment groups. A few prisons have embarked upon the use of group discussions, described variously as group therapy or group counselling, scheduled for the late afternoon and the evening. In spite of the fact that considerable dead or aimless time remains, the leisure time of most prisons in Canada is now somewhat more free of rigid physical control than formerly, and the inmate has more choice in his use of it. But only in a few instances is this relaxation accompanied by the practice of more enlightened socializing techniques. Most frequently it reflects a rather mechanical attempt to keep up with the Joneses in penal practice. Where such relaxation is put into effect without adequate understanding of its implications and without skilful correlation of means and ends, it is to be anticipated that the inmates who are most prison-wise will virtually run the place.[15]

A number of professional services may be regarded by some observers as part of the prison program, possibly because they have grown in importance and taken up an increased proportion of the time in some prisons. These would include casework or counselling activities, chaplaincy services, and psychiatric and other medical or clinical services. It is probably inaccurate to describe them as part of the program: where they exist, although their staff tend to become related to the administrative organization, they can be considered as providing special services to a small number of individuals in response to specific problems or complaints. It is these services that are usually associated with the concept of treatment in the institution, rather than the more customary activities and services that affect the daily life of the inmate.

Even in institutions where the administration is thoroughly committed to the goal of resocializing the inmate for the benefit of both himself and the community, the ratio of professional personnel to inmates does not approach the minimum requirements for adequate service to all who require it. Treatment does not consist only of such services, nor do all prisoners require them; but even the fraction who might appropriately use the competent services of a caseworker, clinical psychologist, clergyman, psychiatrist, neurologist, or other professional worker cannot expect adequate help at the present time. A few prisons employ one or more members of these professions on a full-time basis, but their capacity to provide direct individual service is minimal, partly because of the unfavourable ratio betwen inmates and practitioners. Most prisons retain medical, religious, and other professional services on a part-time or a

---

15Richard R. Korn and Lloyd W. McCorkle, *Criminology and Penology*, New York: Henry Holt and Co., 1959, especially pp. 528-30.

John V. Fornataro

contractual basis. The great majority do not have professionally qualified social workers on their staffs.

These resources, then, where they do exist, tend to be used in response to emergencies or to insistent clamour for attention to some troublesome symptom. Unfortunately, this has at times resulted in the view that the so-called treatment forces are ineffectual except for labelling the emotionally unstable and the mentally ill in the prison and, where possible, suppressing them or transferring them to mental hospitals.

The prevailing inmate culture militates against the appropriate utilization of clinical services. The labelling in prison argot of clinical personnel as 'head-shrinkers' or 'bug-doctors' indicates the bizarre character that both the practitioner and his patient are perceived as possessing. This attitude is a potent deterrent to inmates' taking the initiative in requesting such service, for the importance of acceptance and approval by one's peers is likely to be more crucial in prison than in any of the usual settings in the wider community. The employment of certain less well understood disciplines and procedures, such as casework and some medical specializations, requires a shrewd preparation of both inmates and staff to ensure reasonably consistent support of the services and of those participating in them.

PERSONNEL

The men and women who are employed in prison make up part of its living community. Earlier in this chapter, reference was made to the critical impact that the relative freedom of employees to go outside the walls exerts upon the institution's social structure. Despite possible benevolent attitudes and a desire to assist the inmate to a more satisfying existence, officials, in the view of the inmate group, constitute the opposition.

Personnel are in a paradoxical situation. They form a distinct minority of the total population and are identified with law-abiding behaviour; yet they are expected to exercise authority over a law-violating majority. The minority have loosely articulated authority, not unlike that of a military force in wartime, but the majority are not committed to the rules of the game and the premises under which constituted authority is expected to function. Notwithstanding the seemingly limitless and absolute power that is accorded prison officials, they are part of a complicated, abnormal social system in which sheer physical force becomes a clumsy – even an unwieldy – instrument for ensuring an orderly existence. Professor Sykes examines this limitation of official authority in a chapter that no prison employee should neglect to study with care.[16]

The personnel constitute that segment of the prison population that is expected to give direction, purpose, and focus to the entire organization. Failure on the part of officials to fulfil this function inevitably results in leaving to the inmate part of the community the initiative in determining the goals and the norms of the institution, whether these have formal sanction or not. Moreover, it is clearly unsatisfactory that a small handful of top officials articulate and attempt to execute valid organizational purposes unless the total work force at every level of the hierarchy is deliberately made party to the enterprise.

Canadian prison employees are by no means a homogeneous group. They include some teachers, mechanics, farmers, doctors, engineers, social workers, truck drivers, retired army officers and ex-policemen, and a larger number of persons without any particular vocational competence. Some prison staff are sadistic, some are sentimental; most are between these extremes. Some are venal, some are the soul of integrity; some are indebted to politicians for their jobs, most are not. Their views about the causes and the cures of crime are as varied as those in the outside community. It is no wonder, therefore, that the administering of prisons as distinctly therapeutic and resocializing communities is still far from a reality in Canada.

A search for some kind of intelligible reason for the conglomerate character of Canadian prison personnel seems futile. It appears to be the product of several influences, many totally irrelevant if not hostile to the professed reformative goals assented to by most governments. The presence of personnel trained in such professional disciplines as education, social work, psychiatry, and psychology reflects the stated intention of governments to operate their prison system for the remedy or 'correction' of the offender. In a few institutions, officials with such qualifications occupy key administrative positions. In most, however, they do not hold positions in the direct line of authority, and frequently exert no real influence upon the institution's régime. This is the group commonly called 'treatment staff', as distinct from 'custodial staff'.

The security requirements of prisons have traditionally enjoyed priority of the highest degree. Personnel recruitment has reflected this preoccupation, particularly in some jurisdictions that place a premium upon such qualifications as police or military experience. The presumption is that this kind of previous experience equips an officer as an expert in so-called

---

[16]Gresham Sykes, *op. cit.*, Chapter 3.

'man management'; but the conclusion seems inescapable that the principal competence that those possessing such backgrounds are expected to contribute has to do with surveillance and with the mobilization and use of physical resources to enforce conformity.

A number of technical tradesmen and artisans are essential to the efficient operation and maintenance of the institutional plant, and to the basic housekeeping services. While these employees are typically regarded as auxiliary staff whose concern is the efficient physical operation of the institution, they do exert some influence upon the total life of the prison by their supervision of inmate groups who work in some of the most strategic areas of the prison. These officers are in a position to give useful vocational instruction to supervised inmates having sufficient interest and capacity to learn. A few prisons deliberately structure program to capitalize on this.

The great majority of prison officers are recruited from a variety of occupations bearing no special relationship to the alleged purposes of a correctional institution. They are designated as guards, custodial officers, supervisors, or correctional officers. These are the persons who are expected to oversee the inmate population from admission to release, during work and leisure time; their immediate task is the supervision and the good management of prisoners. No class of prison employees is more intimate with the inmate population or in a more strategic position to affect it; yet, paradoxically, no class is less carefully selected and prepared for its work, and less adequately compensated for the responsibility it is expected to bear. As long as this condition remains, and it is typical, we must expect the prison guard to lack genuine public esteem. What is more serious, we must expect instability of personnel and relatively negative results from prison programs. This situation arises from causes that can be understood and changed, and it cannot be dismissed as inevitable or innately bound up with institutions.[17]

The quality of the personnel in the prison constitutes the single most important influence on the day-to-day life inside and on the eventual personal and social adjustment of the prisoner when he is released. There is no more urgent subject, then, for executive attention in the administration of the prison.

In turn, no aspect of personnel management is of more critical importance than the training of staff – *all* staff. The grossly artificial social context of which the officer is an integral – indeed the pivotal – member;

---

[17]For a parallel in mental hospitals, see Alfred H. Stanton and Morris S. Schwartz, *The Mental Hospital*, a study of institutional participation in psychiatric illness and treatment, New York: Basic Books Inc., 1954, pp. 103ff.

the immense variety of sorts of people who make up the work force, which deprives it of cohesiveness; the low status of prison employees in the outside community: all demand a curriculum of training aimed at producing career officials of the highest competence.

Although several jurisdictions in Canada claim to engage in training-programs for their prison personnel, only one (Saskatchewan, in 1953) has instituted a reasonably comprehensive and universal one. The content is covered over a three-year period coincidental with supervised work. At the conclusion of each year's work the student employees write substantial examinations, which they must pass before being permitted to continue. Upon successful completion of the three-year basic training, the officer has his accomplishment recognized by receiving a certificate at an impressive public function. He also receives, in addition to his normal increments, a continuing salary bonus. Successful completion of the course also qualifies him for promotional consideration.

The Saskatchewan training-program should by no means be regarded as a blueprint for other prison systems, but it does suggest the dimensions of a minimal program. The overwhelming majority of prisons have a sink-or-swim approach to new personnel, and many officers receive their most indelible instruction from inmates or from inaccurate deductions made from their own observations. A few institutions offer some degree of orientation to new personnel, often describing this as staff training. Occasionally brief seminars or training-sessions may be provided for limited numbers or for special categories of personnel. In effect, those responsible for these efforts are making a token acknowledgment of the importance of training, without actually undertaking it.

Since 1948 the Penitentiary Service has conducted a centralized staff-training program intended to provide leadership in the training of its prison officers. The first staff-training college was opened in 1952. Until 1962 its classes consisted of about twenty-four penitentiary officers selected from across the nation, except for training or conference sessions designed for sometimes smaller specialized groups such as chief vocational officers, penitentiary administrators, or clerical and typing staff. The 'regular custodial course' was offered three or four times annually and was completed in approximately six weeks. Changes in 1962 have resulted in basic training becoming the responsibility of each penitentiary, the staff college being reserved for special courses. During the year ending 1960, a total of 137 trainees out of a total penitentiary work force of 2,261 participated in the offerings of the Penitentiary Staff College.[18]

18Commissioner of Penitentiaries, *op. cit.*

While these activities may perform useful functions, it is obvious that the systematic and thorough training of a career service cannot be accomplished thus. Whether the local penitentiary's basic training can achieve this goal any better is very doubtful unless it is provided with training officers who are well equipped to supplement the usual teaching of the custodial aspect with material drawn from relevant legal, sociological, social-work, psychiatric, and related sources.

Concomitant with a training-program of intensity and breadth, there must be administrative direction that gives credibility to the concepts communicated in instruction. Elsewhere the author has argued that the content of training-programs must proceed from and give substance to executive decisions concerning purpose and policy.[19] It is of little value, and may be of harm, to teach an officer what is expected of the institution and its various employees if at the same time he sees quite contrary practices and standards applied in his own institution under the authority of his superior officers. The theoretical ideal will certainly not be achieved quickly in most prisons. Despite the relative remoteness of the ideal, however, it should not be regarded as irrelevant. Training, in short, is not an academic exercise, but must be related purposively to the life of the prison, as a basic means of executing policy. The enhanced qualifications of personnel will make an impact upon the institution's whole life.

A well-trained officer has a right to expect his knowledge and his competent performance to be recognized adequately in his salary. Society produces few if any social problems more complex and more resistant to ameliorative efforts than those associated with many prisoners. Men and women who develop competence in their work with persistent offenders, so that society is better protected and troubled human beings find life more satisfying, are unquestionably entitled to financial and moral recognition of a high order. But until personnel are appropriately equipped, they are unlikely to enjoy such rewards.

IS THE 'NEW DEAL' REAL?

The prison occupies a central position in Canada's administration of criminal justice. For many officials and private citizens it seems to be a source of reassurance, a means of protection against the infliction of loss and harm by law violators. Others have come to regard prison as much a part of living as some regard church attendance – either as an occasional event or as a way of life.

---

[19] J. V. Fornataro, 'What are the staff training problems for Canadian prisons?', *The Canadian Journal of Corrections*, October 1963, pp. 292-301.

In recent years Canadians, together with others in the civilized world, have shown signs of feeling not altogether comfortable about simply locking people up and throwing away the key. We are uneasy when disinterested and rigorous examiners, such as the social scientists referred to earlier in this chapter, probe below the surface of the prison and compare it to a totalitarian state or a decadent society. Consequently we have been at some pains to convince ourselves that prisons are centres of study, remedy, and restoration.

The fact is that prisons look better on paper than they are in reality. It will be noted that this chapter is deficient in facts and figures about Canadian prisons and their precise accomplishments. The author's omission in this regard is deliberate. Official statements and reports include negligible quantities of objective data, for there is a neglect of research and even a lack of reliable statistical reporting. Moreover, those reports that *are* available understandably seek to provide the most favourable interpretation of prison activities. The actual life of the prison often bears little resemblance to what is reported, partly because means and ends have not been reconciled. A like observation was reported by the International Penal and Penitentiary Foundation, which undertook to discover, by a survey of their methods, what various countries meant by 'penal treatment'. In the preface to his report, M. Paul Cornil, the Foundation's president, stated: 'The observer finds that most of our prison services appear incongruous and illogical; the purely punitive attitude survives in spite of the attempt to use methods of treatment based on an entirely different philosophy.'[20]

In 1943, C. W. Topping, a Canadian sociologist, commented that 'there seem to be but two statements in praise of Canadian jails that can be made, the first of which is that they are spotlessly clean; the second that few persons escape from within their walls'.[21] On the whole, we have expected prisons to be unpleasant enough to act as a deterrent, constructive enough to 'rehabilitate' – and *quiet*: citizens and officials alike tend to be satisfied and at ease if prisons and their populations are out of the news.

The most elementary observations should disabuse Canadians of their misplaced confidence in prisons as defences against crime. Our demand for prison accommodation has exceeded our prison capacity, and additional penal facilities have been erected across the country continuously

---

[20]M. Paul Cornil, *Modern Methods of Penal Treatment*, Paris: International Penal and Penitentiary Foundation, 1955, p. viii.

[21]C. W. Topping, *Canadian Penal Institutions* (revised), Toronto: Ryerson Press, 1943, p. 92.

since shortly after the Second World War. The rate of increase in prison population has exceeded that in national population. Rates of recidivism are relatively the same as they were at the time of the Archambault Report (1938), and the crimes committed are not less serious in nature. To blame the 'new penology' for not producing positive results is to fail to recognize that in Canada we have done very little more than *talk* about a new approach. Penal administration and legislatures, in the main, have been seriously deficient both in an integrated philosophy of corrections and in imaginatively constructive ideas.

The prisons do form a part of our total national community. Soon or late they exert an influence upon the larger community – historically it has been one of costly disadvantage. If the public's expectations of protection, through the 're-forming' of people, are to be realized, it will be essential to engage first in rigorously honest appraisal of the effects of prison, and in rationally determined approaches to the reorganization of the penal system. Further tinkering will be wasteful and irresponsible. In Canada, prison is a way of life in defiance of the basic principles of humanitarianism, of reason, and indeed of civilization itself.

THE RELEVANCE OF A RATIONAL IDEAL

Mediocrity and resistance to radical improvement in the public services are sometimes thought to be legitimate because of their practicality. By inference, the application of the fruits of rational endeavour and of scientifically deduced insights is regarded as impractical and visionary. It is one of the theses of this chapter that prevailing Canadian penal practices very evidently avoid the implications of rationality and research, and just as evidently have failed to meet the practical requirement of efficient goal attainment.

Although it is outside the scope of this chapter to propose detailed penal revisions or to prognosticate as to the future of Canadian prisons, it may be pertinent to suggest the merest outlines for a more desirable prison model. At the outset it should be recognized that the system of imprisonment for crime should be purposively co-ordinated in the total system of criminal justice. Comprehensive pre-sentence and probation services, within competently manned courts, would unquestionably reduce the numbers of offenders receiving institutional sentences. The universal use of sensible methods for paying fines by instalment, including provision for working them off and for making restitution, would further stem the flow of essentially harmless persons into prison.

Two main functions appear to be appropriate to institutions for offenders. First, institutions are required for the physical restraint of persons who endanger the safety of others in the free community. Prison workers know that these are a very small minority of the current prison population – ten per cent is probably a liberal estimate. Secondly, institutional resources seem to be our best recognized means of providing for the special or the complex needs of those whose behavioural difficulties are beyond the usual reach or capacity of community resources. Of other possible functions, the deterrent effect of imprisonment has obviously been overrated, and Canadians cannot afford such an expensive method of emotional gratification for the vengeful law-abiding.

Considerably more research of a systematic kind should be conducted with a view to determining the most effective criteria for classifying imprisoned offenders. This task, like many other inquiries involved in penal research, needs to be recognized as continuous and experimental in character. Hard and fast answers, valid for all times and conditions are unlikely.

It appears reasonable to hope that different institutions might develop special resources most appropriate to the requirements of specific groups of offenders. These resources would include not merely capital equipment, but personnel, and the social milieu not only of the institution but also of the immediate community outside. Even though these facilities might be administered in different political jurisdictions, there should be no obstacle in policy preventing the timely referral of inmates to the setting in which they could most effectively be treated. Agreements between governments for reciprocal payment for services, and for the ultimate return of inmates to their home jurisdiction (preferably on parole or with after-care service) are practicable; and precedents exist.

Such arrangements, of course, imply willingness to subordinate vested interests to a well co-ordinated system of institutional services. While it seems logical that the federal government should give leadership in the co-ordinating process, there are cogent reasons for allowing other jurisdictions considerable autonomy in the development of programs that appear relevant – or experimentally pertinent – to the needs of local groups of offenders. The special problems of drug addicts may serve as illustration.

Whether or not governments are prepared for such a degree of disinterested collaboration, their correctional institutions should be reasonably consistent in certain vital respects. It should be recognized in every institution that its primary reason for existence is the community's wish for protection against the social and antisocial acts of the institution's resident population. The aggravation of the inmate's original deficiencies

John V. Fornataro

in social adaptation, by the institution's neglect or by deficient handling, deserves to be regarded as failure – and even social sabotage.

Since correctional services are oriented to adequate social functioning in the larger community, each inmate should be deliberately associated with healthy aspects of the community as fully as is consistent with his capacity. Specifically, unless it is patently unsafe either for himself or for members of the community, he ought to be able to visit his family or helpful friends. It should be routine for many to avail themselves of educational and employment resources in the community.

In some instances, of course, the institution cannot extend so much liberty. One of its most crucial obligations is to retrain its inmates in the area of social relationships. This extension of liberty may well be regarded as an end product, necessitating a number of previous steps *en route* in retraining. The less artificial (by dissociation from the outside) the institution is permitted to be, the greater hope for realistic socialization to occur.

What is suggested here is by no means a kind of laissez-faire approach to the resident population, allowing them total determination of their own régime of treatment. (The present course of expediency in prisons tends to leave the actual balance of power with the inmates, and with those inmates least committed to the social values of our society.) Hospitals and schools in the general community provide suggestive models for comparison: in them, the regimen of the total organization for the collective needs of the entire group, as well as for the periodically changing requirements of individual members, is the product of professional judgments made by the administration.

This process of decision-making ought to involve the conscientious securing of relevant facts on a continuous basis, just as medical and educational decision-making is most sound when the fullest cognizance of the facts is taken. And the subjective perceptions, feelings, and attitudes of the residents are highly relevant facts, in view of the institutional goal. It seems inescapable that inmates must be assisted to participate directly in the identification of obstacles (personal and organizational) to adequate social performance, and to participate in the discovery of effective ways of coping with such difficulties. Both the resident and the administration must be prepared to make adaptations consistent with the social objects of the institution. The safeguard against a 'con-run' prison is the professional competence of the administration. While the administration can comfortably involve the inmate in his own re-socialization, they are knowledgeable and detached and are thus capable of recognizing and

324

responding to feelings and attitudes without relinquishing program control.

The approach suggested here would draw the hostile displeasure both of some officials and of prison-wise inmates. The latter, too, have vested interests in the status quo. In view of the complexity of the task, it should be redundant to observe that its direction calls for the greatest personal maturity and professional competence. Nothing less can be trusted.

13

Parole

F. P. MILLER

The writer of this chapter takes no position in the discussion of theories of the causation and correction of crime. He acknowledges only the practical necessity to operate in his own field on what appear to be the most common-sense current beliefs. In this respect, it is felt that elements of deterrence, treatment, and training are interwoven not inconsistently with a concept of individual moral responsibility.

Tappan has said:

> ... the doctrine of moral responsibility has been woven so tight into the fabric of the criminal and penal law that it can be reworked only very slowly, and then only for the most part by an embroidery at the edge that is ill patterned to the cloth. Ideas of partial responsibility, of irresistible impulses, psychopathic personality, and other extenuating circumstances have come to mitigate the full rigors of a retributive justice, but the ancient rationale persists as the essential design.[1]

Members of a parole board and members of their staff are in a unique position to survey the efforts that are being made to treat the offender and to protect society. Daily they have before them the views of the courts, the police, the institutional officials, the after-care agencies, the inmate himself, his friends, and sometimes even his victims.

They are, as it were, the inspectors of a partially finished product, and it is they who must select those offenders who appear to be ready to return to society. They hope, in each case, that the parolee has matured sufficiently so that his rehabilitation will be furthered by the restraints and services provided by parole – full consideration being given to the protection of the public and the administration of justice.

[1]P. W. Tappan, *Contemporary Correction,* New York: McGraw-Hill, 1951.

Parole is the testing period of the whole correctional-treatment process. Certainly it is a testing period in the eyes of the public.

ORIGINS OF PAROLE

Parole is frequently confused with probation, which is dealt with in Chapter 9. There are some similarities, but there are important differences. Their originators, however, do share a common motive: to provide a means of placing the offender in the community while still under sentence.

Parole grew out of the change in the point of view in penal philosophy, from one of retributive punishment to one of reformation. Many people began to believe that the most socially economic way of protecting society is to restore the offender to normal social functioning. This belief led to a view that it might not be either necessary or desirable for a criminal to spend his full sentence in prison.

Three early basic concepts from which parole developed were:
1. Conditional remission of part of sentence;
2. A contract or agreement;
3. Supervision.

Remission of part of a sentence as an act of clemency was an ancient royal prerogative. Frequently such remission was conditional upon the performance of certain stipulated acts such as making restitution or other amends. This forerunner of parole gives it the element of clemency, which continues to cling despite the protests of its modern-day proponents.

The term 'parole', of course, comes from the French 'je donne ma parole' (I give my word). From this sprang the idea of parole as an agreement or contract between the ex-prisoner and the authority that he would conduct himself in accordance with certain specified terms. Supervision was a necessary corollary, since no agreement could be enforced or sanctions imposed without supervision.

Parole in the sense of conditional freedom was well understood in the case of the indentured servant, and the merits of this arrangement were carried forward in developing the idea.

Parole was an easy procedure to follow the transporting of criminals – generally to Australia – which was common penal practice in the seventeenth and eighteenth centuries. Captain Alex Maconochie introduced a 'stage' system of parole in Norfolk Island in 1840. The ticket-of-leave system of Crofton in Ireland followed. Similar efforts were being made in several parts of the world. Indeterminate sentences were introduced in Germany in 1532 and in Spain in 1832.

By 1865 the ticket-of-leave system was well known in the United States. At that stage prisoners' aid societies were active in fostering the idea of parole. The first full-fledged parole system was established after the opening of Elmira Reformatory in New York in 1876.

PURPOSE OF PAROLE AND DEFINITIONS

Parole is a conditional release from prison. It is a method whereby the offender serves part of his sentence outside the prison in the community. As a method of release it usually implies:

1. Selectivity (A goes out and B stays in);
2. Shortening of the term of imprisonment (A does not serve the full sentence of the court in prison).

Consequently it is sometimes difficult to separate parole from clemency and difficult to deny that it is, in a sense, an interference with the sentence of the court in the context of the Canadian sentencing system.

As a process, parole implies:

1. Restrictions or conditions with sanctions;
2. Surveillance of varying degrees;
3. Service and treatment of the offender.

In these ways it is expected that society will be protected and the offender rehabilitated.

Almost anyone today will subscribe to the generalization that 'parole is a good thing', but each may have his own concept of what parole is.

It is frequently justified, however, on several grounds (not all equally convincing):

1. It reduces the damaging effect of imprisonment, if only because it shortens the term.
2. It encourages good behaviour.
3. It encourages the utilization of institutional facilities for treatment and training.
4. It bridges the transition from the restrictions of prison to the freedom of community life.
5. It allows the offender to be a wage-earner, and thus to support his family and contribute to the economic life of the community.
6. It costs less than imprisonment.
7. It allows the state to restrict the activities of the offender.
8. It allows continuing treatment of the offender in a relatively non-punitive setting.

Some people (both theorists and members of the general public) think of parole as treatment and service. Some others think of it as clemency. Still others think of it as a method for further punitive control. With some persons the emphasis is on the act of releasing, and with others it is on the continuation of the sentence after release. In practice, it works out to be a compromise between these several aspects. The actual nature of parole in any given jurisdiction is determined by the law, the practices of the courts, and the policies of the parole authority.

HISTORY OF PAROLE IN CANADA

Parole has a long history in Canada. For years this country shared with the State of California the distinction of preserving for it the historic term 'ticket of leave'. When Canada's first parole legislation was introduced into Parliament in 1898, the term was current in England and the legislators chose to use it; so for sixty years the Canadian Parole Act was known as the 'Ticket of Leave Act'.

Speaking to the new Bill in 1898, the Prime Minister of that day recognized the problem, which faced a discharged inmate of a penal institution, of readjustment to the free community. Conditional liberation was an obvious method to bridge the gap between the control and restraints of institutional life and the freedom and responsibilities of community life. Under the terms of the Ticket of Leave Act, the Governor General of Canada could, on the advice of a minister of the cabinet – usually the Solicitor General – grant a conditional release (parole) to *any* person serving a term of imprisonment. There were no statutory limitations on eligibility, and the Act in effect made all sentences indeterminate with the maximum to be served set by the court. In practice, of course, there were certain departmental rules restricting eligibility to some degree.

Other federal legislation, passed several years later, made provision for a restricted type of parole in two provinces – Ontario and British Columbia – through a system of so-called indeterminate sentences. In these two provinces, provincial parole boards were given jurisdiction to grant parole to an inmate serving an indeterminate sentence when he had satisfied the minimum, or definite, portion of his sentence. In British Columbia, the indeterminate sentence was limited to a selected class of youthful offenders sentenced to classified institutions. This type of parole in Canada will be dealt with in more detail later.

Prior to 1898 some persons were released from custody by order of the Governor General upon the advice of a minister of the Crown. This was possible as an expression of the royal prerogative of mercy. However, most, if not all, of these releases were unconditional, as there was no one to enforce any condition. It is safe to say that such releases were approved mainly, if not exclusively, because of humanitarian considerations and were properly described as exercises of clemency.

The concept of clemency was destined to permeate thinking on parole for many years following the enactment of parole legislation. This is understandable. For lack of basic and reliable information on the inmate, the administrators of the Act for many years could hardly make an assessment of the social risk involved in releasing an offender. For the protection of the public as well as their own, they were inclined to make use of strict rules of practice that were ultimately established. The net result was that for a long time clement features were of paramount importance in decisions rendered.[2]

When the Ticket of Leave Act first came into force, Canada was a new country, sparsely settled across its vast areas, and it was not easy to develop a system of close parole supervision. It is not surprising that policy in the main was conservative down through the years. Much reliance was placed upon a provision in the Act for monthly reporting by the parolee to the local police. But even in the early years, the need for some form of guidance was recognized, and the Salvation Army Prison Gates Section undertook to give assistance in this respect.

In the early days of this century, this section of the Salvation Army was the one active organization in the field of after-care. Not only did the Salvation Army undertake to provide supervision for some of the persons released on ticket of leave, but one of its officers, Brigadier Archibald, joined the staff of the Department of Justice in 1905 as the first Dominion Parole Officer. He was succeeded in 1922 by Robert Creighton, a former warden of Kingston Penitentiary, who retired in 1927. Mr. Creighton was followed by R. F. Harris, who remained until the position was abolished in 1931. The Dominion Parole Officer visited penal institutions, interviewed inmates, and checked up on character references and prospects of employment for prisoners applying for ticket of leave.

This official, however, was apparently not the person responsible for the full investigation of each case or for the direct presentation of advice to the responsible minister. The administration of the Act, as well as the royal prerogative of mercy, was handled by officers in the Department of Justice who finally constituted a section in the Department known as the Remission Branch and later the Remission Service. First head of the Branch, appointed in 1913, was Pierre Côté, followed by J. D. Clarke. M. F. Gallagher, Q.C., who was appointed in 1924, remained in office for twenty-eight years until his retirement in 1952. His successor was A. A. Moffat, Q.C., who was followed by A. J. MacLeod, Q.C., in 1953.

[2]B. Godbout, 'Remission Service Policy and Practice', Paper delivered Regional Conference on After-Care, Moncton, March 12, 1958.

Mr. MacLeod remained as director until the Service was abolished on February 15, 1959.

The years 1924 to 1931 saw a reorganization of the Service, the absorption of the office of the Dominion Parole Officer, and the formulation of rules of practice. This followed a period in which there had been some serious criticism that paroles had been granted too liberally.

In the depression years prison populations increased and the number of tickets of leave increased concurrently. Then during the Second World War, special attention was directed towards what became known as 'the special war purposes ticket of leave' by which selected persons were released to join the armed forces or to work in war industry.

During post-war years there was considerable development in both institutional treatment and after-care of offenders. In penitentiaries and in several provincial institutions many new facilities for rehabilitation came into being. Vocational training and educational courses began fitting many inmates to become productive citizens. Psychologists, social workers, and other trained specialists were helping inmates to understand their personal problems. Group activities, such as those of Alcoholics Anonymous, and group counselling were giving opportunities for self-expression and the sharing of experience. During the same period and since, there has been a great expansion in the services of after-care agencies in the country as a whole, and in probation services in several of the provinces.

It can be easily seen how these improvements in institutional and community services enabled the Remission Service to expand in the field of parole. As the institutions produced better prospects for conditional release and the after-care and probation services offered better facilities for assistance and guidance, it was possible to release more persons on ticket of leave. The Remission Service first recognized the trend in 1949, and it was decided to open two regional offices, one in Vancouver and one in Montreal.

During the years 1950 to 1955, an increasing number of after-care societies recognized the contribution they could make in offering guidance to the person released on ticket of leave. Working arrangements were made with provincial probation services and the Ontario Provincial Parole and Rehabilitation Service to assist in community investigations and parole supervision.

In 1949 there were eighty parole cases in which special qualified supervision through an after-care agency or a provincial probation or parole agency was arranged. In 1955 the number had risen to 768 and in 1959 had reached 1,773.

In 1957 the Remission Service took a major step forward in the opening of four new regional offices, in Winnipeg, Toronto, Kingston, and Moncton. With the two existing offices this made possible the establishment of a regional organization of six divisions.

This and other staff expansion made it possible for the Service to attempt to promote a better integration of all parts of the correctional organization in Canada. During the preceding years a system of more complete investigation and intensified analysis of the cases had been developed. Except for short sentences or cases presenting strongly compassionate features, the Service had ceased to look on tickets of leave as primarily exercises of clemency. In keeping with the original intent of the legislators, tickets of leave were thought of more as authentic parole releases. Consistent with this concept, the Service accepted the responsibility of following the progress of each individual parolee through the supervisors it had appointed.

In anticipation of a legal requirement to do so, the Service built up an interim system of automatic review. This first brought all long-sentence cases under control and was in the process of being extended to all penitentiary cases when the new Parole Act came into force in 1959.

As might have been expected, the apparent 'success rate' was relatively high. One study of 924 parolees released during 1950 revealed that less than four per cent were recommitted during the parole period. At the end of five years, 681 members of the group, or 73.71 per cent, had not violated parole nor been subsequently sentenced to prison on a new offence. This group includes persons under sentences as short as six months and as long as life imprisonment.

Nevertheless, within this policy it was still possible to give much consideration to the recidivist, particularly where good institutional facilities for training and treatment existed, and when the inmate had served sufficient time for the training and treatment to have had their full impact and for some natural maturation to have taken place. Among recidivists are some persons found by the courts to be 'habitual criminals' or 'criminal sexual psychopaths' who are placed under preventive detention for an indeterminate period. (This should not be confused with the so-called indeterminate sentences under the provisions of the Prisons and Reformatories Act, which will be discussed later, and which, despite the name, have fixed limits. The indeterminate period of preventive detention is 'indeterminate to life'.)

Canada's preventive detention law had been in operation approximately eleven years at the time of the repeal of the Ticket of Leave Act in 1959. However, only about seventy-five persons had been committed during this period. Most of these were persons found to be 'habitual criminals', many of them drug addicts. The cases were reviewed at least once in every three years, and up to December 31, 1958, it had been found possible to release twelve men on licence who had been detained for periods ranging from six to eleven years. The periods for which they had been at liberty at that time ranged from a few months to approximately four years. Licences had been revoked in two cases.

For several years the after-care societies had been receiving grants-in-aid from the Penitentiaries Branch for their assistance to discharged prisoners, but by 1954 the department felt that the special services rendered in ticket-of-leave work needed recognition. Consequently, funds were appropriated for distribution, as a grant-in-aid, in proportion to the actual service rendered.

In 1954 also, the Remission Service, in co-operation with the Penitentiaries Service, initiated an annual conference of the several agencies working with the offender. Representatives of the various supervising agencies (government and private) met annually in conference with Remission Service officials, institutional officials, National Employment Service officers, and some police representatives to discuss mutual problems. Four such annual conferences were held on a national basis. Five regional conferences in 1958 made possible a wider representation and the examination of activities at the local level.

Parole in Canada received much encouraging attention following the publication in 1956 of a report of a committee appointed by the Minister of Justice to inquire into this subject. This committee, under the chairmanship of Mr. Justice Gérald Fauteux of the Supreme Court of Canada, reported on the developments under the existing law and made recommendations for further expansion, including the establishment of a national parole board. Specifically in this last matter the committee stated:

> We consider that a number of fundamental principles should be kept in mind in determining what method of parole administration will be best for Canada. The system should take into account, among other things, the large size of Canada, in a geographical sense, and its relatively small size, in terms of population. It should also take into account the division of legislative power and administrative responsibility between one federal and ten provincial governments.
>
> With these matters in mind, then, we suggest that Canada's parole system should be developed in accordance with the following principles:
> (a) it should provide for continued uniformity of parole administration, but at the same time avoid undue rigidity of practice and procedure;
> (b) it should take into account local conditions which may vary in different parts of the country;

(c) it should be designed to assist in the development, as far as possible, of probation services, specialized penal institutions and after-care agencies;

(d) it should, as far as possible, be a simple but efficient system; and

(e) it should be built up from the present system during an appropriate transitional period and not instituted by any sudden, wholesale abandonment of the present system.

We are firmly of the opinion that the parole authority for Canada should be a quasi judicial body rather than, as is presently the case, a Minister of the Crown acting in an exclusively administrative capacity. The parole authority, we believe, should not be one that is liable to be subjected to the external and internal pressures which are, inevitably, brought to bear on Ministers of the Crown. We have no reason to believe that such pressures exert any influence in connection with the granting of Tickets of Leave at the present time. However, we do believe that it is in the best interests of Canada that the parole authority should, at all times, be in a position to say that its judgments can only be based on the merits of the particular case and that it is not open, in any way, to influence by extraneous considerations.

We recommend, therefore, the establishment of a national parole board, with headquarters in Ottawa, to have the jurisdiction indicated hereunder. It has been suggested to us that regional parole boards would be a satisfactory alternative. We reject this suggestion, because we consider that only a national board, having over-all jurisdiction, will be able to develop and maintain a national parole policy and practice, and provide the uniformity of administration that we consider to be so essential in this aspect of the Canadian correctional field.[3]

These recommendations are now in the process of implementation. Canada's new Parole Act came into force on February 15, 1959, bringing to an end a sixty-year phase of Canadian parole history and starting a new era under the National Parole Board.

CANADIAN PAROLE LEGISLATION

Prisons and Reformatories Act

In discussing legislation let us examine this not-too-well-known Act that has a number of hidden sections on parole. Surprisingly enough, it provides several different procedures for parole. It seems to have been made up of a collection of similar Acts that were consolidated for the first time

[3]Committee to Inquire into the Principles and Procedures Followed in the Remission Service of the Department of Justice of Canada, *Report* (Fauteux Report), Ottawa: Queen's Printer, 1956.

in the *Revised Statutes of Canada 1886*. It is divided into ten parts and covers a number of matters such as insecure prisons, employment of prisoners, etc., none of which are of special interest to us. However, Section 43 is of special interest because it provides for the possibility of a parole board in Ontario.

Section 46 provides for the type of sentence with which the parole board can deal. This is the so-called indeterminate sentence.[4] The Ontario Parole Board has jurisdiction to grant parole to an inmate serving an indeterminate sentence when he has satisfied the minimum or definite portion of his sentence. (The value of such sentence will be discussed in a later section.)

Section 147A and Section 147B make a similar provision for indeterminate sentences in British Columbia and the establishment of a parole board in that province. One major difference between the legislation covering British Columbia and that covering Ontario is that the indeterminate sentence applies to a selected class of offenders, namely, young offenders sentenced to particular classified institutions such as the New Haven 'Borstal' and the Haney Institution.

The Ontario system has been in effect since the 1920s. The Ontario Parole Board grants a hearing to each inmate serving an indeterminate sentence, and, under a chief parole officer, maintains a staff of officers based at the institutions and in large urban areas, who are responsible for investigation of cases and supervision of parolees. They utilize to some degree the services of individuals and agencies in the community for assistance in supervision.

In British Columbia, the system of indeterminate sentence was first introduced in 1949 for youthful offenders detained in an institution modelled on the pattern of the English Borstal. New Haven in British Columbia is a Borstal-type institution and maintains a close link with the community through a voluntary association called the 'Borstal Association'. The organization has a full-time executive secretary and its voluntary associates assist in the supervision of parolees. The activities of the board and the association are now extended to youthful offenders in other classified institutions, provided, of course, they are serving indeterminate sentences.

There is an obvious overlapping of jurisdiction between the provincial parole boards and the National Parole Board.

Sections 99, 107, and 166A of the Prisons and Reformatories Act cover special sentences and parole procedures for women sentenced to the Good Shepherd Reformatory, Halifax, Nova Scotia, and the Interprovincial

4See p. 332.

F. P. Miller

Home for Young Women at Coverdale, New Brunswick. These provisions
for releases have not been used so far as the writer has been able to ascertain. Before the establishment of the National Parole Board, releases from
these two institutions by way of parole were by ticket of leave; they have
since been by parole issued by the Board.

The foregoing brief résumé of the parole provisions in the Prisons and
Reformatories Act will explain Section 5 of the Parole Act.

The Parole Act (See Appendix, page 373)

The advantages and disadvantages of the Ticket of Leave Act were discussed at some length in the Fauteux Report. The Parole Act in the main
follows the recommendations of the Fauteux Committee.

Here, briefly, are some interesting – and some even unique – features
of the Parole Act:

1. The Act is short and clear.
2. It gives very broad powers to the Board compared with some other
   Boards in other jurisdictions.
3. The Board does not have to grant hearings (this sets it apart from most
   other parole authorities).
4. Provisions for eligibility are extremely flexible.
5. The Act provides for a procedure known as 'suspension of parole',
   which allows designated persons to issue warrants for the arrest of
   parolees believed likely to violate parole.
6. The provisions that call for the forfeiture of parole eliminate an
   anomaly of the Ticket of Leave Act, in that a conviction on an offence
   committed prior to the grant of parole no longer brings about an automatic forfeiture.
7. The Act makes it mandatory for the Board to review cases of all persons serving sentences of two years or more.

We shall of course refer to the Act again in some detail as we discuss
such problems as eligibility and supervision.

THE NATIONAL PAROLE BOARD

Organization

The Parole Act came into force on February 15, 1959. The National
Parole Board is composed of five members and is assisted by a staff
known as the National Parole Service. Officers in Ottawa are known as
National Parole Officers. Field officers are designated Regional Representatives of the National Parole Service.

The jurisdiction of the National Parole Board extends only to:

336

1. Granting parole to inmates;
2. Revoking or suspending parole;
3. Revoking or suspending any sentence of whipping; and
4. Revoking or suspending any order made under the Criminal Code prohibiting any person from operating a motor vehicle.

The functions of the National Parole Service are to arrange for:

1. The proper investigation of cases and the preparation of material in relation to them for consideration by the Board, and
2. The supervision of parolees.

At the headquarters of the Parole Service in Ottawa, the preparation of material for cases to be presented to the Board is handled by officers called case investigators and parole analysts. The case investigators are responsible for obtaining the basic reports necessary to a consideration of the case. The parole analysts, as the name implies, make written analyses of cases for presentation to the Board.

The work is divided on a territorial basis. To be more precise, at the present time there are three sections known as the eastern, central, and western sections. Each of these is headed by a section supervisor who has the responsibility of supervising the work of the parole analysts and case investigators in his section.

The parole analyst's work normally includes the preparation of requests for special reports, such as a report upon an investigation of home and other aspects of the community situation to which the parolee will be returning, or the redirecting of specific questions to the institutional authorities or to the regional representatives of the Service. When all inquiries necessary have been completed (within a stipulated period of time) the parole analyst prepares his appraisal of the case, which is reviewed by his supervisor and then presented directly to the Board.

The regional officers have their role to play in the case preparation. They visit institutions regularly, interview the inmates whose cases are under consideration, and present comprehensive reports for the use of the Board.

Although the Service maintains twelve regional offices, it does not rely entirely on its own staff for the day-to-day supervision of parolees. The ten regional representatives, with the help of assistants in some offices, are charged with the administration of all local aspects of parole within their regions, including both the parole hearing before release and the administration of the supervision after release.

The direct parole supervision is frequently provided by agencies in the community, such as private after-care societies, provincial probation services and other governmental agencies, and some volunteers. The designation of the supervisor and supervising agency appears as a specific condition of the parole licence. The supervising agency is usually involved in the case during the investigation period, and ordinarily the agency's worker conducts the community investigation and works with the inmate in his pre-release planning. After the release, the parolee reports regularly to the supervising agency, which, in turn, submits periodic progress reports to the regional representative of the Parole Service under whose authority the parolee continues at large.

Procedure
We need not spend much time describing procedure, which changes from year to year. One cannot, however, fulfil a legal obligation to review the case of every person sentenced to two years or more in prison without an elaborate and precisely defined procedure. The following statistics give an idea of the magnitude of the operation:

In 1961
119,740 pieces of mail were received
137,140 pieces of mail were dispatched
8,769 new files were opened
1,339 cases were concluded
7,240 decisions were rendered (not
including a preliminary review
of all penitentiary newcomers)
Briefly the steps in the procedure are:

A. In the cases of penitentiary inmates
    1. Basic reports received automatically;
    2. Preliminary review;
    3. Applications acknowledged;
    4. Special reports received – institution, field officer, and community investigation;
    5. Case analysis;
    6. Board review.

B. In the cases of provincial and local prison inmates no action is taken before an application is received and there is of course no preliminary review but the other steps follow an application.

SELECTION FOR PAROLE
We can deal with the very important question 'how does one decide who is

to be let out and when?' under three headings: eligibility, criteria, and methods.

Eligibility

Eligibility is to be distinguished from suitability. Eligibility ordinarily refers to time, that is, the time at which, according to the law (or other standard), it has been arbitrarily established that a person may be considered for parole.

In some jurisdictions certain *classes of offenders* are not eligible either by statute or in practice. An example of such eligibility is the person convicted of first-degree murder in some states of the United States. Another example used to be the practice of the Remission Service of Canada not to grant parole to drug-addicts. In some American states persons serving sentences of a certain minimum – for example, six months – are not eligible for parole. There are no classes of offenders in Canada sentenced under the Criminal Code who are not eligible for parole. Theoretically a person sentenced to one day would be eligible for parole some time during the day. The time factor is the significant feature.

The basis for any time-eligibility rule is what is considered the practical necessity that the eligibility must in part be determined by an arbitrary minimum period of detention. The method of setting the minimum period varies from one jurisdiction to another.

It is not necessary that the minimum time for eligibility should be set rigidly by a statute or even by a hard-and-fast departmental rule. Most jurisdictions, however, do set the period by statute. Most American states have a minimum period of one year. But there are other ways.

In the California system the parole authority not only decides when the parolee will be eligible and when he will actually get out on parole, but also fixes the full term of the sentence.

Most jurisdictions in the world (notable exceptions are California, South Dakota, Washington, and West Virginia) have left to the courts the power to fix the term of imprisonment, within certain limits. In nearly all countries the sentence passed by the court is later subject to some variation by a parole authority. In fixing the term the court, one assumes, gives consideration to the deterrent, punitive, and reformative values of the sentence. This matter will be discussed from a different point of view under the heading 'Parole and the Sentence Problem'.

Whatever may be the hopes for the success of training and treatment in prison, imprisonment is still punitive in part, if for no other reason than that it is deprivative of liberty. Even though we view parole as the final stage in the correctional process, we must also recognize that a release on parole is to some extent a lessening of the punitive effect of the sentence.

As long as the sentence is regarded as punitive in whole or in part, or is in effect punitive, and as long as the fixing of the sentence is at the discretion of the courts, most countries seem to adopt the view that some provision must be made to ensure that the discretionary power given to the courts is not nullified by an action of the parole authority. As stated above, this provision usually takes the form of a statutory minimum term for parole eligibility.

Institutional and parole officials may be inclined today to think much more in terms of rehabilitation of the criminal than of the punitive content of the sentence and its deterrent effect on the public; but it is argued that a minimum period of imprisonment is necessary so that training and treatment towards rehabilitation can be given. Time eligibility, some people would say, serves this purpose.

The courts, the institutions, and the parole authority are all concerned with the considerations outlined above, but of course a prisoner applying for parole, or someone applying on his behalf, normally has only one concern: early release.

An inmate on a sentence of normal length who accepts a minimum period of detention may be thought of as accepting the reality of his conviction and sentence; from this point one can proceed to constructive efforts towards his rehabilitation in the institution. If he is able to say to himself, 'It is only to be expected that I must serve a reasonable portion of my sentence', he has come a long way. Without eligibility regulations or the setting of a minimum term for elegibility by the parole authority, the inmate's energies would be directed only towards 'getting out' and he would be in never-ending contention with the parole authority.

The Parole Act provides for time eligibility by regulations. (*See* Appendix, page 379.) In effect these regulations set minimum eligibility as follows:

1. One-third of the sentence or four years, whichever is the lesser, in a sentence of a term of months or years;
2. Seven years in a life sentence imposed by the court as the maximum permitted by the Criminal Code; and
3. Ten years in a life sentence commuted from a sentence of death.

Exceptions may be made where, in the opinion of the Board, special circumstances exist. These regulations allow for maximum flexibility in granting parole at an appropriate time, yet provide some order and method to the process.

In summary, a time-eligibility regulation may be described as an administrative method designed to preserve the purpose of the sentence as

340

passed by the court in both its punitive content and its rehabilitation value. It protects the parole authorities from charges that they are assuming the functions of an appeal court. The Parole Act is designed not to be a mere device to shorten sentences but rather to allow for the operation of a successful parole system. Rightly applied, the time rule brings order and a measure of equity to the consideration of parole and reduces the effect of personal whim or undue influence. The regulations, it is believed, do not have the rigidity of statutory provisions found in other jurisdictions; their flexibility should make possible the application of the concept that 'no deserving case shall suffer'. Another method of solving the problem of eligibility is discussed later under the subject of 'Parole and the Sentence Problem'.

Criteria

The various texts on criminology and on parole give outlines of parole criteria. These criteria may be related to factors that help to predict the prisoner's future behaviour, to reliable opinions, to the need to consider particular people in the community, and to other factors.

Everett M. Porter, member of the California authority, has this to say:

> Probably we may assume that every parole board member has some sort of criteria that is used in arriving at a decision to vote for or against granting parole to a particular inmate. Perhaps it would be safe to conclude that in a broad sense each member of a paroling agency votes for or against granting parole after taking into consideration the following general issues:
>
> 1. The nature and gravity of the inmate's offence against society;
> 2. The deviant history of the person seeking parole or the absence of any misconduct in his past life;
> 3. The inmate's total personality as the same reflects the presence or absence of potential and capacity for serious harm to society;
> 4. The likelihood that on release the offender will return, or will not return to a life of criminal conduct and the probable injury society will suffer should the prisoner become a recidivist;
> 5. What efforts have been made, or not made by the prisoner since imprisonment by way of improvements in habits of social conduct – education or skills – to demonstrate an honest desire to live in harmony with society and its laws; and
> 6. How effective or ineffective the efforts of the inmate seem to have been and will probably be when released in aiding him or her toward living a life free of crime.
>
> On examining the foregoing general criteria, one immediately discovers that unless there is some general *a priori* agreement among us on the

philosophy and nature of criminal conduct and identifiable rules for parole readiness and selection, the weight and conclusion drawn from each element of consideration are apt to be largely subjective despite a desire and perhaps a belief that one is objective. Without identifiable rules measurements may be as varied as there are individual members of parole boards. The challenge we face, it seems, is not so much a matter of identifying what elements we will consider in arriving at our decision to vote for or against granting parole, but our great challenge is to delineate, if possible, identifiable rules by which we are guided to the decisions we make in parole selection.[5]

Since 1957 many writers seem to have followed the lead of the manual on *Parole in Principle and Practice*. This is a report from the 1956 Washington conference on parole. The manual makes two major divisions in setting up criteria: the readiness of the inmate for release and the readiness of the community to receive him.

In the matter of when to release, the readiness of both the offender and the community are primary factors to be considered. This dual readiness has far-reaching implications. The institution has responsibility in helping effect this readiness, but the parolee and society also share responsibility. The offender's readiness and willingness to return to his home community is a factor no greater nor less than is society's readiness and willingness to receive the paroled offender, particularly where the case originally received wide publicity.[6]

The American Law Institute's *Model Penal Code* has some very interesting comments on the subject of parole criteria. These parole criteria, of course, apply in a sentencing framework that contemplates release on parole as an integral part of a process. Usually parole criteria are stated in terms of 'requirements to be satisfied' before one can grant parole. The *Model Penal Code* reverses the approach, interestingly enough, and offers its criteria in terms of the grounds upon which a parole board would be justified in refusing to grant parole. In other words, the assumption is that parole will be granted except in certain circumstances. The Law Institute believes that these grounds can be reduced to four:

1. That there is a substantial risk that the prisoner will not conform to the conditions of parole;
2. That his release at that time would depreciate the seriousness of his crime or promote disrespect for law;

---

[5]E. M. Porter, 'Criteria for Parole Selection', Paper delivered to annual meeting, 88th Annual Congress of Corrections, Detroit, Michigan, September 9, 1958.

[6]National Conference on Parole, *Parole in Principle and Practice*, New York: National Probation and Parole Association, 1957, p. 102.

3. That his release would have adverse effect upon prison discipline;
4. That his capacity to lead a law-abiding life will be enhanced if his correctional treatment or vocational or other training is continued to a later time.[7]

It can be seen, then, that there are many different ways to set out criteria. The writer would like to offer a plan that follows the line of the manual on *Parole in Principle and Practice*. In this plan the parole authority, in the examination of a case for a possible parole, could consider the following:

1. The readiness of the inmate for release as revealed by:
   (a) the nature of his offence;
   (b) his total social background including his history of criminal behaviour;
   (c) his progress since conviction in
       (i) self-improvement,
       (ii) self-understanding, and
       (iii) interpersonal relationships;
   (d) an assessment of his personality.
2. The readiness of the community to receive him as revealed by:
   (a) the community's view of his offence;
   (b) moral and economic support from family, friends, or other sources;
   (c) his obligations;
   (d) prospects of employment.

Methods of Assessment

After the criteria by which to measure the case have been established, methods must be found to ascertain the necessary information. In Canada the sources of information are:

1. The fingerprint section of the R.C.M.P.;
2. The police force that investigated the offence;
3. The court that sentenced the offender;
4. The prosecutor's department;
5. The probation officers who prepared the pre-sentence report and who dealt with the offender on probation;
6. Institutions that have dealt with him in the past;
7. The institution that is now dealing with him;
8. The Parole Board's own representative;

[7]The American Law Institute, *Model Penal Code*, Report, 33rd Annual Meeting, May 23-6, 1956.

9. The social agencies that have dealt with him in the past;
10. His friends and relatives;
11. The inmate himself.

Obviously, these are sources of information with varying degrees of reliability.

Let us examine briefly the value of reports from two of these sources, the *police* and the *institution*.

The inmate is in prison because he committed an offence. The Parole Board wants to know about that offence because the offence may reveal the man, or at least the man as he was at the time of the offence. The Board also wants to know about the effect of the offence on the victim and the public. It is of significance whether violence was involved, whether alcohol was a factor, whether the crime was carefully planned, and whether there was economic pressure.

In considering the case of a sex-offender, for example, the Board is particularly concerned to know whether he is a sexual deviate or a person with normal sexual desires, whose actions, although criminal, are not sexually abnormal. The facts of the offence obviously will be revealing.

The police view of the man at the time of sentence may be very important. Against this his apparent progress as an inmate may be measured and the validity of representations later made on his behalf may be tested. This is not to say that his background or his offence damn him; rather these constitute the basis upon which his prospects for the future may be examined in the light of his apparent progress.

Sometimes the police can fill in the man's background: his family, his work record. They may be able to distinguish the property-offender who has committed his offence under economic pressure from the offender who has managed for years to live by his wits.

The incidence of emotionally toned words sometimes casts doubt on the reliability of a police report as it would in a report from any other source. One may be impressed the first time by a report from a police chief who says, 'He's a no-good bum; leave him there!' But if such phrases constantly turn up in the reports from the same official, one begins to wonder.

From the institutions there are a number of specialists who can report: the warden, the guard, the instructor, the psychologist, the psychiatrist, the chaplain. Each has his own picture of the inmate that can be helpful. Each, of course, sees the inmate in a limited setting and each may have his bias.

It seems obvious that the institutional staff, who live with the prisoner day in and day out, are the people who know him best. It is only a partial

344

truth, however. If it were completely true, there would be no need for a separate parole authority; the question of granting parole could be left entirely to the warden of each institution. The institutional people see the inmate only in the controlled setting of the prison. They see him in his adjustment to prison life and are inclined to make their judgment solely in this light. But if an inmate adjusts adequately to prison, it does not follow that he will adjust adequately to freedom.

Nevertheless, the institutional staff's view is extremely important. Only they can supply the parole authority with details about how he is handling his day-to-day problems. The guard can tell how he reacts to the prison discipline and how he gets along with his fellow prisoners. The instructor can tell something about his work-habits and his abilities to earn a living. The psychologist can give an assessment of his intellectual capacity and his emotional health, and of the extent to which he has developed in self-understanding and in bettering his interpersonal relationships; also the psychologist or other professional treatment-officer can interpret the extent to which he is breaking off his identification with the inmate culture.

Most people who have had much to do with prisons are conscious of the constant hostility that is expressed against police, judges, society in general, and the institution itself. This hostility against authority figures is, of course, a continuation of the basic problem that originally sent to prison the individuals who express it, and the expression indicates that little if any change is taking place. The institutional people are in a position to tell to what extent an inmate is modifying his expression of hostility and to what extent he is attempting to dissociate himself from such expressions on the part of others.

The inmate's view and understanding of the parole authority's requirements of him is a possible fruitful area for assessing his readiness for release. Ohlin had this to say of the Illinois system:

> Although prisoners' views on parole selection vary according to their status as parole applicants, there is, however, a rather well-defined body of beliefs in the prison community concerning the actual influences which bring about a favorable or unfavorable parole decision. It is frequently impossible to find any evidence to support these beliefs other than hearsay or the authority of constant repetition. But as long as they prevail they will be reflected in the offender's attitude toward parole selection and the parole situation.[8]

Strathy in his recent survey at the federal institutions in the Kingston area came up with similar findings:

[8]Lloyd E. Ohlin, *Selection for Parole,* New York: Russell Sage Foundation, 1951, p. 24.

345

The fact that the majority of the subjects had no comments, opinions, or ideas regarding those aspects of an inmate's 'make-up' or character which would influence a Parole Board decision indicates the great lack of understanding by the inmates of the importance of internal emotional and mental forces in the determination of an individual's criminal behaviour.

The forms of institutional behaviour which the subjects most highly valued and perceived as facilitating of a favorable Parole Board decision, (good behaviour, co-operation), are not forms of behaviour which are necessarily indicative of a resolution of an inmate's basic difficulties – of those problems which originally led him to engage in criminally deviant behaviour.[9]

It is appropriate at this point to refer to what is frequently called the 'psychological moment for release'. W. F. Carabine of the National Parole Service discussed this concept in his paper 'Parole as an Alternative to Prison' delivered at the Third Canadian Congress of Corrections held in Toronto in June 1961.

While I do not deny that there is an optimum time for release in many cases, I feel that within this concept, there are errors. The first of these errors, I believe, lies in the fact that in many cases the inmate's readiness for *change* is interpreted as readiness for *release.*

I submit that there is a time when certain inmates become ready for and amenable to change, and therefore to treatment. It is at this time of peak motivation that they should be given every opportunity to intensively *prepare* for a forthcoming release.

The second error within this concept seems to lie in an associated idea and that is, that once this psychological moment arrives, the inmate must be released in a great hurry. And if he is not immediately released, then he will lose his motivation for rehabilitation or will become so bitter if refused an early release, that he will be lost to normal society.

I submit that, if at this 'psychological moment', the inmate becomes involved in an ongoing process which *leads* to release – then, neither deterioration nor lessening of desire for rehabilitation occurs. I might add that this is so even if this ongoing treatment process lasts for a year or more.

A question which must be considered is the value of the personal interview or parole hearing in the selection process. In most jurisdictions parole is almost synonymous with parole hearing. Yet members of the National Parole Board of Canada do not conduct parole hearings; an equivalent hearing is conducted by a representative of the Board.

[9]Peter Arthur Strathy, 'The Expectations of the Parole and Parole Supervision Experience Held by Penitentiary Inmates Prior to Their Release on Parole', unpublished Master's Thesis, School of Social Work, University of Toronto, 1961, pp. 133, 134.

What can be accomplished in an interview? Some parole authorities have been criticized for the perfunctory nature of their interviews with applicants for parole. The writer has sat in with some parole boards during hearings and has had reports from people who have sat in on other parole-board hearings. He feels that it is impossible for anyone other than a prophet to report definitively on an offender solely on the basis of a brief hearing. One need not argue the point; it is self-evident. On the other hand, an interview ranging from fifteen minutes up to, if necessary, one or two hours, conducted by an experienced interviewer who is in possession of a well-documented file, can be most useful. A personal interview by an authorized representative or a member of the parole authority is generally regarded as an essential step in the authority's consideration of a case.

A few years ago there was great emphasis on prediction tables in the consideration of parole. One of the outstanding books on the subject was by Lloyd E. Ohlin. There has been a resurgence of interest since about 1961. Ohlin himself defines the use and limits of an 'experience table'.

> The classification of violation risk on the basis of the parole experience table contributes information of similar value for reaching parole decisions. The parole table, like the insurance life table, informs, but does not dictate the final decision. After considering other factors not included in the experience table, the parole board may alter the estimation of the risk involved or may accept the risk in the interests of society and the offender.
>
> The information furnished by the parole experience table can be of considerable advantage to the parole board on two different levels: it can be used to guide the board in weighing the merits of each individual case on the parole docket and to guide parole policy.[10]

Parole prediction devices are simply a formalized utilization of the results of research, and as such are important. They can be handy guides and can help to draw to attention the 'other side' of a case in which reports and representations are biased. Such devices can help reduce the effect of personal whim and prejudice.

The important thing is that the parole authority keep up to date on the results of research. Frequently research disproves popular misconceptions. In discussing research on selection David Dressler says, 'the younger the offender the less his chances of successful completion of probation or parole all else being equal'.[11] Now this is a fact that people working in the

[10]*Op. cit.*, p. 70.

[11]David Dressler, *Practice and Theory of Probation and Parole,* New York: Columbia University Press, 1959, p. 119.

field learn by experience. It is a particularly difficult lesson to learn, because all pressures are on to give the young offender a chance.

The main danger in too slavish use of prediction devices comes from lack of understanding of the statistical analysis on which a prediction is based. For example, some prediction tables give very high rates of success for sex offenders on parole. The sample of such offenders on which the prediction table is based may well include all types of sex offenders, with a normal distribution of the several types. Such a sample would include certain types for which the prognosis for success on parole is extremely poor, or whose failure on parole could have tragic results. Elements such as these can be dealt with only by those in authority considering each case individually in as responsible and careful a manner as possible.

PREPARATION FOR PAROLE

We can regard the entire period of imprisonment, from the date of admission until the date of release, as a period of parole preparation. Throughout this period there will be a waxing and waning of the inmate's interest in the possibility of parole, culminating in intense activity just prior to the time when parole might be considered favourably.

We can distinguish three phases in the period of imprisonment:
1. The phase of institutional training and treatment;
2. The phase of investigation and consideration;
3. The phase of final pre-release preparation.
In discussing each phase, we shall describe generally the characteristics of the phase and indicate the problems.

Phase One: Institutional Training and Treatment

This is the period of the sentence that is normally served in the institution prior to review for parole. In the Canadian system, normally the inmate is considered for parole when one-third of his sentence or four years, whichever is the lesser, has been served. Ordinarily, in penitentiary cases, an application for parole is made about five months prior to the date when the case could be given consideration in accordance with the eligibility date set.

Problems during the First Phase

1. Interpreting parole and parole rules to the inmate and others interested in his welfare;
2. Assisting the inmate in planning and executing his program of training and treatment;

348

3. Maintaining his morale throughout the period, particularly in long sentences.

Phase Two: Investigation and Consideration

This is the period, usually following an application, during which the Parole Service completes its investigation and the case is submitted to the Parole Board for a decision. The period normally extends from three to six months in cases of penitentiary inmates, depending on the difficulties and delays encountered.

The inmate may be interviewed by several people – the classification officer, institutional officials, the after-care agency worker, the National Employment Service visiting officer, the Parole Service field representative. The Parole Board obtains reports from the institution, the after-care agency, the probation services, the field representative, and other sources of information. Frequently relatives and friends apply to the Parole Board on the inmate's behalf.

Problems during the Second Phase

1. Assessing the inmate and his prospects for successful rehabilitation;
2. Assisting him in his planning;
3. Evaluating his plans;
4. Co-ordinating the activities of all participating officials and agencies and of others interested in his welfare;
5. Re-interpreting parole to the inmate and explaining the significance of activities he is now engaged in;
6. Maintaining his morale.

In the course of the investigation and consideration of a case for parole, several persons and organizations, as we have seen, become directly involved with the inmate and in his plans. From the inmate's point of view, these may represent, on the one hand, sources of assistance in his efforts to secure parole, or on the other hand, barriers he must surmount if he is to be released. The fact is, of course, that most persons and agencies involved are fulfilling two functions: they do assist the inmate where possible, but they may also make an assessment of him that directly or indirectly contributes to the final decision in the case.

The situation is further complicated by considerable overlapping in the fields of activity of the various persons concerned. The inmate may think that the same ground is being needlessly covered by several different persons when from his point of view one person would be enough. Conversely, he may himself consciously enlist several people to work on his behalf.

That there are dangers inherent in this situation is obvious. Here are some possibilities:
1. The inmate becomes confused, harried, discouraged, elated, or resentful;
2. He skilfully manipulates the situation to his own advantage;
3. The officials and workers concerned waste valuable time and energy through duplication and even multiplication of effort;
4. Failure to exchange information brings about confusion of planning and assessment or, worse, a serious omission;
5. So much attention is directed towards 'getting out' that the inmate loses all sense of a sentence continuing beyond the date of his release from prison.

Not all of this activity can or should be eliminated, however. Many areas of planning must be explored from more than one point of view.

During this period, it frequently happens that the inmate becomes increasingly anxious concerning the outcome of his parole application. This is considered by some people to be undesirable, and one can suppose that in certain cases the degree of anxiety could become disabling and cause harmful attitudes towards the future. In many cases, however, it is actually helpful in that it is important that the inmate be in a state of tension concerning his future. He must, of course, have help at this time, to deal with this anxiety and to understand its significance.

Phase Three: *Final Pre-Release Preparation*
This is the period from the moment the parole is declared until the moment of actual release. In past years this period has been very short, usually one or two days. In some instances it has been as short as a few hours. The Parole Board, however, has endeavoured to make possible a longer period.

Problems during the Third Phase
1. Helping the inmate to adjust to the fact of his imminent release, dealing with feelings of anxiety, euphoria, etc.;
2. Completing final arrangements, such as securing clothes, writing relatives, arranging appointments;
3. Helping the inmate to understand his future relationship with his parole supervisor and his responsibilities as a parolee, and to face the fact of his continuing sentence;
4. Accepting the fact that new problems will arise.

One of the greatest problems in parole is the difficulty almost everyone concerned has in facing up to the fact that there must be adequate planning for release. Parole workers find from observation that it is only with the greatest self-discipline that the institutional authorities and after-care workers, let alone the parolee himself, are able to deal with realities. It is an unhappy fact that an offender can find himself on the street, facing problems that he himself has never considered and that have never been presented to him.

Prospects for employment are obviously an important factor. So important has the factor of employment been considered by many people that we frequently find that a guaranteed job is a requirement for parole in some foreign parole jurisdictions. Sometimes it is possible for a prospective parolee to have a suitable job guaranteed before his release. However, not all jobs promised are suitable nor are all promises reliable. The general prospects for employment in relation to the season of the year, and the inmate's earning skills as well as his attitude, aggressive or otherwise, towards finding employment are matters to be considered.

In making a community investigation, it is important to ascertain what will be the inmate's actual physical accommodation after release. If he has a home to go to, it is important to know how his family feels about his return. The attitudes of his wife, his children, and his friends are all important. Superficial inquiry frequently offers a rosy picture that unhappily changes in the reality of release.

The inmate should know, as far as possible, the details of planning done on his behalf by others. A parole plan that is not the inmate's own plan, or that has not been worked out carefully with him, has little chance of success.

PAROLE SUPERVISION

Nature and Purposes of Supervision

Each of our definitions of parole contains an idea of direction, guidance, or leadership. Whatever the emphasis, all the variations of this idea are incorporated in the word *supervision*. Parole as we have defined it – or parole as it is conceived of today – is meaningless except in terms of supervision.

There are three basic approaches to parole supervision. These are service, treatment, and surveillance. *Parole in Principle and Practice* has this to say in the matter:

> Despite the variance in terminology defining the several aspects of case-work, there is general agreement over two basic elements: one is primarily concerned with effecting changes in the environment – service; the other aims to assist the individual in handling his personal adjustment prob-

lems – treatment. In the protective and corrective field, a third element is added which is designed to protect the client against himself and to protect the public from him. This watchfulness is known as surveillance.

Service in parole supervision involves the officer's thorough knowledge and skilled use of community resources and special services to assist the parolee and his family. It provides a setting whereby the community can participate directly in the rehabilitative process.

Treatment requires knowledge and skill also in the use of casework methods to discover underlying social and emotional problems, to assist the parolee in gaining insight into his problems, to guide him toward resolving these problems to the best of his ability and to help him obtain specialized professional service for problems with which the officer is not equipped to deal. The parole officer works through field visits, interviews, case recording, and reports.[12]

The above three approaches are employed in varying degrees depending upon the problems of the individual case and usually with a social casework orientation.

The tools of supervision are:
1. The rules, that is, the Parole Agreement (*See* Appendix, page 382);
2. The reporting function, that is, the necessity to account;
3. The interview (and other personal contacts) at the parole supervisor's office, or at the parolee's home or place of employment;
4. Family resources;
5. Community agencies.

Sanctions and Their Use

A parolee is still serving his sentence, albeit in the community, and his liberty continues conditional upon his satisfactory progress. On the basis of a plan he is released before the expiration of his sentence, it is said, primarily because of the hope, based on his apparent desire to reform, that under a measure of control and with assistance his chances for successful rehabilitation will be increased.

Society desires his rehabilitation because of his own worth as an individual and concomitantly for its own protection. At the least we desire above all else to prevent his return to criminal activity. To the extent that this purpose is not fulfilled, the parolee is a failure and his certificate to be at liberty may be revoked.

To define sensitive areas of conduct, certain specific conditions are imposed (*See* Appendix, page 382). If a parolee violates a condition of his parole, he thereby indicates in most cases an unwillingness or an inability

[12]*Op. cit.*, p 129-30.

to meet the prerequisites for successful rehabilitation. Accordingly, he exposes himself to the only logical step in the circumstances, cessation of his parole and a return to prison.

Supervision is intended to assist the parolee in his rehabilitation. If he fails to respond to the supervision in a positive manner and gives cause for concern that he may resort to crime, his return to custody is imperative. The supervisor (while doing all in his power through service and treatment to help the parolee) is alert for signs of failure that may become threatening to society. The supervisor's responsibility in this respect is twofold: to caution the parolee and to report the disturbing behaviour. Minor lapses from good deportment need not necessarily cause concern. One recognizes that a parolee cannot be expected to become an exemplary citizen overnight. That is why he is on parole. Moreover, it is not the function of parole to recast the parolee in the moral mould of any particular class. However, behaviour that does give the supervisor cause for concern, or any violation of a condition of the licence, should be reported immediately to the parole authority. In his report the supervisor sets out the facts along with an assessment of their significance, and, if he so desires, makes a recommendation.

The following are examples of behaviour or violation of conditions that point seriously to failure:
1. Disappearance (whereabouts unknown) – needless to say, this makes supervision impossible;
2. Repeated failure to keep appointments;
3. Persistent action or inaction against the advice of the supervisor (this would include abandonment of an important phase of the parole plan without consultation);
4. Failure to meet family responsibilities;
5. Persistently keeping late hours;
6. Making unauthorized journeys (limits in this respect should be stipulated in the early phase of the parole);
7. Keeping undesirable associations;
8. Excessive drinking (where there is no condition to abstain);
9. Breach of condition to abstain;
10. Any involvement with police, including:
    (a) being checked by police,
    (b) arrest,
    (c) dismissal of charges,
    (d) conviction.
    (*Note*: Conviction for indictable offence brings about automatic forfeiture, but the supervisor's report is still important; for instance,

there may be a possibility of reinstatement if the court awards a fine or a suspended sentence.)

Situations calling for adverse reports fall roughly into two categories:

1. The behaviour causes some serious concern but in the opinion of the supervisor no imminent danger exists, positive factors outweigh negative factors, and there is reasonable expectation of improvement. In such a situation the behaviour in question becomes a learning experience.

2. The behaviour in the opinion of the supervisor constitutes one of the following:

   (a) a threat to society (i.e., the possibility of further criminal behaviour);

   (b) a threat to the parolee himself (e.g., an alcoholic continuing to drink);

   (c) a flagrant breach of parole which, for the proper administration of the Act, cannot be condoned.

PROBLEMS AND ANOMALIES

We like to speak of a 'correctional process' as if there were something continuous and unified in our approach to the crime problem and our disposition of the criminal. This, of course, is patently absurd, as any casual observation of the process will reveal. Actually, changes and progress have been made piecemeal and quite frequently with no consultation or collaboration between the several professional disciplines involved in the development of a philosophy in respect to the treatment of the criminal or between the several divisions of administrative agencies responsible for the actual treatment of the criminal. Consequently, many anomalies are apparent, and these frequently come to the fore at the time of consideration of parole. The Fauteux Committee recognized this problem.

The remarkable thing about the Fauteux Committee is that, although it was asked to report on parole, it devoted the greater part of its report to matters of corrections other than parole. The terms of reference were explicitly to 'report upon the principles and procedures followed in the Remission Service of the Department of Justice in connection with the Exercise of Clemency and to recommend what changes, if any, should be made to those principles and procedures'. The Minister, however, did make it clear to the members that he did not want to restrict their inquiries and it was his hope that they would 'find it possible to examine the entire field of remission and parole'. However, the committee stated: 'We realized very early that it would not be possible for us to inquire fully into, report upon and make effective recommendations concerning principles and procedures followed in the Remission Service without examining the field of Criminal Law in a great many other aspects.'

The first chapter of the report, entitled 'The Problem for Correctional Reform in Canada', sets out the view that the committee had to take. The members discovered that their real problem was not the principles and procedures followed in the Remission Service, but the total problem of correctional reform in Canada.

Out of forty-four recommendations, only eight were specific positive recommendations in connection with parole. There were two others in connection with after-care that could be considered related to parole, and there were some recommendations concerning the exercise of the royal prerogative, but the bulk of the recommendations had to do with the criminal law, sentencing, probation, institutions, and corrections generally.

We can sum up the Fauteux Report in two terms taken from the report itself: *preventive justice* and *integration*. The committee members believed that the community can defend itself against the criminal if it metes out justice to the individual criminal in such a manner as to prevent his return to criminal behaviour; and that only a high degree of integration of the activity of all agencies dealing with the offender will achieve this preventive justice.

The report considers the manner in which an offender may be dealt with: (1) by the courts, (2) in the penal institutions, (3) by the releasing authority, and (4) in the early stages of his return to the community.

The court, to achieve preventive justice, must make the sentence fit the offender as well as fit the crime. To do this the court needs to be well informed about the offender's background and personality. To this end the Fauteux Committee stresses the importance of pre-sentence reports. The offender, whenever possible, should be left in the community to become an economic asset rather than an economic liability. Extensive use of probation and the instalment payment of fines are the methods urged.

The committee makes other recommendations that, if implemented, would assist the court in dealing with the offender. For example, it urges visits by judges and magistrates to penal institutions; the co-operation of attorneys-general of the provinces in implementing provisions in the Criminal Code concerning charges outstanding in another province; and uniform enforcement in all provinces of the provisions of the Criminal Code relating to habitual criminals and sexual psychopaths.

Many offenders, the committee recognizes, must be removed from the community and sent to institutions. For these it recommends '*a concentration of effort on treatment by way of training, rather than the mere im-*

position of punishment . . . especially . . . in the case of special classes of offenders, particularly youthful offenders and persistent offenders'.

The committee believes that this will be more easily achieved by a *'specialization of institutions and specialization of methods of treatment, with a concentration of professional staff in the areas where it is most needed; the development of small open, minimum security institutions'.*

The report endorses parole as the most effective release procedure. Among other considerations parole, like probation, provides continuing treatment at less cost than that of keeping the offender in prison and treating him there, and allows him to become an economic asset to the community. But parole is not effective without 'judicious and individualized consideration in each case', both before and after release. Such consideration is possible only if a strong parole authority has the facilities to gather the information it requires and to provide effective supervision and after-care. Hence the report recommends establishment of a national parole board, expansion of the parole service, and greater utilization and development of the services of voluntary after-care agencies.

The report acknowledges two great needs: the scientific study of criminality and its treatment, and the provision of qualified workers. To help meet these needs it urges assistance to universities for research and for the training of correctional workers.

Throughout the report is an insistence on the interdependence of all agencies dealing with the offender. Integration is vital to the development of an effective correctional system. Some recommendations are apparently particularly designed to bring about a higher degree of integration. For example, the committee recommends:

1. A national parole board rather than regional or provincial boards;
2. Federal jurisdiction in all sentences of imprisonment exceeding six months;
3. The integration of federal correctional services through a senior officer of the department.

In summary the Fauteux Report recommends:

1. Sentences to fit the offender;
2. Institutions to fit the inmate;
3. Release policies and procedures to fit the individual case;
4. The co-ordination of all in a continuous correctional process developed and improved as a result of scientific study and administered by qualified personnel.

The report is a clear exposition of the interdependence of the several parts of the judicial-correctional system.

The Problem of Restitution
The problem of restitution is one of several anomalies in the judicial-correctional system that come to the fore at the time of consideration of parole. At that point many of the ramifications of restitution must be taken into consideration that up to then could be safely overlooked or denied.

Some form of restitution or compensation was actually at the basis of punishment for criminal behaviour when this function was being gradually taken over by the state. In the transition, emphasis shifted, however, to the state's case against the offender, and the question of restitution was removed more and more from the jurisdiction of the criminal courts.

Dr. Stephen Shafer, reader in criminology at the University of Maryland, in his *Restitution to Victims of Crime,* a most interesting comparative study, says

> If one looks at the legal systems of different countries, one seeks in vain a country where a victim of crime enjoys a certain expectation of full restitution for his injury. In the rare cases where there is state compensation the system is either not fully effective, or does not work at all; where there is no system of state compensation, the victim is, in general, faced with the insufficient remedies offered by civil procedure and civil execution.[13]

The Criminal Code of Canada does make provision for compensation and restitution during the criminal-judicial procedure. Sections 628, 629, 630, and 638(2) all deal with certain aspects of the problem. Since these powers are not uniformly used, however, the parole authority must watch carefully that it is not returning to the community someone who is, as it were, living (directly or indirectly) on his ill-gotten gains, while his victim remains uncompensated. Even in doing this, the parole authority runs the danger of meting out inequitable treatment. It may be easy enough to impose prior to parole a condition of restitution on a person known to have a large sum of money on deposit. What, however, is to be done in the case of an offender who has a reasonable sum of money that may be useful in his re-establishment and eventual rehabilitation?

The parole authority may be faced with the problem of determining the amount of restitution or compensation. This seems to be a judicial process. Consequently, if a parole authority is to take on the responsibility it might better be given such power explicitly by legislation.

If restitution should be enforced through instalment payment, problems of collection would arise that might put the parole officer in the role of collection agent. He might tend to give more of his attention to this practical and pressing problem of collection than to his general supervision of

13Stephen Shafer, *Restitution to Victims of Crime,* London: Stevens and Sons, 1960, p. 117.

the parolee. In many cases the amount of money from earnings available for restitution would be so small in comparison with the total loss to the victim as to be meaningless. Yet in some of these cases, increased restitution payments could easily reach a point of pushing the offender over the edge of a feeling of hopelessness. Under existing circumstances as set out above, one can reasonably feel that the parolee is entitled to the same considerations as a person declared bankrupt.

In cases where restitution is feasible, one can take the view that it could be most helpful in rehabilitation. David Dressler says:

> There is nothing prejudicial about this [making restitution a condition of parole]. When the law-abiding individual borrows money, he must repay. If he accidentally injures another, civil law may require him to pay medical bills and perhaps for loss of working time and capacity.
>
> Restitution may have a positive casework connotation. It offers the individual something within reason that he can do here and now, within the limits of his ability, to demonstrate to himself that he is changing. A fine is punitive. A jail sentence is retributive. But restitution makes sense. It is every man's obligation to meet responsibilities of this sort in civil life.[14]

In by far the majority of cases, the question of parole can be considered without any obligation to take into account whether the victim has been properly compensated. From time to time, however, cases appear in which the sum of money stolen and the possible assets of the offender are both substantial; and in these it would appear to be a complete misplacement of interest to release to the community before his sentence is up an affluent offender who has not completely compensated his victim or victims.

It is not the intention of this writer to embark on a full discussion of the question of restitution in our judicial and correctional process. However, it is an important problem that must be faced eventually. Until it is faced and dealt with, it will continue to plague the parole authority.

Parole for the Sake of Supervision

In the common concept of parole – and certainly in the concept we have developed in this chapter – it is a selective process. We think of a parole authority placing on parole only those people who offer the best prospect of successful rehabilitation and who are considered to be no serious threat to society. This is all very well when the true alternative to release on parole is continued detention. The great majority of offenders, however, cannot be detained indefinitely. Their sentences by law have fixed limits and eventually expire. One must, then, decide, not between a release on

[14]*Op. cit.*, pp. 176ff.

parole and continued detention, but rather between a release on parole at some given time and release as a free agent later on.

Not infrequently, therefore, a parole authority receives representations or recommendations that say essentially that 'the offender is such a poor prospect for rehabilitation that he should be put on parole so that some measure of control can be exercised for even a short period of time'. The hope is that some particular desirable object will be achieved, for instance that the offender will go home, or obtain a job, or start a relationship with a social worker or other counsellor.

In a parole system purporting to be selective, one would say that a parole authority should not grant parole to an inmate not considered a good parole-risk by normal standards *unless* the parole authority is satisfied that there is a reasonable chance of achieving a desirable object, so that the granting of parole is actually protective of society. All arrangements in such cases should be as good as possible and certainly better than ordinary. The parole must be a well-planned measure clearly designed for the protection of the public. Not only must its planning and design *be* the best possible for that purpose, but it must also *appear* to be the best possible.

A good principle in these cases would be to keep the inmate in prison as long as possible consistent with steps to provide supervision after release. Take the case of a potentially dangerous offender, on a sentence of, say, twelve years, who could be released as a completely free agent with his sentence expired at a little over eight years, if he earned all good industry remission and lost no statutory remission. He would be subject to no supervision after release. The public would be better protected if the parole authority were to release him after careful preparation at about six months prior to date of expiration, because then, under Section 25 of the Canadian Penitentiaries Act, the period of control over him would include any period of statutory remission standing to his credit – that is, a possible period of three and a half years. During this period, of course, any breach of condition could bring about his return to the prison to serve the balance of his time.

The final answer to this problem has yet to be given. Many solutions have been suggested including what is frequently called *mandatory supervision* or *mandatory parole*. This will be dealt with in a later section.

Parole is sometimes attacked on the ground that it sacrifices the protection of society for the rehabilitation of the offender. Proponents of parole argue that, on the contrary, parole by its very nature, with its elements of restriction and surveillance, is a protection of society. In this respect, Giardini says:

F. P. Miller

Considered in this light, no criminal has a right to parole. It is society that has a right to parole. Society has a right to parole for several reasons, all of which insure a measure of protection. Parole is the service that aids the released prisoner to bridge the gap between the relatively abnormal environment of the prison and the environment of the community. By providing supervision and guidance during the critical early months of parole, reversion to crime may be prevented. Secondly, parole provides a period in the life of the offender when he can be removed from society as soon as he shows indications of dangerous behaviour without waiting until he commits a new crime. Thirdly, it provides legal authority to compel a former offender to live up to certain accepted standards of conduct. Fourthly, it provides for the former offender a period of supervision under normal social conditions, a testing period, before he is completely free.[15]

However, the release on parole does mean that a man who would otherwise be safely out of the way in prison is placed on the street with a considerable degree of freedom. The problem is frequently put this way: as between the rehabilitation of the offender and the protection of society, which is the more important? The obvious answer is, of course, the protection of society.

In by far the majority of parole cases, however, the welfare and rehabilitation of the offender are ends to be achieved simultaneously with the protection of society. In the rare instances where there appears to be any true conflict, one hopes that with wisdom the proper choice may be made. In a given case, people may differ in their answers to the question whether society is better protected by the inmate's release on parole or by his continuation in prison and ultimate release as a free agent.

Parole and Earned Remission

'Earned remission', 'statutory remission', and 'good time' are all expressions that denote a method whereby part of a sentence of imprisonment is remitted on account of the good behaviour or diligent industry (or both) of the prisoner. This is an area of controversy in the field of penology. However, a system whereby some part of the sentence is remitted as a reward has been accepted in the main for many years as a necessity by penal administrators. It is believed that the incentive of early release does bring about good behaviour and diligent industry. In actual practice, many critics point out that the remission is rarely awarded on a positive basis for actual good behaviour and diligent industry; rather, it works in a nega-

[15]G. L. Giardini, *The Parole Process*, Springfield, Illinois: Charles C. Thomas, Publisher, 1959, p. 19.

tive way in that loss of remission is awarded for bad behaviour and poor industry. Ordinarily in most prisons, by far the greater number of inmates can count on receiving all of their remission if they avoid flagrant breaches of prison discipline.

It is not the writer's purpose to discuss here the merits of earned remission as such. It does have a connection with parole, however. First of all, the two are frequently confused. Many people assume that any release from prison, before the full period awarded by the courts has elapsed, must necessarily be a parole. This confusion can easily bring parole into disrepute, and in this writer's opinion does account for much prejudice against it.

A problem arises, too, in attempting to co-ordinate parole eligibility with the effect of 'good time'. Some parole systems arrange things so that any loss of 'good time' brings about a proportionate delay in eligibility, but of course this is workable only if eligibility is a rigid legal requirement. Where such an arrangement does not exist, loss of 'good time' is meaningless with respect to parole consideration except to the extent that it may be taken by the parole authority as an indication that the inmate is unready for release.

A further problem exists if the amount of remission possible is so substantial as to destroy incentive for release on parole. When the parole authority comes to offering a lessened period of imprisonment, it may find itself in competition with the statutory remission. If parole is no longer wanted, it ceases to be a good method of release.

One over-all solution to these problems is to make the period of statutory remission a period of mandatory parole or supervision.

The Problem of Sanctions

A serious problem in parole is that there are so few usable sanctions. In practice they are limited to the following in increasing order of severity:

1. reprimand,
2. increased restriction,
3. suspension of parole followed by continuation of parole,
4. revocation.

Having released an offender to the community under conditions, one must then enforce these conditions if there is to be faith in their efficacy. Parolees, naturally enough, can be expected to test limits. Even those making reasonable progress present a parole authority with violations that cannot go unnoticed. One easily starts off with a warning. However, if repeated warnings are ignored, there is finally only one effective sanction: return to prison. Naturally, since the rehabilitation of the offender and the protection of society are the purposes of parole, this creates a dilemma because a return to prison may bring about a serious regression, whereas continuation in the community offers some prospect of successful rehabilitation.

One cause of this paradoxical situation may be society's unrealistic expectation that the offender, after his release from prison, must live up to even higher standards than are expected of people who have not been convicted of an offence.

Termination of Parole

If a parolee commits a new offence and is duly charged and convicted, most people would agree that his parole should immediately terminate and that he should be returned to prison on his old sentence plus any new term that he may have received. One hastens to add that perhaps certain minor offences should not bring about this automatic reimprisonment. Canada's Parole Act does make such a provision.

The Act stipulates that 'if a paroled inmate is convicted of an indictable offence committed after the grant of parole and punishable by imprisonment for a term of two years or more, his parole is thereby forthwith *forfeited*'. The Parole Board has no discretion in the matter. However, although the limitation set by the statute means that parole is not immediately forfeited if a parolee is convicted of a non-indictable offence or of an indictable offence that it is not punishable by imprisonment for a term of two years or more, such a conviction can and frequently does become grounds for a Board decision to *revoke* the parole. In Canadian parole nomenclature, the word *forfeiture* is used to denote the termination of a parole by law due to a conviction on an indictable offence punishable by imprisonment for a term of two years or more; *revocation* means the decision of the Parole Board to recall the parolee for a return to the prison to serve the balance of his sentence.

Sometimes a new offence may be in the category that automatically brings about forfeiture by law, but the actual circumstances of the offence and the inmate's progress on parole may lead to a conclusion that a return to prison would not be in the best interests of society or the inmate. Such a situation is usually exemplified in the first instance by the trial magistrate's imposing a nominal sentence for the new offence (a fine, a short time in jail, a suspended sentence); this indicates his intention to 'put the man on the street'.

The Parole Board, under the terms of the Act, has power to re-parole; and so it can – and sometimes does – reinstate a parole after a forfeiture.

In the section on supervision, we discussed behaviour on parole that would lead to revocation. Before the Board can make a proper decision whether to revoke, detailed information is required. This calls for full inquiry. In the meantime it may be felt that for the offender's own protection or the protection of society he should be in custody. Consequently, the Parole Act provides for a procedure known as *suspension* that allows the immediate arrest of a parolee if an authorized person 'is satisfied that the arrest of the inmate is necessary or desirable in order to prevent a breach of any term or condition of the parole'.

Parole has generally been accepted in Canada and in many other countries as an act of grace. The view is taken that no person has a right to parole, and that the decision to grant it is vested in a quasi-judicial board that takes the responsibility of allowing the inmate to serve the remainder of his sentence in the community. This decision is taken only when the board is satisfied that the parolee's liberty will be justified by both his rehabilitation and the protection of society. If at any time the board is no longer satisfied that this condition exists, it cannot live up to its responsibility if it does not have the unequivocal right to return the offender to prison. It is sometimes argued that this return should take place only after due process of charge and conviction on a breach of parole with the usual protections. The answer given is that the offender is being returned to prison to serve, not some new period of time, but merely the period that was awarded him by a court for an offence of which he was convicted by due process.

It is incumbent upon a parole authority, nevertheless, to be scrupulous in its decisions of revocation so that no offender can successfully claim unfair treatment. In any event, each offender deserves an opportunity to explain his behaviour. This opportunity is granted in the Canadian process in three ways:

1. Usually a revocation has been preceded by a period of clear warning concerning the behaviour which has ultimately brought about the revocation.
2. In many cases the revocation is preceded by a suspension during which a full investigation is made including interviews with the parolee.
3. Subsequent to revocation, penitentiary inmates are granted an interview by a representative of the Board who reports fully. On receiving the report, the Board may immediately reconsider the question of parole continuation, or may schedule a later date for reconsideration.

PAROLE AND THE SENTENCE OF THE COURT

One cannot consider the question of parole or postulate any theory of

F. P. Miller

parole without considering the question of sentencing and postulating a theory of sentencing. In a logical judicial-correctional system, the system of sentencing and parole would be interdependent, flowing from the same philosophy; otherwise they would defeat each other, or one would dominate and negate the purposes of the other.

In this context, it is not necessary to say whether one system of sentencing or one system of parole is better than another. Nor is it the writer's intention to criticize the Canadian sentencing system in itself or the parole system in itself. The point is that it does not make sense to proceed from a particular philosophy of sentencing that expects to protect society by the imposition of particular sentences, and then have the anticipated effect apparently nullified by a parole authority that shortens the term of imprisonment on criteria different from those which brought about the sentence in the first instance. Similarly one cannot expect a parole system based on criteria of selection that call for certain periods of detention and certain periods of supervision to be fully effective if the sentence is so short as to preclude any impact of imprisonment, any time for investigation, and any time of consequence for supervision on release. And again parole will not be possible if the sentence imposes a mandatory period of detention that allows, in effect, no time for parole.

Jaffary shows the interdependence of the courts and the parole authority when he says:

> The sentencing power, as has been shown, is a shared power. The legislative branch of government defines the offences and sets maximum limits of punishment in the Criminal Code. The court, on a plea or verdict of guilt, prescribes a sentence within the statutory limits. If the sentence is to imprisonment, the duration of the term in the prison, the release from the institution, and the supervision of the remaining part of the sentence are responsibilities of the administrative authority – the National Parole Board. This sharing of sentencing power implies that the court, when sentencing to imprisonment, should have knowledge not only of the man and his offence, but also of the institution to which he may go and the parole authority under whose control he may later be. Under this rationale of correction the magistrate becomes a member of a partnership which has the common purpose of the protection of the community.[16]

It is fair to say that in Canada sentences seem at times to be imposed without contemplation of the possibility of parole as an integral part of a judicial-correctional process.

[16]Stuart King Jaffary, *Sentencing of Adults in Canada*, Toronto: University of Toronto Press, 1963, p. 9.

A court that sentences a persistent offender to a term of six months (for whatever good reason) makes it impossible for the paroling authority to use its power to assist in the rehabilitation of the offender, and to place him under restrictions. From this point of view the Board has had no chance to accept its responsibility to protect society. On the other hand, releases on parole often seem to some people to be mere sentence-shortening for no apparently good reason. An obvious example of this occurs when the paroling authority releases on parole at two years an offender, under sentence of six years, who has embezzled several thousands of dollars. The Board may rightly feel that he has derived the maximum benefit of imprisonment and that his rehabilitation can be enhanced by parole. Nevertheless, in the eyes of many members of the public, the Board appears to interfere with the sentence of the court. Undoubtedly, the court had in mind what are considered to be the very important values of deterrence and respect for the law.

The usual proposal for sentencing in a system where release by way of parole is contemplated is the so-called indeterminate sentence. There are, of course, several variations of this. The concept and history of the indeterminate sentence is exhaustively covered in the United Nations publication on the subject. The concept is a confused one and means different things to different people, as the following extracts will indicate:

> The expression 'indeterminate sentence' itself seems to have been invented by Brockway, the American who introduced the system and founded the famous Elmira Reformatory. He proposed it to the Cincinnati Congress of the American Prison Association as early as 1870. It caught on, but has been frequently and, on the whole, justly criticized. Critics have pointed out that the penalty, not the sentence, is indeterminate; and one may even add that in fact the penalty itself is not and cannot be indeterminate. The indeterminateness relates only to the duration of the penalty, and really exists only when the duration is to be determined later in time than the court's sentence.
>
> Between conditional release and the indeterminate sentence there are a number of technical differences. They are dominated by the concept which, for example, so eminent a criminologist as Sutherland advances when he says that indeterminate sentence presupposes that the exact period of custody is not fixed before the custody begins. Whereas, parole implies that a portion of the period of custody may be spent outside the institution. Conditional release may be defined with stricter legal precision as the power given to the executive authority to exempt a person sentenced to a penalty deprivative of liberty from the need to serve part of that sentence as determined by the judge, in the cases and on the conditions laid down by statute. Indeterminate sentence, on the other hand, should

mean a penalty or measure deprivative of liberty in which the time of release is not fixed in advance by the judge, who merely fixes a minimum or maximum penalty (relative indeterminateness), or orders the offender to be placed at the disposal of the competent authority for an indefinite period (absolute indeterminateness).

These differences certainly exist and should be emphasized in order to avoid any confusion. However, an objective study of the systems actually in force is bound to point out that in the penitentiary practice of today the two institutions tend to come close together and sometimes to be indistinguishable.[17]

Essentially, the indeterminate sentence was brought into being as a device to ensure that a period of custody is sufficiently long to have a rehabilitative effect and to permit a release to take place at the optimum time of readiness, and as a means of providing adequate restraints and assistance following release. These purposes have not always been achieved.

In the present system of sentencing in Canada, when the courts pass a so-called definite sentence, it is subject to modification by virtue of the Parole Act, and so is in fact an indeterminate sentence. The Parole Board regulations govern the time of eligibility. This is not a discretionary power of the courts. On the other hand, the sentence of the court does affect the parole eligibility to some degree in that the parole regulations set eligibility more or less in proportion to the length of the sentence.

The several types of indeterminate sentence in use depend on various combinations of several factors. These factors are: minimum and maximum terms, fixing category of offenders to whom the sentence may apply, utilization of institutional facilities, and method of release. One cannot deal with all the combinations; it will suffice for present purposes to give three examples of indeterminate sentencing.

1. The court has absolute discretion in respect to fixing *definite* term (that is, minimum period of detention before parole eligibility) and *indefinite* term (that is, maximum period of detention) and absolute discretion as to whom the sentence may apply. This is the type of sentencing provided for in the Prisons and Reformatories Act. It has not always achieved its purpose through the very fact that it leaves too wide discretion in these matters to the court. It is in fact a denial of the concept of the indeterminate sentence as a tool of treatment.

The court, given complete freedom in setting the minimum and maximum periods, has been faced with three difficulties:

[17]*The Indeterminate Sentence,* New York: United Nations, Department of Social Affairs, 1954, pp. 4, 5, 6.

(a) It has traditionally felt compelled to take into account the concept of the 'appropriate punishment for the offence'. From the viewpoint of rehabilitation the danger here, in this writer's opinion, is that the total sentence will be, not too long, but rather too short. The writer does not suggest that a man should get a sentence longer than he deserves, but rather suggests that the monetary value of something he has stolen cannot in itself be the true measure of his 'deservingness' and certainly not of his need. Moreover, this is not to say that there is no place for short sentences, but that there is no place for a short sentence that contemplates parole.

(b) The court cannot know within narrow limits at the time of sentence the suitable period of incarceration and the appropriate time of release.

(c) The courts cannot maintain a uniformity of sentencing practice that will both preserve an equity in terms of punishment and provide a suitable period for reformative training and treatment.

In connection with the application of the sentence to a particular person, the court *can* most certainly, with proper information at hand, decide within narrow limits whether the sentence is suitable to the subject. This may be the essential job of the court in respect of an indeterminate sentence. If a statute does not define the wider limits, however, the court may very well be at a loss. Without such wider limits, we find the following situations:

(a) Prisoners of all ages from sixteen to seventy serving indeterminate sentences.

(b) Prisoners serving indeterminate sentences that seem to bear no relationship to previous records of crime and to other indications of potentiality for successful rehabilitation.

(c) Prisoners serving indeterminate sentences of such varying lengths as to present great difficulties for the institutional authorities, who are expected to carry on a program of training and treatment.

A particular jurisdiction may have an excellent system of classified institutions, but the authorities will not be able to cope with this situation.

The Parole Board in such a situation has a difficult task:

(a) It may feel compelled to refuse parole to recidivists who are not ready for release although the sentence was passed presumably to provide for a period of supervision.

(b) To preserve some semblance of equity, it may feel compelled to grant parole to first offenders with good conduct records, even though the period of training has been insufficient.

367

(c) It must frequently either refuse to grant parole when only a short period remains, or grant parole knowing that the period available is likely to be of little use from a rehabilitative point of view or from the point of view of protection of the public.

This is not to quarrel with the general argument that the court should have discretion in sentences. Rather it is to say that this type of indeterminate sentence does not truly offer the flexibility claimed for it.

In contrast, let us look at another type of indeterminate sentence.

2. The total sentence is set by statute at four years; application of sentence is at the discretion of the court within defined limits; the minimum period of detention is set by statute. The prototype is the English borstal-type sentence.

This type of sentence achieves its purpose for the following reasons:

(a) All subjects receive exactly the same maximum sentence: four years. The maximum period in the institution (three years) is long enough for effective training in all but the worst cases, but not so long as to be psychologically incomprehensible to the subject.

(b) The period of release eligibility (nine months to three years) provides a wide range to allow for individual differences.

(c) Supervision for one year after release is assured even if the subject stays the maximum period allowed in the institution.

(d) The statute defines the class of persons to which the sentence may apply: namely, youthful offenders between the ages of sixteen and twenty-three who have failed to benefit from either probation or short imprisonment and who seem likely to benefit from the borstal training.

(e) The statute provides for assistance to the court in its application of the sentence by requiring a pre-sentence report.

Here we have the court left with the final discretion in the decision to pass the sentence. In passing sentence the court has reasonable assurance that adequate facilities exist for training and that the release will take place at the most appropriate time under suitable conditions of supervision, etc.

3. 'Indeterminate to life' is a third type of which the Canadian preventive-detention sentence is an example. It obviously should apply only to a special class of persons. The Criminal Code describes two groups (habitual criminals and dangerous sexual offenders) within narrow limits and provides for periodic reviews of sentences. These precautions no doubt are a protection against capricious lifelong detention. It is question-

able whether an indeterminate-to-life sentence could safely be allowed to apply to any broader classifications of offenders.

These three examples purport above all to include the concept of parole in the philosophy of sentencing. On the other hand a philosophy of sentencing which makes the *sole* objective of sentencing the deterrence of the community at large leaves no room for parole except as a pure exercise of clemency. Even if deterrence is not the sole objective of the sentence but is considered to be the primary objective, the feasibility of parole in the so-called process becomes questionable. In this writer's opinion, sentencing systems can be devised – and in fact the present Canadian law already provides for such a system – that make possible proper emphasis on deterrence and yet allow for the possibility of parole.

If the state feels justified in taking an individual and using him as a means to an end – namely, the re-education of society by deterrence – then it should feel no compunction in interfering with his life to the extent of endeavouring to re-educate him to become a more useful citizen.

VARIATIONS AND SPECIAL USES

Gradual Release

One variation of parole that has been used in recent years is what is known in England as the 'Bristol Experiment'. In Canada we have experimented on this principle with what is called 'gradual release', a procedure designed to assist particularly the long-term prisoner in his progressive adjustment to community life. The inmate to be released is allowed to leave the prison daily and sometimes overnight, during a period that may be as short as one week or as long as three months, just prior to final release on parole or at expiration of sentence.

At its minimum, gradual release usually includes shopping-trips, opening bank accounts, registration at the National Employment Service, attendance at church, visits to private homes, and recreational activities such as movies and athletic events.

In some cases, local employers have provided temporary full-time employment for periods of a few weeks. The inmate leaves the prison each morning on his own recognizance to do his day's work. In a few instances, prisoners have been permitted to go out each day on their own to look for permanent employment. Sometimes an inmate on gradual release, in civilian clothes, assists a prison officer in duties in the neighbouring city. On occasion, an inmate has accompanied prison officers of his own faith attending a retreat at a religious institution. Inmates have been allowed a 'home parole' for a few days.

369

The method has also been used for intensive casework with certain disturbed inmates nearing their discharge dates. These inmates, on the face of it, were not good subjects for parole, but it was felt that every effort should be made to give them whatever assistance was possible for their own reclamation and for the protection of society.

Members of the prison staff and workers in after-care societies make the arrangements for activities during gradual release and provide supervision when required.

Experience to date has shown that a great deal of time must be taken in each individual case and that it is important that competent persons be free to conduct the program. Such a variety of benefits has been revealed that some danger has developed of confusion as to the purpose of gradual release. The possible negative aspects need to be examined before a sound philosophy can emerge.

Halfway House

One logical future extension of parole is with that group of men who are institutionalized or inadequate to such an extent that even the restraints imposed by an ordinary parole, including gradual release, are not sufficient to guarantee a reasonable chance of success. For members of this group, a 'halfway house' or hostel could provide a solution. There are, of course, probation homes already in existence, and the reasons for their existence are well accepted. Certain agencies provide for a limited number of parolees in a hostel type of accommodation that offers the security so essential to this group. This writer believes, however, that the group is large enough to justify extending the present facilities.

If they were so located, some gradual release, as we understand it today, might even take place directly from such hostels, because their location would be convenient for resocialization, job-hunting, and the other activities of gradual release. This would remove some of the burden of gradual-release activities from the limited facilities of the smaller cities and towns in which some of the major institutions are situated.

THE FUTURE OF PAROLE

The fact that parole is one of the youngest and best-loved children of modern correction has had an inevitable effect on evaluations of the subject. When parole is discussed, it is frequently assumed that (1) it will function as an incentive to inmates to improve themselves while in confinement; (2) it will provide a bridge over which the offender can negotiate his way to a good personal and social adjustment; (3) it enables a correctional system to implement the individualized treatment process;

(4) it provides protection for the public against the criminal and at the same time increases the likelihood that social resources will be constructively utilized in his behalf.

Little concrete evidence exists to demonstrate which, if any, of these hopes and aspirations have been realized. The lack of research in this area should be a source of concern to every citizen.[18]

Throughout this chapter the writer has offered his own opinion and the opinion of others that 'parole is a good thing'. The words of Korn and McCorkle quoted above, therefore, are intended to place forcibly before the reader the reality that these opinions are no more than *a priori* judgments. There has been little empirical study of the efficacy of parole. We hope, but we do not know, that parole does in fact assist in the rehabilitation of the offender and in the protection of society.

This truth notwithstanding, the preponderance of opinion is that parole logically should be the best method of release from prison. The laws of most countries now incorporate it as an integral part of the legal method of dealing with offenders. Consequently, we can say that parole is here to stay, or at least will be here for a long time. This should not stop us from subjecting our parole concepts and practices to constant and serious scrutiny and empirical study.

We may find on closer examination that parole should be used in many forms and many variations to suit particular needs. The 'white-collar criminal', for example, may need it, but perhaps it should be of a more punitive and restrictive character, in a different setting from the casework setting that we usually consider essential in our present concept. Similarly we may conclude that the many 'accidental criminals' require little attention of any sort; perhaps for them parole is in effect mere sentence-shortening.

Parole, like almost all other phases of modern correctional practice, has been built around the needs of the male offender. We should not be surprised, therefore, that the female offender does not respond in the same manner as the male offender to the common parole techniques. Perhaps we should develop something entirely new for the female offender.

Already, in experiments in the United States and in Canada, we are finding that parole may be useful in the treatment of drug addicts but that it is unlikely to be useful if the traditional restrictions of parole are imposed.

Much work has been done in parole prediction based mainly on pre-institutional factors. The philosophy of parole, however, is in the main

[18]Richard R. Korn and Lloyd W. McCorkle, *Criminology and Penology*, pp. 624-5.

based on a belief that human beings can and do change. If this belief is valid then it should be able to pass a test. Study should be made of the predictive value of factors based on institutional treatment, training, and adjustment, and factors based on parole plans and types of supervision.

If we are able finally to establish that in fact 'parole is a good thing', then we may have to conclude that all releases from prison should be by way of parole (in some form or other). The future of parole undoubtedly calls for careful examination of methods for mandatory parole or mandatory supervision. This will pose new and complicated problems. What degree of restriction should be imposed, and how much assistance should be given? What types of offenders should be the subjects of the variety of methods of release that might be available?

In Canada, the parole authority traditionally has not considered that it has any role in revision of sentences. However, this aspect of the total problem of sentencing may have to be reconsidered if the courts continue to look upon the function of the Parole Board as sentence-shortening.

The final words in the conclusion of the Fauteux Report seem especially fitting to conclude this chapter:

> No matter what may be the diversity and the quality of preventive measures designed and adopted in this branch of operation of criminal justice, there will undoubtedly continue to be criminals and recidivists. These are truths as permanent as human nature. *The necessity and the duty remain nonetheless to meet the problem.* The failure of a relatively few offenders to respond to the hopes of the courts, the penal institutions, the Remission Service and after-care agencies affords no justification for a failure by society to attempt to salvage, reform and rehabilitate the majority of those who have offended the laws of the country.

This is the recurring challenge.

Appendix

PAROLE ACT

An Act to provide the Conditional Liberation of
Persons Undergoing Sentences of Imprisonment
(*Assented to 6th September*, 1958)

HER MAJESTY, by and with the advice and consent of the Senate
and House of Commons of Canada, enacts as follows:

SHORT TITLE

rt title.   **1.**   This Act may be cited as the *Parole Act*.

INTERPRETATION.

initions.   **2.**   In this Act,

)ard."   (a) "Board" means the National Parole Board established by this Act;

mate."   (b) "inmate" means a person who has been convicted of an offence under an Act of the Parliament of Canada and is under sentence of imprisonment for that offence, but does not include a child within the meaning of the *Juvenile Delinquents Act* who is under sentence of imprisonment for an offence known as a delinquency;

agistrate."   (c) "magistrate" means a justice or a magistrate as defined in the *Criminal Code*;

rrole."   (d) "parole" means authority granted under this Act to an inmate to be at large during his term of imprisonment;

roled ate."   (e) "paroled inmate" means a person to whom parole has been granted;

role ervisor."   (f) "parole supervisor" means a person appointed by the Board to guide and supervise a paroled inmate; and

gulations."   (g) "regulations" means regulations made by order of the Governor in Council.

BOARD ESTABLISHED

rd blished.   **3.**   (1) There shall be a board, to be known as the National Parole Board, consisting of not less than three and not more than five members to be appointed by the Governor in Council to hold office during good behaviour for a period not exceeding ten years.

irman and e-Chairman.   (2) The Governor in Council shall designate one of the members to be Chairman and one to be Vice-Chairman.

373

Temporary members.	(3) The Governor in Council may appoint a temporary su stitute member to act as a member in the event that a member absent or unable to act.
Quorum.	(4) A majority of the members constitutes a quorum, a a vacancy on the Board does not impair the right of the remaini members to act.
Rules of procedure.	(5) The Board may, with the approval of the Governor Council, make rules for the conduct of its proceedings and t performance of its duties and functions under this Act.
Head office.	(6) The head office of the Board shall be at Ottawa, b meetings of the Board may be held at such other places as t Board determines.
Seal.	(7) The Board shall have an official seal.
Remuneration.	4. (1) Each member of the Board shall be paid such remune tion for his services as is fixed by the Governor in Council, and entitled to be paid reasonable travelling and living expenses incurr by him while absent from his ordinary place of residence in t course of his duties.
Staff.	(2) The officers, clerks and employees necessary for t proper conduct of the business of the Board shall be appointed accordance with the provisions of the *Civil Service Act.*
Chief executive officer.	(3) The Chairman is the chief executive officer of the Boa and has supervision over and direction of the work and the staff the Board.

POWERS AND DUTIES OF BOARD

Jurisdiction of Board.	5. Subject to this Act and the *Prisons and Reformatories A* the Board has exclusive jurisdiction and absolute discretion to gra refuse to grant or revoke parole.
Review of cases.	6. (1) The Board shall at the times prescribed by the regu tions

    (a) review the case of every inmate serving a sentence of i prisonment of two years or more, whether or not an appli tion has been made by or on behalf of the inmate, and

    (b) review such cases of inmates serving a sentence of impris ment of less than two years as are prescribed by the regu tions, upon application by or on behalf of the inmate.

Decisions.	(2) Upon reviewing the case of an inmate as required subsection (1) the Board shall decide whether or not to grant paro
Regulations.	7. The Governor in Council may make regulations prescribi

(a) the portion of the terms of imprisonment that inmates shall serve before parole may be granted,

(b) the times when the Board shall review cases of inmates serving sentences of imprisonment, and

(c) the class of cases of inmates serving a sentence of imprisonment of less than two years that shall be reviewed by the Board upon application.

8. The Board may

(a) grant parole to an inmate if the Board considers that the inmate has derived the maximum benefit from imprisonment and that the reform and rehabilitation of the inmate will be aided by the grant of parole;

(b) grant parole subject to any terms or conditions it considers desirable;

(c) provide for the guidance and supervision of paroled inmates for such period as the Board considers desirable; and

(d) revoke parole in its discretion.

9. The Board, in considering whether parole should be granted or revoked, is not required to grant a personal interview to the inmate or to any person on his behalf.

10. Where the Board grants parole it shall issue a parole certificate, under the seal of the Board, in such form as the Board prescribes, and shall deliver it or cause it to be delivered to the inmate and a copy to the parole supervisor, if any.

11. (1) The sentence of a paroled inmate shall, while the parole remains unrevoked and unforfeited, be deemed to continue in force until the expiration thereof according to law.

(2) Until a parole is revoked, forfeited or suspended the inmate is not liable to be imprisoned by reason of his sentence, and he shall be allowed to go and remain at large according to the terms and conditions of the parole and subject to the provisions of this Act.

SUSPENSION OF PAROLE

12. (1) A member of the Board or any person designated by the Board may, by a warrant in writing signed by him, suspend any parole and authorize the apprehension of a paroled inmate whenever he is satisfied that the arrest of the inmate is necessary or desirable in order to prevent a breach of any term or condition of the parole.

(2) A paroled inmate apprehended under a warrant issued under this section shall be brought as soon as conveniently may be

Appendix

before a magistrate, and the magistrate shall remand the inmate
custody until the Board cancels the suspension or revokes the paro

Review by
Board.

(3) The Board shall forthwith after a remand by a magistra
under subsection (2) review the case and shall either cancel t
suspension or revoke the parole.

Effect of
suspension.

(4) An inmate who is in custody by virtue of this secti
shall be deemed to be serving his sentence.

Forfeiture of Parole

Forfeiture.

13.   If a paroled inmate is convicted of an indictable offence, co
mitted after the grant of parole and punishable by imprisonment f
a term of two years or more, his parole is thereby forthwith forfeit

Apprehension upon Revocation or
Forfeiture of Parole

Apprehension.

14.   (1) If any parole is revoked or forfeited, the Board may,
warrant under the seal of the Board, authorize the apprehension
the paroled inmate.

Recom-
mitment.

(2) A paroled inmate apprehended under a warrant issu
under this section, shall be brought as soon as conveniently may
before a magistrate, and the magistrate shall thereupon make (
his warrant under his hand and seal for the recommitment of f
inmate as provided in this Act.

Execution of Warrant

Warrants for
apprehension.

15.   A warrant issued under section 12 or 14 shall be executed
any peace officer to whom it is given in any part of Canada, a
has the same force and effect in all parts of Canada as if it had be
originally issued or subsequently endorsed by a magistrate or otl
lawful authority having jurisdiction in the place where it is execut

Recommitment of Inmate

Place of
recommit-
ment.

16.   (1) Where the parole granted to an inmate has been revok
he shall be recommitted to the place of confinement to which
was originally committed to serve the sentence in respect of wh
he was granted parole, to serve the portion of his original term
imprisonment that remained unexpired at the time his parole v
granted.

Idem.

(2) Where a paroled inmate, upon revocation of his par
is apprehended at a place not within the territorial division to wh
he was originally committed, he shall be committed to the c
responding place of confinement for the territorial division witl

376

which he was apprehended, to serve the portion of his original term of imprisonment that remained unexpired at the time his parole was granted.

ct of
eiture.

17. (1) When any parole is forfeited by conviction of an indictable offence the paroled inmate shall undergo a term of imprisonment equal to the portion of the term to which he was originally sentenced that remained unexpired at the time his parole was granted plus the term, if any, to which he is sentenced upon conviction for the offence.

m to be
ed.

(2) The term of imprisonment prescribed by subsection (1) shall be served as follows:

(a) in a penitentiary, if the original sentence in respect of which he was granted parole was to a penitentiary;

(b) in a penitentiary, if the total term of imprisonment prescribed by subsection (1) is for a period of two years or more; and

(c) in the place of confinement to which he was originally committed to serve the sentence in respect of which he was granted parole, if that place of confinement was not a penitentiary and the term of imprisonment prescribed by subsection (1) is less than two years.

viction
offence
mitted
ng parole.

(3) Where a paroled inmate is, after the expiration of his parole, convicted of an indictable offence committed during the period when his parole was in effect, the parole shall be deemed to have been forfeited on the day on which the offence was committed, and the provisions of this Act respecting imprisonment upon forfeiture of parole apply *mutatis mutandis*.

ADDITIONAL JURISDICTION

ocation
uspension
ertain
ishments.

18. (1) The Board may, upon application therefor and subject to regulations, revoke or suspend any sentence of whipping or any order made under the *Criminal Code* prohibiting any person from operating a motor vehicle.

nency.

(2) The Board shall, when so directed by the Minister of Justice, make any investigation or inquiry desired by the Minister in connection with any request made to the Minister for the exercise of the royal prerogative of mercy.

MISCELLANEOUS

er, etc.

19. An order, warrant or decision made or issued under this Act is not subject to appeal or review to or by any court or other authority.

Appendix

Evidence. **20.** Any order, decision or warrant purporting to be sealed w the seal of the Board or to be signed by a person purporting to a member of the Board or to have been designated by the Board suspend parole is admissible in evidence in any proceedings in a court.

Expenditures. **21.** All expenditures under or for the purposes of this Act sh be paid out of money appropriated by Parliament therefor.

Super-annuation. **22.** The members and staff of the Board shall be deemed to employed in the Public Service for the purpose of the *Public Serv Superannuation Act*.

Transfer of staff. **23.** Notwithstanding subsection (2) of section 4, the Goverr in Council may by order transfer persons who prior to the co mencement of this Act were members of the staff of the Depa ment of Justice to the staff of the Board.

Repeal. R.S. 1952, c. 264. **24.** (1) The *Ticket of Leave Act* is repealed.

Licence under former Act deemed parole. (2) Every person who at the coming into force of this Ac the holder of a licence issued under the *Ticket of Leave Act* to at large shall be deemed to have been granted parole under this *A* under the same terms and conditions as those under which **t** licence was issued or such further or other conditions as the Boa may prescribe.

Revoked or forfeited licence. (3) Every person who was issued a licence to be at la₁ under the *Ticket of Leave Act*, whose licence was revoked or f feited and who at the coming into force of this Act is unlawfully large may be dealt with under this Act as though he were a paro inmate whose parole had been revoked or forfeited.

Reference. (4) A reference in any Act, regulation or document t conditional liberation or ticket of leave under the *Ticket of Le Act* shall be deemed to be a reference to parole granted under t Act.

Habitual criminals. (5) The powers, functions and duties of the Minister Justice under section 666 of the *Criminal Code* are hereby tra ferred to the Board, and a reference in that section to permiss to be at large on licence shall be deemed to be a reference to par granted under this Act.

Coming into force. *25. This Act shall come into force on a day to be fixed by proc mation of the Governor in Council.

*Note – Proclaimed in force as of February 15, 1959.

PAROLE REGULATIONS
P.C. 1960 – 681
(as amended)

REGULATIONS MADE UNDER THE PAROLE ACT

1. These Regulations may be cited as the *Parole Regulations*.

2. (1) The portion of the term of imprisonment that an inmate shall ordinarily serve, in the cases mentioned in this subsection, before parole may be granted, is as follows:
   (a) where the sentence of imprisonment is not a sentence of imprisonment for life or a sentence of preventive detention, one-third of the term of imprisonment imposed or four years, whichever is the lesser, but in the case of a sentence of imprisonment of two years or more to a federal penal institution, at least nine months;
   (b) where the sentence of imprisonment is for life but not a sentence of preventive detention or a sentence of life imprisonment to which a sentence of death has been commuted, seven years.

(2) Notwithstanding subsection (1), where in the opinion of the Board special circumstances exist, the Board may grant parole to an inmate before he has served the portion of his sentence of imprisonment required under subsection (1) to have been served before a parole may be granted.

(3) A person who is serving a sentence of imprisonment to which a sentence of death has been commuted, shall serve the entire term of the sentence of imprisonment unless, upon the recommendation of the Board, the Governor in Council otherwise directs.

(4) The Board shall not recommend a parole, in a case coming within subsection (3), until at least ten years of the term of the imprisonment have been served.

3. (1) In the case of every inmate serving a sentence of imprisonment of two years or more, the Board shall
   (a) consider the case of the inmate as soon as possible after the inmate has been admitted to a prison, and in any event within six months thereof, and fix a date for his parole review;
   (b) review the case of the inmate in order to decide whether or not to grant or recommend parole and, if parole is to be granted, the date upon which the parole is to commence, on or before
      (i) the date fixed for the parole review pursuant to paragraph (a), or

(ii) the last day of the relevant portion of the term of imprisonment referred to in subsection (1) of section 2,

whichever is the earlier; and

(c) where the Board, upon reviewing the case of an inmate pursuant to paragraph (b) does not at that time grant or recommend parole to the inmate, continue to review the case of the inmate at least once during every two years following the date the case was previously reviewed until parole is granted or the sentence of the inmate is satisfied.

(2) Where an application for parole is made by or on behalf of an inmate who is serving a sentence of imprisonment of less than two years, the case shall be reviewed upon completion of all inquiries that the Board considers necessary but, in any event, not later than four months after the application is received by the Board.

(3) Nothing in this section shall be construed as limiting the authority of the Board to review the case of an inmate at any time during his term of imprisonment.

4. (1) Where the Board receives an application to suspend or revoke a sentence of whipping, the Board shall

(a) determine forthwith if the sentence should be suspended pending further investigation and, if it was so determined, issue an order accordingly;

(b) conduct such investigation as appears to be warranted in the circumstances; and

(c) as soon as possible after completing the investigation, if any, referred to in paragraph (b)

(i) revoke the sentence,

(ii) refuse to revoke the sentence,

(iii) suspend the sentence for any period the Board may deem applicable,

(iv) refuse to suspend the sentence, or

(v) cancel the order of suspension, if any, made pursuant to paragraph (a).

(2) An order of suspension made pursuant to subsection (1) expires ten days before the expiration of any term of imprisonment to which the convicted person, to whom the sentence of whipping relates, has been sentenced unless, before that day, the Board revokes the sentence of whipping.

5. Where the Board receives an application to suspend or revoke an order made under the *Criminal Code* prohibiting a person from operating a motor vehicle, the Board shall

(a) conduct as quickly as possible such investigation as appears to be warranted in the circumstances; and

(b) determine as soon as possible if the order should be suspended or revoked and, if it so decides, issue an order accordingly.

6. Where the Board suspends or revokes an order made under the *Criminal Code* prohibiting a person from operating a motor vehicle, the suspension or revocation may be made upon such terms and conditions as the Board considers necessary or desirable.

PAROLE AGREEMENT

I clearly understand that I am still serving the sentence imposed but I am being granted parole to permit me to resume my activities as a citizen at large in the community, under supervision. Therefore, in consideration of parole being granted to me, I solemnly agree:

1. To remain, until the expiry of my sentence, under the authority of the National Parole Service Regional Representative in ....

2   To forthwith proceed directly to ....
    ....and, immediately upon arrival and at least once a month thereafter, to report faithfully to ....

3. To accept the supervision and assistance of my supervisor ....

4. To remain in the immediate area of ....
    .... or as designated by the Regional Representative and, if I have good cause to leave this area, to obtain permission beforehand through my supervisor.

5. To endeavour to maintain steady employment and to report at once to the Regional Representative through my supervisor, any change or termination of employment or any other change of circumstances such as accident or illness.

6. To secure advance approval from the Regional Representative, through my supervisor, if at any time I wish to:
    (a) purchase a motor vehicle;
    (b) incur debts by borrowing money or instalment buying;
    (c) assume additional responsibilities, such as marrying;
    (d) own or carry fire-arms or other weapons.

7. To abide by all instructions which may be given by my supervisor or by the Regional Representative through my supervisor, and especially with regard to employment, companions, hours, intoxicants, operation of motor vehicles, medical or psychiatric attention, family responsibilities, court obligations.

8. To abide by these special conditions: ....

9. To forthwith communicate with the Regional Representative, through my supervisor, if I am arrested or questioned by peace officers regarding any offence.

10. To obey the law and fulfill all my legal and social responsibilities.

I have read, or have had read to me, and fully understand and accept the conditions, regulations and restrictions governing my release on parole. I will abide by and conform to them strictly. I also understand that if I violate them in any manner, I may be recommitted.

....
                      (*name*)   (*number*)

Witnessed:...

....
              (*title*)

Date of leaving...

14

After-Care and the Prisoners' Aid Societies

A. M. KIRKPATRICK

Prisons are places that men leave. A few die, a few are executed, and a few become insane; but it is an important fact that they do not remain in prison. When prisoners are held in custody, instead of being killed or transported as in past centuries, they must eventually be returned to the community. It is then that their second punishment very often begins.

Citizens concerned about the lot of the deprived and disinherited began to see, a full century ago, that men and women coming from prisons had to face very serious problems of readjustment. On both humanitarian and religious grounds, they began to render such help as they could on a voluntary and usually individual basis. Such response to human need usually does not develop in any orderly or systematic pattern, and the work of the prisoners' aid societies, which developed in Canada from these early volunteer efforts, has been no exception. Since it is patently impossible to describe the work of the after-care societies in detail, this chapter discusses their work in general terms only, while recognizing the variation in their policy and practice.

Every province in Canada has after-care services, frequently called prisoners' aid societies, available to the ex-inmate. These services have developed in different ways. Not all are specifically organized as prisoners' aid societies, and some perform other welfare or religious functions in their communities.

The Correctional Services Department of the Salvation Army is organized on a national basis and provides coverage in all provinces as part of the total religious and humanitarian service of the Salvation Army in Canada. Its services include court attendance to give counsel, advice, and

384

general assistance to accused persons. Ex-inmates in the care of the Salvation Army may utilize hostels, rehabilitation centres, and the institutions that deal with the problem of alcoholism. Spiritual therapy is an important aspect of such programs and is in the historic tradition of the founder, William Booth.

> In 1890 the first 'Prison Gate Home' in Canada was opened [by the Salvation Army] in Toronto. It provided not only food and shelter but also employment in the woodyard, the boot-and-shoe shop, and the bakery. The stream of derelicts flowing into the first Prison Gate Home widened every week, until twenty, thirty, fifty human wrecks had found a haven . . . . In recent years the name of the department has changed from 'Prison and Police Court Work' to 'Correctional Services'. This change conforms to the general usage of 'corrections' by the Department of Justice and after-care agencies. The term has come into use to describe the total process by which society attempts to correct the anti-social attitudes and behaviour of the law-breaker.[1]

Quebec has the Société d'Orientation et de Réhabilitation Sociale in Montreal and the Service de Réadaptation Sociale, Inc., in Quebec City. In a recent development in that province, the Diocesan Societies, which specialize in family and child welfare throughout the province, began to serve not only the families of those in prison, but also former inmates. In British Columbia, the Borstal Association gives individual care for the younger age-group. In Ontario, a parole and after-care service is carried on by the Department of Reform Institutions, in addition to the work of the private agencies. The Catholic Rehabilitation Services and the Church Army of the Anglican Church are active in some Canadian centres. The Elizabeth Fry Societies, which work with women, have branches in several provinces and are in some cases closely associated with the John Howard Societies. The latter are provincially organized in all provinces, and in many cases have branches in the larger urban centres.

The John Howard Society of Canada was organized in February 1960, at a meeting in Ottawa. Representatives of all but one of the provincial John Howard Societies were present and were able to give immediate ratification to the Articles of Agreement drawn up at the meeting. During the same month, it was reported that preliminary steps had been taken to bring about an association of Quebec after-care societies.

The John Howard Society of Quebec, which operates in Montreal, claims the longest continuous history of prisoners' aid work in Canada. It dates from 1892, when it was organized within the Anglican Church.

[1]*The Law Breaker and the Salvation Army*, Toronto: Salvation Army, 1961.

The aims of the founders were stated as 'reformation of offenders, their welfare when discharged, to watch the law courts to the interest of offenders under arrest, the prevention of crime, and prison reform'.[2] In actual fact, the earliest Canadian record of prisoners' aid work goes back to 1867, when a group of church workers in Toronto first began to bring spiritual consolation to inmates of the jail. The first prisoners' aid society began in Toronto in 1874, but the development was sporadic and there were gaps in the provision of service. The present John Howard Society of Ontario has been in existence under different names since May 1929. The first use of the name John Howard Society was in 1931 by the British Columbia group under the leadership of Rev. J. Dinnage Hobden.

With the post-war appointment of Major-General Ralph B. Gibson as Commissioner of Penitentiaries for Canada and Joseph McCulley as his Deputy-Commissioner, there came a readiness in the Canadian federal service to recognize the development of prisoners' aid work. At that time, J. Alex. Edmison, Q.C., was the Executive Director of the John Howard Society of Ontario and also the President of the Canadian Penal Association. He travelled across the country, stressing the need for aid to ex-inmates, and largely as a result of his leadership, various societies were formed. About 1946, at his suggestion, the name John Howard Society came into general use.

It is probably fair to say that the punitive nature of the penal practices of the time produced this type of response from sensitive and interested citizens. Certainly there has been a dramatic growth in prisoners' aid societies since then, which indicates the interest not only of the general public but also of both federal and provincial governments. The federal government has provided financial support for the work done for ex-prisoners, and some societies have received provincial government grants. It should be clear, however, that these societies are formed of voluntary groups of citizens expressing the community's concern for the returning offender. Although they receive government support through *ex gratia* grants, they are mainly financed through Community Chests. Thus they provide an example of the combining of government and citizen action, both philosophically and financially, to provide necessary social services. While they operate in the closest co-operation with the government departments, they are, none the less, private social agencies responsible to their communities through elected boards of directors.

2Ellen Prince, 'A History of the John Howard Society of Quebec, Inc.', (M.S.W. Thesis, McGill University, 1956).

AID ON DISCHARGE TO AFTER-CARE

Obviously, the societies' fundamental responsibility is in the re-establishment of ex-inmates in their communities. It is now generally accepted that the social services of all major communities should make provision to help the returning prisoner. Most of the prisoners' aid societies have developed casework services interrelated with the other social agencies in their communities and closely related to the various governmental correctional services.

This represents a marked change in approach from merely 'aid on discharge' to individualized and specialized after-care on a sustained basis, which necessitates the employment of professionally trained social workers to provide the casework service. The professional has by no means replaced the volunteer: a number of the branches of the various prisoners' aid societies are entirely voluntary in their organization, though they may operate under the guidance of and in consultation with a professional staff.

The change in approach has resulted, in the larger centres particularly, in continuous service based on prior investigation, individual attention, and prolonged contact between the offender and the worker. The personal contact and the relationship that is built up are, along with his own motivation, the essential ingredients of the inmate's progress towards re-establishment. The social worker must combine objectivity and sympathy, but he must insist on getting to know his client well enough to diagnose his problems even if this produces discomfort in the initial stages. The importance of such close contact is obvious when it is realized that many of the problems faced by the ex-inmate are of a deep emotional nature.

Particular reference to marital reintegration has been made by E. V. Shiner, formerly of the staff of the John Howard Societies of Quebec and Ontario:

> Marriage is obviously the closest of all adult human relationships. In it the personalities of the husband and wife impinge directly and constantly upon one another. Regardless of the external factors which affect the marital adjustment it can be seen that the individual's capacity to love and his ability to handle hostility are at the core of the marriage relationship. Negative feelings exist in every marriage, for their roots lie in frustration, the natural by-product of a union of different personalities. We have noted that both inter-personal relationships and impulse-control are impaired in the group from which our clients appear. One must be on the alert for signs of stress in the offender's marriage. We know that the seeds of potential destructiveness are sown in one of the marriage partners, and consequently some form of marital imbalance

may be present. These factors probably exist in the marriage situation of most releasees returning to their families. Superimpose upon this potentially unstable marriage the trauma of separation and the negative by-products resulting from incarceration, and one begins to appreciate the difficulties faced by the married offender.[3]

But there is also the ex-inmate's immediate need to bridge the gap between institutional maintenance and self-maintenance in the competitive economic and social community. The prisoners' aid societies exist to meet both the emotional and socio-economic needs by offering help to those who wish to profit from it and who show some indication of being able to use it constructively. This counselling service expresses the community's charitable intentions towards the ex-inmate.

Essentially, the worker in the after-care agency seeks out the strengths inherent in every human being. He helps the ex-inmate adjust to earning his living by these strengths and not by his weaknesses. His attitude, therefore, must be one that accepts, though it does not condone, past crimes or the possibility of future crime. Moralizing is of little use, and blaming a man for failure, trivial or great, adds no strength to his struggle. The agency's service must be accommodated as much as possible to the man's need. This must be done within agency policy, however, and also within agency resources, but inventiveness and initiative make it possible to draw on many other resources that are available in the community.

It is essential that the service given an ex-inmate be related to the experience he has had in prison, and that the probable effect of his imprisonment on his chances of re-establishment in the community be taken into account. Though funds are used for material assistance on a planned basis, the prisoners' aid societies have developed policies and practices, based on long experience and observation, that preclude their acting as a relief agency. Personnel have a good knowledge of the prisons and of the criminal population. They are in and out of the institutions frequently, know the staffs and many of the inmates, have studied the penal system and participated in its growth and development, and have developed considerable skill in the work of parole and after-care.

While in this chapter we mostly speak in terms of male offenders, it is important to remember that a relatively small proportion of women offenders pose a most difficult treatment problem, both in the institutions and on release in the community. There are, of course, enough successes with women, as well as with men, to justify the effort. But the crux of the

---

[3]E. V. Shiner, 'Return of the Married Offender to His Family', *Proceedings*, Canadian Congress of Corrections, Montreal, 1957.

community's responsibility is expressed by Miss Phyllis G. Haslam, Executive Director of the Toronto Branch of the Elizabeth Fry Society:

> Many of those with whom we work are not doing well. We take the attitude that if we can be of assistance to a girl who is or has been an offender we should give what help we can, realizing that there are many times when we can do little more than letting the girl know that we care. Certainly with our lack of experience we do not have enough knowledge yet to know with any certainty which person will succeed and which will fail. Even when we have more knowledge there would seem to be a place in the community for an agency working with the offender where the main concern will be with the person and not primarily with her success or failure.[4]

PRE-RELEASE REFERRAL SERVICES

With the development of the modern approach in the period following the Second World War, it was realized that it is essential to any proper program of individual rehabilitation that offenders be interviewed in the institution before release. With few exceptions, the prisoners' aid societies have set up pre-release services, in some cases with specially designated workers, to bring about referral of the offender from the institution and to provide some picture of him before he returns to the community. Such services, by providing knowledge of the institutional program and an assessment of the inmate, allow continuity of treatment or training. Assessment of the individual ideally includes an account of his strengths and weaknesses, his plans and resources, his personality and social handicaps, his relationships in the community, his chances of finding work, and any other factors that could help in devising a plan to be worked upon co-operatively by the man himself and the representative of the prisoners' aid society.

The services of the various agencies are explained to the inmate by the institutional staff. If he wishes to accept such service, he himself takes the next step and requests help. Most of the agencies believe that it is important that he take this step himself.

The John Howard Societies of British Columbia and of Quebec have initiated counselling with groups of wives in the community prior to the release of their imprisoned spouses. Their experience shows that such intensive preparation is helpful emotionally to the resumption of family life and reduces the feeling of social isolation. They regard this group experi-

[4]Phyllis G. Haslam, *Annual Report, 1956*, Elizabeth Fry Society, Toronto Branch.

ence not as a substitute for individual casework, but as a most desirable added item to their service practices.

D. C. S. Reid, formerly of the staff of the John Howard Society of Ontario and now Executive Director of the Alberta Society, lists four main aspects of the pre-release interview that follows a prisoner's request for help: the introduction, which develops the request; presentation to the inmate of a brief outline of agency service; decision by the inmate to use the referral service; a more detailed interpretation of agency service, standard post-release problems, and community attitudes.

He goes on to list the following series of standard post-release problems, which he compiled for ready use during such interviews:

1. Employment:
   (a) An inability to use constructively the job-placing services in the community such as the National Employment Service,
   (b) Disillusionment about the employment situation, i.e., lack of job, and length of job-hunting process,
   (c) Inability to find work, to sell oneself to an employer,
   (d) When in employment, inability to face up to employer and barter for the best working arrangements,
   (e) General feelings of insecurity in employment, such as fear of employees, someone coming in off the street and facing him, and fear of police visit to the employer.
2. Economic insecurity over the period from release to first pay.
3. The securing of accommodation.
4. Recovery from the initial period of confusion, depression, and mental disorientation.
5. The resumption of normal family and marital relationships and the difficulties that ensue.
6. The pressure to acquire material effects, particularly clothing.
7. The establishment of social relationships.
8. The constructive use of leisure time.
9. The fear of finding himself back with the 'rounders'.
10. Handling his drive for acceptance.
11. Dealing with returning cycles of depression and lack of progress as first planned, and frustration in some cases at being unable to make any headway.
12. Hostile attitude towards authority, particularly the police.
13. Pre-conviction debts, both financial and social.
14. Problems of fantasy thinking and fabrication, such as inability to tell a straight story to employers, after-care workers, family and friends.
15. How to use counselling effectively.
16. How to handle the over-confidence that comes with the first pay.
17. Bonding and licensing.

18. The doldrum period.[5]

Some indication of the extent of this pre-release service is shown in the *Report* of the Commissioner of Penitentiaries, 1960, in which a table of activities of welfare organizations is displayed.[6] This table indicates that the various societies made a total of 1,440 visits to the penitentiaries during the year and had 10,065 interviews with inmates. When it is noted that during the same year there were 6,344 inmates on the registers of the various penitentiaries, it will be seen that this was, in itself, a fairly broad coverage of the inmate population. The numbers of visits and the numbers of inmates interviewed in the various provincial reformatories and jails are not known, but they would increase this total very materially.

FINANCIAL ASSISTANCE

Rev. W. E. Hart of the John Howard Society of New Brunswick expresses the financial problem:

> How does society treat the prisoner on release? Put yourself in the shoes of a young man twenty-three years old who had spent the last three years in Dorchester Penitentiary. You are a free man again. The prison door is shut behind you but the world you go out into is strange and un-friendly. You have a new outfit of street clothes but no work clothes, and $10 in your pocket. Suppose you have no home, no friends, and no job and you cannot easily get work, and prison routine has made it difficult for you to adapt yourself to a normal life.[7]

Fundamental to the casework service provided by most of the agencies is the use of financial assistance. The earnings of prisoners in the penitentiary system were increased in 1964, but are still quite low, and the effect of the change has not been fully realized, though it is now estimated that a man may have about $17 per year of sentence. The discharge gratuities paid by the various provincial institutions vary, but are also quite small. For example, in Ontario, the gratuity is two dollars per month up to a maximum of $20 on discharge. Hence, the ex-inmate meets financial problems when he 'hits the street'. It has long been one of the clichés of the prisoners' aid societies that 'you can't counsel a man on a hungry stomach'. It seems socially immoral to encourage him to look for work

[5]D. C. S. Reid, 'After-Care Pre-Release Preparation of Prison Inmates', *The Canadian Journal of Corrections*, vol. 1, nos. 1 and 2.
[6]Commissioner of Penitentiaries, *Report*, Ottawa: Queen's Printer, 1960, pp. 58-9.
[7]William E. Hart, *What is a John Howard Society?*, Ottawa: Canadian Welfare Council, 1952.

and try to re-establish himself in the community, unless some provision is made to help maintain him even at the lowest level of subsistence while he awaits his first pay from gainful employment.

The prisoners' aid societies obviously want the ex-inmate to find a job speedily, primarily for his own sake, but also because in many cases they are providing material assistance for him. This money is to enable him to survive while he seeks employment and until he gets his first pay and is, of course, for necessities such as food, lodgings, work-clothing, and work-tools. Since he is almost insolvent when he reaches the community, the securing of food and shelter are immediate necessities. It is of great importance that his ability to maintain himself should develop quickly and that opportunities should be made available for him to find his niche as a socially and economically productive person in society.

In a recent article, Louis Zeitoun of the John Howard Society of Ottawa says: 'The tradition of private agencies pioneering in social service development has been true also in the field of prisoner rehabilitation, and, today, in Canada it is primarily the private agency which meets the need of our ex-prisoners. Since a term in prison is not a qualification for public welfare assistance, the giving of material aid has become an important part of private agency service to be administered as part of a total casework plan.' He is referring here to the crux of the problem, namely, that because they have been in prison for a long time, many inmates find it difficult to establish that they are eligible for welfare assistance. He continues: 'Ideally, the prison dischargee should be eligible for public welfare assistance, with the function of the private agency focused upon the giving of a casework service to help with psychological and environmental problems, but providing material assistance where necessary for specific reasons as part of this process.'[8]

The old concept was to advise, assist, and befriend, and these functions are still essential elements. But it is important to realize the main difference between the occasional help of the volunteer and the organized effort resulting in continuous supervision. 'The social worker, both in the field of group-work and in that of casework, is no longer concerned only with the task of alleviating material distress, but is engaged also in the more difficult job of helping the individual to adapt himself to the problems of the world in which he lives.'[9]

---

[8]Louis Zeitoun, 'Material Assistance Given by After-Care Agencies in Canada', *American Journal of Correction*, vol. 21, no. 1, p. 15.

[9]John Spencer, 'The Place of the Social Worker in the Prison Systems', *The Howard Journal*, 1951, p. 87.

EMPLOYMENT

It is obvious that in re-establishing the ex-inmate in the community, employment is a fundamental factor. We are fortunate in Canada to have a National Employment Service, which has a Special Services Department to handle handicapped people. By regulation, ex-inmates are considered to fall within this category for a period of thirty days, and are entitled to the help of the Special Services officers. These men and women have a record of very excellent service to ex-inmates, and the societies co-operate most closely with them in matters of employment.

The National Employment Service specializes in finding jobs and placing suitable individuals in them, whereas the prisoners' aid societies specialize in counselling in that they endeavour to support and encourage the newly released offender through the rebuffs that he inevitably receives in job-seeking. The National Employment Service maintains its own pre-release service in some institutions where its representatives visit the inmates.

Most prisoners realize that employment is the direct avenue to self-maintenance, and are anxious to get a job in the belief that this is the only thing they need to guarantee success. Materially this may seem true because, of course, survival is fundamental; but, when some of the emotional factors involved in re-establishment are taken into account, it is not surprising that many are not able to hold jobs when they first return to the community.

Many are afraid that their records will become known by their employers or their fellow employees. Others find it difficult to follow the discipline of employment, which involves the acceptance of direction, regular hours, steady consistent effort, good work habits, and co-operative effort with other employees at common tasks. Some feel unable to bargain for proper workloads and pay, and may be imposed on by unscrupulous employers or foremen. Thus the ex-inmate may fail at a number of jobs before one works out and he can settle down.

The following, an actual case, is an example of the perils that lie in wait for an ex-inmate. A man employed in a supervisory position received a pay increase and was told that, in addition, he was to be promoted. Unexpectedly, all employees of the firm were instructed to obtain a certain credential. Knowing that he could not obtain this credential without his record becoming known to his employer, he went to the caseworker of the prisoners' aid society. After considerable discussion, he realized that the best thing for him to do would be to go to his employer and disclose his record himself. In the short run, it would have been easier for him if the caseworker had gone to the employer and made the disclosure; but in the long run, it was better for his development and for his relationship with his employer that he face the situation himself. This is what he did, and the employer immediately telephoned the caseworker, who then went to the employer's office to discuss the matter. The employer had not known that he was employing an ex-convict and was greatly concerned; but after discussion he agreed that the man was the same employee whom he had known an hour before, whose pay he had increased and whom he had decided to promote. He agreed also that the fact of the man's prison record did not really make any difference to the discharging of his duties.

THE STIGMA OF THE 'EX-CON'

Many large firms and even some governments still carry on their employment application-forms the question, 'Have you ever been convicted of a criminal offence?' Seeing this, the ex-inmate has to decide whether he will reveal his record or deny that he has one. He knows, from his own experience and that of others, that if he indicates he has had a criminal conviction, someone else is almost sure to appear better qualified for the job. He also knows that if he does not reveal the record himself, it may be discovered later through the process of bonding or in some other way, and at that time he is likely to be discharged for having falsified his employment application.

Speaking generally, the employment opportunities for ex-inmates are best when employers are prepared to look at them and at their problems in an individual way, and to base their decisions on good personnel practices rather than on prejudice. Even in these, as in less favourable conditions, the big questions still stand. 'Will the employer be told the truth at the risk (imaginary or not) of the job being given to another applicant equally qualified but with no prison record?' 'Will the prison record be suppressed, and references and an immediate job history be fabricated, in order that a job may be secured?' 'Will falsification ultimately lead to disclosure, with the loss of the job, references, and such goodwill as may have been achieved?' These are questions hotly debated among inmates, and each man has to determine for himself how he will deal with them.

Because 'blanket bonding' of employees is becoming very prevalent, the areas of employment open to ex-inmates are gradually shrinking. Today many delivery men, truckers, and warehouse employees are bonded. When the bonding company refuses to bond an employee, an explanation is necessary, and it is very likely that the ex-inmate will be seeking new employment.

Again, an actual case will serve as an illustration of what happens.

A man out of prison for three years worked at wages insufficient to support his family. He obtained a much better job as a factory shipper, but did not declare his criminal record at the time of application. After six weeks, following the usual inquiry, the bonding company refused to bond him and his criminal record was divulged to the employer. During these six weeks, however, his work and loyalty had been of the highest order. His socially minded employer wished to retain him, and so transferred him to a non-bonded position, a routine labouring job. Since the wage-level was again too low to permit him to support his family, he became once more a frustrated man looking for work at a rate of pay adequate for his needs.

The licensing of trucks and certain kinds of stores and businesses is controlled to ensure that these enterprises are conducted with regard to the public safety and interest. Licences to ex-inmates are rigorously curtailed in some jurisdictions on the ground of protection of the public. The reluctance of police commissions and of bonding companies to license or bond ex-inmates indiscriminately can be understood. All applicants, whether or not they have a criminal record, are carefully screened. But when a man has demonstrated over a period of years that he is living a responsible life, free from criminal activity or association, he is being most unfairly discriminated against if he is denied an opportunity to advance himself or to pursue a chosen avenue of employment.

Ex-inmates are truthfully in the position of second-class citizens as far as employment is concerned. Many, who, as individuals, have excellent intelligence, aptitude, and training, are forced into the ranks of unskilled labour. This is particularly true of men who have had vocational training in the prisons and who seek to have this training recognized for purposes of apprenticeship. In some jurisdictions and in some trades, prison vocational training is not rated the same as similar training on the outside, nor are the men accepted and given opportunity to qualify as tradesmen. With the development of programs of training in the institutions, this matter assumes major importance.

It is only fair, however, to say that ex-inmates are at times their own worst salesmen. They are no angels, any more than are ordinary citizens, and temptation and frustration sometimes prove too strong. On occasion an employer who has hired an ex-inmate finds himself badly let down. Few employers in such circumstances feel like turning the other cheek. Many say, 'Once bitten twice shy', and the approach becomes more difficult for the next ex-inmate. But many employees who are not ex-inmates also succumb to temptation and frustration of various kinds. Unfortunately the belief is widespread that the ex-inmate will probably prove to be dishonest, that he is in any case inevitably a bad risk, and even that he is a worse risk than people with a bad employment record who have not been in prison.

EMOTIONAL AND RELATIONSHIP PROBLEM

The work of the prisoners' aid societies is not done in a vacuum. Where possible, the resources of the family should be gathered around the ex-inmate. Other services such as family agencies, municipal welfare agencies, and medical and psychiatric facilities should be used where their specialized resources can be drawn upon to bring about the offender's re-establishment. By every means possible, ex-inmates must be helped to get some insight into the reasons why they have been in conflict with society and the criminal law, and in many cases, why they have been unable to form or maintain workable human relationships with relatives, friends, neighbours, or employers.

The emotional problems experienced on release from prison are very great. The newly free individual needs to regain a concept of his role as a free and contributing citizen, to re-develop emotional roots, to achieve a lessening of the feelings of hostility bred by the heightened frustrations of prison life, to secure acceptance by other people, and to be or to become tolerant enough himself to accept other people – particularly, perhaps, a family who may have learned to get along without him.

There is an immediate return to the responsibilities of self-maintenance and the exercise of choice, so that simple actions such as purchasing, ordering meals, opening doors, and handling money become matters for major decisions. There is always the danger of mistaking liberty for licence in the first flush of freedom. Some go on a luxury spending spree; others on a drinking spree. Such conduct is neither to be condoned nor moralized about, but rather to be accepted and worked with. Many men have said that they are afraid to move into community groups lest they be recognized and identified as criminals, rejected, and further hurt. A prison experience does not render a man impervious to emotional hurt.

A man who came to see a prisoners' aid society worker one Monday morning is typical. He was broke, he had a hangover, and he was full of remorse. He spoke with great feeling of his terrible loneliness and said that on Saturday he had gone down to 'the corner', where he had met some of the men he had known in prison. His comment was, 'I knew they weren't good friends down there. But poor friends are better than no friends.'

An urge to acquire the visible symbols of success – watches, cars, a 'good front' – is often obvious. Unless things 'break right', the temptation to revert to previous habits is very hard to resist. There is sometimes a 'chip on the shoulder' – an expectation of discrimination – with constant guardedness lest some remark or action reveal the recent prison experience.

The very pace of life on the outside becomes disturbing, often in relation to fast transportation. Anxieties may arise from the ex-inmate's fear of meeting people, and he may tend to escape into inner isolation. Having lived apart from women and children for a long time, he has to adjust to dealing with them again. This is particularly hard for the man who returns to his own family and has to resume parental relationships. The control of his children, whom he may not have seen for years, can be a very difficult problem.

Many feel a great need to make up for time lost in prison. They desire fast action, to get things done in a hurry. This is the problem of immediacy that seems to relate to the loss of normal time-sense during imprisonment. A man 'doing time' has to forget time and the normal planning of activities. When he returns to the community, he may be so conscious of the awful gap in his life that he will develop a compelling urge to catch up with relatives and neighbours whose gainful employment has advanced their status and resources during his absence.

SUPERVISION OF PAROLEES

In 1947, a Committee for the Adult Offender, of which the late Dr. Stuart Jaffary of the School of Social Work of the University of Toronto was chairman, stated in its report:

> The return to the community should be a conditional one. The parole authority must be aware of the needs of the offender – for employment, for home life or companionship, for decent recreation – and see that he has a chance to have these needs satisfied. This implies a parole and rehabilitation service, which is available for his re-establishment, for as long as he cares to use it. The beginnings of such a service are now available in such agencies as the Salvation Army, the Church Army, the John Howard Society and others, and the work of these agencies needs expansion and strengthening. Eventually, more responsibility for this service must be undertaken by the central authority itself, as an integral and final step of the treatment process, whose goal is the rehabilitation of the offender.[10]

Recent years have brought important developments in the use of the

[10]Dr. Stuart Jaffary, *Report*, Committee for the Adult Offender, Welfare Council of Toronto, 1947.

prisoners' aid societies by the National Parole Board in supervising men on parole. The provincial Parole Boards also have used their services.[11]

In describing parole, Patrick Deehy of the John Howard Society of Quebec says:

> Parole is a psycho-social situation which has come into being as a result of decisions taken by the inmate and by an authority group. It is in a sense a contract between two parties although it is something of a one-sided contract in that it lays down more in the way of obligations for the parolee than for the paroling authority and is in essence merely a changing of venue for the serving of a sentence. The parolee is not a completely free man. This contractual element in parole and the relative restriction of freedom, no matter how small, becomes of great importance when we consider the picture in relation to the family as a whole.[12]

In 1950, social agencies provided supervision in only eighty-seven cases for persons released on parole. In 1955, such supervision was arranged in 786 cases and almost entirely through prisoners' aid societies. During these years, the annual number of tickets of leave granted increased from 754 to 1,309, and the annual failure rate – revocation, forfeiture, or subsequent sentence to penal institution – fell from 23.5 per cent to 7.1 per cent.[13] These figures suggest that the supervision provided by the prisoners' aid societies was a significant factor in reducing the failure rate. It is important to note that, though the inmate is released under the *authority* of the regional representative of the Parole Board, he is under the *supervision* of the prisoners' aid society.

A person whose sentence has expired, unlike a parolee, is completely free. He is under no obligation to ask for service, nor does he have any legal requirements to fulfil. He can be brought into a relationship with a caseworker only through the latter's effectiveness, the ability of the agency to meet his needs, and his own willingness and motivation to seek help. But in spite of the formalities of legal requirements and supervision in the case of the parolee, a true relationship with him is also impossible unless the caseworker is effective and the parolee's needs can be met. Relationship is a matter of content, not of periodic reporting.

With many men on full-term release, the contact may be very brief, since once they have succeeded in getting on their own feet, they generally wish to become anonymous and to break all links with the prison past,

11For a more extensive discussion of parole, see p. 326.
12Patrick Deehy, 'The Impact of Parole Upon the Family', *Canadian Journal of Corrections*, July 1961.
13*Report*, Committee on Release Procedures (Fauteux Report), Ottawa: Queen's Printer, 1956, pp. 100-1.

including that with the after-care agency. With men on parole, however, the contact must be maintained as a condition of their release. Sufficient time is thus made available for developing a relationship, often one with very real content and far greater depth than a short period would have allowed. Some parolees are so hard-shelled that this type of relationship does not come into existence; yet most of these satisfactorily observe the conditions of their parole and refrain from criminal activity. A few refuse to abide by the conditions, and thus make their paroles liable to revocation by the Parole Board. The society must report to the Parole Service all circumstances concerning a parolee, provide a review of his attitudes and activities, and make it possible for the service to intervene if necessary at any stage of the parole period.

A. K. Couse of the John Howard Society of Ontario writes: 'Like probation, parole supervision provides a unique and genuine opportunity to individualize the treatment of the person under care. We are convinced that parole supervision must necessarily entail a face-to-face relationship between two people within which the supervisor consciously continues the process of treatment which began with the sentence and which was carried on during incarceration.' [14]

He goes on to say:

> The supervisor should make very clear to the parolee the nature of the contact which is required with the agency. Within this contact we are concerned that parole supervision should provide an opportunity for the parolee to enter into a relationship with one particular person. This person should know as much as possible of the parolee's life and penal experiences, his attitudes and his potentialities. The relationship should provide for the free expression of need and feeling upon the part of the parolee. It should encourage self-help, decision making, self-direction and self-discipline, where there is capacity for such activity. It may involve the setting of firm limits, stimulation to change or the holding of the parolee to reality. It should also include the elements of support, encouragement and acceptance in a climate where moral judgment is not expressed though further anti-social behaviour is not condoned.

Obviously this involves the use of authority even to the extent of legal sanctions. Although the prisoners' aid societies are voluntary non-governmental bodies, the workers operate as parole supervisors but without the status of peace officers held by probation officers or government parole officers. They seem to experience little difficulty through lack of peace-officer status. All social work carries its own authority, legal, economic,

[14]A. K. Couse, (Unpublished staff paper, February 18, 1958).

or social; in this case the legal responsibility delegated to the worker differs only in degree from the different type of responsibility embodied in other aspects of social work. The workers, however, are keenly aware that the public demands protection. They know it must not be assumed that the authority of the Parole Service automatically guarantees this protection. There cannot be protection of society unless there is within the supervisory process an effort to achieve self-awareness on the part of the offender, by exploring with him his attitudes, his feelings, and his reactions to and experiences with authority now and in the past.

'In our opinion,' says Mr. Couse, 'the parole supervisor stands in a unique position between the ex-offender and society. On the one hand he represents the authority of society and so must do all that he can to protect society against those unwilling or unable to adjust to the normal demands of the community. Simultaneously he must enable those who are anxious to re-establish themselves to make a productive contact with the community. The supervisor's role cannot be that of the passive, completely accepting caseworker who only works with a client who has asked for help. Part of his role is to exert control and at the same time help the parolee build controls within himself.[15]

GRADUAL RELEASE

Because it was known from experience that many long-sentence prisoners returning to the community are completely 'fogged' and unable to cope with the problems that immediately beset them, the idea was developed, first at Kingston Penitentiary, of releasing them on a daily basis prior to their final release. The first inmate in Canada to experience gradual release was a woman from the Women's Prison at Kingston, who was placed under the supervision of the Elizabeth Fry Society of Kingston in 1955. The first habitual offender allowed gradual release was placed under the supervision of the John Howard Society of Ontario, Toronto Office, in 1957. These were most significant occurrences, since they necessitated a great deal of co-operation by the social workers and the institutional staffs, and because the results of careful observation of the actual experiences have proved of great value as the program has subsequently developed.

In a broad sense, gradual release, now generally practised across the country, is a method whereby the warden of a penitentiary may release an inmate for daily periods, with or without an escort, for whatever reason the warden may consider advisable. The purpose is to promote the

[15]*Ibid.*

inmate's reintegration in the community and resocialization, and to aid his ultimate re-establishment. The method has been used with men being released on parole or on expiry of sentence. Considerable authority has now been vested in the warden by the Commissioner of Penitentiaries to authorize programs of gradual release, co-ordinated by the classification department of the penitentiary and usually operated with the co-operation of one of the prisoners' aid societies.

'At its minimum, "gradual release" usually includes shopping trips, opening bank accounts, registration at the National Employment Service, attendance at church, visits to private homes, and some recreational activities – movies, athletic events, etc.' [16]

Such a program helps the inmate to become familiar with the idea of living in a community again, while still maintaining the security of residence provided by the institution. But this is not enough. It is now generally considered desirable that there should be a gradual-release hostel ouside the walls of the penitentiary and that the inmate should be sent there before he embarks on the program. At present, when the inmate returns to the penitentiary after a spell of freedom, a number of security problems arise. He may be carrying notes and contraband, or he may have to return to his cell after lock-up, and so create some disturbance. Psychologically, he suffers tension in that he must return from the freedom of the community to the cell block, where he is 'bugged' by other inmates to talk about his experiences on the outside. A more definite break with the prison experience should be available, but the prisoner still needs a secure base of maintenance. A gradual-release hostel could provide this, and its staff should plan, co-ordinate, and supervise the inmate's program. Community release centres should be developed in the metropolitan communities to serve a similar function for the last few weeks of sentence.

Such programs must be designed to discover the problems that the inmate is likely to encounter in the community, and to help him resolve them. Later he will have to face these problems without supervision by any overt authority. It is best that his weaknesses as well as his strengths be noted and worked with as he enters the community under guidance.

Gradual release is primarily a program of community re-socialization rather than employment, since most of the penitentiaries are in relatively small communities where the opportunities for employment in competitive industry are few. In any event, it is apparent from experience that employers do not wish to hire men on a short-term basis except for casual

16F. P. Miller, 'Parole in Canada'. *American Journal of Correction*, vol. 21, no. 1, p. 11.

labour. It costs money to orient and train a new worker, and naturally they do not want to spend the money on employees who are not going to be permanent. This difficulty would not apply in release-centres in larger communities, where opportunities for employment would be available and desirable.

Another problem arises from the danger of releasing ex-inmates into the community where the institution is located at a higher rate than the community's own normal return-rate, with consequent association of ex-inmates leading to further criminal activity.

In order to avoid idleness during the period of gradual release, inmates should be employed in institutional work outside the walls when they are not actually engaged in community activities connected with their programs. The plan for eventual gainful employment should be worked out individually on the assumption that the inmate will return to his home community. His family, if any, should remain, until his final release, in their own community where their legal residence and eligibility for assistance is established. It is then that the threads of family, employment, and community life on a completely non-institutional basis should be picked up.

SOME DIFFICULTIES ARE NOTED

The various prisoners' aid societies work in very different ways, mainly because of geographical location. For example, the British Columbia Society can easily visit the British Columbia Penitentiary as often as desirable because it is within the Vancouver city-limits, but the Vancouver Island Society must cross the Strait of Georgia to do so. The Quebec penitentiaries are very close to Montreal. In Alberta, the prisoners' aid workers had to travel several hundred miles to do their pre-release visiting, and have now joined with the Saskatchewan Society to maintain an office close to the penitentiary. In the Maritimes, visiting is done at frequent intervals. In Ontario, it has been found essential by the John Howard Society to set up a pre-release service at Kingston where three men's prisons have a combined population of close to 2,000 persons.

Setting standards and establishing common practices is always difficult. A conscientious endeavour has been made, however, to develop a common body of policies and practices. This effort was facilitated for a number of years by an annual conference held under the auspices of the Department of Justice at the Penitentiary Staff Training College at Kingston. Here for a week the representatives of the government services and the after-care agencies worked together to integrate their services in order to make them as helpful as possible to ex-inmates returning to the community. After a lapse of a few years, these conferences were resumed in 1964 with results that will prove beneficial to the service to inmates in prison and to those who have been released.

The development of after-care on a referral basis presents a problem. Inmates have an opportunity of obtaining pre-release service in the institution. Should they, then, be served when they come in unreferred 'off the street', and to what extent? In a sense, to serve such people nullifies the effort to provide pre-release service and to see that constructive plans are developed before the prisoner leaves the institution. There is, however, the obligation to maintain the prisoners' aid tradition, which is to help someone who appears ready to seek and use help; the community expects the after-care society to provide such help.

It is inevitable that inmates and institutional staffs should sometimes confuse pre-release service with an institutional service. This is particularly likely to happen if the after-care workers assume the role of institutional social workers. Some societies like to perform various general welfare services for the inmates while they are still in prison, in the hope that the inmates will as a result be disposed to seek their services prior to release. Others feel that with so much to be done in pre-release work, with such limited resources, they must restrict themselves to the actual pre-release kind of service. Some feel it is important to undertake demonstration projects in the hope that these will eventually be taken over by the government service. Others believe that one of their roles is to help with inmate welfare by supplying reading materials, handicraft materials, recreational facilities, and entertainment.

Most societies attempt to interpret themselves and their objectives to the public through films, material provided for radio programs and newspaper articles, addresses and lectures given to community groups, and briefs on a variety of subjects submitted to the various government departments responsible for corrections. In addition, representations are made, in person and by correspondence, to government bodies and commissions concerned with matters of interest in the correctional field. These activities not only serve the purpose of interpretation but they also constitute an unremitting endeavour by the prisoners' aid societies to serve as the conscience of the community in correctional affairs and to maintain the heritage and tradition of John Howard and Elizabeth Fry in penal reform.

NATIONAL ORGANIZATION

At this stage in the development of the prisoners' aid societies, no comprehensive national federation or association exists. The John Howard

Society of Canada and the Correctional Service of the Salvation Army are organized nationally and are able to speak on a national basis. But there is a considerable body of opinion that the time has now come when the non-governmental agencies that concentrate all or most of their efforts on prisoners' aid work should form some kind of federation or association to make broad representation possible, and to bring about planning with the federal government on a truly national scale. This view was strengthened by the report of the Fauteux Committee, which recommended increased grants to prisoners' aid societies.[17] Implementation of this recommendation could entail some form of financing on a concerted or co-operative basis. The Committee also recommended the development of additional societies to provide service more widely throughout the country, and suggested procedures of certification to ensure that prisoners' aid societies achieve certain standards if they are to continue to be used by the Parole Service for the supervision of people on parole.

COMMUNITY RESPONSE

It is a far cry from the days in 1835 at Kingston Penitentiary when the rules and regulations for this first penal institution in Canada were established. The section having to do with the discharge of convicts was very short and read as follows:

> . . . a discharged convict shall be clad in a decent suit of clothes, selected from the clothing taken from new convicts. . . . He shall then be supplied with money, according to the distance of the district where he was tried and sentenced, but not exceeding the sum specified in the law – one pound. As the time when the convict is about to be discharged is favourable for eliciting truth, with a view to obtaining facts which may be useful, the chaplain will endeavour to obtain from him a short history of his life, his parentage, education, temptations, and the various steps by which he was led into a course of vice and crime, and commit the same to writing, for the information of the Inspectors; after which, the convict shall be discharged with a suitable admonition and advice. . . .

The late John Kidman, one of the early workers in the prisoners' aid field in Canada, reported in his book *The Canadian Prison* that the first prisoners' aid association was established by those who, a few years earlier, had formed a Sunday School in the local jail. He said that 'these workers discovered what all such workers do, that it was useless to preach to men and women in prison unless their material needs on release are also given attention'. [18]

17*Op. cit.*
18John Kidman, *The Canadian Prison,* Toronto: Ryerson, 1947.

Lack of money has plagued the prisoners' aid societies. Often there has been official apathy, and sometimes opposition. During the early years, the work was sometimes sporadic with groups becoming incorporated and later dying out. The societies now appear to be strongly organized and deeply rooted in their communities as a result of their acceptance by Community Chests and United Appeals, which provide the major part of their financing. This acceptance is a tangible recognition by the community of its responsibility for the return of the offender, and of the citizen's stake in law enforcement and the correctional process. It is in the community that the ex-inmate will either return once more to crime or find himself a new role and a new responsibility as a productive citizen.

There is economic justification for the relatively small cost to the community of maintaining after-care services as part of the war against crime, since it costs over $2,000 a year to maintain a man in prison. The Archambault Commission of 1938 found that it cost over $25,000 to commit and maintain a repeater, which in today's terms would be about $50,000. But the greater justification and reward for those engaged in this work is the knowledge that human values have been conserved and that former offenders have been productively re-established in our communities. There is today a new happiness in many lives that were formerly wasted and ruined by past misdeeds, and abounding evidence of increased usefulness to friends, relatives, and society as a whole.

Appendix

JOHN HOWARD

John Howard, who lived from 1726 to 1790, was the son of a moderately wealthy London tradesman. When he was 16 years old his father died and he inherited his estate and fortune. In 1755 he decided to travel to Lisbon to help care for the thousands who had been made homeless by an earthquake. The ship on which he sailed was captured by a privateer. Howard was confined in Brest with many other prisoners in a dark, damp, filthy dungeon. It seemed that the hardships he endured here gave birth to his decision to become socially useful. After being moved to various prisons along the French coast he managed to obtain an exchange prisoner and he was permitted to return to England.

In 1773 Howard was appointed Sheriff of Bedford. This was an honorary post but he chose to do the work himself. One of his first tasks was to get county officials to pay gaolers a salary. He spent much time and individual effort persuading the prison keepers to institute changes which removed many of the abuses and shocking conditions of that day. In

1784 Howard was able to bring the matter of prison reform before Parliament. As a result public hearings were established and he was called as a key witness. The facts brought out in the hearings were a great surprise to Members of Parliament. Prior to these hearings he had carefully documented his experience and observations. These were published in two volumes on *The State of the Prisons*. They were printed at his expense and most of them given away to interested people.

In 1785 he turned his attention to investigating the best methods of treating the plague which was rampant in Europe at that time. In 1789 Howard left England to pursue his investigations in Russia. While helping to nurse the sick he himself became ill. After a number of attacks of fever he died on January 20, 1790. On his tomb at Cherson in England the following is inscribed: [19]

JOHN HOWARD

WHOEVER THOU ART, THOU STANDEST AT

THE TOMB OF THY FRIEND

1790

ELIZABETH FRY

Elizabeth Fry was an Englishwoman who lived in the late eighteenth and first half of the nineteenth century. She was a member of the Society of Friends (Quaker). She believed that she should demonstrate her belief by action, and this action took the form of working with and on behalf of the woman offender. Her greatest concerns were to establish useful and remunerative activities for women in custody, to work for adequate segregation of first offenders from those with long records, to provide adequate accommodation, food, and necessities for those in custody and those who were deported to the colonies, and to provide education and activities for children who were in custody with their mothers.

Her methods were to use volunteers to visit women in prison as friends, to use her and her husband's influence directly with those in positions of authority to have changes made in conditions and legislation, and to consult with those in custody regarding changes which they felt would result in their rehabilitation.[20]

Further Reading

ADAMS, E. 'The Toronto Elizabeth Fry Society', *Food for Thought*, Toronto: Canadian Association for Adult Education, February 1954.

[19]*News Bulletin*, John Howard Society of Saskatchewan, November 1961.
[20]Phyllis Haslam, (Contributed notation).

APPLEBY, E. 'Rehabilitation Services for the Female Offender in the Province of Ontario'. M. S. W. Thesis, University of Toronto, 1948.

ARNOTT, J. 'Culture and Rehabilitation', *Canadian Welfare*, September 1953.

CANADA. *Report* of the Royal Commission to Investigate the Penal System of Canada (Archambault Report). Ottawa: King's Printer, 1938.

————. *Report* of the Committee to Inquire into the Principles and Procedures Followed in the Remission Service of the Department of Justice of Canada (Fauteux Report). Ottawa: Queen's Printer, 1956.

CANADIAN WELFARE COUNCIL (Delinquency and Crime Division). 'After-Care of Discharged Prisoners'. *Brief* to the Select Committee on Reform Institutions of Ontario, 1954.

COUSE, A. K. 'Power and Authority in Treatment', *Social Worker*, January-February 1963.

DEEHY, P. 'The Impact of Parole Upon the Family', *Canadian Journal of Corrections*, July 1961.

EDMISON, J. A. 'Civil Rehabilitation', *Canadian Bar Review*, November 1949.

HARRIS, D. 'Citizen Participation in Prisoner Rehabilitation', *Social Worker*, July-August 1953.

HART, W. E. *What is a John Howard Society?* Ottawa: Canadian Welfare Council, 1952.

HASLAM, P. 'The Damaged Girl in a Disturbed Society', *Canadian Welfare*, March 15, 1961.

JACKSON, J. 'Rehabilitation After Prison'. M. S. W. Thesis, University of Toronto, 1957.

JAFFARY, S. *Committee for the Adult Offender.* Toronto: Welfare Council of Greater Toronto, 1947.

JOHN HOWARD SOCIETY OF ONTARIO. *Thirty Years On,* 1959.

KIRBY, A. J. 'Would You Hire an Ex-Convict?', *Plant Administration*, Toronto: Maclean-Hunter, July 1960.

KIRKPATRICK, A. M. 'After-Care in the Canadian Correctional Treatment Plan', *Canadian Penal Association Proceedings*, 1953.

————. *Gate Money.* Chicago: John Howard Association, 1953.

————. 'Issues in the Rehabilitation of Prisoners', *Social Worker*, March 1954.

————. 'They Don't Die in Prison', *Royal Canadian Mounted Police Gazette,* December 1956.

————. 'Human Problems of Prison After-Care', *Federal Probation*, September 1957.

————. 'Their Second Punishment', *American Congress of Corrections Proceedings,* 1958.

————. 'Prison Detour – Road Block', *Canadian Personnel and Industrial Relations,* July 1959.

————. 'Prisoners' Aid Societies in Canada', *American Journal of Correction,* January-February 1959.

————. 'Prisoners' Aid and Penal Reform', *Crime and Delinquency,* October 1960.

————. 'Re-Establishment Problems of Prisoners in Canada', *Société Internationale du Criminologie,* Paris, 1962.

KLARE, H. *Human Salvage from Prison Stock Piles.* Toronto: John Howard Society of Ontario, 1959.

LAVELL, A. *The Convicted Criminal and His Re-Establishment as a Citizen.* Toronto: Ryerson Press, 1926.

LAW, J. M. 'The Kingston Elizabeth Fry Society', *Food for Thought,* Toronto: Canadian Association for Adult Education, February 1954.

LAYCOCK, S. R. *Pastoral Counselling for Mental Health.* Toronto: Ryerson Press, 1958.

LEMMON, W. 'Ex-Prisoner Rehabilitation in Canada', *Canadian Welfare,* September 1953.

MALONEY, A. *Human Beings Within the Law.* Toronto: John Howard Society of Ontario, 1959.

MELCHERCIK, J. *Employment Problems of Former Offenders.* Ottawa: Canadian Welfare Council, 1955.

MILLER, F. 'Parole and the After-Care Agency', *Canadian Welfare,* December 1956.

MILLER, F. 'Parole in Canada', *American Journal of Correction,* January-February 1959.

NAGEL, H. 'Employment Problems of Male Offenders on Parole'. M. S. W. Thesis, University of Toronto, 1957.

NEVILLE, F. 'Social Casework in Correctional After-Care', *Canadian Welfare,* March 1957.

PRINCE, ELLEN. 'A History of the John Howard Society of Quebec, Inc.' M. S. W. Thesis, McGill University, 1956.

REID, D. C. S. 'After-Care Pre-Release Preparation of Prison Inmates', *Canadian Journal of Corrections,* October 1958 and January 1959.

R.C.M.P. *Law and Order in Canadian Democracy.* Ottawa: King's Printer, 1949.

SALVATION ARMY. *The Law Breaker and the Salvation Army,* 1961.

SHINER, E. V. 'The Return of the Married Offender to His Family', *Canadian Congress of Corrections Proceedings,* Ottawa: Canadian Welfare Council, 1957.

SMITH, J. 'Whose Job?', *Food for Thought,* Toronto: Canadian Association for Adult Education, March 1955.

STRATHY, P. 'Expectations of the Parole and Parole Supervision Experience'. M. S. W. Thesis, University of Toronto, 1961.

ZEITOUN, L. 'Material Assistance Given by After-Care Agencies in Canada', *American Journal of Correction,* January-February 1959.

———. 'Parole Supervision and Self-Determination', *Federal Probation,* September 1962.

15

Treatment

GORDON W. RUSSON

WHAT IS TREATMENT?

In the field of corrections, the term 'treatment' is given many different interpretations. No single one would be sufficient to satisfy all interests and meanings. The word appears more and more frequently in correctional literature, and it is doubtful if there is any other word with a less distinct or more misleading application. It is a legitimate request to make of any person using it that he identify clearly the meaning he wishes to attach to it.

Some of the confusion in the uses of terms seems to arise from an attempt to equate legal and therapeutic concepts; but, as in the familiar example from algebra class, one cannot add apples and oranges. In this discussion, for instance, it appears preferable to use the word delinquent in a generic sense, indicating the predominant attitude of the person involved. The terms 'crime' and 'delinquency' refer essentially to different degrees of seriousness of the same phenomenon; in studying the individual criminal or delinquent it is preferable to refer to him as an offender.

The term 'offender' must in its turn be used with the awareness that it identifies the individual as a person who is subject to social disapproval, but does not necessarily describe him in any way as a personality. Indeed, the only way in which offenders are certain to be like one another is in the fact that each has committed an offence. Because of variations in laws and in the circumstances surrounding behaviour that is unlawful and therefore considered offensive, this item of similarity does not have any consistent psychological value. Offenders who become 'clients' of various correctional services, whether in prison or in the free community, are usually alike also in the fact that they have been apprehended and convicted. These similarities, however, cannot be assumed to be certainties,

410

as consideration has been given in some areas to the provision of services, including incarceration, that would accommodate voluntary requests by offenders, or by those who fear becoming offenders. Perhaps such consideration was prompted by the once-popular belief that delinquency was an illness like any other illness, and that prisons were rapidly becoming comparable in function to hospitals. Requests for such services are not numerous. Groups of offenders do have other similarities by means of which they can be classified and studied as psychological types. Subsequent work is then based on a knowledge of the individual's psychological nature, not on the fact that he is an offender.

The offender undergoing treatment may sometimes legitimately be called a 'patient'. This terminology, however, implies that there is a medical context, and such is not always the case. It seems appropriate to refer to the offender as a 'client', regardless of the details of the therapeutic situation, and to refer to the person from whom he seeks help of a remedial nature as the 'therapist'.

Treatment in its most general and least useful sense refers to everything that happens to a person in prison or under some sort of supervised program. The use of the term in this sense is, of course, perfectly legitimate; but so used it does not imply any remedial value. General treatment of offenders has historically gone through several phases, including cruelty, indifference, neglect, and humaneness – not necessarily in that order. The humane approach to work with offenders is tremendously important and the brevity of its description here should not be taken as an index of its worth; but its consideration as a type of treatment needs little further comment. It is more appropriately identified under such headings as custodial care, control, handling, maintenance, or management. A diligent effort is needed to keep it free of factors likely to have a negative effect on its clients, as well as adequate for maintaining a good standard of health – physical, psychological, and social.

In this meaning – or group of meanings – the application of a band-aid is treatment, a visit from a member of the community is treatment, a beating is treatment. The effect on the offender's personality may be negligible, or even harmful. It can readily become a practice in a correctional program to speak of things as treatment that undeniably are so in some contexts, but are not in others – medical and dental care, psychotherapy, and various types of education and skill-training, for instance. However, unless these can be demonstrated specifically to have a mitigating influence on the offender's pattern of delinquency, a false impression is created by calling them treatment.

In a second or intermediate level of application of the term, treatment

411

refers to activities deliberately used to foster improved concepts of citizenship. These activities encourage the establishment of patterns of living considered to be psychologically and socially healthy, and include teaching and training, recreation, participation in group projects, and a large part of counselling both individually and in groups. The term 'treatment program', as generally understood, probably has its origin in this meaning. Essentially, the logic of this approach is derived from a deficiency-oriented interpretation of the sources of criminality. Where lack of education has played a major role in the individual's committing an offence, upgrading will undoubtedly reduce his likelihood of repeating. Social retardation, poor work-habits, and poor sportsmanship all may be similarly implicated, and the appropriate raising of the individual to a more satisfactory level will have an obvious remedial effect.

This approach, hailed in recent years as a revolutionary method of penology, has had some heart-warming successes and some dismal failures. Its surface beauty has been marred by observations that penetrate to the resistant nature of many an offender's personality. Programs of education and training have been criticized on the grounds that they do not automatically rehabilitate; they may simply produce a better trained criminal. An inmate who succeeds in the educational department may progress only from being a forger with Grade Ten education to being a forger with Grade Twelve.

The frequent and rather glib use of the phrase 'treatment program' must be surveyed rather critically. At times the phrase becomes a cliché by which inmates express their poor opinion of a prison situation, as when they refer to their own conformity as 'getting the program'. There is perhaps reason to consider that the two words 'treatment' and 'program' are in some ways contradictory, whereas 'training-program' and 'educational program' are semantically correct. Programs tend to become stable, and clients are forced to accommodate to them. Stabilized programming may at times be the antithesis of treatment. Probably many activities currently labelled as treatment programs should be called training programs or educational programs.

Both humane, generalized care and this activity programming will benefit some offenders. The results are neither surprising nor unpredictable. The benefit will be to those offenders whose delinquency can be traced to the effects of misfortunes that may be counteracted by either or both of these types of treatment. Some sick people in hospital recover simply because of the clean, warm, cheerful, and otherwise healthy surroundings; some improve because of good nursing care, selected diet, and programs of re-training. But the hospital, prison, probation, or parole clients whose illnesses or disorders are not automatically responsive to supportive surroundings, but require specific intervention, will remain un-improved or will get worse at an unchanged rate unless their individual remedial requirements are provided for.

In its third level of use, treatment is specifically designed to suit the requirements of the individual. It is perhaps better identified by the word therapy and must proceed from an accurate and complete diagnosis of the individual's disorder and from knowledge of what is likely to bring about positive change. Specific therapy properly related to the offender's dis-order is penology's newest and apparently least accepted offspring. It seems at times to be less enthusiastically defended than are custody, capital punishment, and corporal punishment. A discussion of this mean-ing of treatment as a part of correctional activities is essentially in the realm of corrections-yet-to-come. At the same time attention must be drawn to the fact that outstanding work is being done by individuals and groups in both correctional research and treatment.

The unqualified use of the word treatment can give the impression of meaning any or all of the above, leaving the user uncommitted to a bind-ing definition. This potential for abuse has by no means been neglected in correctional literature.

One of the least sophisticated and perhaps most tenacious concepts of specific treatment is illustrated by the saying that a wrong-doer must 'take his medicine'. This expression can, of course, be used as an ironical joke making a parody of treatment; but it is often used quite seriously by some-one who derives his point of view from the once widely held belief that the most unpleasant-tasting medicines are the most effective. By this strange parallel, the very unpleasantness of the punishment guarantees its curative effect.

Punishment is still hotly defended as a form of treatment. Usually, arguments in its favour are based on the need for strong measures, and those against it are based on humanitarian principles. The humanitarian argument, no matter how attractive philosophically, is probably the least convincing. Whether or not punishment has any corrective value, either positively or negatively, is an issue that must be cleared on technical, not emotional grounds. Technically the arguments in support of punishment are weak and unsupported by valid research.

There are two distinct errors inherent in the insistence on the use of punishment as a method of correction. The first would be an error in con-nection with any method expected to have remedial value, and it arises out of placing emphasis on method rather than on what is to be treated. The second arises from a preoccupation with what offenders do rather than with what they are. As for what offenders are, psychology has not yet succeeded in defining this; we have only superficial generalizations. Thus the demand for punishment usually arises from the nature of the offending behaviour rather than the likelihood of reform. Although it is true that some forms of punishment have a deterrent effect on some offenders, insistence upon punishment seems, in the main, to be an expression of the frustrations of those who demand its application, and is therefore not really oriented to the nature of the offender at all.

It is a mistake to place more emphasis on method than on the purpose that the method is intended to accomplish. To do so compels the hapless individual to conform to the method rather than the method to the individual. A discussion of treatment is therefore not primarily one of techniques. In fact, except in the detailed study of specific problems, the discussion of techniques, whether one wishes to include punishment or not, is out of order. What is required is the fundamental mapping of principles on which to base treatment. The lack of firmly established and generally accepted principles of treatment is at present one of the most serious lacks in corrections. No method is, in itself, therapeutic; it becomes so only when appropriately applied to a particular problem. A plaster cast is wonderful for a broken leg, useless for measles. The nature of the offender's disorder should be the cornerstone of remedial activity; yet in modern correctional practice it often seems that the offender is forgotten.

Any process, group, or facility that presumes to be designated as therapeutic must be able to refer to a well-disciplined and consistent frame of reference for its authority. Authority in this context is appropriately vested in knowledge, not in persons. Such a frame of reference must include a comprehensive and accurate diagnostic system, an accurate and complete interpretation of diagnostic categories, and resources for therapy adequately designed and proven through experience to be effective for the disorders encountered. Failure by correctional staff to work within such a frame of reference is likely to be due to their desire to hide their uncertainty behind a cloud of protective vagueness. To say that an offender is being treated for his delinquency or for his inadequate socialization is to say no more than that a person in hospital is being treated for his unhealthy condition. To have any but the most superficial of meanings, treatment in any context must be directed towards a definite objective – an illness, an injury, a functional handicap – that it is designed to remedy. It can cure, relieve, or improve, but it must have a direct bearing on a consistently identified clinical entity.

The potential for criticism of the current use, or misuse, of the term treatment is perhaps less than this presentation might imply. Eagerness to bring about changes and the putting into practice of new ideas are not things to be scorned. One pointer to the source of difficulty is that correctional programs tend to proceed in a cart-before-the-horse manner. Institutions are erected and programs instituted; commitments are thus made to patterns and practices that cannot be altered for years to come. Yet all this is done before an adequate research effort has been made to find the nature of the problem that necessitates the activity. We are faced with the fact that as yet there is no generally accepted psychological definition of delinquency and no generally accepted theory to explain its occurrence and thus lead to its remedy, and that there are no really effective methods of therapy proven to have had more than a fringe effect on the large core-group, chronic repeaters, that constitutes the major part of prison populations.

Efforts to date seem to have been directed to all types of disturbance except the specific phenomenon of delinquent behaviour *per se*. It has been assumed that delinquency could be explained satisfactorily as the logical consequence of such misfortunes as illiteracy, neurotic conflict, unemployment, facial disfigurement. The fact that these are often associated with delinquency is not proof that they cause it. Many times the associated phenomenon is a correlate only, not a cause. Assumptions cannot be substituted for diagnosis.

If an offender does have a neurotic conflict that can be demonstrated by adequate evidence to be the origin of his delinquent behaviour, if his conflict is amenable to therapy, if there is a therapist available to treat his neurosis, and if he accepts the therapy, then he can indeed be helped, and in all probability the resolution of his conflict will remove the likelihood of further delinquency. Such a happy result seems to be possible for and available to only a small percentage of offenders.

Elaborate programs can be based on premature generalizations that lack of education, poor training, and emotional distress are in themselves the well-springs of delinquency; but in fact they are not. Their presence may favour the manifestations of delinquency, but their effect in such cases is supportive not causative. The best of methods fail if they are applied inappropriately. The legitimacy of describing any activity as treatment, unless it is consequent upon a proper diagnosis, is questionable. The first thing that must be appreciated is that the identification of delinquent behaviour does not constitute a diagnosis.

As a community or national problem, it may be appropriate to consider delinquency as a disease or illness. Here again, however, we must ask whether it is a basic condition from which other evils spring or whether it is a manifestation, a sign, of some more fundamental disorder. Poverty,

415

unemployment, ignorance, superstition, broken families, can all give the appearance of being related causatively to delinquency; but the search too often has been for scapegoats, including comic books and television, rather than for knowledge based on scientific research. Not all poor people are delinquents; not all delinquents are victims of poverty. But all delinquents do have in common an attitude or frame of reference that, at the final moment of choice, permits the operation of an offence-giving pattern of behaviour.

The search to identify everything that is basically delinquent and thereby to understand more clearly the nature of the offender's attitude would be relatively simple, if it were only a matter of more and better studies of known offenders. But progress towards better understanding of the nature of delinquency-prone attitudes is impeded by an apparent reluctance on the part of many correctional workers to look directly at that which constitutes the giving of offence to others. He who searches for truth must look also within himself; failure to do so leads inevitably to the development of self-protective 'blind spots' and to the focusing of attention only upon those who have been caught. The point of view that is psychologically basic to offending has a much more widespread distribution than is manifested by legally defined offenders alone. For instance, many people proceed to break traffic speed-laws if no police patrol is in sight, even though they are fully aware that to do so is illegal. Most people would agree that it is wrong to hit another person for the sake of winning an argument, yet to many parents it is proper to do so if the other person is one's own child. Telling lies is wrong and causes offence, but 'white lies' that supposedly hide painful truths from tender ears are widely accepted as being justified. Yet these acts and the attitudes from which they spring are part of the society we create; they are the garden in which the weeds of delinquency grow. For the ultimate sources of delinquency, we must explore deeply and perhaps painfully into the complexities of our everyday life, into the beliefs and practices of our society.

Organized communities have done and are doing tremendous work to combat local delinquency by providing educational and recreational facilities, encouraging the constructive outlet of energy, and generally becoming conscious of the responsibilities of citizenship. The success of these efforts demands the dedicated participation of whole communities, and it can be maintained only so long as the basic attitude towards responsibility governs at least the majority of citizens.

The expanding scope of correctional services and the involvement of increasing numbers of professional workers are bringing us in the direction of a more complete handling of the problems of delinquency. The services are, however, not yet enough, either quantitatively or qualitatively; crime marches on, recidivism rates remain staggeringly high, and new prisons must be erected. We return repeatedly to the awareness of our present lack of knowledge.

No discussion of treatment would be complete without some mention of prevention. But prevention, although it is based on similar principles and has similar objectives to those of treatment, cannot occur until that which is to be treated is thoroughly understood. Only when the processes that bring about offending behaviour have been identified will it be possible to work toward their prevention. Historically, prevention of disease has been consequent upon extensive efforts aimed at treatment. Prevention, then, appropriately comes under the heading of control.

WHAT IS TO BE TREATED?

The comment that the offender must be treated with understanding as a human being with dignity has been made so often that it has become rather trite. But it is a comment that is pertinent only to the therapist's attitude, not to the technical requirements of his practice.

Should the whole person be treated? Only if adequate study provides evidence to indicate such an approach. Is the necessary approach that of character-training? Again, only if the evidence indicates it. Is casework the answer, or work-camps, or fewer prisons, or tougher prisons? The same answer is always at hand, that therapy can be appropriately directed only in a manner and toward the objectives determined by thorough clinical study and accurate diagnosis.

The starting-point in the whole process of treatment is the identification and location of the problem to be treated. It is not appropriate in this discussion to go beyond generalities and attempt a detailed interpretation of the pathology of the individual offender; this is the realm of those responsible for clinical study of offenders and the planning of therapy. Each offender's behaviour arises from a pattern of maladjustment that is unique to him. Modification of his behaviour is dependent upon his ability to recover from his own particular disorder. For some disorders the prognosis is extremely poor. We return once again to the necessity to study further and to seek through research the answers we do not know.

Legal definitions of delinquency are not suitable as cornerstones of psychological theory. Psychology based on assessment of the individual apart from his patterns of social interaction is seriously handicapped since it tends to miss some vital issues. The broadening concept of social psychology seems to offer promise with its focus on the person in society and

417

the phenomena of interpersonal relationships – for delinquency can be described only in terms of a relationship between persons or, at least, between a person and some other person's property or welfare. It has no meaning in terms of the individual alone.

Since delinquency is a form of behaviour representative of a relationship between offender and offended, it is not correctly described as a disease of the individual. The term 'causes of delinquency', while it may be appropriate to the general consideration of delinquency as a social evil, is not appropriate to the study of the individual offender. Saying that delinquency must be understood as a sickness rather than as a badness, and assuming that one has simply to find the causes, apply something called treatment, and thus bring the problem under control, is both an over-simplification and an improper application of a medical concept of disease. The search for 'causes' of delinquency as though it were a disease is useless. Certain basic disorders of personality, frequently identified in offenders, may correctly be called diseases; some of these are amenable to efforts called therapy, but knowledge in this area is still quite meagre. Offending behaviour can be described as a developed pattern of adaptation, sometimes expressive of a whole philosophy of life; as such, its nature can be understood better as a phenomenon similar to the language we speak. It has origins, is subject to various influences, is taught, learned, and practised, and has certain well-defined and commonly found characteristics. It also serves at times as a means of communication expressing the psychological distortion and distress of the individual.

Delinquent behaviour as a psychological phenomenon can be defined as that which constitutes an actual or a potential offence to others. For the purposes of this interpretation, it does not matter whether or not the offender is apprehended and convicted. Giving of offence has its origin in the attitude of the offender, and it is in this attitude that the offender is characteristically different from persons who deliberately plan their activities to avoid bringing trouble and danger to others. The offender is the person who, under conditions of perhaps the slightest stress, is likely to choose a path of action that will have as a major feature the giving of offence. Giving offence may be a deliberate act, or it may occur from neglect and lack of adequate measures to avoid offence.

We can therefore profitably study an offender with no mention of his actual offence. Studying his attitude and its origins will bring better results than studying the details of his crime. It is in those factors that are basic to his attitude towards both himself and others that the pathology lies. For treatment purposes he is neither thief nor murderer, neither cheque artist nor sex offender.

418

Closely correlated with delinquent behaviour is an attitude of irresponsibility, sometimes pervading the whole personality, sometimes exhibited in a fairly selective fashion. Is irresponsibility the same as delinquency? Perhaps not, but it is a close companion. It springs from a lack of full appreciation of the rights and privileges of others, and appears to be consistent with an impaired sensitivity (originally to one's own rights and privileges). Often the sensitivity of psychologically disturbed persons is heightened rather than reduced. People who are properly diagnosed as disturbed persons would seem, therefore, to have some anti-delinquency insurance. Some delinquents are disturbed, it is true, but the predominant attitude in which delinquency flourishes is one of numbness and callousness. Correctional workers after an initial period of orientation to the field often express a wish that their offender-clients were a little more disturbed.

The plausibility of a claim to emotional disturbance is frequently exploited by offenders who have learned that such an approach meets with reasonable success. 'When people push me, I get upset and then I'm liable to do anything. Someone is bound to get hurt.' In the face of a persistent lack of effort to do anything about the liability to become upset, the exploitation and the basically irresponsible attitude become apparent. The ready verbalization is 'I can't do anything about it'. Others are: 'If I commit suicide it will be your fault'; 'I've been used to doing what I liked all my life'; 'If I can't cancel the deal, I'm liable to do damage to the car. So I'll get a year in jail; I can't help it. I'll at least have the satisfaction of getting even.' A chronic forger, during one of several periods in a mental hospital, had the rather jolting experience of being told by the psychiatrist to face up to himself as a master pretender and acknowledge his 'phoney' nature. During the subsequent prison sentence, he said that he could now accept being 'phoney' and could see that this probably explained his habits of forgery. He could do nothing about it, however, since he claimed he was 'probably born that way'.

In such manner, emotional disturbance, parental rejection, alcohol, and a host of other 'causes' have been used as pawns to protect the elusive king that is the desire to evade responsibility. The main effort seems to go into the search for a non-self agent or a depersonalized agent of the self for which one cannot be held responsible. 'Is it my subconscious that makes me do these things Doc?' 'I figure it's all due to my early childhood.' 'When I get mad everything goes black, and I can't remember anything I do.' The belief in the right to shed responsibility at whatever cost to personal integrity becomes apparent. It is in fact this resistance against the taking of responsibility for his own offending actions that is characteristic of the chronic offender's psychological functioning.

Before we proceed further on this theme, it should be pointed out that the success of one's efforts at treating offenders cannot be measured by simply recording the number of interviews conducted or the number of cases processed. Such records describe the behaviour of the therapist, not that of the client, and to emphasize them continually is to have fallen into the old trap of placing emphasis on the method instead of on the purpose it is supposed to serve.

Delinquency then is a form of behaviour; it is behaviour that expresses a particular and definite attitude. It is the chosen behaviour of persons whose capacity to contemplate and choose non-offensive patterns is impaired.

In whom is this capacity impaired? Certainly, emotional distress accounts for some impairment. Severe anxiety, fear, or depression exerts a constricting influence on our capacity to think. They do not, however, automatically induce delinquent behaviour. The capacity to choose more acceptable alternatives is impaired in those who have too little general experience to know better – in all probability a very small percentage of offenders. It is impaired in those whose way of life is essentially parasitic, who care little for anyone else and expect the world to gratify their wishes. It is impaired in those who have been deliberately taught that delinquency is not wrong as long as one is not caught. It is impaired in the mentally defective and in the mentally ill. It is impaired in those who, because of lack of education, training, and skill, already have a limited range of choices. In the final analysis, however, we are left with the unavoidable conclusion that whatever extenuating circumstances surround the offence, it is committed because of a force no more nor less powerful than the choice of the offender.

The remarkable thing is that in so many instances it is difficult even by stretching a point to identify one plausible extenuating circumstance. The automatic assumption that the committing of an offence must have been due to conflict or emotional upset is rapidly becoming a tired and over-beaten horse. Much of the time it has no basis except in sheer speculation. The lack of adequate explanation and the apparent foolishness of the offence are often no more obvious to anyone than they are to the offender himself. This mystery about the self and about the reasons for one's actions is part of the phenomenon of offence-giving; it frequently makes the question to the offender, 'Why did you do it?' quite out of order. He cannot provide an explanation.

Offenders themselves often ask the question, 'Why do I do these things?' This approach is becoming popular as a means by which, through posing as a person who is delinquent without knowing why, the offender can acquire a plausible explanation. One prison inmate said, 'I didn't need to steal the car. In my business I owned four already!' The ease with which interpretations can sometimes be worked out after one interview and a short series of tests makes the dangers of accepting plausible explanations obvious. Perhaps the most frequently used explanation of 'excuse-value' is that of intoxication at the time of offence, 'I never steal when I'm sober'. It is often a correlated finding that the individual makes no effort to choose the obvious course of abstinence from alcohol.

The explanation that alcohol is mainly responsible for their delinquencies is presented by many prison inmates. Its use appears to be partly due to the frequency with which these people have committed offences while intoxicated, and partly due to the popularity of prison Alcoholics Anonymous groups, which in some institutions have been the pioneers of group work-programs. Many inmates are ready to accept the interpretation that dependence on alcohol is a disease, and to cling to it as a way of accounting for their behaviour. Often an inmate will accept, from other inmates more readily than from the staff, the interpretation that alcohol does not cause, but only permits, and that by blaming his actions on alcohol he is really seeking to excuse himself from responsibility. Such an interpretation can stir up considerable uneasiness, particularly if the individual has found comfort in the belief that he has a disease on which he can blame his behaviour and over which he has no control.

Undoubtedly some offenders' behaviour can be explained adequately by one of the extenuating circumstances mentioned above. But with a great many offenders, perhaps the majority, the behaviour that constitutes the offences is perfectly logical in their whole frame of reference; in these there can be found no evidence of a bona fide disturbance, and the presence of other factors often considered to be the causes of delinquency, such as poverty, unemployment, and bad companions, appears to be largely a coincidence.

When delinquency is a response to intolerable stress, the offence is part of a deviant pattern, an exception, or a flaw, and we may realistically speak of rehabilitation. Where a stressful circumstance such as poverty or insanity has been largely responsible for the emergence of relatively weak potential for delinquency, the treatment of the economic or mental situation will constitute an effective remedy.

The strength of motivating factors varies, and it can readily be understood that where there is only a mild proneness to delinquency a severe stress may be necessary for delinquency to occur. Where the proneness is strong, it needs little if any support. In people whose standards of citizenship are high and consistent, the likelihood of becoming delinquent is extremely small or non-existent.

With those whose delinquency is inseparable from the stabilized personality, there is no return to a healthy state. Our concept of what must change must also change. A great many offenders – the majority of prison populations – offend for no reason more simple to state or more horrifying to comprehend than that delinquency is part and parcel of a well-integrated pattern of social interaction, normal and real to the person pursuing it. Treatment for these people must encompass an entire way of life. It is the whole personality that is sick, or deformed, or stunted. The labelling of medical care, exploration of conflicts, group living, and various training-efforts as treatment is only a pretence, for these things serve no purpose more curative than an aspirin does for a brain tumor. Therapy here faces the stupendous task of reshaping whole personalities. Whether or not this is possible is yet to be demonstrated; certainly success cannot be expected in the space of a pre-determined period of months or under any but the best of circumstances or under the direction of any but the most skilled personnel.

Some offenders seem capable of little constructive thinking. It is not necessarily that they are unintelligent, but rather that their mental capacity is not put to use. One can tell that a brain is present but there is not much evidence of a mind. For a brain and a mind are not the same thing: they bear the same relationship to one another as do hands and skill. Treatment to be successful in these cases must awaken the dormant mentality; this is a task for a long period of patiently guided experience.

Some offenders appear to be lacking in emotion, particularly emotion in respect of relationships with other people. It is as though other people do not exist for this type of offender except in terms of the least possible appreciation. The popular interpretation that emotional disturbance is the source of various psychological difficulties and illnesses and of some forms of delinquent behaviour is based on the assumption that there is, in the suffering individuals, an emotionality of considerable strength. However, the experiencing of strong emotions that are important in terms of interpersonal relationships is something that occurs in a very complex state of living, and some people who are offenders – and some who are not – simply do not appear to experience such emotions. In non-professional terms, such people are described by those who know them as shallow, emotionally cold, unfeeling. While it is true that active emotional upheaval is one type of psychological pathology, it is a professional error to attempt to explain all deviations from healthy psychological functioning in these terms. Interpretations of emotional crippling or stunting would be more correct. Attempts at therapy based on an assumption of normal emotional capacity are therefore falsely oriented.

CONDITIONS NECESSARY FOR TREATMENT

A discussion of conditions conducive to adequate therapy would probably be expected to include a list of facilities, equipment, programs, and personnel. There can be no denying the importance of any of these; but their significance is superseded by four conditions, without which treatment cannot occur and which are often sufficient in themselves. These are: (1) the readiness of the client for treatment, (2) the competence of the therapist, (3) the availability of the necessary time, and (4) the opportunities in the treatment situation for creative real-life experiences.

The importance of the individual therapist as a person charged with the responsibility of therapeutic management is highlighted here because of the present trend to see all such activities as a function of a 'team' or of a rather vague entity called 'the program'. The hazard of spreading the work too far and too thin is that in the long run no one actually takes any responsibility. In fact, such an arrangement often precludes individuals' assuming responsibility where it would be in the interests of good treatment for them to do so. The ease with which responsibility can thus be dissipated is disturbing when we compare it with the ready evasion of responsibility by the offender. The competence of the therapist is closely tied in with his preparedness to shoulder responsibility for his client's progress, for the conditions under which he himself works, and for his mistakes. Team approaches probably have a legitimate and singular value in therapy; they probably do not have anything near the value that is so freely ascribed to them. Only if the requirements for proper therapy can be translated into team action, and if it is necessary to do so, is the team approach the method of choice. Otherwise its value is questionable.

Readiness for treatment on the part of the offender is the most important factor and the one most likely to be ignored. All other conditions are of secondary importance. Perhaps the reason it tends to be forgotten is that in other areas of service and therapy, where clients voluntarily seek help, the readiness is practically always present so that it is taken for granted. But the offender in prison or on probation is usually in the situation against his will. If not openly resentful, he may be astutely congenial, following the principle that discretion is the better part of valour.

Readiness for therapy is based on a readiness to tolerate, if not to welcome, change in one's self. It is dependent upon at least two factors: (a) awareness of personal difficulty producing distress of some kind, such as pain, or anxiety, or regret, and (b) awareness of the fact that at least some of the trouble originates within the self. Readiness for therapy is, therefore, not necessarily assured by a request for interview or for treatment, much less by a passive acceptance of help offered by a therapist. Some requests are expressions of chronic over-dependency; some are made to gain advantage or to create an impression. The therapist must make his own assessment of the validity of the request; even initially it should carry some indication of a search for a new outlook, and of a preparedness to do something about one's problems beyond simply talking about them.

Readiness for change can be identified by evidence that the client is actually investing time and effort in an attempt to improve himself. Included would be a consistent and prolonged adherence to standards imposed upon the self and an absence of motives of secondary gain. Attempts at therapy without this ingredient of readiness for change are a waste of time and are possibly a self-deception on the part of the would-be therapist. A number of offenders are not eligible for therapy because they see no reason why they themselves should change, but expect the world to adapt to them as they are. It is also important to understand that a lack of readiness for change is not simply an absence; it is an indication that an active resistance to change exists, capable of defeating all efforts from outside the self. This single factor of readiness, if accompanied by a reasonable intellect and a reasonable capacity for self-assessment, can suffice. Offenders with these qualifications can and do work out their own reform without help from anyone else, sometimes in the face of remarkable obstacles. They are not many in number, however. Their small representation emphasizes how vain was the hope of reformation in the old penitentiary idea that required the prisoner to contemplate the error of his ways in solitude, and expected that at the end of a measured period of time, decided by someone else, he would arrive back in the free community with an improved philosophy of life. Few people can achieve this remarkable reformation of character under ideal circumstances. The present expectation that inmates will learn a lesson through confinement in isolation has little logical support.

Readiness for therapy can be influenced by circumstances outside the self, particularly if it is a somewhat hesitant readiness. It is essentially an outgrowth of the urge to take responsibility, normally vigorous in healthy people. The desire to take responsibility often begins to show itself through the making of an increasing number of decisions by the offender. The survival of this budding but perhaps reluctant plant is endangered on all sides. The court decides the type, location, and duration of sentence, and the conditions under which it is to be served. In prison, decisions about what the offender eats and when, what he wears, where or even if he works, with whom he associates, when he rises and when he goes to bed, are essentially taken over by others. Even the thing called treatment may be instituted by someone else. So much responsibility is lifted from the inmate that the concept of re-growth of personality is at times rather blurred. For this 'program' not only relieves him of responsibility, it also teaches him to avoid it. Since many offenders adapt with chameleon-like patterns, the prison routine encourages their already flourishing conviction that the taking of responsibility is not a proper function to be included in their way of life.

The therapist's competence may not necessarily be determined by the nature of his profession or by his status among colleagues. It is based on his capacity for uncompromising honesty in his appraisal both of the client and of his own efforts, and on his ability to respond to the requirements of the situation without being dislodged by external pressure or by his own prejudice. The therapist must have both adequate skill and confidence in it. In addition he must realize his own limitations and know where he cannot tread. In our enthusiasm to treat and to do, we can only too easily forget the first rule to do no harm whether or not one can do good. The therapist's authority must be consistent with the responsibility he is expected to assume. It is not possible, with the type of disorders most frequently encountered in prison, to treat properly unless the therapist has authority for the total management of his clients.

Time is needed for the establishment of a suitable relationship between client and therapist – a great deal of time, if there are problems of personality pattern. Abandoned avenues of thought and feeling have to be reopened. Reflection and change come slowly. Rapid and dramatic cures are extremely rare outside of fiction. At the beginning of treatment, no one can tell how much time may be needed for it to become effective, though it may be possible to make general estimates in months or years. Regardless of what other considerations may justify the practice, it is illogical from a therapeutic standpoint for a legal body, the court, to decide beforehand how long a prison sentence or period of probation shall be in which adequate treatment can occur.

On a similar theme, something of a cold war has been waged in recent years between those who believe a prison is primarily a place of custody and those who wish to carry the torch of therapy into its darkened recesses. The would-be therapist who works with a client (offender) in the free community faces a parallel, albeit less tangible, problem in that any offender-client, whether within the prison or on the street, is in the begin-

425

ning a captive participant. Custody of one sort or another is a very real part of the situation.

Custody for its own sake can become the object of unrealistic veneration, unless its constructive value can be included in a newer philosophy. Loss of liberty alone has no proven rehabilitative value for the inmate, protects society only for the period of incarceration, which is often relatively brief in comparison to the offender's criminal career, is a deterrent to a minority of offenders only, and often leads to the offender's becoming a bitter, more hardened, and more determined social menace. Neither the offender nor society, therefore, is guaranteed any real protection. Perhaps custody has at times been defended as an end in itself, because the older prison practice had nothing else to offer.

Advocates of treatment sometimes forget that if the physical body were not restrained and kept within reach, by the forces of prison custody or other court sanction, there would be no client with whom to work. An unwilling offender may be reached if he can differentiate the therapist from the authority under which the therapist works; but the offender must be on hand for some time, even against his will, if he is to learn to make this distinction.

Perhaps those who favour custody and those who favour treatment can reach a compromise at some future date when a realistic evaluation has been made of the nature and purpose of each. Custody must remain, for without its authority in some situations there would be no control; but it cannot remain as an end in itself. If treatment is to gain permanent acceptance, it must be accorded its proper place and must be diligently used. But custody must be in support of therapy, with general acceptance that the offenders are apprehended and either allowed to remain in the free community under supervision or kept apart from the larger society for whatever time is necessary, in each case essentially in order that remedial work be done. Custody therefore is justified as a means of detaining offenders long enough for some research and, if possible, for some corrective therapy to take place. Anything less than this amounts to neglect and an evasion of responsibility by society; and evasion of responsibility is close to delinquency.

There may be some doubt, however, that an institution primarily designed to serve only as a custodial unit can be transformed into a therapeutic setting. Unrealistic expectations seem to have stemmed from at least two possible sources: (a) the belief that the most severe distortions of personality can be favourably altered by such methods as group activities, trades-training, counselling, and recreational programs, all of which are applied, as it were, from the non-self world, and (b) a disregard for the harmful elements inherent in the prison setting that can in the long run effectively neutralize any beneficial elements.

Disorders of the personality pattern remain as little understood and as difficult to treat as cancer – perhaps more so. Successful methods of treatment, if they are to be found and put into practice, will require no less than a complete reshaping of correctional philosophy and the efforts of the most highly skilled personnel.

Opportunities for creative real-life experiences constitute the fourth indispensible condition for treatment. An interview in which one's past, present, and future life is discussed is not divorced from reality; it is a down-to-earth working situation in which the client learns to do something new or at least to do something better than he did it before. It must never be allowed to drift into a detached sort of reverie or reflection in which one's present behaviour, conclusions, and attitudes become irrelevant.

Discussion of personal problems, self-study, and the achievement of insight constitute an approach suitable for a small proportion of offenders only. It is frequently stated that this should not be contemplated as the future pattern of corrections, simply because there would not be enough trained therapists to provide the service. It has perhaps not been realized that there may not be enough offenders amenable to this approach for it to be used except on a limited and selective basis.

One-to-one interviews, however, are not the only possible pattern for therapeutic relationships. Bush-camp experiences, involvement in sports, combined efforts on a work-bench project, and a host of other experiences that the therapist can share are available, waiting only to be exploited constructively by imaginative therapists and equally imaginative administrative and budgetary authorities. The therapist must be prepared to rise from his cushioned swivel-chair, leave his polished desk, and establish a more flexible concept of therapy, which may require getting his feet wet – literally, not figuratively – and his hands greasy.

Therapist and client must go through the experience of combining forces in striving toward an objective, whether this be the traditionally envisioned goal of insight or the building of a piece of furniture. Neither the work of one alone, nor the making of the furniture, nor any other methods have any intrinsic therapeutic value. They are useful only in that they set the stage for a rewarding and growth-fostering experience in human relationships.

When the courts limit their function to the factual proof of offence, when there is a clearly understood science of behavioural pathology, when both confinement in prison and supervision in the free community are oriented primarily to the adequate treatment of the offender, and when

427

staff are so thoroughly skilled that they can remedy the deformities of personality that underlie the offender's way of life – then, and not before then, will it be possible to say that treatment is being provided.

Further Reading

BROMBERG, W. *Crime and the Mind*. Philadelphia: Lippincott, 1948.

————. 'The Treatability of the Psychopath', *American Journal of Psychiatry*, vol. 110, no. 8 (February 1954).

CIALE, J. 'Problems in Establishing a Therapeutic Relationship in a Prison Community', *Canadian Journal of Corrections*, vol. 1, no. 4 (July 1959).

CLECKLEY, H. *The Mask of Sanity*, 2nd Edition. St. Louis: Mosby, 1950.

CORMIER, B. 'Some Rights, Duties and Responsibilities in Penology and Suggested Changes', *Canadian Journal of Corrections*, vol. 1, no. 4 (July 1959).

CORMIER, B., M. Kennedy, J. Sangowicz, and M. Trottier. 'Presentation of a Basic Classification for Clinical Work and Research on Criminology', *Canadian Journal of Corrections*, vol. 1, no. 4 (July 1959).

————. 'The Natural History of Criminality and Some Tentative Hypotheses on its Abatement', *Canadian Journal of Corrections*, vol. 1, no. 4 (July 1959).

EGAN, M. 'Changing Concepts in Working with the Pre-Delinquent', *Canadian Journal of Corrections*, vol. 3, no. 3 (July 1961).

FROMM, E. *The Sane Society*. New York: Rinehart (Toronto: Clarke, Irwin), 1955.

GREENACRE, P. *Trauma, Growth and Personality*. New York: Norton, 1952.

HENDERSON, D. *Psychopathic States*. New York: Norton, 1939.

JONES, M. *Social Psychiatry*. Springfield: Charles C. Thomas (Toronto: Ryerson), 1962.

KARPMAN, B. (chairman). 'The Psychopathic Delinquent Child', *American Journal of Orthopsychiatry*, vol. 20, no. 2 (April 1950).

————. 'Psychopathic Behaviour in Infants and Children: A Critical Survey of the Existing Concepts', *American Journal of Orthopsychiatry*, vol. 21, no. 2 (April 1951).

OURSLER, F., and W. Oursler. *Father Flanigan of Boys Town*, 1st Edition. Garden City, New York: Doubleday, 1949.

PIAGET, J. *The Construction of Reality in the Child*. New York: Basic Books, 1954.

REDL, F., and D. Wineman. *Children Who Hate*. Glencoe, Illinois: The Free Press, 1951.

————. *Controls From Within*. Glencoe, Illinois: The Free Press, 1952.

RUSSON, G. 'A Design for Clinical Classification of Offenders', *Canadian Journal of Corrections*, vol. 4, no. 3 (July 1962).

SILVERBERG, W. *Childhood Experience and Personal Destiny*. New York: Springer, 1962.

SULLIVAN, C., M. Grant, and J. Grant. 'The Development of Interpersonal Maturity: Applications to Delinquency', *Psychiatry*, vol. 20, no. 4 (November 1957).

SUTTIE, I. *The Origins of Love and Hate*. New York: Julian Press, 1952.

SZASZ, T. *The Myth of Mental Illness*. New York: Hoeber-Harper, 1961.

16

Special Problem Groups: Alcoholics, Drug Addicts, Sex Offenders

J. D. ARMSTRONG AND R. E. TURNER

Introduction

It may well be a reflection of our social attitudes that the subjects of this chapter are commonly referred to as alcoholics, drug addicts, and sex offenders. Alcoholic is an adjective used as a noun, a practice to which many purists object with some justification; but this same language adaptation is often used to describe people with certain types of illness. We often speak of cardiacs, diabetics, asthmatics, which puts the alcoholics at least in respectable medical company. On the other hand when we refer to the sexual offender, we are clearly suggesting a matter of law, justice, and consequent penalty. Somewhere in between are the addicts to a host of drugs other than alcohol, some of whom, such as those habituated to tobacco or coffee, are of no interest to the law unless the collection of a tax is involved; others for a variety of reasons command the attention and vigour of a complex enforcement machine, the courts, and a substantial portion of our penal organizations.

The alcoholic is, of course, the victim of a drug of modest danger, a drug historically entrenched in our society and almost universally accepted. The sexual deviate, on the other hand, is perceived as a misfit in a society that is confused, bewildered, disorganized, and in disagreement in its approach to those universal forces in human behaviour that will not be denied. In the area of sexual expression, our legal system tends to regard

*Dr. Armstrong was formerly the Medical Director of the Alcoholism and Drug Addiction Research Foundation, Toronto.

variations from a poorly defined norm as illegal. So confused is the situation that almost any form of sexual activity could, under certain circumstances, be considered illegal and result in some form of official sanction.

The ordinary task of the physician or the psychiatrist is to understand human function and dysfunction, health and disease, but in writing this chapter we are concerned only with those manifestations of disease that are, of themselves, subject to legal action and not with the underlying causal problem. This limitation is imposed on us by the fact that, while the three areas to be covered here point to certain patterns of human behaviour as manifestations of disease, our society has decided that certain of these manifestations will be subject to criminal charges and that others will not. There are, of course, many aspects of illness subject to legal regulations, for example, infectious diseases and many types of serious mental illness. But here we are only concerned with those aspects of disease that result in actions prohibited by the criminal law.

In this situation our definitions must be tailored to compromise between the understanding of the physician, that of the enforcement officer, and, of course, that of those concerned in rehabilitation.

Statistics also may have little meaning. Even if we could discover what percentage of arrests under the Ontario Liquor Control Act, for example, represented individuals with categorizable problems of alcoholic disease, there would still be differences from community to community, depending on the prevailing attitudes to drinking, to social position, to public drunkenness, and so on.

Yet there is no question that, with or without statistics and verifiable facts, our society expects firm measures to be taken against the outcasts – the sex offender and the drug addict – looking with suspicion on any relaxation of strict confinement and control. In contrast, our society is often reluctant to impose effective controls on the alcoholic until it is too late, although he may be deliberately punished rather than treated time after time for acts arising from his illness – being drunk, for example, or assaultive. Such punishments are usually brief and provide no solution to the underlying problem. Unfortunately we cannot give comprehensive answers to such problems here. Much research and study is needed before an effective solution can be reached.

It should also be recognized that, although the three problem groups are dealt with separately, many combinations are encountered in practice. A man may be using both alcohol and barbiturates excessively at the same time. Another may change from dependence on alcohol to dependence on narcotic drugs as a new response to the same basic psychopathology. Alcohol or other drugs may be used to relieve the anxiety

431

created by a deviate sexual pattern – or the drugs may act as a complete defence against unconscious deviate sexual drives – so that the use of the drug may itself represent a pattern of sexual perversion.

Alcoholics

ARRESTS, ALCOHOLICS, AND ALCOHOLISM

In Court G (which handles all offences of drunkenness for the city) in Toronto during the year ending October 31, 1961, there were 18,280 appearances of people on charges of being drunk in a public place under the Liquor Control Act of Ontario.[1] More than 17,000 of these resulted in convictions, and in most cases the sentence was a fine with alternative imprisonment. The fine was paid in only 5,581 cases. Following new provincial legislation early in 1961, 267 cases were sent to the Alex G. Brown Clinic at Mimico, Ontario, for treatment, and 1,017 of the offenders were given suspended sentences.

Approximately 8,700 individuals accounted for the 18,280 appearances. A maximum of 6,000 were appearing for the first time in the twelve months; 1,560 appeared for a third or subsequent time.

At the time of writing, it is not known what percentage represented examples of various types of the disease that we call alcoholism, but a careful research study of this question is being carried out by the Alcoholism and Drug Addiction Research Foundation at the request of the Attorney-General of Ontario. It is expected that a formal report of this study will be published in 1965 and will provide a useful basis for understanding and dealing with the so-called 'chronic drunkenness offender', who now occupies so much of the time of our courts and reform institutions. Many indications suggest that alcoholic disease underlies numerous offences in which its presence is only vaguely hinted at by those concerned, or not realized at all. It has been estimated that up to sixty per cent of the population of certain Ontario reformatories have abnormal dependence on alcohol, although the fact may not have been in any way evidenced in the circumstances of arrest. It is also estimated that there are more than 20,000 alcoholics in the Toronto area, most of whom never or rarely come into the courts.

The word alcohol appears daily in our news, in accounts of motor accidents, murders, and other tragedies. Case-books of lawyers, physi-

---

1The authors admit here to local bias, and apologize for quoting statistics of their own community and province somewhat more frequently than others, in the belief that these are, with minor variations, illustrative of a general situation.

cians, and social workers contain this word over and over again in relation to disease, destruction, and other social disturbances. In many,
perhaps most, such cases we are not dealing just with the man or
woman who had one too many and was unfortunate enough to get into
trouble. All too often the person involved is known to his family, his
employers, his doctor, his friends, even to the courts, as a heavy drinker,
one who has been depending on alcohol for many years – depending to
such a degree that his personality has changed, his attitudes to those
around him have altered, his behaviour has become increasingly irresponsible. He has been unreliable, difficult, and resistant to suggestion.
He has deteriorated physically, mentally, socially, and morally. Tragedy
has been almost inevitable, but those who were aware of this could not or
did not prevent it.

Schmidt and Smart have recently reported a study indicating that a
large proportion of persons convicted of drunken driving are alcoholics
who have at some time been under treatment for alcoholism.[2] How much
greater is the chance that alcoholic disease underlies crimes more violent
and less commonplace than those of the drinking driver? It seems fair to
speculate that the alcoholic driving dangerously, fighting, being destructive, or in murderous or suicidal acts, may do much more damage to his
community than either the drug addict or the sex offender. Despite the
fact that we accept alcoholism as a disease more readily than we do drug
addiction or a sexual offence, when the alcoholic does misbehave we tend
to punish arbitrarily and ineffectively, disregarding the part illness may
play in the offence.

In 1960 it was estimated that there was a minimum of 228,650 alcoholics in Canada.[3] It was also estimated that only about ten per cent of
these had ever received treatment from any source and no guess at all
could be made as to the effectiveness of treatment.

In alcoholism, as in drug addiction and in sexual perversions, or for
that matter in any other behavioural disorders such as murder or suicide,
the manifestation we observe that results in social action will commonly
be a symptom of underlying personality disorder. There is undoubtedly
a difference between the man who goes through a red light and the man
who plunges a knife into his sweetheart, even though neither action might
have taken place had the individuals concerned not been significantly
impaired in judgment and ability through the action of alcohol. Yet a

[2]W. Schmidt and R. Smart, 'Problem Drinking as a Factor in Drinking-Driving
Offences', *The Canadian Journal of Corrections*, vol. 3, no. 2 (1961), pp. 1-6.
[3]Alcoholism and Drug Addiction Research Foundation, *Annual Report*, 1962, Appendix
III, pp. 75-83.

man who runs his car into a tree while under the influence of alcohol may be representing only one of a variety of conditions underlying the obvious behaviour. True, he may be just a healthy young man in the careless high spirits of a night out, but more likely he is a neurotic or ineffective person depending on alcohol to produce a sense of well-being, or a man depressed and not caring to live, or a man angry and giving vent to his rage, or a man using his car to provide him with the power he does not have otherwise.

UNDERLYING PSYCHIATRIC DISORDERS, AND CLASSIFICATION

Any of the usual psychiatric illnesses may provide a basis for the unhealthy use of alcohol, but more commonly we find a personality disorder, a psychoneurosis,[4] or even a depression,[5] and less commonly a schizophrenic[6] or organic mental disorder; occasionally the basis is the discomfort of chronic physical disease, for which relief is sought. But the drinking patterns and their duration in individuals have contributed to form a variety of types into which alcoholics may be classified apart from the underlying psychiatric disorder. Jellinek describes five main types.[7] The *alpha* alcoholic, although drinking heavily and regularly, remains at the symptomatic stage in which his drinking provides relief for an underlying social, psychiatric, or physical problem, without irreversible dependency, loss of control, or other indications of habituation or addiction. The *beta* type is the person who by custom regularly drinks so much that the continued toxic action of alcohol or its congeners, or the effects of chronic malnutrition, eventually cause repeated drunkenness or one or more of a variety of physical disasters. The *gamma* type of alcoholic represents a further development from the alpha state and shows evidence

[4]*Psychoneurosis*: a psychological disorder characterized by any of a variety of symptoms, for example, feelings of anxiety, depression, disturbed physical functions, and so on, that are not appropriately warranted by the stress being experienced at the time. The individual retains insight, in that he is aware that his reactions are the product of illness.

[5]*Depression*: a state of illness characterized by feelings of dejection, with slowing of thinking and body functions, voluntary and involuntary, and expression by the patient of agitation and worry. The dejection may be profound enough to permit gross distortion of thinking processes (delusions).

[6]*Schizophrenic disorder*: any of a large group of disorders characterized by certain thought processes being completely dissociated or broken away from other components of the individual's apparent intellectual and real experiences. This condition is demonstrated by various kinds of inappropriate behaviour, or patterns of belief, or false perceptions of sound, sight, feeling, etc., all of which the patient finds consistent with his own concept of himself and his world.

[7]E. M. Jellinek, *The Disease Concept of Alcoholism*, New Haven, Conn.: Hillhouse Press, 1960.

of true dependence on alcohol, particularly in his being unable to control his intake whenever he starts to drink, so that he always proceeds to intoxication and undesired behaviour patterns. The *delta* type is also an habituated drinker who may commonly emerge from the beta group. Drunken episodes are less characteristic of this type, and loss of control may not be demonstrated, but any attempt to withdraw from alcohol results in discomfort to a degree that varies with individuals. The delta type cannot get along without alcohol. The *epsilon* type is a victim of one of a number of episodic types of alcoholism.

MANAGEMENT

The variation in types and in the underlying disorders implies variation in management from case to case. Attempts to diagnose and understand the individual problem could and should apply as much to persons brought to attention through legal processes as to those reporting voluntarily to various treatment agencies for assistance. The sad fact is, however, that there are not enough facilities available to deal with alcoholic problems in the community, even for voluntary patients, and that most alcoholics in custody are ignored as treatment problems.

In Switzerland, Sweden, Holland, and some other European countries, legislation permits a court, in a case involving alcohol, to direct the offender to a resource for examination and treatment. Furthermore, he may be required to remain in treatment until he is considered well. There are, of course, many variations in administration. In Sweden separate 'temperance courts' investigate complaints regarding an individual's drinking habits. Treatment clinics or institutions are in many cases operated in conjunction with such courts. In Holland the treatment centres are quite separate and under no jurisdiction of the courts, but there are considerable out-patient and in-patient facilities. Roughly fifty per cent of the patients who attend the Alcoholism Bureau Clinics, of which there were seventeen throughout the country in 1960, attend under the direction of a court.

In the State of Massachusetts, the approach has been to encourage a therapeutic attitude among the staffs of the penal institutions. In addition there is legislation providing a minimum mandatory sentence for certain offences involving alcohol, such as repeated drunkenness, to be followed by an indeterminate sentence to provide both a minimum exposure to treatment plus an opportunity to grant parole at the most suitable time.

CANADIAN FACILITIES

In Ontario, the Alex G. Brown Clinic in the Mimico Reformatory has

435

been operated by the Department of Reform Institutions for some years to provide treatment for alcoholic prisoners, but it can accommodate only a small number of those presumed to have alcohol problems. Legislation passed in 1961 in Ontario provides for a thirty-day mandatory sentence or a voluntary ninety-day commitment for any 'third offender' found guilty of being drunk in a public place, the purpose being to allow time for treatment. One additional institution of approximately 125 beds, also at Mimico Reformatory, has already been opened to meet the needs created by this legislation.

In Alberta, as in Ontario, there is a unit in the reformatory system (Belmont Rehabilitation Centre, near Edmonton) devoted to providing a short-term treatment program for individuals sentenced to the provincial reformatory and found to be suffering from alcoholism.

One encouraging aspect, in favourable contrast to the situation in the problem of dealing with narcotic addiction, is the increasing number of public clinics throughout Canada devoted to the treatment of alcoholism, and the increasing acceptance of alcoholism as a problem to be dealt with by physicians, general hospitals, mental-health clinics, and mental hospitals. This development provides the courts with some latitude, even with present legislation, in determining the sentence of those in whose offences alcohol has played some role. Treatment may be included as a condition of probation with some hope that such treatment will be available in the community. The probation officer may assist the probationer in finding a treatment facility or may accept arrangements the probationer makes privately.

In all Canadian provinces except New Brunswick and Newfoundland, governmental agencies are now established to determine the need for treatment, research, and education in the field of alcoholism, and to recommend or implement policies respecting their provision. Under the auspices of these agencies, treatment facilities are available in British Columbia, Alberta, Saskatchewan, Manitoba, and Ontario. The addresses of all eight provincial agencies follow. These agencies can provide information regarding facilities throughout their provinces as well as those they may operate themselves.

British Columbia: The Alcoholism Foundation of British Columbia,
175 West Broadway Street,
Vancouver 10, British Columbia.

Alberta: The Alcoholism Foundation of Alberta,
9929 – 103rd Street,
Edmonton, Alberta.

	737 – 13th Avenue, S.W., Calgary, Alberta (Branch Clinic).
Saskatchewan:	Bureau On Alcoholism, Department of Social Welfare and Rehabilitation, Health and Welfare Building, Regina, Saskatchewan.
Manitoba:	The Alcoholism Foundation of Manitoba, 124 Nassau Street, Winnipeg 13, Manitoba.
Ontario:	The Alcoholism and Drug Addiction Research Foundation, 24 Harbord Street, Toronto 5, Ontario. Branches in Ottawa, Hamilton, London, Fort William, and Sudbury.
Quebec:	Study and Information Committee on Alcoholism, Parliament Building, Quebec City, Quebec.
Nova Scotia:	Alcoholism Research Commission, 5639 Spring Garden Road, Halifax, Nova Scotia.
Prince Edward Island:	Physical Fitness and Alcohol Education, Provincial Building, Charlottetown, Prince Edward Island.

In each province there is, in addition, some provision to deal with alcoholic patients in the mental-hospital system.

It is to be hoped that in time further changes in legislation will take place that make it possible to examine and identify the offending alcoholic at an earlier stage, thus ensuring early help both for his own benefit and that of the community.

Ontario has much legislation that limits the behaviour of the drinker; aside from various provisions of the Liquor Control Act,[8] there are the Indian Act, [9] and the Highway Traffic Act.[10] Yet none of these recognizes

[8]Liquor Control Act, *Revised Statutes of Ontario, 1960*, Chapter 217, with Amendments to May 1, 1962, Toronto: Queen's Printer.

[9]Indian Act, *Revised Statutes of Canada, 1952*, Chapter 149, Ottawa: Queen's Printer.

[10]Highway Traffic Control Act, *Revised Statutes of Ontario, 1960*, Chapter 172, Toronto: Queen's Printer.

clearly the possible state of illness of the drinker. Such recognition occurs only in the provisions of the Mental Hospitals Act that deal with habitués[11] and the legislation permitting treatment in the Mimico Reformatory as already mentioned. It is still quite possible in Ontario for an assaultive alcoholic to serve his sentence and return to his community, having received little or no treatment, or for an impaired driver to have his licence restored after a prescribed period of time without having to provide any proof of recovery, despite the fact that a state of illness was the basic reason for his restriction in the first place.

The Ontario Mental Hospitals Act does provide for the emergency apprehension for examination of any mentally disturbed person, without certificate or a warrant; for committal of habitués for periods of up to thirty days on the certification of two physicians; and for committal of habitués for periods of up to two years on presentation of evidence to a county court judge, who hears the case in chambers, that is, in private.

An additional problem is posed when a jury attempts to determine guilt and a judge attempts to pass sentence in a criminal case in which the defendant is socially and mentally so deteriorated, as a result of disease-drinking, that he is governed by less rigid standards than previously or in which he was so impaired at the time of his offence that he could not apply proper judgment in governing his action, or in aiming at a specific intent, or in applying deliberation or planning to his actions. Such factors are of great concern in determining the degree of responsibility in a case of homicide. Even when the act is already attributed to an individual, the verdict might be capital murder, non-capital murder, manslaughter, self-defence, or not guilty by reason of insanity as a result of the degree of intoxication at the time of the offence, this in turn being influenced by the extent of damage – social, psychological, and physical – resulting from habitual heavy drinking.

TREATMENT

It should be clearly recognized that there is no readily available, certain method of treatment that can be applied to identified or legally controlled alcoholics. There is a certain body of evidence that controlled confinement under skilfully directed conditions will result in a gradual change in attitude and behaviour, which will permit the individual eventually to return to society with little danger of a recurrence of his former symp-

11Habitué Act, Mental Hospitals Act, *Revised Statutes of Ontario, 1960*, Chapter 236, Part V, Sections 49-54, Toronto: Queen's Printer.

toms.[12] On the other hand there is also evidence that some degree of organic brain deterioration is extremely common in alcoholic disease where there has been any degree of prolonged uncontrolled or heavy drinking.[13] One has the uncomfortable feeling too that the methods of diagnosis employed are very clumsy and do not identify such deterioration until it is moderately advanced. The rehabilitation of persons so affected is extremely difficult since their capacity for insight and new learning is considerably restricted. This problem is only one of many in which considerable research is needed. In the development of any program in an institution, as part of a rehabilitation scheme, serious thought should be given to answering effectively the unsolved questions; only thus can we continue to develop a sound basis for therapy.

Treatment at the present time, whether under controlled or voluntary conditions, essentially includes the following steps:

First, one must deal with the immediate state of physical or toxic disturbance, which may be due to the alcohol, or to the response to its withdrawal (in its severe state, delirium tremens), and which in either instance is contributed to by prolonged dietary disturbance.[14] Treatment requires the use of drugs, usually of the tranquilizer type, to allay the tremors and anxiety, and the restoration of the disturbed metabolic state, usually by attention to diet, supplemented by necessary vitamins and minerals.

Then one must carry out adequate investigation to determine the degree of physical damage and the nature of emotional disturbance.[15] Here the physician involves his colleagues in psychiatry, psychology, social work, and nursing. Treatment may include re-education through individual psychotherapy,[16] but for many cases, group methods seem more

[12]P. G. Aungle, 'The Care and Treatment of Psychopathic Offenders in Norway, Sweden, and Denmark', *The Journal of Mental Science*, vol. 105, no. 439 (April 1959), pp. 428-39.

[13]A. E. Bennett *et al.*, 'The Diagnosis of Intermediate Stage of Alcoholic Brain Disease', *American Journal of Psychiatry*, vol. 116, no. 8 (1960), pp. 705-11.

[14]M. P. Hoover, 'Management of Acute Alcoholic Intoxication', *Canadian Medical Association Journal*, vol. 83 (December 24, 1960), pp. 1352-5.

[15]J. D. Armstrong, 'The Special Clinic for Alcoholism', *Canadian Medical Association Journal*, vol. 83 (December 24, 1960) pp. 1359-61; and 'Psychiatric Theories of Alcoholism', *Canadian Psychiatric Association Journal*, vol. 6, no. 3 (1960), pp. 140-8.

[16]*Psychotherapy*: 'a form of treatment for problems of an emotional nature in which a trained person deliberately establishes a professional relationship with a patient with the object of removing, modifying or retarding symptoms, of mediating disturbed patterns of behaviour, and of promoting positive personality growth and development.' L. R. Wolberg, *The Technique of Psychotherapy*, New York: Grune and Stratton, 1954, p. 3.

effective, especially superficial types of group therapy permitting re-education and insight at the patient's own pace. Occupational therapy permits further exploration and development of insights.

On discharge from hospital most patients require long-term supervision on an out-patient basis. Here again one may use individual interviews with professional staff or continue a program of group psychotherapy.

An additional approach to treatment here is the use of the drugs antabuse and temposil.[17] These are commonly referred to as protective drugs. Their usefulness depends on the fact that they have no effect observable to the patient until he takes a drink containing alcohol. Shortly after doing so, he develops a number of short-lived but unpleasant symptoms (including flushing, headache, pounding pulse, shortness of breath). The fear of this reaction, or the experience itself, dissuades the person from further drinking. Hence the drugs protect him from the serious complications of drinking.

Newer forms of treatment are under investigation. These include the use of drugs, such as lysergic acid, which produce states of mental distortion that are believed to provide some insight through recall of previously forgotten or poorly understood experience. Other methods under investigation involve a technique known as 'conditioning'. Here the patient is subjected to a very disturbing experience such as inability to breathe (brought about by the administration of a temporarily paralysing drug), coincidentally with having an alcoholic drink. Subsequently, any further attempt to drink will result in the same disturbing reaction, even though the paralysing drug is not given. Thus the patient should be deterred from further drinking.

Drug Addiction

An old Persian tale tells of three travellers arriving at a city after the gates had been locked for the night. One was an alcoholic, one an opium addict, and the third a smoker of hashish (which we know as marihuana). The alcoholic said 'Let us break down the gates'; the opium user said 'No, let us lie down and sleep till morning'; but the hashish smoker said, 'I am going to slip through the key-hole.'

This parable effectively demonstrates the belligerence of the alcoholic, the escapism of the opium user, and the fantasy of the hashish or marihuana smoker. Yet, as indicated in the introduction to this chapter, the

---

[17]J. D. Armstrong, 'The Protective Drugs in the Treatment of Alcoholism', *Canadian Medical Association Journal*, vol. 77 (August 1, 1957), pp. 228-32.

latter two are almost always thought of in relation to criminal or penal situations, while the first, despite his belligerence, has been more publicly accepted as the victim of an illness.

In this section we are largely concerned with persons addicted to various narcotic substances, or to substances with a lesser but comparable capacity to produce a state of addiction.

ADDICTION

By a state of addiction we mean that a drug, for whatever reason it was first taken, has been so satisfying that the person has continued to use it, over and over again, until he has become dependent on it, sometimes to reproduce not only the initial satisfaction but other satisfactions as well.

Actually the physical response may be almost identical on repeated use, changing only over a period of time as the individual develops a tolerance. The psychological reasons for wanting to escape into the drug-induced realms of fantasy may be quite varied, however, and may include anger, depression, anxiety, and the other common emotional states, any one of which may predominate and consistently cause the victim to turn to a drug for a solution. In using a drug to allay one emotional discomfort, he may discover that it serves him equally well in dealing with others.

The body adjusts to the drug, so that increasingly larger doses are required to obtain the desired effect. After this tolerance, as it is called, has developed, if the drug is withdrawn the organism experiences symptoms that vary according to the drug used. Alcohol seems to have relatively mild addiction-producing properties, but seems able to release aggressive or other drives ordinarily kept under control, hence possibly attracting to its use those who need to release such drives. The user of marihuana probably does not become addicted at all. He gets from his drug-induced reveries an enjoyment that reduces the need for behaviour that has destructive or other antisocial implications. He becomes psychologically dependent on the drug since he finds himself seeking its special pleasures over and over again. The heroin addict is very definitely addicted, but the pleasurable action of the drug leads not to violence but to an indescribable, heightened sense of well-being. He becomes a criminal, if he was not one before, mainly because of the high cost of obtaining his drug through the illegal market. To obtain money for heroin, many men turn to petty theft and many women to prostitution.

Presumably our extreme legal and social sanctions against opium derivatives and comparable synthetic drugs are based on the belief that a high percentage of the population is susceptible to addiction, with result-

ing social deterioration.[18] There is some evidence that the degree of
mental and physical destruction caused by addiction to these drugs may
not be nearly as great as in alcohol addiction.

Marihuana is not an addiction-producing drug in the physiological
sense, but a psychological dependence can undoubtedly be developed.
Furthermore, marihuana is sometimes used by traffickers to introduce
people to the pleasures of using drugs, a fact that explains its inclusion in
the schedule of drugs attached to the Narcotic Control Act of Canada.
In any case a person under its influence is of questionable responsibility,
and since this state can be induced very quickly it is reasonable to regard
the drug as dangerous, even if not addicting.

THE PROBLEM IN CANADA

The largest group of narcotic-drug addicts is made up of those who get
their supplies through criminal channels, that is, those whose possession
of narcotic drugs is illegal, and who are willing to transgress social boundaries in the initiation and maintenance of their habit. The second largest
group is made up of people whose professions bring them into contact
with the drugs – doctors, druggists, nurses, veterinarians; and the third
comprises those who have become addicted through having a drug administered for medical reasons. These are commonly referred to as the
criminal, professional, and medical groups of addicts. The criminal group
far outnumbers the other two groups put together, accounting for nearly
3,000 of Canada's approximately 3,500 narcotic addicts.

It should be emphasized that an addict is unfortunately labelled criminal simply by the fact of illegally possessing the drugs he uses. This means
that a narcotic addict who is not professional (having drugs available
through his profession) or medical (being addicted in the process of
treatment for another illness) is automatically criminal. Many addicts,
however, are persons who have criminal records or tendencies in any case.

The above classification, arbitrarily determined by laws and regulations
that may or may not be realistically related to the problems of the addicted person, is justifiable in terms of the control of the problem of drug
addiction from the social and public-health point of view. But a doctor
interested in this problem would prefer to see in use classification systems that would recognize the psychiatric and medical concomitants of
the addiction and any special characteristics of addicted groups themselves.

18An Act to Provide for the Control of Narcotic Drugs, *Revised Statutes of Canada,*
Ottawa: Queen's Printer, 1961, Chapter 35.

There are, of course, a host of other drugs that may be involved, varying considerably in their actions and in the ways their users regard them. Certain barbiturate drugs, of which increasing doses lead to a state similar to alcoholic intoxication and to growing incompetence, may be used both by persons whose neurosis is manifested by anxiety and insomnia, and by persons on the fringe of the criminal group of society who take them as a source of 'kicks' and call them 'goofballs', 'yellow jackets', and so on. In the one case the drug is probably obtained legally through prescription and in the other case illegally. There is increasing evidence of the illegal use of various drugs, particularly barbiturates and amphetamines, which while under special controls for sale and distribution nevertheless find their way into unauthorized hands for improper use. The amphetamine group of drugs (methedrine, benzedrine, etc.) is equally high-addicting and claims victims haphazardly among professionals, neurotics, and the criminal fringe; the essential effect of these drugs on the central nervous system is to excite, rather than to depress as do alcohol and the barbiturates.

It must not be forgotten that, with the possible exception of marihuana, all the drugs that can lead to addiction are most useful medically. Conflict arises when the medical use prepares the ground for addiction as it does in the case of narcotics, barbiturates, amphetamines, and others, or when the legal controls seriously interfere with the availability of the drug for medical use, as in the case of heroin.

MANAGEMENT

In planning a program for treatment of narcotic addiction, it is important to recognize the social background from which the patient comes. For instance, the physician who is addicted may have a reasonably high degree of social motivation and accept treatment either voluntarily or with a minimum of persuasion. In such cases the neurotic or personality problem may not have manifested itself so clearly in antisocial behaviour as in some others.

Persuasion and pressure seem to be required to inspire motivation to obtain help in most types of addict, including the alcoholic. However, in various inadequate personalities, especially those who commonly become involved in the criminal use of drugs, the satisfaction of the drug is of such an order, and the addiction so readily and thoroughly established, that only the most consistent type of coercion should be expected to work. By this, one does not imply that punishment, as such, is desirable, but that certain conditions of restriction of freedom may be required to assist in the establishment of motivation.

443

One may argue that such restriction interferes with the individual's right to control his own destiny. However, two points should be kept in mind: first, that the illness itself influences a person's ability to exercise his judgment as he might otherwise, and second, that the impact of the illness on his family and his community is such that a measure of control is commonly desirable.

The United States Public Health Service has, for some years, operated hospitals at Lexington, Kentucky, and at Fort Worth, Texas, for treatment of drug addictions. Addicts who are inmates of federal penitentiaries may be transferred to these hospitals for treatment, and can be held there for the remainder of their sentences. In fact, nearly ninety per cent of admissions are voluntary. This may be a technicality since in many, if not most instances, the addicts seek treatment only to avoid legal action, which would be more stringent than hospitalization. Except for persons who are under sentence and released on parole, there is no means of keeping patients under continuous out-patient supervision.

A few years ago a voluntary unit was set up in Detroit to provide treatment for the many narcotic addicts in that community.[19] Although some 510 patients were seen in three years, the unit's effective results were abysmally low. A modified program is now being introduced in conjunction with an amended Mental Health Act of the State of Michigan that will permit committal of patients for treatment and continuing compulsory follow-up for an indefinite period after discharge from hospital.[20] Dr. Herbert Raskin, director of the clinic, recommends that this plan should not be permitted to discourage the voluntary admission and treatment of addicts in other clinics. In order to get the greatest possible number of addicts to take treatment, it is necessary to operate both voluntary and compulsory systems of admission.

Much is said about the so-called British system. A report by Larimore and Brill sums up very well the contrasts between British and United States methods.[21] There is little essential difference in the law (this observation applies also to Canada), but statistics indicate that there is a relatively small addiction problem in Britain. Voluntary treatment by physicians is clearly allowed, and the physician carrying out treatment is expected, as in any other aspect of his practice, to meet certain defined

[19]H. A. Raskin, 'Narcotic Addiction, Method of Herbert A. Raskin, M.D.', *Current Therapy*, Wayne State University, Detroit, Mich., 1960.

[20]Department of Mental Health Act, *Statutes of State of Michigan*, Act 271, 1945 (Revised 1960).

[21]G. W. Larimore and H. Brill, 'The British Narcotic System', *New York State Journal of Medicine*, vol. 60, no. 1 (January 1, 1960), pp. 107-15.

ethical standards of care. These standards limit the circumstances in which he can provide drugs to known addicts except for withdrawal in hospital, and the amount he can allow. Reports of favourable results from voluntary treatment on an out-patient basis such as that by Frankau and Stanwell[22] suggest that it would be desirable for physicians in Canada, as well as Britain and the United States, to examine more closely their potential role in being able to treat narcotic addicts, assuming that this can be done with the permission and co-operation of law-enforcement agencies.

Lady Frankau's approach essentially consists of prescribing adequate doses of the patient's addicting drug until a therapeutic relationship is well established between the patient and the therapist. The addict has become thoroughly estranged from most humans outside his 'addict world'. It is essential that he come to accept, trust, and understand the therapist. This process cannot be hurried, nor can the manipulation of his drug requirements. Only when a satisfactory relationship is established can the process of withdrawal be begun. The withdrawal may still have to be completed in hospital. Such a procedure is legally permissible in Canada under the Narcotic Control Act of 1961.

The British Columbia Narcotic Addiction Foundation, under the direction of Dr. Robert Halliday, has successfully demonstrated that addicts can be withdrawn from their drugs while under out-patient care.

In 1963 the Alcoholism and Drug Addiction Research Foundation of Ontario established a unit for out-patient care of narcotic addicts in Toronto.

Diskind reported in 1960 on a project in New York State in which intensive rehabilitative supervision is provided for parolees with addiction problems, even to the extent of permitting the parolee to remain out of an institution and on parole despite evidence of relapse.[23] The implication was that after the period of relapse, rehabilitation could continue without starting again from the beginning. Any such treatment program unquestionably requires prolonged out-patient supervision and probably also repeated admissions to hospital.

There is some suggestion that without treatment or punishment of any kind, the process of the illness, like certain other kinds of problems manifested by disturbed social behaviour, simply burns out, and that the

---

22I. M. Frankau and P. M. Stanwell, 'The Treatment of Drug Addiction', *The Lancet*, no. 7165 (December 24, 1960), pp. 1377-9.

23W. H. Diskind and R. F. Hahinan, 'Specialized Supervision of Parolees Having a History of Narcotic Addiction', P.C.1, Final Report of The Special Narcotic Project, New York State Division of Parole, Albany, N.Y., 1960.

addiction loses its hold on the older person. Because at present we cannot estimate the effects of this burning-out, nor even be sure it exists, it is difficult to evaluate the success of any treatment program.

CANADIAN LEGISLATION

The Canadian federal legislation known as the Narcotic Control Act, 1961,[24] if effectively implemented, may well be a model plan for management of the criminal addict who is incapable of volunteering for treatment or remaining voluntarily long enough for effective recovery. It provides penalties for those found in illegal possession of, or trafficking in, or importing certain drugs, as set out in the schedule appended to the Act. Several sections deal with persons found to be in possession of, or trafficking in, or importing, who on examination are also found to be narcotic addicts. Such a person may be remanded on request from counsel for the Crown, or on his own request or that of his counsel, for observation and examination for a period not exceeding seven days (Section 16).

In passing sentence the judge is to consider the result of such examination including evidence of at least one duly qualified medical practitioner. If the court is satisfied that the person is a narcotic addict it may, notwithstanding provisions of other sections of the Act to do with trafficking, possession, or importing, sentence him to custody for treatment for an indefinite period, instead of any other sentence that might be imposed for the offence for which he was convicted. Such a person is to be confined for treatment in an institution maintained and operated under regulations of the Penitentiary Act (Section 18(1)). A person who is sentenced to custody for treatment for an indeterminate period is subject to the Parole Act and during confinement will be considered an inmate according to the meaning of the Act. On release, under certificate of the Parole Board, he will be a paroled inmate within the meaning of that Act (Section 18(2)). The sentence of custody for treatment is to expire within ten years from the date of his release on parole, which may be fixed by the Parole Board, unless by that time his parole is forfeited or revoked.

Obviously no purpose will be served if addicts are sentenced to penitentiary for an indeterminate term unless adequate facilities and a program for treatment are available. It is expected that some time in 1965 an institution will be opened at Matsqui, about forty miles from Vancouver, British Columbia, to deal with narcotic addicts, most of whom will be referred through the provisions of the Narcotic Control Act. The

24An Act to Provide for the Control of Narcotic Drugs, *op. cit.*

British Columbia location reflects the large percentage of addicts in the Vancouver area.

Sexual Offenders

DEFINITION

The sexual offender is a person convicted of committing a sexual act forbidden by, or contrary to, the law.

There is confusion frequently between the terms 'sexual offender' and 'sexual deviate'. Sexual deviation means sexual conduct other than sexual intercourse with an adult of the opposite sex, which is performed for sexual gratification and is persistently preferred to normal genital coitus. Clinically, it is extended to such conduct in fantasy as well as in overt behaviour. The conduct must provide complete satisfaction. The term should not be applied to sexual activity that is substituted for preferred but unavailable heterosexual activity, nor 'deviant acts' performed in foreplay to normal genital coital activity. Not all sexual offenders, then, are sexual deviates. For instance, a man who has sexual intercourse with a female 'of previously chaste character' aged fourteen or more and under sixteen has committed a sexual offence under the Criminal Code of Canada, Section 138 (2), but not a deviant act.

It must be realized, too, that not all sexual deviates are sexual offenders. Practice of the deviation known as fetishism, for example, is not an offence, though it may lead to one.

Further, a person may be charged with a non-sexual offence which, on examination, is found to arise out of sexual deviation; that is to say, the criminal behaviour has sexual psychopathology[25] as its basis. Examples of this type of offence are: breaking and entering a home to steal female underclothing for fetishistic purposes, or stealing it from a clothes-line; shop-lifting or kleptomania[26] in which a person, frequently a female, steals some object for symbolic sexual gratification rather than for gain; arson due to pyromania;[27] assault arising out of a homosexual encounter; murder arising out of sadism; sending poison-pen letters; making obscene telephone calls; some offences in connection with obscene literature. East states that such non-sexual offences are essentially sexual in origin if the offence has for its immediate purpose the immediate or delayed gratification of normal or abnormal sexuality.[28]

[25]*Psychopathology*: abnormal mental functions or processes, in developmental terms.
[26]*Kleptomania*: pathological compulsion to steal.
[27]*Pyromania*: pathological compulsion to set fires.
[28]Sir N. East, *Society and the Criminal*, Springfield, Illinois: Thomas, 1951.

Lastly, sexually deviant behaviour may be secondary to alcoholism, psychopathy,[29] mental retardation, psychosis, or organic brain disease.

THE PROBLEM

Three manifestations of sexually deviant conduct concern society: violent and dangerous acts; behaviour that constitutes a nuisance, or is performed in a public place; and acts involving young and possibly impressionable persons that may have traumatic consequences. Society's basic concern in all these cases is morality.

The sexual offender poses many problems in respect of causation, of the administration of justice, of correction (including treatment), and of the protection of the public. These problems have to be considered against a confused background of preconceived and rigidly prejudicial ideas of sexuality, different standards in different social strata, actual sexual behaviour, and ignorance (though there may be more enlightened opinions

---

[29]*Psychopathy*: K. G. Gray and H. C. Hutchison surveyed Canadian psychiatrists for their opinions of psychopathic personality in descriptive terms (*The Canadian Psychiatric Association Journal,* vol. 9, no. 6 (December 1964), pp. 452-61). The ten traits or features most commonly listed as significant were: inability to profit from experience; lack of sense of responsibility; inability to form meaningful relationships; lack of control over impulses; lack of moral sense; chronic or recurrent antisocial behaviour; failure to alter behaviour as a result of punishment; emotional immaturity; inability to experience feelings of guilt; self-centred attitude.

The Mental Health Act of England (1959) makes special provision for the compulsory treatment of offenders who have 'a persistent disorder or disability of mind (whether or not including subnormality of intelligence) which results in abnormally aggressive or seriously irresponsible conduct on the part of the patient, and requires or is susceptible to medical treatment'. This is the first legal definition of psychopathy.

Sir David Henderson describes psychopaths as constituting 'a rebellious, individualistic group who fail to fit in to their social milieu, and whose emotional instability is largely determined by a state of psychological immaturity which prevents them from adapting to reality and profiting from experience. They may be adult in years, but emotionally they are so slow and backward and uncontrolled that they behave like dangerous children. They lack judgment, foresight and ordinary prudence. It is the sheer stupidity of their conduct which is so appalling.' (Sir David Henderson and R. D. Gillespie, *Textbook of Psychiatry,* 9th Edition, revised by Sir David Henderson and Ivor R. C. Batchelor, London: Oxford University Press, 1962, p. 318.)

Psychosis: 'A severe emotional illness in which there is a departure from normal patterns of thinking, feeling, and acting. Commonly characterized by loss of contact with reality, distortion of perception, regressive behaviour and attitudes, diminished control of elementary impulses and desires, abnormal mental content including delusions and hallucinations. Chronic and generalized personality deterioration may occur. May require commitment to a mental hospital.' (From 'A Psychiatric Glossary', by the Committee of Public Information, American Psychiatric Association, 1957.) This term coincides approximately with the legal and lay concept of insanity or mental illness.

amongst the public than is generally appreciated). Sexual behaviour and attitudes hinge upon social morality and historical religious doctrines. The criminal law attempts to maintain standards of behaviour that are considered to be necessary for the welfare of the community. It is concerned with the grosser forms of sexual misconduct, which, on account of their abnormal character, associated violence, or the immaturity or mental disability of the victim, can be controlled only by the criminal law.

The task in the treatment of crime seems to be two-fold – the protection of society and the rehabilitation of offenders. Obviously, rehabilitation of offenders would go a long way towards protecting society. In some instances strictly punitive methods have proven inappropriate and ineffective. In certain cases, however, compulsory detention may be a necessary part of a correctional treatment program.

Since in Canada the Criminal Code applies to the entire country, we are spared one problem which causes great difficulty in the United States. In that country a particular sexual act may be considered an offence in one jurisdiction and not in another.

The aims of sentence are (1) punishment, (2) deterrence, and (3) rehabilitation or reformation. It is not known to what extent the punishment of sexual offenders deters them from repeating their acts, or deters potential offenders, but it is clear that often they have not considered the law at all before committing their offences, and even if they have, that they have been so overwhelmed by their urges that they have proceeded anyway. Some do not appreciate that the act is against the law (as, for example, in the case of an adolescent boy attempting to look at the genitals of a young girl).

The rehabilitative or reforming aspects of sentence may include psychiatric treatment. The question is where such treatment ought to take place. Is the particular offender best suited for treatment in an out-patient psychiatric setting, in a mental hospital, in a custodial institution? If in a custodial institution, then in what type – penitentiary, reformatory, maximum security within the penal system, maximum security within a medical system?

There is a question too concerning how sexually deviant female offenders should be dealt with, for instance, lesbians and some prostitutes. It is recognized that far fewer females than males suffer from disorders of sexual deviation. One would therefore expect to find fewer females as sexually deviant offenders in court. Spencer notes that the male to female ratio for sexual offences in Canada is 221:1.[30] In 1959, the Metropolitan

---

[30] J. Spencer, presented at the Canadian Congress of Corrections, Toronto, May 1961.

Toronto Police statistics indicated that of 369 sexual offences prosecuted, only five were offences by females (two gross indecency, two incest, and one indecent act).[31] These figures exclude charges, such as vagrancy, that deal with the problem of prostitution. But in prostitution the sexual act is usually not deviant under our definition nor is the act as such an offence.

INCIDENCE

It is not known to what extent sexual acts forbidden by law are committed.[32] Some do not come to notice, some are not reported, others are reported but the offender is not apprehended or not convicted. The incidence of non-sexual offences that are the result of sexual aberration (discussed on page 447) is also unknown. Finally, the number of offenders apprehended and convicted varies according to community attitudes and the vigilance and efficiency of the police.

Sexual offences constitute a small proportion of indictable offences, 3.5 per cent as compared with 36.9 per cent for theft. (The male/female ratio for theft is 13:1.) Spencer notes that a comparison between England and Canada shows no consistent increase in sexual crimes in Canada such as has appeared in England since the war.[33] In England, the percentage of all indictable crime represented by sexual crime has now risen to the Canadian figure of 3.5 per cent.

The reports of the Dominion Bureau of Statistics do not permit adequate analysis since not all jurisdictions report consistently.[34] In 1960, D.B.S. reported 42,613 persons charged under the Criminal Code with indictable offences, of which 38,193 were convicted. There were 6,926 persons charged with offences against the person, and 5,606 persons were convicted (16.3 per cent and 14.7 per cent respectively). Among sexual offences, indecent assault on a female was the most common one, involving 572 persons charged and 460 convicted. Buggery, bestiality, and gross indecency, which are grouped together, accounted for 412 persons charged and 384 convicted. Other offences listed were: sexual intercourse and attempt – 151 persons charged, 125 convicted; rape – 95 charged, 56 convicted; indecent assault on male – 93 charged, 79 convicted; incest – 56 charged, 44 convicted. Other offences were attempted rape and seduction. All sexual offences together involved 1,406 persons charged of which 1,168 were convicted. This represents 3.3 per cent of all persons

[31]Metropolitan Toronto Police Department, *Statistical Reports*, 1959.

[32]*Sexual Offences*, A Report of the Cambridge Department of Criminal Science, London: Macmillan, 1957.

[33]Spencer, *op. cit.*

[34]Dominion Bureau of Statistics, *Eighty-Sixth Annual Report of Statistics of Criminal and Other Offences*, Ottawa: Queen's Printer, 1961.

charged and 3.1 per cent of those convicted. In terms of offences against the person, sexual offenders constitute 20.3 per cent of the persons charged in this group and 21.1 per cent of those convicted.

TABLE I

PROSECUTIONS FOR SEXUAL OFFENCES, ONTARIO*

	1958		1959		1960		1961	
	No.	Convicted	No.	Convicted	No.	Convicted	No.	Convicted
Buggery	6	5	1	1	7	3	4	4
Carnal knowledge and attempted carnal knowledge	38	29	39	26	42	25	32	15
Gross indecency	12	9	7	5	18	15	10	8
Incest	8	6	13	11	21	12	14	10
Indecent act or exposure	28	21	24	21	33	25	37	26
Rape and attempted rape	45	2	32	8	43	4	41	14
Seduction	3	0	8	4	3	1	—	—
Loitering near school	—	—	2	2	—	—	—	—
Total	140	72	126	78	167	85	138	77

Population of Ontario: about six million.

*Compiled from the *Annual Reports* of the Commissioner of the Ontario Provincial Police, Toronto: Queen's Printer, 1958, 1959, 1960, and 1961. The figures do not include statistics for cities that maintain their own police forces.

TABLE II

PROSECUTIONS FOR SEXUAL OFFENCES, METROPOLITAN TORONTO*

	1958		1959		1960		1961	
	No.	Convicted	No.	Convicted	No.	Convicted	No.	Convicted
Indecent assault	140	93	155	86	209	135	238	179
Carnal knowledge	10	3	12	7	21	12	43	33
Attempted carnal knowledge	2	2	4	1	3	3	—	—
Gross indecency	182	176	55	51	91	76	187	178
Incest	3	2	12	6	3	2	6	6
Indecent act or exposure	89	76	100	77	135	109	155	139
Rape and attempted rape	25	8	26	18	21	9	36	25
Seduction	4	2	1	1	1	1	—	—
Sodomy	7	3	4	3	12	9	14	11
Total	462	365	369	250	496	356	679	571

Population of Metropolitan Toronto (1961): 1,595,809.

	1958		1959		1960	
	No.	Convicted	No.	Convicted	No.	Convicted
All criminal and general offences except traffic and vehicular offences.	43,830	36,810	51,868	42,667	63,861	52,716

*Compiled from the Metropolitan Toronto Police Department *Statistical Reports,* 1958, 1959, 1960, and 1961.

J. D. Armstrong and R. E. Turner

Table I shows that in Ontario there were 140 prosecutions for sexual crimes in 1958, 126 in 1959, 167 in 1960, and 138 in 1961, with 72, 78, 85, and 77 convictions respectively. Table II provides the corresponding figures for Metropolitan Toronto.

There is no evidence to suggest that the incidence of sexual offences is increasing at an alarming rate, or, indeed, keeping in mind the increase in population, that it is increasing at all. In fact, the rate each year varies inconsistently with the size of the population.

One way of examining the extent of the sexual-offender problem is to study the number of persons in various penal institutions who have been convicted of sexual offences. The figure usually quoted for Canadian penitentiaries is 8 per cent of the total number of inmates. Mohr's survey of sexual offenders in Kingston Penitentiary indicated that they numbered 63, or 6.4 per cent of the 980 inmates.[35] The greatest number of these had been convicted of rape or attempted rape. There were 22 persons with such convictions, about a third of the sexual offenders. Six had been convicted of being criminal sexual psychopaths (see p. 455). It is noteworthy that incest, contributing to juvenile delinquency, and gross indecency showed a high representation of older offenders, whereas abduction, sexual intercourse with females (under fourteen, and between fourteen and sixteen), and rape included mostly younger offenders.

In another study by Mohr of sexual offenders in Millbrook Reformatory, an institution of a maximum-security type where most of the sexually deviant offenders sentenced to the Ontario reformatories are committed, it was found that in May 1961 there were 66 sexually deviant offenders, of whom 52 had committed sexual offences, 4 had committed arson, and 10 had committed other criminal offences but had been found to be sexually deviant after committal.[36]

In 1960, 340 sexual offenders were committed to Ontario reform institutions. They made up 3.8 per cent of all offenders committed for indictable offences during the same time, about the same percentage as the number of sexual offenders among those committed for indictable offences in all of Canada (3.5 per cent). More than one-third of these Ontario offences were connected with prostitution. Among the others, the most common charge was indecent assault, and the next most common was contributing to juvenile delinquency. Of all offenders committed to jail in

[35]J. W. Mohr, 'A Short Survey of Sexual Offenders in Kingston Penitentiary', *Canadian Journal of Corrections*, vol. 5, no. 3 (July 1963).
[36]J. W. Mohr, 'A Short Survey of Sexual Offenders in Ontario Reformatory, Millbrook', *Canadian Journal of Corrections*, vol. 5, no. 3 (July 1963).

452

Canada in 1960 (50,671), approximately 750 were sexual offenders, constituting only about 1.5 per cent. If one considers that more than half of the jail population of Canada consists of persons convicted of liquor offences (which are usually not indictable), one arrives at the same figure mentioned earlier, 3.5 per cent.

The provincial mental hospital at Penetanguishene has a maximum-security unit (Oak Ridge), which in 1962 contained 260 patients. These had been admitted from the reform institutions, Kingston Penitentiary, Ontario Hospitals, and general hospitals, as well as through the courts and by other admission. Of the sexual offenders, two had been committed there by warrant of the Lieutenant-Governor (one for obscene telephone calls, the other for indecent exposure); two by warrant of the Minister of Justice (both for incest); seven had been referred from the reform institutions (two each under conviction for gross indecency, indecent assault on a male person, and indecent act, and one each for buggery and carnal knowledge); three had been referred directly from the courts without legal documentation (one each for indecent assault on a male, for buggery, and for rape); and three had been referred from other Ontario mental hospitals (two under conviction for indecent assault and one for attempted rape).[37]

The Forensic Clinic of the Toronto Psychiatric Hospital, in the six years from May 1956 to the end of April 1962, had 329 sexual offenders referred from the courts (chiefly magistrates' courts) and the probation service for complete psychiatric examination in an out-patient setting.[38] Their offences were indecent act, contributing to juvenile delinquency, gross indecency, indecent assault on a male person, indecent assault on a female person, and incest.

LEGISLATION

Part IV of the Criminal Code, which concerns sexual offences, public morals, and disorderly conduct, lists the offences classed as sexual offences under the Act. The following are indictable offences:

37C. K. McKnight, J. W. Mohr, and B. B. Swadron, 'The Mentally Ill Offender in the Oak Ridge Hospital Unit', *Criminal Law Quarterly*, vol. 5. no. 2 (1962).

38More information on the work of the Forensic Clinic may be found in *Annual Reports*, Forensic Clinic, Toronto, 1958, 1959, 1960, 1961, 1962, 1963, 1964; R. E. Turner, 'The Forensic Clinic, Toronto', *Criminal Law Quarterly*, vol. 2, no. 4 (February 1960); and R. E. Turner *et al.*, 'The Forensic Clinic of the Toronto Psychiatric Hospital', *Canadian Journal of Corrections*, vol. 1, no. 1 (October 1959).

Section 135 (136)	– rape
Section 137	– attempt to commit rape
Section 138 (1)	– sexual intercourse with female under four-teen
(2)	– sexual intercourse with female over four-teen and under sixteen
Section 140	– sexual intercourse with feeble-minded, in-sane, idiot, or imbecile
Section 141	– indecent assault on female
Section 142	– incest
Section 143	– seduction of female between sixteen and eighteen
Section 144	– seduction of an unmarried female person of previously chaste character under promise of marriage
Section 145 (1)	– illicit sexual intercourse with step-daughter, foster daughter, or female ward
(2)	– illicit sexual intercourse with female em-ployee under twenty-one of previously chaste character
Section 146	– seduction of female passengers on vessels
Section 147	– buggery or bestiality
Section 148	– indecent asault on male
Section 149	– acts of gross indecency
Section 155	– parent or guardian procuring a female per-son to have illicit sexual intercourse
Section 156	– owner, occupier, or manager of premises, permitting a female under eighteen to have illicit sexual intercourse with a particular male person or persons on the premises
Section 157	– adultery or sexual immorality in the home of a child, endangering the morals of the child, or rendering the home an unfit place for the child
Section 184 (1)	– procuring
Section 234	– abduction of a female

The following are summary convictions:

| Section 158 | – indecent act |
| Section 164 (1) (c) | – common prostitution or night-walking |

Section 164 (1) (e) – loitering near a school, playground, public park, or bathing-area, by a person who has been convicted of certain sexual offences[39]

Mewett made a plea for 'a somewhat more rational approach to the whole complex matter of sexual acts as crimes in modern society'.[40] He noted that there is really 'not much in the way of sexual activity which a person can definitely do without at least the possibility of running counter to some section or other of the Criminal Code'. Rodgers analysed federal legislation governing sexual behaviour.[41] The *Report* of the Royal Commission on the Criminal Law Relating to Criminal Sexual Psychopaths (the McRuer Commission) reviewed the provisions of the Criminal Code relating to sexual offences and presented criticism of the substantive law and procedure.[42] The report continued on the insufficiency of the law, the disposition of the prisoner, the problem of the sexual offender, treatment of sexual offenders, and release. It reviewed treatment in other countries and the law in New Jersey and California. This report resulted in a significant change in the Criminal Code. By assent of Parliament on July 13, 1961, an Act was passed to amend the Criminal Code, which in part concerned the sections of the Code pertaining to the criminal sexual psychopath. Section 659 of the Code is repealed and paragraph (b) of that section now reads as follows:

'Dangerous sexual offender' means a person who, by his conduct in any sexual matter, has shown a failure to control his sexual impulses, and who is likely to cause injury, pain or other evil to any person, through failure in the future to control his sexual impulses or is likely to commit a further sexual offence, . . .[43]

Section 661 (1) remains the same. It provides that where a person is accused of an offence under Sections 136, 138, 141, 147, 148, or 149, or of an attempt to commit an offence under one of these sections, the court

---

[39]This concerns persons convicted of one of the offences listed in section 661 (1) (a) or (b), namely, rape, carnal knowledge, indecent assault on female, buggery or bestiality, indecent assault on male, or gross indecency.

[40]A. Mewett, 'Sexual Offences in Canada', *Criminal Law Quarterly*, vol. 2, no. 1 (May 1959), p. 21.

[41]R. S. Rodgers, *Sex and Law in Canada*, Ottawa: Policy Press, 1962.

[42]Royal Commission on the Criminal Law Relating to Criminal Sexual Psychopaths (The Honourable J. C. McRuer), *Report*, Ottawa: Queen's Printer, 1958.

[43]The previous wording of this section read as follows: 659 (b) ' "Criminal sexual psychopath" means a person who, by a course of misconduct in sexual matters, has shown a lack of power to control his sexual impulses and who as a result is likely to attack, or otherwise inflict injury, pain or other evil on any person. . . .'

shall, upon application by the Crown, before passing sentence, hear evidence as to whether the accused is a dangerous sexual offender. On the hearing of an application, 'the court shall hear any relevant evidence, and shall hear the evidence of at least two psychiatrists, one of whom shall be nominated by the Attorney General'.[44]

This new Section (661) continues that

> where the court finds that the accused is a dangerous sexual offender it shall, notwithstanding anything in this Act or any other Act of the Parliament of Canada, impose upon the accused a sentence of preventive detention in lieu of any other sentence that might be imposed for the offence of which he was convicted or that was imposed for such offence, or in addition to any sentence that was imposed for such an offence if the sentence has expired.

Section 666 requires

> that where a person is in custody under a sentence of preventive detention, the Minister of Justice shall, at least once in every year, review the condition, history, and circumstances of that person for the purposes of determining whether he should be permitted to be at large on licence, and if so, on what conditions.[45]

One can do no better than quote from the foreword by Gray in Rodgers' book.

> ... the overall impression is that our sex laws are a legal jungle, without much rhyme or reason. The compilation of scientific data on a large scale about sexual deviation is relatively recent. Comparison of data compiled in different jurisdictions shows that some definite generalizations may be drawn. There is no question that the increasing volume of research in this field will yield even more important generalizations in the immediate future. The application of these findings to our criminal law may provide the legislator with the rational basis which is so often lacking in present attempts at a legislative solution.[46]

CLINICAL ASPECTS OF THE SEXUAL OFFENDER

To understand the sexual offender, it is necessary to examine the sexual

---

[44]Previously this read 'on hearing of an application under sub-section (1) the court may hear any evidence that it considers necessary, but shall hear the evidence of at least two psychiatrists, one of whom shall be nominated by the Attorney General'.

[45]This section previously read that 'the Minister of Justice shall, at least once in every three years, review the condition, history, and circumstances ... '.

[46]Rodgers, *op. cit.*, p. 5.

deviate and the aspects of his behaviour that may come into conflict with the law.[47]

Homosexuality is sexual attraction to persons of the same sex. It is the commonest deviation though it does not represent the commonest sexual offender. The homosexual is generally charged under Section 149 of the Criminal Code – gross indecency. This usually applies to males, but lesbians (female homosexuals) may also be charged with acts of gross indecency. This section refers to an act of gross indecency with another person. Some homosexual offenders are charged under Section 148, that is, with indecent assault on a male, or indecent assault on a male with intent to commit buggery. It is beyond the scope of this chapter to give details about homosexuality. There are many excellent references available.[48]

Early research findings concerning the homosexual offender at the Forensic Clinic, Toronto, indicate that the peak ages at which offences occurred appeared to be in the late twenties and the late forties. The acts which led to the charges were mostly masturbation and fellatio.[49] The offences usually took place in the person's car, in a park, or in public washrooms. Most partners were strangers. Most were charged with gross indecency, the remainder with indecent assault, contributing to juvenile delinquency, and indecent exposure. The homosexual offenders showed the lowest number of recidivists when compared with exhibitionists and pedophiles, only four per cent repeating the offence in the follow-up period of three years. (It is noteworthy that three of these repeaters also committed non-sexual offences.)[50]

[47]Sexual deviation is studied in greater detail in A. Ellis and R. Brancale, *The Psychology of Sex Offenders*, Springfield, Illinois: Thomas, 1956; F. S. Caprio and D. R. Brenner, *Sexual Behaviour: Psycho-Legal Aspects*, New York: The Citadel Press, 1961; E. Glover, *The Social and Legal Aspects of Sexual Abnormality*, London: The Institute for the Study and Treatment of Delinquency, 1956; R. E. Turner, 'The Sexual Offender', *The Canadian Psychiatric Association Journal*, vol. 9, no. 6 (November-December 1964).

[48]D. J. West, *Homosexuality*, London: Duckworth, 1955; G. Westwood, *A Minority. A Report on the Life of the Male Homosexual in Great Britain*, Toronto: Longmans, 1960; I. Bieber *et al.*, *Homosexuality*, New York: Basic Books, 1962; A. Leitch, 'Male Homosexuality as a Medico-Legal and Sociological Problem in the United Kingdom', *International Journal of Social Psychiatry*, vol. 5, no. 2 (autumn 1959); D. Curran and D. Parr, 'Homosexuality: An Analysis of 100 Male Cases Seen in Private Practice', *British Medical Journal*, vol. 1 (April 6, 1957); E. Glover, *The Problem of Homosexuality*, London: Institute for the Study and Treatment of Delinquency, 1957; and 'Homosexuality' (Editorial, and 'The Other Side'), *Canadian Medical Association Journal*, vol. 86 (1962).

[49]*Fellatio*: sexual stimulation of the penis by the mouth.

[50]Reported at Forensic Clinic Seminars, September 13, 1960, February 7, 1961, and November 1961, by Dr. J. W. Mohr.

The *exhibitionist* is one who receives sexual arousal and gratification by exposing his genitals, and having them viewed by another individual.[51] Exhibitionism is probably the commonest sexual offence. Offenders are charged under Section 158 of the Code – indecent act (indecent exposure). Of the 54 offenders in a group analysed, 31 exposed exclusively to adults, 17 exclusively to children, and 6 to both adult women and female children.[52] The exhibitionistic act is often committed in such a way that detection and arrest are easy. The majority of exhibitionists are in their twenties. It is notable that the age of onset of this symptom shows two peaks, in the mid-teens and the mid-twenties. Exhibitionists over the age of thirty-five more commonly have associated problems of alcoholism, other deviations, or organic deterioration. The act ranges from the showing of the penis, with or without an erection, to open masturbation, and is occasionally accompanied by obscene language. In some offenders, the urge appears to come on suddenly and compulsively; in others it increases gradually until it overcomes inhibitions. It is extremely seldom that there is any attempt to establish closer sexual contact with the victim. All the exhibitionist seems to want is a reaction by the viewer to the sight offered. The offence is committed most commonly from a private vehicle, on the street, in a public building, or through the window of a store or house. It is important for treatment considerations to ascertain to whom the person exposes, whether to adult women or female children. The victim is usually a stranger. Pedophilic urges are present in a number of those who expose to children. In the findings of the Forensic Clinic, Toronto, exhibitionists showed the highest number of recidivists (20 per cent). In those treated, recidivism appeared to be much higher among exhibitionists who exposed exclusively to children than among those who exposed exclusively to adult women. Those who exposed to both adult women and children showed an even higher recidivism rate.

The *voyeurist* is the 'peeping tom'. Voyeurism is manifested by efforts to see someone undressed, to see a person's genitals, or to observe a couple in the act of intercourse. Offenders often can be charged under trespassing or vagrancy sections. Voyeurism may be closely associated with exhibitionism. Many exhibitionists have voyeuristic tendencies and some voyeurs have exhibitionistic thoughts.

The *pedophile* is one who is sexually attracted to children, that is to

---

[51]*See also* N. K. Rickles, 'Exhibitionism', *Journal of Social Therapy*, vol. 1 (1955); and F. H. Taylor, 'Observations on Some Cases of Exhibitionism', *Journal of Mental Science*, vol. 93, no. 392 (1947).

[52]J. W. Mohr, R. E. Turner, and M. B. Jerry, *Pedophilia and Exhibitionism, A Handbook*, Toronto: University of Toronto Press, 1964.

those who have not reached or completed puberty. A group of 55 has been studied, consisting of 27 who were involved with female children, 23 with boys, and 5 with both. Twenty-five per cent of the pedophiles were drunk or to some extent affected by alcohol when they committed their offence. Heterosexuals made up more of this 25 per cent than did homosexuals. The homosexual pedophile showed the greatest rate of recidivism; the heterosexual the lowest. There were three age-peaks, in the late teens, in the late thirties, and in the late fifties. The act usually involved fondling the victim, sometimes included a mouth-genital contact, and sometimes included exposing in a pedophilic context. Most heterosexual pedophile victims were in the age-group of eight to eleven years and most homosexual pedophile victims were twelve to fifteen years of age. Of 17 heterosexual pedophiles treated in an out-patient setting, only one repeated the offence; of 15 homosexual pedophiles similarly treated, three repeated.[53]

Pedophiles are charged with contributing to juvenile delinquency (Section 33 of the Juvenile Delinquents Act) and indecent assault.

The heterosexual pedophile generally involves himself with a girl whom he knows and to whom he may be related, and who resides near his own home. The homosexual pedophile is less likely to be acquainted with his victim; and even if he does know him, the boy is not likely to be from his own neighbourhood.

The other sexual deviations are as follows:

1. *Sadism* is sexual arousal and gratification by thought of, observation of, or infliction of cruelty.
2. *Masochism* is sexual arousal and gratification by the infliction of cruelty, pain, or humiliation upon the deviate himself.
3. *Transvestism* (or cross-dressing) is the deviation in which a person dresses in the clothing of the opposite sex for sexual gratification.[54] Charges of theft can often be laid.
4. *Fetishism* is the deviation in which a person makes use of some body part, or some article of clothing of the opposite sex, directing the sexual drive towards that object. As in transvestism, charges of theft are often laid.
5. *Bestiality* is sexual involvement with animals. This is covered in Section 147 of the Code.

---

[53]J. W. Mohr, 'Pedophilia', *Canadian Psychiatric Association Journal*, vol. 7, no. 5, October 1962.

[54]*See* N. Lukianowicz, 'Survey of Various Aspects of Transvestism in the Light of Our Present Knowledge', *Journal of Nervous and Mental Diseases*, vol. 128, no. 36 (January 1959); and J. B. Randell, 'Transvestism and Trans-sexualism', *British Medical Journal*, vol. 2 (December 26, 1959).

Sexual deviation may be associated with mental deficiency, psychopathy, psychosis, psychoneurosis, epilepsy, alcoholism, organic brain disease, or other character disorders.

Sexual offenders cannot be assessed as a homogeneous group of offenders.[55] Generally speaking, they do not progress from minor to major sex crimes, although a very small percentage may commit both. A measurable proportion are likely to be persistent in their particular offences, and they do not change from one type of offence to another. Frequently they constitute more of a nuisance than a danger.

It should be noted that a 'child victim' is not always an unwilling partner. The juvenile sometimes participates willingly in the sexual activity, although in law the responsibility rests with the adult partner. The effect on the child victims or partners varies considerably from case to case, depending on the child's psychological make-up, the manner in which the case is dealt with by parents, police, and others concerned, and whether or not it is presented in court. Psychological harm to the child is more likely determined by the reaction of others around him than by the act itself, unless he is physically harmed.[56]

Two articles published in 1960, one by D. J. Atcheson[57] and one by D. T. Maclay,[58] are particularly useful references in respect of juvenile sexual offenders.

TREATMENT

One can no more write in a general way about the treatment of the sexual offender than one can so write of the sexual offender himself. The considerations involved may be summed up by asking: What types of sexual offenders should be offered psychiatric treatment and where? Which sexual offenders should be offered treatment as part of the rehabilitation program? Should the suggested treatment be undertaken in a psychiatric out-patient clinic with or without probation, in a mental hospital, or in one of the types of custodial institution? What special legal procedures are required, particularly in order to protect the public from the few

[55]M. S. Guttmacher and H. Weihofen, *Psychiatry and the Law*, New York: Norton, 1952.
[56]This subject is treated more thoroughly in E. R. Rogers and J. Weiss, *California Sexual Deviation Research: Study of Sex Crimes Against Children* (Darwin M.), Part 2, January 1953; and 'Sexual Assault on Children', by Our Legal Correspondent, with Editorial, *British Medical Journal*, vol. 2 (December 16, 1961).
[57]D. J. Atcheson, 'Social Aspects of Sexual Behaviour', *Criminal Law Quarterly*, vol. 3, no. 4 (February 1961).
[58]D. T. Maclay, 'Boys Who Commit Sexual Misdemeanours', *British Medical Journal*, vol. 1 (January 16, 1960).

sexual offenders who are dangerous? Finally, should treatment continue on parole or final release for those who have had to be incarcerated? What of continuing after-care when formal treatment has been completed?[59]

The report of the McRuer commission offers some answers to these questions in its chapter on treatment.[60] It reviews legislation in several countries as well as pointing out the deficiencies and difficulties of the situation in Canada.

As indicated in the next section much detailed research is necessary before definite statements can be made about treatment of each type and sub-type of sexual offender. Treatment has a poor chance of success if the offender's motivation is weak or non-existent, but even this factor varies from one case to another.

Treatment consists of:

1. Assisting the offender-patient to acquire control over his deviant behaviour so that his law-breaking activities will cease.
2. Modifying the underlying psychopathology, thus permitting the person to become better adjusted to the restraints and demands of living in a community.
3. Readjusting his personality problems so that he can live in better harmony with himself, his family, and his community.[61]

It is not too optimistic to believe that many sexual offenders can be cured. It has become clearer that various forms of individual psychotherapy can be of considerable use. At present, however, such methods are practicable only at the out-patient psychiatric clinics where they are being developed and exercised. They are available, therefore, only to offenders who are able to remain in the community. Such treatment can be long and arduous, requiring skilled personnel. Part-time professional persons in institutions cannot hope to provide psychotherapy effectively and economically. Superficial and supportive psychotherapy and casework, provided by workers such as probation officers, psychiatric social workers, and psychologists, can be useful in assisting disturbed offenders and those in institutions and, perhaps, in preparing the latter for further and more intensive treatment on release. Group therapy has become a

---

[59]For further consideration of these questions, see P. D. Scott, 'Assessing the Offender for the Court', *British Journal of Criminology*, vol. 1, no. 2 (October 1960), and 'Psychiatric Reports for Magistrates' Courts', *British Journal of Delinquency*, vol. 4, no. 2 (October 1953); and R. E. Turner, 'Psychiatric Considerations for Remand and Diagnostic Centres', *Canadian Journal of Corrections*, vol. 6, no. 4 (October 1964).

[60]*Op. cit.*, p. 49.

[61]M. Schmideberg and R. H. Orr, 'Psychiatric Treatment of Offenders', *Mental Hygiene*, vol. 43, no. 3 (July 1959).

promising method of psychotherapy. It is believed that some offenders actually do better with group treatment, and of course it is a considerable saving of time to be able to treat a number of persons simultaneously.[62]

Another promising method is reciprocal inhibition therapy.[63] Aversion therapy can be useful.[64] In these procedures, the patient is taught to think of pleasant or unpleasant feelings whenever he has impulses to carry out an offending act. This combination helps him to reduce the strength of the impulses, and bring about greater control.

Drugs in the form of tranquilizers, sedatives, and anti-depressants are useful under highly controlled conditions. Hormonal medication has not shown impressive results. Some merits have been claimed for castration, but apart from the question of effectiveness, castration is a controversial subject in English-speaking countries.[65]

Knowledge in the field of treatment of the sexual offender is not yet far advanced, but progress is being made. Even in the present state of treatment, however, the low rates of recidivism among those who have been treated indicate that treatment should be considered in all but the seriously disturbed and dangerous sexual offenders.[66] Pessimism is simply not warranted.

[62]Group therapy is treated more thoroughly in the following publications: R. E. Turner, 'Group Treatment of Sexual Deviations', *Canadian Journal of Corrections*, vol. 3, no. 4 (October 1961); V. Hartman, 'Some Observations of Group Psychotherapy with Paedophiles', *Canadian Journal of Corrections*, vol. 3, no. 4 (October 1961); and V. Hartman, 'Group Psychotherapy with Pedophiles', *Criminal Law Quarterly*, vol. 7, no. 4 (February 1965).

[63]*See* I. K. Bond and H. C. Hutchison, 'Application of Reciprocal Inhibition Therapy to Exhibitionism', *Canadian Medical Association Journal*, vol. 83, no. 1 (July 2, 1960); and S. Rachman, 'Sexual Disorders and Behaviour Therapy', *American Journal of Psychiatry*, vol. 118, no. 3 (September 1961).

[64]*See* M. J. Raymond, 'Case of Fetishism Treated by Aversion Therapy', *British Medical Journal*, vol. 2 (October 13, 1956); B. James, 'Case of Homosexuality Treated by Aversion Therapy', *British Medical Journal*, vol. 1 (March 17, 1962); J. R. Ball and J. J. Armstrong, 'The Use of L.S.D. 25 in the Treatment of Sexual Perversions', *Canadian Psychiatric Association Journal*, vol. 6, no. 4 (August 1961).

[65]For those interested in the merits of castration, useful reference can be found in Report of the Royal Commission on the Criminal Law Relating to Criminal Sexual Psychopaths, *op. cit.*; 'Castration of Sex Offenders – Editorial', *British Medical Journal*, vol. 1 (April 9, 1955); J. Bremer, *Asexualization*, New York: Macmillan, 1959; and P. W. Tappan, 'Treatment of the Sex Offender in Denmark', *American Journal of Psychiatry*, vol. 108, no. 4 (October 1951).

[66]Further information may be found in Mohr, Turner, and Jerry, *op. cit.*; Mohr, 'Pedophilia', *op. cit.*; and R. E. Turner, 'Treatment of the Sex Offender', *Criminal Law Quarterly*, vol. 3, no. 4 (February 1961).

RESEARCH

The need for research is the theme of this chapter on special problem groups, as well as of the entire book.[67] Without detailed and extensive research in the matters pertaining to corrections, most ideas are, at best, respectable only in a theoretical sense.

The report of the McRuer commission states that there is a great necessity for concentration on ways and means of clinical study and experiment to arrest the development of sexual deviation, and that the responsibility for this extends far beyond the jurisdiction of the courts, and even of the legislative bodies. It recommends that all known effective measures be taken to effect such an arrest. It pleads for the organized scientific study of offenders committed to serve indeterminate sentences and for the extension of such a study to all sexual offenders serving sentences in penitentiaries. It recommends that diagnostic centres be established in conjunction with special institutional treatment under the direction and auspices of universities, and that these centres should operate in a close relationship with the courts. The report states that there is an urgent need in Canada for research in all aspects of sexual deviation, with a view to the development of means of correction and prevention. It recommends that the government of Canada make provisions for special grants to the universities, both for developing special research schemes to determine the causes of sexual abnormality and for improving the methods of treatment. It suggests that special clinics be set up, in co-operation with the courts and the penal institutions, to which a person found guilty of any sexual offence may be required to report for study and treatment.

Until these recommendations are implemented, it is not likely that the reformation of sexual offenders will be successfully effected on a large scale.

Summary

In this chapter we have briefly considered three problems of illness with related criminal and other legal implications. We have briefly described some of their clinical aspects and some aspects of treatment.

Treatment of a patient ordinarily requires that he be in hospital, or

[67]More detailed comments on the need for research may be found in J. W. Mohr, 'The Contribution of Research to the Selection of Appropriate Alternatives for the Sexual Offender', *Criminal Law Quarterly*, vol. 4, no. 3 (January 1962); 'Potentialities for Research in a Remand and Diagnostic Centre', *Canadian Journal of Corrections*, vol. 6, no. 4 (October 1964).

attend an out-patient clinic or a doctor's office. A person who has broken the law, however, may be placed in a custodial institution or only permitted to be at large under some form of parole or probation. The problem in dealing with the sick person who commits a criminal act, or whose illness in itself is considered an offence against society, is in ensuring that although legal sanctions are applied when necessary for society, maximum opportunity for recovery is allowed at the same time. Sometimes we fail to recognize that even a therapeutically oriented prison may not be as useful as a custodial hospital. The institution to which the offender is sent must maintain a high standard of careful clinical investigation and apply exemplary methods of therapy involving medical, psychiatric, social, and psychological disciplines. There must be adequate facility for therapeutic follow-up; it is equally important, though often disregarded, that there be opportunity for research into every aspect of the illness under consideration.

Further Reading

FRIEDMAN, P. 'Sexual Deviations', *American Handbook of Psychiatry*. New York: Basic Books, 1959, Chapter 29, p. 589 ff.

GUTTMACHER, M. S. *Sex Offences*. New York: Norton, 1951.

MARGETTS, E. L. 'Sex Deviations', *McGill Medical Journal*, vol. 19, no. 49 (February 1960).

MOHR, J. W., R. E. Turner, and M. B. Jerry. *Pedophilia and Exhibitionism: A Handbook*. Toronto: University of Toronto Press, 1964.

PACHT, A. R., *et al.* 'Diagnosis and Treatment of the Sexual Offender: a Nine Year Study', *American Journal of Psychiatry*, vol. 118, no. 9 (March 1962).

SCOTT, P. D. 'The Treatment of Sex Perversions', *Maudsley Bequest Lecture*, London, February 9, 1959.

THOMSON, P. G. 'Sexual Deviation', *Canadian Medical Association Journal*, vol. 80 (March 1, 1959).

UNITED STATES. *Federal Probation* (a journal of correctional philosophy and practice, published monthly by the Administrative Office of the United States Courts in co-operation with the Bureau of Prisons of the Department of Justice, Washington, D.C.), September 1950.

17

Penal Reform and Corrections

A. M. KIRKPATRICK

When prisoners were killed, transported to the penal colonies, or sent to the galleys there was no need for a correctional system. It was necessary only to maintain fortress-like jails in which they could be held while awaiting trial and either the execution of the sentence or, for the more fortunate, release. Debtors and political prisoners were an exception in that many of them spent weary years in jail seeking to discharge their financial obligations or awaiting the royal pleasure.

It was in these punitive bastilles than John Howard and Elizabeth Fry began their humanitarian work. Because of his personal experience as a French prisoner of war in the prison hulks in the harbour of Brest, Howard had become concerned about the lot of civil prisoners. He laid the foundation of penitentiary science with his broad survey of British prisons, *The State of the Prisons in England and Wales,* published in two volumes in 1777.

Jeremy Bentham paved the way for a penological approach in his *Rationale of Punishment* (1775). 'Montesquieu perceived the necessity of a proportion between offences and punishments. Beccaria insists upon its importance. But they rather recommend than explain it; they do not tell in what that proportion consists. Let us endeavour to supply this defect, and to give the principal rules of this moral arithmetic.'[1] Thus Bentham rephrased the ideas expressed by Montesquieu in his *Lettres Persanes* (Persian Letters, 1721), and Beccaria in his *Dei Delitti e delle Pene* (On Crimes and Punishments, 1764) into his 'criminal prophylaxis'. This depicted the prevention of crime as a balance between those measures designed to direct the individual's pattern of living into socially

[1] J. Bentham, *The Theory of Legislation* (edited by C. K. Ogden), London: Routledge and Kegan Paul Ltd., 1950, p. 324.

accepted ways and those broad social programs designed through law to restrain the development of criminal behaviour and activity. His principle of relating specific punishments to various orders of offences has been described as a 'tariff system of sentencing'; but more important are his utilitarian concepts of punishment as related to the social good. At the beginning of the nineteenth century, Sir Samuel Romilly's public pressure for the revision of the criminal law began to link juristic thinking to penal experience and practice. Public interest, in the study of human society and man as its basic component, received continuing stimulus through the writings of Darwin, Comte, and Spencer.

John Howard in his *State of the Prisons* describes the early beginnings of detention prisons at San Michele in Rome and La Casa di Corregione in Milan. But the Quakers of England and America were in the forefront of this movement and gave it practical effect by the introduction of custodial prisons, the first of which was the adaptation of the Walnut Street Jail in Philadelphia in 1790. These prisons came as a reform against the harshness of contemporary punishment. Their management was based on the belief that solitary and silent confinement, solitary work, reflection, and the reading of the Bible would induce penitence.

But the custodial prison was still intended to be a deterrent and it spread throughout the world in different forms. Auburn Prison in New York State (1821) adopted congregate work, recreation, and dining, but endeavoured to prevent communication by the 'rule of silence'. The assumption was retained that the rougher the treatment, the greater the deterrence. Thus the inhumanities of former days persisted, only in different form, in the early era of prisons and penology.

It was in Italy that the scientific study of criminology began. The leader was Francesco Carrara, who, in 1873, 'regarded criminal law as a changing social institution and crime as a product of individual disposition and environmental forces'.[2] As the leader of the 'positivist' school of thought and an eminent criminal lawyer, he challenged the legal profession: 'Former lawyers bade men study justice, but Lombroso bade justice study man.'[3] Lombroso, who died in 1909, laid stress on knowing the individual to understand his offence and the necessary correction.

The French School also made an important contribution. Raymond Saleilles in his book *L'Individualisation de la Peine* (Individualization of Punishment, 1898) discussed the adaptation of penalties not only to the gravity of the offence but to the personality of the offender. Gabriel

[2]Leon Radzinowicz, *In Search of Criminology*, London: Heinemann Books, 1961, p. 3.
[3]*Ibid.* p. 168.

Tarde developed the concept that the individual should be held responsible before the courts for his violations of the law. His objective in formulating this legalistic argument was to make possible the satisfactory working of the Criminal Code, which required some such assumption underlying judgment and sentencing. Tarde was less concerned about the philosophical argument of free will or determinism, which also sought to throw light on the nature of responsibility.

The belief was widely held in the early nineteenth century that pain, suffering, deprivation, strict discipline, and the performance of useless and unpleasant tasks would not only deter but also bring about repentance, remorse, and reformation. From this point of view such treatment was not really vindictive or cruel but utilitarian and, as such, humanitarian in its purpose and in its intended result.

Fear and the law-enforcement traditions of deterrence and custody ruled the prisons. But the idea that something more was needed slowly gained acceptance throughout the nineteenth century. Criminologists, penologists, jurists, politicians, and the common man began to see, from different points of view, that the aim should be correction. It became self-evident that it is useless to send men away from society to learn how to live in society; they will learn only how to live in a prison.

When prisoners are held in custody, instead of being killed or transported, the problem of their ultimate disposal arises. They must eventually be released back to the community. The public began to realize that prisons are not only places to which we consign law-breakers; they are also places whence they return to the community.

It became clear that changing the attitudes of the law-breaker and creating in him positive motivations for social living should be the new goal of the penal system. Such a process would cost less, would be more humane, and would protect the public better than a system under which prisoners merely 'did time'.

This correctional idea, which gained stature in the early years of our century, found sustenance in the developments in the social and medical sciences and in the contemporary understanding of human nature and of the nature of society itself. It owed much to the studies carried out by criminologists, to the experience and findings of progressive penologists engaged in the prison service, and also to the representations made to government bodies by the prisoners' aid societies and by religious groups in reports and public hearings. Developments in the Commonwealth countries show the influence of the series of British 'Blue Books' representing the great variety of statements by royal commissions and select and departmental committees that, from the middle of the eighteenth century on, examined all aspects of penal policy and practice, and sought to link them with developments in criminal justice. The thoroughness and integrity of these public investigations are unsurpassed.

Canada has had several such inquiries, the best known of which were made by the Archambault Commission in 1938 and the Fauteux Committee in 1956. There have been various provincial inquiries, usually of a more specific and limited nature.

In the United States around the turn of the present century, there was, as there had been a hundred years previously, a surge of penal ideas and experiments; but they were very different from the uninspiring and rigid ideas of solitary confinement of the previous century. New leads had come from, among others, Alexander Maconochie in Norfolk Island, Australia. In 1840 he developed a 'task sentence' rather than a 'time sentence'. This was really the beginning of the indeterminate sentence: 'When a man keeps the key of his own prison, he is soon persuaded to fit it to the lock.' Walter Crofton, in Ireland, developed in 1835 a mark system of five classes, the last of which led to conditional release in the community. The reformatory idea had been initiated in 1876 at Elmira in New York State and shortly after, around the turn of the century, the juvenile court and the beginnings of the probation system came into being.

These new services showed a radical change from the traditional concept of custodial punishment and gave vent to a social conscience newly awakened to the stigma of penal servitude and its apparent ineffectiveness. The process of penal reform had thus preceded the findings of criminologists, illustrating that these do not always proceed at the same pace and that the former may frequently anticipate the latter, as an expression of changed social values, humanitarianism, and practical experience linked to utilitarian policies and practices.

Public and political thinking had so far progressed in England in 1944 that Mr. Herbert Morrison, the Home Secretary, said on the question of penal reform:

> The first principle . . . is to keep as many offenders as possible out of prison. In the 1860s it was laid down in plain terms that the sole object of imprisonment was punitive deterrence with the emphasis on the punitive. Just that. And so for a generation we had the most strictly deterrent penal system ever devised. The experiment had to be made at some time. The belief in the efficiency of severe punishment is always cropping up and without the devastating failure of this experiment we might never have known better. The failure was so complete that a departure to fresh principles became essential.[4]

[4]From a speech made on March 28, 1944, on Penal Reform.

468

As indicated earlier, there was opposition to the dictum of deterrence of 1860, but it expressed the official view of the prison commissioner of the day.

Progressive correctional administrators and treatment staffs have been employed and funds provided for developing progressive programs, for retraining and educating staff members, and for modern specialized institutions. But all these developments are still within the custodial framework. There has been no basic change in the warrant of committal given to the prison warden that he hold the offender in secure custody till the expiration of his sentence. He is not ordered to treat him; he is not ordered to retrain him; he is ordered simply to hold him. But progressive administrations have sought by policy and instruction to modify the exclusive function of custody.

Long-needed change is now invigorating the penal institutions across Canada. Except in some provincial systems, these institutions have in past years been of maximum or near maximum security, regardless of the offence, penal record, security risk, or personality-type of the inmates. There has been a lack of diversity and flexibility, not only in security but also in programs of individualized treatment and training.

Encouraging efforts have been made to change imprisonment from an experience that has often been a static, and in some cases a negative, process to a more positive program with a dynamic aimed at personality change and the acquisition of social, vocational, and educational skills.

It now appears to be accepted philosophically, though not in actual practice, that to build more maximum-security, 'escape-proof' institutions is unnecessary, except in the case of certain specialized types. We still note efforts to perpetuate a concept of imprisonment that is unrelated to any true correctional philosophy and causes grievously heavy drains on the public purse – and therefore on the individual taxpayer. It remains to be truly accepted that more pertinent and positive values may be achieved, both humane and economic, by the application of more money to correctional personnel and services, and less to custodial staff, buildings, and routines, with the consequent development of a program that will be devoted to treatment of the offender.

Treatment is a word frequently used and abused, but rarely defined. According to whether there is an inherent or congenital deficiency, or whether some acquired impairment of function exists, the objective of treatment should be either remedial or restorative. In the correctional field, treatment is the variety of processes used within a hospitable milieu to create or restore, to the greatest possible degree, the ability of the individual to establish desirable goals and to perceive not only his individual

469

role but also his social responsibility to live acceptably and productively in his community, thus enabling him to function at his best capacity in his interpersonal and community relationships.

Correctional treatment deals only with identified law-breakers. To bring about their correction, it is necessary to deal with difficult problems both of motivation and causation. The forces for good and evil seem to battle constantly not only in the offender but in every human being. The Chinese expressed the conflicting forces of darkness and light as the *Yin* and *Yang*. Dynamic psychology views the inner turmoil as a conflict between 'libido' and 'super-ego', with the 'ego' as mediator and integrator. Regardless of nomenclature, each individual seems to be a mixture of attitudes, good and evil, any of which may possess his behaviour at any particular time and, if evil, produce antisocial or criminal results.

It becomes of paramount importance to understand the individual if treatment is to take place. Many scientific tests have been developed to measure intelligence, aptitudes, various degrees of tolerance, and general stability of personality; but it has proved most difficult to make a satisfactory appraisal of basic motivations and attitudes and a prognosis of future conduct, both of which are so essential in determining sentence, treatment, and eventual parole.

With the development of the probation service has come the pre-sentence report which provides a social history of the offender, based on knowledge of his occupation, avocations, associates, and family. This personality profile is important but may be subjective, depending on the points of view and attitudes of those who provide the information, and may lead to faulty interpretation of the data. Though varying techniques may be used, those who deal with the offender are constantly faced with the problem of attempting to assess the inner motivations and attitudes of those they wish to help.

Research into the causation and prevention of crime and delinquency is confronted by a complex range of problems, since the important and determining factors appear to reside in the permutations and combinations of both hereditary and environmental processes. These processes in turn are bound into the meanings that experiences have for each personality and are subject to the tension, stress, and strain that are unique to the development of each individual. Crime and delinquency must, therefore, be viewed in the context of the society in which they occur. Social morbidity reflects its community. Both the immediate neighbourhood and the broad society itself are prerequisites to the individual's illegal reactive behaviour which we call delinquency or crime.

It is clear that research concerning the offender cannot be expected to result in prescriptions for his treatment that, if placed on a card and run through the computer, would provide the requisite formula for a restored human being. Much of any success depends not merely on research, but also on the sound training of the practitioner or therapist and the personal investment made by him. This must be reinforced by empathy on his part, and he must be governed by intuitive appraisal, based on experience, of the way the offender presents himself and the material he produces during the interview. The offender himself provides the most effective clues to his own problems and treatment.

In the correctional field it is necessary to make choices, but not at random or by hunch. Decisions have to be made responsibly, with intelligence, humaneness, and genuine humility, because of and despite the lack of guidance from precise and definitive research about the individual or about the correctional services.

We are still confronted not only with the question of the physical, mental, and social attributes of individual criminals, but also with that of the categories or classifications into which we may place such apparently heterogeneous individuals for purposes of study and treatment. In Canada there has been no change in the definitive juridical or legislative determination that the criminal law should be based on the doctrine of free will and individual responsibility. Should this be qualified by the concepts of dynamic psychology, which reveal the irrational nature of the motivation for much of human behaviour?

While the sentence is intended to have effect as a deterrent, as a moral lesson, and as a means of maintaining public confidence in the legal order, should it recognize only that a penal offence has been committed? Should the punishment be meted out only in relation to the gravity of the specific offence, or should it be related also to the personality and recidivistic potential of each offender? In the latter case, how can the prognostication of recidivism be made with sufficient accuracy to serve as a guide to sentencing, treatment, and parole? Where are the clinical services to be found to implement such a philosophy? How effective, in themselves, are the processes of probation, institutional treatment, and parole, and with what groupings of offenders have these processes the greatest potential as curative and protective measures? How should the jail, reformatory, and penitentiary systems be integrated and diversified for maximum treatment potential? How should the offender's re-establishment into society be best planned to eradicate the penal stigma and to prevent recidivism?

The fundamental problems in need of research relate to causation, or why people commit offences, to the methods by which they can be prevented from offending, and to the processes of retraining or treatment by

471

which their behaviour may be changed to avoid repetition of criminal activity.

Basic to a consideration of these problems is the development of sound statistical data to enable all the relevant factors to be measured and assessed in their interrelationships.. The Dominion Bureau of Statistics has recently revised its methods of tabulation and presentation. Recognizing that data are no more valid than their source, the Bureau has also made a major revision of its methods of collecting and reporting criminal offences. It is anticipated that historical tables will soon be made available and will give not only absolute figures but also rates related to the relevant age-populations.

The importance of this development and its continued refinement should not be underestimated. At present it is impossible to determine how many *different* persons commit offences in a given year, since a tabulation of individual offenders is made only for indictable offences. The number of different citizens who have at any time been in a penal institution is not known, and so we have no satisfactory basis for the calculation of a true recidivist rate. It is still impossible to determine with accuracy the number of different persons who go to penal institutions in a year.

From this it can be seen that present recidivist rates are most inaccurate yardsticks with which to measure the success or failure of the correctional programs. They have in fact tended to divert attention from the core of the problem, which lies in the actual treatment process. Is there anything specific in probation, institutional treatment, or parole that enables the offender to change or is there something inherent in these processes as a whole? Is the change in the individual due really to the shock and exposure of arrest, conviction, and sentencing, rather than to the treatment service that then ensues? Is it correct to judge whether a program has been a success or a failure on the basis of the reconviction rates of the participants? Is it accurate to compare the recidivist rates of the probation, institutional, and parole services? To what extent are variations in rates due to the selective processes that apply in differentiating the types of offenders who are placed within the scope of these varying methodologies? Is it valid to compare statistics from different jurisdictions without making appropriate allowance for the differences in law, sentencing practices, types of treatment services available, administrative organization, and collection and presentation of data?

British statistics are often compared with their Canadian counterparts and most improperly, in most cases, because of the differences between them. The Home Office provides one integrated correctional service in Britain, in which the number of different offenders is recorded. Canada has a federal and ten provincial correctional services with another being developed for the Yukon and the Northwest Territories. These various correctional services are not federally and provincially integrated, and often not integrated even within their own jurisdictions.

Treatment obviously cannot flourish within a static concept or milieu; but much may become possible through the development of a dynamic relationship between the offender and all the people with whom he comes in contact. His immediate environment, with the significant controls and modifications it exerts on his conduct, provides the offender with either a receptive or rejective milieu for such social re-education.

It is still true that the very nature of the setting in prisons of the maximum- and medium-security type militates against treatment as a dynamic process in which the milieu is part of the restorative or remedial process. To construct any building means to create conditions in which people will necessarily live in one way rather than another. Of great significance then are the criteria to be followed in the design, construction, and even in the location of these institutions. The need is for small institutions, differentiated as to program and the nature of custody, less permanent and massive in structure, and located close to the major urban centres, which not only provide the majority of prison populations but present greater opportunities and facilities for program both for inmates and staff.

In our major institutions there is a line drawn between the inmate group and the administration. While there is a marginal 'no man's land' of debatable co-operation, an emotional and psychological barrier exists between the custodians and those in custody. The new inmate may withdraw psychologically and isolate himself. He may co-operate with the administration at the risk of losing face with the inmate population and being considered a 'stool pigeon', with resulting silent or punitive treatment. He may and usually does choose to identify himself with the inmate population, this seeming to be the wisest and most practical solution. Experienced institutional personnel feel that these barriers increase the difficulties of developing effective treatment in the prisons as they are at present operated and organized.

The prison environment has its own norms and its own code of ethics, largely developed from the criminal backgrounds of the majority of those incarcerated. All prisons are fundamentally the same in the characteristic cultural attributes they maintain, but each is essentially different in the way in which these attributes are expressed in the inmate group. Among these ways are attitudes of deceit in relation to authority, suspicion of those who would help, and hostility to those outside the inmate group.

473

There is exposure to asocial and antisocial behaviour and, with normal sexual outlet denied, there is often aberrant sexual behaviour. Most inmates reject the latter; but many accept and perpetuate this heritage of criminal tradition.

Summing up the prison paradox, James V. Bennett, Director of the United States Bureau of Prisons, says:

> But even our modern system is proceeding on a rather uncertain course because its administration is necessarily a series of compromises. On the one hand, the prisons are expected to punish; on the other, they are supposed to reform. They are expected to discipline rigorously at the same time that they teach self-reliance. They are built to be operated like vast impersonal machines, yet they are expected to fit men to live normal community lives. They operate in accordance with a fixed autocratic routine, yet they are expected to develop individual initiative. All too frequently, restrictive laws force prisoners into idleness despite the fact that one of their primary objectives is to teach men how to earn an honest living. They refuse the prisoner a voice in self-government, but they expect him to become a thinking citizen in a democratic society.[5]

Fortunately, Canada has experienced an active development in probation as an alternative to imprisonment and in parole, as a selective device for terminal community treatment, in lieu of continued imprisonment till expiry of sentence. This development constitutes a recognition of the weaknesses of the prison system and a realization that in selected cases the protection of society is as adequately ensured by individualized treatment of the offender in the community.

While the purposes, methods, and techniques of probation and parole are similar, the demands and controls vary since a significant difference arises because of the time-interval that imprisonment imposes in the case of parole. Both follow conviction and both work towards the re-establishment of the offender, but parole follows a period of incarceration that may have affected the individual's personality significantly, depending on his capacity to adjust to it. Changes may have been produced in the imprisoned offender that will differentiate the problems of the parole supervisor from those of the probation officer.

The parolee usually presents significant problems arising from his removal from his family and society, and the loss of his job and his freedom. He has experienced a period of social isolation and rejection, during which his imagination has revised his pre-prison experiences. Often, as shown by cell pictures and prison writing, there is an idealization of his relatives and former associates. This is based on static recollection; in

[5]*Federal Prisons*, Washington: United States Department of Justice, 1948. p. 3.

fact, both he and the world outside are changing, usually in different ways. Obviously, the longer he stays in prison the greater the disparity between actuality and mental image.

Then, too, among family and friends there is often an idealization of the offender as they last saw him. When the prisoner returns, each may find the other different from what had been imagined; they may indeed have become strangers. Thus there is a very serious problem of interpreting these idealizations in the pre-release work with prisoners in the prisons, and with their intimates in the community, in order to lay the groundwork for the emotional impact of the actual reunion.

These problems usually do not arise with the probationer, who is normally in custody for only a short time before trial, and then only if bail is not allowed. His exposure has been to a police lock-up or a jail, and during this time, in many cases, he has been in a condition of emotional upheaval and shock relating to his arrest and the exposure of his alleged offence. The court, by putting him on probation, indicated that he merits trust; this is the type of stimulus likely to encourage him and produce eagerness to 'make good' and prove himself worthy of such trust. In addition he has been selected because he is likely to succeed under probation supervision. Most probationers accept supervision as a fortunate alternative to imprisonment.

Though parole is not a legal right, the inmate usually feels that if he achieves certain standards, behaves himself in prison, and attempts to better himself, he will be granted parole as a reward, unless his record is bad. He realizes that he was not trusted by the court nor considered suitable for probation. Hence, his attitude is not likely to be as positive about the court as that of a probationer. He may leave prison on parole with the conviction that he has earned his release and that he is, therefore, under less obligation to authority; and so he may resist the efforts of his parole supervisor.

Because of these distinctions, those working with probationers and parolees can expect a difference in their attitudes. While the difference may appear to be basically a psychological one, it has sub-cultural aspects, since the parolee has been exposed to the inmate culture of the prison community where there has been general acceptance and adherence to the 'code' of the underworld with its evasion, manipulation, and opposition to authority. The parolee is emotionally scarred in a way that marks him as significantly different in respect of the type of service he will require, and in respect of his probable expectations and the demands he will make upon his supervisory officer at varying stages of the relationship, as well as those which the supervisor will make upon him.

It is not trite to suggest that the point of arrest by the police should, in fact, mark the beginning of the criminal offender's rehabilitation. His treatment in the police lock-up, the way in which statements are taken, the manner in which evidence is presented, the sentencing process, and the eventual disposition of the case all have an important bearing on the attitudes to social authority that will be evidenced in any program to re-establish him. Every effort should be made by the police to allay and, if possible, reduce the hostility to authority that so many offenders exhibit in indirect as well as direct action.

It is probably nonetheless true to suggest that the sentencing process should mark the beginning of the formal corrective process. It has long been a prerogative of the Bench not only to determine guilt or innocence but also to mete out the sentence. In past generations this latter function was performed with primary reference to the nature of the crime, the community's attitude, and the sentence prescribed by law. Historically, this method has resulted in each court's evolving its own scale of norms, with the consequence of different sentences in different courts in different jurisdictions. Wide variations of punishment have given substance to the belief of the offender that, no matter how carefully his sentence is weighed by the individual magistrate, the end result is derived from a capricious sentencing process.

Sentencing should take into account the needs of the offender in addition to the factors mentioned above. The consequence would be an individualization of sentencing that would be based on treatment considerations and designed to produce a socially and economically productive citizen rather than the recidivist that so frequently results. In this context, sentencing should attempt to reconcile the rights of society and the needs of the offender in his reintegration in society. Such a sentencing process would call for the proper involvement of disciplines such as medicine, social work, and psychology in the preparation of a clinical assessment and social history of the offender. Through the pre-sentence report this would help the Bench in weighing the most effective disposition of the case.

Individualizing of sentencing in keeping with a proper corrective design is seen in action when, after careful clinical and community assessment, three men are sentenced differently for participation in the same offence: one to probation, one to a short spell in reformatory, and one to a long term in penitentiary. This kind of sentencing is already being practised by magistrates and judges who are convinced of the value of relating sentencing and correction. Some sections of the public and of inmate populations may protest and fail to understand; but there is growing acceptance of such individualization, particularly when the Bench makes known the reasons for it.

But the correction of the offender depends on a series of administrative functions operated municipally, provincially, and federally with, in some cases, more than one department involved. Thus the problem of securing any kind of integration or even co-ordination is exceedingly difficult. Each service has tended to function in its own sphere, to do its own part of the job within its own framework of public responsibility, and to assume that the other services will do the same.

Law enforcement, the administration of justice, and the correctional process have for too long been regarded as separate entities. In the complex industrial society that our nation has achieved, it has become essential that their objectives and practices be integrated in recognition that the entire process should lead towards correction of the offender.

All the services described in this volume are concerned with the protection of society from the law-breaker. Traditionally, each has tended to operate without much knowledge of the functions and procedures of the others, even without knowing much about the nature of criminality or the dynamics of criminal conduct. At the time of writing, there is still no formal mechanism for co-ordinating these services, though there have been some meetings and some informal attempts at co-operation and interrelationship.

The Canadian Corrections Association is of national scope and embraces all the correctional services. It has done much to integrate correctional development through problem-centred study committees. Wide reporting and discussion of practice and research has been made possible through its biennial congress and its publication, *The Canadian Journal of Corrections*.

Other integrating associations of a more unitary nature, but of great importance in correctional development, are the Criminal Law Section of the Canadian Bar Association, the Criminal Justice Section of the National Commissioners for Uniformity of Legislation, the National Association of Canadian Chiefs of Police, provincial magistrates' and probation officers' associations, provincial corrections associations and various inter-disciplinary institutes and seminars. There has also been increased interest and participation in correctional affairs by colleagues from the universities, professional groups, and bodies such as the Canadian Mental Health Association.

Integration in the broad social interest is highly important since there is, in fact, a continuity involved in all the apparently differentiated correctional processes. This is provided by the object of their efforts, the offender himself. He should be able to find some reasonable rationale for what each does to him. He should be able to assess how the effect of each relates positively to the ultimate objective of his correction and eventual re-establishment in the community.

The existing situation is further complicated by the mobility and transiency of many offenders who become enmeshed, at one and the same time, in these services in different municipalities or provinces throughout the country. Criminal records of indictable offences are centrally maintained by the R.C.M.P. in Ottawa, but often sentence is passed for summary offences, and on occasion, for indictable offences, before the record becomes available. There is a National Parole Board, which, it is suggested, will ultimately relieve the two existing provincial parole boards of their responsibilities. There is one Criminal Code for all of Canada; but this is administered by the provinces. This implies continued consultation by the Attorney-General of Canada with the Attorneys-General of the provinces to ensure a reasonably similar standard of enforcement. There is need for a probation compact so that probationers may be transferred, with enforceable sanctions, from one jurisdiction to the other, and so that the status of probation may be known to the court in any province prior to sentence. Study of the chronological history of criminal careers shows that there is a need for sentencing to follow some *sequence*, in most cases from probation to penal institution. The institutions require reorganization as to function and as to custody to make such progression a practical and effective procedure. There is need for the development of probation and institutional services across Canada to bring all provinces to a uniformly high standard. This could be achieved by establishing a federal advisory and consultative service and providing federal grants to assist in meeting defined and progressive criteria.

The offender initially encounters the police and the courts. He may, if convicted, be fined or put on probation; otherwise he is given an institutional sentence. Ultimately he may experience parole and be offered after-care service. But the responsibility for imprisonment is, generally speaking, arbitrarily divided between federal and provincial jurisdiction according to length of sentence. Under a sentence of less than two years, he may go to a county jail, a reformatory, an industrial farm, or a farm-camp, depending on the provincial services available. Under a lengthier sentence he will be sent to the penitentiary system and may go to a maximum-, medium-, or minimum-security prison or to a farm-camp.

In either case he is really sentenced to the particular penal authority, which then classifies him as to the type of institution believed to provide the custodial security and program of training or treatment most appropriate for him. Thus the court, which does the sentencing, does not control the progression of the inmate throughout the prison system. Obviously, it would be most difficult for judges and magistrates to have enough knowledge of the many institutions and their programs and of the continuous personality development of the inmates to enable them to perform effectively the function of designating the institution and the program to be followed. They should, however, be encouraged to voice their opinions concerning the offender and the type of treatment likely to benefit him. These opinions would help the institutional authorities in their initial classification.

A proposal has been made by the Fauteux Committee, and seems to be generally accepted by federal and provincial authorities, that all adults sentenced to more than a year of imprisonment become the jurisdictional responsibility of the federal correctional system. It has also been proposed and apparently accepted that no sentences between six months and a year be permitted. This would mean that, except for longer sentences imposed under certain provincial statutes, the provincial jurisdiction would cease at six months.

Just how the judiciary will view these changes is difficult to estimate. Will the Bench be generally reluctant to sentence to more than a year in a federal institution? Will six months in a provincial institution be considered too short for institutional treatment? Will the shorter sentence tend to be looked upon as a warning, perhaps following probation? Will the longer sentence to a federal institution be expected to be more effective for retraining or long-term treatment?

Count Gleispach, an Austrian, speaking at the Penitentiary Congress in London in 1925, and penologists and royal commissions since that date, have urged magistrates to visit the penal institutions to obtain some insight into the future of those they sentence to them. Many magistrates now do this and also attend conferences on sentencing practices in order to share their views with their professional colleagues.[6]

But perhaps it is through the development of probation that the magistrate has met post-sentence problems most intimately. Through the probation officers attached to his court, he has been able to follow closely the course of convicted offenders and to assess the effectiveness of his judgment. It is still his duty to decide between fine, probation, or institutional treatment; this is a grave individual and social responsibility.

Magistrates are becoming increasingly aware of the parole board's responsibility to review the progress and behaviour of each prisoner and

6Leon Radzinowicz, *op. cit.*, p. 24.

assess his potential to complete satisfactorily an appropriate residual portion of his sentence under supervision in the community. Parole does not in any sense imply a negation of the original sentence, but rather constitutes, under sound legislative sanction, the fulfilment of its reformative aspect. Experience indicates that it should be increasingly relied on as the method of release. Development is needed, therefore, of prediction methods to assist what is essentially a judgment process about the individual's potential for re-establishment in the community. The offender on parole is still not free, even though he is living in the open community under certain conditions including supervision. Usually the supervision is provided by the after-care societies, such as the John Howard and Elizabeth Fry Societies, by the Salvation Army correctional services, by provincial probation officers, or by the regional representatives of the National Parole Service.

Morale, incentive, and employer-employee relationships are as important in public institutions as they are in business enterprises. Services, structures, and programs will be no more effective than the personnel employed in them. Inasmuch as the objectives of the correctional services in Canada have been changing and are developing in relation to training and treatment principles, it follows that staff must also change and must be able to understand and employ new methodologies.

Great credit must be given to those who have been manning these services for many years and who are now expected to adapt to new ideas and ways of operating. Their experience must be utilized and built upon during the periods of shift and change, which may easily precipitate disturbances and tensions, particularly in the isolated and controlled settings of the penal institutions.

When the traditional régimes and disciplines are changed in a penal institution, they must be replaced by a positive program that re-defines the relation of inmate to staff, inmate to inmate, and staff to staff. Self-discipline must replace external control. Without question a man may be forcibly put in prison and controlled physically. But his ideas about the kind of life he intends to lead on release cannot be shaped by force. External conformity can be exacted as long as the sanction is present, and its application may be necessary with some offenders. But it is now realized that, in general, society expects from the correctional services a self-aware and self-disciplined citizen.

Since guards must become correctional officers, they should be recompensed by salaries and working conditions commensurate with such responsibility and such an enhanced concept of their role. Obviously recruiting and selection will have to recognize these new requirements, and staff training of an intensive nature must transform the attitudes and capacities of those already in the service.

In-service training of staff at all levels has already been generally accelerated. It should be directed not only to competence in performance of specific and routine functions but also to the development of proper motivation and attitude. For those who show capacity and are marked for promotion into the management group, special training is essential to develop a broad grasp of correctional philosophy and an understanding of the contributions made to corrections by various professional disciplines such as psychiatry, sociology, social work, psychology, theology, and education.

Correctional managers should be taught how to utilize the contributions of professional workers and how to create the kind of setting in which they can function effectively. The universities are challenged to interpret and make known the needs and opportunities of the correctional services and to establish practice and research relationships. Such relationships would expose students to the setting and would encourage them to dedicate themselves to correctional practice in positive and productive programs.

> Reform of any institution must come generally from those who know of it and are free to speak of it. Prison reform in Canada has been held back, first, because those responsible for the administration of the system would not in many cases admit its weaknesses, and second, because the inmates who could speak, do not generally care to make known, after freedom, that they are ex-convicts, and even if they waive that feeling, their word is discounted, owing to their record.[7]

Sensitive citizens since the time of John Howard and Elizabeth Fry have been concerned with the lot of the deprived and disinherited. They observed that men and women coming from prison have tremendous problems of readjustment as well as valuable potential for re-establishment. They looked inside the prison to seek amelioration of the conditions of penal servitude. But through prison visitation and after-care in the community, the prisoners' aid workers gradually began to arrive at a penal philosophy.

They asserted their views and pressed for the acceptance of a penal program based on the principle of reformation. They expressed the belief that man can change if attention is given to the cause of his behaviour, and they called for processes of treatment based on an individualized and

[7]John Kidman, *Penal and Prison Reform in Canada*, Public Affairs Press, December 1937, p. 65.

therapeutic approach. This philosophy was developed outside the penal system as was the pressure to implement it. In the early days following Howard, the reformer spoke vigorously and publicly of the defects of the penal system as he saw them. Naturally, the proposed objectives and methods met with some resistance.

The resistance was basically a result of conflict in views about punishment. Prisons represented tradition, law enforcement, deterrence, custody. Essentially they were identified with the community's fear of the criminal. The after-care societies and religious groups, notably the Quakers, represented humanitarianism and the developing views of the social sciences. They were identified with the conscience of the community in regard to the treatment of prisoners and their needs on returning from the prisons.

The belief slowly gained acceptance that the interests of society would be served best by a penal system with objectives of reformation. Its tenets are worthy of re-statement. It became obvious that it is less expensive and more humane, and that it ultimately provides better protection to the public to see that imprisonment results in some change for the better within the offender in regard to his conflict with society rather than merely to compel him to 'do time'. Experience indicated that this was a realistic point of view.

A recognition of shared objectives has been growing as the correctional services have matured. The services are acquiring the ability to change from within and occasionally to seek constructive suggestions from without. But there are many back-waters and eddies in this stream of correctional progress. Constant community awareness and external pressure are necessary in support of developing progressive ideas and the appropriation of funds.

While the after-care societies are still concerned about matters of penal reform, perhaps their fundamental work today is with ex-inmates in the community and it is from this relationship that they draw their knowledge of new needs and problems within the penal system as a whole. The after-care workers and the correctional staffs have stopped saying, in effect, to one another: 'Your prisons – your community'. Each group has come to the realization that whereas we can punish the mass we can reform only the individual, and that the needs of ex-inmates returning from incarceration to their communities are manifold and different from those of any other group of citizens.

A service relationship, in fact a partnership, between the after-care workers and the correctional staffs has resulted from giving the former access to the institutions to develop service relationships with inmates.

Through service to the inmates a consciousness of shared objectives has resulted. This has been centred on the offender as an individual returning to society. The only reason for the existence of the after-care society as a service organization is the man or woman who walks in the front door seeking help. Essentially, the only reason for existence of the correctional service is the same man committed to custody by law.

Amenities and welfare measures ameliorate the purely punitive aspects of the prison, facilitate improved function of prisoners and staff as individuals, induce positive behaviour, prevent the onset of new personality disturbances, and retard the progress of any such disturbances already existing. Provision of effective individual treatment, and of conditions and measures conducive to mental health, is based on a belief in and recognition of the worth, dignity, and potentiality of man, and on the further belief that crime is not necessarily chronic and irreversible.

John Mabbott said succinctly in one of his articles on the criminal law: 'If our sentimentalists cry "coddling of prisoners" let us ask them also to come out clearly into the open and incorporate whatever starvation and disease and brutality they think necessary into the sentence they propose.'[8]

We must work in the shadow of past error; do what we can with the situation as we find it. We cannot stay outside and cast aspersions. By shared effort, the errors of various views will gradually be diminished and constructive solutions will emerge. These in turn will represent error to those who, in the future, fall heir to them and to the problems that produced them. The true speed of penal reform is not that of headlong precipitancy but of the unremitting energy that wastes no time.

The work of the after-care societies has developed in the ordinary citizen a greater interest and participation in corrections. It is only natural to want to evaluate the success and failure of work in this field. In thinking of standards, however, we should realize that there is a standard inherent in the actual performance of the service, and not place too much emphasis on the formulation of criteria to measure the quality of performance.

The worth of beliefs in the correctional process must at present be demonstrated in a context in which they cannot yet be given a fair trial. This is true in the institutions because, no matter how much improved physically, prisons are still prisons. It is true in the community, because attitudes to ex-offenders vary from frank acceptance and support to utter cynicism.

8J. Mabbott, *Justice and Social Policy*, New York: Prentice-Hall, 1961, p. 54.

A. M. Kirkpatrick

In spite of the development of integration and interdependence in the work of government departments and private and professional agencies, all will have been in vain unless there is created in the minds of the offenders themselves a realization and acceptance of the objectives. This recognition, along with genuine and interested participation in the program, is increasingly evident, though general resistance to authority and acceptance of the inmate sub-culture remain as basic barriers. Continued and steady progress, with some evidence of its application, must reach the individual inmate, or the measure of acceptance already achieved will give place to cynical apathy. This could well thwart, for a time, the best of effort and intention.

There is growing recognition by the community of its responsibility to the offender on his return. The citizens' greatly increased interest in law enforcement and the correctional process is significant since it is back in the community that the ex-inmate will either return once more to crime or find himself in a new role of social and economic responsibility. Governments and Crown corporations should show greater sensitivity to this problem than they do now, by paying more attention to the possibilities of employing ex-inmates who are properly qualified and suitable for positions open to competition or appointment.

The attitudes of the public still tend to fluctuate from one extreme to the other in regard to punishment and the treatment of the offender. Hence, programs of public education must be unremitting in their extent and intensity. Correctional workers have travelled a long and arduous road along with the offender; but gains must be maintained and new challenges must be met. It is not enough merely to delineate the problems of the ex-inmate or of the correctional services that work with him. It is essential that we interpret broadly in the community the worth and dignity of every human being, including the offender against the criminal law.

> Recently an ex-inmate said to an after-care worker: Prison life is an unrealistic experience. A man loses complete contact with reality. He comes to feel that life will be very easy when he hits the street. He comes to feel and to believe that his former difficulties (conflict with wife, unemployment), will not present a problem. It is a terrible shock for the first few days back on the street when he encounters reality.

Further Reading

BRAITHWAITE, J. W. *A Community Focussed Prison.* Calgary: John Howard Society of Alberta, April 1960.

CANADA. *Report* of the Royal Commission to Investigate the Penal System of Canada (Archambault Report). Ottawa: King's Printer, 1938.

———. *Report* of the Committee to Inquire into the Principles and Procedures Followed in the Remission Service of the Department of Justice of Canada (Fauteux Report). Ottawa: Queen's Printer, 1956.

CITIZENS' FORUM. *Should Drug Addicts Go to Jail?* Toronto: Canadian Association for Adult Education, October 1959.

———. *Crime and Punishment.* Toronto: Canadian Association for Adult Education, March 1960.

———. *Can Prisons Reform Criminals?* Toronto: Canadian Association for Adult Education, October 1955.

COUGHLAN, D. 'At the Court Level', *Canadian Penal Association Proceedings,* October 1953.

EDMISON, J. A. 'The Eternal Problem of Crime and Criminals', *Queen's Quarterly,* vol. LX, no. 2 (1953).

———. 'Progress in Canada', *Canadian Welfare,* September 1953.

EDWARDS, J. L. J. 'Canadian Teaching and Research in Criminology', *University of Toronto Law Journal,* vol. XIII, no. 2 (1960).

FULTON, HON. E. D. 'Recent Developments in Canada's Correctional Services', *Canadian Journal of Corrections,* vol. 3, no. 2 (July 1961).

———. 'The Limits of our Imagination Alone Restrict the Effective Contribution that the Private Citizen Can Make', *Canadian Journal of Corrections,* vol. 2, no. 3 (July 1960).

JOHNSTONE, W. F., and B. W. Henheffer. 'History of Treatment in Canadian Penitentiaries', *Canadian Welfare,* September 1952.

JAFFARY, S. K. 'Saskatchewan Examines Penal Reform', *Canadian Bar Review,* December 1946.

———. *Sentencing of Adults in Canada.* Toronto: University of Toronto Press, 1963.

KIDMAN, J. *The Canadian Prison.* Toronto: Ryerson Press, 1947.

KIRKPATRICK, A. M. 'Personnel Needs in the Correctional Field', *Social Worker,* June 1957.

———. 'The Birth of Prison Reform', *Canadian Welfare,* May 1959.

———. 'Mutual Objectives of Private and Public Correctional Agencies', *Social Worker,* January 1960.

———. 'Correcting Corrections', *Criminal Law Quarterly,* February 1960.

————. 'New Views on the Narcotic Problem', *Canadian Medical Association Journal*, June 1960.

————. 'Prisons and Their Products', *Canadian Journal of Corrections*, vol. 4, no. 3 (July 1962).

LAVELL, A. *The Convicted Criminal and His Re-establishment as a Citizen.* Toronto: Ryerson Press, 1926.

MACDONALD, R. ST. J. 'Narcotic Drug Addiction in Canada', from *Current Law and Social Problems.* Toronto: University of Toronto Press, 1960.

MCCULLEY, J. 'Rehabilitation from the Point of View of the Administrator', *American Prison Association Proceedings,* 1951.

MCGRATH, W. T. 'The New Criminal Code', *Queen's Quarterly*, vol. LX, no. 2.

NEW BRUNSWICK. Department of the Attorney-General, *Report* of the Commission on the Gaol System (Dickson Report). Fredericton: King's Printer, 1951.

OUTERBRIDGE, W. R. 'Authority – Its Use and Misuse in Probation', *Canadian Journal of Corrections,* vol. 2, no. 3 (July 1960).

SASKATCHEWAN. *Report* of the Saskatchewan Penal Commission. Regina: King's Printer, 1946.

STEVENS, E. 'Recent Developments in Adult Corrections in British Columbia', *Social Worker,* April 1952.

TOPPING, C. W. *Canadian Penal Institutions.* Toronto: Ryerson Press, 1929.

Pamphlet Series, John Howard Society of Ontario.

EDINBOROUGH, A. *Public Opinion, Crime and Correction.* March 1961.

FAUTEUX, HON. G. *Preventive Justice.* June 1957.

GARNEAU, J. *Treatment in Canadian Penitentiaries.* March 1961.

GROSSMAN, HON. A. *Taking a Fresh Look at Correctional Institutions.* February 1964.

MACLEOD, A. J. *The Citizen and the Correctional System.* March 1958.

————. *The Changing Canadian Prison.* March 1962.

————. *Training the Prisoner to Live in Freedom.* March 1963.

MCCULLEY, J. *Some Present Problems in Corrections.* March 1958.

————. *Now is the Time.* March 1960.

MCGRATH, W. T. *Planning Canada's Correctional System.* April 1960.

WARDROPE, HON. G. C. *Trends in Correctional Planning.* March 1961.

APPENDIX

Adult Correctional Institutions in Canada

FEDERAL PENITENTIARIES

EASTERN REGION, comprising the Provinces of Nova Scotia, New Brunswick, Prince Edward Island, and Quebec
DORCHESTER PENITENTIARY, Dorchester, N.B.
Maximum-security institution for males
SPRINGHILL INSTITUTION, Springhill, N.S.
Minimum-security institution for males
DORCHESTER FARM ANNEX, c/o Dorchester Penitentiary
Minimum-security institution for males
BLUE MOUNTAIN CORRECTION CAMP, Gagetown, N.B.
Minimum-security institution for males
ST. VINCENT DE PAUL PENITENTIARY, St. Vincent de Paul, Quebec
Maximum-security institution for males
ST. VINCENT DE PAUL INDUSTRIAL ANNEX, St. Vincent de Paul, Quebec
Medium-security institution for males
ST. VINCENT DE PAUL FARM ANNEX, c/o St. Vincent de Paul Penitentiary
Minimum-security institution for males
FEDERAL TRAINING CENTRE, St. Vincent de Paul, Quebec
Medium-security institution, specializing in vocational training, for males up to 25 years of age
GATINEAU CORRECTIONAL CAMP, Ste. Cécile de Masham, Quebec
Minimum-security institution for males
LECLERC INSTITUTION, St. Vincent de Paul, Quebec
Medium-security institution for males, specializing in industrial training and production
VALLEYFIELD INSTITUTION, Valleyfield, Quebec
Minimum-security institution for males, industrial program for pre-release inmates

CENTRAL REGION, comprising the Provinces of Ontario and Manitoba
KINGSTON PENITENTIARY, Kingston, Ontario
Maximum-security institution for males

PRISON FOR WOMEN, Kingston, Ontario
Maximum- and medium-security institution for females
COLLINS BAY PENITENTIARY, Kingston, Ontario
Medium-security institution for males, specializing in vocational and industrial training
BEAVER CREEK CORRECTIONAL CAMP, Gravenhurst, Ontario
Minimum-security institution for males
LANDRY CROSSING CORRECTIONAL CAMP, Petawawa, Ontario
Minimum-security institution for males
COLLINS BAY FARM ANNEX, c/o Collins Bay Penitentiary, Kingston, Ontario
Minimum-security institution for males
JOYCEVILLE INSTITUTION, Kingston, Ontario
Medium-security institution for males, specializing in industrial training and production
JOYCEVILLE FARM ANNEX, c/o Joyceville Institution
Minimum-security institution for males
MANITOBA PENITENTIARY, Stony Mountain, Manitoba
Medium-security institution for males
MANITOBA FARM ANNEX, c/o Manitoba Penitentiary
Minimum-security institution for males

WESTERN REGION, comprising the Provinces of Saskatchewan, Alberta, and British Columbia

SASKATCHEWAN PENITENTIARY, Prince Albert, Saskatchewan
Maximum-security institution for males
SASKATCHEWAN FARM ANNEX, c/o Saskatchewan Penitentiary, Prince Albert, Saskatchewan
Minimum-security institution for males
BRITISH COLUMBIA PENITENTIARY, New Westminster, British Columbia
Maximum-security institution for males
WILLIAM HEAD INSTITUTION, Vancouver Island, British Columbia
Minimum-security institution for males
AGASSIZ CORRECTIONAL CAMP, Agassiz, British Columbia
Minimum-security institution for males
MOUNTAIN PRISON, Agassiz, British Columbia
Special institution for Doukhobour inmates, males and females

PROVINCIAL INSTITUTIONS

ALBERTA
BELMONT REHABILITATION CENTRE, P.O. Box 6057, Station C, Edmonton, Alberta
Male alcoholics
THE BOWDEN INSTITUTION, Box "R", Innisfail, Alberta
Male offenders 16-25; also section for boys under 16
PROVINCIAL GAOL, P.O. Box 490, Lethbridge, Alberta
Males 16 and up
CALGARY PROVINCIAL GAOL, P.O. Box 250, Station "B", Calgary, Alberta
Males 16 and up
PROVINCIAL GAOL, Bag 10, Fort Saskatchewan, Alberta
Males 16 and up; females 18 and up

BRITISH COLUMBIA

OAKALLA PRISON FARM, Drawer "O", South Burnaby, B.C.
Male offenders with sentences less than two years. Four pre-release forestry camps situated on the Chilliwack River, each having a capacity for sixty inmates selected on a pre-release basis from Oakalla Prison Farm

WOMEN'S GAOL, Twin Maples Farm, B.C.
A farm in Maple Ridge Municipality for selected females; program is community centred

ALOUETTE RIVER, 21st Ave., Haney, B.C.
A fifty-man unit for alcoholics serving short terms

NEW HAVEN, Burnaby, B.C.
A Borstal-type institution for selected male offenders between 16 and 23, selected by the Central Classification Unit in Vancouver

HANEY CORRECTIONAL INSTITUTION, Box 1000, Haney, B.C.
Vocational training institution for selected male offenders with sentences less than two years; inmates are classified for transfer from Oakalla Prison Farm to Haney Correctional Institution

GOLD CREEK CAMP
Minimum-security forest camp situated on Alouette Lake for male offenders selected on a pre-release basis from Haney Correctional Institution

PINE RIDGE CAMP
Minimum-security honour camp situated near Haney Correctional Institution; for male offenders selected from Haney Correctional Institution

PROVINCIAL GAOL, Kamloops, B.C.
Local prisoners, male and female, with sentences under six months (mostly minor offences)

CLEARWATER FOREST CAMP
Minimum-security forest-camp program for selected male offenders and pre-release inmates from the Prince George and Kamloops provincial jails

PROVINCIAL GAOL, Prince George, B.C.
Local male prisoners with sentences up to two years less a day

CHILLIWACK FOREST CAMPS, Box 320, Chilliwack, B.C.
Consisting of four camps situated on the Chilliwack River, each camp having a capacity for sixty selected inmates, selected by the Central Classification Unit at Oakalla Prison Farm

VANCOUVER ISLAND UNIT, 4216 Wilkinson Road, Victoria, B.C.
All male offenders, from the Vancouver Island area, with sentences of less than two years

SNOWDON AND LAKEVIEW FOREST CAMPS, Box 1387, Campbell River, B.C.
Two camps situated near Campbell River on Vancouver Island, B.C., both with a capacity of sixty inmates selected by the Central Classification Unit of Oakalla Prison Farm

MANITOBA

GAOL FOR WOMEN, Portage la Prairie, Manitoba
GAOL FOR WOMEN, P.O. Box 1320, The Pas, Manitoba
PROVINCIAL GAOL, Headingley, Manitoba
PROVINCIAL GAOL, Brandon, Manitoba
PROVINCIAL GAOL, Dauphin, Manitoba
PROVINCIAL GAOL, The Pas, Manitoba

Appendix

NEW BRUNSWICK

NEW BRUNSWICK CENTRAL REFORMATORY, R.R. No. 6, Fredericton, N.B.
Selected male offenders over 16 serving a sentence of less than two years
THE INTERPROVINCIAL HOME FOR YOUNG WOMEN (PRIVATE), Coverdale, N.B.
Selected Protestant women prisoners from New Brunswick, Nova Scotia, and Prince Edward Island

Selected Roman Catholic adult female prisoners are sent to the Good Shepherd Reformatory for Females at Halifax, Nova Scotia. Other adult prisoners – male and female – are held under the regulation of the Department of the Attorney-General. The Municipalities are responsible for administration costs although some assistance is received through a provincial subsidy.

NEWFOUNDLAND

HER MAJESTY'S PENITENTIARY, St. John's, Newfoundland
Both male and female prisoners
SALMONIER PRISON CAMP
Operated in conjunction with Her Majesty's Penitentiary

Adult prisoners in Newfoundland who receive a sentence of two years or more, and who would normally be held in a federal penitentiary, are held in the provincial institution under the terms of an agreement signed at the time of Confederation. The Federal Government pays a fixed per diem rate for each such prisoner.

NOVA SCOTIA

Adult prisoners and some female prisoners are held in local prisons and county jails operated by municipal authorities and subject to regulation by the Department of the Attorney-General. Selected female prisoners are committed to the Interprovincial Home for Women at Coverdale, New Brunswick, and to the Good Shepherd Reformatory for Females at Halifax, Nova Scotia.

GOOD SHEPHERD REFORMATORY (PRIVATE), 6183 Quinpool Road, Halifax, N.S.
Catholic women

ONTARIO

ONTARIO REFORMATORY, Guelph, Ontario
Male offenders between 16 and 19 inclusive, and male offenders 20 years of age and over; medium security with academic, vocational, industrial, and agricultural training
FORESTRY CAMP, Camp Hendrie, Ontario
Minimum-security forestry camp for selected inmates from Ontario Reformatory, Guelph
ONTARIO TRAINING CENTRE, Brampton, Ontario
Minimum-security training-centre, providing academic and vocational training for selected prisoners 16 to 25
ONTARIO TRAINING CENTRE (BURTCH), Brantford, Ontario
Minimum-security academic and vocational training-centre for males of limited ability and aptitude, between the ages of 16 and 25

490

FORESTRY CAMP, McCreight's Dam, Ontario
Minimum-security forestry camp for selected inmates from Ontario Reformatory, Elliot Lake
ONTARIO REFORMATORY, Mimico, Toronto 14, Ontario
Medium-security, with industrial and agricultural training, for short-term male repeaters 20 years of age and over, many of whom are alcoholics
FORESTRY CAMP, Hillsdale, Ontario
Minimum-security forestry camp for selected inmates from Ontario Reformatory, Mimico
ONTARIO REFORMATORY, Millbrook, Ontario
Maximum-security for intractable-type inmates, sex offenders, drug addicts and arsonists; treatment, industrial training, and braille printing
DURHAM CAMP
Work camp, short-term male prisoners, situated on the outside grounds of Ontario Reformatory, Millbrook
BURTCH INDUSTRIAL FARM, Brantford, Ontario
Male recidivists, 20 years of age and over with maximum sentence of twelve months; minimum security, industrial and agricultural training
RIDEAU INDUSTRIAL FARM, Burritt's Rapids, Ontario
Minimum security, for male recidivists 20 years of age and over with maximum sentences of twelve months; industrial and agricultural training
INDUSTRIAL FARM, Monteith, Ontario
Minimum security, for male recidivists 20 years of age and over with maximum sentences of twelve months; agricultural training
INDUSTRIAL FARM, Fort William, Ontario
Minimum security, for male recidivists 20 years of age and over with maximum sentences of twelve months; agricultural training
BURWASH INDUSTRIAL FARM
Two integrated camps and a main institution, ranging from minimum to medium security; male recidivists 20 years of age and over with sentences up to two years; training in agriculture, lumbering, and industry

ANDREW MERCER REFORMATORY FOR WOMEN, Toronto, Ontario
Medium security for females 16 years and up; academic, household science, commercial and industrial training
ONTARIO WOMEN'S GUIDANCE CENTRE, Brampton, Ontario
Minimum-security training and guidance centre for selected young female offenders 16 years and over; academic, vocational, and household-science training
ONTARIO WOMEN'S TREATMENT CENTRE, Brampton, Ontario
Training and treatment centre for selected female offenders 16 years and over who volunteer for admission

DISTRICT JAILS
In Northern Ontario the eight district jails of Algoma, Sudbury, Thunder Bay, Parry Sound, Kenora, Temiskaming, Rainy River, and Nipissing are operated by the Department of Reform Institutions.

Thirty-five county jails and two city jails are owned and maintained by their respective jurisdictions, but are inspected and supervised by the Department.

PRINCE EDWARD ISLAND

PRINCE COUNTY JAIL, Summerside
QUEEN'S COUNTY JAIL, Charlottetown
KING'S COUNTY JAIL, Georgetown

Appendix

QUEBEC
SHERIFF

DISTRICT	OFFICE
Abitibi	Amos
Arthabaska	Arthabaska
Beauce	St-Joseph-de-Beauce
Beauharnois	Valleyfield
Bedford	Sweetsburg
Bonaventure	New Carlisle
Chicoutimi	Chicoutimi
Drummond	Drummondville
Gaspé à Percé	Percé
Gaspé à Ste-Anne-des-Monts	Ste-Anne-des-Monts
Gaspé à Hâvre-Aubert	Hâvre-Aubert, Iles-de-la-Madeleine
Hauterive	Baie Comeau
Hull	Hull
Iberville	St-Jean
Joliette	Joliette
Kamouraska	Rivière-du-Loup
Labelle	Mont-Laurier
Mégantic	Thetford Mines
Montmagny	Montmagny
Montréal	Montréal
Nicolet	Nicolet
Pontiac	Campbell's Bay
Québec	Québec
Richelieu	Sorel
Rimouski	Rimouski
Rimouski à Matane	Matane
Roberval	Roberval
Rouyn-Noranda	Rouyn
Saguenay	La Malbaie
St-François	Sherbrooke
St-Hyacinthe	St-Hyacinthe
St-Maurice	Shawinigan
Témiscamingue	Ville-Marie
Terrebonne	St-Jérôme
Trois-Rivières	Trois-Rivières

In particular, attention is called to these three institutions:
PRISON DE MONTREAL (BORDEAUX), 800 ouest, boulevard Gouin, Montréal, Québec
PRISON DES FEMMES, 11,000, rue Tanguay, Montréal, Québec
PRISON DE QUEBEC, Parc des Champs de Bataille, Québec

SASKATCHEWAN

PROVINCIAL CORRECTIONAL INSTITUTION, Box 617, Regina, Saskatchewan
Younger male offenders, mainly 16 to 25
PROVINCIAL CORRECTIONAL INSTITUTION, Prince Albert, Saskatchewan
Older male offenders, 26 and up
PROVINCIAL CORRECTIONAL INSTITUTION, Prince Albert, Saskatchewan
Female offenders

492

Index

Adult court, 136-208
Aeronautics Act, 93
After-care, 384-406
  aid on discharge to, 387-9
  community response, 404-5
  concern for, 384-5
  development, 384-6, 405
  emotional problems, 396-7
  employment, 393-6
  financial assistance, 391-2
  growth, 386
  and the juvenile offender, problems, 262-3
  juvenile-workers: heavy case-load, 262
  pre-release referral services, 389-91
    assessment of inmate, 389
    need for, 389
  referral basis, problem, 403
  role of social worker, 392
  supervision of parolees, 397-400
  women offenders, difficulties, 388-9
  see also Parole; Prisoners' aid societies
Alberta, probation in, 232-3
Alcohol, as 'excuse-value' in delinquency, 421
Alcoholics, 432-40
  arrests, 432
  drunken driving, 433
  facilities for, 435-8
  legislation:
    lack of recognition of alcoholism as illness, 437-8
    problem of determining responsibility, 438
  management, 435
  numbers in Canada, 433
  reluctance of society to impose effective controls, 431, 433
  treatment, 438-40
    drugs, 440
    no sure method, 438-9
    steps towards, 439-40
  types of, 434-5
  underlying psychiatric disorders and classification, 434-5
Alcoholics Anonymous, 225, 331, 421

Alcoholism, symptom of underlying personality disorder, 433-4
Alcoholism and Drug Addiction Research Foundation, 433n
Alex G. Brown Clinic, 432, 435-6
Allen, C. K., 110n
American Law Institute, on parole criteria, 342
Anglican Church: Church Army, 385
Appellate courts:
  appeals taken (1961), 170-1
  importance of work, 171-2
  powers, 172
Archambault Commission: see Royal Commission to Investigate the Penal System of Canada
Armstrong, J. D.:
  on protective drugs in the treatment of alcoholism, 440n
  on psychiatric theories of alcoholism, 439n
  on the special clinic for alcoholism, 439n
  on special problem groups: alcoholics, drug addicts, 430-47
Atcheson, D. J., on social aspects of sexual behaviour, 460
Atlantic Provinces:
  code of criminal procedure, 140
  conservative outlook of criminal courts, 173
Attorney-General and department, 180-6
  agents, 181-3
  coroners, 183-5
  duties, 180-1, 182-3, 184, 196; probation, 231, 232, 234, 236, 238
  justices of the peace, 185-6
  responsible for law enforcement, 115-16
Aungle, P. G., on the care and treatment of psychopathic offenders in Norway, Sweden, and Denmark, 439n
Austin, John:
  on concept of sanction, 17n
  on law as it is and as it ought to be, 29n

Index

Bail, 194

Banking and Commerce Committee, 107

Barnes, Harry Elmer, and Negley K. Teeters, on new horizons in criminology, 34n

Beattie, R. H., on problems of criminal statistics in the United States, 62n

Beccaria, Cesare, on crimes and punishment (1764), 465

Bell, M.: see Chute, C. L.

Bennett, A. E., et al., on the diagnosis of intermediate stage of alcoholic brain disease, 439n

Bennett, James V., on the prison paradox, 474

Bentham, Jeremy, on rationale of punishment, 465

Bonding, problem to ex-prisoner, 394-5

Borstal Association, 385

Borthwick, J. Douglas, on history of Montreal prisons, 283n

Boscoville School (Quebec), 251

Bracton, Henry, on law, 110

Brill, H., on the British narcotic system, 444n

'Bristol experiment', 369

British Columbia, probation in, 231-2

British North America Act, 1, 94, 138, 140, 141, 177-8, 215
  appointment of judges, 167
  criminal law, 91
  jurisdiction of penal administration, 302
  organization and jurisdiction of law-enforcement agencies in Canada, 112

Bronner, Augusta F.: see Healy, Wm.

Brown, George, report on prisons (nineteenth century), 287

Cairns, Huntington, 17

Caldwell, Robert G.:
  on criminology, 109n
  on the police, 132

Canada Evidence Act, 144, 185; distinguishing feature, 144-5

Canada Shipping Act, 178

Canadian Association of Chiefs of Police, 125

Canadian Bar Association, 107, 477

Canadian Bill of Rights, 119, 138-9

Canadian Corrections Association, 2, 32, 62, 477
  on the child offender and the law, 278n

criticism of juvenile delinquency legislation, 31-2

Canadian Mental Health Association, 477

Canadian Police College, 124

Capital punishment, 39-40

Carabine, W. F., on parole as an alternative to prison, 346

Carrara, Francesco, 466

Catholic rehabilitation societies, 385

Cattell, R. B., on personality, 42n

Causation theories:
  biological determinism, 42-7
  body-type theory, 45-7
  conclusions, 56-8
  heredity and environment, 41-2
  physical defects, 44-5, 47
  physiological factors, 42-8
  psychological factors, 48-51
    application of psychological testing to delinquents, 48-51
    emotional disturbance, 50-1
  sex and age, 47-8
  sociological factors and theories, 52-6
    ecological factors, 52-3
    the family, 53
    gang activity, effect on delinquent behaviour, 53-4
    social disorganization, 54-5
    social norms, 54
    white-collar crime, 55-6

Cavan, Ruth Shonle, and Eugene S. Zemans, on marital relationships of prisoners in twenty-eight countries, 306n

Cavenagh, W. E., on the child and the court, 35n

Chiffins, R. I., on punishment and treatment, 17n

Child Welfare Act, Newfoundland (1944), 210

Child Welfare and Youth Protection Act, Sweden (1924), 31

Children of Unmarried Parents Act, 215

Children's Bureau, United States Department of Health, Education and Welfare, on training-school discipline, 263n

Children's Protection Act, 215

Children's Protection Act, Ontario (1893), 31

Church of England Temperance Society, 223

Chute, C. L., and M. Bell:
  on Augustus John, 223n
  on crime, courts, and probation, 236n

Index

Crime and correctional services, 1-11
Crime and delinquency, rates 59-90
 another approach to criminal statistics, 89-90
 calculation of, 65-6; fallacy of per-
  capita rates, 65-6
 by country of birth, 83-4
 changes in rates of convictions for
  three major classes of indictable
  offences (1900-60), 68-70
 criminal statistics as samples, 62-4
 for indictable offences, five-year averages (1901-60), 68
 juvenile delinquency, five-year averages (1926-60), 67
 ratios of court, police, and institutional statistics, 63-4
 sources of Canadian statistics, 59-62;
  selected offences 'known to the
  police' of Montreal, Toronto,
  Vancouver (1960, 1961), 60-1
 variations, 66-89
  age differences, 74-5; by sex, 74-5
  country-of-birth differences, 83-5
  differences over time, 66-70
  educational differences, 78-80; by
   type of offence, 79-80
  provincial differences, 85-9; correlated with heavy urban growth-
   rate, 86-7; correlated with
   other 'social problems', 89;
   standardized for rural-urban
   distribution, 85-6
  religious differences, 80-2
  sex differences, 70-5; by age, 74-5;
   by province, 70-1; by type of
   offence, 72-4
  urban-rural distribution, 75-8; by
   province, 75-7; by type of
   offence, 77-8
Crime and society, 13-40
 broad principles, need for, 16
 conclusions, 38-40
 crime and corrections, unsuitability of
  present definitions, 13-15
 criminal law, how to reduce the scope
  of, 21-2
 definitions and concepts, 13-24
 deterrent laws and the reign of terror,
  39-40
 the effect of double morality on
  children, 35-6
 exploitation of criminals, for peace
  and morality, 39
 humanitarian laws and the principles
  of welfare reunited, 40

juvenile delinquency:
 Canadian legislation, criticism of,
  31-3
 deterrence, the uses and limits of,
  33
 legislation and enforcement of welfare, 31
 the limits of retribution, 32-3
juvenile justice abroad, 33-4
juvenile laws: moral exhortation and
 hypocrisy as backbone of, 34-5
the law, moral purpose of, 23-4
law and jurisprudence, need for reduction of principles, 16-17
law and welfare in the modern state,
 38
law as it is and law as it ought to be,
 29-30
legal and social concepts of crime,
 conflict between, 17
morality versus social purpose of law,
 23-4
morals, enforcement of, 24-31
 criticized, 25
 introduction, 24-5
 the nature of morals, 27-8
 public morality and individual
  freedoms, 25-6
 public morality and public opinion,
  28
 public order versus private morality,
  26-7
 social consequences of illegal acts,
  28-9
offender as a part of social system,
 19-20
prediction and individual prevention,
 dangers, 36-7
psychopathology, uses and abuses,
 20-1
sanctions, 22; effectiveness, 23
sentencing:
 legal and social functions, 14-15
 multiple aims, 15
separation of law and morals, 30-1
the trial as a morality play, 20
welfare, the enforcement of, 31-40
welfare and punishment in one definition of crime, 18; consequences,
 18-19
Criminal Code of Canada, 91-108
 passim, 118-24 *passim*, 178, 230,
 478
 and the 'citizen's arrest', 126-7
 common-law principles, 144ff
 and criminal statistics, 61-2

Elizabeth Fry Societies, 385, 400, 403, 406, 480

Elizabethan Poor Law, 311

Elkins, W., on the English penal system, 245n

England, early probation work, 222-3

Exchequer Court of Canada, 141, 146, 147; jurisdiction, 176

Ex-prisoners:
emotional problems, 396-7
employment, 393-6
bonding problem, 394-5
licensing problem, 395
perils, 393-4
financial assistance, need for, 391-3
relationship problem, 396-7
self-maintenance, return to responsibility, 396-7
standard post-release problems, 390-1
stigma, 394-6

Extradition Act, 106

Fagan, R. F., on Canadian political prisoners in Tasmania, 284

Family and Children's Court Act (B.C.), 231

Family court:
administration, 219
conclusions, 219
function, 218
legislation, 218-19

Fauteux Committee: see Committee to Inquire into the Principles and Procedures Followed in the Remission Service

Fellatio, definition, 457n

Female offender and parole, 371

Ferri, Enrico, on the concept of social defence, 19

Ford Foundation, on teachers of tomorrow, 275n

Forensic clinic, Toronto Psychiatric Hospital, 453

Fornataro, John V.:
on Canadian prisons today, 302-25
on the staff-training problems for Canadian prisons, 320n

Frankau, I. M., on treatment of drug addiction, 445n

Fromm, Erich, on the origin of ethics, 28

Frym, Marcel, on what psychiatry can do for criminology, 37n

Fugitive Offenders Act, 106

Fuller, Lon L., on positivism and fidelity to law: a reply to Professor Hart, 29-30

Gang activity: effects on delinquent behaviour, 53-4

Giardini, G. L., on the parole process, 359-60

Gibson, Major-General Ralph B., 386

Giffen, P. J., on rates of crime and delinquency, 59-90

Gleispach, Count, 479

Glueck, Sheldon and Eleanor, 37n, 46-53 *passim*
on juvenile delinquents grown up, 48
physique and delinquency, 46
on unraveling juvenile delinquency, 37n, 49, 50, 52, 53

Godbout, B., on remission service policy and practice, 330n

Goffman, Erving, on the characteristics of total institutions, 306

Goring, Charles, on the English convict, 44-5

Gradual release, 400-2
difficulties, 401-2
reasons for, 401

Grunhut, M., on juvenile delinquents, 252

Grygier, Tadeusz, 13-40
on the chronic petty offender, 38n
on the concept of the state of delinquency, 31n, 34n
on crime and society, 13-40
on the likes and interests test, 36n
on social and psychological consequences of deterrent and other oppressive measures, 33n
on the teaching of criminology, 37n

Guttmacher, M. S., on psychiatry and the law, 460n

Habeas corpus, 194-5

Habitual criminal, 104; possibility of parole, 332-3, 368-9

Hahinan, R. F., on specialized supervision of parolees having a history of narcotic addiction, 445n

Halfway House, 370; experiment with, 263

Hall, Jerome, on reason and reality in jurisprudence, 17n

Halliday, Robert, 445

Hart, H. L. A., 26
on positivism and the separation of law and morals, 14, 29-30

Index

Mercy, prerogative of, 101-4
  commutation of sentence of imprison-
    ment, 103
  free pardon, 102
  ordinary pardon, 102
  remission of corporal punishment,
    103-4
  remission of fines and forfeitures, 103
  remission of sentence of imprison-
    ment, 102
  restoration of driving privileges, 103
Mewett, Alan:
  on the proper scope and function of
    the criminal law, 16n
  on sexual offences in Canada, 455
Mill, John Stuart, on liberty, 26
Miller, F. P.:
  on parole, 326-83
  on parole in Canada, 401n
Mittermaier, C. J. A., 28
Mohr, J. W., on pedophilia, 459n
  on a short survey of sexual offenders
    in Kingston Penitentiary, 452n
  on a short survey of sexual offenders
    in Ontario Reformatory, Mill-
    brook, 452n
Mohr, J. W. *et al.,* on pedophilia and
  exhibitionism, 458n
Montagu, Ashley, on the biologist looking at crime, 43n
Montreal Legal Aid Bureau, 188
Montreal Transcript, on prisons (1838),
  281
Moodie, Susanna, 299n
Morals:
  effect of double morality on children,
    35-6
  enforcement, 25-30
  nature, 27-8
  public morality and individual free-
    doms, 25-6
  public morality and public opinion, 28
  public order versus public morality,
    26-7
  separation of law and morals, 30-1
  social consequences of illegal acts,
    28-9
Morrison, Herbert, on penal reform,
  468
Morton, J. D., 21
  on crime and the law, 16n
  on the crisis in criminal law, 20, 23
  on the function of the criminal law,
    16n
Moylan, J. G., contribution as inspector

of penitentiaries (nineteenth century), 294-7

Narcotic Control Act, 106, 144, 442,
  446-7; search, persons and property,
  120, 121
National Association of Canadian Chiefs
  of Police, 477
National Commissioners for Uniformity of Legislation, 477
National Conference on Parole:
  on parole in principle and practice,
    342n
  on parole supervision, 352
National Defence Act, 141
National Employment Service, 333, 401;
  Special Services Department, 393
National Parole Board, 162, 179, 231,
  238, 336-48, 398, 478
  establishment of, 333-4
  jurisdiction, 336-7
  organization, 336-8; supervision, 337-8
  procedure, 338
National Parole Service, 336ff, 480
New Brunswick:
  probation in, 238
  qualifications of magistrates, 143
Newfoundland:
  code of criminal procedure, 140
  juvenile delinquency legislation, 145
  probation in, 239
Newman, Donald J., on legal aspects of
  juvenile delinquency, 34n
Nova Scotia:
  probation in, 238
  qualifications of magistrates, 143
Nyquist, Ola, on juvenile justice, 31n

O'Connor, Maurice, on impressions concerning adaptation to imprisonment, 307
Official Secrets Act, 144
Ohlin, Lloyd E.:
  on selection of parole, 345
  on the use of prediction tables in the
    consideration of parole, 347
Ontario:
  average numbers convicted of indict-
    able offences, 158-9
  code of criminal procedure, 140
  diversification of penal institutions,
    310
  persons tried on charges of indictable
    offences (1961), 157
  probation in, 236-7

502

Santayana, George, 21
Saskatchewan:
Dept. of Social Welfare and Rehabilitation, Corrections Branch, manual of policies and procedures, 222n
prison personnel training-program, 319
probation in, 233-4
Saskatchewan Bill of Rights, 138
Schizophrenia, definition, 434n
Schmideberg, M., on psychiatric treatment of offenders, 461n
Schmidt, W., on problem drinking as a factor in drinking-driving offences, 433
Schools for the Protection of Youth Act (Quebec), 64
Schwartz, Mildred: *see* Vallee, Frank G.
Schwartz, Morris S.: *see* Stanton, Alfred H.
Seeley, John R., 21; on society, social pathology, and mental ills, 19n
Sentencing, beginnning of formal corrective process, 476
Service de Réadaptation Sociale Inc., 385
Sexual offenders, 447-63
clinical aspects, 456-60
exhibitionist, 458
homosexuality, 457
other sexual deviations, 459
pedophile, 458-9
voyeurist, 458
and the Criminal Code, 449
the dangerous, 104-5
definition, 447-8
incidence, 450-3
numbers in penal institutions convicted of sexual offences, 452-3
rates, 450-3
legislation, 453-6
male-female ratio, 449-50
the problem, 448-50
prosecutions for sexual offences:
Metro Toronto, 451-2
Ontario, 451, 452
research, 463
treatment, 449, 460-3
Sexual psychopathology, definition, 447n
Shafer, Stephen, on restitution to victims of crime, 357
Shaw, Clifford R., *et al.*, on delinquency areas, 52-3

Sheldon, Wm. H., body-type theory, 45-7; *et al.*, on varieties of delinquent youth, 45n
Shiner, E. V., on return of the married offender to his family, 387-8
Sinclair, D., on training-schools in Canada, 244-78
Smart, R., on problem drinking as a factor in drinking-driving offences, 433
Social norms, breakdown, 54
Social system in prison, 307-8
Société Canadienne de Criminologie, 2
Société d'Orientation et de Réhabilitation Sociale, 385
Sociological theories of causation, 52-6
Special problem groups: alcoholics, drug addicts, sex offenders, 430-64
combinations of, encountered in practice, 431-2
facilities for, 435-8
introduction, 430-2
management persuasion and pressure, 443-4
summary, 463-4
underlying psychiatric disorders, and classification, 434-5
see also Alcoholics; Drug addicts; Sexual offenders
Spencer, John, on the place of the social worker in the penal system, 392n, 449
Stanton, Alfred H., and Morris S. Schwartz, on the mental hospital, 318n
Stanwell, P. M., on the treatment of drug addiction, 445n
Stott, D. H., on the prediction of delinquency from non-delinquent behaviour, 37n
Strathy, Peter Arthur, on inmate's view of parole, 345-6
Summary Jurisdiction Act of 1879 (England), 222
Supreme Court of Canada:
appeal to, on a point of law, 156
appeals from provincial courts, 151-2
appointments to, 143
available to appellate courts for summary offences, 156
characteristics of jurisprudence, 172
court of appeal, 141
court of last resort, 179-80
importance of judgments, 171-2
organization, 142

Sutherland, Edwin H.:
theory of criminal behaviour, 'differential association', 54-5
on white-collar crime, 54-5
Sutherland, Edwin H., and Donald R. Cressey:
on principles of criminology, 47, 55n
on sex differences in crime, 70n
Sykes, Gresham, on the society of captives, 306, 307n, 317n

Tappan, Paul W.:
on contemporary corrections, 220, 326
on crime, justice, and corrections, 50, 54, 57
on juvenile delinquency, 34
Tarde, Gabriel, on individual responsibility, 466-7
Teeters, Negley K.: *see* Barnes, Harry Elmer
Territorial waters, application of criminal law, 175-6
Thrasher, F. M., on the gang, 53
Ticket of Leave Act, 329, 336; repeal of, 332
Topping, C. W., on Canadian penal institutions, 321
Towle, Charlotte, on common human needs, 224
Traill, Catherine Parr, 280
Training-schools, 244-78
administration, 244-8
changing concepts of institutional care, 248-52
changes in community attitudes, 248-9
child analysis, contributing factor, 249
segregation of child offender, 248
the children in, 252-6
four classes that should be committed, 254
mis-placement, reasons for, 253-4
multiplicity of maladies, 252
staff, difficulties in coping with, 252
two basic groups, 253
classification by sex and religion, 254-6
conformity, undue emphasis on, 275
early history, 248
facilities, 256-8
factors determining release from, 261
function, 273
government-administered, control of intake lacking, 254

groups committed to, 245
jurisdiction in each province, 247-8
legislation, 244-8
maximum-security institutions, 256-7
need for classification program, 254
need for variety of institutions, 251-2
neglected children:
the case for separating, 245
versus young offender, 245
privately administered, control of intake, 254
programs, 258-63
academic, 259
atmosphere needed for, 260-1
fivefold nature, 258
recreational and social education, 260
treatment, 258-63
vocational training:
boys, 259-60
girls, 260
punishment and discipline, 263-73
controls, 270-1
'firm and fair', use of, 271
sanctions for, 270-1
definition, 270
forms, 266-70
corporal, 266-7
deprival of privileges, 269
group, 266
merit and demerit system, 267-8
'punishment group', 268
segregation, 268-9
senior children applying corrective measure, 266
importance of personal relationships, 265, 269-70
problems, 263-5
staff and children, relationship between, 271-3
consistency as a prime factor, 272-3
importance, 271-3
the use of authority, 273
who should handle, 269-70
staff, 273-7
conflict between trained specialist and untrained supervisor, 250-1
shortage of high-calibre supervisors, 275-6
supervisor, work of, 274
supervisors, numbers of, 274-5
training, 275-7
conflict between trained specialist and untrained supervisor, 277